D1191157

Emerging Capital Markets in Turmoil

Emerging Capital Markets in Turmoil

Bad Luck or Bad Policy?

Guillermo A. Calvo

The MIT Press
Cambridge, Massachusetts
London, England

MIT Press books may be purchased at special quantity discounts for business or sales promotional use. For information, please email special_sales@mitpress.mit.edu or write to Special Sales Department, The MIT Press, 55 Hayward Street, Cambridge, MA 02142.

This book was set in Palatino on 3B2 by Asco Typesetters, Hong Kong and was printed and bound in the United States of America.

Library of Congress Cataloging-in-Publication Data

Calvo, Guillermo.
  Emerging capital markets in turmoil : bad luck or bad policy / Guillermo A. Calvo.
    p. cm.
  Includes bibliographical references and index.
  ISBN 0-262-03334-8 (alk. paper)
  1. Financial crises. 2. Capital market. 3. Financial crises—Developing countries.
  4. Capital market—Developing countries. I. Title.
HB3722.C35   2005
332′.09172′4—dc22   2005047152

To all those who dare think outside the box, but are prudent in expressing their ideas.

Contents

Preface

This book contains papers on capital market issues in Emerging Market economies (EMs). These issues caught the public's eye during Mexico's Tequila crisis in 1994–95 and have not ceased to grab the headlines since then. Over the last fifteen years EMs have been pleasantly raised by the tide of capital inflows, only to be rudely thrown back to the ground by a crisis in which credit stops and exchange rates jump out of control. These episodes have hit everyone, saints and sinners alike.

When Mexico and Argentina were hit during the Tequila episode, many observers attributed the crisis to low saving rates and simply saw it as a replay of the crises of the early 1980s. However, this view got a serious jolt in 1997 when several East Asian economies suffered similar crises despite displaying awe-inspiring high saving rates. Finally, all conventional views held prior to 1994 were thrown into disarray after the Russian crisis in 1998. Russia represents a tiny share of the world's output, commerce, and finance. However, the Russian default resulted in a massive collapse of EM bond prices even though it entailed only a partial repudiation of Russia's *domestic* debt.

The issues raised by the above episodes are still hotly debated. Thus, it seemed to me that the time was ripe for putting several of my crisis papers between two covers. I thought too that the collection should contain not only the most refined version of an idea, but also papers in which the idea was taking shape. This has the advantage of presenting the issues from the "front lines." This may be especially valuable for younger generations that have not lived through these episodes. The papers cover a wide range of topics, from a search for stylized facts to formal theories focusing on a narrow but relevant issue. However, the introductions to the book and to each of the first four parts motivate and outline the main issues covered by the papers and, in some cases, provide context to the discussion.

A book like this is not produced in a vacuum. To begin with, several of the papers in this collection are coauthored with a group of first-rate scholars: Allan Drazen, Alejandro Izquierdo, Leo Leiderman, Enrique Mendoza, Rick Mishkin, Carmen Reinhart, and Ernesto Talvi. These scholars and many other friends and colleagues have helped me shape a veritable morass of fact and opinion into (I hope) simple ideas and stylized facts; besides, I have learned a lot from their own research.

To be sure, what remains from a decade of thinking and research is, in essence, very little. However, paradigm change is, as a general rule, based on what initially appears to be a slight change of focus. I do not claim that my effort has resulted in a paradigm change, but I sense that the research that has taken place in the last decade—while still short of earth-shaking results—has laid the ground for a major revision of the way we think about financial crises and policymaking in Emerging Market economies. That is why, through several years of thinking and writing on these issues, I have experienced first-hand the difficulty of articulating and "selling" new ideas. In order for new concepts to take root, first they must be accepted by a select group of individuals who are prepared to think "outside the box." I was very fortunate to find such a group with a predisposition to help me nurture "baby" ideas, while ensuring that the babies followed the straight and narrow path of logical and factual consistency. Moreover, being a member of a group with those characteristics was instrumental in enhancing the persuasiveness of the new concepts, and leveling the playing field in the battle against outdated concepts that stubbornly refuse to go away. In this respect I cannot help but cite John Maynard Keynes in (the last sentence of) the preface to his *General Theory*: "The difficulty lies, not in the new ideas, but in escaping from the old ones, which ramify, for those brought up as most of us have been, into every corner of our minds."

The production of this book would have been very hard without the help of Pilar Bilecky. Pilar has been my guardian angel at the Inter-American Development Bank for more than three years, helping me to find the time for this task in a busy schedule, and efficiently monitoring the gestation of this book through all the stages of production.

I am also thankful to the institutions that housed me while these papers were written: the International Monetary Fund, the University of Maryland, and the Inter-American Development Bank. The first and the last gave me a view of the battleground that would have been inaccessible from the ivory tower; they also provided me with a keen sense

of the relevant policy issues. Finally, the University of Maryland gave me the opportunity to write and speak without fearing the rage of some powerful bureaucrat or politician.

By now I have clearly established that my debts are multiple and large, but there is still one collaborator who has remained unmentioned and for whom I cannot find the words to express my boundless gratitude: Sara Calvo. Sara has been my companion for over twenty years. She singlehandedly lifted me from the dark caves of the Nibelungs to the thin air of Valhalla. While covering my back, she provided invaluable professional expertise and knowledge, helping me not to get easily distracted by the lovely rainbow, and to pay more attention to the wise voice of Erda. The equilibrium that Sara brought to my life has kept my mind focused on the exciting issues covered in this book while holding steady my fingers on the keyboard.

Emerging Capital Markets in Turmoil

Introduction

This book is about the financial crises that have raged through Emerging Market economies (EMs) from Mexico's 1994–95 (Tequila) crisis to the present.[1] In this section I will highlight the sequence of central events and debates, and the evolution of relevant ideas during that period, both in academia and policy circles. In particular, I will argue that crisis theory has progressed from focusing mainly on variables like fiscal deficit, debt sustainability and real currency overvaluation to stressing the role of the *financial sector*, especially balance-sheet mismatches (e.g., foreign-exchange-denominated liabilities vis-à-vis domestic-currency-denominated assets, or short-term obligations vis-à-vis long-term assets). Focusing on the financial sector has led to stressing *stocks*, as opposed to flows, and the role of *credibility*—an elusive concept to pin down empirically—which also has a stock dimension.

Let me start from the beginning, the Tequila crisis. The year 1994 was a very dramatic one for Mexico. It was an election year, and devaluation was in the air. Devaluation had been a *gift* of the incumbent to the new administration many times in the past (Mexicans even had an expression for it: *La Maldición del Sexenio*). Moreover, several prominent analysts insisted that the peso was overvalued and in urgent need of an overhaul (e.g., Dornbusch and Werner [1994]). This put upward pressure on peso interest rates during the year, which authorities tried to offset by expanding domestic credit from the central bank and changing the composition of public debt from pesos to U.S. dollars; the subsequent expansion of domestic credit resulted in a loss of international reserves. In addition, the political front suffered two major shocks, namely, the Chiapas uprising and the assassination of the leading presidential candidate, Luis Donaldo Colosio.

Interestingly, the international community seems to have taken all of this in stride. Interest rate spreads on Mexico's dollar debt, for instance, were low by EM standards. This may have been partly due to expectations that Mexico would join NAFTA and become a member of the OECD. But another possible reason, not to be overlooked, is that Mexico received highly visible accolades from the Multilateral Financial Institutions. For instance, in the IMF/World Bank 1994 Spring meetings held in Madrid, the Mexican economy was portrayed as exemplary. This may have sent a strong message that those institutions were ready to bail out bondholders in case of a speculative attack (as actually happened).[2]

The devaluation debate attracted international attention. In April 1994, the Brookings Institution organized a panel on the Dornbusch-Werner (1994) paper. Stan Fischer and I were the discussants, and on that occasion it became apparent to me that the conventional analysis was leaving out of the picture several issues that seemed central to me, such as debt maturity and denomination, and credibility. A central policy issue in the debate was the possibility of correcting the perceived currency overvaluation in Mexico by a 20 percent devaluation, as advised by Dornbusch and Werner. I was afraid that the remedy could be worse than the disease because a one-step unscheduled devaluation might breed distrust in investors' minds and lead to a run on all Mexican obligations. This would result in a balance of payments crisis because the government had no reserves to repay obligations coming due in the short run, a large portion of which were in U.S. dollars. As a result, a 20 percent devaluation might result in a major crisis and destabilize the whole domestic financial system. Unfortunately for Mexico, I turned out to be right. Instead of obediently staying within the 20 percent ceiling dictated by the government, the exchange rate went wildly out of control and overshot the 100 percent mark.[3]

Old ideas die hard. For new ideas to win the day, the mind (individual and collective) has to absorb a new model or paradigm in which the new ideas are inserted. This is not easy, especially for the practitioner whose training years are long behind him; but, more interestingly, old ideas die hard because new ideas have to receive sufficiently broad support for them to be adopted in policy circles.[4] Policy decisions require a large degree of actual or potential *consensus*. Otherwise, they cannot be implemented. Thus, under these circumstances, new ideas are ignored until they have permeated deep enough into the relevant institutions.

One implication of the above phenomenon was that the Tequila crisis sent policy circles in frantic search for an explanation based on first-generation models (e.g., Krugman [1979]), even though not all of the pieces fit together. Since in the end only Mexico and Argentina suffered sizable crises, and both economies had undergone BOP crises in the early 1980s owing (as commonly believed) to unsustainable fiscal deficits, it did not take long for policy circles to conclude that these crises were the result of fiscal indiscipline, either actual or potential.[5]

Fortunately, academic circles were not completely indifferent to these events. Papers produced around the time of the Tequila episode, for example (e.g., chapters 4, 7, and 10 in this book, and Cole and Kehoe [1996]), suggest that the Tequila crisis could have stemmed from vulnerabilities in the financial sector. As noted above, a striking vulnerability in the case of Mexico was the existence of dollar-denominated, short-maturity public sector liabilities (e.g., *Tesobonos*). Thus, a possible scenario is that the controlled one-step devaluation engineered by the government in December 1994 raised suspicions that the government would fail to honor *Tesobonos* and induced a run on public sector liabilities in Mexico. The stock of *Tesobonos* was not large relative to GDP (less than 8 percent), but it greatly exceeded the stock of international reserves. Here is where short-maturity matters.[6] Given the shortfall of reserves, the options were: (1) an unrealistically large fiscal adjustment, (2) debt rollover, or (3) open debt repudiation.[7] Debt rollover without crisis would have been difficult because, in the lack-of-credibility scenario, the impasse is triggered by Mexico's insufficient creditworthiness. Therefore, the only realistic option would have been (3) open debt repudiation, which, of course, results in a balance-of-payments (BOP) crisis. If the debt had been denominated in domestic currency, and not in U.S. dollars, the central bank could have serviced the debt by issuing domestic money. This probably would have resulted in a large price increase, but, under flexible exchange rates, the BOP crisis would have been avoided. It is worth noting that foreign-exchange-denominated debt or "Liability Dollarization" has become a focal theme in this literature. Liability Dollarization played a key role in several later crisis episodes (Korea and Indonesia 1997, Turkey 2001, and prominently in Argentina 2001, which will be discussed in chapter 6).

In addition, focusing on financial vulnerabilities brings up the possibility of multiple equilibria. Thus, for example, under liability dollarization and short-maturity public debt, the expectation that the currency will suffer a large devaluation may trigger a run on such debt, inducing a devaluation of the currency. Models exhibiting self-fulfilling crises are called second-generation models. An early example is Obstfeld (1986). More recent examples are chapter 7 in this book, Cole and Kehoe (1996), and Obstfeld (1996). An attractive feature of these models is that a crisis could strike "out of the blue," thus rationalizing situations in which agents are taken by surprise. However, an inherent problem with self-fulfilling prophecy models is that they do not tell us how a particular equilibrium is selected. Thus, the literature shows some efforts to find extra constraints for recovering equilibrium uniqueness. I discussed this issue in Calvo (1996, introduction to part II) and argued that, although adding more constraints could restore uniqueness, the equilibrium solution could be highly sensitive to "irrelevant" parameters. A recent attempt along these lines, which has received considerable attention, is the elegant paper by Morris and Shin (1998), where a mechanism of expectations-of-expectations under imperfect and heterogeneous information results in a unique equilibrium, even though with shared information the economy would display equilibrium multiplicity.[8] Thus, the equilibrium now depends on the peculiarities of the information transmission mechanisms that are seldom observed by the econometrician and thus empirically hard to test. Moreover, the Morris-Shin approach is not fully convincing because currency runs are highly visible in this Media Age of instant information. Long lines of panicky depositors trying to get their money out are quickly aired on TV screens. Thus, under crisis-prone situations, information is likely to become substantially more homogeneous and public, bringing back the problem of equilibrium indeterminacy.

Multiple equilibria models are interesting not only because they help to model highly unexpected crises, but also because they help to rationalize large changes in key variables like the current account, which is a salient characteristic of recent EM crises. By definition, the current account is the difference between income and expenditure (or absorption). Thus, unless there are large supply shocks, or changes in temporal or inter-temporal prices, the standard representative-individual model predicts that the current account displays a very stable pattern (e.g., in continuous-time, nonstochastic models the prediction is that the current account is a continuous function of time). In contrast, the current account could exhibit large changes across equilibria. Prior to a crisis, for example, the current account might exhibit a large deficit as a result of expected high income growth; but, if the economy switches to crisis mode, future prospects become dimmer, inducing higher saving rates and, thus, a sharp contraction in the current account deficit (CAD).

A related phenomenon is sudden stop (of capital inflows). Let us recall that, abstracting from errors and omissions, we have the following accounting identity:

$$KI = CAD + \Delta R, \tag{1}$$

where KI and ΔR denote capital inflow and reserve accumulation, respectively. A sudden stop is usually defined as a large contraction in KI. Clearly, then, a large current account reversal and a sudden stop are closely linked. As shown in Edwards (2004), however, these two concepts are far from being identities in practice. In my work I have preferred to focus on Sudden Stop because *external shocks* are likely to be more directly reflected in KI than in CAD. For example, if an economy's creditworthiness is lowered as a result of a crisis in another economy (a situation usually referred to as *contagion*), then one will more likely observe the shock first in KI. CAD will eventually reflect the shock as well, but policymakers usually react to such a shock by releasing international reserves in an attempt to delay adjustment in aggregate demand, given the latter's usually dire consequences in terms of unemployment and financial disruption. Interestingly, most EM crisis episodes exhibit sudden stop, while in advanced market economies the incidence of sudden stops is much less frequent (see Calvo, Izquierdo, and Mejia [2004]).[9]

Another fact that has become apparent is the *bunching* of sudden stop episodes in EMs, that is, simultaneity of sudden stop crises. Bunching, incidentally, is much less pervasive in advanced market economies (see Calvo, Izquierdo, and Mendoza [2004]). A popular convention is that bunching may be the result of *contagion* or the presence of a common factor.[10] Chapter 12 contains a model in which asset prices are hit by margin calls in the central capital market, a common factor. The model can be utilized to show the possibility that several EMs are hit at the same time because their funding has similar sources, and this conjecture has in fact received empirical support (see Kaminsky and Reinhart [2004], and Broner, Gelos, and Reinhart [2002]). Bunching was especially dramatic in connection with the 1998 crisis in Russia, and the impact on EM bond prices was very large in a number of countries. This caused major confusion at the time because Russia has a very small presence in international trade and finance markets, and none of the available models could account for this phenomenon.[11] My conjecture, incidentally, is that the Russian crisis also revealed the bunching phenomenon in a dramatic way, which increased the perceived correlation of returns across EM securities. The latter may have turned out to be a key factor behind the unraveling of the EM bond market, possibly causing the sequence of EM financial crises that took place after 1998.

1   Conventional Analytical Tools before 1995

Previous discussion shows that since 1994, and as crises erupted, the intellectual climate has increasingly favored models in which balance-sheet vulnerabilities (e.g., Liability Dollarization) and multiple equilibria took center stage. As noted, prior to the Tequila crisis the conventional wisdom was centered on Krugman (1979). But there were other pieces of analysis that played an important role. Many of these have not been superseded and are highly relevant. Thus, it is worth spending a little time summarizing the main analyses—and their limitations. I will discuss two separate but complementary strands of the literature: Krugman (1979) and early warning indicators (debt sustainability analysis and currency overvaluation).

Krugman (1979)

This is an elegant model, which is capable of rationalizing a sudden attack on a central bank's reserves, even though the driving force behind the crisis, that is, the fiscal deficit, is constant over time. The key for the sudden attack on reserves is that policy exhibits a large, though subtle, discontinuity. The latter takes place at crisis time as authorities abandon the exchange rate peg and finance the deficit by issuing domestic money. This leads to a discontinuous jump in the rate of inflation, causing a discontinuous collapse in the demand for money and a run on international reserves. Therefore, the proximate cause for the BOP crisis is a contraction in the stock of real monetary balances (where money is defined as the money base). As noted in chapter 3 in this book, Flood, Garber, and Kramer (1996), and Kumhof (2000), however, this is not how most recent BOP crises have evolved. What typically happens is that domestic credit from the central bank exhibits a sudden increase, while the money base remains largely undisturbed. As shown in, for example, Velasco (1987) and chapter 7 of this volume, Krugman (1979) can be supplemented in such a way that domestic credit from the central bank sharply expands to cover contingent expenses—but the simple notion that a BOP crisis is just a run on domestic money cannot be salvaged. Moreover, once contingent obligations are taken into account issues like the health of the banking system (Velasco [1987]), short-term debt and Liability Dollarization come to the fore (chapter 7 of this book).

Krugman (1979) implies that a crisis can be prevented or quickly resolved by increasing the fiscal primary surplus. However, for the fiscal recipe to work, the government must be expected to follow through with fiscal adjustment in the future, and deficits must not be hidden through the use of "creative" accounting, for example. Thus, even in the simple Krugman (1979) world, *credibility* of policy announcements is a critical ingredient in policy effectiveness.

Early Warning Indicators

This approach attempts to identify factors that may help to anticipate crisis. The methodology is highly empirical, although informed by theory. I will discuss two indicators that occupied center stage prior to the Tequila crisis (and still do in many quarters): debt unsustainability and currency overvaluation.

Debt Sustainability Analysis

The idea is to be able to detect cases in which the expenditure of some key sector of the economy follows a path such that, if not subject to a sharp correction, the sector will be subject to a sudden stop. To illustrate, I will focus on net foreign indebtedness for the economy as a whole. Thus, denoting by b net foreign indebtedness as a share of GDP, we have:

$$\dot{b} = cad - b\eta, \tag{2}$$

where a dot on a variable denotes its time derivative, *cad* stands for the (constant) current account deficit as a share of GDP, and 0 for the (constant) growth rate of GDP. Given *cad* and 0, (2) is a stable differential equation in b. Clearly, at steady state

$$b = \frac{1}{\eta} cad. \tag{3}$$

Although the system is stable, steady-state b may be so large that the country as a whole may prefer to default on its international debt obligations. For the sake of simplicity, suppose that there is a critical debt level B such that if $b \# B$ debt is paid in full, while if $b > B$ debt will be totally repudiated. Hence, the maximum *cad* consistent with full debt repayment is, by equation (3), equal to $B0$. If *cad* exceeds $B0$, then there will come a time when b reaches B and the country will suffer a sudden stop.

Several analysts pointed to the high current account deficit in Mexico during 1994 (about 8 percent of GDP)—and the prospects of even higher deficit in 1995—as a signal that a large expenditure contraction was needed. At the time, Mexico exhibited very low growth rates. Thus, it would not have been implausible to assume that the relevant output growth rate for Mexico, 0, was around 2 percent per annum. Hence, by equation (3), the implied steady-state debt-to-GDP ratio would be about 400 percent of GDP. This debt level could not be expected to be sustainable, because even if interest rates on Mexico's debt were unrealistically low, say 5 percent per annum, debt service would be around 20 percent of GDP, giving rise to irresistible default incentives.

Why would a country reach unsustainable debt levels, eventually forcing individuals to undergo draconian cuts in consumption and investment? One possible explanation is government profligacy, especially if citizens do not fully internalize the government budget constraint. However, that is not a convincing argument for the 1990s because policymakers appear to have learned the lesson of the 1980s, and there is no clear sign of fiscal unsustainability.[12] Another explanation is high rate of time preference. If individuals' subjective discount rate exceeds the international rate of interest, then debt will eventually hit the upper bound. However, in this case the sudden stop would be fully anticipated and should not, in principle, be associated with a sharp fall in consumption and output (a typical fact in crisis episodes); see Atkeson and Rios-Rull (1996). In sum, debt sustainability analysis is a useful instrument to assess the need for fiscal or expenditure adjustment, but it falls short of an explanation for some of the key characteristics of recent crises, in particular the devastating effects of sudden stops.

Currency Overvaluation

This is a very slippery concept. In principle, in the absence of foreign exchange controls, the real exchange rate—defined as, for example, the ratio of a relevant external price level (*times* the free market exchange rate) to a relevant domestic price level (e.g., the CPI)—is presumed to be at equilibrium. However, what lies behind the notion of overvaluation is comparison of the current real exchange rate with that which would prevail along a sustainable path. To illustrate, if the *cad* is unsustainable according to previous analysis, then the current real exchange rate is likely to be lower than under a smaller sustainable *cad*. Therefore, overvaluation is tantamount to unsustainability. This does not make the analysis superfluous, because estimates of currency overvaluation provide an assessment of how much the real exchange rate should rise when the economy switches to a sustainable path. The greater is the implied relative price change, the greater the damage to the financial system, especially if the change is sudden and largely unanticipated (i.e., if it occurs in the context of a sudden stop; chapter 6 discusses these issue for several Latin American countries).[13] The question remains, however, of why the private sector would so badly fail to anticipate large changes in relative prices. Overvaluation analysis is mute on this key issue.

2   Conventional Wisdom before 1995

Here I will be mostly referring to the conventional wisdom in Washington, particularly the IMF, where I worked during 1988–1992. I think it is fair to say that conventional wisdom with respect to crisis prevention prior to the Tequila crisis boiled down to the following: Put your house in order and the rest will follow suit. Putting one's house in order, however, essentially meant "ensure fiscal sustainability." Thus, when the Mexico crisis erupted in 1994–95, Washington went around looking for skeletons in the fiscal closet that could provide evidence for an unsustainable fiscal deficit. And, sure enough, some skeletons were found (e.g., loans from development banks had increased substantially during the election year), but it was not enough to justify a fall in Mexico's output of more than 6 percent in 1995 (see chapter 4).

Argentina provided the other major crisis episode of 1995. This case was an even bigger challenge for the conventional wisdom because Argentina's economy had exhibited much more vigorous growth than Mexico's, and it was thus harder to argue that debt or fiscal sustainability was at stake.

Conventional wisdom is hard to change because, as noted, old ideas die hard. Moreover, before dying, old ideas try to mutate in order to survive.[14] This phenomenon became evident after the Mexico-

Argentina crisis episodes. All of a sudden, Washington woke up to the low-savings phenomenon and, as a result, a crusade was launched to stimulate saving in Latin America.[15] However, as if nature abhorred feeble-minded arguments, the 1997 East Asian crisis quickly dealt a fatal blow to this mutation of the previous conventional wisdom; East Asia is the world region with the highest saving rates. Thus, the death knell had been sounded for the old conventional wisdom, and the time was ripe for a new, or at least richer, policy paradigm.

3 Groping for a New Conventional Wisdom after 1997

Mutations continued after the East Asian crisis of mid-1997. Having thrown the low-saving explanation out the window, the exchange rate—that ubiquitous variable—reentered the stage and morphed into a view that still holds some sway, namely, the polar view of exchange rate regimes. Fortunately, fresh variables and concepts also found their way into conventional wisdom, two of the most salient being the role of short-term and foreign-exchange-denominated debt (liability dollarization). I will briefly discuss these topics below.

The Polar View

This view states that there are only two types of foreign exchange regimes that are crisis-proof: (i) free floating and (ii) irrevocably fixed exchange rates (e.g., full dollarization, adopting a foreign currency like Panama; or a watertight currency board à la Hong Kong). The definition of irrevocably fixed exchange rates is clear enough, but what is a regime of free floating exchange rates? Any Econ 101 student knows that the value of money depends on money *supply*. Free floating, as interpreted in policy circles, says nothing about how money is generated and, thus, free floating would be consistent with very different *monetary* regimes. For example, it would be consistent with quantitative money targets, like Friedman's x% rule, or inflation, interest-rate, or real-exchange-rate targeting! Thus, taken at face value the polar view would support Irrevocably Fixed exchange rates and be critical of foreign exchange controls in any other regime (because exchange rates would not be free to float). That is all. However, advocates of the polar view had something very different in mind. They were really after *soft pegs*, i.e., temporary and unsustainable predetermined exchange rate systems, the type adopted by all crisis countries before crisis struck.

The polar view is a clear example of the "soft thinking" that runs in policy circles, and how easily conventional wisdom converges to incomplete ideas that at best signify a rejection of what failed the last time around, without subjecting them to a modicum of serious analysis. A dangerous thing, indeed!

Short-Term Bonds and Liability Dollarization

The East Asian crises confirmed the relevance of an issue that had already surfaced in the context of the Mexican crisis, namely, the risk associated with short-term debt obligations, especially when they are denominated in terms of foreign exchange (liability dollarization). This is discussed in chapter 6; see also Rodrik and Velasco (2000). Debt rollover can generate a BOP crisis if the rollover takes place when interest rates are high or prohibitive. Though this is not a new phenomenon, what was new was its virulence and frequency in EMs. Presumably if financial markets are deep and information is good, debt rollover, especially when the amounts are not large, should proceed smoothly, as it does every week in the United States when the Treasury rolls over treasury bills. However, recent EM crises show that those preconditions are not so common in EMs and, as a result, debt rollovers may throw an EM into crisis. This fact was soon internalized by the IMF and is now part of the new conventional wisdom. This went hand in hand with another major change of focus. Domestic debt started to be considered as not too dissimilar from external debt; this represents a recognition that financial globalization has mostly done away with bond market segmentation.

As stated at the outset, the current views of crisis in EMs place a great deal of emphasis on balance-sheet considerations and the structure of financial systems. In a way, the analysis in the last ten years has revealed that "putting your house in order" must include setting up effective *institutions*. Moreover, since the financial sector is at center stage, quality, timeliness and reliability of information are of utmost importance. In a world of global finance, information involves both domestic and foreign individuals and firms. Thus, there is a clear need for international cooperation in this respect. In addition, if crises occur because of informational gaps that are apparent to international regulators or monitors but not to a significant number of market participants, a case could be made for giving International Financial Institutions the ability to act quickly in order to prevent unnecessarily negative consequences. This can partly be done in the context of the current International Financial Architecture, but more global and effective instruments and institutions may have to be developed (see chapter 18 in this book for a discussion of an emerging market fund, or EMF).

4   Are We There Yet?

After almost ten years of crises and a good number of new insights, have we succeeded in making EMs any safer from financial crises? My answer is an emphatic "no." If the international community had internalized the important role played by financial considerations, would they have abandoned Argentina to its historic crisis in 2001? A popular argument for the no-bailout policy is that Argentina followed a lax fiscal policy and, thus, new money would go down the drain and increase even further Argentina's debt with international financial institutions. However, as discussed in chapter 6 in this volume, much of the fiscal deterioration since 2000 was due to low growth and the increase in the interest-rate spread that low growth produced as investors started to question debt sustainability (despite a major fiscal adjustment undertaken during 2000).[16] If the international financial community had understood the few lessons that I tried to convey above, it would have realized that a central problem faced by highly dollarized Argentina was the lack of a lender of last resort; and if that had been well-understood, the financial community would have put much less emphasis on fiscal adjustment, and much more emphasis on providing the necessary foreign-exchange liquidity (as was later done for Uruguay).[17]

Another instance that, at the very least, reveals incomplete learning of crisis lessons is how debt obligations are treated in HIPCs (highly indebted poor countries). As a condition for substantial debt forgiveness, these countries are constrained *not* to borrow in the international market—but they are free to borrow domestically. This condition only makes sense if one thinks that domestic debt is like a tax on domestic residents, that is, it will never be repaid. Aside from giving governments perverse incentives (e.g., borrow from domestic pension funds with the intention of never paying back), this lopsided constraint ignores financial globalization. Actually, the regulation has been so ineffective that some HIPCs are already at the brink of defaulting on their *domestic* debt.

5   Sketch of the Book

The book is divided into five Parts. Part I, Early Rumblings, contains a set of papers written before the Tequila crisis that led us (my co-authors and I) to the conjecture that a sharp rise in U.S. interest rates might result in a balance-of-payments crisis, especially in Latin America. The key point of these papers is that *external factors matter*, and matter a lot. This message defied the prevailing conventional wisdom in multilateral financial institutions, and it still does today when those institutions are on automatic pilot. Part II, The Beast Awakens, contains papers mostly written in the heat of the Tequila, Russia 1998, and Argentina 2001 crises. The core of these papers is a narrative of crisis episodes on the basis of simple theory and reduced-form econometrics. Thus, parts I and II contain the inspiration and empirical evidence that lay the groundwork for the theory later presented in the book.

Part III, In Search of a Theory, contains the main theoretical papers, written with the professional economist in mind. This part can be skipped without loss of continuity, but I prefer to believe that it contains substantive material for the graduate student and the active researcher in the field. Part IV, The Exchange Rate and All That, goes back to a more empirical stance and focuses on the exchange rate issue, which is always at the forefront of the debate. The IMF, for example, seems to have taken a firm stance in favor of flexible exchange rates inspired (it appears) by the fact that prior to crisis all economies followed some form of *soft peg* or *very dirty float*. The papers in part IV make a simple central point: Typically, EMs are far from being pure floaters because floating is hard and possibly disrupting. In turn, floating is hard or disrupting because of weak institutions and poor credibility. Thus, blindly advising flexible exchange rate to an EM is like a doctor giving a prescription without checking its possibly serious side effects. I hasten to say, however, to avoid possible misunderstanding, that the IMF is conscious of these difficulties *in practice* and, as a general rule, has not succumbed to the official mantra.

The book closes with part V, which consists of some reflections on facts, theory, and policy.

Notes

1. I am grateful to Sara Calvo and Ernesto Talvi for very useful comments.

2. Some observers claim that the Mexican bailout induced excessive lending in other EMs and was partly responsible for the 1997 East Asian crises (see Meltzer [2000]). This conjecture is discussed and dismissed in chapter 18 of this book.

3. Incidentally, to the surprise of most analysts educated in the Krugman (1979) tradition, money supply (in none of its familiar definitions) showed a significant reduction. Thus, *prima facie* it cannot be claimed that the Tequila crisis stemmed from a run against domestic money. This issue is further discussed below.

4. Old ideas die hard everywhere, academia included. However, there is greater resistance to new ideas in policy circles, perhaps because *originality* is less prized than *consensus*.

5. Were the crises of the 1980s that different from the more recent ones? Was fiscal unsustainability a key factor behind those crises, as commonly believed, or did financial factors of the kind seen in recent crises also play a central role? These are still open questions that deserve further study. Ernesto Talvi and I are planning to make some progress in this respect in a forthcoming book.

6. Moreover, some observers have noted that repos between domestic banks and Wall Street financial institutions, plus weak domestic banks' balance sheets, considerably shortened the (residual) maturity of Tesobonos.

7. Notice that currency devaluation would do nothing to relieve the debt burden because Tesobonos were U.S. dollar liabilities.

8. It is interesting to note that Keynes (1936) thought that expectations-of-expectations was itself a source of equilibrium multiplicity (for a recent version of the view see Frydman and Phelps [1983]), while expectations-of-expectations is a key mechanism to ensure uniqueness in Morris and Shin (1998).

9. Roughly speaking, Calvo, Izquierdo, and Mejia (2004) define sudden stop as a contraction in KI that exceeds by two standard deviations the mean of changes in KI in the past. Thus, the intuition behind this definition is that sudden stop contains a large unanticipated component.

10. Forbes and Rigobon (1999) are critical of the contagion hypothesis.

11. The feeling in capital markets could be described by the word "panic." People enter into panic when they are hit by a large shock and they do not know where it came from. It should be noted, though, that one explanation that quickly surfaced at the time was reverse moral hazard, which was presumably caused by the refusal of the IMF to bail out Russia. See chapter 18 in this book for a discussion.

12. However, Burnside, Eichenbaum, and Rebelo (2004) claims that bank bailouts and other contingent government obligations were large enough to question fiscal sustainability. Notice, however, that unsustainability holds if crisis occurs. This is not the case otherwise, though, because contingent government expenses are conditional on crisis occurring. Thus, this view of the Asian crisis implies assuming existence of multiple equilibria. What kicked Asia out of Paradise? That is the unanswered question.

13. See Goldfajn and Valdes (1999) for an empirical analysis of the link between real exchange rates and crises.

14. This is consistent with the previous discussion that old ideas die hard. Mutation economizes on learning and speeds up consensus.

15. Incidentally, except for tasteless contrarians who have no regard for diplomatic etiquette, nobody would have dared to say that the United States is a low saver too!

16. I was critical of the fiscal adjustment at the time, because neither the president (De la Rúa) nor the finance minister (Machinea) seemed to believe in it. They seemed not to understand a basic fact, namely, that the effectiveness of fiscal adjustment is a function of its perceived *durability*—the latter requiring that policymakers are prepared to stake their reputations to sustain them.

17. To be fair, the IMF's inactivity in the case of Argentina could, to a large extent, be explained by the fact that the institutional constraints prevented the Fund from engaging in massive bailouts unless the bailout was strongly supported by some G7 shareholders (as in the Tequila crisis). Actually, the IMF showed clear signs of having learned the crisis lessons when it pushed forward the CCL (contingent credit line) proposal.

References

Atkeson, Andrew, and Jose-Victor Rios-Rull, 1996, "The Balance of Payments and Borrowing Constraints: An Alternative View of the Mexican Crisis," *Journal of International Economics* 41:331–349.

Burnside, Craig, Martin Eichenbaum, and Sergio Rebelo, 2003, "Government Finance in the Wake of a Currency Crisis," presented at the VI Workshop in International Economics and Finance at University T. Di Tella.

Broner, Fernando, Gaston Gelos, and Carmen M. Reinhart, 2004, "When in Peril, Retrench: Testing the Portfolio Channel of Contagion," presented at the Conference on Emerging Markets and Macroeconomic Volatility, San Francisco Federal Reserve and University of Maryland, San Francisco, CA, June 4–5.

Cole, Harold, and Timothy Kehoe, 1996, "A Self-Fulfilling Model of Mexico's 1994/95 Debt Crisis," *Journal of International Economics* 41 (November): 309–330.

Dornbusch, Rudiger, and Alejandro Werner, "Mexico: Stabilization, Reform, and No Growth," *Brookings Papers on Economic Activity* 1:253–297.

Edwards, Sebastian, 2004, "Thirty Years of Current Account Imbalances, Current Account Reversals, and Sudden Stops," NBER Working Paper no. 10276.

Flood, Robert, Peter Garber, and C. Kramer, 1996, "Collapsing Exchange Rate Regimes: Another Linear Example," *Journal of International Economics* 41, no. 3–4: 223–234.

Kumhof, Michael, 2000, "Quantitative Explanation of the Role of Short-Term Debt in Balance-of-Payments Crises," *Journal of International Economics* 51, no. 1: 195–250.

Forbes, Kristin, and Roberto Rigobon, 1999, "No Contagion, Only Interdependence: Measuring Stock Market Co-Movements," NBER Working Paper no. 7267.

Frydman, Roman, and Edmund S. Phelps, 1983, *Individual Forecasting and Aggregate Outcomes: "Rational Expectations" Examined*, Cambridge: Cambridge University Press.

Goldfajn, Ilan, and Rodrigo O. Valdes, "The Aftermath of Appreciation," *Quarterly Journal of Economics* 114:229–262.

Kaminsky, Graciela, and Carmen M. Reinhart, 2004, "The Center and the Periphery: The Globalization of Financial Turmoil," presented at the IMF Conference in Honor of G. Calvo on April 16, Washington, DC.

Keynes, John M., 1936, *The General Theory of Employment, Interest and Money*, London: Macmillan & Co.

Krugman, Paul R., 1979, "A Model of Balance-of-Payments Crises," *Journal of Money, Credit, and Banking* 11 (August): 311–325.

Meltzer, Allan H., 2000, *Report of the International Financial Institution Advisory Commission*, Senate Committee on Banking, Housing, and Urban Affairs.

Morris, Stephen, and Hyun Song Shin, 1998, "Unique Equilibrium in a Model of Self-Fulfilling Currency Attacks," *American Economic Review* 88:587–597.

Obstfeld, Maurice, 1986, "Rational and Self-Fulfilling Balance-of-Payments Crises," *American Economic Review*, March, 72–81.

Obstfeld, Maurice, 1996, "Models of Currency Crises with Self-Fulfilling Features," *European Economic Review* 40:1037–1047.

Rodrik, Dani, and Andres Velasco, 2000, "Short-Term Capital Flows," *Annual World Bank Conference on Development Economics*.

Part I

Early Rumblings

Introduction to Part I

The chapters in this part were written while my collaborators and I worked at the IMF; Leo was visiting the Research Department, while Carmen and I were full-time staff there. These chapters carry a straightforward message, namely, that Latin American economies are highly sensitive to news from the U.S. economy. My intuition about the existence of a significant linkage with the U.S. economy was inspired by a trip around several Latin American countries in 1992. At that time capital flow to EMs was running at full steam, bringing about accumulation of international reserves and output expansion—all good news. The capital inflow phenomenon was not well understood, however, and observers came up with idiosyncratic explanations that, given the phenomenon's relatively recent origin, could not be subjected to serious empirical testing.

When empirical evidence is shaky, explanations have a tendency to become self-serving. Thus, policymakers and multilateral financial institutions interpreted these facts as reflecting the success of the Brady Plan, and that several countries in the region had embraced the path of economic reform. However, I did not find this argument fully convincing, as many countries were undergoing a similar experience even though their reform efforts varied greatly in some cases.

On my return to Washington, Carmen, Leo, and I sat down to discuss this puzzling similarity of outcome despite the divergence of objective conditions. It soon became obvious to us that, if there were common factors, they must lie outside the region, and the natural candidate was the U.S. economy. The papers in this part show that we were on the right track, as empirical tests confirm that U.S. variables explain a large portion of regional variance.

I will let the papers speak for themselves, and rather say a few words on how these papers were received at the IMF. I believe I would not be exaggerating if I said that the reception was cold and, if any-thing, unsympathetic. This took us by surprise because we thought the papers were full of useful insights. For example, they showed that EMs could be vulnerable to crisis even though they followed traditional Fund advice. At the time we were especially concerned about a pos-sible sharp rise in U.S. interest rates, and one of our key findings was that U.S. interest rates were important in the determination of capital flows to Latin America—increasing when interest rates were low, and vice versa. Thus, our research suggested the possibility of a sharp capital flow reversal (which later materialized in the Tequila crisis when the Fed finally raised interest rates by about 300 basis points in 1994)—a shock that both the IMF and EMs should prepare themselves to confront. Could anyone think of a better use of research time?

We were, of course, very naïve. As pointed out in the Introduction to this book, old ideas die hard. In this case, it is clear why. New ideas could put at risk the credibility of policymakers and multilateral insti-tutions. What if residents realized that the region's incipient success was in great part due to sheer luck? Would the IMF risk its influence and partnership with the region's policymakers by openly accepting the results of an empirical study that, quite possibly, would be rejected by the next nerd who hit a computer?

Understandable as it is, it always strikes me how little empirical evi-dence is required to keep old ideas and conventions on their lofty ped-estals. Keynes's genius always comes to mind in this respect: "Worldly wisdom teaches that it is better for reputation to fail conventionally, than to succeed unconventionally" (Keynes [1961], chapter 12). The main lesson that I extract from this is that there exists a great distance from discovery to application, even in economics. My feeling is that most of us occupy extreme points of the spectrum: either we work on discovery, or we work on applications. The road between these two points is home for a small band of adventurers who run the risk of being dismissed by the other two groups as outsiders, or worse. Fortu-nately, this market imperfection has been internalized by some multi-lateral financial institutions, like the IDB, where research on those desolate points in-between is encouraged.

References

Keynes, John M. 1961. *The General Theory of Employment, Interest and Money*. New York: Macmillan & Co.

1

Capital Inflows and Real Exchange Rate Appreciation in Latin America: The Role of External Factors

Guillermo A. Calvo, Leonardo Leiderman, and Carmen M. Reinhart

The revival of substantial international capital inflows to Latin America is perhaps the most visible economic change in the region during the past two years. Capital flows to Latin America, which averaged about $8 billion a year in the second half of the 1980s, surged to $24 billion in 1990 and $40 billion in 1991. Of the latter amount, 45 percent went to Mexico, and most of the remainder went to Argentina, Brazil, Chile, Colombia, and Venezuela. Interestingly, capital is returning to most Latin American countries despite wide differences in macroeconomic policies and economic performance across the region. In most countries, the capital inflows have been accompanied by an appreciation in the real exchange rate, booming stock and real estate markets, faster economic growth, an accumulation of international reserves, and a strong recovery of secondary-market prices for foreign loans.

Without a doubt, an important part of this phenomenon is explained by the fundamental economic and political reforms that have recently taken place in these countries, including the restructuring of their external debts. Indeed, it would have been difficult to attract the amount of foreign capital mentioned above without these reforms. Nevertheless, although domestic reform is a necessary ingredient for reviving capital flows, it only partially explains Latin America's forceful reentry into international capital markets. Domestic reforms alone cannot explain why capital sometimes flowed to countries that did not undertake reforms and conversely why it sometimes did not flow, except until recently, to countries where reforms were introduced well before 1990. For domestic reforms alone to explain the co-movement of capital inflows across countries in the region, one would have to posit the existence of strong reputational externalities (or "contagion" effects): reforms in some countries give rise to expectations of future reforms in others.[1]

This chapter maintains that some of the renewal of capital flows to Latin America results from external factors and can be considered an *external shock* common to the region. We argue that falling interest rates, a continuing recession, and balance of payments developments in the United States have encouraged investors to shift resources to Latin America to take advantage of renewed investment opportunities and the region's increased solvency;[2] economic developments outside the region help to explain the universality of these flows. The present episode may well represent an additional case of financial shocks in the center affecting the periphery—an idea stressed by Diaz-Alejandro.[3]

International capital inflows affect the Latin American economies in at least four ways.[4] First, they increase the availability of capital in the individual economies and allow domestic agents to smooth out their consumption over time and investors to react to expected changes in profitability. Second, capital inflows have been associated with a marked appreciation of the real exchange rate in most of the countries. The larger transfer from abroad has to be accompanied by an increase in domestic absorption. If part of the increase in spending falls on non-traded goods, their relative price will increase—the real exchange rate appreciates. Third, capital inflows have an impact on domestic policy-making. The desire by some central banks to attenuate the real exchange rate appreciation in the short run frequently leads them to intervene, purchasing from the private sector part of the inward flow of foreign exchange. Moreover, the attempt to avoid domestic mone-tization of these purchases has often led the monetary authorities to sterilize some of the inflows, a policy that tends to perpetuate a high domestic-foreign interest rate differential and that gives rise to in-creased fiscal burdens. The extent to which the inflows are sustain-able also concerns the authorities. The history of Latin America gives reason for such concern: the major episodes of capital inflows, during the 1920s and 1978–81, were followed by major economic crises and capital outflows, such as in the 1930s and the debt crisis in the mid-1980s.[5] Fourth, capital inflows can provide important—though ambiguous—signals to participants in world financial markets. An increase in capital inflows can be interpreted as reflecting more favor-able medium- and long-term investment opportunities in the receiving country. But capital may also pour in for purely short-term speculative purposes, when lack of credibility in a government's policies leads to high nominal returns on domestic financial assets. In fact, several such episodes have occurred in Latin America, where lack of credibility and a short-term financial bubble have been associated with large inflows of "hot money" from abroad. Although it remains to be seen which one of these two scenarios best fits the present picture, the strong recovery in secondary-market prices of bank claims on most of these countries (figure 1.1) and various other indicators of country risk provide some support for the first, more favorable, scenario.[6]

In sum, this chapter has three main objectives, which are developed from data for ten Latin American countries.[7] The first is to document the current episode of capital inflows to Latin America. The second is to assess the role of external factors in accounting for the observed capital inflows and the real exchange rate appreciation. The third is to elaborate on the implications of capital inflows for economic policy. In this paper, the first section deals with basic concepts about capital flows and the relationship between capital inflows, the accumulation of reserves, and the gap between national saving and investment. The stylized facts about capital inflows to the region are documented in the second section. A third section provides a quantitative assessment of the role of external factors on the accumulation of reserves and on real exchange rate appreciation in the ten countries considered. The implications of capital inflows for domestic economic policy are discussed in a concluding section.

I   Accounting of Capital Flows

International capital flows are recorded in the nonreserve capital account of the balance of payments (BOP). This account includes all international transactions involving assets other than official reserves, such as transactions in money, stocks, government bonds, land, and factories. When a national agent sells an asset to someone abroad, the transaction enters the agent's country's balance of payments as a credit on the capital account and is regarded as a capital inflow. Accordingly, net borrowing abroad by domestic agents or a purchase of domestic stocks by foreigners are considered capital inflows, representing debt and equity finance respectively.

The simple rules of double-entry accounting ensure that, excluding statistical discrepancies, the capital account surplus, or net capital inflow (denoted by KA), is related to the current account surplus (denoted by CA) and to the official reserves account (denoted by RA) of the BOP through the identity:[8]

$$CA + KA + RA \equiv 0.$$

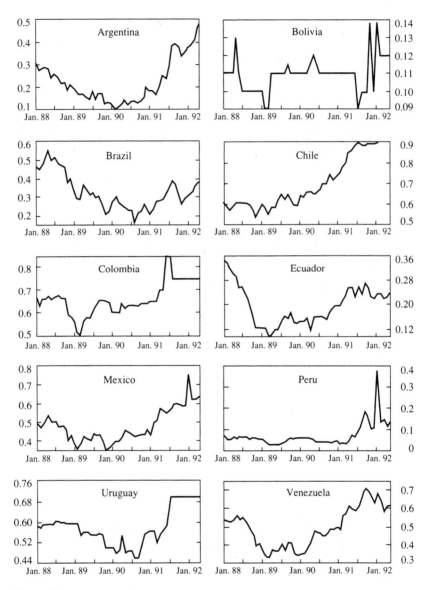

Figure 1.1
Secondary-market prices for loans, January 1988–1992 (In percent of face value). Source:
Salomon Brothers, *LDC Debt Report* (various issues).

A property of the current account is that it measures the change in an economy's net foreign wealth. A country that runs a current account deficit must finance this deficit either by a private capital inflow or by a reduction in its official reserves. In both cases, the country runs down its net foreign wealth. Another characteristic of the current account is that national income accounting implies that its surplus equals the difference between national savings and national investment ($CA \equiv S - I$). Accordingly, an increase in the current account deficit can be traced to either an increase in national investment, a decline in national savings, or any combination of these variables that results in an increased investment-savings gap. Finally, the official reserves account records purchases and sales of official reserve assets by central banks. Thus, the account measures the extent of official foreign exchange intervention by the authorities and is often referred to as the official settlements balance or the overall balance of payments.

The foregoing discussion indicates two polar cases of how a central bank might respond to increased capital inflows. If a central bank chooses not to intervene in response to a capital inflow, the increased net exports of assets in the capital account finances an increase in net imports of goods and services in the current account—capital inflows would *not* be associated with changes in the central bank's holdings of official reserves. At the other extreme, if the domestic authorities actively intervene and purchase the foreign exchange brought in by the capital inflow, the increase in *KA* is perfectly matched by an increase in official reserves. In this case, the gap between national savings and national investment does not change, nor does the net foreign wealth of the economy. The capital inflow would be perfectly correlated with changes in reserves.

In reality, foreign exchange market intervention does not occur on a scale that would produce a one-to-one relationship between *RA* and *KA*. The observed increase in capital inflows to Latin America has been partly matched by an increase in the region's current account deficit and partly by an increase in the central banks' official reserves.

II   Stylized Facts

In this section, we quantify some key aspects of the current episode of capital flows to Latin America and related underlying macroeconomic developments.[9] To document the regional aspects of this phenomenon, we aggregate annual data and focus on Latin America as a whole.[10]

Monthly data for individual countries are used to provide greater detail. We also elaborate on the role of external developments, especially those in the United States.

Anatomy of Capital Inflows

Table 1.1 presents a breakdown of Latin America's balance of payments into three main accounts. The capital inflows appear as surpluses in the capital account: about $24 billion in 1990 and about $40 billion in 1991. A substantial fraction of the flows has been channelled to reserves, which increased by about $33 billion in 1990–91. About 63 percent of the inflow in 1990 was matched by an increase in official reserves, leaving the rest of the inflow to finance the deficit in the current account. Yet, the latter increased markedly in 1991, accounting for 59 percent of the capital inflow. Considering the 1990–91 period as a whole, the net capital inflow was divided equally between a widening current account deficit and higher official reserves. The former suggests that capital inflows have been associated with an increase in the gap between national investment and national savings. In countries like Chile and Mexico, an important part of the inflows has financed increases in private investment; yet, in countries like Argentina and Brazil, there has been a marked rise in private consumption.[11] The increase in official reserves, in turn, indicates that the various monetary authorities met the capital inflow with a heavy degree of foreign exchange market intervention.

Part of the increased capital inflows represents repatriation of previous flight capital, but Latin America is also attracting new investors.[12] As table 1.2 reports, an increase in net external borrowing accounts for about 70 percent of the capital inflow in 1990–91. The increase is primarily due to borrowing by the private sector from foreign private banks.[13] Increased external borrowing reflects the restoration of access to voluntary capital market financing after the debt crisis.[14] Portfolio investment and foreign direct investment also increased. The latter amounted to about $12 billion, $4 billion of which resulted from privatizations.[15]

Since there has been a substantial degree of central bank intervention in the face of capital inflows, there is an important degree of comovement between official reserves and capital inflows. In fact, if one is interested in monthly developments, for which direct data on capital inflows are not available, changes in reserves are a reasonable proxy

Table 1.1
Latin America: Balance of Payments, 1973–91

Year	Balance on goods, services, and private transfers[a]		Balance on capital account[a]		Balance on capital account plus net errors and omissions[a]		Overall balance[b]	
	Billions of dollars (1)	Percent of GDP (2)	Billions of dollars (3)	Percent of GDP (4)	Billions of dollars (5)	Percent of GDP (6)	Billions of dollars (7)	Percent of GDP (8)
1973	−4.7	−2.4	—	—	8.5	4.4	3.8	2.0
1974	−13.5	−5.3	—	—	13.3	5.2	−0.2	−0.1
1975	−16.3	−6.1	—	—	14.7	5.5	−1.6	−0.6
1976	−11.8	−3.8	—	—	16.9	5.4	5.1	1.6
1977	−11.6	−2.7	19.8	4.6	16.4	3.8	4.8	1.1
1978	−19.4	−4.0	30.5	6.2	27.4	5.6	8.0	1.6
1979	−21.7	−3.8	35.0	6.2	32.9	5.8	11.2	2.0
1980	−30.3	−4.3	47.0	6.7	34.0	4.9	3.7	0.5
1981	−43.5	−5.5	59.4	7.4	41.9	5.3	−1.6	−0.2
1982	−42.2	−5.5	45.1	5.9	23.0	3.0	−19.2	−2.5
1983	−11.6	−1.7	22.4	3.2	13.6	1.9	2.0	0.3
1984	−3.2	−0.5	15.5	2.3	12.5	1.8	9.3	1.4
1985	−4.4	−0.6	6.7	0.9	5.5	0.8	1.1	0.2
1986	−18.9	−2.6	14.2	1.9	12.3	1.7	−6.6	−1.0
1987	−12.0	−1.6	14.5	1.9	15.3	2.0	3.3	0.4
1988	−12.4	−1.5	8.2	1.0	4.7	0.6	−7.7	−0.9
1989	−10.0	−1.1	15.7	1.7	12.1	1.3	2.1	0.2
1990	−8.8	−0.8	24.1	2.3	23.9	2.3	15.1	1.4
1991	−22.3	−2.1	38.1	3.8	39.8	3.9	17.5	1.7

Source: IMF, *World Economic Outlook* (various issues).
a. A minus sign indicates a deficit in the pertinent account. Balance on goods, services, and private transfers is equal to the current account balance less official transfers. The latter are treated in this table as external financing and are included in the capital account.
b. Column (7) equals the sum of columns (1) and (5). A positive entry in column (7) indicates the accumulation of international reserves by the monetary authorities.

Table 1.2
Latin America: Items in the Capital Account, 1973–91
(In billions of U.S. dollars)

Year	Net external borrowing	Non-debt-creating flows	Asset transactions (net)[a]	Errors and omissions[a]	Total
1973	6.0	2.5	—	—	8.5
1974	11.1	2.2	—	—	13.3
1975	11.4	3.3	—	—	14.7
1976	14.2	2.7	—	—	16.9
1977	19.4	2.8	−2.5	−3.4	16.4
1978	28.0	4.9	−2.5	−3.1	27.4
1979	30.2	7.2	−2.4	−2.1	32.9
1980	43.1	6.8	−3.0	−13.0	34.0
1981	61.0	8.2	−8.9	−17.5	41.9
1982	45.7	7.2	−7.7	−22.1	23.0
1983	18.7	4.6	−0.9	−8.8	13.6
1984	14.1	4.5	−3.1	−3.0	12.5
1985	6.2	6.1	−5.4	−1.4	5.5
1986	11.3	4.3	−1.3	−1.9	12.3
1987	10.0	6.0	−1.2	0.5	15.3
1988	3.8	8.8	−4.3	−3.5	4.7
1989	10.9	6.9	−2.1	−3.6	12.1
1990	28.0	8.6	−12.5	−0.2	23.9
1991	17.3	14.1	6.7	1.7	39.8

Source: Data for western hemisphere from IMF's *World Economic Outlook* (various issues).
a. These two categories are included in net external borrowing and non-debt-creating flows for the 1973–76 period.

for these inflows. Figure 1.2, which depicts monthly data on official international reserves for the countries in our sample, shows a pronounced upward trend in the stock of official reserves starting from about the first half of 1990. In 1991, the year with the highest capital inflows to the region, the accumulation of reserves accelerated as the monetary authorities reacted to the inflows by actively increasing their purchases of foreign assets constituting international reserves.[16]

Real Exchange Rate Appreciation

Figure 1.3 provides evidence on the behavior of real effective exchange rates.[17] At least two regularities emerge from the figure. First, with the exception of Brazil, all countries have been experiencing a real

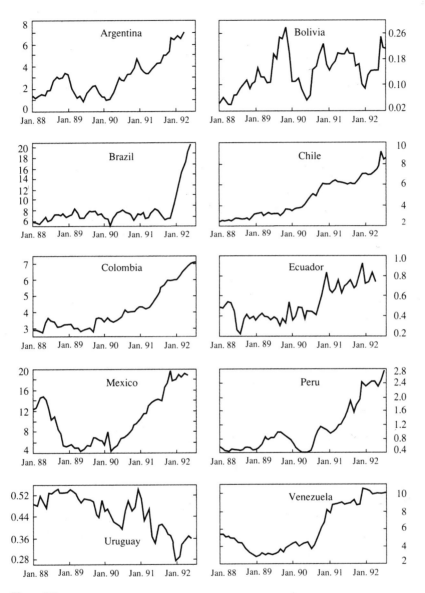

Figure 1.2
Total reserves minus gold, January 1988–July 1992 (Billions of U.S. dollars). Source: IMF, *International Financial Statistics* (various issues).

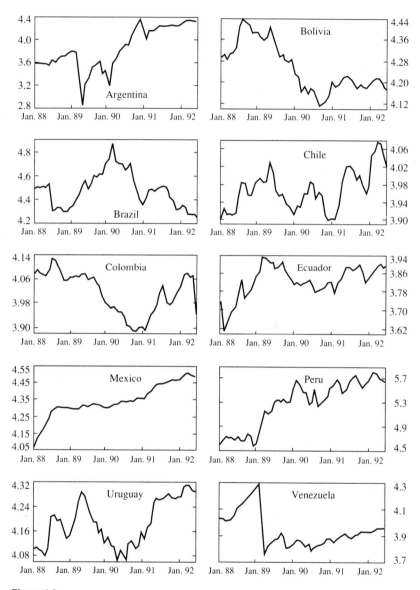

Figure 1.3
Real effective exchange rates, January 1988–July 1992. Source: IMF, Information Notice System (database). Note: An increase in the index denotes real exchange rate appreciation.

exchange rate appreciation since January 1991. In half of the cases, the appreciation began before January 1991. Second, even within a small sample of monthly observations, considerable evidence points to the cyclical behavior of real exchange rates. Leading examples of this phenomenon are Brazil, Chile, and Uruguay. Although some of these cycles can be attributed to fluctuations in capital inflows, they are also the result of other shocks, such as changes in the terms of trade and in domestic monetary, fiscal, and exchange rate policies. Combining the evidence from figures 1.2 and 1.3 indicates an important degree of co-movement in these variables across countries, despite their wide differences in policies and institutions.

Rates of Return Differentials

Expected rates of return on available assets play a key role in investors' decisions about whether or not to move capital internationally. Since data for expected returns are not readily available, and depend on how one models expectations, we first look at actual returns. As shown in figure 1.4, there was a large increase in the U.S. dollar stock prices on major Latin American markets in 1991.[18] Argentina's market exhibits the biggest single annual return of almost 400 percent, while Chile's and Mexico's register returns of about 100 percent each.[19] The marked increases in stock market prices have resulted in similar rises in the prices of country and regional market funds traded in the United States and elsewhere. According to the investment bank Salomon Brothers, $850 billion of foreign investment entered Brazil's stock market in the last four months of 1991 and about $600 million entered the Argentine market in 1991.[20] However, as the numbers indicate and figure 1.4 confirms, the stock market booms and the attendant high returns materialized *after* capital had begun to flow into the region. It would thus be difficult to argue that high differentials on stock market returns were responsible for attracting the first wave of capital.

Figure 1.5 provides evidence on the lending and deposit interest rate spreads between U.S.-dollar-equivalent domestic interest rates in Latin American countries and interest rates in the United States. Since in some countries interest rates are regulated, and since capital mobility is imperfect, spreads across the various countries cannot be compared in a straightforward manner. In addition, as figure 1.5 highlights, the variability in domestic interest rates differs markedly across countries; as such, the scales in the figure vary from country to country, with

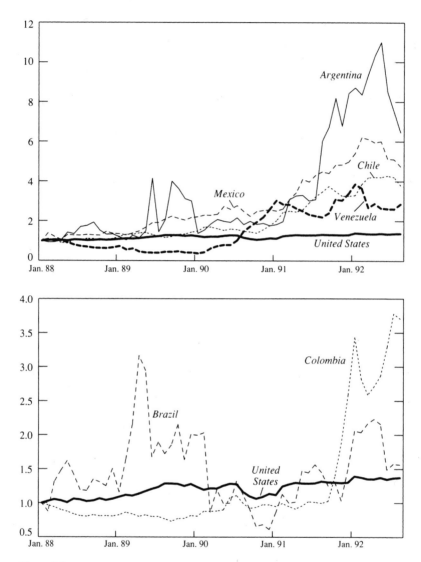

Figure 1.4
Stock market performance, January 1988–August 1992 (Stock price indices in U.S. dollars, January 1988 = 100). Sources: Standard & Poor's (S&P) *Analyst Handbook* and International Finance Corporation, *Quarterly Review of Emerging Stock Markets*. Note: The S&P 500 index was used for the United States.

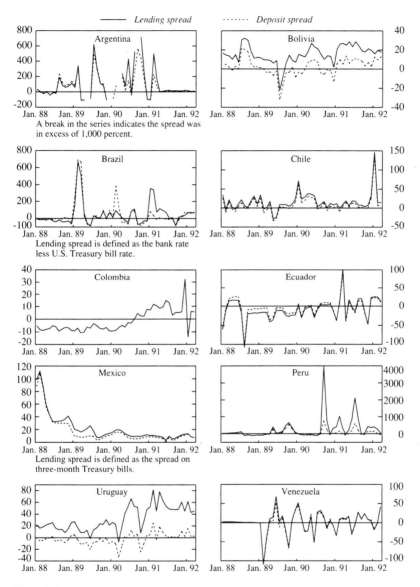

Figure 1.5
Interest rate spreads, January 1988–March 1992 (Dollar equivalent of domestic rate less U.S. rate, annual percentages rates). Sources: IMF, *International Financial Statistics,* and various central bank bulletins. Notes: Deposit spreads are based on interest rates on certificates of deposit; lending spreads are based on loan rates charged by banks less the interest rate on U.S. commercial paper.

Argentina and Peru having the broadest ranges and Bolivia and Colombia the narrowest. With these caveats in mind, the dominant impression from figure 1.5 is that of relatively high interest rate differentials in Latin America in the 1990–91 period. It is also evident from the figure that the pattern of spreads varies considerably across countries, an unsurprising result since the monetary authorities in these countries have not reacted uniformly to the capital inflows and since the timing of regulatory changes has also varied considerably across the sample countries. Although the relatively high differential rate of return on Latin American assets has been associated with a marked rise in capital inflows to the region, the inflows have not arbitraged away the large differentials. In some countries, such as Argentina, the interest rate differential decreased sharply as capital poured in; in others, such as Chile, interest rate differentials displayed a less pronounced response to the inflows (see figure 1.5). As argued later in this chapter, these different patterns may reflect cross-country differences in the authorities' use of sterilized versus nonsterilized intervention.

In sum, three main stylized facts emerge with regard to interest rate differentials. First, there is little co-movement in domestic interest rates, and hence in spreads, across the countries in our sample. Second, the "noise-to-signal ratio" of the domestic dollar rates varies substantially across countries. As figure 1.6 illustrates, countries offering the highest returns also had the greatest volatility of returns.[21] Third, despite sizable capital inflows, the positive differentials have not been fully arbitraged away. The persistence and size of this wedge between domestic and foreign rates also appear to vary markedly across countries.

Other Macroeconomic Developments

Selected macroeconomic indicators are reported in table 1.3. Consider how developments in 1991, the year when capital inflows grew to about $40 billion, differ from those in earlier years. First, economic growth revived. After three years of stagnation, real GDP increased by almost 3 percent in 1991. However, gross capital formation as a percent of GDP remained at about the same level as in the second half of the 1980s, suggesting a more efficient utilization of resources. At the same time, the rate of inflation dropped markedly (though it nevertheless remained at a three-digit level for the region), and central government fiscal deficits came down significantly.

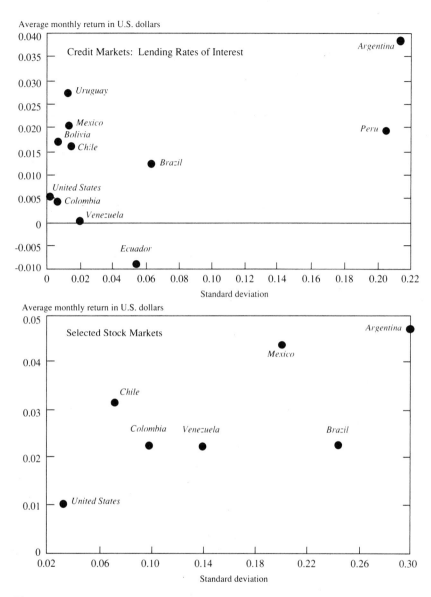

Figure 1.6
Risk and returns. Sources: IMF, *International Financial Statistics;* various central bank bulletins; International Finance Corporation, *Quarterly Review of Emerging Stock Markets;* and Standard & Poor's *Analyst Handbook.*

Table 1.3
Latin America: Macroeconomic Indicators, 1973–91

Year	Growth of real GDP (percent change)	Gross capital formation[a] (percent of GDP)	Consumption[a] (percent of GDP)	Inflation (percent)	Central govt. fiscal balance (percent of GDP)	Commodity prices (percent change)	Terms of trade (percent change)	External debt (billions of dollars)	External debt to exports (ratio)	Debt service (ratio)	Reserves (billions of dollars)	Reserves to imports (ratio)
1973	8.4	29.3	74.5	32.1	—	47.4	6.5	44.4	176.2	29.3	12.0	35.1
1974	6.9	24.4	75.8	37.5	—	20.9	-7.0	58.2	163.4	27.9	11.9	21.7
1975	3.1	24.7	77.7	52.0	—	-12.5	-7.5	68.6	195.8	32.2	10.0	17.5
1976	5.5	23.5	79.6	66.1	—	23.0	12.2	82.0	204.1	31.4	15.2	25.8
1977	5.3	25.1	79.0	49.9	-2.2	27.9	8.0	124.6	192.6	28.2	28.5	28.5
1978	4.1	24.8	78.6	41.9	-2.0	-12.6	-9.4	154.9	215.7	37.1	35.5	35.5
1979	6.1	23.2	79.6	46.5	-0.7	14.0	5.0	187.2	196.8	38.8	42.7	42.7
1980	5.3	23.7	79.7	53.7	-0.6	11.8	7.9	229.4	181.8	33.0	40.3	40.3
1981	1.0	23.0	79.7	58.2	-3.0	-15.3	-5.2	285.6	207.7	40.6	39.6	39.6
1982	-0.9	20.9	80.1	64.6	-4.0	-11.0	-5.0	325.5	264.7	50.4	28.1	28.1
1983	-3.2	17.9	81.2	98.6	-3.7	0.8	-2.7	340.2	288.0	40.7	29.3	29.3
1984	3.6	17.2	79.0	124.2	-4.1	-0.8	4.2	360.3	275.1	40.5	40.5	30.2
1985	3.4	18.4	76.2	128.2	-4.0	-8.3	-5.4	368.2	293.7	42.1	41.2	31.7
1986	4.3	18.2	78.9	79.4	-5.2	5.5	-10.2	381.9	347.9	46.1	33.3	25.6
1987	2.2	19.9	75.1	117.8	-7.0	-0.8	-5.4	419.1	341.4	38.5	38.0	27.7
1988	0.4	20.9	72.7	243.2	-5.8	21.2	-0.6	409.3	294.7	42.7	30.8	20.0
1989	1.0	19.6	72.6	434.2	-6.3	-2.3	0.2	408.9	262.2	30.2	33.0	19.4
1990	-0.1	19.6	77.0	647.8	-0.3	-7.2	-0.1	422.1	251.6	26.9	47.8	26.3
1991	2.9	20.7	—	162.5	-1.0	-5.6	-4.9	440.7	264.8	32.8	65.3	33.5

Sources: Data for western hemisphere from IMF's *World Economic Outlook* and *International Financial Statistics* (various issues).
a. This column includes private and government consumption.

The changing economic conditions in Latin America are also reflected in the region's debt and solvency indicators. At $441 billion, the region's external debt amounts to 2.6 times its exports of goods and services. Although still high, this ratio has decreased markedly from the 3.5 figure in 1986. Since most of Latin America's external debt to commercial banks is still in terms of floating rates, the drop in short-term U.S. interest rates and the drop in the debt-to-export ratio have translated into a rapid decline in the external debt service ratio over the past two years. In fact, the level of the debt service ratio in 1991 (32.8 percent) is about the same as the levels that were observed before the capital inflow episode of the late 1970s.

These developments represent only part of the changing environment in Latin America in the early 1990s. In addition, the move toward privatization and deregulation, the introduction of financial reforms, and the restructuring of existing external debt have all contributed to returning Latin America to the list of viable investment locations in world financial markets.

External Factors

It is difficult to point to a single dominant external factor that would account for the recent capital inflows to Latin America, as several external developments have converged to stimulate such flows. First, there has been the sharp drop in U.S. short-term interest rates to about half their level two years ago, their lowest levels since the early 1960s. By reducing the external debt service on floating-rate obligations, this decline in U.S. interest rates has improved the solvency of Latin American debtors. For a given level of interest rates in Latin America, these developments provide incentives for the repatriation of capital held in the United States and for increases in borrowing by Latin American agents from capital markets in the United States. Beyond short-term interest rates, returns from other investments in the United States have decreased as well, such as in the real estate market.[22]

Second, several external factors probably contributed to the increase in Latin America's current account deficit and to the need to finance this deficit by increased capital inflows. Two such factors are the continuing recession in the United States and in other industrialized countries and the continued decline in Latin America's terms of trade throughout the past decade—which mainly reflects a decrease in the prices of petroleum and other commodities. In principle, a decline in a country's terms of trade can be expected to result in a larger current account deficit (the Harberger-Laursen-Metzler effect) and, in the absence of major intervention by the national authorities, in a larger capital inflow to finance this deficit. However, the changes in the terms of trade in 1990–91 are too small to account for the sharp increase in capital inflows: Latin America's terms of trade only decreased by 1.2 percent in 1990 and by 5.2 percent in 1991. This pattern contrasts with earlier episodes in which terms of trade changes were probably the main shocks explaining fluctuations in the capital account; Diaz Alejandro (1983) documents that between 1928/29 and 1932/33, there was an average decline of about 48 percent in the terms of trade of five Latin American countries.[23] In short, autonomous shocks to international capital flows seem to play a larger role than terms of trade shocks in accounting for the most recent capital inflows.

Third, during both of the most recent episodes of capital inflows to Latin America—1978–82 and 1990–91—there were sharp swings in the private capital account of the U.S. balance of payments in the form of increased outflows and reduced inflows (table 1.4). In fact, the years 1990 and, even more so, 1991 register the first net capital outflows from the United States after eight consecutive years of net inflows![24] That this change is associated with changes in the capital account of Latin America is clear from table 1.5, where it is shown that about 60 percent of the increased capital inflows in 1991 are directly associated with increased private capital outflows from the United States to Latin America, as recorded in the U.S. BOP accounts. Similarly, the relatively large capital inflow of 1978–81 to Latin America was matched by increased private capital outflows from the United States, and the U.S. capital inflow episode of 1983–89 was matched by increased capital outflows from Latin America.[25] In other words, the data appear to support the notion that swings in private capital outflows from the United States play a key role as external impulses affecting the size of capital inflows into Latin America.

A fourth external factor was the important regulatory changes to occur in the capital markets of industrial countries in 1990, changes that reduced the transactions costs for agents accessing international capital markets from Latin America and other developing countries.[26] Perhaps, the most salient changes were the approval of "Regulation S" and "Rule 144A" in the United States, which reduced transaction and liquidity costs faced by developing countries in approaching capital markets there.

Table 1.4
United States: Balance of Payments, 1973–91
(In billions of U.S. dollars)

Year	Current account	Capital account	Capital account plus net errors and omissions	Overall balance
1973	7.07	−9.71	−12.30	−5.23
1974	1.94	−9.25	−10.75	−8.81
1975	18.06	−28.67	−22.71	−4.65
1976	4.18	−25.24	−14.68	−10.50
1977	−14.49	−18.46	−20.55	−35.04
1978	−15.40	−30.63	−18.08	−33.48
1979	0.20	−14.53	9.75	9.95
1980	1.20	−35.91	−10.26	−9.06
1981	7.26	−28.07	−8.50	−1.24
1982	−5.86	28.79	7.89	2.03
1983	−40.18	24.72	36.13	−4.05
1984	−98.99	72.52	99.71	0.75
1985	−122.25	108.18	128.05	5.80
1986	−145.42	95.78	111.64	−33.78
1987	−162.22	98.68	105.36	−56.86
1988	−128.99	101.05	92.72	−36.27
1989	−106.41	104.91	123.34	16.93
1990	−92.16	−4.60	58.90	−33.26
1991	−8.66	−18.20	−21.30	−29.96

Sources: IMF, *International Financial Statistics* and U.S. Department of Commerce, *Survey of Current Business* (various issues).

Table 1.5
Changes in Capital Accounts
(In billions of U.S. dollars)

Periods compared	Private capital account of western hemisphere (1)	Private capital account of United States with western hemisphere (2)
1978–81 against 1976–77	17.4	−9.9
1983–89 against 1978–81	−24.4	30.1
1991 against 1983–89	30.1	−17.5

Note: Positive entries in column (1) indicate an increase in net private capital flowing into the western hemisphere. A negative entry in column (2) indicates an increase in the net private capital outflow from the United States to the western hemisphere.

III   Role of External Factors: Econometric Analysis

In this section, monthly data for ten Latin American countries covering the period January 1988 to December 1991 are used to analyze key features of the recent capital inflows. The analysis begins by establishing the extent of co-movement of official reserves and real exchange rates among these countries since they proxy for capital flows. We then develop and estimate a model designed to assess the relative importance of external shocks in the reserves accumulation and real exchange rate appreciation.

Co-Movement of Reserves and the Real Exchange Rate

Given the lack of monthly data (and, for a number of countries in the sample, quarterly data) on capital inflows, we examine the joint behavior of international reserves and the real exchange rate, two variables that have been closely associated with the recent inflows. The previous section revealed an important degree of co-movement in reserves and real exchange rates across countries, which could be interpreted as reflecting the effects of a common external shock to Latin American countries (figures 1.2 and 1.3). Accordingly, a first task in this section is to examine this issue quantitatively by using principal components analysis. Principal components analysis can describe the co-movement in data series.[27] We begin with ten time series, recording reserves for each country, and then construct a smaller set of series, the principal components, to explain as much of the variance of the original series as possible.[28] The higher the degree of co-movement existing among the original ten series, the fewer is the number of principal components needed to explain a large portion of the variance of the original series. If the ten series are identical (perfectly collinear), the first principal component will explain 100 percent of the variation of the original series. Alternatively, if all ten series are perfectly uncorrelated, it will take ten principal components to explain all of the variance in the original series; no advantage would be gained by looking at common factors, since none exists.

The procedure begins by standardizing the variables, so that each series has a zero mean and a unit standard deviation. This standardization ensures that all series receive uniform treatment and that the construction of the principal components indices is not influenced disproportionately by the series exhibiting the largest variation.

Table 1.6
Establishing the Co-Movement in Macroeconomic Series

	1988:1 to 1991:12	1988:1 to 1989:12	1990:1 to 1991:12
Real exchange rate			
Cumulative R^2 for:			
First principal component	0.44	0.41	0.58
Second principal component	0.73	0.78	0.79
χ^2 (45 df)	...	302.01	286.31
Probability value	...	(0.00)	(0.00)
Reserves			
Cumulative R^2 for:			
First principal component	0.61	0.48	0.67
Second principal component	0.77	0.69	0.80
χ^2 (45 df)	...	204.97	297.23
Probability value	...	(0.00)	(0.00)
Domestic inflation rate (12-month percent change)			
Cumulative R^2 for:			
First principal component	0.37	0.60	0.45
Second principal component	0.57	0.88	0.64
χ^2 (45 df)	...	475.94	306.40
Probability value	...	(0.00)	(0.00)

Note: The cumulative R^2 gives the percentage of the variance of the original series explained by the indicated principal components.

We construct the principal components indices for the period from January 1988 to December 1991. In addition, for comparative purposes, two subperiods are considered: 1988–89 and the capital inflow episode of 1990–91. As figure 1.2 has shown and table 1.6 confirms, the extent of co-movement in reserves during the capital inflow period of 1990–91 is considerable, higher than in the preceding two years. The first principal component explains 67 percent of the variation in reserves, and the second principal component explains an additional 13 percent of the variation. Accordingly, 80 percent of the variance in the ten reserves series is captured by two indices indicating a sizable degree of co-movement. More formally, we tested the null hypothesis that the ten reserves series are linearly independent and found that this hypothesis could be rejected at standard significance levels.[29]

Applying the same procedure to ten data series describing the real exchange rate indicates that the degree of co-movement across countries in the region has also increased in the recent capital inflow episode. The fraction of real exchange rate variance explained by the first principal component during 1990–91, 58 percent, is substantial, although somewhat lower than for reserves. The first two principal components explain a sizable 79 percent of the variance of the real effective exchange rate. A number of factors, such as cross-country differences in exchange rate regimes and in the degrees of wage and price flexibility, are likely to account for the lower degree of co-movement observed in the real exchange rate when compared with reserves.

As for the increased covariation of reserves and the real exchange rate in the recent period, it may well reflect the effects of an external shock common to the region in the past two years. Interestingly, when we examined the principal components of the domestic inflation rate, a variable less obviously linked to external factors, we found that the extent of covariation among the inflation rates of these ten countries had diminished rather than increased in the recent period.[30]

The correlations between the first principal component of reserves and the individual country reserves series tend to confirm the evidence in figure 1.2. The regional index does quite well in accounting for reserve fluctuations in eight of the ten countries. For the real exchange rate, the results are anticipated in figure 1.3.[31]

The first principal components (plotted in figure 1.7) could be interpreted as regional exchange rate and reserves indices. Purged of country-specific idiosyncracies, they could reflect the influence of unobservable external factors common to the region as well as any coordinated internal developments in the region. To explore the possible role of external factors, table 1.7 shows the correlation between the first principal components for the reserves series and the real exchange rate series and a set of variables from the United States. The latter includes the nominal rates of return on real estate, stock and bond markets, short-term deposit and lending rates of interest, and detrended real disposable income.

As discussed earlier, it seems plausible to hypothesize that a fall in U.S. interest rates, stock market returns, real estate returns, and economic activity would be associated with an increase in the flow of capital to Latin America, which would at least be partly reflected in an increase in the regional indices for reserves and the real exchange rate (the latter indicating a real exchange rate appreciation). Indeed, most of the evidence on simple pairwise correlation coefficients is in this direction (table 1.7). Notice that the correlations of the U.S. variables

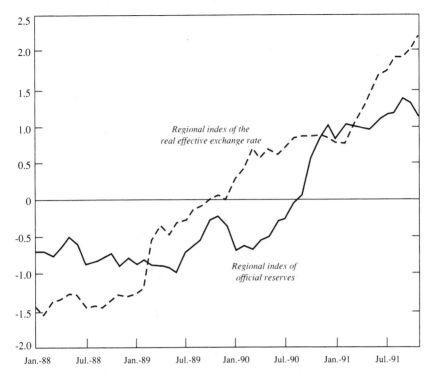

Figure 1.7
First principal components, January 1988–December 1991. Notes: An increase in the real effective exchange rate index denotes an appreciation. Principal components indices are constructed to have a zero mean and unit variance.

with the real exchange rate index are lower than those of the reserves index, although they are still substantial.

Having assessed the degree of cross-country co-movement in reserves and the real exchange rate, we next examine the dynamic interaction between these two variables in each country. Combining figures 1.2 and 1.3 indicates a pattern of co-movement in which the increase in reserves precedes the real appreciation in the exchange rate.[32] This temporal pattern differs from what would have emerged had there been a shock to the external terms of trade, or to the real exchange rate, followed by accommodating reserve accumulation. In order to investigate this issue more formally, we performed Granger causality tests for each of the ten countries using monthly data from January 1988 to November 1991.[33] On balance, the results characterize the recent episode as one in which the reserve accumulation preceded the real exchange rate appreciation.[34]

Table 1.7
Contemporaneous Correlations of the Regional Variables with Selected U.S. Indicators, 1988–91

U.S. variables	First principal component of reserves	First principal component of the real exchange rate
Treasury bill rate	−0.922	−0.603
Certificate of deposit	−0.928	−0.694
Commercial paper	−0.926	−0.691
Treasury long bond	−0.696	−0.668
One-month capital gain in S&P 500	0.001	−0.107
12-month capital gain in S&P 500	−0.086	0.136
One-month capital gain in real estate[a]	−0.095	−0.041
12-month capital gain in real estate[a]	−0.445	−0.707
Deviations from trend in real disposable income	−0.939	−0.730

Sources: IMF, *International Financial Statistics,* and data from Data Resources Incorporated.
a. Measured using prices of existing homes.

Quantifying the Role of External Factors

In this section, the analysis proceeds in two stages. First, we construct indices of the unobserved external factors (or impulses), which are then incorporated into a structural vector autoregression (VAR). Second, we perform tests of exclusion restrictions on the foreign factors to determine their statistical significance, and we compute variance decompositions to quantify their relative importance in accounting for forecast error variance of reserves and real exchange rates. Impulse response functions show how reserves and real exchange rates react to an external shock.

In modeling the external impulses, one could consider a whole vector of variables that could affect Latin American economies. Here we opt for an unobserved index model, where the constructed index is correlated with the observed time series for the United States, which appear in table 1.7. Specifically, we construct and use the first and second principal components of these series. Figure 1.8 illustrates how closely the first principal component captures the joint movement of the various interest rates and economic activity in the United States. The second principal component captures swings in returns on the equity and real estate markets. Having a measure of external impulses,

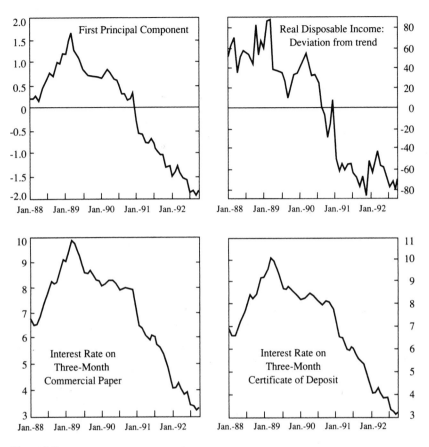

Figure 1.8
External variables, January 1988–October 1992. Sources: Board of Governors of the Federal Reserve System, U.S. Department of Commerce, and the authors. Note: Principal components indices are constructed to have a zero mean and unit variance.

we then embed them in a structural VAR. Defining $PC1_t$ and $PC2_t$ as the first and second principal components of the U.S. variables and denoting the logs of reserves and the real exchange rate by RES_t and REX_t, respectively, the reduced form of the system is given by

$$PC1_t = \alpha_1 + \gamma_1 t + \sum_{i=1}^{n} \beta_{1i} PC1_{t-i} + \sum_{i=1}^{n} \beta'_{1i} PC2_{t-i} + u_t^{PC1},$$

$$PC2_t = \alpha_2 + \gamma_2 t + \sum_{i=1}^{n} \beta_{2i} PC1_{t-i} + \sum_{i=1}^{n} \beta'_{2i} PC2_{t-i} + u_t^{PC2},$$

$$RES_t = \alpha_3 + \gamma_3 t + \sum_{i=1}^{n} \beta_{3i} PC1_{t-i} + \sum_{i=1}^{n} \beta'_{3i} PC2_{t-i} + \sum_{i=1}^{n} \delta_{3i} RES_{t-i}$$

$$+ \sum_{i=1}^{n} \delta'_{3i} REX_{t-i} + u_t^{RES},$$

$$REX_t = \alpha_4 + \gamma_4 t + \sum_{i=1}^{n} \beta_{4i} PC1_{t-i} + \sum_{i=1}^{n} \beta'_{4i} PC2_{t-i} + \sum_{i=1}^{n} \delta_{4i} RES_{t-i}$$

$$+ \sum_{i=1}^{n} \delta'_{4i} REX_{t-i} + u_t^{REX}. \tag{1}$$

As equation (1) illustrates, we allow for dynamic interaction between the foreign factors but impose temporal exogeneity on them by not including lagged values of the endogenous variables (reserves and the real exchange rate) in their respective equations ($\delta_{1i} = \delta_{2i} = \delta'_{1i} = \delta'_{2i} = 0$). Hence, we impose structure on the temporal relationships between these variables.[35] Each equation in the system includes a constant and a time trend. Since the number of lags included in the right hand side of each equation could affect the tests, and given that we had no strong priors on this issue, we used the Akaike and Schwarz criteria to select among one-, three-, six-, nine-, and 12-month lag profiles.[36] These criteria, unless otherwise noted, yielded three lags as optimal.

The reduced-form residuals, the u_t, depend on the structural errors, denoted e_t, and the contemporaneous relationships among the endogenous variables, specifically $u_t = e_t \mathbf{A}$. So next, we consider the structure of the matrix $\mathbf{A}$, which describes the contemporaneous relationships among the variables. In the general case, a causal ordering amounts to assuming that the endogenous variables enter the system in a triangular form, with the first equation containing one endogenous variable, the second two variables, and so on, giving a specific form to the $\mathbf{A}$ matrix. Instead, we follow the methodology of Bernanke (1986) and Blanchard (1989): *a priori* (structural) restrictions are imposed on the identifying matrix. Specifically, since the foreign factors are presumed exogenous, we do not allow for feedback from the shocks to the domestic variables to the reduced-form error of the first and second principal components of the foreign variables. In addition, we impose the restriction that the principal components indices are orthogonal by construction, so that they depend on their own shocks, as in equations (2) and (3),

$$PC1_t = e_t^{PC1}, \tag{2}$$

$$PC2_t = e_t^{PC2}, \tag{3}$$

while reserves are affected by the structural shocks to the foreign variables and by a shock to reserves themselves,

$$RES_t = a_{31}PC1_t + a_{32}PC2_t + e_t^{RES}, \tag{4}$$

$$REX_t = a_{41}PC1_t + a_{42}PC2_t + a_{43}RES_t + e_t^{REX}. \tag{5}$$

The real exchange rate is allowed to respond to all of the shocks.[37]

After the system is estimated using monthly data from January 1988 to November 1991, we test for the significance of the foreign factors. Table 1.8 summarizes the results of the tests for exclusion restrictions, tests that involve the temporal relationships. The null hypothesis being

Table 1.8
Tests for the Significance of Foreign Factors, 1988–91

Country	Test for exclusion restrictions Chi-squared statistic	Contemporaneous relationships a_{31}	a_{32}	a_{41}	a_{42}
Argentina	14.981	0.091	−0.451	−0.225	−0.140
	(0.242)	(0.243)	...	(0.405)	...
Bolivia	16.167	−0.092	−0.533	−0.011	−0.041
	(0.184)	(0.170)	(0.045)	(0.030)	...
Brazil	23.224	−0.045	0.481	0.043	0.323
	(0.026)	(0.011)	...	(0.327)	...
Chile	29.527	−0.031	−0.246	−0.018	0.545
	(0.003)	(0.041)	(0.026)	(0.152)	...
Colombia[a]	31.548	−0.014	−0.048	0.009	0.024
	(0.002)	(0.157)	...	(0.176)	...
Ecuador	17.285	−0.230	0.668	−0.070	1.359
	(0.139)	(0.139)	(0.082)	(0.376)	...
Mexico	23.203	−0.136	−0.324	−0.056	−0.063
	(0.026)	(0.216)	...	...	(0.627)
Peru	25.058	0.121	0.150	0.022	0.203
	(0.015)	(0.061)	(0.017)	(0.128)	...
Uruguay	11.275	−0.042	0.197	−0.050	0.076
	(0.505)	(0.042)	(0.012)	(0.153)	...
Venezuela	9.342	−0.045	−0.280	0.003	0.743
	(0.673)	(0.266)	...	(0.054)	...

a. According to the Akaike and Schwarz criteria, the optimal lag length was six months.

tested is that the foreign variables do not affect reserves and the real exchange rate. The high χ^2 statistics and low probability values indicate that in eight of the ten countries, one can reject the null hypothesis at a 75 percent level of confidence or higher.[38] Only in half of the sample countries is there any evidence of a significant contemporaneous relationship between the foreign factors and reserves or the real exchange rate.

Although table 1.8 provides evidence on only the statistical significance of the relationships among the variables, it is also useful to assess the relative importance of the foreign impulses. For this purpose, we examine variance decompositions and the impulse responses of the real exchange rate and official reserves. Two observations are worth noting from the results of the variance decompositions of real exchange rate forecast errors presented in table 1.9. First, for most countries, foreign factors account for a sizable fraction (about 50 percent) of the monthly forecast error variance in the real exchange rate. Second, a pattern appears among the countries considered. Foreign factors explain the greatest share of the variance of the real exchange rate in countries that experienced no major changes in domestic policies in the period under consideration, 1988–91: Bolivia, Colombia, Chile, and Ecuador implemented their stabilization programs well before our sample started.[39] Foreign factors explain the least for Argentina, Brazil, Mexico, and Venezuela, all countries where significant changes in domestic policy took place during the sample period.[40]

Foreign factors also account for a sizable fraction of the forecast error variance in monthly reserves in most of the countries considered, as is clear from the variance decompositions presented in table 1.10. It turns out that the explanatory power of the foreign factors is least for Argentina and Venezuela and most for Chile, Colombia, and Ecuador.

Last, we turn to impulse response functions, figures 1.9 and 1.10 depict for the ten countries in our sample the response of reserves and the real exchange rate to a one-standard-deviation shock to the first principal component of the foreign variables. As indicated earlier, and as illustrated by figure 1.8, a positive shock to the first principal component of foreign variables could be interpreted as an increase in short-term U.S. interest rates. If this shock is associated with a decreased capital outflow from the United States, then it could be associated with a permanent decrease in reserves and a real exchange rate depreciation in Latin America.[41] For most countries, evidence in the figures supports this hypothesized pattern. There are exceptions, however. In

Table 1.9
Decomposition of Variance: Real Exchange Rate

Country	Months	Standard error	Foreign factor	Reserves	Real exchange rate
Argentina	1	0.706	36.331	3.096	60.573
	6	0.917	28.141	12.881	58.978
	12	0.949	30.350	12.772	56.878
	24	0.974	33.668	12.185	54.146
Bolivia	1	0.059	50.275	0.012	49.713
	6	0.128	57.185	2.245	40.570
	12	0.134	57.732	2.126	40.142
	24	0.139	61.239	1.958	36.803
Brazil	1	0.629	50.796	0.000	49.204
	6	1.253	48.370	0.529	51.101
	12	1.414	48.600	0.546	50.855
	24	1.477	49.166	0.547	50.288
Chile	1	0.292	51.208	0.024	48.768
	6	0.461	53.343	0.022	46.635
	12	0.468	53.395	0.027	46.578
	24	0.468	53.400	0.028	46.572
Colombia	1	0.344	51.697	0.013	48.290
	6	0.715	53.234	0.064	46.703
	12	0.797	53.250	0.052	46.697
	24	0.827	53.495	0.048	46.456
Ecuador	1	0.728	50.747	0.006	49.247
	6	1.125	50.861	0.013	49.126
	12	1.131	50.952	0.013	49.035
	24	1.133	51.093	0.013	48.894
Mexico	1	0.609	47.346	0.142	52.512
	6	1.163	46.439	0.231	53.330
	12	1.242	46.342	0.249	53.409
	24	1.252	46.442	0.250	53.308
Peru	1	0.224	45.589	0.512	53.898
	6	0.302	42.408	3.065	54.527
	12	0.339	47.796	3.694	58.510
	24	0.373	55.599	3.313	41.088
Uruguay	1	0.293	50.547	0.008	49.445
	6	0.563	51.202	0.059	48.739
	12	0.578	51.074	0.099	48.827
	24	0.581	51.229	0.100	48.671

Table 1.9
(continued)

Country	Months	Standard error	Foreign factor	Reserves	Real exchange rate
Venezuela	1	0.246	49.910	0.006	50.083
	6	0.347	47.950	1.730	50.320
	12	0.372	48.748	2.503	48.749
	24	0.383	49.985	2.922	47.092

particular, reserves rise in Brazil and Uruguay in response to the shock, and Ecuador experiences a sustained real appreciation.

Furthermore, the response pattern most common in figure 1.9 (for Argentina, Colombia, Ecuador, Mexico, and Peru) is one in which reserves decline as capital flows out. When capital ceases to leave, reserves stabilize at a lower level. In figure 1.10, the most common response of the real exchange rate to a positive shock to the first foreign principal component (for Argentina, Bolivia, Chile, Colombia, Mexico, Uruguay, and Venezuela) is a permanent real depreciation.[42] This finding confirms that, in most of the cases considered, an increase in interest rates abroad induces a capital outflow from these countries. Reversing the exercise to fit recent developments, the evidence from the impulse responses indicates that a decline in U.S. interest rates would, all else being equal, generate an accumulation of official reserves and an appreciation of the real exchange rate in most of the countries, although puzzling exceptions remain.

IV Policy Implications

The foregoing empirical analysis suggests that external factors have played a role in recent developments in Latin America. These capital flows, in turn, have contributed to the accumulation of foreign reserves and the appreciation of real exchange rates.[43] Using these observations as background and taking into account the possibility that external factors could reverse their course and result in capital outflows from Latin America, we turn to the next relevant set of issues, concerning the form and timing of appropriate policy responses to capital flows.

Given that the 1980s were a period of capital shortage for Latin America, it follows that the first question when discussing policy is how should policymakers respond to the recent inflows. Several

Table 1.10
Decomposition of Variance: Official Reserves

Country	Months	Standard error	Foreign factor	Reserves	Real exchange rate
Argentina	1	0.457	46.939	53.061	0.000
	6	0.917	28.141	12.881	58.978
	12	0.965	23.908	48.220	27.873
	24	1.005	29.242	44.649	26.109
Bolivia	1	0.235	3.583	96.417	0.000
	6	0.513	38.860	37.467	23.673
	12	0.569	45.647	30.533	23.820
	24	0.570	45.794	30.393	23.813
Brazil	1	0.219	50.421	49.579	0.000
	6	0.504	51.428	11.183	37.389
	12	0.508	51.806	11.053	37.140
	24	0.511	52.482	10.893	36.625
Chile	1	0.064	26.316	73.684	0.000
	6	0.317	52.475	6.984	40.541
	12	0.514	54.327	2.780	42.893
	24	0.559	54.621	2.353	43.026
Colombia	1	0.300	49.594	50.406	0.000
	6	0.399	48.426	34.939	16.635
	12	0.433	51.639	29.657	18.704
	24	0.464	56.270	25.818	17.912
Ecuador	1	0.214	21.531	78.469	0.000
	6	0.577	53.184	13.929	32.886
	12	0.643	54.415	11.242	34.343
	24	0.668	57.760	10.413	31.827
Mexico	1	0.416	43.950	56.050	0.000
	6	1.753	43.856	4.498	51.646
	12	2.176	46.022	3.041	50.936
	24	2.264	48.266	2.822	48.912
Peru	1	0.090	15.758	84.242	0.000
	6	0.447	43.682	13.199	43.119
	12	0.539	49.176	10.681	40.143
	24	0.620	58.030	8.645	33.325
Uruguay	1	0.066	24.936	75.064	0.000
	6	0.222	51.478	10.499	38.023
	12	0.287	52.592	6.304	41.104
	24	0.303	54.672	5.688	39.640

Table 1.10
(continued)

Country	Months	Standard error	Foreign factor	Reserves	Real exchange rate
Venezuela	1	0.092	21.038	78.962	0.000
	6	0.267	31.511	24.542	43.947
	12	0.301	29.796	25.532	44.672
	24	0.323	30.139	25.209	44.652

countries in the region are concluding successful negotiations with their creditors and effectively coming to grips with their fiscal imbalances. Thus, at what point do capital flows—into countries like Chile and Mexico, which have financed increases in private investment—become undesirable?

There are three types of concerns that policymakers tend to voice about capital inflows: (1) since capital inflows are typically associated with real exchange rate appreciation and with increased exchange rate volatility, they may adversely affect the export sector; (2) capital inflows—particularly when massive—may not be properly intermediated and may therefore lead to a misallocation of resources; and (3) capital inflows—especially the "hot money" variety—may be reversed on short notice, possibly leading to a domestic financial crisis. These concerns are not new. Indeed, the depth of the debt crisis in the 1980s certainly contributed to the magnitude and sudden reversal of international capital flows. The remainder of this section examines the foundations of these concerns and their policy implications.[44]

Evidently the development of the export sector has laid the foundations for technological advancement and economic growth in most Latin American countries. Moreover, in highly indebted countries, the behavior of exports has been an important indicator of creditworthiness. Thus, changes in exports associated with capital inflows may have economywide effects, and hysteresis effects, that are not fully internalized by the private sector—thus providing a rationale for policy intervention.

In turn, improper intermediation could be the result of speculative "bubbles," improperly priced (explicit or implicit) government insurance, lack of policy credibility, market failure (such as externalities, economies of scale, and nominal wage or price rigidity), or some combination of the above. Although the bubbles hypothesis is a highly

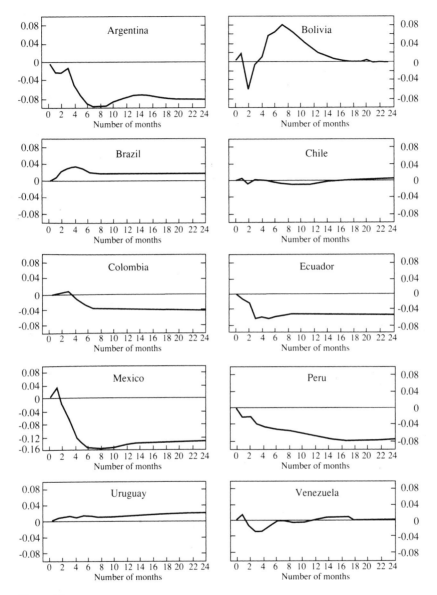

Figure 1.9
Response of official reserves to a one-standard-deviation shock in the first foreign factor

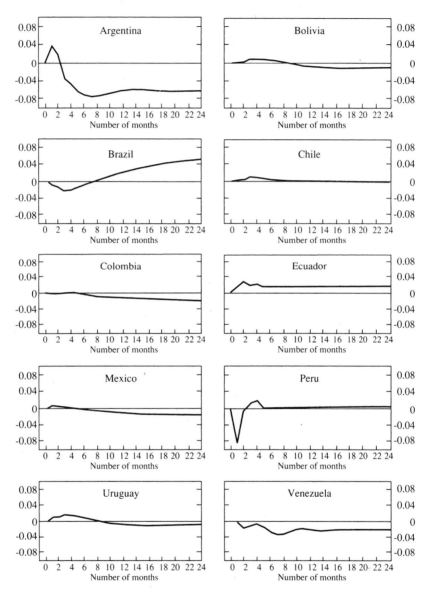

Figure 1.10
Response of the real exchange rate to a one-standard deviation in the first foreign factor

appealing one in policy circles,[45] it does not immediately follow that a bubbles equilibrium (leaving aside its empirical foundations) calls for government intervention. A clear case for intervention could be made if the government had better information than private agents and could thus prevent the creation of a speculative bubble. This proposition is doubtful, however. Hence, intervention could be ineffective and even counterproductive. Another case for intervention is when the speculative bubble is driven by the expectation that government will bail out speculators when the bubble bursts. Because these bubbles are associated with improperly priced insurance and a lack of policy credibility, they are not *pure* bubbles. Optimal policy to prevent this type of bubble could simply mean the setting up of appropriate mechanisms to prevent government from bailing out speculators. It may be optimal to make a credible commitment that *government will not intervene* if the bubble bursts.

In practice, however, governments may be unable to make such commitments credible, especially when they involve the possibility of bank failures. As recent experience in the United States and Latin America shows, it may not be possible to state credibly that bank deposits are not fully guaranteed by the government if banks run into financial difficulties. As a result, banks may end up receiving free deposit insurance.[46] Thus, a natural proposal is to require banks to join a mandatory deposit insurance scheme. Such a scheme, however, must be highly sophisticated—indeed, much more sophisticated than those prevailing in some industrialized countries. For example, such a scheme would have to take into account the probability of a massive withdrawal of funds if external conditions reverted. Consequently, in the short run it may be more practical simply to preclude banks from intermediating much of the new capital inflow by increasing required reserve ratios. Regulations could also make banks less vulnerable to speculative bubbles in other markets (like equity and real estate markets) that are the by-product of massive capital inflows. In particular, by limiting the investments of banks in these markets, the banking system would be better insulated when the bubble bursts.[47]

As pointed out above, a third rationale for policymakers' concerns about capital inflows is based on the fear of a quick reversal of the inflows. Such a reversal may exacerbate the negative effects of improper intermediation, or actually *give rise* to improper intermediation. In an environment characterized by asymmetric information, a sudden capital outflow may lead lenders to conclude that the country has suffered a negative supply shock, even when no shock has occurred. The sudden capital flight, in turn, may bring about the discontinuation of efficient investment projects. Thus, if start-up costs for these projects are significant (because of increasing returns to scale or market failure, using two examples), their discontinuation provokes a deadweight loss, which, from the lenders' point of view, may be observationally equivalent to an exogenous negative supply shock. Consequently, the expectations that gave rise to these detrimental capital outflows may *become* rational. Thus, this example of a self-fulfilling prophecy gives another reason for intervention. The example also shows that policy intervention may be called for even when the funds are channelled to investment projects.

Based on the foregoing discussion, we consider five interventionist policies: (1) a tax on capital imports; (2) trade policy; (3) fiscal tightening; (4) sterilized and nonsterilized intervention by the central bank; and (5) a rise in the marginal reserve requirements on bank deposits and more regulated bank investments in equity and real estate markets.

Taxes on short-term borrowing abroad have been used in some countries—Israel in 1978 and Chile in 1991. Although this policy is effective in the short run, experience suggests that the private sector is quick in finding ways to dodge these taxes, by over- and under-invoicing imports and exports and by increased reliance on parallel financial and foreign exchange markets.

Trade policy measures can help to insulate the export sector from real exchange rate appreciation. One possibility in this area is to pay higher export subsidies. However, this policy distorts resource allocation between exportable and importable goods, and the fiscal cost could be substantial. For example, to offset a 20 percent overvaluation of the real exchange rate through export subsidies would increase fiscal expenditures by about 4 percent of GDP, given that the average export-to-GDP ratio for Latin America hovers around 20 percent. Alternatively, the authorities could increase both export subsidies and import tariffs in the same proportion—to avoid creating further relative discrepancies between internal and external terms of trade—*and* announce that these subsidies and tariffs will be phased out in the future. Indeed, if the private sector perceives these measures as transitory, agents are likely to substitute future expenditure for present expenditure, thus cooling off the economy and attenuating the real exchange rate appreciation. The fiscal cost of this package need not be large, particularly if the trade deficit is small. Furthermore, static distortions are not increased, since such trade policy does not change initial relative price distortions between exports and imports. However, this policy can be criticized on two grounds. First, its effectiveness depends on the private sector believing that those subsidies and tariffs will be phased out; otherwise, individuals will do little to lower present expenditure. Thus, the effectiveness of the policy depends very strongly on *credibility*—both the credibility of policy and the credibility of price forecasts. Second, this policy deviates from the present global trend toward commercial liberalization and free trade agreements.

Another policy reaction to greater capital inflows is to tighten fiscal policy through higher taxes or through lower government expenditure. This policy, although not likely to stop the capital inflow, may lower aggregate demand and curb the inflationary impact of capital inflows.[48] Toward this end, higher taxes may be less effective than lower government expenditure. Often when credit is widely available—as when the country is subject to massive capital inflows—individuals' expenditures can be largely independent of their tax liability. This is especially true if higher taxes are expected to be transitory—a somewhat plausible expectation since the higher taxes would be associated with the transitory capital inflows. By contrast, lower government expenditure—particularly when directed to the purchase of nontraded goods and services—has a direct impact on aggregate demand, which is unlikely to be offset by an expansion of private sector demand. However, a contraction of government expenditure is always a sensitive political issue. Overall, it is hard to find a strong case for adjusting fiscal policy—which is usually set on the basis of medium- or long-term considerations—in response to short-term fluctuations in international capital flows. However, if the authorities plan a tightening of the fiscal stance, the presence of capital inflows may call for earlier action in this respect.

Sterilized intervention has been the most popular policy response to the present episode of capital inflow in Latin America. Leading examples of this policy are provided by Chile in 1990–91 and Colombia in 1991. With capital inflows, this type of intervention amounts to the sale of government bonds by the central bank in exchange for foreign currencies and securities.[49] This policy does not necessarily stop private agents from engaging in international loan transactions, but, if successful, it does insulate the stock of domestic money from variations associated with capital mobility. If effective, sterilization tends to increase domestic nominal and real interest rates, lower aggregate demand, and mitigate the appreciation of the real exchange rate.[50]

There are, however, two main difficulties with sterilized intervention. First, sterilization leads to an increase in the differential between the interest rate on domestic government debt and international reserves, thus creating a fiscal (or quasi-fiscal) deficit. Second, by preventing a fall in this differential, sterilization tends to perpetuate the capital inflow, thus exacerbating any problems caused by the inflow. The impact of sterilization on the interest differential can be seen in figure 1.11, which compares cases of sterilization in Chile and Colom-

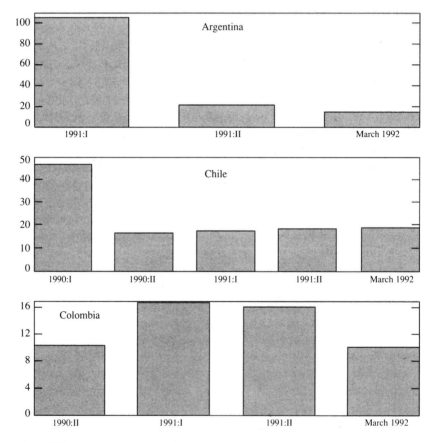

Figure 1.11
Domestic lending rates in U.S. dollars (quarterly and monthly averages). Sources: IMF, *International Financial Statistics,* and various central bank bulletins.

bia against a case of nonsterilization in Argentina. It is seen that in the recent capital inflows episode, the domestic interest rate exhibits a much smaller decline (or an actual increase) in sterilizing versus nonsterilizing countries. The recent experience of Chile and Colombia indicates that sterilized intervention has not reduced capital inflows, yet the increase in the fiscal deficit may be quite substantial. For example, Rodriguez (1991) estimates the fiscal burden of sterilized intervention in Colombia during 1991 at about 0.5 percent of GDP. Consequently, serious doubts can be cast on the desirability of sterilized intervention when countries are still attempting to solve domestic debt difficulties and when public sector budgets require further trimming.[51]

Alternatively, the central bank could opt for nonsterilized intervention, whereby the central bank purchases the foreign exchange brought in by the capital inflow in exchange for domestic money—as under a fixed exchange rate. This policy can help avoid nominal exchange rate appreciation and is likely to narrow the domestic-foreign interest rate differential; however, it is likely to generate an increase in the domestic monetary base beyond the central bank's target. The latter development, in turn, could fuel inflationary pressures and contribute to real exchange rate appreciation. It is at this point that credibility regarding a fixed nominal exchange rate comes into play. In this connection, floating exchange rates have an advantage, because the required real exchange rate appreciation does not necessarily mean that inflation must accelerate. Furthermore, floating rates allow the domestic central bank to operate as a "lender of last resort." By contrast, under fixed rates and fractional-reserve banking, preventing liquidity-type financial crises—particularly, when capital starts flowing out—may require the central bank to hold a large stock of international reserves, which is a costly if not unfeasible undertaking.[52] The credibility-related considerations, therefore, give some support to a regime of floating exchange rates when the economy is subject to substantial capital flows.[53]

As discussed earlier, attempting to insulate the banking system from short-term capital inflows is an attractive goal when most of the flows take the form of increased short-term bank deposits. In these circumstances, a sudden reversal of capital inflows may quickly result in bank failures. Marginal reserve requirements could be sharply raised such that they become higher as the maturity of deposits shortens; in fact, a 100 percent required reserve ratio could be imposed on deposits with the shortest maturity. Although this scheme would impose a burden on the banking system and could result in some disintermediation of the capital inflows, it has the advantage of decreasing banks' exposure to the risks of capital flow reversals. In addition, regulation that limits the exposure of banks to volatility in equity and real estate markets would further insulate the banking system from the bubbles associated with sizable capital inflows.

To summarize, there are grounds to support a mix of policy intervention based on the imposition of a tax on short-term capital imports, on enhancing the flexibility of exchange rates, and on raising marginal reserve requirements on short-term bank deposits. Given the likely fiscal costs, it is hard to make a strong case in favor of sterilized intervention, unless countries exhibit a strong fiscal stance and capital inflows are expected to be short-lived. In any case, we believe that none of the above policies will drastically change the behavior of real exchange rates or interest rates. The choice of appropriate policies, however, could decidedly attenuate the detrimental effects of sudden and substantial future capital outflows.

Notes

The authors wish to thank the participants at these seminars, numerous colleagues, and, in particular, Michael Bruno, Sara Calvo, Peter Clark, Eduardo Fernández-Arias, and Miguel Kiguel for their helpful suggestions.

1. For a theoretical framework that would accommodate this expectations hypothesis and that finds broad empirical support in developing countries, see Ghosh and Ostry (1992).

2. Latin America is not the only region to experience increased capital inflows in 1991. Similar developments occurred in Asia and the Middle East. At the same time, there was a marked rise in capital outflows from the United States and Japan.

3. See Diaz-Alejandro (1983, 1984).

4. For a recent study of the effects of capital movements, see International Monetary Fund (1991). On the role of reforms and capital account liberalization, see Mathieson and Rojas-Suarez (1992).

5. For a comparison of the current episode with the late 1970s, see Calvo, Leiderman, and Reinhart (1992).

6. For the evolution of individual country ratings, see *LDC Debt Report* by Salomon Brothers.

7. The countries included in our sample are Argentina, Bolivia, Brazil, Chile, Colombia, Ecuador, Mexico, Peru, Uruguay, and Venezuela.

8. Notice that $RA < 0$ implies the accumulation of reserves by the monetary authority.

9. See also *Financial Times* (1992), Kuczynski (1992), and Salomon Brothers (1992).

10. For the purposes of the present section, Latin America includes the same set of countries included under western hemisphere in the IMF's *World Economic Outlook* and *International Financial Statistics*.

11. These figures, which are available from the authors, express investment and consumption as shares of GDP and rely on preliminary national income accounts data for 1991.

12. On the role of various policy measures to reverse capital flight—such as amnesties, capital account liberalization, and introduction of foreign-currency-denominated domestic instruments—see Collyns and others (1992) and Mathieson and Rojas-Suarez (1992).

13. Some of this increased borrowing may represent hidden repatriation of flight capital.

14. See, for instance, El-Erian (1992) and Collyns and others (1992, chapter III).

15. For a comprehensive discussion of the composition of the inflows in the recent episode and how it compares to that of the inflows of the late 1970s, see Collyns and others (1992).

16. Uruguay is an exception to this pattern: capital inflows were not accompanied by an increase in reserves.

17. The IMF indices of the real effective exchange rate are used; hence, an appreciation is represented by an increase in the index.

18. The surge in stock prices during 1991 was followed by a moderate decline in 1992.

19. The price-earnings ratio in Argentina increased from 3.1 in 1990: IV to 38.9 in 1991: IV; in Chile it increased from 8.9 in 1990: IV to 17.4 in 1991: IV; and in Mexico it moved from 13.2 in 1990: IV to 14.6 in 1991: IV. These figures are from Emerging Markets Data Base, International Finance Corporation.

20. See Salomon Brothers (1992).

21. An implication of this discussion is that from the investor's perspective the information content of a drop in U.S. interest rates is different from that of an equal rise in the domestic interest rate—although in both cases the interest rate differential would change by the same amount.

22. Also, there was a 4 percent decrease in U.S. corporate profits, while corporate profits in other regions (including Latin America) increased by 10 percent in dollar terms.

23. The countries are Argentina, Brazil, Colombia, Cuba, and Mexico.

24. Some examples of this development follow. First, there has been an increase in the amount of investments in foreign securities by mutual funds in the United States. As of May 1992, the assets of stock funds that invest largely outside the United States stood at $41.8 billion, more than twice the level at the end of 1988, and assets of global funds have soared to $28.5 billion from just $3 billion in 1988. Second, in 1991, the sale of foreign shares in public and private deals doubled, to a record $9.8 billion. Bond deals rose 48 percent to $55.3 billion. Third, new foreign investment in U.S. companies and real estate plummeted 66 percent in 1991. See *The New York Times* (July 5, 1992).

As indicated earlier, private capital outflows from Japan also increased sharply in 1991, by $36 billion.

25. It is useful to recall how sizable these inflows to the United States were in the mid-1980s (table 1.4). From net capital outflows of about $20 billion a year in the late 1970s,

the private capital account turned into surpluses (capital inflows) that peaked at $128 billion in 1985. These inflows, which mainly took the form of increased borrowing from abroad, were mostly used to finance high and increasing current account deficits, which rose well above $100 billion in the second half of the 1980s.

26. Our discussion here draws heavily on El-Erian (1992).

27. For an exposition of principal components analysis, see Dhrymes (1970). Swoboda (1983), in an application that is close to ours in spirit, used this approach to examine economic interdependence across different exchange rate regimes for six of the Group of Seven countries.

28. The analysis that follows uses the logs of reserves and logs of the real exchange rate.

29. The test statistics, which are distributed as a χ^2 with 45 degrees of freedom, and the attendant probability values are presented at the bottom of table 1.6.

30. Applying a different methodology, Engle and Issler (1992) find significant co-movement in the per capita GDP of several Latin American countries, as these countries share common trends and common cycles.

31. Notice that, as shown in figure 1.3, Brazil's real exchange rate depreciated through most of the sample period and its upturn came fairly late. Thus, it is not surprising to find that the regional exchange rate index, the first principal component, does poorly in capturing its fluctuations. In effect, the correlation is negative. These details are available upon request.

32. Morande (1988) noted this pattern of interaction for the case of Chile in the previous capital inflow episode of 1977–82.

33. The tests are performed on the logarithms of the levels of the variables, and each equation includes a constant and a time trend.

34. These results are not reported but are available upon request. The contemporaneous relationship between reserves and the real exchange rate, about which Granger causality tests are silent, is explored in the next section.

35. Our procedure is similar to the DYMIMIC models associated with Watson and Engle (1983) and Stock and Watson (1989). One key difference in the approaches is that here we adopt a two-step procedure by first constructing the unobserved factor index (indices) and then incorporating that factor(s) in a dynamic model.

36. For simulation evidence on the efficacy of these criteria, see Lütkepohl (1985).

37. Alternative orderings are explored. One alternative imposes that there be no contemporaneous relationship between reserves and the real exchange rate, while another treats reserves as the most "endogenous" variable in the system. The results do not differ appreciably from those presented here.

38. Evidence suggesting the importance of U.S. economic developments on the Latin American business cycle is presented in Engle and Issler (1992).

39. Bolivia's program began in August 1985; Colombia had programs in 1985–86; Chile's stabilization dates to the Tablita program of 1978.

40. Argentina has had three stabilization plans during the period considered; Brazil has had four. The Mexican plan began in December 1987 and has continued throughout the period. Venezuela floated its exchange rate in January 1989.

41. Had we considered, instead of levels, the change in reserves (a flow) and the rate of change of the exchange rate, the impact of the shock would be expected to die out.

42. The depreciation is sometimes followed by a short-lived appreciation, as in the cases of Argentina, Bolivia, Chile, Mexico, and Uruguay.

43. In terms of economic agents in Latin America, it is also possible to interpret these developments as originating in a portfolio shift away from foreign (dollar-denominated) financial and physical assets toward domestic assets. For a model in which such a portfolio shift leads to a temporary appreciation of the real exchange rate and to the accumulation of reserves by the central bank, see Calvo (1983).

44. For a discussion of these issues from the perspective of Chilean monetary and exchange rate policies, see Zahler (1992).

45. Professional opinion is divided on this issue (see Stiglitz (1990)).

46. Actually, unless banks are forced to pay for deposit insurance, free market forces may not generate a privately based deposit insurance scheme. This happens because the expectation of free insurance if banks run into financial difficulties may make any privately based deposit insurance scheme unprofitable.

47. The above point about market failure will not be discussed here. An important example, however, is associated with the export sector, which, as shown before, is likely to produce externalities in the rest of the economy.

48. In addition, to the extent that it reduces the government's need to issue debt, a tighter fiscal stance is also likely to lower domestic interest rates.

49. For a more detailed discussion of the role of central bank intervention (sterilized or nonsterilized), see Mussa (1988) and Obstfeld (1991).

50. A necessary condition for these outcomes, and for the effectiveness of sterilized intervention, is that domestic and foreign bonds are imperfect substitutes in agents' portfolios. Casual observation suggests that this is the case in Latin America. Cumby and Obstfeld (1983) produced econometric results for Mexico in the 1970s in support of imperfect substitutability between peso-denominated assets and foreign assets. For industrial countries, Obstfeld (1991) concludes that sterilized intervention is a weak instrument of exchange rate policy and that monetary and fiscal policies, and not intervention per se, have been the main policy determinants of exchange rates in recent years.

51. See also Calvo (1991), who provides an example in which social welfare always declines with sterilization and in which the effectiveness of sterilization relies on its worsening the credibility of a stabilization program.

52. The problem is exacerbated when, like in most Latin American countries, the liabilities of the banking system are heavily biased toward short-term deposits, enhancing the chances of a run against the domestic banking system.

53. When the system is not subject to big swings in international capital flows, the opposite conclusion can be reached: fixed rates may dominate. See Calvo and Végh (1992).

References

Bernanke, Ben S., "Alternative Explanations of the Money-Income Correlation," *Carnegie-Rochester Conference Series on Public Policy*, Vol. 25 (Autumn 1986), pp. 49–100.

Blanchard, Olivier Jean, "A Traditional Interpretation of Macroeconomic Fluctuations," *American Economic Review*, Vol. 79 (December 1989), pp. 1146–64.

Calvo, Guillermo A., "Trying to Stabilize: Some Theoretical Reflections Based on the Case of Argentina," in *Financial Policies and the World Capital Market: The Problem of Latin American Countries*, ed. by Pedro Aspe Armella, Rudiger Dornbusch, and Maurice Obstfeld (Chicago: University of Chicago Press for NBER, 1983), pp. 199–220.

———, "The Perils of Sterilization," *Staff Papers*, International Monetary Fund, Vol. 38 (December 1991), pp. 921–26.

———, and Carlos A. Végh, "Currency Substitution in Developing Countries: An Introduction," IMF Working Paper 92/40 (Washington: International Monetary Fund, May 1992).

Calvo, Guillermo A., Leonardo Leiderman, and Carmen M. Reinhart, "Capital Inflows to Latin America: The 1970s and the 1990s," IMF Working Paper 92/85 (Washington: International Monetary Fund, October 1992).

Collyns, Charles, and others, *Private Market Financing for Developing Countries*, World Economic and Financial Survey Series (Washington: International Monetary Fund, 1992).

Cumby, R. E., and M. Obstfeld, "Capital Mobility and the Scope for Sterilization: Mexico in the 1970s," in *Financial Policies and the World Capital Market: The Problem of Latin American Countries*, ed. by Pedro Aspe Armella, Rudiger Dornbusch, and Maurice Obstfeld (Chicago: University of Chicago Press for NBER, 1983), pp. 245–76.

Dhrymes, Phoebus J., *Econometrics: Statistical Foundations and Applications* (New York: Springer-Verlag, 1974).

Diaz-Alejandro, Carlos F., "Stories of the 1930s for the 1980s," in *Financial Policies and the World Capital Market: The Problem of Latin American Countries*, ed. by Pedro Aspe Armella, Rudiger Dornbusch, and Maurice Obstfeld (Chicago: University of Chicago Press for NBER, 1983), pp. 5–35.

———, "Latin American Debt: I Don't Think We Are in Kansas Anymore," *Brookings Papers on Economic Activity*, Vol. 2 (1984), 335–89.

El-Erian, Mohamed A., "Restoration of Access to Voluntary Capital Market Financing," *Staff Papers*, International Monetary Fund, Vol. 39 (March 1992), pp. 175–94.

Engle, R., and J. Issler, "Common Trends and Common Cycles in Latin America," mimeo (1992).

Financial Times, "Latin America Finance and Investment," April 6, 1992.

International Monetary Fund, Research Department, *Determinants and Systemic Consequences of International Capital Flows*, IMF Occasional Paper No. 77 (Washington: International Monetary Fund, 1991).

Ghosh, A., and J. Ostry, "Do Capital Flows Reflect Economic Fundamentals in Developing Countries?" (unpublished; Washington: International Monetary Fund, 1992).

Kuczynski, P. P., "International Capital Flows into Latin America: What Is the Promise?" paper presented at the World Bank Annual Conference on Development Economics, Washington, D.C., April 30, 1992.

Lütkepohl, Helmut, "Comparison of Criteria for Estimating the Order of a Vector Autoregressive Process," *Journal of Time Series Analysis*, Vol. 6 (1985), pp. 35–52.

Mathieson, Donald J., and Liliana Rojas-Suarez, "Liberalization of the Capital Account: Experiences and Issues," IMF Working Paper 92/46 (Washington: International Monetary Fund, June 1992).

Morande, Felipe G., "Domestic Currency Appreciation and Foreign Capital Inflows: What Comes First? (Chile, 1977–82)," *Journal of International Money and Finance*, Vol. 7 (December 1988), pp. 447–66.

Mussa, Michael, "The Role of Official Intervention," in *The Merits of Flexible Exchange Rates: An Anthology*, ed. by Leo Melamed (Fairfax, VA: George Mason University Press, 1988).

Obstfeld, Maurice, "The Effectiveness of Foreign-Exchange Intervention: Recent Experience," Discussion Paper No. 1452 (Cambridge, Mass.: Harvard Institute of Economic Research, September 1989).

Purcell, John F. H., *Private Capital Flows to Latin America* (New York: Salomon Brothers, Sovereign Assessment Group, February 1992).

Rodriguez, C., "Situación Monetaria y Cambiaria en Colombia" (unpublished manuscript; Buenos Aires, Argentina: CEMA, November 1991).

Stiglitz, Joseph E., "Symposium on Bubbles," *Journal of Economic Perspectives*, Vol. 4 (Spring 1990), pp. 13–18.

Stock, J. H., and M. W. Watson, "New Indexes of Coincident and Leading Economic Indicators," *NBER Macroeconomics Annual 1989* (Cambridge: MIT Press, 1989), pp. 351–93.

Swoboda, Alexander K., "Exchange Rate Regimes and U.S.-European Policy Interdependence," *Staff Papers*, International Monetary Fund, Vol. 30 (March 1983), pp. 75–102.

Watson, Mark W., and Robert F. Engle, "Alternative Algorithms for the Estimation of Dynamic Factor, Mimic and Varying Coefficient Regression Models," *Journal of Econometrics*, Vol. 23 (December 1983), pp. 385–400.

M. Zahler, Roberto, "Política Monetaria en un Contexto de Apertura de la Cuenta de Capitales," *Boletin Mensual*, Banco Central de Chile, Vol. 65 (May 1992), pp. 1169–80.

2 Capital Inflows to Latin America: The 1970s and 1990s

Guillermo A. Calvo, Leonardo
Leiderman, and Carmen M.
Reinhart

1 Introduction

For the first time since the onset of the debt crisis in the summer of 1982, capital began to return to Latin America during 1990 and 1991; a phenomenon analyzed by Calvo, Leiderman, and Reinhart (1993). In general, Latin America's re-entry into the international capital markets, as noted by El-Erian (1992), was perceived as a positive development. However, policy-makers in the region have also voiced some concern about the less favourable side-effects of these capital inflows. First, it was feared that the real exchange rate appreciation that often accompanies these inflows would adversely affect the international competitiveness of the export sector. Second, there was concern that the inflows could be reversed abruptly, possibly doing considerable damage to the domestic financial system in the process. The fear of reversal was based on the experience of the debt crisis, which followed on the heels of the "capital bonanza" of 1978–81.

This chapter compares the recent capital inflows experience with that of the late 1970s. The analysis examines the differences and similarities between the two episodes over three broad areas:

1. Domestic macroeconomic conditions in the recipient countries at the outset of both episodes.

2. The behaviour of the external factors that influence the international allocation of capital.

3. The response of key macroeconomic variables, such as the real exchange rate, reserves, and stock prices to the inflow of capital.

The chapter assesses the vulnerability of these economies to an unexpected swift reversal in capital inflows, and whether there are signs that the vulnerability has changed appreciably over time.

The chapter is organized as follows. Section 2 reviews some basic empirical characteristics of capital inflows during the episodes of the late 1970s, together with the more recent experience of 1990–1. The section also examines quantitatively the extent to which these capital inflow episodes were a regional phenomenon as opposed to a country-specific event. Section 3 reviews various indicators of initial conditions in both episodes. Section 4 examines the role played by external factors, such as interest rates and capital account developments in the USA, which affect the pattern of capital flows in these economies. This section draws heavily on our previous work, Calvo, Leiderman, and Reinhart (1993). Final remarks and some policy implications are discussed briefly in Section 5.

2   Empirical Regularities

First we shall discuss the anatomy of capital inflows, then turn to the responses of various macroeconomic variables to the inflows, and finally compare the degree of regional co-movements in the previous and current episodes.

2.1   Broad Evidence

While the recent capital inflows to the region were sizeable, amounting to US$24 billion in 1990 and about US$40 billion in 1991, to date these magnitudes remain well below those observed during the previous episode of 1978–81.[1] As table 2.1 highlights, the orders of magnitude, in US$, are quite similar to those observed during 1978–9, the first two years of the earlier episode.[2] However, when measured relative to the gross domestic product (GDP) it is clear that the recent inflows do not match the experience of the late 1970s. The same applies to the transfer of resources to Latin America, defined as net capital inflow minus net payment of profits and interest, which in each year of the earlier episode was about double the value of the inflows in 1991—US$12 billion a year in the late 1970s compared to US$6 billion in 1991 (see Griffith-Jones *et al.*, 1992).

Figure 2.1 provides country-specific evidence of some of these developments. It shows that net capital inflows were larger in the recent episode only in Bolivia and Mexico, where the capital account balance as a share of GDP in 1991 reached 3.6 and 7.6 percent, respectively. For Argentina, the net inflows amounted to 1.7 percent of GDP in 1991, or

Table 2.1
Latin America: Balance of Payments, 1973–91

Year	Balance on goods, services and private transfers[a] US$ billion (1)	% of GDP (2)	Balances on capital account[a] US$ billion (3)	% of GDP (4)	Balance on capital account plus net errors and omissions[a] US$ billion (5)	% of GDP (6)	Overall balance[b] US$ billion (7)	% of GDP (8)
1973	−4.7	−2.4	—	—	8.5	4.4	3.8	2.0
1974	−13.5	−5.3	—	—	13.3	5.2	−0.2	−0.1
1975	−16.3	−6.1	—	—	14.7	5.5	−1.6	−0.6
1976	−11.8	−3.8	—	—	16.9	5.4	5.1	1.6
1977	−11.6	−2.7	19.8	4.6	16.4	3.8	4.8	1.1
1978	−19.4	−4.0	30.5	6.2	27.4	5.6	8.0	1.6
1979	−21.7	−3.8	35.0	6.2	32.9	5.8	11.2	2.0
1980	−30.3	−4.3	47.0	6.7	34.0	4.9	3.7	0.5
1981	−43.5	−5.5	59.4	7.4	41.9	5.3	−1.6	−0.2
1982	−42.2	−5.5	45.1	5.9	23.0	3.0	−19.2	−2.5
1983	−11.6	−1.7	22.4	3.2	13.6	1.9	2.0	0.3
1984	−3.2	−0.5	15.5	2.3	12.5	1.8	9.3	1.4
1985	−4.4	−0.6	6.7	0.9	5.5	0.8	1.1	0.2
1986	−18.9	−2.6	14.2	1.9	12.3	1.7	−6.6	−1.0
1987	−12.0	−1.6	14.5	1.9	15.3	2.0	3.3	0.4
1988	−12.4	−1.5	8.2	1.0	4.7	0.6	−7.7	−0.9
1989	−10.0	−1.1	15.7	1.7	12.1	1.3	2.1	0.2
1990	−8.8	−0.8	24.1	2.3	23.9	2.3	15.1	1.4
1991	−22.3	−2.1	38.1	3.8	39.8	3.9	17.5	1.7

Notes:
a. A minus sign indicates a deficit in the pertinent account. Balance on goods, services and private transfers is equal to the current account balance less official transfers. The latter are treated in this table as external financing and are included in the capital account.
b. Column (7) equals the sum of columns (1) and (5). A positive sign in column (7) indicates accumulation of international reserves by the monetary authorities.
Source: World Economic Outlook, IMF, various issues.

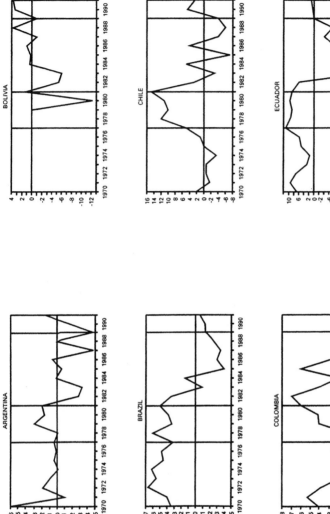

Figure 2.1
Selected Latin American countries: balance on capital account, 1970–91, percentage of nominal GDP, in US$.
Notes: Positive entries denote capital inflows; capital account balance includes errors and omissions; vertical lines denote the beginning and end (when applicable) of capital inflows episodes. Source: IMF, *World Economic Outlook*, various issues.

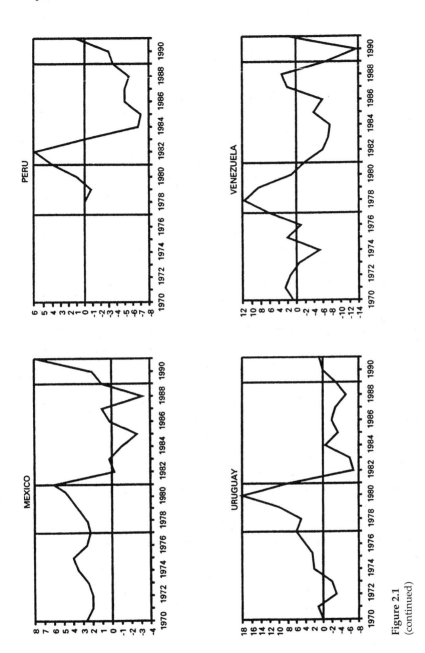

Figure 2.1
(continued)

about half the 3.3 percent peak of 1979. In the case of Chile, net capital inflows in 1990 were about 6 percent of GDP, well below the level of 15 percent in 1981, the year of the largest inflows in the earlier episode. Similarly, capital inflows to Brazil, Ecuador, Uruguay and Venezuela during the current episode were small in comparison to those of the previous episode.

An important difference between the two episodes of capital inflows is evident from columns (7) and (8) of table 2.1. For the region as a whole, capital inflows have financed less of the current account deficits and more of the reserves accumulation in the present episode than in the earlier episode, as analyzed by Calvo, Leiderman, and Reinhart (1993).

Table 2.2 presents a breakdown of the types of capital flow to Latin America. While net external borrowing is the key item in the capital account of the region both in the late 1970s and early 1990s, as Collins *et al.* (1992) suggest, the composition of capital inflows is markedly different in the two episodes. First, they note that private-sector borrowing through bank loans and bond issues was significantly lower in the recent episode. Second, foreign direct investment was much higher in 1991,—reaching US$14 billion—than in the late 1970s, and included cash inflows of US$3.5 billion from the privatization of state-owned enterprises, particularly in Argentina, Brazil, Mexico, and Venezuela. These inflows as a result of privatization are a relatively new phenomenon; they were not present in the 1970s. Third, the 'errors and omissions' item was much smaller compared to the early 1980s. This may well indicate that current capital flight was considerably smaller than in the earlier episode as discussed by Mathieson and Rojas-Suarez (1992).[3] Put differently, net external borrowing represents a larger percentage of total capital inflows in the earlier episode than in the present one, and the opposite is true for the relative size of non-debt-creating flows.

How did the region respond to the capital inflows? Consider first the behaviour of official reserves, as depicted in figure 2.2. It shows that in real terms the accumulation of official reserves in the current episode matched or exceeded those of the previous episode for most countries. Reserve accumulation was substantial in Argentina, Bolivia, Ecuador, Mexico, and Venezuela, about the same in Brazil, Colombia, Peru and Uruguay, and in Chile smaller in the current episode than in the earlier one.

Capital inflows are typically accompanied by real exchange rate appreciation. According to figure 2.3, the recent real exchange rate ap-

Table 2.2
Latin America: Items in the Capital Account 1973–91, US$ Billion

Year	Net external borrowing	Non-debt creating flows	Net asset transactions[a]	Errors and omissions[a]	Total
1973	6.0	2.5	—	—	8.5
1974	11.1	2.2	—	—	13.3
1975	11.4	3.3	—	—	14.7
1976	14.2	2.7	—	—	16.9
1977	19.4	2.8	−2.5	−3.4	16.4
1978	28.0	4.9	−2.5	−3.1	27.4
1979	30.2	7.2	−2.4	−2.1	32.9
1980	43.1	6.8	−3.0	−13.0	34.0
1981	61.0	8.2	−8.9	−17.5	42.8
1982	45.7	7.2	−7.7	−22.1	23.0
1983	18.7	4.6	−0.9	−8.8	13.6
1984	14.1	4.5	−3.1	−3.0	12.5
1985	6.2	6.1	−5.4	−1.4	5.5
1986	11.3	4.3	−1.3	−1.9	12.3
1987	10.0	6.0	−1.2	0.5	15.3
1988	3.8	8.8	−4.3	−3.5	4.7
1989	10.9	6.9	−2.1	−3.6	12.1
1990	28.0	8.6	−12.5	−0.2	23.9
1991	17.3	14.1	6.7	1.7	39.8

Notes:
a. These two categories are included in net external borrowing and non-debt creating flows for 1973–6.
Totals may not tally due to rounding.
Source: Data for western hemisphere, IMF, *World Economic Outlook*, various issues.

preciation was similar to that observed in 1978–79, although the recent level of the exchange rate remains well below the levels of the late 1970s and the early 1980s.[4] The appreciation of the real exchange rate is now somewhat greater in Argentina, Ecuador and Venezuela, but about the same in the remaining countries. When comparing the timing of reserves accumulation and real exchange rate appreciation, most of the evidence in *both* episodes suggests that the accumulation of reserves *precedes* real exchange rate appreciation.

Capital inflows are also often associated with stock market booms. Figure 2.4 indicates that the booms in the stock markets of Argentina, Brazil, Chile, and Mexico are roughly comparable.[5] While a part of these booms can be accounted for by the same fundamental factors

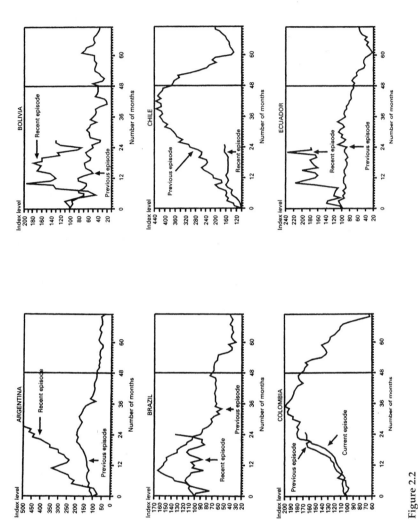

Figure 2.2
Total official reserves, US$ billion at 1985 constant prices. Notes: Total reserves minus gold (in U.S. dollars) deflated by U.S. Consumer Price Index. Recent episode: January 1990 = 100. Previous episode: January 1978 = 100. Vertical line denotes January 1982. Source: *International Financial Statistics*.

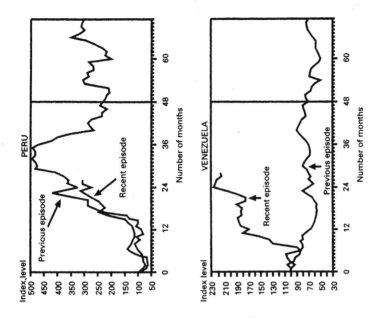

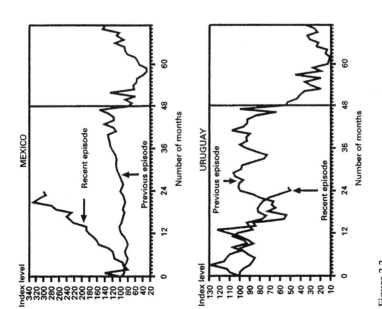

Figure 2.2
(continued)

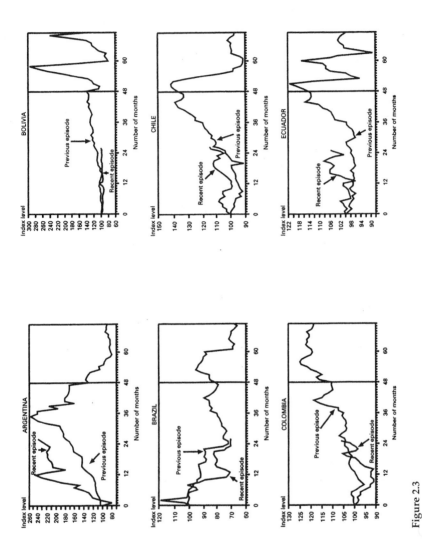

Figure 2.3
Real effective exchange rates. Notes: An increase in the index denotes a real exchange rate appreciation. Recent episode: January 1990 = 100. Previous episode: January 1978 = 100. Vertical line denotes January 1982. Source: IMF Information Notice System.

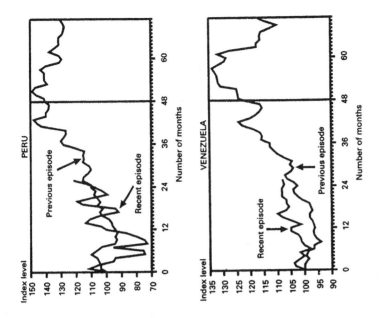

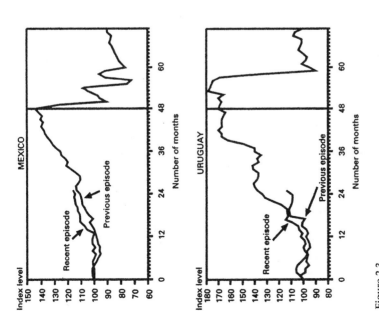

Figure 2.3
(continued)

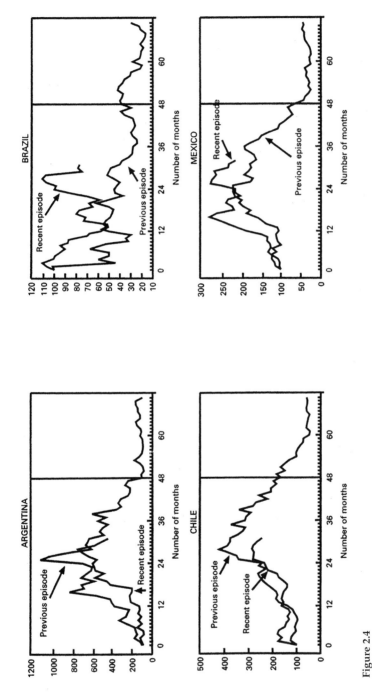

Figure 2.4
Real stock prices. Notes: Stock prices in U.S. dollars, deflated by U.S. Consumer Price Index. Recent episode: January 1990 = 100. Previous episode: January 1978 = 100. Vertical line denotes January 1982. Source: International Finance Corporation, *Quarterly Review of Emerging Stock Markets*.

that give rise to capital inflows, "speculative bubbles" may also have played an important role.

2.2   Regional Co-movements: Then and Now

Despite wide differences in policies and conditions, there is an important degree of *co-movement* across countries in the bahaviour of capital inflows, official reserves, the real exchange rate, stock market returns, and interest rate differentials illustrated in figures 2.1 to 2.4. Indeed, in an earlier paper, Calvo, Leiderman, and Reinhart (1993) we provided statistical evidence in support of the notion that the recent episode of capital inflows embodied a key common component that was of a *regional*, rather than a country-specific nature. The presence of a strong common element across countries in the region was interpreted as being the result of a common external shock affecting Latin America.[6] In this sub-section we examine whether the previous (1978–81) episode, shared this regional dimension.

In order to assess quantitatively the extent of co-movement among the various economic time series considered, we used 'principal components' analysis. We began by taking an individual time series—say the official reserves for each of the ten countries and then constructed a smaller set of series of the principal components, to explain as much of the variance of the original series as is possible.[7]

In principle, it would have been desirable to use direct data on capital inflows. However, for most of the countries in our sample these data were only available on an annual basis. Consequently, we analyzed the extent of co-movement in the official reserves and the real exchange rates for which monthly data are available, as proxies for capital inflows. In addition, using monthly data, the extent of co-movement in inflation rates was examined.

The periods considered were: the previous capital inflows episode, running from January 1978 to December 1981, and, for comparison purposes, the following four years, that is, January 1982 to December 1985. Similarly, we considered the recent episode, running from January 1990 to March 1992, and for comparison purposes the period immediately preceding it, from January 1988 to December 1989. The analysis that follows uses the logs of reserves and the real exchange rate. The inflation rate is the 12-month difference in the log of the consumer price index.

Table 2.3
Establishing the Co-movement in Macroeconomic Series, Previous and Recent Episodes

	Previous episode Jan. 1978– Dec. 1981	Debt crisis years Jan. 1982– Dec. 1985	2nd episode Jan. 1988– Dec. 1989	Recent episode Jan. 1990– Nov. 1991
Real exchange rate				
First principal component	0.81	0.51	0.41	0.58
Second principal component	0.96	0.71	0.78	0.79
Chi-square (45)	1274.55	470.50	302.01	286.31
Probability value	(0.0000)	(0.0000)	(0.0000)	(0.0000)
Reserves				
First principal component	0.58	0.50	0.48	0.67
Second principal component	0.77	0.74	0.69	0.80
Chi-square (45)	645.28	431.26	204.97	297.23
Probability value	(0.0000)	(0.0000)	(0.0000)	(0.0000)
Domestic inflation rate				
(12-month percentage change)				
First principal component	0.57	0.53	0.60	0.45
Second principal component	0.81	0.78	0.88	0.64
Chi-square (45)	744.82	783.49	475.94	306.40
Probability value	(0.0000)	(0.0000)	(0.0000)	(0.0000)

Note: The cumulative R^2 gives the percentage of the variance of the original series explained by the first principal component, the first two principal components, and so on.

The key results that emerged from examining the extent of co-movement across countries in reserves, the real exchange rate and inflation are presented in table 2.3 and summarized in words:

1. The extent of co-movement in reserves and the real exchange rate across countries is markedly greater in the previous capital inflows episode from January 1978 to December 1981 than in the debt crisis years, that is, January 1982 to December 1985. Similarly, the degree of co-movement in reserves and the real exchange rate across countries is greater in the recent capital inflows episode of January 1990 to March 1992 than in the previous two years. Increased co-movements under capital inflows could possibly be explained by external shocks that are common to the region.[8]

2. The degree of co-movement in reserves across countries is greater in the recent episode. Two possible explanations are: (a) greater intervention in the recent episode, aimed at either avoiding exchange rate

appreciation or at increasing reserves as a cushion against possible adverse future shocks; or (b) an attempt to bring the reserve-to-imports ratios back to their "long-run" values—which seems plausible given that in the recent episode eight of the ten countries were below their "long-run" reserve-to-imports ratios, as discussed in greater detail below.

3. The co-variation in real exchange rates was much greater in the January 1978 to December 1981 period than in any period since. Possible explanations may be: (a) since there was less intervention at that time, the exchange rate was allowed to react to the inflow more uniformly; and (b) the exchange-rate-based stabilizations (or *tablitas*) in the Southern Cone during the earlier period were better synchronized than the stabilization programmes of the last two years considered.

4. The extent of co-movement in the domestic inflation rate, a variable less obviously linked to external factors, diminished in the recent episode of capital inflows relative to that of the previous two years, 1988 and 1989; whereas in the previous episode the extent of co-movement was about the same as that which characterized the following four years.

3 Initial Conditions

Initial conditions may play a key role in determining the economic performance and response to capital inflows. They may also determine the vulnerability of a given economy or region to a reversal of those flows. Accordingly, we focus on comparing some of the similarities and differences in the initial conditions in the Latin American countries under study. Initial conditions are represented by various indicators for the region for 1977–8 and 1988–9, the two periods immediately preceding both episodes of capital inflows; these are discussed in the next section.

The main results from this comparison are summarized below:

1. External debt indicators suggest that most of these countries were more vulnerable to an adverse external shock, for example, in the form of an increase in world interest rates, in the 1990s after the debt crisis, than in the 1970s. While the sharp declines in US and other international interest rates have gone a long way towards reducing the debt-servicing burdens of these ten heavily-indebted countries, external debt ratios were sharply higher, as shown in table 2.4, at the outset of the current capital inflow episode. Further, as shown in table 2.4, the

Table 2.4
Initial Conditions: External Debt and Reserves Indicators

Country	Floating-rate debt as a percentage of total long-term debt		Ratio of total external debt to exports of goods and services		Official reserves as a ratio of nominal imports in US$	
	1977	1989	1980	1989	1977	1989
Argentina	39.4	83.2	242.4	511.3	0.9	0.4
Bolivia	30.9	22.3	258.2	433.8	0.4	0.3
Brazil	54.6	71.0	304.3	295.0	0.6	0.5
Chile	17.5	69.6	192.5	174.6	0.2	0.5
Colombia	9.1	46.0	117.1	208.3	0.9	0.8
Ecuador	45.5	63.7	203.1	386.8	0.4	0.3
Mexico	53.1	79.4	259.2	250.0	0.3	0.3
Peru	30.3	32.3	207.7	415.7	0.2	0.4
Uruguay	21.4	73.1	104.1	161.3	0.7	0.5
Venezuela	60.2	87.3	131.8	205.1	0.8	0.7

Sources: IMF, *International Financial Statistics* and *World Economic Outlook*; and World Bank, *World Debt Tables*, various issues.

proportion of external debt carrying a variable interest rate is much higher now in most of the sample countries.

2. In eight of the ten countries considered, the ratio of official international reserves to imports was higher at the outset of the previous episode, and closer to its long-run average, as illustrated in table 2.4. The fact that reserves at the outset of the present episode were, more often than not, below their long-run averages may explain why reserve accumulation has been greater in the current episode.

3. Vulnerability to terms-of-trade shocks has been a common characteristic of most Latin-American economies. This vulnerability can be partially assessed by examining the structure of merchandise exports, which provides an idea as to the extent of diversification in the export base of these countries. Table 2.5 presents a breakdown of exports into broad groupings for the years 1977 and 1989. The picture that emerges is mixed. Some countries—notably Brazil, Chile, Colombia, and Mexico—have made considerable progress in diversifying their export base since the late 1970s. Others have not appreciably changed the structure of exports and remain vulnerable to the vagaries of international commodity prices.

4. The public sector was larger and showed weaker budgetary discipline in the first episode. As table 2.5 indicates, government

Table 2.5
Selected Indicators: Merchandise Exports and Public Consumption, Percent

	1977				1989			
	Fuels, minerals and metals[a]	Other primary commodities[a]	Manu-factures	Public consump-tion[b]	Fuels, minerals, and metals[a]	Other primary commodities[a]	Manu-factures	Public consump-tion[b]
Argentina	1	75	24	9	4	64	32	8
Bolivia	79	17	4	13	80	15	5	11
Brazil	10	64	26	9	15	33	52	14
Chile	83	10	7	15	57	33	10	10
Colombia	4	77	19	8	26	49	25	11
Ecuador	50	48	2	15	49	48	3	9
Mexico	32	39	29	11	41	14	45	8
Peru	47	45	8	15	55	26	19	7
Uruguay	1	60	39	12	0	61	39	14
Venezuela	97	1	2	15	91	1	8	10

Notes:
a. Percentage share of merchandise exports.
b. Nominal public consumption as a percentage of nominal GDP.
Sources: Export merchandise from World Bank, World Development Report (various issues). Public consumption from national income accounts in IMF, International Financial Statistics and World Economic Outlook (various issues).

consumption as a share of GDP is markedly lower in the recent episode for the majority of countries, with the exception of Brazil and Colombia. The stronger commitment to reduced government intervention in the recent episode is also evident in the volume of privatization in a number of the countries. For example, during 1991, Argentina, Brazil, Mexico and Venezuela raised about US$15 billion through the privatization of state-owned enterprises; as indicated earlier, US$3.5 billion of this was cashed as inflow from abroad. Financial markets have also been liberalized in a number of countries. The reduction in the size of government and the move towards privatization and deregulation suggest that the resurgence of capital inflows during 1990–1 may be taking place against a backdrop of stronger fiscal policy fundamentals.

5. Despite these positive developments, the debt burden in the public sector is larger now than it was in the earlier episode as shown in table 2.6. Thus, from 1976–7 to 1987–8 the ratio of domestic public debt to GDP increased in Argentina from 4.6 percent to 17.1 percent; in Brazil from 10 percent to 18.6 percent; in Chile from 2.1 percent to 11.7 percent, and in Mexico from 3.2 percent to 11.3 percent. This is one of the legacies of a decade of fiscal deficits. Combining these developments with those in item 1. above indicates that between the 1970s and the 1990s there was a marked increase in both the external and the internal public debt of Latin America.

Table 2.6
Selected Indicators

	Domestic debt excluding central bank as percentage of GDP		
	1976–7	1981–2	1987–8
Argentina	4.6	6.0	17.1
Bolivia	0.0	0.0	0.0
Brazil	10.0	12.8	18.6
Chile	2.1	1.9	11.7
Colombia	3.7	3.5	6.4
Ecuador	0.1	—	—
Mexic	3.2	2.7	11.3
Peru	1.0	0.3	0.1
Uruguay	5.5	3.5	21.7
Venezuela	1.7	5.5	8.6

Source: Guidotti and Kumar (1991).

6. Because part of the capital inflows is monetized through non-sterilized central bank intervention, for example in Argentina, it is useful to assess the inflationary potential of these flows. If monetization were met by an increase in the quantity of real money balances demanded, then there would be no inflationary pressures arising from the inflows, so we examined the velocity of circulation of M1 and found evidence of increased levels of velocity in most countries. Some of the increased monetization could have contributed to reducing velocity towards earlier levels; such a move would be consistent with the reduction in the rate of inflation observed in most countries and with the re-activation of the real sector.

7. Turning to the real sector, initial conditions during the earlier episode were more favourable than in the current one. Between 1976 and 1977, real GDP in Latin America grew at a rate of 5.4 percent a year. In contrast, in 1988–9 real GDP growth in the region was less than 1 percent a year. At the start of the previous episode the ratio of investment to GDP was relatively high—about 21 percent for the region as a whole. Relatively high levels were observed for both the public and private sector investment components. These relatively high ratios were maintained, and even slightly increased, during the earlier inflows of 1978–81. However, all these investment ratios were markedly reduced during the debt crisis years, thereby leaving weaker initial conditions for the present episode. Are the present capital inflows being used to finance increases in investment? Our examination of the data suggests that in most cases, no major changes in investment ratios were observed during 1991. The exceptions appear to be Chile and Mexico, where some increases were observed. For the region as a whole, however, it is safe to conclude that so far the present capital inflows have not financed major increases in private or public sector investments. Thus, questions can arise as to how the Latin-American countries will generate the resources required to repay the new external debts associated with the recent capital inflows.

8. Latin-American stock markets are typically shallow, volatile, and particularly vulnerable to developments in international capital markets. While market capitalization has universally increased in the recent past for all the larger Latin-American markets,[9] it is primarily driven by soaring stock prices. To gauge if these markets have deepened during the past decade, it may be necessary to look at other indicators, such as measures of volatility and the number of companies

listed in the stock exchanges. In fact, the number of companies listed in the largest stock exchanges in these countries, appears to be falling. In 1980, 278 companies were listed on the Buenos Aires stock exchange and 265 companies on Chile's Santiago exchange. However, by 1989 the number of companies had fallen to 178 and 213, for Argentina and Chile respectively. The trend is similar for Venezuela and Colombia, while the number of companies in the Mexican stock exchange is about the same now as it was in the early 1980s. Brazil provides the exception, as the number of listings there rose from 426 in 1980 to 592 in 1989.[10] Overall, stock markets appear to be at least as vulnerable now as they were at the start of the earlier capital inflows episode.

Summing up, several important indicators point to weaker initial conditions in the current capital inflows episode than in the earlier one. In particular, there is now a higher burden of domestic and external public debt; a larger portion of the external debt is now subject to variable rates; reserves are now lower relative to imports, and growth and investment as a percentage of GDP are now lower than in the earlier episode. Moreover, in most of the sample countries current capital inflows have not been used so far to finance any marked increase in investment. However, other indicators work in the opposite direction. Namely, there are leaner public sectors after the debt crisis, that is, structural deficits are lower; there is a strong commitment to lower budget deficits and inflation and to the reform and privatization of the various economies—all of which suggests future capability to deal with debt repayments.[11] These positive developments have probably dominated the overall outlook of the region, as reflected in the recent restoration of voluntary capital market financing for Latin-American countries.

4   External Factors

Our earlier work maintained that some of the renewal of capital inflows to Latin America in the 1990s was due to external factors, which could be considered an external shock common to the region. A comparison with the 1970s suggests that similar considerations applied then as well, as shown in table 2.7. The main external factors at work in both episodes are as follows.

1. There was a decline in nominal and real interest rates in the USA. In 1975–7 nominal US interest rates were 30 percent lower than in

Table 2.7
External Factors: Selected U.S. Indicators

	Annual average				
	1972–81	1982–91	1978–81	1982–9	1990–1
Balance of USA with Latin America and other western hemisphere countries on:					
Current account (US$ m)	5642	−7955	11676	−8060	−7535
Private capital account (US$ m)	−7864	15724	−8434	15620	16140
Private capital account incl. statistical discrepancy* (US$ m)	−6201	7637	−10766	7809	6947
3-month treasury bill rate (%)	7.8	7.6	10.7	7.1	6.5
Inflation (% change)	8.5	4.1	10.7	4.0	4.8
Ex-post real interest rate (%)	−0.7	3.5	−0.0	3.9	1.7
Real GDP growth (%)	2.8	2.4	2.4	2.9	0.1
Real capital gains/losses					
real estate (%)	−0.1	3.6	−0.8	5.1	−2.7
S&P500 index (%)	−4.6	7.5	−3.4	9.1	1.5

Notes:
* The statistical discrepancy will normally include capital flight.
a. Real equity and real estate prices obtained by deflating the nominal indices by the consumer price index (CPI).
b. The price of existing homes was used as the indicator for the real estate market.
c. A minus sign on the capital account denotes a capital outflow from the USA to Latin America.

1972–4, and in 1991 they were 50 percent below 1989 levels. In both episodes, *ex post* real interest rates were relatively low; and even negative between 1974 and 1980, as shown in table 2.8. By reducing the external debt service on floating rate debts, the recent decline in US interest rates has improved the solvency of Latin-American debtors; as reflected in a rise in the secondary market prices for their loans.

2. The value and purchasing power of Latin-American exports markedly increased before or at the start of the capital inflow episodes. As detailed in table 2.8, real export earnings expanded at a healthy rate in all ten countries during 1972–81. Thus, despite heavy borrowing to finance current account deficits, ratios of debt to exports remained stable. Between 1975–6 and 1977–8, the value of Latin-American exports rose by 40 percent and the purchasing power of exports increased

Table 2.8
Real Export Earnings—Percentage Change

	Average		
	1978–81	1982–9	1990–1
Argentina	7.7	−1.0	10.6
Bolivia	12.9	2.8	4.0
Brazil	0.7	7.7	−9.0
Chile	8.7	9.5	−0.4
Colombia	−2.4	9.3	9.2
Ecuador	6.2	1.8	0.6
Mexico	32.5	0.0	8.3
Peru	11.4	−2.4	−7.9
Uruguay	5.9	5.9	1.5
Venezuela	12.8	−5.2	6.8

Source: IMF, World Economic Outlook.

by 13 percent. Similarly, between 1986–7 and 1988–9 the value of Latin-American exports increased by 29 percent and the purchasing power of exports rose by 14 percent. These developments cannot be accounted for by fluctuations in the terms of trade alone. In fact, the terms of trade were rising at the start of the earlier episode, but were decreasing at the start of the recent one; their level during the latter was about 20 percent lower than at the start of the previous episode. Interestingly, it is precisely at times of improved export performance that Latin-American countries borrow more from abroad.

3. In both episodes of capital inflows, external conditions resulted in an increase in the availability of loanable funds in international capital markets. In this respect, the recycling of petro-dollars played an important role in the 1970s. However, as industrial countries drifted into recession, the funds were loaned elsewhere, and Latin America was one of the main recipients. In this connection, Sachs (1989) indicates that during the two years 1980 and 1981, total bank exposure to the major debtor countries nearly doubled compared with 1979. In the two years 1980 and 1981, after the rise in real interest rates, the commercial banks made about as many net loans to the major debtors as during the entire period 1973–9. Similar considerations apply to the 1990s, in that in addition to low interest rates, there were weak performances in equity and real estate markets in the USA, as was seen in table 2.7. Real stock prices were somewhat stronger in the current episode than during

most of the 1980s, while real estate was weaker. In both cases it is clear that the investment climate in the USA was relatively unattractive, and investors had incentives to seek opportunities elsewhere, for example, in Latin America. This reallocation of international capital flows is evident from table 2.7, which shows a marked rise in capital outflows from the USA to Latin America during both episodes.

When these foreign factors are quantified in the form of principal components—as in Calvo, Leiderman, and Reinhart (1993)—it is found that they account for a sizeable fraction—about 50 percent—of the forecast error variance of official reserves and real exchange rates of the ten countries in our sample. Thus, while the economic and political reforms in a number of these countries have been instrumental in the re-entry of Latin America to the international credit markets—and indeed there is a significant statistical residual to be accounted for— the evidence suggests that economic conditions in the USA may also have played an important role in shaping the patterns of capital inflows into Latin America in both these episodes.[12]

5 Concluding Remarks

The restoration of voluntary access to international credit markets is, without doubt, a positive development for Latin America. However, given that the previous episode of capital inflows ended in the debt crisis of the 1980s, there is well-founded concern that the present trends could be reversed. The reversible nature of the inflows would be particularly marked if a sizeable share of the capital inflows were 'hot money'. It is therefore necessary to assess the extent to which these economies are vulnerable to a sudden withdrawal of international capital.

In some areas Latin-American countries are better placed now than in the late 1970s. For example, governments have reduced their spending and structural deficits; policies are oriented towards privatization and deregulation; and inflation is being brought under control in a number of countries in the region. In addition, during the decade of the 1980s most of these countries learned to cope with adverse terms-of-trade shocks and successfully maintained growth in real export earnings through the expansion of the volume of exports. There is evidence too that some of these countries were successful in further diversifying their export base. This scenario contrasts with the late

1970s, when the buoyant export performance was largely due to favourable terms of trade. As the experience of the 1980s shows, the external shock was fully reversed in an abrupt manner. It appears that much of the aggressive lending by commercial banks during 1979–81 was based on the expectation that the favourable terms of trade environment would persist.

While these economies have become more resilient in a number of important areas over the past decade, there are other areas where their vulnerability has increased. As the key debt ratios show, external and internal public sector indebtedness remains at levels sharply above those of the late 1970s. Further, the proportion of variable rate debt is now much greater. Taken together, the facts suggest that these economies are now more vulnerable to an increase in world interest rates than they were during the late 1970s. Stock markets have not deepened to any significant extent since the boom–bust cycle of the late 1970s and early 1980s; in fact, some of the evidence suggests the opposite. As a consequence, these markets are quite susceptible to speculative inflows that could be reversed at short notice. The banking system also remains vulnerable to a sudden withdrawal of deposits, particularly if investments are anything less than fully liquid, and if reserve requirements on short-term deposits are low. Thus, while the renewed optimism about the reintegration of Latin America in world capital markets is warranted, some of the stylized facts and economic indicators of these countries suggest that optimism should be tempered by caution.

Notes

1. See also Kuczynski (1992), Salomon Brothers (1992), and Griffith-Jones *et al.* (1992).

2. Here we refer to columns 5 and 6 of table 2.1, which include errors and omissions. This calculation of the capital account balance, we believe, provides a more accurate reading of the extent to which the external indebtedness of the region is changing, as, particularly in the previous episode, sizeable and rising capital flight coexisted with the increasing inflows. It thus appears that a sizeable portion of the funds that were borrowed in international capital markets were finding their way back to financial institutions in the USA and elsewhere, in the form of flight capital.

3. Notice that in 1991 the 'net errors and omissions' item became positive for the first time in several years. This may indicate the unrecorded return of capital that might have previously gone abroad.

4. The latter is not surprising, as the terms of trade for almost all the countries in the region have deteriorated markedly since the late 1970s, with many countries registering declines in the 40–50 percent range. According to Khan and Ostry (1992), a terms of trade

decline of 10 percent is likely to produce a median decline (depreciation) in the equilibrium real exchange rate of about 4 percent.

5. Also comparable are the domestic/foreign interest rate differentials in both episodes.

6. On the role of external shocks, see Diaz Alejandro (1983 and 1984).

7. For an exposition of principal components analysis, see Dhrymes (1970).

For an application that parallels ours see Swoboda (1983), who used this approach to examine economic interdependence across different exchange rate regimes for six of the G7 countries.

8. In all cases we tested the null hypothesis that the ten series are linearly independent and found that we could reject this hypothesis at standard significance levels. The test statistics, which are distributed as with 45 degrees of freedom and the attendant probability values, are presented in table 2.2.

9. Argentina, Brazil, Chile, Colombia, Mexico and Venezuela are the six largest equity markets in the region.

10. A striking contrast is Korea, where the number of companies listed more than doubled during the 1980s. The source for the data cited is International Finance Corporation (IFC), Emerging Stock Markets Handbook.

11. Moreover, it could be argued that there has been a learning process throughout the debt crisis.

12. This proposition is formally, tested for the recent episode in Calvo, Leiderman, and Reinhart (1992). The results indicate that in nine of the ten countries considered, the external factors were significant in explaining the behaviour of reserves and the real exchange rate.

References

Calvo, G. A., Leiderman, L., and Reinhart, C. (1993) "Capital Inflows and Real Exchange Rate Appreciation in Latin America: The Role of External Factors," *IMF Staff Papers*, vol. 40, pp. 108–51.

Collins, C. (ed.) (1992) "Private Market Financing for Developing Countries," *World Economic and Financial Surveys* (Washington, DC: IMF).

Dhrymes, P. J. (1970) *Econometrics: Statistical Foundations and Applications* (New York: Springer-Verlag) pp. 42–64.

Diaz Alejandro, C. F. (1983) "Stories of the 1930s for the 1980s," in Aspe Armella, P., Dornbusch, R. and Obstfeld M. (eds), *Financial Policies and the World Capital Market: The Problem of Latin American Countries* (University of Chicago Press for the NBER).

Diaz Alejandro, C. F. (1984) "Latin American Debt: I Don't Think We Are in Kansas Anymore," *Brookings Papers on Economic Activity*, no. 2, pp. 335–89.

El-Erian, M. (1992) "Restoration of Access to Voluntary Capital Market Financing," *IMF Staff Papers*, vol. 39 no. 1, pp. 175–94.

Griffith-Jones, S., Marr, A., and Rodriguez, A. (1992) "The Return of Private Capital to Latin America; the Facts, an Analytical Framework and Some Policy Issues," Interamerican Development Bank (mimeo).

Guidotti, P. E., and Kumar, M. S. (1991) "Domestic Public Debt of Externally Indebted Countries," Occasional Paper no. 80 (Washington, DC: IMF) (June).

International Financial Statistics Yearbooks (Washington, DC: IMF).

Khan, M. S., and Ostry, J. D. (1992) "Response of the Equilibrium Real Exchange Rate to Real Disturbances in Developing Countries," *World Development* (September).

Kuczynski, P. P. (1992) "International Capital Flows into Latin America: What is the Promise?" (Presented at the World Bank Annual Conference on Development Economics, Washington, DC (April).

Mathieson, D. J., and Rojas-Suarez, L. (1992) "Liberalization of the Capital Account: Experiences and Issues," IMF Working Paper WP/92/46, (June).

Sachs, J. (1989) "Conditionality, Debt Relief, and the Developing Country Debt Crisis," in Sachs, J. (ed.), *Developing Country Debt and the World Economy*, (University of Chicago Press for the NBER, pp. 275–84.

Salomon Brothers (1992) *Private Capital Flows to Latin America*, Sovereign Assessment Group (February).

Swoboda, A. K. (1983) "Exchange Rate Regimes and European–U.S. Policy Interdependence," *IMF Staff Papers*, vol. 30, pp. 75–102.

Part II

The Beast Awakens

Introduction to Part II

This part contains four chapters. Chapters 3 and 4 deal with the Tequila crisis, and chapter 5 presents my early reaction to the 1998 Russia crisis before I developed a formal apparatus (chapter 12) to check for logical consistency. Finally, chapter 6 discusses the recent 2001–2 Argentina crisis episode. The only major episode missing here is the 1997 South East Asia crisis.

In chapters 3, 4, and 5 the reader will find few references to topics like current account deficit, currency overvaluation, and fiscal deficit. Instead, the discussion there is focused on financial issues like insufficient backing of M2 and short-term foreign exchange liabilities with international reserves, and world capital markets that become dysfunctional after a liquidity squeeze. The explanation for the bias is that these papers were an attempt to show the importance of financial variables for either triggering a crisis or intensifying its effects. At the time, economists tended to ignore financial variables. This had a long history stemming from the many years that the private capital market was virtually closed to what we now call emerging market economies. Thus, for example, in order to assess whether a country held sufficient international reserves, the IMF used to look at the ratio of reserves to average monthly imports. This is a relevant statistic if international reserves are mostly held to ensure that imports will not collapse if the country faces a deterioration of its terms of trade, for example. The situation is quite different, however, if the government is also responsible for ensuring a working domestic banking system and securing the repayment of short-term debt when faced with adverse international financial conditions (e.g., a sudden stop in capital inflows). Under those circumstances, ratios like international reserves to M2 (or M2 *plus* short-term financial liabilities) are also relevant, particularly (although not exclusively) in a currency-peg regime.

The last chapter in this part (chapter 6) integrates the traditional variables into the analysis, but it does so while keeping a sharp focus on the financial sector. For example, chapter 6 shows that a large current account deficit (relative to the output of Tradables) could magnify the effects of a sudden stop if the economy exhibits high liability dollarization (i.e., foreign-exchange denominated debt). The reason is that typically during sudden stop episodes the current account deficit is pushed down to near zero. The latter implies that if the current account deficit is high, aggregate demand will exhibit a sharp contraction, lowering the relative price of nontradables relative to tradables (i.e., provoking a *real* depreciation of the currency). This may create serious financial difficulties in the nontradables sector if it is subject to high liability dollarization. Thus, the current account deficit comes back into the picture, but in a different role. Instead of being a signal of debt unsustainability, it returns as a signal of potential financial trouble. I personally believe that financial considerations are at the heart of recent crises. True, debt unsustainability cannot be dismissed out of hand, but if not for the intrusion of financial problems, debt unsustainability could be managed in a smooth and non-disastrous way—very far from the debacle scenarios that most recent crises have brought about.

Before closing this section, I would like to direct the reader's attention to short chapter 5. It contains important insights that only recently have been subject to empirical analysis showing that a relevant transmission channel provoking EMs crises may have been the capital market itself (see Broner, Gelos, and Reinhart (2004) and Kaminsky and Reinhart [2004]). I sense that this is an area of research that is relatively underdeveloped and is very promising in terms of insights and global financial policy implications. For instance, from this perspective, in trying to anticipate the shock waves of a given country's crisis, one should learn about the portfolio composition of the major holders of that country's liabilities. This is so because the shock waves will reach countries whose liabilities are in the hands of the same investors. This view also has important implications for the design of a new global financial architecture. For example, the shock waves could be contained if there was a global Lender of Last Resort. Under this view, a Lender of Last Resort should be much more effective than sending Fund missions to all the countries involved in a global collision provoked by a dysfunctional capital market.

References

Broner, Fernando, Gaston Gelos, and Carmen M. Reinhart, 2004, "When in Peril, Retrench: Testing the Portfolio Channel of Contagion," presented at the Conference on Emerging Markets and Macroeconomic Volatility, San Francisco Federal Reserve and University of Maryland, San Francisco, CA, June 4–5.

Kaminsky, Graciela, and Carmen M. Reinhart, 2004, "The Center and the Periphery: The Globalization of Financial Turmoil," presented at the IMF Conference in Honor of G. Calvo on April 16, Washington, DC.

3

Capital Flows and Macroeconomic Management: Tequila Lessons

Guillermo A. Calvo

Introduction

The Mexican financial debacle and its aftermath, i.e., the *Tequila* effect, have left most analysts reeling and searching for an answer to the question: why was the punishment so much greater than the crime? An answer to this question is especially pressing given that, just a few months, if not days before the collapse, there was strong consensus that Mexico had finally "graduated" into the first world. In the first world, devaluation is not a "crime" but an effective instrument for addressing balance of payments problems. Actually, in the first world refusing to devalue when one's currency is under heavy speculative attack, might be a "crime," as shown by the European currency turmoil in 1992 (see Goldstein *et al.*). So, what was so wrong about Mexico's devaluation, and why did Mexico's problems distabilize other markets around the world, particularly in countries that had shown, up until then, an impeccable and enviable track record for an extended period of time, like Malaysia and Thailand?

The central objective of this paper is to pick up the pieces from the Mexico/Tequila episode, try to give an answer to the above question, and draw lessons for macroeconomic management under international capital volatility.

The paper is organized as follows. A summary of my research on this topic (heavily drawing on Calvo, 1995; Calvo and Goldstein, 1995; Calvo and Mendoza, 1995) will be summarized in the next section. The section after will present a more in-depth analysis of the issues concerning the making of a crisis and the crisis itself. The "Tequila" effect and the role of banks will be discussed and the main findings summarized. Finally, the main policy lessons, will be discussed.

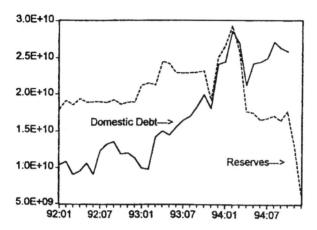

Figure 3.1
Mexico: domestic debt (CETES plus Tesobonos) in US$ and international reserves

Mexico and All that: The Latin American Chapter

The recent crisis in Mexico has made it evident that balance-of-payments crises are not only provoked by "flow" type disequilibria, like current account or fiscal deficits, but are also, and perhaps fundamentally, linked to financial vulnerabilities. I will illustrate this point by briefly reviewing some features of the recent experience in Mexico, Argentina, Brazil and Chile.[1]

Economists will debate the origins of the Mexican crisis for a long time to come. However, there are some factors that are unquestionably associated with the crisis. One such factor is the large holdings of Tesobonos (short-term dollar denominated debt issued by the Mexican Treasury)—far exceeding international reserves at the central bank (see figure 3.1)—that could not be refinanced under reasonable financial conditions after the unscheduled 20 December devaluation of the peso.

A large maturity mismatch between assets and liabilities like the one prevailing in Mexico by the end of 1994 makes the country prone to speculative attacks. This is even more likely if those bonds are mostly held, as in the case of Tesobonos, by institutional investors who derive no special liquidity services from such holdings and, thus, are highly sensitive to changes in expected returns.

A speculative attack of the type that took place in Mexico may or may not be successful. A speculative attack is not successful if the country could quickly find new investors who are willing to roll over its debt. The latter is likely to happen if the country is perceived as just undergoing a liquidity crisis and its solvency is not at risk. Unfortunately, however, solvency is very much like honesty: it can never be fully certified, and proofs are slow to materialize. The problem is especially complex if, in addition, current bond holders refuse to roll over maturing debt, since this may be taken by the other investors as a *signal* that the country is actually suffering from solvency difficulties. Since solvency takes time to prove, other investors may also refuse to refinance, making the run successful, at least in the short run.

Why would a liquidity crisis escalate into a prolonged solvency crisis? A liquidity crisis forces the government to adopt stopgap measures which could be highly counterproductive. For example, the country may react by imposing taxes that are easy to collect in the short run, like higher public goods prices, but which have a deleterious effect on output. Or the new taxes may fall on labour, lowering take-home wages and inducing labour strikes, again resulting in negative output effects. Thus, stopgap measures themselves may end up causing an insolvency crisis (see Calvo, 1995). As a result, it is not inconceivable that, if left to its own devices, a country like Mexico in 1995 would have been thrown into a solvency crisis like the one following the August 1982 moratorium.[2]

In terms of the central thread of this section, the above discussion points to the possibility that the Mexican crisis had a lot to do with the fact that the country was financially vulnerable, a phenomenon that is in principle independent of whether its current account deficit was large or small.

Before turning to other aspects of Mexico's financial sector, it is worth comparing Mexico with other countries in the region with respect to the size of the public debt maturing in 1995. Figure 3.2 (a) shows public sector debt service, excluding debt amortization, as a share of exports for the period 1992–1994. The difference between Mexico and the other three countries (Argentina, Brazil and Chile) is striking. Figure 3.2 (b) differs from figure 3.2 (a) in that debt amortization is added to public sector debt service. The ratios are, therefore, larger than in figure 3.2 (a) but still Mexico stands at the top, with a ratio reaching almost 160% in 1994.

However, figure 3.2 (b) reveals some interesting new information. Compared with figure 3.2 (a), Brazil leaves the low-ratio pack to join Mexico at the top, and even exceeds Mexico's ratio in 1994. This reflects the fact that a large share of Brazilian public sector *domestic* debt is of

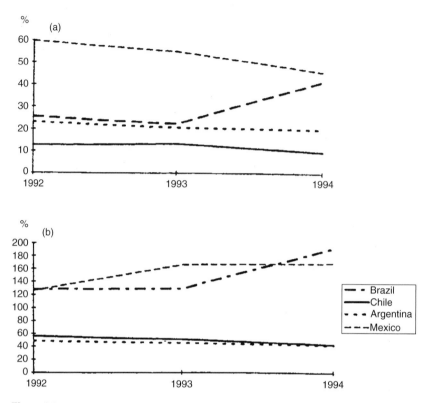

Figure 3.2
(a) Scheduled and (b) potential public sector debt service/exports ratio (foreign and domestic) for selected countries 1992–1994. The scheduled ratio assumes rollover of all amortizations

very short maturity. Furthermore, the ratios for Argentina and Chile remain below 60%, showing that not much debt was scheduled to mature during those years.

Figure 3.2 (b) raises at least two relevant questions. First, what kept Brazil from the kind of financial trouble experienced by Mexico, given that their ratios (including amortization) were so similar? My conjecture is that it may be linked to the type of debt holder. Brazilian domestic debt (outside the central bank), in contrast with the Tesobonos, was largely in the hands of Brazilian commercial banks or firms, with commercial banks being the dominant holders until recently.

If public debt is held by banks, then the ultimate holders are largely depositors who place high premium on liquidity services and, hence, may be much less interest-sensitive than pure Tesobonos-type foreign

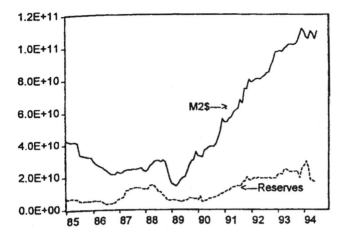

Figure 3.3
Mexico: M2 (in US$) and International Reserves

investors. On the other hand, if the debt is held by Brazilian firms, then chances are that it is being utilized for "repurchase agreements" or "repos" which enhance firms' liquidity. Hence, again, interest-sensitivity may not be large, lowering the chances of a Tesobonos-type run.

A second question raised by figure 3.2 (b) is, why did Argentina run into serious difficulties—requiring emergency help from the Fund—and not so Chile, when Chile and Argentina were in the same ballpark as far as the debt service ratio is concerned? To answer this question we need to examine monetary aggregates and exchange rate systems prevailing in these countries. This will also help us to give a better answer to the first question.

Figure 3.3 shows M2 deflated by the peso/dollar exchange rate (henceforth denoted M2$) in Mexico, and gross international reserves (in US dollars). M2$ increases sharply since 1989 prompted partly by banking reform that liberalized bank interest rates and eventually lowered reserve requirements to zero. Another factor was the existence of substantial capital inflows since 1989 (see Calvo and Mendoza, 1995), which tended to increase monetary aggregates for at least two reasons: (1) higher expenditure, and (2) some of the capital inflows involved a relocation of bank accounts from offshore to local banking institutions, which was most likely prompted by high interest rates in Mexico.[3]

Before the 20 December devaluation, M2$ represented almost five times the maximum level gross international reserves ever achieved in

Mexico. This ratio far exceeds the ones observed in Brazil—where the ratio of M2$ to gross international reserves hovers around 3—and it is vastly larger than in Chile, where it is around 1.5. I feel that the relatively high ratio for Mexico is a relevant factor behind the country's financial difficulties.[4]

By December 1994 Mexico's currency was virtually pegged to the US dollar, while US short-term interest—a key determinant of capital flows in Latin America, see Calvo *et al.* (1993)—had shown a clear upward trend since the first quarter of 1994. Therefore, capital flows decelerated during 1994, which tended to puncture the money bubble shown in figure 3.3 (see Calvo and Mendoza, 1995). Given the exchange-rate peg, a fall in M2 would have created a serious liquidity squeeze in Mexico or interest rates in Mexico would have risen more than was acceptable for Mexican authorities.[5] Thus, not surprisingly, during 1994 the Bank of Mexico followed an active credit expansion policy to offset deposit withdrawals. This policy was successful in preventing a fall in M2 but created the vulnerability conditions for a run against Tesobonos shown in figure 3.1 (see Calvo and Mendoza, 1995, and the next section).

Turning now to the second question raised above ("why was Argentina and not Chile so close to serious financial turmoil"), I would like to advance two complementary hypotheses: (1) the relevant monetary aggregate for Argentina (M3 which includes US dollar-denominate deposits) as a share of gross international reserves was not very different from that in Mexico (hence it was "large"), and (2) monetary aggregates in Argentina grew considerably faster than gross international reserves, while in Chile both series moved almost in tandem. Thus, even if both economies were to be hit by capital outflows, Chile was stronger and had not increased its bank vulnerability (as measured by the ratio of the monetary aggregate to gross international reserves) as sharply as Argentina.

Furthermore, bank vulnerability was higher in Argentina than in both Brazil and Chile because Argentina is committed to a currency board which limits the central bank's ability to operate as lender of last resort, whereas the other countries have made much less binding monetary/exchange rate policy commitments.

In Search of Deeper Roots I: The Road to Crisis

The above evidence suggests that financial considerations may play a key role in macroeconomic crises, especially when the economy faces external or exogenous shocks. However, although financial statistics like the ratio of M2 to international reserves, M2\$/Reserves, appear to convey some useful information on financial vulnerability for some key Latin American countries, straightforward extensions to European countries, for example, could be seriously misleading. We illustrate this point by examining the case of Austria and reexamining that of Mexico prior to the December crisis.

Over the last two decades Austria has exhibited high macroeconomic stability. However, (1) the Austrian Schilling, AS, has been unilaterally pegged to the DM for the last 15 years, (2) there is no formal arrangement between the two countries to support the AS; (3) the fiscal deficit has averaged more than 2% of GDP during the period of the peg, *and* (4) the M2\$/Reserves ratio never fell below 10 since 1960. Contrary to Mexico, however, on average, the current account has not exhibited large disequilibria, and the currency has been relatively stable in real terms (see Hochreiter and Winkler, 1995). Thus, the Dornbusch *et al.*, 1995, symptoms of "good health" are present, while one of our key symptoms of financial vulnerability, i.e. M2\$/Reserves, appears to be excessively high—more than twice the maximum ever observed in Mexico. Does this imply that, after all, financial factors are less relevant than Dornbusch *et al.*, factors? In what follows, I will argue that financial vulnerability depends essentially also on the *stability* of monetary aggregates. Furthermore, I will argue that Mexico's monetary instability is partly a reflection of capital flows volatility.

Consider the cases of Austria and Mexico, and let us focus on the stock of real M2 (i.e. M2 divided by the CPI), M2r. For these countries, and as a rough approximation, one cannot reject the hypothesis that the log of M2r, indicated by LM2r, follows a *random walk*.[6] Thus, for example, estimation results allow us to compute the probability that M2r will fall by more than a certain percent in the next few months. This information can be applied to estimate the probability of running down the stock of international reserves due to a contraction in the monetary aggregates in a given period of time (i.e. the probability of a balance of payments crisis in a given period of time), given the exchange rate. Other things being equal, the probability of running down the stock of reserves increases with the *volatility* of M2r (see the precise definition in endnote 6 above).

Estimation results show that the volatility of M2r is about four times larger in Mexico than in Austria.[7] Thus, the same M2\$/Reserves ratio carries greater risk of a balance of payments crisis in Mexico than in

Austria. For example, if Mexico had the high M2$/Reserves ratio exhibited in Austria, then the above methodology implies that the probability of a balance of payments crisis within a 6-month interval in Mexico would be around 13%, while it would be negligible in Austria (4×10^{-7}%!).

However, a more relevant question is, according to this methodology, was Mexico following a very risky strategy in allowing the M2$/Reserves ratio to climb up to about 5 (before the crisis started to develop in February/March 1994)? The answer is, in my judgement, "no." Starting from a ratio of 5, the probability of running a balance of payments crisis within a 6-month period is only about 1%. After the second half of 1994, the M2$/Reserves ratio climbed to more than 7. However, even if the M2$/Reserves ratio equals 8, the above-mentioned probability of a balance of payments crisis would rise to about 8%, which does not appear to presage impending crisis.[8]

The above analysis has completely abstracted from external factors. In Calvo et al. (1993) it is argued that external factors have played a prominent role in the determination of capital flows in Latin America. In particular, it is shown that as the interest rate on US treasury bill falls, it sets in motion capital inflows into Latin America; conversely, capital outflows from Latin America take place in response to a rise in the US T-bill rate. Furthermore, lower US T-bill rates are associated with current account deficits and a boom in domestic expenditure (especially in consumer durables).

In addition, if the demand for monetary aggregates is an increasing function of expenditure, then M2r would rise during capital-inflow periods and, conversely, fall during periods of capital outflows. Thus, one should expect that the stock of monetary aggregates in a country like Mexico is a negative function of the US T-bill rate. This conjecture is tested in Calvo and Mendoza (1995). The paper shows, using quarterly data, that the short-run semi-elasticity of the demand for M2r is approximately equal to -2, while in the long run[9] it is approximately equal to -5. Thus, the 2% (plus) rise in the US T-bill rate that took place during 1994 should result in a decline of M2r of about 4% in the short run, climbing up to about 10% in the long run (and 6% after 2 quarters).

Therefore, the rise in the US T-bill rate during 1994 added an extra downward push to Mexican M2r, bringing us closer to a quantitatively plausible explanation of Mexico's balance of payments crisis. However, this is still far from a fully satisfactory explanation because, starting from an M2$/Reserves ratio of 5, the full effect of the observed rise in US T-bill rates would have resulted in an M2$/Reserves ratio of about 9 (if the central bank did not intervene by increasing domestic credit, and the exchange rate was held constant). Thus, the probability of a balance of payments crisis in 6 months time would have risen to about 11% (which, again, does not impress me as very large). Besides, if the central bank had not intervened, Mexico's deposit interest rates may have increased further, possibly causing M2r to fall by less than observed, helping to prevent or, at least, postpone the crisis.

The latter observation highlights the fact that a fully-fledged explanation of a balance of payments crisis needs to take into account the *policy response.* This point was brought up in the previous section, but has so far been neglected in the present one. Before turning to the policy response issue, however, it is worth summarizing our findings.

I have argued that despite the apparent high-risk financial strategy followed by Austria, its banking policy has been noticeably more prudent than the one followed by Mexico. However, our discussion has not identified factors that are clearly sufficient to rationalize the balance of payments crisis in Mexico. To be true, empirical evidence suggests the demand for monetary aggregates in Mexico fell in 1994 as a consequence of the rise in US short-term interest rates. However, the latter effect was not large enough to run down international reserves. Besides, even if one takes into account the "natural" volatility of monetary aggregates in Mexico, the probability of a balance of payments crisis does not look impressively high.

Turning to the discussion of policy response, we start by noting that both statistical analysis and explicit statements by the monetary authority in Mexico reveal that as the demand for M2r fell during 1994 (due to the above-mentioned factors combined with the negative political shocks), Mexico's central bank expanded domestic credit (see figure 3.4, and Banco de Mexico, 1995). I will now argue that credit expansion from the central bank is the final key piece of the crisis build-up puzzle.

Credit expansion succeeded in stabilizing M2r before the crisis, but at the cost of generating a gradual loss of international reserves (see figure 3.4). Interestingly, however, standard demand for money functions do not *explicitly* contemplate the existence of an effect on money demand stemming from the expansion of domestic credit. Such is also the case with the Calvo–Mendoza demand for money reported above. Hence, these types of demand for money are unable to account for the

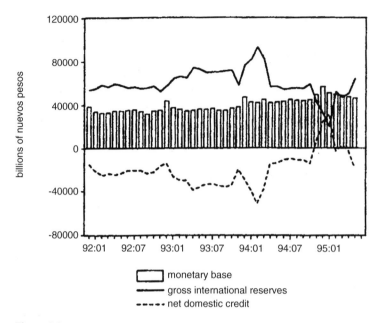

Figure 3.4
Monetary base, foregin reserves and net domestic credit to the Bank of Mexico

stability of M2r during 1994, since they cannot support the conjecture that credit expansion succeeded in raising M2r *directly*. However, some indirect evidence is available. For example, the forecast error of the Calvo–Mendoza demand-for-money equation is significantly positive for all of 1994, while domestic credit from the central bank exhibits a sharp increase over the same period (figure 10 in Calvo and Mendoza 1995).[10]

I will now offer a possible rationale for the existence of a positive association between domestic credit expansion and the stock of monetary aggregates. Consider the following scenario. There are two types of economic agents: the "rich" and the "poor." For simplicity, let us assume that the "rich" and the "poor" have the same marginal propensity to consume out of wealth (inclusive of government subsidies); however, the "poor" are subject to a "cash-in-advance" technology, while the "rich" are not. Consider now an expansion of domestic credit by the central bank which is used to increase subsidies to the "poor" (which, incidentally, is not an implausible assumption in an election year). We assume that this is perceived as a transfer from the "rich" to the "poor" and, thus, perceived total wealth is unchanged.

By previous assumptions, total consumption remains unchanged, but the demand for monetary aggregates goes up. In addition, if the "poor" have a higher propensity to consume out of wealth than the "rich," then this income-transfer scheme will expand aggregate expenditure, worsening the current account deficit, and increasing the demand for money even further. The higher activity level will likely increase the demand for *bank deposits* by firms. In this fashion, the fall of M2r could be slowed down. Moreover, the expansion of bank deposits generated by the rise in domestic credit helps to cushion the fall in bank credit induced by the hike in international interest rates.

Notice that the demand for money rises as the above transfers to the "poor" are activated. This implies that the loss of reserves during the "transition" is lower than if the demand for money would not have been affected by the transfers. However, once the demand for money stabilizes at its higher level, the loss of reserves may exhibit a sharp increase. Besides, if these types of transfers are discontinued, the fall in reserves could be catastrophic because of the associated fall in the demand for money by the "poor" (and the corresponding negative impact on the demand for bank deposits by the "rich"). This helps to explain why the loss of reserves may not be as large as the initial credit expansion (but may be exacerbated when credit expansion stops).[11]

In Mexico, domestic credit (12-month average) from the central bank (in real terms) is 12% higher in 1994 than in 1993, and represents nearly 100% of the loss in international reserves. Thus, a superficial reading of the evidence might lead us to conclude that the balance of payments problem in Mexico is, to a large extent, explained by a sudden urge of the monetary authority to increase domestic credit (due, possibly, to electoral considerations).

However, our analysis suggests a deeper cause, namely, domestic credit expansion may have been prompted by trying to cushion the economy from the deflationary effects of a rise in international rates of interest.[12] This explanation is especially interesting for our discussion here because it is applicable to all economies which are highly sensitive to a contraction in bank credit, independently of their political cycles. I will have more to say about the credit-sensitivity issue later.

In Search of Deeper Roots II: Crisis

While roads leading to crises offer us some empirical evidence which can be examined under the lens of standard econometric methods, crises themselves develop very quickly and, thus, could be subject to the same empirical methods only if there is a good number of crises that share similar characteristics. This fact has left crisis theories largely untested, making the field ripe for conflicting theories, since they are hard to reject on the basis of standard econometric methods.[13]

This section will not attempt to settle this scientific predicament. Instead, it will focus on the recent crisis in Mexico and try to obtain some "lessons."

The first lesson is that the popular Krugman (1976) model can be easily extended to accommodate several features of the Mexican crisis, but it still leaves a lot to be desired as a complete explanation.

The basic Krugman model assumes an exchange rate rule according to which the exchange rate is fixed if the stock of international reserves exceeds a certain minimum "tolerable" level. Otherwise, if keeping a fixed exchange rate would imply running down reserves below their "tolerable" minimum, the exchange rate is allowed to float freely. In a no-growth context with perfect capital and goods mobility (the latter implying PPP), it is assumed that the government runs a constant fiscal deficit which is fully monetized (i.e., the central bank extends non-sterilized credit to government). Under these circumstances, standard demand for money functions imply that, during the fixed-rates period, real monetary aggregates are constant over time. Thus, the expansion of nominal money generated by the fiscal deficit is immediately offset—in the fixed exchange rate regime period—by an equal loss of international reserves. Clearly, then, sooner or later the "tolerable" minimum reserves level will eventually be reached creating a balance of payments crisis.

The intellectual success of Krugman (1979) owes much to the way the crisis materializes in the model. As noted, the moment a crisis happens, the fixed exchange rate regime is abandoned, and is replaced by one of floating exchange rates. Hence, what was *reserve loss* during the fixed-rates period, becomes *inflation* under floating. Thus, if the demand for money falls with inflation (or the nominal interest rate), as in standard money-demand models, then when crisis hits, the demand for money takes a dive. Moreover, in Krugman's model, individuals are endowed with perfect foresight, preventing the exchange rate from jumping during a crisis. Thus, when crisis hits, the fall in the demand for money takes the form of a fall in the *stock* of international reserves. This dramatic acceleration of reserve losses—which is a hallmark of balance of payments crises—is, in my opinion, the jewel in the crown for this model.

This framework has been highly influential in establishing the point of view that crises are rooted in fiscal imbalances. Even though a fiscal imbalance is a *flow* imbalance, it causes a *stock* imbalance (i.e., the sudden loss of reserves) due to the fall in the demand for money when international reserves reach their minimum "tolerable" level.

As shown in Calvo (1995), there are many simple ways to patch up Krugman's model so as to have it render more realistic results. For example, in his model, international reserves fall continuously during the fixed-exchange-rate regime, something which is hardly observed in practice. This is easily taken care of, though, by assuming that the monetary authority is able to sterilize the growth of domestic credit by issuing central bank certificates of deposit, for example.

The assumption of perfect foresight—which prevents the existence of risk premia on domestic interest rates—can also be easily relaxed by introducing random shocks and rational expectations. Results are essentially the same as in Krugman's model, except that the time of the crisis is now stochastic and there is room for risk premia. This extension is especially relevant for Mexico, given that, as argued in the previous section, Mexico's demand for money has an important random component. In addition, the demand for money in Mexico depends on the US interest rate which also has a random component.

Other evidence that random factors played a relevant role in Mexico is that Wall-Streeters seemed to have been taken by surprise by the 20 December devaluation. Apparently, they expected the central bank to fight the loss of international reserves by adopting a tighter monetary stance (e.g. raising interest rates on Tesobonos and/or CETES). Irrespective of whether or not this strategy would have been successful, one could translate the Wall-Streeter befuddlement as reflecting surprise at the policy response.

A translation of the latter into Krugman's model—which does not do full justice to the verbal story—might be to say that from the point of view of the private sector, the policy response of the Mexican monetary authority reflected an upward shock to the minimum "tolerable" level of international reserves: Mexico stopped the fixed-rates game when reserves were around US$ 6 billion, while the market previously expected them to tolerate much lower levels. This is, incidentally, a plausible conjecture because Mexico had obtained an automatic credit

line from its NAFTA partners of about US$ 8 billion, i.e. Mexico stops
the game with about US$ 14 billion in gross international reserves, a
substantial amount.

Neither is a valid criticism of Krugman's approach to point to the
fact that in Mexico monetary aggregates did not fall at the time of the
crisis, as predicted by the simple model, and that the "speculative attack" came from Tesobonos' holders rather than money holders. First,
I have already shown that it is not difficult to rationalize a policy-
induced increase in monetary aggregates.[14] Secondly, one can show
that the attack from bondholders may take place in a Krugman-type
model (with bonds added, see Calvo, 1995), if bonds earn an interest
rate which exceeds that on international reserves.

However, for bondholders to rundown (totally or partially) their
stock of bonds during a crisis, and to refuse to refinance them at reasonable rates of interest, it is necessary that they believe the country is
experiencing a *solvency* crisis (i.e. the country is unable or unwilling to
pay). Here is where a Krugman-type model begins to look seriously incomplete, because there is no compelling evidence that Mexico was
close to insolvency prior to 20 December 1994.

To be sure, in 1994 the current account deficit was around 8% of
GDP and was expected to climb to 9% in 1995, and the fiscal deficit
had increased to about 4% of GDP (if loans from the development
banks are counted as fiscal expenditure) in 1994. But these are "flow"
variables that usually worsen before presidential elections and, thus,
their deterioration need not be deemed "permanent." Why would this
temporary deterioration lead to a massive speculative attack for fear of
insolvency? What are the "obvious" reasons that led private investors
to expect that Mexico was unable to get back on track and make the
necessary fiscal adjustment after 1995?

I have no altogether satisfactory answer to those questions. However, I feel that a polar opposite explanation to that implied by Krugman's model holds a great deal of interest, namely, the view that a
balance of payments crisis may *itself* be the cause of insolvency.

Let us take last section's discussion as a foundation and start from
the following stylized facts: (1) during 1994, external and internal factors lead to a lower demand for money; (2) to offset these factors, the
central bank pumps in more credit; (3) as a result, monetary aggregates
do not fall, but international reserves are lost (without necessarily
reaching their minimum tolerable or critical level); (4) towards the end
of 1994, a large gap between short-term government obligations and

international reserves (even including the credit line from NAFTA partners) is created; (5) an unscheduled devaluation takes place on 20 December.

Assuming that the country is solvent and "willing to pay," then a possible outcome is "no run." However, if investors expect that other investors—particularly, Tesobonos' holders—will try to cash in their Mexican assets, then the situation might be quite different. In the first place, Tesobonos had to be redeemed in the short run. Thus, for the country not to default, it was necessary for it to get fresh new funds on very short notice.

In contrast, if no refinancing was forthcoming, Mexico had to (1) engage in draconian, perhaps unfeasible, short-run fiscal adjustment, and/or (2) obtain official support. Under option (1), policy measures could have negative economic/political consequences, while, under option (2), the consequences would be less dreadful although they would also be negative in the short run because official support is likely to involve tough fiscal conditionality. Thus, under this scenario, a balance of payments crisis may make Mexico's investment projects look a lot less attractive. Does this imply that rational investors would refuse to refinance Tesobonos?

Clearly, if we are prepared to assume that no refinancing has *per se* *serious* negative consequences for Mexico, then there is no need to look any further. But, as argued by Calvo (1995), a run against domestic assets could be provoked by "small" shocks if there is sufficiently large portfolio diversification. Intuitively, diversification allows investors to select mutual funds with very small variances, making them approximately safe bets. Thus, if one of the investment projects in the mutual fund is expected to have a lower return, it is not very costly to drop it entirely from the fund, since the fund's total variance will exhibit, if anything, only a slight rise, while its expected return will fall by less than if the project had not been dropped.[15]

Consequently, the private sector refusal to refinance Tesobonos would be fully rational even if the negative effect of the crisis on the profitability of Mexican projects was relatively modest. In turn, (the good news is that) this would imply that if the damage to the Mexican economy caused by the run is small, access to the capital market might be fully reactivated after an also modest perceived recovery.

The above argument relies on the existence of multiple equilibria, given that the run may or may not take place depending on whether individuals expect the run to happen or not to happen. Furthermore, and more interestingly, in this example multiple equilibria depend on short-term liabilities exceeding international reserves by a wide margin. If instead of Tesobonos, Mexican official liabilities had been entirely composed of long-term debt obligations, for example, then a run against government debt would simply result in a drop of its market price, without provoking a distortionary policy response. But, in the absence of a negative effect from distorionary policy response, the only rational expectations equilibrium would be "no run."[16]

What was the role of the 20 December devaluation? Previous analysis is totally silent on exchange rates since, according to the above interpretation, the crisis occurs just because investors believe so.[17]

However, once the crisis scenario is set in motion, the new equilibrium is associated with lower capital inflows and, therefore, lower expenditure. As argued in the previous section, the demand for money is an increasing function of expenditure. Thus, lower capital inflows could lead to lower real monetary aggregates. Since international reserves fell to minimum tolerable levels as a consequence of the run against Tesobonos, the decline in the demand for money could not be accommodated by a further loss of reserves and, thus, the exchange rate took the full brunt of adjustment.

In this context, the "managed" devaluation of 20 December was a naive attempt to avoid exchange rate overshooting, perhaps in the expectation that disequilibria was of a "flow" nature and would disappear once variables like the *real exchange rate* were gently positioned at their long-run equilibrium levels. But the value of a currency in terms of another currency—especially during a currency crisis—is preeminently determined by "stock" considerations—like the fall in the demand for money highlighted earlier—and overshooting is the rule. Mexico was no exception.

In sum, the conjecture that fiscal factors played a key role in generating Mexico's balance of payments crisis has some merit. However, it is not convincing as the *sole* explanation for the crisis, unless one is prepared to believe that Mexico was perceived as insolvent, and unable to reform itself within an orderly, no-crisis, framework. An alternative explanation (which I will can "capital-markets led") for the crisis is that international reserves suffered sizeable losses as a result of trying to prop up declining monetary aggregates by means of domestic credit expansion. The lower stocks of international reserves, coupled with a relatively large stock of short-term government debt obligations, created the conditions for a balance of payments crisis. The latter gave rise to distortionary policy response and, in turn, to Mexico's insolvency, validating the rationality of the speculative attack.

"Tequila" Effect and the Role of Banks

The previous section should not give the impression that "simple" models or explanations will be able to rationalize fully capital markets problems in emerging markets. Models offer a framework in which logically consistent discussion can be carried out but the (unreal) "real" world always remains elusive and constantly challenges our dearest models. As argued before, crisis models are particularly susceptible to these challenges because we rely on a weak data base. This is even more so for the "Tequila" effect—namely, the negative effect and tension that the Mexican crisis brought about in other emerging markets, particularly their stock markets and banking systems.

In this section we will first discuss the "Tequila" effect and, then, the role of banks in a crisis scenario.

"Tequila" Effect

The "Tequila" effect is especially disconcerting because many affected countries had few direct links with Mexico, and had not patterned their policy regimes after Mexico's. Thus, in other words, it is hard to find "fundamentals" that could account for the "Tequila" effect.

Clearly, a Krugman-type model is no great help in this respect. However, the alternative view—i.e. the capital-market led view of crises outlined above—holds considerable promise. A possible story along these lines is that Mexico's events drove investors to think that other emerging markets might run into similar difficulties, and tried to be the first to get out. This behaviour may be fully rational since Mexico had revealed the possibility of "another" equilibrium at which investing in emerging markets becomes a less attractive proposition.

The speculative attack was somewhat successful in Argentina (where international financial support and a tight fiscal programme had to be implemented), but failed everywhere else. The stock market recovered quickly in countries in Latin America and Asia that were able to exhibit solid financial sectors (like Chile, Hong Kong and Thailand)—which is again consistent with the capital-market led crisis view.

Nevertheless, forecasting errors were made. Forecasting errors, of course, do not immediately imply irrationality. However, one would feel more reassured if some rationale could be found for such errors. This is by no means a trivial task. If the market operated under full information, for example, no such rationale would be available because investors would know *ex ante* which speculative attack would succeed and which one would not.

The emerging markets phenomenon involves a search process in which investors gradually discover new financial instruments that help to diversify portfolio risk. However, as these instruments take the form of different countries' assets and debt obligations, the costs of following a full-information strategy may become increasingly costly, given that a full-information strategy would call for detailed country-specific and highly frequent information, ranging from production shocks to policy decisions. Furthermore, the payoff of the full-information strategy falls off with the number of diversification opportunities, especially if countries are hit by idiosyncratic shocks which are largely uncorrelated across countries. Thus, the higher portfolio diversification associated with the emerging markets phenomenon may have *induced* investors to operate under low information.[18] This sets the stage for a "Tequila" effect, since just the suspicion that a "bad" equilibrium may exist, together with the suspicion that the other players may feel the same, might provoke a run, even though "fundamentals" are virtually unchanged.

To sum up, the "Tequila" effect gives further support to the view that the speculative attacks may stem *from* the capital market and not just be merely reflected in it. Moreover, the Tequila episode itself may be intimately associated with the higher portfolio diversification that took place in the last few years as a result of capital inflows in emerging markets (see Calvo *et al.*, 1994).

The Role of Banks

Standard macroeconomic theory has paid relatively little attention to banks. For example, in the literature about flexible versus fixed exchange rates, banks and, more specifically, bank loans are entirely ignored. To illustrate this point, consider the well-known proposition that, under perfect capital mobility, fixed dominates flexible exchange rates if random shocks are entirely *nominal*, e.g. only affect the demand for money (see Aizenman and Frenkel, 1985). This proposition relies on the observation that under fixed exchange rates shifts in the demand for money, for example, will automatically be accommodated since, otherwise, the exchange rate would not remain fixed. Normally, bank deposits are highly (positively) correlated with money demand. Thus, a fall in money demand implies, ceteris paribus, a fall in the stock of bank loans. In standard models the latter has no effect on output because these models assume that the cost of new funds is independent of whether firms obtain them from domestic banks or, say, from the Eurodollar market.

In practice, however, the cost of loanable funds is not independent of their source. Few firms have access to the Eurodollar market, and even those that do, find it difficult to tap that market for short-run working capital purposes. Hence, under those circumstances, the mechanism that ensures instantaneous accommodation of money supply under fixed exchange rates is no longer without costs. A fall in the demand for money, for example, causes a fall in bank loans and could, thus, have a negative impact on output and investment.

Bank lending is the dominant source of funds for firms in underdeveloped countries (for evidence on Latin America, see Rojas-Suárez and Weisbrod, 1994). Therefore, cuts in bank loans have an immediate and usually serious impact on economic activity.[19] Taking this fact for granted, we will now return to discuss the role of banks in capital market crises.

So far, our discussion on financial vulnerability has focused on the level of international reserves that would ensure the sustainability of a fixed or quasi-fixed exchange rate regime. The above remarks, however, point out the possibility that fluctuations in the demand for monetary aggregates may also have an impact on economic activity. This may help to rationalize the policy reaction of monetary authorities in Mexico during 1994 which, as shown above, resulted in an expansion of domestic credit. For, if the latter had not taken place, bank credit would have contracted and possibly caused a decline in output and employment. In this context, even a benevolent social planner, devoid of any electoral agenda, may have followed an expansionary credit policy.

This adds an important facet to the crisis discussion. To illustrate, let me focus on the case in which there is no social tolerance for a cut in bank loans. Thus, if, for example, international interest rates rise, leading to a fall in the demand for bank deposits, then, for bank loans to remain unchanged, either deposit interest rates must rise and/or domestic credit from the central bank will have to expand. If deposit interest rates do all the work, there is a risk that lending interest rates will skyrocket and non-performing loans will soon start to rise to dangerous levels (recall Sweden 1992). Thus, we can conceivably find cases in which an enlightened monetary authority prefers a policy mix in which domestic credit from the central bank is allowed to expand in some states of nature.

As noted in the previous section, credit expansion could conceivably keep monetary aggregates higher than otherwise, but the medicine may have to be taken daily, implying that, other things being equal, this type of policy might result in a *continuous* loss of international reserves. Hence, even though initial fiscal deficit is low and does not threaten the viability of the fixed exchange rate regime, the *induced* fiscal (or quasi-fiscal) deficit (associated with the expansion of domestic credit to prevent bank credit contraction) can increase and make the exchange rate regime unsustainable (in Krugman-type fashion).

In other words, when the monetary authority is highly sensitive to cuts in bank credit, a decrease in the demand for money may result in a balance of payments crisis along the lines of Krugman's model. An unsustainably large fiscal deficit becomes the proximate cause of crisis, but the fiscal deficit is an *endogenous* variable, and rises as monetary aggregates show a tendency to contract. Thus, a deeper cause for the crisis lies in monetary/financial variables although, on the surface, it may appear that the cause is simply lack of fiscal discipline.

Recapitulation

As noted in the Introduction, the main challenge posed by the Mexico/ Tequila episode is explaining why seemingly minor shocks could result in major macroeconomic disruption. Our analysis strongly suggests that aside from standard solvency considerations—conventionally expressed in terms of flow variables like fiscal and current account deficits—financial variables play an important role. However, our discussion has also revealed that financial variables alone do not suffice to rationalize a crisis. Something else must trigger a major crisis.

The case of Mexico suggests that financial vulnerability at the end of 1994 made it possible for a run against Tesobonos to bring Mexico to the brink of default. However, we argued that the latter would not have taken place if Mexico's solvency was not in question. Otherwise, new Tesobonos' holders could have been found.

Thus, a satisfactory explanation must show that financial turmoil changes expectations as to the country's solvency. Solvency, it could be argued, lies in the eye of the beholder. Solvency considerations involve the *future*, and since the future has no reality but in man's imagination, perceptions on a country's solvency are bound to reflect current and past events.

Professional economists and practitioners are well aware of the connection between present/past events and expectations. But a specific conjecture from the above analysis is that perception of a country's solvency may be strongly predicated on the state of financial variables.

Establishing a connection between financial variables and solvency is only a first step. A satisfactory explanation needs to go further. It must be able to show why small peccadillos result in major capital-markets punishment. Our analysis suggests that Mexico departed from a sustainable path in 1994, but the departure was neither unusual nor unreasonable. An adjustment was probably necessary but, why was it so large and so socially costly?

Our analysis suggests that in a global financial world, investors may be very sensitive to the perception of small negative shocks. An example of the latter might be the unscheduled peso devaluation, coupled with policy announcements that did not involve significant cuts in government spending. I think the shock was small because it was bound to have increased the probability of default in some, perhaps unlikely, states of nature. However, in a globalized financial world the investors' response may have been disproportionately large, at least initially.

Under normal circumstances, the initial stock market collapse would give rise to expectations of capital gains, luring back reluctant investors. This did not happen in Mexico, which leads me to a main conjecture, namely, that emerging-markets economies are likely to exhibit more than one equilibrium. Thus, taking equilibrium-multiplicity for granted, the initial investor's retreat from the Mexican stock market—including Tesobonos—may have pushed the Mexican economy into a "bad" equilibrium in which the marginal productivity of capital in Mexico suffered a sharp decline compared with the pre-crisis situation.

According to our analysis, Tesobonos and other dollar-denominated short-term debt (which includes banks' dollar-denominated negotiable obligations) played a key role in pushing the economy into a "bad" equilibrium. Had capital inflows been fully invested in the Mexican stock market, the speculative attack would not have required major help from the US Treasury and multilateral institutions. Hence, Mexico would not have been forced into medium-run costly fiscal adjustment which, in this interpretation, *validated* the "bad" equilibrium.

This interpretation also provides an easy rationale for the Tequila effect. The "bad" Mexican equilibrium appears to have taken the capital market by surprise. Capital market newsletters and low interest rate premia on Mexican dollar-denominated short-term debt prior to the crisis indicate, quite decisively, that market participants were taken largely by surprise by the extent of the Mexican crisis. However, investors were quick learners and, thus, guessed that the same phenomenon might take place in other emerging markets. Arguably, then, the Tequila effect is just a reflection of panicky "animal spirits" in search of the nearest exit.

Policy Implications

The picture emerging from the above discussion is very different from the conventional one in which financial factors are a veil rather than a major forcing variable. Therefore, the present section will be devoted to a discussion of aspects that the new reality calls for special attention. It should be pointed out, however, that there is no attempt to provide a full taxonomy of cases, or a full coverage of all relevant issues.

Exchange Rate

Mexico's crisis has revealed that devaluation could be costly for economies that are financially vulnerable. For example, before 20 December, one might have expected that a devaluation would not have triggered a run against dollar-denominated liabilities. However, Mexico's key lesson is that if there is a 'bad' equilibrium lurking in the background, a devaluation—especially, an unscheduled devaluation—could coordinate expectations and help push the economy to the "bad" equilibrium.

This observation tilts the balance against fixed exchange rates (including narrow bands) but should not be taken to *imply* that flexible rates are optimal, because the above-mentioned problem with fixed exchange rates could be remedied by lowering financial vulnerability.

Actually, the main lesson from our analysis is that the optimal exchange rate essentially depends on the prevailing financial structure. Only if high financial vulnerability is inevitable, should a country be strongly advised to adopt a system of flexible exchange rates.[20]

Several factors lie behind financial vulnerability, some of which will be highlighted in the ensuing discussion. However, it should be noted that financial vulnerability increases with volatility of both real *and* monetary variables. Thus, in contrast with the standard literature on exchange rates, floating exchange rates could become attractive even though the main source of structural volatility stems from the demand for money, for example, a *nominal* variable *par excellence*. This is a relevant point because emerging markets are likely to exhibit high nominal volatility.

It is worth noting, however, that when shocks are preponderantly "nominal," fixed exchange rates combined with active reserve-requirements regulations may dominate exchange rate flexibility. This combination was successfully tested in Argentina during the Tequila episode. It consists of lowering reserve requirements when the demand for money falls, and raising them when the opposite takes place. In this fashion, bank credit could be insulated from fluctuations in the demand for money.

The main difficulty of the above policy is that, in practice, it is not easy to determine when the demand for money has suffered a sufficiently permanent shift that warrants a change in reserve requirements. Furthermore, while lowering reserve requirements is likely to be welcomed by both banks and the private sector, increasing them may face political flak. Thus, this policy may have a bias towards low reserve requirements which, for reasons discussed earlier, could unduly increase financial vulnerability.

Public Debt

Debt maturity and currency denomination are important characteristics of public debt instruments. This became evident during the Mexican crisis, although it had already been explored in the academic literature (see Guidotti and Kumar, 1991).

Short-maturity debt is dangerous because it may trigger a self-fulfilling balance of payments crisis. Moreover, the existence of these self-fulfilling prophecies is more likely, the more difficult or costly it is for the debt to be repudiated. A good example in this respect are Teso-bonos which were denominated in dollars.

On the other hand, hard-to-repudiate debt obligations ensure against a moral hazard or time-inconsistency and are, therefore, useful to nail down "good" equilibria. Thus, the main difficulty lies with short maturities.

The situation is different, however, if debt is easy to repudiate like, for example, when debt is denominated in local currency and the stabilization plan is not fully credible. In this case, short-term debt may be desirable because it reduces the temptation to liquidate its real value through devaluation.[21]

One reason countries choose short-maturity public debt is the occasionally exorbitant steepness of the term structure of interest rates. This is, however not the only reason. Countries are sometimes led to "short-termism" in their attempt to fulfil ambitious price stabilization targets. For example, authorities may have made fiscal policy announcements that could only be carried out if short-maturity debt, with its attendant low interest rates, is issued.

Another reason is that policy is sometimes made counting on good, albeit transitory, news to be permanent. This behaviour was observed during the 1970s' oil boom (see Little *et al.*, 1993), and it came back to life with full force during the recent capital-inflows episode. When temporariness is revealed by the disappearance of former bountiful circumstances, policymakers are driven to adopt stopgap policies, among which "short-termism" takes the place of honour.

Extending debt maturity may not be an easy task and could involve heavy costs. The latter, however, should be a warning signal to policymakers that credibility is slim. Thus, the main line of attack should be to build credibility by, for example, adopting IMF-endorsed tighter (but efficient) fiscal policy. Furthermore, to discourage "short-termism," rules could be adopted limiting the issue of short-term debt. Thus, for instance, in a regime of fixed exchange rates, the stock of short-term bonds (plus some fraction of M2 which could be determined on the basis of the methodology discussed earlier) may not be allowed to exceed the stock of gross international reserves.

Another relevant characteristic of public debt is the type of holder. In Mexico a large share of short-term debt (mostly Tesobonos) was in the hands of non-Mexicans, who are likely to be more interest-sensitive than their local counterparts (recall the discussion earlier). This situation sharply contrasts with that in Brazil, where most short-term public debt is held by domestic banks and firms.

Brazil, it should be recalled, was able to devalue in March 1995 and announce further devaluation in May the same year without causing a Mexican-type debacle.

Therefore, it appears that foreign holdings of short-term public debt are particularly volatile. It should, thus, be advisable to endow short-term debt with characteristics that make it somewhat unappealing to foreign holders. There is no sure-fire solution here but a partial one may be to denominate short-term debt obligations in terms of domestic currency.

International Reserves and Banks

International reserves help to cushion the effects of fluctuations in monetary aggregated and debt refinancing difficulties. Thus, an alternative to the policies discussed in the previous subsection is for the central bank to amass a sufficiently large stock of international reserves.

Reserves adequacy is conventionally measured by the equivalent number of months worth of imports. However, while this was an appropriate measure in the Bretton Woods world of low capital mobility, our discussion reveals that complementary, if not more relevant, indicators should take into account financial considerations. Thus, as noted earlier, one should pay more attention to ratios of monetary aggregates to reserves.

The relevant monetary aggregate may differ across countries, but short-term public debt should always be part of these aggregates. However, the weight attached to public debt should depend on the type of holder, currency denomination and the explicit or implicit exchange rate regime. Thus, in a currency board system like that in Argentina, short-term public debt in pesos should be given full weight, because it is equivalent to a dollar-denominated debt. On the other hand, in a country like Colombia where a regime of exchange rate bands is being adopted, domestic debt could be valued at the highest exchange rate (i.e. the exchange rate corresponding to maximum scheduled devaluation) within the band.

As noted above, banks play a very sensitive role in a crisis. Time and again we have learned that announcements of tough banking rules, like the absence of bank bailouts, are seldom enforced. Thus, bank liabilities are, to some extent, contingent fiscal liabilities that come due during a banking crisis. To lower their incidence, one can think of three possibly complementary ways of action: (1) high bank (remunerated or unremunerated) reserve requirements; (2) large share of international banks endowed with automatic international credit lines; and (3) effective swap agreements with other central banks.

Solution (1) takes its extreme form in Simons' (1936) proposal of 100% reserve requirement on sight deposits. Clearly, under those circumstances a run against sight deposits will never result in a banking or credit crisis. The main drawback of Simons' (1936) proposal, however, is that it promotes disintermediation or leads banks to mask sight deposits under a different, but essentially equivalent, form—like "offshore" sight deposits.

The second type of solution (international banks) consists of attracting money-centre banks to operate in the domestic market. A successful example of this sort is Hong Kong. In this fashion, a liquidity squeeze originating in banks' domestic operations (e.g. an across-the-board deposit withdrawal) could be quickly and painlessly offset by drawing liquidity from banks' foreign branches or headquarters.

This solution requires a significant presence of money-centre banks in the domestic market. The latter, however, may require a drastic overhaul of the current system. Thus, for example, Argentina has a free-entry policy in the banking sector but its banking industry is still largely dominated by local banks.

International banks appear to be particularly reticent to participate in retail banking. This may be due to cultural considerations but, I suspect, the presence of large state banks with a wide net of national branches may be a contributing factor. State banks are normally expected to receive fiscal support, making competition much harder for new entrants. Thus, encouraging a significant presence of money-centre banks may entail a major downsizing of state-owned banking institutions.

Finally, swap agreements with other monetary authorities are possible and have been put into effect, but the sums involved were usually dwarfed in comparison with the support required in times of crisis. Mexico, for example, had a swap agreement with the Fed of about US$2 billion, while the rescue package ended up hovering around US$50 billion.

Capital Inflows, Cool Heads and Signals

The recent capital inflows episode has shown how easily policymakers mistake transitory for permanent positive shocks. An unfortunate characteristic of these inflows is that they may last for relatively extended periods of time, and exhibit infrequent occurrence. Hence, in addition to the customary credulity of policymakers (particularly, as concerns the success of their own policies), these episodes can cause objective observers wrongly to infer that capital inflows have an unrealistically high permanent component. This mistake is especially easy to make if a country has undertaken well-advised structural reforms, as in the cases of Argentina, Chile and Mexico. For, in that case, capital inflows are partly linked to those reforms (which have a relatively permanent character), making the statistical inference problem especially difficult.

A sour lesson of the Mexico/Tequila episode is that capital markets are quick to forget good structural reform and, as argued above, may be unduly impressed with short-run financial turbulence. In addition, even in the case in which capital inflows are highly permanent, benefits from capital inflows may be significantly lower than the costs associated with comparable outflows. Therefore, a key lesson is that it is better to err by underestimating than by overestimating the permanence of capital flows and, at any rate, policymakers would be well advised to keep a "cool head" and restrain the fervour of "animal spirits" during capital-inflow episodes.

The above considerations provide a rationale for running a positive fiscal balance during capital-inflow periods. This has the advantage of cooling off the economy, and generating public sector savings that could be utilized during capital-outflow periods to increase aggregate government expenditure (for Keynesian or unemployment compensation purposes). These extra savings would be especially valuable if during those periods the country is rationed out of the capital market (due, for instance, to "contagion" effects).

In addition, Talvi (1995) has recently shown that fiscal accounting under high capital flows volatility is an important and less-than-trivial issue. For example, as a general rule, tax revenue is an increasing function of expenditure. Thus, capital-inflow periods are characterized by higher-than-average fiscal revenue, while the converse holds true when capital flows out. Hence, this provides another rationale for fiscal tightening during capital-inflow episodes (and fiscal relaxation when capital flows out).

Credible signals are important. In this respect, multilateral institutions can be very effective, because emerging markets are "small" and have little direct influence on the management of those institutions. Therefore, agreements between emerging-market countries and multilaterals are less suspect of credibility-enhancement tricks. In this respect, the agreement between Argentina and the Fund early this year is a relevant example. The sums involved in the agreement were not high enough to prevent a successful bank run, but the Fund's presence was able to enhance credibility and, thus, stabilize the situation overnight.[22]

Mexico's experience also suggests that "easy" policies, like currency devaluation, cannot stand on their own. For credibility's sake they should be accompanied by short-run socially-costly measures. Otherwise, the government might become suspect of being prone to adopt easy time-inconsistent solutions which involve reneging on past explicit or implicit commitments.

Acknowledgments

This is a revised version of a paper presented at the Seminar on Implications of International Capital Flows for Macroeconomic and Financial Policies, organized by the International Monetary Fund, and held in Washington, D.C., December 11–15, 1995. I am grateful to Sara Calvo, Jacob Frenkel, Ernesto Hernández-Catá, and Ernesto Talvi for useful comments.

Notes

1. The reader should be warned, however, that the following remarks are highly tentative, and are intended to set the stage for the ensuing discussion.

2. This appears to have been the view of the US Treasury in orchestrating the rescue package for Mexico.

3. Arguably, high market-determined Mexican interest rates reflected, in part, the active sterilization policy pursued by the monetary authority during the stabilization plan.

4. This point will be further discussed in the following section.

5. Mexican authorities appear to have been reluctant to let bank interest rates fully bear the brunt of adjustment. A possible explanation for this high-interest aversion is that interest rates on mortgages were linked to short-term rates.

6. Variable x follows a random walk if $x_{t+1} = \alpha + x_t + u_{t+1}$, where α is a constant and the u_ts are a set of identically independently distributed (i.i.d.) random variables, which we further assume to be normally distributed. Volatility of x is measured by the estimated standard deviation of u.

7. These estimates are based on monthly observations. Data is taken from the International Financial Statistics, IMF. M2 is the sum of "money" and "quasi-money." The period for Austria is 1960:01 to 1994:12. For Mexico the period is 1990:01 to 1993:12. In this fashion, we leave out high-volatility periods for Mexico, associated with bank restructuring in 1989 and the political events of 1994. Furthermore, we assume that the relevant M2$/Reserves ratio for Austria is 10.

8. Financial vulnerability could be much greater, however, if monetary authorities were sensitive to cuts in bank credit. This important topic will be taken up later.

9. For monthly data, the short-run semi-elasticity falls to -1, but the long-run semi-elasticity is still around -5.

10. The contemporaneous correlation of these two series for 1994 is only weakly positive on a monthly basis. However, I do not see this as invalidating the conjecture that expan-

sion of domestic credit prevented monetary aggregates from falling to the levels predicted by the Calvo–Mendoza equation, since the dynamic configuration of this process is likely to be complex. There are leads and lags that cannot possibly be detected on 12 months data.

11. For Mexico, however, the coordination between domestic credit and international reserves is very striking, see figure 3.4.

12. Of course, this does not deny that electoral considerations may have increased the monetary authority's sensitivity to an economic downturn.

13. Recent progress on this issue is reported in Frankel and Rose (1996) and Kaminsky and Reinhart (1996).

14. For a discussion of this issue and an alternative extension of Krugman's model to account for the stability of monetary aggregates in the face of a speculative attack, see Flood et al. (1996) and Calvo (1996).

15. Enrique Mendoza (personal communication) shows, based on simulations that take into account estimated variance-covariance matrices, that the degree of portfolio diversification need not be high for these effects to be large.

16. This shows, incidentally, the advisability of generating a pattern of uniformly-staggered bond maturities, a subject that will be taken up later in the paper.

17. However, it could be argued that the unscheduled devaluation may have sent a signal that Mexico had been hit by, at least a small negative shock.

18. Analytical results supporting this view can be found in Calvo (1995).

19. This is a topic that deserves further analysis. For a discussion focusing on the US economy, see Bernanke and Gertler (1995).

20. An often-heard advice after Mexico's crisis is for emerging-market economies to adopt a "dirty float" regime. In my opinion, this is a promise-nothing-and-do-what-you-please system which, in practice, only constrains government to unified exchange rates. It is, thus, an invitation to engage in time-inconsistent, socially costly, games.

21. However, this case is not very relevant for economies where price stability is highly valued, as in present-day Argentina.

22. This opinion is not universally shared. Some analysts believe that Mexico's March stabilization programme played a key role for the credibility of Argentina's IMF programme.

References

Aizenman, J., and Frenkel, J. A. (1985) Optimal wage indexation, foreign exchange intervention, and monetary policy, *American Economic Review*, 75, 402–423.

Bernanke, B. S., and Gertler, M. (1995) Inside the black box: the credit channel of monetary policy transmission, *The Journal of Economic Perspectives*, 9(4), 27–48.

Banco de México (1995) *Report on Monetary Policy*.

Calvo, G. A. (1995) Varieties of capital market crises, Working Paper No. 15, Center for International Economics, University of Maryland at College Park, November.

Calvo, G. A. (1996) On the resilience of money demand under duress: notes from the bop crisis front. Manuscript, February.

Calvo, G. A., and Goldstein, M. (1993) Crisis prevention and crisis management after Mexico: what role for the official sector? Manuscript, September.

Calvo, G. A., Leiderman, L. and Reinhart, C. M. (1993) Capital inflows and real exchange rate appreciation in Latin America. *IMF Staff Papers*, 40, 108–151.

Calvo, G. A., Leiderman, L. and Reinhart, C. M. (1994) The capital inflows problem: concepts and issues' *Contemporary Economic Policy*, XII, 54–66.

Calvo, G. A., and Mendoza, E. G. (1995) Reflections on Mexico's balance-of-payments crisis: a chronicle of a death foretold, *Journal of International Economics*, forthcoming.

Dornbusch, R., Goldfajn, I. and Valdes, R. (1995) Currency crises and collapses. MIT manuscript, August.

Flood, R. P., Garber, P. M. and Kramer, C. (1995) Collapsing exchange rate regimes: another linear example. *Journal of International Economics*, forthcoming.

Frankel, J. A., and Rose, A. K. (1996) Exchange rate crashes in emerging markets: an empirical treatment. *Journal of International Economics*, forthcoming.

Guidotti, P. E., and Kumar, M. S. (1991) Domestic public debt of externally indebted countries. *IMF Occasional Paper* No. 80, June.

Hochreiter, E., and Winckler, G. (1995) The advantages of tying Austria's hands: the success of the hard currency strategy. *European Journal of Political Economy*, 11, 83–111.

Kaminsky, G. L., and Reinhart, C. M. (1995) The twin crises: the causes of banking and balance of payments problems. Working paper. Presented at the Conference on Speculative Attacks in the Era of the Global Economy, held during 1–2 December, at the Center for International Economics, University of Maryland.

Little, I. M. D., Cooper, R. N., Corden, M. and Rajapatirana, S. (1993) *Boom, Crisis, and Adjustment: The Macroeconomic Experience of Developing Countries*. Published for the World Bank by Oxford University Press.

Rojas-Suárez, L., and Weisbrod, S. R. (1994) Financial market fragilities in Latin America: from banking crisis resolution to current policy challenges. IMF Working Paper WP/94/117, International Monetary Fund, Washington, DC.

Simons, H. C. (1936) Rules versus authorities in monetary policy. *Journal of Political Economy*, 44, 1–30.

Talvi, E. (1995) Exchange-rate based stabilization with endogenous fiscal response. Manuscript, Inter-American Development Bank, September.

4

Petty Crime and Cruel Punishment: Lessons from the Mexican Debacle

Guillermo A. Calvo and
Enrique G. Mendoza

Before December 1994, Mexico was hailed as the prime example of success of market-oriented reforms. It was widely believed that, despite the year's serious political shocks, the country was poised for ascending to a sustainable high-growth, low-inflation equilibrium. There was debate over the bloated current-account deficit and overvalued real exchange rate, and the need for some correction prior to the "ascension," but the strength of the country's fundamentals was rarely questioned.[1] The devaluation itself was welcomed by many as a necessary adjustment. For instance, Stanley Fischer argued that "the exchange rate adjustments ... will help reinforce the economic recovery that has been evident since early 1994 and secure the viability of Mexico's external position" (International Monetary Fund, 1994). Thus, the severe crisis that followed and its global spillover were met with shock and disbelief.

After two severe speculative attacks in March and November, Mexico attempted a devaluation of 15 percent on December 20. The markets' response was dramatic. A final attack pushed foreign reserves well below the Bank of Mexico's "tolerable minimum" of U.S. $10 billion, and in the subsequent days stock markets in Mexico, South America, and other "emerging" regions of the world plummeted. For Mexico the consequences were catastrophic. The government could not refinance its dollar-denominated, short-term bonds ("Tesobonos") at any reasonable interest rate, while the private sector lost access to global capital markets. The country was forced to float the exchange rate. Interest rates rose sharply, and the subsequent liquidity squeeze resulted in Mexico's worst recession in modern times, putting the already weak banking system at the brink of collapse.

The sudden and violent financial crash helped to correct the imbalances highlighted by most analysts: the trade deficit running at about U.S. $1.5 billion per month by the end of 1994 turned into a surplus in less than two months, and the real exchange rate fell back to its end-of-1990 level. However, this failed to trigger an early recovery in 1995, and after stabilizing around M$6.40 per U.S. dollar for several months, in November the exchange rate fell sharply to about M$7.7 per U.S. dollar. Thus, this evidence casts serious doubts on the relevance of conventional explanations, which rely on current-account deficits and real currency appreciation (e.g., Rudiger Dornbusch and Alejandro Werner, 1994). Moreover, it is surprising that capital markets in countries seemingly unrelated to Mexico and without any of its vulnerability symptoms were also hit by the Mexican crash.

Our research suggests that the heavy punishment capital markets inflicted on Mexico is characteristic of a new kind of crises in the global-markets era. Punishment appears to be especially harsh on countries committed to fixed exchange rates. Rather than a crisis due to conventional current-account sustainability or real overvaluation (i.e., "flow") problems, Mexico's crash was primarily a capital-account crisis of "stocks," to some extent similar to the balance-of-payments crises studied by Paul Krugman (1979). The Mexican crisis, however, differs in that it was not caused by monetization of a fiscal deficit. To the contrary, for the first time in the postwar period the peso collapsed without the pressure of clearly expansionary policies. Instead, the peso became extremely vulnerable because of (a) large imbalances between money balances, short-term debt, and gross reserves caused in part by the effects of global markets on the financial system, and (b) the tendency of global investors in the complex world economy, in which information is costly to acquire, to neglect fundamentals and display herding behavior. We believe that these two elements are necessary to explain key features of the crisis. A theory of "fundamentals" explains the increased vulnerability reflected in the money and debt imbalances, while a theory of herd behavior justifies the massive capital flows triggered by the devaluation. The "stock" problems we highlight here have thus revealed their potential to be as dangerous as conventional "flow" problems—hence the interest in studying them and in designing mechanisms to anticipate and correct them.

I   Vulnerability Warnings and the Peso Collapse

The vulnerability of the peso was exhibited in two key imbalances relative to the stock of international reserves (see figure 4.1), which were clearly noticeable before the collapse. First, there was a *monetary-*

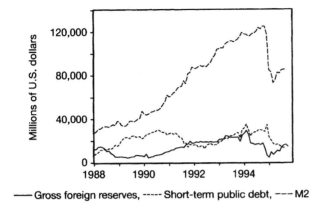

Figure 4.1
Mexico: Money and debt imbalances

aggregates imbalance: real money balances (in dollars or in CPI units) largely exceeded gross foreign reserves, making the peso vulnerable to negative and persistent money demand shocks. If such shocks occurred, a given pre-crisis rate of net domestic credit expansion would be rendered inconsistent with the fixed exchange rate, even under unchanged fiscal policy. This imbalance gradually built up during 1988–1993, as Mexico experienced a surge in foreign capital inflows and booming private expenditures (which suggests a positive link between real balances and aggregate demand, as postulated in cash-in-advance models). The monetary aggregates imbalance was further fueled by far-reaching financial reform that *inter alia* eliminated reserve requirements, credit controls, and restrictions to global capital flows. This was accompanied by a worsening of banks' balance sheets, which in turn severely limited the central bank's ability to rein in the growth of monetary aggregates.

Second, there was a *debt* imbalance: private holdings of short-term public debt, measured in dollars, grew much larger than foreign reserves, and a large portion was converted to Tesobonos. The stock of debt was 5.5 times larger than the stock of reserves just before the collapse. We claim that this large imbalance resulted from the policy response in early 1994 to shocks that threatened to cause a sharp and sudden deceleration in the rapid growth of demand for liquid, peso-denominated assets experienced in previous years (e.g., the rise in U.S. interest rates, the slowdown in GDP growth in 1993, and the perception of a major political crisis).

The run on reserves in the aftermath of the Luis Donaldo Colosio assassination (March 23, 1994) reflected a run on government bonds by both the private sector and commercial banks, revealing a widening differential between interbank interest rates and those paid on government bonds. Faced with increased banking fragility, the central bank (a) expanded domestic credit to "sterilize" the effect of the fall in reserves on the monetary base, and (b) slowed down the decline in public-debt holdings by offering Tesobonos in exchange for short- and long-term peso-denominated bonds (Cetes, Bondes, and even the CPI-indexed Ajustabonos). This second policy converted most public debt to Tesobonos, with a large fraction taken by foreign investors. Thus, vulnerability to runs on government bonds worsened considerably as average bond maturity shortened, bonds were dollarized, and bondholders without transactional or liquidity needs became major holders.

International reserves fell sharply in April and then stabilized. However, short-term debt was already nearly 40-percent larger than gross reserves, reversing the situation of 1992–1993 and signaling the growing fragility of the currency peg. By November, before the second attack on reserves, the debt imbalance showed private debt holdings (mostly Tesobonos) 2.2 times larger than reserves. Pedro Aspe (1995) argues that the authorities responded to this second attack by repeating sterilized intervention, aiming to avoid large adjustments to interest rates or the exchange rate because of political uncertainty one week before the end of the Salinas term. Aspe's account of the policy debate shows no indication that the authorities worried about their ability to roll-over existing Tesobonos or place additional debt. Eventually, however, the government found it increasingly difficult to place Tesobonos, and the collapse arrived in December, when markets refused to roll-over Tesobonos falling due and the attempt at the managed devaluation failed with a final bonds-led attack on reserves.

To understand why the imbalances described above foretold the collapse of the Mexican peso we consider an extension of the Krugman (1979) model presented in Calvo (1995). The extension does not rely on obvious fiscal-policy laxity. A particular example consistent with the Mexican experience is one in which surging capital inflows, combined with radical financial liberalization, induce a lending boom in a setup prone to financial fragility. Fragility results from the perverse incentives given to credit markets by the currency peg and an explicit or implicit commitment by the central bank to act as lender of last resort. In an extreme case, with short-term bonds financing long-term loans, one can show under fairly general conditions that the size of the speculative attack increases with the size of the expected banking-system bailout, and that the attack occurs earlier than in a standard Krugman model.

Still, models like this only begin to explore the complex interaction among the global capital market, financial asset demand, and vulnerability of currency pegs in developing economies. Several important questions remain unanswered. In Mexico's case, for instance, monetary aggregates as measured in the data during 1994 do not show the sharp decline predicted both by conventional models of speculative attacks and econometric studies of Mexico's money demand (see section II). One possible interpretation is that the government employed credit expansion to finance net transfers to voters prior to an election. If these households consumed most of the transfer, and if consumer-goods firms maintained real balances in proportion to their capacity utilization, one could explain the downward inflexibility of real monetary aggregates in the early stages of a balance-of-payments crisis. The danger is that, as the policy is reversed and the inertia of the original weakening of money demand takes over, the fall in money demand and, hence, the loss of reserves at the moment the peg is abandoned are magnified.

II Econometric Evidence: Money Growth and the Transmission Mechanism

Our econometric analysis of money-demand models for M2 in Mexico (see Calvo and Mendoza, 1996) provides unambiguous evidence that (a) the global capital market influences the growth of M2, (b) M2 and expenditures are closely related, and (c) real M2 should have declined sharply in 1994. Using error-correction specifications of real M2 money demand, we identify large and significant effects of world capital markets on Mexico's M2, represented by a negative effect of the interest rate on 3-month U.S. Treasury bills (T-bills) and a positive effect of inflows of foreign reserves. We also show that private consumption and investment expenditures provide additional information for explaining money demand not included in the traditional scale variable represented by GDP.

This money-demand analysis predicts a large decline in the stock of real M2 for 1994 (equivalent to about U.S. $12.6 billion) on account of the rising T-bill rate, and the slowdown of GDP and aggregate demand

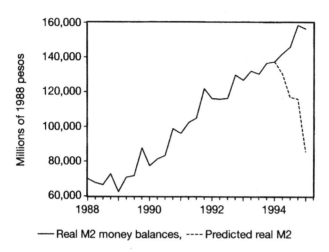

— Real M2 money balances, ---- Predicted real M2

Figure 4.2
Mexico: Actual and predicted real M2 money balances

a year before (see figure 4.2). Contrary to this prediction, actual real M2 continued to grow in 1994. The policy response described in section I implied such a large structural change that if the M2 equations are reestimated adding only the second quarter of 1994, the coefficients on the T-bill rate, foreign reserves, and expenditures become statistically insignificant.

In Calvo and Mendoza (1996), we also examine comovements of cyclical components of real M2, private expenditures, GDP, the 28-day Cete rate, and the real exchange rate based on different detrending methods. We find further evidence of a positive link between M2 and private expenditures. Multivariate causality tests show, in addition, that M2 causes GDP and expenditures, and not vice versa (in line with a cash-in-advance model in which money carried over from the past is used in current transactions) and that the Cete rate (the main instrument of monetary policy at the time) Granger-causes M2, GDP, and expenditures without feedback.

Further analysis based on a parsimonious VAR system provides additional evidence in favor of our view and illustrates the key role of the Cete rate as a policy instrument for the duration of the currency peg. In sharp contrast with similar studies for industrial countries, particularly the United States (see Christopher A. Sims, 1992), the Cete rate is clearly identified as the policy instrument, with the expected effects on real and nominal variables. Impulse-response analysis shows that upward adjustments in the Cete rate were very effective in lowering real money balances, bringing down inflation, and slowing the growth of GDP and private expenditures. Finally, impulse-response functions also show large effects, consistent with the intuition developed above, resulting from sudden inflows of foreign capital (e.g., innovations to real M2 or expenditures).

III "Optimal" Herding Behavior in the Global Marketplace

Several important events in the aftermath of Mexico's currency collapse showed how sensitive world markets are to the arrival of news that may not be directly related to the fundamentals driving asset returns in a particular country and, hence, suggest that global investors may be susceptible to exhibiting "herding" behavior. First, in the days after the currency collapse, Mexico was unable to attract holders to roll-over maturing Tesobonos despite offerings at high interest rates, and the stock market fell sharply as foreign and domestic investors chose to reduce their exposure. Guillermo Ortiz (1995) noted that "after the devaluation, financial markets for Mexico virtually disappeared, and there was a true stampede, in which all Mexican public and private debt instruments where literally thrown out." Second, since the collapse, Mexican markets have remained extremely vulnerable to wild rumors originating at home or abroad, as vividly illustrated by the sharp fall in the peso on November 3, 1995, on unfounded rumors of a military coup and the resignation of the finance minister. A Reuters cable quoted a trader as saying "the day has been one of total anguish, we dropped as low as 7.72 pesos per dollar but now the rumors have been denied, the market breathes again." Third, in the days after the Mexican crash, emerging markets worldwide also fell as the "Tequila effect" propagated, and global investors reacted to the news on Mexico by suddenly changing their views on the merits of investments in all emerging markets. (Sara Calvo and Carmen M. Reinhart [1995] provide statistical evidence of strong contagion effects.)

This kind of "herding" by the global investor does not necessarily reflect any irrational behavior and does not require sophisticated theories to be justified. To the contrary, in Calvo (1995) and Calvo and Mendoza (1996) herding is a feature of the simplest of portfolio-choice models, the mean-variance model. In this model, investors balance optimally the trade-off between diversification and costly information-gathering as opportunities to diversify rise. As a result,

(a) portfolio allocations to a single country become highly responsive to very small changes in perceived expected returns, and (b) the benefits of gathering country-specific information to firm up beliefs with regard to those returns diminish. Thus, diversification encourages ignorance, and in this environment even frivolous rumors may trigger massive capital flows that are seemingly inconsistent with a country's "fundamentals."

However, high sensitivity to rumors does not fully explain the persistence of the Mexican recession. By the same logic of this model, the recession could have been avoided, or quickly reversed, by a slight fall in stock prices or rise in Tesobonos' interest rates.

The last model in Calvo (1995) provides the missing link. The model assumes that fiscal adjustment is socially costly. Thus, if the initial run against Tesobonos forces the government to undertake very tough fiscal adjustment, a new "bad" equilibrium could appear. Notice that, according to this interpretation, the initial run has to prompt tighter and socially costly fiscal policy. If, in contrast to Mexican experience, investors had been willing to refinance maturing Tesobonos (at possibly slightly higher interest rates), then no official reaction may have been called for. The run would likely have been reflected in lower stock prices, but lacking the disruptive policy response, the price decline would have been no larger than a "technical adjustment."

IV   Conclusion: Lessons for Avoiding Cruel Punishment

This chapter argues that the harsh punishment that world capital markets dealt Mexico (and emerging markets in general) following the country's attempt at a modest devaluation reflects the substantial risks embodied in the volatile capital flows characteristic of the global world economy. Despite conventional-wisdom arguments favoring the devaluation as the best "medicine" for a large current-account deficit and an overvalued real exchange rate, and despite the devaluation's effectiveness at addressing these problems, the attempt at correcting the misalignment of the exchange rate triggered a deep and protracted economic crisis and caused continued weakness in Mexico's currency and stock markets. It follows from the analysis that the warning signals given by traditional vulnerability indicators (such as the size of the current-account deficit and the stock of reserves) need to be complemented by indicators of financial vulnerability such as monetary and debt imbalances.

Still, this analysis also suggests that volatility is an inescapable feature of the global economy that comes along with its advantages for risk-diversification, transfers of technology, and enhanced efficiency in resource allocation. Balancing the pros and cons is difficult, but domestic policy and international institutions can play a key role in moderating the risks. Domestic policy could ameliorate the impact of capital-market volatility by, for example, lengthening the maturity of public debt and helping to strengthen the banking system through, for instance, higher liquidity requirements and mandatory capital/deposit ratios. International institutions, on the other hand, could take the role of lender of last resort, which, given sufficient commitment and resources, can reduce the risk of sudden stampedes in capital markets. Also, publicly available "surveillance" studies, with an emphasis on financial vulnerability, can provide information as a public good and lessen the risk of herding behavior triggered by rumors (see Calvo and Morris Goldstein, 1995).

The phenomena studied here also pose challenges for international economics. It is important that we advance our understanding of the channels of transmission by which global integration affects real and financial variables, and that we learn more about how economic policies interfere with these channels. We hope to make progress in these areas in future work.

Notes

Center for International Economics, Department of Economics, University of Maryland, College Park, MD 20742, and International Finance Division, Board of Governors of the Federal Reserve System, Washington, DC 20551, respectively. This paper was written while Mendoza was a visiting scholar at the Center of International Economics of the University of Maryland. We thank Andy Atkeson, Dave Backus, Bill Gruben, Steve Kamin, John Rogers, Andres Velasco, and the participants at the conference Speculative Attacks in the Era of the Global Economy for helpful comments. The views expressed here are not those of the Board of Governors of the Federal Reserve System.

1. The current-account deficit at the end of 1994 stood at 8 percent of GDP. The real exchange rate had appreciated by more than 55 percent since the beginning of the December 1987 stabilization plan.

References

Aspe, Pedro. "Mexico en 1994: Las Razones de la Politica Cambiaria." *Reforma: Corazon de Mexico* (Mexico City), 14 July 1995, (587), p. 2A.

Calvo, Guillermo A. "Varieties of Capital Market Crises." Mimeo, University of Maryland, 1995.

Calvo, Guillermo A. and Goldstein, Morris. "Crisis Prevention and Crisis Management after Mexico: What Role for the Official Sector?" Mimeo, University of Maryland, 1995.

Calvo, Guillermo A. and Mendoza, Enrique G. "Mexico's Balance of Payments Crisis: A Chronicle of a Death Foretold." *Journal of International Economics*, 1996, *41*, pp. 235–264.

Calvo, Sara and Reinhart, Carmen M. "Capital Flows to Latin America: Is there Evidence of Contagion Effects." Mimeo, World Bank, Washington, DC, 1995.

Dornbusch, Rudiger and Werner, Alejandro. "Mexico: Stabilization, Reform, and No Growth." *Brookings Papers on Economic Activity*, 1994, (1), pp. 253–315.

International Monetary Fund. "IMF Supports Mexico's Exchange Rate Action." News Brief No. 94/18, 22 December 1994.

Krugman, Paul. "A Model of Balance of Payments Crises." *Journal of Money, Credit, and Banking*, August 1979, *11*(3), pp. 311–25.

Ortiz, Guillermo. Statement to the American Chamber of Commerce, quoted from *La Jornada* (Mexico City), 26 July 1995, p. 1A.

Sims, Christopher A. "Interpreting the Macroeconomic Time Series Facts: The Effects of Monetary Policy." *European Economic Review*, June 1992, *36*(5), pp. 975–1000.

5 Capital Market Contagion and Recession: An Explanation of the Russian Virus

Guillermo Calvo

This chapter will offer a brief overview of the role information gathering plays in international financial markets for emerging market (EM) economies. It will then offer a hypothesis of how structural weaknesses make this system susceptible to local viruses that the system itself then transmits and magnifies rapidly into international contagion.

I will begin with four general observations about what makes information gathering unique in financial markets for EMs.

First, a prominent difference between advanced and emerging capital markets is the much higher cost that investors face in assessing the economic prospects of EM countries.

Second, information costs are higher in emerging markets for several reasons (each of which may not apply to all economies). They include a narrow production base of tradable goods (e.g., copper for Chile, oil for Venezuela), short and sometimes not very successful track records in capital markets, young democracies, or political systems that are prone to polarization (e.g., the presidential campaign of Cardoso versus Lula da Silva in Brazil). And the list goes on.

Third, information costs are high in the following two senses: Entry costs are large and informational value decays rapidly. This implies that information gathering is subject to *large economies of scale*. Consequently, there are a few clusters of international (rather than local) specialists that are on top of events in EMs. The rest of the capital market remains blissfully ignorant.

Finally, these informational economies of scale, in combination with other economic and political factors, induce the formation of *specialist* clusters that are knowledgeable about whole regions, e.g., Asia, Latin America. Sometimes a cluster encompasses the whole spectrum of EMs. These clusters are the operators of those mutual funds, hedge funds, etc., which focus on *large* EM subsets.

The Logic of the Russian Virus and Sudden Stops

How does this structure set the stage for contagion? In particular, what role might it have played in spreading the Russian virus of 1998? Suppose that a large EM defaults on debt obligations held by these funds. As a result, and in line with fundamentals, the funds' market value shrinks by exactly their capital losses on the defaulted debt. This shock, however, could be magnified and spread to other EMs by contagion mechanisms like the two that follow.

Default Rumors

Upon observing Russia's default, investors raise their subjective probability that other EMs will follow suit. One explanation for the fear of additional defaults is that the G7 sent a signal by letting Russia collapse that they would not be ready to bail out other EMs in case of financial stress, increasing suddenly the exposure risk of investors elsewhere. Another line of reasoning is that Russia's default lowered the credit market stigma on defaulting. Such conjectures are very difficult to assess in the short run due to the high costs and short-lived nature of information. As Calvo and Mendoza (1998) explain more fully, a rational investor could choose to believe the worst-case scenario and play it safe, causing a fall in EMs' security prices.

The Lemon Problem

If the funds are leveraged and get margin calls because of Russia's default, they will be forced to sell some of their long positions. In perfect information markets, the price of those assets need not change as a result of the sale. Money from loans that were withdrawn as a result of margin calls will be invested in the securities sold by EM specialists. However, if *most* specialists in Russian debt are subject to margin calls, then these securities will have to be sold *outside* the specialists' circle. The latter investors are less informed than the specialists and, therefore, will be willing to buy only if the securities are sold at large price discounts (a situation that echoes Akerlof's celebrated Lemon Problem). Moreover, given that, as argued above, Russian investment funds may likely hold other EM paper as well, these holdings will also suffer a substantial price decline.

As long as the contagion problem is not resolved, EMs will face much higher interest rates or outright exclusion from the capital market, causing a "sudden stop" in capital inflows. As a result, aggregate demand will suffer a sudden collapse, which will likely cause a sharp output slowdown. This might be the "kiss of death" for EMs *because it would tend to validate the uninformed investor's fear that EM financial obligations are actually Lemons.* Consequently, interest rates will remain high and the possibility of deep recession will arise because there would be no end in sight for the sudden stop (for a discussion of sudden stops, see Calvo, 1998).

To sum up, then, the logic of the Russian virus outlined here does not rely on multiplicity of equilibria. The liquidity problem faced by specialists due to Russia's default, for example, kicks them out of the game at the margin. Therefore, prices *are* set by the uninformed, or blind, investor. These, in turn, are willing to hold EMs' paper only if traded at deep discounts (due to the Lemon Problem), which provokes a sudden stop in EMs. Under those circumstances, the "blind" investors have every reason to continue thinking that EM financial obligations could be lemons. Therefore, the fundamental exogenous shock to the system is Russia's default, which, in turn, provokes a loss of *effective* human capital in financial markets—causing a negative output shock in other EMs.

Lessons

What conclusions can we draw from this?

First, emerging markets far from the source of the initial shock can be victims even though they are *innocent bystanders*. Because contagion is possible and even likely for EMs, the costs of capital market contagion could be major.

Second, *lemons are worse than rumors*. False rumors have a short life span (although false rumors may not fade so quickly when elections are impending). In contrast, the Lemon Problem is much harder to uproot. To stop this type of contagion, one or more steps may have to be taken. Specialists could reenter the market, but this is unlikely since it presupposes the Federal Reserve will restore EMs' paper liquidity. A new set of specialists could also step up to the plate and enter the market, but that is unlikely to occur fast enough to halt the contagion. Or the G7 could organize a massive bailout operation for EMs, which is also unlikely.

Third, regional financial coordination is required. EMs must realize that the risk of capital market contagion makes them interdependent. Therefore, they should devise ways to discourage individual countries from following risky financial policy. This can initially be implemented through existing free-trade blocs. If such mechanisms were in place, Brazil might not be running such a biased short-term maturity structure.

Finally, the G7 countries have a major role in stabilizing EMs. This is perhaps a good time to start thinking about a World Central Bank.

References

Calvo, G. 1998. "Capital Flows and Capital Market Crises: The Simple Economics of Sudden Stops." In a forthcoming *Journal of Applied Economics*.

Calvo, G., and E. Mendoza. 1998. "Rational Herd Behavior and the Globalization of Securities Markets." Forthcoming in a National Bureau of Economic Research book edited by Sebastian Edwards.

6 Sudden Stops, the Real Exchange Rate, and Fiscal Sustainability: Argentina's Lessons

Guillermo A. Calvo, Alejandro Izquierdo, and Ernesto Talvi

1 Introduction

The fall of the Convertibility Program (i.e., the currency board regime) in Argentina has stirred a lively discussion about the causes for its collapse. Several explanations have been offered. The most popular one relates to the unholy combination of a fixed exchange rate and large fiscal deficits that led to a rapid growth in public debt, severe fiscal sustainability problems, and eventually, a loss of access to the credit markets. Another popular view stresses the impact of a fixed exchange rate regime coupled with devaluation by Argentina's major trading partners as an important cause of real exchange rate (RER) misalignment, which reduced profitability in the tradable sector. This, in turn, slowed down investment and led the economy into a protracted recession as it deflated away the RER disequilibrium.

The purpose of this chapter is to provide a different interpretation of the collapse of Convertibility, which places special emphasis on two key structural characteristics of Argentina's productive and financial structure and on political economy considerations.

Our point of departure is the Russian crisis of August 1998, which drastically changed the behavior of capital markets. We believe that developments at the center of capital markets were key to producing an unexpected, severe, and prolonged stop in capital flows (hereon referred to as Sudden Stop, SS) to Emerging Market economies, and Latin America was no exception.

We will argue that in the case of Argentina two considerations played a crucial role in magnifying the effect of the sudden stop in capital flows and in creating the fiscal and financial problems that eventually Argentina had to confront, namely:

a) A relatively closed economy, i.e., an economy with a small share of tradable goods output (more specifically, output that could swiftly be transformed into exports) relative to domestic absorption of tradable goods;

b) Liability Dollarization (more specifically, large financial currency-denomination mismatches) in both the private and public sector.

Being closed implies that the Sudden Stop (SS) may call for a sharp increase in the equilibrium real exchange rate, RER (i.e., real depreciation). Liability Dollarization, in turn, entails foreign-exchange-denominated debt in "peso producing" sectors (mostly non-tradables) including the government, which implies large balance sheet effects when the RER rises. Thus, these two factors represented a dangerous financial cocktail for both the private sector and the government.

Argentina's Fall from Paradise could be rationalized by its commercial closed-ness, and penchant for dollar indexation in the corporate sector. In that sense, the tragedy needs no fisc to grab one's imagination. Under liability dollarization the need for a sharp (equilibrium) real devaluation in the aftermath of the SS hit first and foremost corporate balance sheets. Perhaps more importantly, it lowered the collateral of non-tradable sectors, which, by and of itself, brings about a *stock* retrenchment of credit to the non-tradable sector (see, for example, Izquierdo, 1999[1]). Hence, to the first exogenous Sudden Stop, a second round follows, which validates and likely deepens the impact of the first.

This kind of shock can only be met by a sale of assets, financial restructuring or the initiation of bankruptcy procedures. No flow "belt tightening" of the corporate sector could probably do the trick. The problem here, though, is that the shock hits a whole sector, not just an individual firm. Prospects for individual firms are hard to assess when they belong to a network immersed in financial difficulties. Thus, assets can only be sold at rock-bottom prices, and financial restructurings and bankruptcy procedures are especially hard and time consuming, which precipitate the economy into a protracted recession. Under these circumstances, cries for help will likely rise from every corner, and it will be politically very difficult for the government to stay put and wait for the dust to settle—thus, unavoidably bringing into play strong and complex political economy factors.

A strong fisc could have come to the rescue by *effectively* socializing private debts or providing additional collateral (like in Korea's IMF-orchestrated bank negotiations with external creditors in 1997, which eventually resulted in a rise in public debt equivalent to more than 30 percent of GDP). As argued in Calvo, 2002b, the government can play an important role in cases in which the economy is hit by *low-probability* shocks, like the aftermath of the Russian 1998 crisis.[2] However, and this is when the fisc kicks in, given the financial structure of the public sector, Argentina's government was also exposed to exactly the same financial problems as the private sector following the SS and the RER rise. The government thus became part of the problem rather than (as in Korea) part of the solution. But our view departs from the fiscalist view of the Convertibility's demise. Argentina was fiscally weak (i.e. vulnerable to a Sudden Stop) not because it had an unreasonably large current (flow) fiscal deficit—which it did not— inconsistent with the fixed exchange rate regime. Argentina's fiscal weakness lay in that the government was unable to offset the fundamental vulnerabilities associated with the country's closed-ness and Liability Dollarization, the latter impinging upon both public and private debt.

Adding together private and public debt, and computing its share in GDP after the Sudden Stop (involving a higher RER), it is clear that Argentina's debt was dangerously high, as early as 1999. For the sake of the argument, consider the case in which the government socializes the larger GDP-equivalent debt incurred by corporates after such change in the RER (which, as will be argued, hovers around 60 percent). Under those circumstances, we will argue that the government would have been required to produce a permanently larger primary surplus in excess of 3% of GDP. *Permanently* is a key word. Sustaining higher levels of debt by implicitly collateralizing it with future flows of primary surpluses is an extraordinarily difficult task since, for starters, future flows depend on future governments. If credibility on future surpluses is at stake, the ability to roll over the stock of debt would be severely hampered, creating a *stock* retrenchment problem for the government, potentially as severe as that suffered by the private sector. To illustrate this point, it is sufficient to say that a failure to produce such an adjustment of the primary surplus on a permanent basis would have implied a 75% haircut on the existing debt.

To avoid a painful default, Argentina had to permanently and credibly raise its primary surpluses. This could only occur by raising taxes or reducing primary spending. Raising taxes is particularly problematic when the corporate sector itself is under severe financial stress and arrears with the public sector become very significant as a source of financing.[3] As a result, raising taxes on the non-corporate sector and/or reducing primary expenditures were the only options available, absent debt restructuring.

The government was thus forced to engage in *wealth redistribution* policies across sectors. This is where politics kicks in with full force, and phenomena like War of Attrition among different groups in society develop. Wealth redistribution sets in motion a tug-of-war in which decisions are *delayed* and, as the War of Attrition literature shows (see Sturzenegger and Tommasi, 1998), can be highly disruptive. Thus, unless a supranational entity generates a *cooperative* equilibrium, the impasse may take a long time to resolve and may seriously deepen the extent of the crisis. Since no positive rate of return can match losing a chunk of capital to the taxman's ax, this impasse in resolving which sectors would ultimately sustain the losses, brought about a grinding stop to all investment projects, except for those few that could be safely shielded from the bloodbath (e.g., black-market transactions). Under these circumstances, tax revenue falls, further weakening the government's fiscal situation. This, in turn, increases the expected devaluation and sets in motion a new wave of credit cuts.

At this stage, politically feasible solutions were inevitably going to involve spreading the cost of adjustment among all players, making some type of debt restructuring inevitable. In turn, expectations of debt restructuring would severely hit the banking system to the extent that most of its assets consisted of government debt and dollar loans to non-tradable sectors. It should therefore come as no surprise that a bank run materialized as a corollary of the Sudden Stop.

Finally, a word on the role of the Convertibility regime itself. Argentina's adherence to its hard peg to the dollar probably made things worse, but for reasons not necessarily related to competitiveness. As argued in Talvi (1997), incomplete but inevitable adjustments can mask the gravity of the underlying fiscal situation. In the case of Argentina, maintaining the peg and delaying the inevitable adjustment of the RER may have contributed to conceal the true nature of its financial problems for a long period of time, leaving politicians and the general public largely unaware of the gravity of the financial situation, a factor that might have contributed to undermine the political support for the necessary fiscal and financial adjustments. Furthermore, maintaining the peg left Argentina without a valuable instrument of the adjustment package, namely, inflation, which has proven, time and again, to be a very powerful tool for lowering government expenditure (in real terms).

The chapter is organized as follows: Section 2 examines capital market trends in Latin America following the Russian crisis of 1998 and provides a rationale for Sudden Stop behavior. Specifically, we show that the nature of Sudden Stops has typically been large and persistent. Section 3 dwells on conditions under which Sudden Stops lead to a sharp depreciation of the RER, and ranks a set of Latin American countries in terms of vulnerability to these shocks. Section 4 focuses more closely on Argentina. It discusses fiscal sustainability and determines the sources of vulnerability to swift changes in the RER, and computes how those changes affected Argentina's fiscal position. Section 5 dwells on the effects of RER adjustment on the materialization of contingent liabilities (particularly those arising from currency-denomination mismatches in the corporate sector). We compute how Argentina's fiscal position would have deteriorated even further under the assumption that the government would attempt (as it eventually did) to bail out the corporate sector. Section 6 briefly touches upon the concealment of the financial problems under Argentina's hard peg, and analyzes likely performance under a floating exchange rate regime following a Sudden Stop. The chapter concludes with some policy lessons for Latin America that emerge from Argentina's experience, and an Appendix that reviews the policies followed by Argentina.

2   The World Scene after Russia

Russia's August 1998 crisis represents a milestone in the development of emerging capital markets. Massive capital inflows that set sail to Latin America in the early 1990s, financing high growth rates and large current account deficits, came all of a sudden to a standstill following Russia's partial foreign debt repudiation in August, 1998. It was hard to imagine how a crisis in a country with little if any financial or trading ties to Latin America could have such profound effects on the region. This puzzle seriously questioned traditional explanations for financial crises (based on current account and fiscal deficits) and led analysts to focus on the intrinsic behavior of capital markets. Thus, it was argued that prevailing rules for capital market transactions may have been responsible for the spread of shocks from one country to other regions (Calvo, 1999).[4]

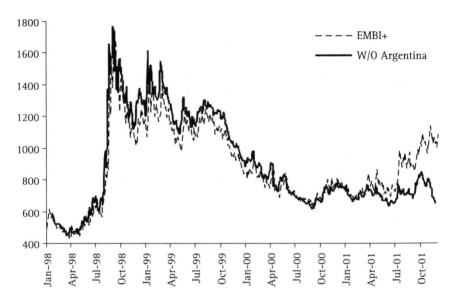

Figure 6.1
External financial conditions (EMBI+, Spread over U.S. Treasuries). Source: JP Morgan Chase.

Table 6.1
Difference in Bond Spreads with Minimum Pre-Crisis Levels

	1999	2000	2001
EMBI+	666	307	393
EMBI+ w/o Argentina	757	315	259

Source: JP Morgan Chase.
Note: Values are yearly averages.

In figure 6.1, spreads measured by the EMBI+ index show a dramatic increase following the Russian crisis. Although they have since decreased, spreads exhibit a substantial gap compared to pre-crisis levels, exceeding 250 basis points for 2001.[5] This gap was much higher for 1999 and 2000 (over 700 basis points and 300 basis points, respectively, see table 6.1).

Latin American markets were not the only ones hit by the higher cost of capital. For most EMs higher interest rates were accompanied by a large reduction in capital inflows. Figure 6.2 and table 6.2 show that for the seven biggest Latin American economies the decline was sharp, particularly for portfolio flows, mimicking the sharp interest rate hike. The fact that the root of this phenomenon lied in Russia's

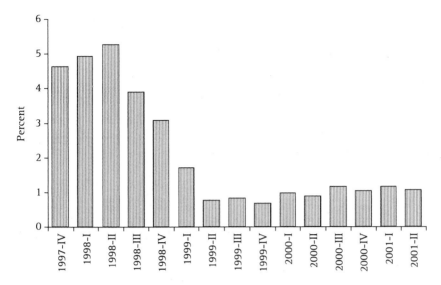

Figure 6.2
Sudden stop in LAC (captial flows, % of GDP). Includes Argentina, Brazil, Chile, Colombia, Mexico, Peru, and Venezuela. Source: Corresponding Central Banks.

Table 6.2
Capital Flows, % of GDP

	1998.II	2001.III	Reversal
Capital Flows	5.6	1.6	−4.0
Non-FDI Capital Flows	2.0	−0.9	−2.9
FDI	3.6	2.5	−1.1

Source: Corresponding Central Banks.
Note: Includes Argentina, Brazil, Chile, Colombia, Mexico, Peru, and Venezuela.

crisis indicates that the capital-inflow slowdown contained a large *un-expected* component. "Large and highly unexpected" are the two defining characteristics of what the literature calls Sudden Stop (see Calvo and Reinhart, 2000). New information that a standstill in the capital account can materialize for rather exogenous reasons (and for a whole region) such as the Russian crisis, generating drastic effects on government sustainability (either because of debt revaluation effects or the emergence of contingent liabilities), may reduce the appetite for holding assets of countries that may be subject to big swings in the RER and are highly dollarized in their liabilities. Thus, this realization could bring the capital account to a lengthy standstill.

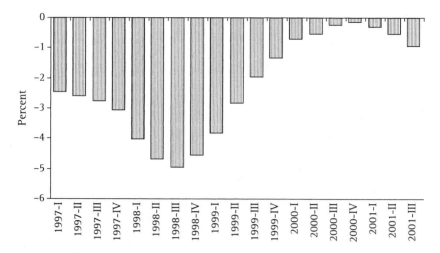

Figure 6.3
Sudden stop and the current account in LAC (4 quarters, % of GDP). Includes Argentina, Brazil, Chile, Colombia, Mexico, Peru, and Venezuela. Source: Corresponding Central Banks.

Sudden Stops usually lead to a significant cut in current account deficits. Starting in the fourth quarter of 1998, key Latin American countries showed a steady decline in their current account deficits, which eventually reached a zero balance by the end of 2000.[6] This adjustment of the current account was on average equivalent to 5 percentage points of GDP for the seven biggest Latin American economies (see figure 6.3).

3   Sudden Stops and Real Exchange Rate Adjustment

So far we have made a case for the large external component accounting for the observed fall in capital inflows. But what are the consequences of this event in terms of RER behavior and debt sustainability analysis? Two key elements in this discussion are the unexpected component of the Sudden Stop and its duration. It is clear that expectations prevailing before the Russian crisis are unlikely to have factored in the widespread effects on EMs that followed, so the unexpected element required for a Sudden Stop is met. A different question is whether this shock was perceived as temporary or highly persistent, which is quite relevant from a policy perspective. With the benefit of hindsight it is easy to argue that the shock had a large permanent component, since the stalling in capital inflows has lasted more than three years now.

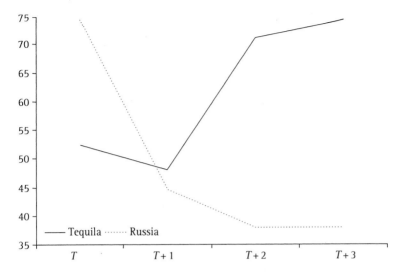

Figure 6.4
Sudden stop in LAC (net private capital flows, US$ billions). Note: "LAC" refers to Western Hemisphere countries, according to IMF definition. "*T*" denotes the year of occurence of the crisis. Source: World Economic Outlook (IMF), December 2001.

But it is not clear that it was perceived as such from the very beginning (this is an important point that we will revisit when we discuss Argentina in greater detail). Indeed, investors and policymakers had witnessed a quick recovery of capital flows following the Mexican (Tequila) crisis in 1995, which could have led them to expect a similar quick recovery after the Russian collapse. But things turned out differently. Figure 6.4 shows that two years after the Mexican crisis there was more than a complete recovery of capital flows, whereas there has been no recovery in capital flows to the region since 1998 following the Russian crisis.

Sudden stops are also typically accompanied by large contractions in international reserves *and* declines in the relative price of nontradables with respect to tradables (i.e., real currency depreciation). By way of illustration, consider the case of a small open economy that experiences a current account deficit before a Sudden Stop takes place. By definition:

$$CAD = A^* + S^* - Y^*, \tag{1}$$

where *CAD* is the current account deficit, A^* is absorption of tradable goods, S^* represents net non-factor payments to foreigners, and Y^* is the supply of tradable goods. If financing of the current account deficit

Table 6.3

Current Account Balance, US$ billions

	ARG	BRA	CHL	COL	ECU
1998	−14.5	−33.4	−4.1	−5.2	−2.2
1999	−11.9	−25.4	−0.1	0.2	0.9
2000	−8.9	−24.6	−1.0	0.3	0.7
2001	−5.6	−23.2	−0.9	−2.1	−0.8

Current Account Change, % of 1998 Imports

	ARG	BRA	CHL	COL	ECU
1999 vs 1998	6.1	10.6	18.8	31.3	49.0
2001 vs 1998	21.1	13.5	14.9	18.0	21.3

Source: World Economic Outlook (IMF), April 2002.

is stopped, the full amount of that imbalance needs to be cut. Table 6.3 shows that current account adjustment can be sharp. Indeed, it is not uncommon to see an abrupt adjustment towards current account balance within a year following the Sudden Stop.

A measure of the percentage fall in the absorption of tradable goods needed to restore equilibrium is given by:

$$\eta = CAD/A^* = 1 - \omega, \tag{2}$$

where ω is a measure of the un-leveraged absorption of tradable goods, defined as:

$$\omega = (Y^* - S^*)/A^*. \tag{3}$$

Notice that this measure captures the share of absorption of tradable goods that is financed by the domestic supply of tradable goods.[7] The lower this value, the higher will be the share of absorption of tradables financed from abroad. In other words, relatively closed economies with a small supply of tradable goods running a current account deficit will be highly leveraged. As we will see later, this is an important consideration regarding RER behavior after a sudden stop in capital flows.

In order to obtain an estimate for η that can be used for cross-country comparisons, we proxy A^* by imports. We use the observed current account adjustment for different periods, taken as a share of imports at the time of the crisis, in order to illustrate the observed percentage fall in absorption of tradable goods that was required to accommodate the change in the current account. Results are shown in table 6.3 for 1999 and 2001. Countries like Chile, Colombia, and Ecuador, where the percentage fall ranged anywhere from 18.8 to 49 percent, experienced a quick and substantial adjustment in absorption of tradable goods by 1999. Adjustment in Brazil and Argentina has taken longer, a phenomenon that we will analyze in more detail later.

Having shown that the percentage fall of tradable goods absorption can be substantial after a Sudden Stop, we now consider effects on non-tradable goods. A common assumption in the literature is that preferences are homothetic, implying that the income expansion path of tradable vis-a-vis non-tradable goods is linear. Under this assumption, for a given RER, consumption of non-tradable goods is therefore proportional to that of tradable goods.[8] As a result, a decline in demand for tradable goods of size η must be matched by a proportional fall of equal size in the demand for non-tradable goods. Now consider the effects of this fall in demand on the RER. Given that the price of tradable goods is determined from abroad, all we need to take into account is the behavior of the non-tradable goods market. Define demand for non-tradables as:

$$h = a - \chi p, \tag{4}$$

where h is (the log of) demand for non-tradable goods, p is (the log of) the relative price of non-tradable to tradable goods, i.e., the inverse of the RER, χ is a parameter, and a captures the income effect. Then, for a given RER, the fall in demand following a Sudden Stop is simply:

$$da = \eta = 1 - \omega. \tag{5}$$

Assuming, for simplicity, that the supply of non-tradable goods is fixed (so that $dh = 0$), then the required percentage change in the real exchange, after differentiation of (4), is given by:

$$-dp = (1 - \omega)/\chi; \tag{6}$$

That is to say, the higher is the leveraged absorption of tradables, i.e. the lower is ω, the higher the impact on the RER needed to restore equilibrium after a Sudden Stop. The intuition for this result is that, in the short run, the ability to generate purchasing power in terms of tradables is exports minus debt service. Thus, a Sudden Stop that requires a larger *proportional* sacrifice in absorption in terms of tradables, the smaller is ω. Another element that affects our measure of

Table 6.4
Un-leveraged Absorption Coefficient (ω)

BRA	ARG	ECU	COL	CHL
0.56	0.66	0.66	0.70	0.81

Source: World Economic Outlook (IMF), and own estimates.
Note: Values are given for 1998.

absorption leverage is non-factor payments (S^*), typically composed of interest payments, which implicitly captures indebtedness levels. High external indebtedness therefore reduces available resources to finance absorption of tradable goods, requiring greater RER realignment following the elimination of the current account deficit. Given these characteristics, ω is a good summary statistic to measure the impact on RER realignment. A further simplifying assumption we make is that the supply of tradable goods can be measured by exports whereas, as earlier noted, imports serve as a proxy for absorption of tradables.[9] Table 6.4 contains a list of Latin American EMs ranked by this measure in 1998. Chile clearly leads the ranking in terms of un-leveraged absorption. Argentina, although not the lowest ranked in the group, stands 15 percentage points below Chile, indicating that it would need greater RER realignment following a Sudden Stop.

Another key element in determining the size of the required change in the RER is given by the price elasticity of the demand for home goods, χ. Estimates for developing countries are typically much lower than those for industrial countries, implying that Sudden Stops can be much more devastating for EMs. Thus, not only are Sudden Stops a much more common feature of developing countries (see Calvo and Reinhart, 2000), but their effects can be more dangerous as well. Actually, the higher vulnerability of EMs to Sudden Stops could partly explain their higher recurrence.

Given this framework, we next ask what should be the size of RER realignment following a Sudden Stop that requires a full adjustment of the current account deficit, using 1998 as a starting point. To compute this, we make use of equation (6), taking a value of $\chi = 0.4$ (the lowest point estimate in the literature). Given that we measure the RER as the inverse of (antilog of) p, the rate of depreciation is $-dp$. Obviously, these figures should not be taken at face value, but as a way of ranking the effects of a Sudden Stop across countries.[10] Table 6.5 shows the results. As it stands, this exercise indicates that Argentina would have needed to depreciate its RER by 46 percent in order to bring down its

Table 6.5
Required % Change in Equilibrium RER

BRA	ARG	ECU	COL	CHL
52.5	46.2	46.1	43.0	32.4

Source: World Economic Outlook (IMF), and own estimates.
Note: Values are given for 1998.

current account to zero, whereas Chile, for example would only have needed to depreciate its RER by 32 percent. This means that Argentina would have needed to depreciate its RER about 43 percent more than Chile in order to close the current account gap.

Moreover, since the Russian crisis, between 1998 and 2001 Chile depreciated its currency vis-à-vis the dollar by about 45 percent in real terms, and closed a current account gap of almost 19 percent of imports. Chile's current account deficit was equivalent to 6 percent of GDP in 1998 and fell to zero in 1999. In this respect, it would look like Chile's adjustment was larger than that of Argentina, whose current account deficit fell from 4.9 percent of GDP in 1998 to 2.4 percent of GDP in 2001. However, if Argentina's reduction in the current account gap is measured as a share of imports (the relevant measure from our perspective), the reduction was also 19 percent, similar to the adjustment observed in Chile. According to our model, Argentina's depreciation should have been at least as large as that of Chile (45 percent), clearly indicating that the depreciation of the RER that effectively took place in Argentina (around 14 percent) was far from sufficient given the underlying adjustment in the current account.[11] The slow adjustment of RER observed in Argentina can be explained by the combination of a fixed exchange rate and price stickiness (a relevant feature given the weight of public wages and public utility fees in price behavior), which retarded the adjustment of the RER.

4   Debt Valuation and Fiscal Sustainability

We now turn our attention to the effects of RER depreciation on fiscal sustainability. It is not uncommon to find countries where public sector debt is largely denominated in terms of tradables (see table 6.6) and government revenue comes to a large extent from non-tradable activities. This introduces a currency mismatch in the public sector balance sheet, which makes any sustainability analysis highly susceptible to RER swings.

Table 6.6
Public Sector Debt Mismatch Measure

	ARG	ECU	COL	BRA	CHL
B/eB^*	0.08	0.02	0.59	1.76	1.30
Y/eY^*	8.63	2.94	6.36	12.34	2.85
$(B/eB^*)/(Y/eY^*)$	0.01	0.01	0.09	0.14	0.45

Source: Own estimates.
Note: Values are given for 1998.

Consider the typical sustainability calculation, where the size of the primary surplus necessary to keep a constant ratio of debt to GDP is computed, given a cost of funds, and a growth rate for the economy. Take the standard asset accumulation equation:

$$b_{t+1} = b_t \frac{(1+r)}{(1+\theta)} - s_t, \tag{7}$$

where b is the debt to GDP ratio, r is the real interest rate on debt, θ is the GDP growth rate, s is the primary surplus as a share of GDP, and t denotes time. To obtain a constant debt to GDP ratio ($\bar{b}$), the budget surplus must satisfy, assuming constant r and θ:

$$s = \bar{b}\left[\frac{(1+r)}{(1+\theta)} - 1\right]. \tag{8}$$

Key to this analysis is the initial debt to GDP ratio ($\bar{b}$), which, in turn, depends on its denomination in terms of tradables and non-tradables. This ratio can be expressed as:

$$\bar{b} = \frac{B + eB^*}{Y + eY^*}, \tag{9}$$

where e is the RER (defined as the price of tradables relative to non-tradables), B is debt payable in terms of non-tradables, B^* is debt payable in terms of tradables, Y is output of non-tradables, and Y^* is output of tradables. Obviously, debt composition, as well as output composition, matter a great deal for sustainability analysis, because mismatches between debt and output composition can lead to substantial differences in valuation of the debt/GDP ratio following a real currency depreciation. For example, consider the limit case in which $b = eB^*/Y$, where all valuation effects take place on debt only. This is the worst scenario in which RER depreciation hits fully on sustainability. Another case that is particularly relevant is that in which $(B/eB^*)/(Y/eY^*) = 1$, i.e., when the composition of debt and output is perfectly matched. When this condition holds, a change in the RER has no effect on fiscal sustainability. Table 6.6 shows how countries ranked in terms of mismatch at the time of the Russian crisis.[12] A value of 1 would indicate a perfect match, and a value of zero would indicate the highest degree of mismatch. Clearly, the highest mismatch holds for Argentina. On the other side of the spectrum lies Chile, the best-matched economy, with a value of 0.45.

For comparison purposes, we consider the effects of a RER rise of 50 percent on debt valuation and fiscal sustainability for all the countries we selected, as of 1998. The results are presented in table 6.7[13]. We see clearly that under this scenario, Argentina, together with Ecuador, would be the hardest hit economy in terms of debt revaluation. Just because of the relative price adjustment (holding the assumption that interest rates on public debt and GDP growth remain unchanged), Argentina's debt/GDP ratio would jump from 36.5 percent of GDP to 50.8 percent of GDP, an increase of nearly 40 percent on impact. Quite

Table 6.7
Fiscal Sustainability under a 50% RER Depreciation

	ARG	BRA	CHL	COL	ECU
(a) Base Exercise					
Observed Public Debt (% of GDP)	36.5	51.0	17.3	28.4	81.0
Real Interest Rate	7.1	5.8	5.9	7.3	6.3
Real GDP Growth	3.8	2.0	7.5	3.6	2.6
Observed Primary Surplus (% of GDP)	0.9	0.6	0.6	−3.0	−0.2
i. Req. Primary Surplus (% of GDP)	1.2	1.9	n.a.	1.0	2.9
(b) Change in Relative Prices					
Real Exchange Rate Depreciation	50.0	50.0	50.0	50.0	50.0
Imputed Public Debt (% of GDP)	50.8	58.1	18.7	34.9	107.2
Real Interest Rate	7.1	5.8	5.9	7.3	6.3
Real GDP Growth	3.8	2.0	7.5	3.6	2.6
ii. Req. Primary Surplus (% of GDP)	1.6	2.2	n.a.	1.2	3.9
NPV of $ii - i$ (% of GDP)	14.3	7.1	n.a.	6.5	26.3
Corresponding Debt Reduction (%)	28.2	12.2	n.a.	18.7	24.5
$ii - i$ (% of Government Expenditures)	2.3	1.0	n.a.	1.3	4.5

Source: Own estimates.
Note: Values are given for 1998. n.a.: Not applicable given that the real interest rate is smaller than the growth of GDP, so sustainability is not a concern.

a different scenario plays out for Chile, where the debt revaluation effect is minimal: public sector debt as a share of GDP increases from 17.3 percent to 18.7 percent. It is interesting to see that in the case of Brazil, a 50 percent rise in the RER only affects the debt/GDP ratio by 14 percent. As we shall see later, in our view this was a key element, together with a substantial adjustment in the primary surplus, to explain Brazil's success in controlling its fiscal position after the real currency depreciation it experienced in 1999.

We also consider the effects on the required primary surplus following a rise in the RER. Making use of equations (8) and (9), we calculate the required primary surplus after revaluation of the debt/GDP ratio.[14] It is important to note that these calculations implicitly assume that the shock is permanent. Had the shock been temporary, the effects on sustainability would be a lot less and, consequently, the need for adjustment would be smaller. But as it became apparent after the 1998 Russian crisis, this shock was highly persistent, implying that the adjustment in the RER and its effect on debt valuation was large as well. Of course, this was not clear at the time of the crisis, which led to underestimating the necessary fiscal adjustment.

Taking as a benchmark the case in which the RER depreciation is permanent, we estimate changes in the required primary surplus needed for sustainability. The biggest correction is for Ecuador (about 1 point of GDP). Argentina, for example, would require an adjustment of 0.4 points of GDP. In order to assess the significance of this adjustment, we estimate the net present value of the difference between the required primary surplus before and after the RER depreciation, which is equivalent to the change in debt before and after the shock, measured in percentage points of GDP.[15] This figure would be equivalent to 14.3 points of GDP for Argentina, and as much as 26.3 points of GDP for Ecuador. Besides, these figures only represent changes in the required primary surplus, and, in most cases, countries had much lower observed primary surpluses than those required, meaning that the need for adjustment was much higher. In summary, once again we see that highly indebted, dollarized and closed economies are bad candidates to accommodate RER swings that will be fiscally sustainable.

Given that we have used exports as a proxy for tradable goods output in these calculations, we run the risk of overestimating the effects of RER depreciation because tradable goods output will typically be higher than exports. In order to assess the significance of this shortcut, we compare results against a more thorough measure of tradable out-

Table 6.8
Fiscal Sustainability under a 50% Depreciation

	ARG	BRA	CHL	COL	ECU
(a) Base Exercise					
Observed Public Debt (% of GDP)	36.5		17.3	28.4	81.0
Real Interest Rate	7.1		5.9	7.3	6.3
Real GDP Growth	3.8		7.5	3.6	2.6
Observed Primary Surplus (% of GDP)	0.9		0.6	−3.0	−0.2
Req. Primary Surplus (% of GDP)	1.2		n.a.	1.0	2.9
(b) Change in Relative Prices					
Real Exchange Rate Depreciation	50.0		50.0	50.0	50.0
Imputed Public Debt (% of GDP)	47.2		18.1	32.3	98.9
Real Interest Rate	7.1		5.9	7.3	6.3
Real GDP Growth	3.8		7.5	3.6	2.6
Req. Primary Surplus (% of GDP)	1.5		n.a.	1.1	3.6
NPV of $i - ii$ (% of GDP)	10.7		n.a.	3.9	17.9
Corresponding Debt Reduction (%)	22.7		n.a.	12.1	18.1
$i - ii$ (% of Government Expenditures)	1.7		n.a.	0.8	3.1

Source: Own estimates.
Note: Values are given for 1998.

put typically used for this calculation. This measure defines a category of output as tradable when imports plus exports of goods similar to those produced in that category exceeds output by more than 5 percent. This is performed for categories defined by the national accounting system at a one-digit level. Results are shown in table 6.8.[16]

As can be seen by comparing table 6.8 with table 6.7, although there are some differences in debt to GDP ratios, the required primary surplus following an adjustment in relative prices does not change substantially, implying that our first approximation is indeed a good one to evaluate the effects of a Sudden Stop.[17]

Now that we have provided examples of the effects on the RER of closing the current account gap, and examples of debt revaluation for a given depreciation of the RER, we put both pieces together for the case of Argentina, and analyze the effects of a sudden stop in capital inflows in 1998 (results are summarized in table 6.9). In our example, following a Sudden Stop, Argentina's RER would have to rise by about 46 percent. Had this depreciation occurred, the country would have displayed a debt/GDP ratio of 49.7 percent, a considerably larger value than that observed in 1998 (which was 36.5 percent of GDP).

Table 6.9
Fiscal Sustainability in Argentina under Alternative Scenarios in 1998

	Debt to GDP Ratio (%)	i. Adjustment in Prim. Surplus[a]	NPV of i. (% of GDP)	i. (% of Gov. Expenditures)	Debt Reduction (%)
(a): Baseline[b]	36.5	0.3	9.3	1.5	25.6
(b): Change in Relative Prices to close current account deficit (RER depreciation of 46.2%)	49.7	0.7	22.6	3.6	45.4
(c): (b) + 200 BPS Increase in Real Interest Rate	49.7	1.7	32.8	8.3	66.0
(d): (c) + 1% Reduction in Real GDP Growth	49.7	2.2	35.6	10.8	71.7
(e): (d) + Contingent Liabilities	58.6	2.7	44.5	13.5	75.9

Source: Own estimates.
Notes: a. The observed primary surplus for 1998 was 0.9 percent of GDP.
b. The baseline scenario assumes a long run rate of growth of 3,8% and a 7,1% real interest rate.

Under favorable growth and interest rate assumptions,[18] the *permanent* primary surplus needed to sustain the new (and higher) debt/GDP ratio would have been equivalent to 1.6 points of GDP, 0.7 percentage points of GDP higher than the observed figure (0.9% of GDP).

The above analysis only considers valuation effects, but table 6.9 also examines two other factors associated with the Sudden Stop: interest rates and economic growth. On the one hand, if our hypothesis that the Russian crisis changed investors' perceptions about the risk associated with EM bonds is correct, then interest rates are likely to rise. On the other hand, the fact that GDP growth rates fell all over Latin America may have increased expectations of much lower growth than originally expected.

Re-computing our estimates under the assumption that interest rates remain 200 basis points higher than in 1998 (an increase similar to the observed increase in EMBI spreads in 2001 compared to pre-Russian crisis levels) and growth estimates fall by one percent, the primary surplus needed to achieve fiscal sustainability following a Sudden Stop, goes all the way to 3.1 percent of GDP, or about 2.2 percent of GDP above the observed value for 1998 (see table 6.9). The needed adjustment is equivalent to 13.5 percent of total expenditures, a large figure from a political perspective. Alternatively, the size of debt reduction required for sustainability in the absence of a fiscal adjustment, exceeds 75 percent once we factor in all the different elements of a Sudden Stop that affect the fisc. From a credit risk perspective, this is also a large figure that helps us understand why under imperfect credibility on future primary surpluses, the ability to roll over the existing stock of debt was severely hampered after the Sudden Stop. It is worth noticing that under the 1998 baseline scenario[19] it is not evident that Argentina's fiscal position was out of control. Indeed, standard sustainability analysis indicates that the difference between the required and observed primary surplus was 0.3 percentage points of GDP at prevailing RER, growth and real interest rate levels (see table 6.9). Undoubtedly, Argentina was quite vulnerable to RER swings, but it was not clear before the Russian crisis that Argentina's fiscal position was out of hand in the absence of a Sudden Stop.[20] This warns about the need to obtain risk-weighted measures of fiscal sustainability that account for the occurrence of events such as a Sudden Stop. This type of tool could prove beneficial to internalize the need for more conservative fiscal policy.

This experience highlights two relevant aspects pertaining debt: both debt levels and indexation clauses are crucial in determining the effects

of Sudden Stops on sustainability. High debt levels imply little room
for cushioning valuation effects. Higher debt service, in turn, may
imply higher RER swings. And dollarization (or indexation to the
dollar) can trigger substantial valuation effects that may compromise
solvency.

It is useful to contrast the Chilean and Argentine experiences in
terms of sustainability. Chile was subject to a Sudden Stop that forced
the country to bring the current account to almost a zero balance, an
adjustment equivalent to 18.8 percent of imports. Yet, it fared much
better in terms of fiscal sustainability. Chile differed from Argentina in
two respects. First, as we already argued in the previous section, Chile
required a smaller RER realignment given the country's openness and
low indebtedness position. Second, recalling our exercise on the valuation effects of a rise of 50 percent in the RER (close to Chile's effective
depreciation of 45 percent) described in table 6.7, it is clear that Chile's
debt/GDP ratio remained almost unchanged. Chile's relatively high
share of tradables in GDP, and relatively low ratio of debt in tradables
to total debt, helped dampen the effect of the rise of the RER on sustainability. Thus, very little changed in terms of sustainability for Chile
after the Sudden Stop. Moreover, the RER shift was successful in
switching production to tradables (an effect that we do not consider
in our model), thus compensating in part for the standstill in capital
flows. Table 6.10 shows the change in exports relative to the change in
the current account deficit observed one year and three years after the
Russian crisis, as an indication of the contribution of exports in closing
the current account gap. It clearly shows that Chile was highly successful in switching production to tradables, something that did not occur

Table 6.10

Exports Change/Current Account Change, %

	ARG	BRA	CHL	COL	ECU
1999 vs 1998	−127.5	−47.6	11.1	8.7	8.0
2001 vs 1998	−1.8	82.7	79.1	43.8	41.8

Exports Change, %

	ARG	BRA	CHL	COL	ECU
1999 vs 1998	−10.6	−6.5	2.4	3.5	5.0
2001 vs 1998	−0.5	14.3	13.4	10.2	11.3

Source: World Economic Outlook (IMF), April 2002.

in Argentina, in part because the RER misalignment was providing little incentive to do so.

Another interesting case to contrast with Argentina is that of Brazil. Why was the rise in the RER in Brazil successful? Three factors contribute to its explanation. First, by 1999, the country's adjustment of the current account was equivalent to only 10.6 percent of imports, far below the 44.2 percent that would have occurred had the current account deficit been completely eliminated. So what made Brazil avoid a bigger adjustment? Contrary to the experience of other countries, the Sudden Stop in Brazil was short-lived and quickly compensated by FDI flows, which increased 80 percent in dollar terms between the second quarter of 1998 and the second quarter of 2001. According to our view, this prevented an even larger currency meltdown.[21] Second, Brazil's level of indebtedness was quite high in 1998 (51 percent of GDP) and a sustainability analysis along the lines presented here would have shown that large fiscal adjustment was also needed. After the 1999 crisis and in contrast to Argentina, Brazil responded with a severe fiscal adjustment, which increased its primary balance considerably by 3.5% points of GDP in 1999. This adjustment proved to be politically feasible and long lasting, two factors that are crucial in explaining Brazil's success in weathering the Sudden Stop, something that was unattainable by Argentina. And third, a crucial difference with Argentina is that by 1998, although Brazil's public debt was higher as a share of GDP than in Argentina, it was only partially dollarized, as table 6.6 shows. Since the level of dollarization was also relatively low in the private sector, contingent liabilities were kept in check, an issue we will discuss further in the next section. Therefore, revaluation effects of real currency (i.e., a rise in RER) over the public debt/GDP ratio were not substantial.

5 Real Exchange Rate Adjustment and Contingent Liabilities

So far we have not discussed another issue that further raises the hurdle for any type of sustainability analysis following a Sudden Stop, namely, the existence of contingent liabilities of the public sector, originated in the corporate and banking sectors. Here the financial system becomes an element of extraordinary importance. It is not uncommon, as was the case of Argentina recently (and cases like Thailand, for example, in previous crises), to find that commercial bank loans are heavily dollarized, whereas a large proportion of bank debtors obtain income from non-tradable activities. This currency mismatch between debtors' revenues and liabilities can easily lead to financial distress following large swings in the RER, as balance sheets deteriorate dramatically with the increased value of loans, which usually render these sectors bankrupt. To the extent that expectations concur that the public sector is willing to bail out banks and/or the corporate sector in the event of a crisis (another common feature of recent crises), then this bailout ought to be added to the sustainability analysis of the fisc. The combination of big RER swings, highly dollarized public debt, and the materialization of contingent liabilities of this sort can send debt/GDP ratios to skyrocketing levels, rendering public sector accounts bankrupt. Argentina suffered from all of these. Rough estimates of the bank bailout yield anywhere between US$7bn and US$13bn, and this excludes previous rediscounts and repos placed with public banks to finance their deposit losses equivalent to about US$6bn. Putting it all together yields an additional burden of US$13–19bn, which raises the debt/GDP ratio after the shock to anywhere between 55.8 and 58.6 percent, almost two thirds higher than the pre-crisis 1998 measure!

Obviously, public debt surges of this magnitude are the prelude to a wealth redistribution conflict given the size of the required adjustment. Once all elements triggered by the Sudden Stop are factored in,[22] the primary balance needed to regain sustainability would have exceeded 3% of GDP, a figure never attained by Argentina in its recent history (see table 6.9). In order to achieve this, the government would have needed to come up with new sources of financing or a cut in expenditures. It is evident from our previous discussion that the corporate sector could not be considered a good candidate for taxation, given that it was facing the same balance sheet breakdown and credit crunch confronted by the government. Thus, abstracting from default, the government was left with basically two alternatives: taxing consumers or reducing expenditures via wage cuts. Both instruments were to some extent used by different ministers during the de la Rua administration, but they proved to be politically very tricky because both were mostly placing the burden over the shoulders of the middle class, de la Rua's main political constituency. Besides, these loosing groups in the wealth redistribution game eagerly challenged the implicit decision of the government to leave external creditors unscathed. The redistribution conflict gave rise to a war of attrition in which decisions were delayed, deepening the extent of the crisis and the credibility of the public sector in terms of its ability to generate fiscal surpluses of the magnitude needed to regain sustainability. This, of course, closed any remaining open doors to government financing from abroad, thus making it clearer that the solution to this conundrum would most likely involve debt restructuring, something that lay at the heart of the bank run experienced in 2001. Most bank assets comprised loans to the private sector (most of them exhibiting currency mismatch) as well as government bonds. Both stocks would be severely hit at the time of the crisis. This realization precipitated a run by depositors in order to avoid the expected confiscation of their deposits.

In summary, when judging sustainability by taking into account the valuation impact of a Sudden Stop and the cost of a bail out of the corporate sector on the balance sheet of the government, it would become apparent that by late 1999 Argentina had acquired a large debt problem as summarized in table 6.9. To "fix" this problem would have required very large cuts in government expenditures at a time when the fixed peg to the dollar left Argentina without a valuable instrument, i.e., inflation, to engineer large government expenditure reductions which are politically very costly to implement in an explicit way.

Once we take into account the standards set by the new equilibrium RER, the de la Rua administration was facing an uphill battle in order to restore creditworthiness. The fair question to be asked is whether adjustments of such magnitude would have been feasible with standard fiscal policy instruments. Under lack of credibility, Argentina was definitely facing a stock problem, which can hardly be resolved with a tool such as the public sector deficit, which represents a flow, unless it is expected to be long-lasting. This was a tall order given the weak political structure underlying de la Rua's administration. Indeed, at this stage it would have been extremely difficult for any government to search for a solution that did not involve some form of debt restructuring.

Before concluding this section, let us revisit the issue of the expected duration of the Sudden Stop and expectations about Argentina's lack of fiscal sustainability. As it has already been argued, all sustainability calculations presented here were made under the assumption that the shock was permanent, but it is not clear that the shock was initially perceived as such by capital markets. Figure 6.5 shows Argentina's public bonds' spread measured by the EMBI index relative to the EMBI average for emerging markets. The fact that for the period starting with the Russian crisis through early August of 2000, Argentina's

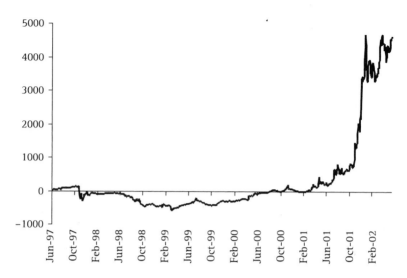

Figure 6.5
Argentina: Relative external financial conditions (EMBI Arg—EMBI+). Source: Bloomberg.

relative spread was lower than the average spread, indicates that the market had not yet declared Argentina insolvent.

Although private capital flows had already dried up by early 1999 (see figure 6.6), two factors may have contributed to avoiding bankruptcy expectations. First, it was not clear that the shock would be permanent (introducing uncertainty about the size of the required adjustment in relative prices), and therefore, it was not clear that Argentina's position would become unsustainable. But to the extent that investors updated expectations about the duration of the shock based on past and present behavior of capital flows, the observed persistence of the initial Sudden Stop deteriorated expectations about Argentina's fiscal solvency, thus contributing to the increase in spreads. Second, although lower output levels resulting from the private sudden stop in capital flows impacted directly on tax collection, putting additional strain on fiscal accounts, multilaterals provided financing to the public sector during this period. Had the shock been temporary, this additional financing would have been sufficient to cover the government deficit and avoid default since there would be no underlying sustainability problem. But as time went by and it became clear that capital inflows were not returning, real currency depreciation (i.e., a rise in RER) was unavoidable and sustainability was at stake.

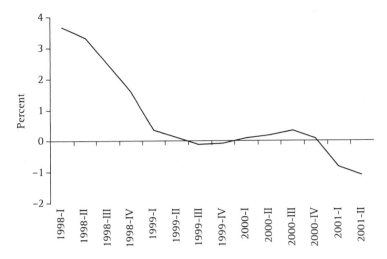

Figure 6.6
Sudden stop in Argentina (Private capital flows, % of GDP). Source: Central Bank of Argentina (BCRA).

6   Nominal Exchange Rate Issues

We now briefly turn to the implications of having kept a fixed exchange rate regime in place when the sudden stop in capital flows hit Argentina (requiring substantial changes in the RER), and contrast this against a scenario where the exchange rate is allowed to float. The Argentine experience shows that under certain conditions, fixed exchange rates can help to conceal fiscal disequilibrium. In particular, if prices are sticky, the RER may take time to reach its new equilibrium, revealing very little about the true magnitude of the necessary fiscal adjustment. The problem is that under those circumstances, it would be politically very hard to justify the need for a substantially larger fiscal retrenchment. This would be true even if we assume (unrealistically) that the International Monetary Fund and policymakers were aware of the yawning misalignment. The fact that the true magnitude of the fiscal adjustment was not evident may also be relevant in explaining the political turmoil that took place in 2000 in Argentina. Faced with the dilemma of deciding whether it was necessary or not to proceed with fiscal adjustment, the ruling alliance experienced substantial tension. This may very well have been the underlying force behind the resignation of several cabinet members and its implicit breakup following the vice-president's resignation. Even if sluggish

RER adjustment was concealing the need for fiscal adjustment, one may ask whether other variables such as central bank reserves could have revealed that information. Under a fixed exchange rate regime, reserve loss would be a signal for adjustment. But this variable can be a very noisy signal. For example, to the extent that the crisis is anticipated, consumption will be higher before than after the crisis (see Calvo, 1986), and so will money holdings and reserves in a cash-in-advance model. Thus, reserves may actually conceal the need for adjustment. Also, to the extent that reserves are supported by multilateral loans, they may mask the needed corrections (for a discussion of reserves as noisy signals, see Talvi, 1997 and Calvo, 1998).

These considerations immediately raise the question: Would it have been very different had Argentina floated its exchange rate instead in January 2000? Leaving any initial overshooting aside, the floating rate may have revealed that Argentina was in the dumps. The de la Rua administration would have faced some of the same difficulties currently faced by Duhalde's administration, such as dealing with a banking system bailout. However, remedial measures may have been taken then, avoiding the costly financial engineering that was undertaken later in 2001. Moreover, the alliance was supported by a strong popular vote. This power endowment would have been instrumental in finding an expedient resolution to the crisis, something that the current administration would very much relish.

However, the above scenario is unrealistic. Authorities would likely have been reluctant to let the exchange rate go as far up as required to reach equilibrium RER. Be it because of high liability dollarization, high pass-through from the exchange rate to inflation, or lack of credibility, the authorities would likely have suffered from "fear of floating" (see Calvo and Reinhart, 2002). For these reasons, we conjecture that devaluation would have gone only half way. Thus, although the RER would have adjusted more rapidly at the beginning, interest rates would have exhibited a sharp increase. Surging interest rates are the result of incomplete devaluation and, thus, the expectation of more devaluation to come (*peso problem*). Higher future devaluation could bring about an Indian Summer in aggregate demand but, eventually, boom gives way to bust. The lower price of consumption today vis-à-vis the future may lead to an increase in aggregate spending, but inevitably this gives way to bust in the future as the wealth constraint binds. Therefore, it is unclear that a more flexible exchange rate system would have successfully cleared the air in 2000. Even if the nominal exchange rate had been allowed to float freely, results would not have been much different. Argentina's high vulnerability to big swings in the RER following a Sudden Stop and its detrimental effects on corporate balance sheets and fiscal sustainability were there to stay regardless of whether the exchange rate regime was fixed, or allowed to float.

On the other hand, it is clear that floating the exchange rate was indeed a solution to the problem of nominal wage inflexibility faced by the government in the last few months before the collapse of Convertibility, a key element in bringing down real expenditure levels through inflation.[23] But this clear benefit in "facilitating" the fiscal adjustment would probably have been insufficient to compensate for the balance sheet breakdown caused by Liability Dollarization. As result, a debt restructuring process to resolve the dynamics set in motion by the Sudden Stop became inevitable.

7 Lessons and Policy Issues

We now take stock and use what we have learned to list a set of lessons/policies for Latin America that are derived from our analysis of vulnerability to Sudden Stops. An overview of the specific attempts made in Argentina to escape the crisis, and the reasons why we believe they failed, are left for the Appendix.

Argentina was extremely vulnerable to a sudden stop in capital inflows such as the one that followed the Russian crisis due to three characteristics: extremely closed to international trade (C), highly indebted (D), a high degree of *de facto* dollarization both in the public and private sector and, as a result, large financial currency mismatches (M). For future reference we will call an economy with these characteristics a *CDM* economy. Without any pretense of being exhaustive, in what follows we list the main policy lessons that logically emerge from our analysis:

1. *CDM* economies are vulnerable to changes in international conditions that require an adjustment in the current account deficit since they may require correspondingly large increases in equilibrium RER.

2. In *CDM* economies, large changes in the RER could generate deep financial distress in the corporate sector and/or turn a sustainable fiscal position into an unsustainable one, leading to financial problems for the public sector as well.

3. A banking crisis may be the inevitable corollary, either because banks are themselves exposed to RER changes and/or because they are exposed to the public sector through large holdings of public debt.

Exchange Rate Policy

4. CDM economies are vulnerable, regardless of the exchange rate regime that is adopted. Sudden Stops are shocks to credit that generate real effects, with long-run outcomes that are independent of nominal exchange rate arrangements (although short-run dynamics can vary substantially depending on nominal arrangements).

5. Exchange rate flexibility could play a useful role if the C, D or M are dropped (as was the case of Chile). It may be particularly useful if nominal wage inflexibility in the public sector is an issue. Otherwise, however, exchange rate flexibility could give rise to non-transparent policies, which might do more harm than good. In the short run, the C is hard to drop, and dropping D or M could be traumatic (as exemplified by Argentina's default and pesofication).

Fiscal Policy

6. Prima facie, in CDM economies it is dangerous to have high levels of public indebtedness. Governments should decide on lower debt levels (based on their degree of openness and Liability Dollarization) that create the necessary space for the public sector to respond in times of crisis while securing sustainability.

7. Dealing with an unsustainable fiscal position involves wealth redistribution across sectors. The way and the speed at which that redistribution is made are crucial in determining how fast a crisis is resolved. Ideally, wealth redistribution should be contracted ex-ante.[24]

Trade Policy

8. Increasing trade openness (i.e., dropping the C) may be relevant not just because it reduces the size of RER swings after a Sudden Stop, but also because, from a financial perspective, a higher share of tradable sectors in output composition may reduce the risk of currency mismatches in private sector balance sheets. This effectively reduces the vulnerability of the banking sector following RER swings,

as well as the size of potential bailouts that may worsen the fiscal position. Although the literature has focused on the benefits of openness for growth, the financial channels described above may be equally important.

Debt Management Policy

9. Efforts should be made to create markets for the issuance of debt in domestic currency not indexed to the exchange rate (i.e., dropping M).[25] Any debt contract that is contingent on RER fluctuations could be highly beneficial, not only because it may soften valuation effects, but because it specifies ex-ante the redistribution process generated by a Sudden Stop, thus avoiding the costly resolutions and the associated political turmoil. But this must be done in such a way that two common weaknesses are avoided: First, debt should be issued under terms that eliminate incentives to inflate it away through money creation (such as CPI indexing). Second, issuance should be made at sufficiently long maturity to avoid vulnerability to liquidity shocks. Typically, attempts to issue debt with these characteristics have not been successful. But a recurrent characteristic of these attempts has been the fact that issuance was made under domestic law instead of international law. Thus, there may be a significant difference in risk other than that associated with exchange rate risk, which may further complicate currency-matching strategies.

APPENDIX

Domestic Policies in Argentina under the Perspective of the Sudden Stop

Here we will present, and briefly discuss policies that were pursued in Argentina prior to the fall of the Convertibility Program.

Fiscal Policy

From the previous discussion, it is clear that fiscal restraint introduced during end-1999/early-2000, although in the right direction, was not sufficient to cope with the sustainability demands raised by the new equilibrium RER and the expected bailout of the private sector, making it difficult for the government to sustain the higher levels of debt, thereby creating a stock problem. The Fund was not immune to this misunderstanding. Under the assumption that Argentina was facing a liquidity problem, the initial program agreed upon with the de la Rua administration was followed by the *blindaje*.[26] Fiscal policy was relaxed and the original program was buttressed by a larger package. This failed, as the program was now shooting in the wrong direction. This mistake in diagnosis could be key in understanding why there was a lack of consensus about the degree of fiscal adjustment needed to re-store credibility. When the size of adjustment reaches the magnitude required by the Sudden Stop, it is easy to see why a heterogeneous po-litical alliance can break up. This was exacerbated by the fact that econ-omists did not offer a clear explanation to politicians about the reasons and urgency for adjustment, and particularly about the need to regain solvency if the capital flow standstill was ever to be reversed. This conceptual and political maelstrom was a clear source of uncertainty for the private sector about the future. In this respect, it is not sur-prising that investment projects were suspended, resulting in higher unemployment.

An attempt to introduce a fiscal package in early 2001 by a new minister[27] (which again would not have been sufficient to recover sol-vency) was quickly ruled out given that an agreement could not be reached either with some members of the alliance or with the opposi-tion party. After this failed attempt, fiscal adjustment was rejected by the new incoming minister[28] (a big error in a situation in which sus-tainability was at stake), and replaced by a bewildering variety of stimulating fiscal arrangements (competitiveness plans), which were subject to several changes (another big error regarding credibility). Fis-cal policy was swiftly changed in mid-2001, when it became clear that no additional external financing was going to materialize, by adopting a zero-deficit rule, and cutting transfers to provincial governments. Both measures put the political system to the test, and came too late to stop the crisis. Even though these announcements were made in an at-tempt to send a signal of improved sustainability, they were probably not credible inasmuch as political support was dim and the wealth re-distribution struggle previously alluded to was already developing.

Debt Management

On the debt management side, under the perception that the country was only facing liquidity problems, the government engineered a massive debt swap in June 2001 to extend the maturity of the debt profile, but ended up validating extremely high interest rates which, in turn, confirmed expectations about an unsustainable fiscal position. This quickly led to expectations of a balance of payments crisis, which in the case of Argentina would be much more devastating given the existence of highly dollarized liabilities in the banking system.

Another measure aimed at improving the fiscal position was the "voluntary"[29] debt exchange introduced in late 2001, which reduced interest rates and extended debt maturity. But even if it was the right way to go because this policy was addressing the debt stock problem by reducing its present value, such measures should have been introduced much earlier. By then, the attack on the banking system and reserve loss were underway.

Exchange Rate Policy

To correct for RER misalignment, the *convergence factor* was introduced in mid-2001, basically a peg to a basket composed of dollars and euros in equal proportions[30] that would become effective for all transactions when the parity between these currencies reached one. For trade transactions, though, dollars were exchanged at the ongoing dollar/ euro basket rate, which amounted to a (fiscal) devaluation of about 8 percent. Unfortunately, the prevailing view was that misalignment stemmed exclusively from trade factors like the devaluation of the Real and the euro—which ignored misalignment due to country risk considerations. From the previous analysis, it is clear that the peso's real depreciation obtained through fiscal devaluation, although in the right direction, was far from enough to correct the existing misalignment. The implementation of the convergence factor also had implications for exchange rate policy that may have contributed to the deposit run that would take place later, and the emergence of contingent liabilities that would further compromise the fiscal position. The *convergence factor* was mired in messy implementation, as there was no clear indication about when this new rule would become operational for all transactions. All that agents knew was that it would materialize whenever the dollar and the euro reached a parity of one to one. Moreover, this policy signaled to the market that the government was ready to loosen the shackles of the currency board and devalue. Fearful of the detrimental effects on bank assets that devaluation would cause via massive bankruptcies, depositors figured out that their assets (even if dollarized) were at stake, particularly given that the burden of a bank bailout was probably perceived as too big for the government to handle with its own resources. In this context, the signal given by the change in the currency board worsened expectations, something that would later lead to a massive deposit withdrawal and even larger loss of international reserves.

Monetary Policy

Perhaps the policy that most swiftly precipitated the balance of payments crisis (which, in turn, would weaken the fiscal position even further with the materialization of contingent liabilities), was the expansionary monetary stance held by the administration, even when the Currency Board kept the exchange rate firmly tied to the dollar.[31] Expansionary reserve requirement policies were introduced,[32] but quickly compensated for as a result of IMF pressure. The second tool available was domestic credit to commercial banks, which was sharply increased (see figure 6.7). Central bank credit expansion explains about

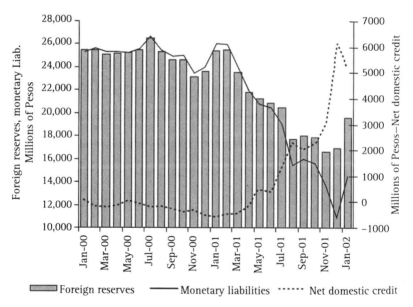

Figure 6.7
Increase in domestic credit and foreign reserves loss. Source: Central Bank of Argentina (BCRA).

53 percent of the staggering loss of reserves that took place from April to December 2001.[33] As discussed in Calvo, 2002a, under a Sudden Stop, a Central Bank will have incentives to hand its reserves to the credit constrained non-tradable corporate sector via credit expansion (a strategy that requires keeping a fixed exchange rate); but this may be a risky policy because it is not at all clear that reserves will end up in the hands of those who need them the most. There is a high chance that the sectors more likely to receive the proceeds from credit expansion (the public sector and prime borrowers with access to international markets, who represent a lower risk to banks) will end up unwinding their dollar debts, something that could be highly beneficial in light of upcoming devaluation. Thus, reserves are lost and there is little relief for those originally targeted by the Central Bank.

Not all credit expansion reflected the heterodox monetary position. As it turns out, soon after the government gave these expansionary signals, deposits began to decline sharply (about 18 percent between April and December 2001), which allegedly demanded central bank intervention in order to prevent a massive crash of the banking system. But, in any case, the question still remains as to what led the central bank to accommodate deposit withdrawal so swiftly, when the dominant theory was that foreign-owned banks would provide the necessary liquidity.

As crisis brewed, deposits fled the system and composition changed in favor of private banks, most of which are foreign-owned. Thus, depositors seem to have bought the theory—which constituted the intellectual basis behind bank denationalization since at least 1995—that foreign-owned banks would not let their subsidiaries go under. The central bank responded by providing support to the official sector. Deposits in those banks far exceeded international reserves. Thus, the realization that the central bank was ready to bail out state-owned banks reinforced the expectation that the currency board's days were numbered. To further complicate matters, the central bank increased the reserve requirement of deposit-receiving banks in order to sterilize credit expansion (marginal reserve requirements were set at 75 percent). This sent a clear signal to foreign banks that they might be differentially treated, and their assets eventually confiscated, completely neutralizing the "lender of last resort" role that those banks were supposed to play.[34]

Notes

We want to thank Ricardo Caballero, Enrique Mendoza and Rick Mishkin for very useful comments and Luis Fernando Mejía for excellent research assistance. The views expressed in this document are the authors' and do not necessarily reflect those of the Inter-American Development Bank.

1. This model assumes that non-tradable collateral is accepted by foreign creditors. In other models, such as Caballero and Krishnamurty, 2003, where only tradable collateral is accepted and assumed to be fixed, falls in the price of non-tradables do not have an effect on output because tradable collateral remains unaffected. Even if this were the case, crises of this magnitude, which bring along fiscal un-sustainability, could also alter the amount of tradable collateral since the tradable sector may be exposed to confiscation from the public sector.

2. The Russian crisis was not a low probability event. Savvy investors knew that sooner or later a crisis was likely to erupt. Our claim, however, is that it was hard to even imagine, ex ante, that a crisis in a country that represents less than 1 percent of world output would have such devastating effect on the world capital market.

3. Moreover, under the corporate bailout scenario assumed above, this option would simply not be available.

4. As the argument goes, to the extent that there exist large fixed costs (relative to the size of projects) in obtaining information about a particular country, resulting economies of scale lead to the formation of clusters of specialists, or informed investors, who lead capital markets. These investors leverage their portfolios to finance their investments and are subject to margin calls in the event of a fall in the price of assets placed as collateral. Remaining investors, the uninformed, observe transactions made by informed investors, but are subject to a signal-extraction problem, given that they must figure out whether sales of the informed are motivated by lower returns on projects or by the informed facing margin calls. As long as the variance of returns to projects is sufficiently high relative to the variance of margin calls, uninformed investors may easily interpret massive asset sales as an indication of lower returns and decide to get rid of their holdings as well, even though the cause for informed investors' sales was indeed due to margin calls.

5. We compare the lowest 1998 pre-crisis spread level to yearly averages of the spread measure in following years.

6. Although FDI flows fell on average in the aftermath of the Russian crisis, they did increase significantly in Brazil, where FDI flows rose 80 percent in dollar terms from the second quarter of 1998 to the second quarter of 2001. We follow up on this fact because it may be an important element behind the resumption of capital flows to Brazil. A possible explanation is that higher interest rates led to sharp declines in domestic collateral, adding to the perception that this asset class was more risky than expected. Thus, domestic firms found it more difficult to finance the current operations and expansion plans, further depressing their plants' market value. This may have opened attractive investment opportunities for G7-based firms whose collateral was insulated from EM financial turmoil, leading to a sharp increase in FDI.

7. Net of non-factor payments.

8. In what follows we abstract from investment. This is indeed a major omission, which is, however, likely to be less misleading in a steady state context such as the present one. Catena and Talvi, 2001, reach similar results in terms of a full-fledged dynamic model.

9. A scenario that is makes sense in the short run.

10. Here we have made several strong assumptions, such as that the supply of both tradable and non-tradable goods are constant, and that the price elasticity of demand of non-tradables is low and the same across countries. Again, these figures do not attempt to match observed figures, but to illustrate the main transmission channels behind Sudden Stops.

11. Had Argentina reduced its current account balance to zero, the required adjustment should have been higher than that of Chile, as illustrated in table 6.5.

12. We proxy output of tradable goods (Y^*) with exports. This measure is particularly relevant in the short run, although it could underestimate tradable output in the long run.

13. Calculations were made assuming that debt is issued either in terms of tradable goods, or in terms of non-tradable goods. When debt is issued in domestic currency, the relevant price index for valuation purposes is the consumer price level, which typically includes a share of tradable goods in the basket it values. In this respect, real depreciation should affect the valuation of domestic-currency-denominated debt through the tradable component of the price level, making the effects of a RER rise larger than estimated here. This can be interpreted as the case where a portion of this debt is issued in terms of tradable goods, so that the valuation effects of RER depreciation are larger.

14. Assuming interest rates and GDP growth remain at initial levels, which underestimates the required primary surplus.

15. This is computed as $(s^* - s)(1 + \theta)/(r - \theta)$, where s^* is the required primary surplus after the rise in RER (real currency depreciation), s is the required primary surplus before the rise in RER, r is the real interest rate, and θ is the growth rate of the economy. This is obtained by solving (7) forward and taking the difference between the stream of flows valued at s^* with respect to the stream of flows valued at s. In other words, it measures the change in debt (in percentage points of GDP) that corresponds to the permanent increase in the primary surplus.

16. Results for Brazil could not be computed, given that national accounts data is not split according to standard classification.

17. Even more thorough measures that split national accounts data at two or more digit levels may yield different results, but that information was not available for all countries in our sample, so we rely on calculations at a one digit level only.

18. The growth rate used for this exercise is the geometric average of the previous 10 years. Interest rates are average rates on public debt prevailing in 1998. Both measures do not account for the fact that following a sudden stop in capital flows interest rates typically increase and growth prospects decline. Thus, sustainability calculations are less demanding than those that would prevail had these additional effects been incorporated. We account for this later on.

19. That is when we take the prevailing average interest rate, growth rate and RER instead of imputed post-shock levels.

20. This assertion is made without considering the possibility that the RER was appreciated by 1998.

21. One can only conjecture that to the extent that FDI flows were due to opportunities facing foreign investors given the low valuation of Brazilian firms after the devaluation of the Real (a one time shot), Brazil should be ready for additional fiscal adjustment in case FDI flows do not proceed at the previously observed pace.

22. That is, valuation effects, interest rate increases, growth slowdown and the emergence of contingent liabilities.

23. A floating exchange rate regime is a solution to a fixed exchange rate regime facing serious difficulties, such as a Sudden Stop. But this does not necessarily point to floating exchange rates as a better regime, since the advantages of such a regime should be evaluated ex-ante.

24. For example, Brazil sold exchange rate insurance to private firms (and its cost was budgeted). This avoided a costly redistribution process by the time Brazil faced devaluation in 1999.

25. Indeed, this is just one instrument to insulate the economy from the effects of external shocks. Other instruments, contingent on indicators of external shocks (such as main export commodity prices), could be just as beneficial. For more on this, see Caballero (2002).

26. A package of about US$40bn provided by official creditors.

27. Mr. Ricardo Lopez-Murphy, a respected macroeconomist known for being fiscally strict was appointed to the Ministry of Economy.

28. Mr. Domingo Cavallo, the father of the convertibility plan introduced in 1991, who had been highly successful in the fight against inflation and making the economy grow fast during the first presidency of Carlos Menem.

29. Banks and pension funds were the main bondholders of the debt to be exchanged. Banks were persuaded to enter the exchange under pressure that their assets would otherwise have to be marked to market, something that could threaten their net worth position. Pension fund limits for holdings of public debt were increased to allow for placement of additional bonds.

30. But surprisingly, not the Real, which would have been a key price to include if the main reason behind this change was to increase trade competitiveness.

31. This policy was implemented after the dismissal of the central bank president, Pedro Pou. Although Convertibility required that the monetary base be backed by foreign assets, a share of these foreign assets could be composed of government paper in foreign currency, thus providing room for expansionary monetary policy.

32. Bank excess reserves were accepted as part of reserve requirements, implying an expansion of lending capacity, but this was compensated for by increases in reserve requirement rates.

33. Reserves are net of US$4 billion in IMF loans.

34. Although many feared that foreign banks typically would not behave as shock smoothers, bringing along necessary resources to finance a bank run, the case of Uruguay may be relevant proof that when rules of operation are not changed and contracts are not repudiated, foreign banks may have incentives to come up with the necessary resources.

References

Caballero, R. (2002) "Coping with Chile's External Vulnerability: A Financial Problem" [online paper], URL: http://web.mit.edu/caball/www/Chile_11Jan2002.pdf

Caballero, R., and A. Krishnamurthy (2003) "A 'Vertical' Analysis of Monetary Policy in Emerging Markets" [online paper], URL: http://web.mit.edu/caball/www/verticalaer .pdf

Calvo, G. A., (2002a) "Explaining Sudden Stop, Growth Collapse, and BOP Crisis: The Case of Distortionary Output Taxes" [online paper], URL: http://www.imf.org/external/pubs/ft/staffp/2002/00-00/pdf/calvo.pdf

Calvo, G. A., (2002b) "Globalization Hazard and Delayed Reform in Emerging Markets," *Economia*, Spring 2002, (2) 2.

Calvo, G. A., and C. Reinhart, (2002) "Fear of Floating," *Quarterly Journal of Economics*, (117) 2:379–408.

Calvo, G. A., and C. Reinhart, (2000) "When Capital Flows come to Sudden Stop: Consequences and Policy," in P. K. Kenen and A. K. Swoboda (Eds.) Reforming the International Monetary and Financial System, International Monetary Fund: 175–201.

Calvo, G. A., (1999) "Contagion in Emerging Markets: When Wall Street Is a Carrier" [online paper], URL: http://www.bsos.umd.edu/econ/ciecrp8.pdf

Calvo, G. A., (1998) "Growth, Debt, and Economic Transformation: The Capital Flight Problem", in F. Coricelli, M. Di Matteo and F. Hahn (eds.) *New Theories in Growth and Development*, Palgrave Macmillan: 251–69.

Calvo, G. A., (1986) "Temporary Stabilization: Predetermined Exchange Rates," *Journal of Political Economy*, (94) December:1319–1329.

Catena, Marcelo, and Ernesto Talvi, (2001) "Sudden Stops in a Dynamic General Equilibrium Model: an Application to Latin American Countries," mimeographed document.

Izquierdo, A., (1999) "Credit Constraints, and the Asymmetric Behavior of Output and Asset Prices under External Shocks," Ph.D. dissertation, University of Maryland.

Sturzenegger, F., and M. Tommasi, (1998) "The Political Economy of Reform," Cambridge, MA: MIT Press.

Talvi, E., (1997) "Exchange Rate Based Stabilization with Endogenous Fiscal Response," *Journal of Development Economics*, (54) October:59–75.

Part III

In Search of a Theory

Introduction to Part III

On December 20, 1994, the news struck the wires like a thunderbolt: Mexico had devalued! It was a 14.7 percent devaluation, modest by EM standards, but still significant enough to capture one's imagination. The official voice of international financial institutions did not take long to make itself heard. Predictably, the message was: "Nothing to worry about, this is just a correction." But there was a great deal to be worried about. The exchange rate went through the roof, and output fell by more than 6 percent. Wall Street cried foul, and after only a few days the shock wave spread over EMs—even South East Asian economies that were believed to be immune to this type of crisis—and some feared that it could spread to the US. I had been warning about a meltdown in Mexico in the event of a currency devaluation (see Calvo [1994]), but the spreading of the crisis across EMs took me—and everybody I know, including financial institutions—almost completely by surprise. The papers in this section try to make sense of these new phenomena that were to be repeated in the 1997 South East Asia crisis, and most shockingly in the 1998 Russian crisis—not to mention the tremors that shook up EMs after the Turkish, Brazilian, and Argentinean crises that were to follow. I will now say a few words about the central themes covered.

Chapter 7 ("Varieties of Capital-Market Crises") was written in the heat of the Tequila crisis. As I recall, a first draft was finished before the end of January 1995. The title reveals the first tremors of a paradigm shift. It does not say Balance of Payments or Currency crises, which would have been the natural title at the time, but Capital Market crises. The objective of the paper was to take stock of what we knew at the time, to extend some of the models (specifically Krugman [1979]), and to offer new vistas, all of which turned out to be perspectives on the credit market—thus the title. Extensions of Krugman (1979) show several subtle ways in which policymakers can momentarily hide unsustainable situations and, most importantly, generate *contingent* central bank liabilities. Typically these liabilities are linked to banks requiring financial support during bank runs or when banks are unable to roll over expiring debt obligations.

As discussed in chapter 11, Krugman's framework is incomplete because it cannot account for the steep output fall and large currency devaluation that has accompanied most recent crises (Brazil 1999 is an exception). To be sure, large currency devaluation could be accounted for by incorporating large random shocks into the Krugman (1979) model. However, that would take much of the appeal away from the model because its explanatory power would rest on the exogenous random shock. These considerations played a role in the search for alternative explanations. One of them, pioneered by Obstfeld (1986), highlights equilibrium multiplicity, and it is explored in chapters 7, 9, and 10. As pointed out in the Introduction, the drawback is that unless more constraints are imposed, there is nothing in those models that pins down equilibrium, making them an imperfect tool for positive economics. Equilibrium-multiplicity models have thus been appended with extra details that succeed in yielding uniqueness.

An example appears in chapter 13 of this book. The model in chapter 13 is capable of producing several key features of recent crises without having to rely on large random shocks. Actually, the model presented there is non-stochastic, but a salient characteristic is that the mapping from fundamentals to the set of equilibria is discontinuous. Thus, a small change in fundamentals could result in a large change in equilibrium values. This implies that a small random shock would be able to cause a major impact on the economy. This type of magnifying effect is very interesting, especially because of the high incidence of Sudden Stops, i.e., large capital account reversals (see Calvo, Izquierdo, and Mejía [2004]).

Another magnification channel is imperfect information. Imperfect information is a fundamental characteristic of capital markets, which, when combined with market frictions, for example, could yield large magnification effects. This subject is explored in chapters 7, 9, and 12. Chapter 12, for instance, combines imperfect information with margin calls (i.e., constraints on portfolio leverage). This insight was inspired by the Russian 1998 crisis, which spread like wildfire through EMs, even though no traditional fundamental could be singled out as a possible cause. Chapter 12 shows that a shock that triggers margin calls—and thus causes liquidity problems in the capital market, as was widely reported in the press at the time of the Russian crisis—has the potential of creating confusion among investors, ion, driving them to dump EM securities. What is interesting about this example is that, while traditional fundamentals may be intact, EMs could suffer severe credit-access problems as a result of market confusion.

Chapter 8 is an intermediate input for the architecture of crisis models. It does not directly refer to crises, but shows that the effects of regime-change expectations vary depending on market completeness. In particular, if credit contracts are not state-contingent, then expectations of future regime change lead to equilibrium outcomes with interesting dynamics—even in the case in which the conditional expectation of a regime change (conditional on the regime change not having taken place) is constant over time. This is relevant for EMs because (1) crises are usually accompanied by some regime change, and (2) state-contingent credit contracts are still rare. In fact, the standard practice is for international loans to EM to be non-state-contingent and denominated in foreign exchange (liability dollarization).

My sense is that theoretical developments after the Tequila crisis (a vast literature that I am not surveying, although most of the topics are represented in this volume) have revealed the relevance of concepts like *vulnerability*, somewhat to the detriment of traditional concepts like *sustainability*. To be sure, the two are connected. A vulnerable economy is unlikely to be sustainable for a long time (in the sense that a regime change is likely to occur). However, the shift of emphasis has put researchers on the track of cataloguing vulnerabilities and identifying those that are more likely to cause major damage. If successful, this research agenda will provide the practitioner with a fresh menu of warning indicators and suggest structural policies to prevent financial crises and attenuate their harmful effects.

References

Calvo, Guillermo A., 1994, "Mexico: Stabilization, Reform, and No Growth" Rudiger Dornbusch and Alejandro Werner, eds., *Brookings Papers on Economic Activity*, comment, vol. 1, pp. 253–315.

Calvo, Guillermo A., Alejandro Izquierdo, Luis F. Mejia, 2004, "On the Empirics of Sudden Stops: The Relevance of Balance-Sheet Effects." NBER Working Paper 10520, May.

Krugman, Paul R., 1979, "A Model of Balance-of-Payment Crises," *Journal of Money, Credit, and Banking*, vol. 11, no. 3, August, pp. 311–325.

Obstfeld, Maurice, 1986, "Rational and Self-Fulfilling Balance-of-Payments Crises," *American Economic Review*, March, 72–81.

7 Varieties of Capital-Market Crises

Guillermo A. Calvo

1 Introduction

"It is to be noticed that the position of a country which is preponderantly a creditor in the international short-loan market is quite different from that of a country which is preponderantly a debtor.[1] In the former case, which is that of Great Britain, it is a question of reducing the amount lent; in the latter case it is a question of increasing the amount borrowed. A machinery which is adapted for action of the first kind may be ill suited for action of the second" Keynes (1924, p. 18).

The recent currency turmoil in Latin America has brought home the fact that in this postmodern world of high capital mobility, countries are being disciplined, and their "noses" occasionally twitched, by the anonymous capital market. Wall Street has become as much a presence in democracies as the median voter. One view of the situation—I would dare to say, the prevalent view among economists—is that Wall Street gets into your hair because you are running an unsustainable economic programme and crises are bound to happen. An elegant rendition of this view is the balance of payments model in Krugman (1979).

Another polar view is that countries are at the mercy of the capital market—see Flood and Garber (1984) and, especially, Obstfeld (1986) which focuses squarely on this issue. If investors deem you unworthy, no funds will be forthcoming and, thus, unworthy you will be. Despite the appeal of this view in the popular press, however, this point of view has not yet made a significant dent in the profession's conventional wisdom, which is still dominated by the Krugman model.[2]

This chapter attempts to bring under one roof these two views, putting special emphasis on balance of payments crises, and to offer some new policy-relevant examples. Section 2 reviews Krugman's model under the assumption that after the balance of payments crisis, the fiscal deficit is entirely financed by the inflation tax. Section 3 introduces domestic banks and discusses the implications of having a "lender of last resort." Examples are shown in which this new feature either speeds up the crisis or contributes to macro risk or confusion.

Section 4 brings in the capital market by examining the case in which public debt is issued in order not to lose international reserves in the short run. It is shown that the 'bonds trick' could backfire by bringing forward the balance of payments crisis, or by eventually generating higher inflation. More interestingly, however, it is shown that the outcome may depend on bond-holders' expectations—Wall Street comes into your living room not just as a perceptive accountant, the accountant's expectations now *do* matter.

Section 5 shows that even though the source of all problems is the fiscal deficit, the latter may behave in a confusing way. An example is developed from first principles in which a balance of payments crisis is preceded by a period of fiscal balance. Such balance is obtained as a result of the private sector's running a current account deficit which, in turn, is provoked by the expectation that the exchange rate policy is unsustainable (and it is!). This example reveals the fallacy of the view—associated with the names of Nigel Lawson and E. Walter Robichek—that all is well if the fisc behaves.

Section 6 changes gears and considers the possibility that crises are provoked by international investors themselves even in the absence of radical changes or fiscal disequilibrium. Models are developed in which it is rational for individuals to be highly sensitive to "news", especially when portfolios are highly diversified. As a result, massive reallocation of funds takes place on just the hint that a given country is a better or a worse investment prospect. The paper argues that the equilibrium outcome could be highly detrimental to the welfare of local or home factors. This point is further nailed down by examining a case in which sudden capital outflows could cause real damage.

Section 7 concludes with some policy implications and suggestions for further research.

2 Krugman's Model

The standard theory of balance of payments crises is predicated on the assumption that the fiscal stance is inconsistent with exchange rate policy. A canonical example is provided in Krugman (1979) and will be briefly outlined here.

The exchange rate is assumed to be fixed if there are enough reserves to sustain the value of the domestic currency (that is, if reserves are above or at their critical level, which we assume to be zero); otherwise, exchange rates are allowed to float freely. Furthermore, the government is assumed to run a fiscal deficit which is fully monetized. (The latter, as will be seen, turns out to be a crucial assumption.) Assuming perfect capital mobility, no uncertainty, and perfect foresight, the domestic interest rate is equal to the international one during the fixed-rates phase, and to the international interest rate *plus* the rate of devaluation, during the floating-rates phase.

Let the demand for real monetary balances function be denoted by $L(i), L'(i) < 0$, where i is the domestic nominal interest rate. Assuming purchasing power parity (PPP) and no international inflation, we can identify the domestic price level with the exchange rate E. Let the government run a fiscal deficit which is fully financed by the central bank. Denoting the deficit in real terms by d, and the stock of international reserves at the central bank by R, we have:[3]

$$\dot{R}_t = -d \tag{1}$$

during the fixed-rates régime. This is so because the demand for money (monetary base in the present example) in real terms is constant at level $L(i^*)$, where i^* denotes the international interest rate. Equation (1) states that credit to government will result in reserves loss because the additional flows of domestic money that it entails are not demanded by the public. Given PPP, excess money supply cannot result in higher prices. Thus, there is no *internal* mechanism to get rid of excess money supply at equilibrium. But there exists an *external* mechanism, that is exchanging excess money for international reserves—which is the implication of equation (1).[4]

Equation (1) is an important building block in Krugman's model but not its clincher, which actually is showing that the loss of reserves will take a steep plunge down to their critical level exactly at the time the system switches from fixed to floating exchange rates (hereon referred to as "switch time"). This is so for the following reasons.

First, after reserves are exhausted the mechanism implied by equation (1) will not be available. Thus, the *external* mechanism for getting rid of excess money will no longer be operative. However, since the exchange rate is allowed to float, prices will now be able to rise in line with currency devaluation. Let the inflation rate (equal to the rate of devaluation, due to PPP) be denoted by π. Then, at steady state during the floating-rates phase, we have:[5]

$$\pi L(i^* + \pi) = d. \tag{2}$$

In other words, flow seigniorage from money creation is used to finance the fiscal deficit which, of course, requires the inflation rate to be positive, implying an abrupt jump in the domestic nominal interest rate at switch time. Hence, as the economy switches to the floating exchange rate régime, the demand for money takes a precipitous fall.

Krugman argues that (in the continuous-time version of the model) under perfect foresight the exchange rate cannot jump at any time because, if it did, individuals would be able to reap unbounded arbitrage profits (recall the assumption of perfect capital mobility). Thus, at switch time the exchange rate exhibits no appreciation or depreciation.

Therefore, at switch time—which sooner or later has to arrive given the constant drain on reserves implied by equation (1)—we have:

Loss of reserves at switch time $\equiv \Delta R = L(i^*) - L(i^* + \pi) > 0.$ (3)

A typical Krugman balance of payments crisis is depicted in figure 7.1. Reserves are steadily lost during the period from 0 to T when reserves

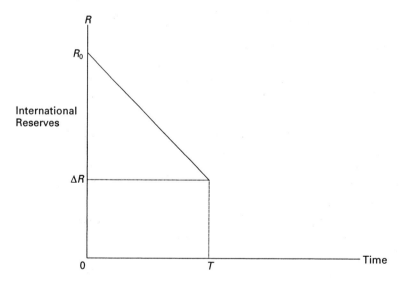

Figure 7.1
Krugman Crisis

reach level ΔR. At that point in time, there is a run against domestic money and reserves fall to zero (that is, a balance of payments crisis takes place). After time T, reserves remain at zero and inflation is positive—and constant, due to our steady-state assumptions.

The most remarkable feature of a Krugman crisis is the sudden loss of reserves at time T even though individuals have perfect foresight and, thus, nobody is taken by surprise. Therefore, the model has the ability of rationalizing, in a perfect-foresight context, an often-observed feature about balance of payments crises, namely, a speculative attack on the currency leading to the abandonment of fixed exchange rates.

3   Hidden Bonds: The Financial Trap

The recent Mexican crisis has once again shown that the financial sector could significantly contribute to the timing of a balance of payments crisis. It does so, though, in a way that is easily missed by policymakers, and becomes evident only after the crisis is set in motion. A typical scenario involves a capital inflows episode in which part of the inflows are channeled through the banking system. In the case of Mexico, for example, M2 divided by the exchange rate more than doubled in the period 1990 to 1993, even though output grew by much less.

If depositors believe that the central bank will operate as lender of last resort, they will have little incentive to monitor the quality and characteristics of bank loans. In particular, they will not be concerned by the existence of a mismatch of maturities whereby loans exhibit longer maturities than deposits. At the same time, if bank managers share the same belief, they are likely not to offer conditions that are attractive enough for long term deposits given that, as a general rule, interest rates are an increasing function of maturity. This incentive structure gives rise to the type of maturity mismatch mentioned above.

Therefore, as M2 rises a central bank which, implicitly or explicitly, operates as lender of last resort would *de facto* be acquiring short term obligations. Under those circumstances, a bank run would force the central bank to issue high-powered money to bail out banks. Thus, for example, in terms of Krugman's model the loss of reserves at switch time (equation (3)) would be augmented by the bailout.

Consider the following simple example. Money is just high-powered money as in Krugman's model but we now introduce banks whose liabilities (deposits) are pure bonds generating no *liquidity*. Bank deposits are denominated in the local currency. Thus, assuming no operations costs and no reserve requirements, a competitive perfect-foresight equilibrium (with no default) implies that the loan interest rate = deposit interest rate = international interest rate = i^* (before switch time), and $i^* + \pi$ (after switch time).

Let the initial stock of deposits be zero. We assume that a new plot of land is discovered, requiring tractors to till it. Hence, profit maximization implies that tractors will be imported until their price-adjusted marginal productivity equals the international interest rate. Let the real sums involved be denoted by Z. Funds are intermediated through the banking system which, say, extends an infinite-maturity loan to buy those tractors at the above-mentioned variable interest rate, financed by instant maturity deposits yielding the same interest rate.[6] A bank run is defined as a situation in which depositors withdraw their entire stock of deposits and buy international reserves. For this to be possible, the central bank provides the necessary high-powered money in exchange for the entire banks' portfolio.

Hence, after a bank run, condition (2) above becomes:

$$\pi L(i^* + \pi) = d - Zi^*. \tag{2'}$$

Compared to the previous example, the fiscal deficit is now reduced by the yield on the original bank loan, that is Zi^*. Furthermore, equation (3) now takes the following form:

$$\text{Loss of reserves at switch time} \equiv \Delta R = L(i^*) - L(i^* + \pi) + Z > 0. \tag{3'}$$

Interestingly, the effect of a higher Z is ambiguous because, by (2'), it reduces the fiscal deficit and, thus, inflation after switch time is lower. The latter implies, by (3'), that the fall in the demand for money at switch time is smaller. Therefore, by (3'), the loss of reserves at switch time is subject to two opposing forces: (a) a negative force represented by the increase in the demand for money after switch time, and (b) a positive force represented by the higher Z.

We will now highlight the case in which the direct effect of Z dominates. This would clearly be the case if $i^* = 0$ because, by (2'), inflation after switch time is not affected by Z. Thus, by continuity, one can show that an increase in Z will increase the switch-time fall in reserves if the international interest rate is sufficiently small.

Since equation (1) still holds, figure 7.1 remains valid for the present analysis. In particular, it is clear from the figure that the switch time is smaller (that is T is smaller) the larger is the switch-time loss of reserves (that is, ΔR). Therefore, we have shown an example of an endogenous bank run associated with the 'good news' of higher land productivity (and higher capital inflows). The bank run speeds up the timing of the balance of payments crisis.

The above analysis has left several loose ends. For example, why would there be a bank run? Banks offer competitive interest rates and, thus, no depositor gains by fleeing the domestic system. The problem is that if there were a bank run the banking system would not have enough liquid resources to meet its obligations. This triggers the central bank to act as lender of last resort, which prompts a loss of international reserves as shown above.[7]

We defined a bank run as complete depletion of bank deposits. What if only a share, φ, is withdrawn at switch time? If no further bank runs are anticipated, this will affect the timing of the crisis, but not the central message of this section, namely, that the existence of a central bank ready to operate as lender of last resort could change and, conceivably, bring forward a balance of payments crisis. However, if φ is arbitrary and/or bank runs occur in several stages, a multiple-equilibrium situation would arise, suggesting that the existence of a lender of last resort could contribute to macro risk if not sheer confusion.[8]

4   Deficit Cover-up: Domestic Debt

In many instances, countries attempt to mask the loss of reserves before the balance of payments crisis by issuing domestic debt.[9] This masking operation is aided by the convention—adopted by the IMF, for example—whereby domestic debt is not taken into account (as a negative item) in computing *net* international reserves.

Let us assume that government finances the fiscal deficit by issuing short-maturity domestic debt.[10] Let the real stock of domestic debt be denoted by b. Therefore, equation (1) is now replaced by:

$$\dot{b}_t = d + i^* b_t. \tag{4}$$

In this fashion, international reserves R need not change as a result of the budget deficit. However, domestic debt will accumulate without bound and transversality-type conditions will not be satisfied.

In order to be specific let us assume that the government will not renege on its domestic debt. Thus, assuming government debt to be of instant maturity (a close approximation being overnight repos), the government will be ready to exchange bonds for cash on a par basis at any time. Consider now Krugman's scenario in which the exchange is fixed unless it can no longer be sustained by the central bank.

Clearly, equation (4) cannot hold forever because the government is paying debt with debt. Assuming a constant international interest rate, i^*, the present discounted value position of the government equals $b_0 + d/i^*$. The latter is a positive number—that is, the government would be spending beyond its means—if initial government debt is zero (which we assume to make this example comparable with the previous one).

Suppose that in the event of a balance of payments crisis the government will stop issuing domestic debt and will finance the fiscal deficit (including service on the domestic debt) by means of seigniorage. Thus, after the crisis, equation (2) becomes:

$$\pi L(i^* + \pi) = d + i^* b_{T+} \tag{5}$$

where b_{T+} denotes the stock of bonds at time T after bond redemption at time T (more on this later).

We will now show that, under the present circumstances, the timing of the speculative attack and its inflationary consequences are functions of the amount of bonds that will be redeemed at switch time. The latter is a decision that lies with speculators and may not be pinned down by "fundamentals" (see, however, the discussion at the end of this subsection). Therefore, masking reserve losses by issuing government bonds may put policy even more at the mercy of whimsical market sentiments.

To illustrate, we will examine two polar cases: (1) all bonds are redeemed, and (2) no bond is redeemed at switch time. Consider, first, the case in which all bonds are redeemed at switch time. Then, inflation after T will have to be just enough to finance the fiscal deficit d, which implies that equation (2) holds also for this case, and, hence, inflation after crisis is the same as before. However, reserve loss is larger because in addition to the drop in the demand for money—the same as before—individuals are assumed to redeem their bonds in their entirety.

More formally, by equation (4), and recalling that $b_0 = 0$, we have:

$$b_T = \frac{d}{i^*}(e^{i^* T} - 1). \tag{6}$$

At switch time, the loss of reserves must be equal to the initial level, R_0, because by assumption the central bank has lost no reserves during the fixed-rates phase. By a similar argument as in Krugman (1979), one can show that the equality condition between the loss of reserves and R_0 is a necessary condition for an equilibrium. If reserves were positive after the attack, then money holders would have made a mistake because nominal interest rates would fail to rise as expected. On the other hand, if reserves were not enough for the attack, then speculators would have made a mistake—they should have staged the attack earlier—a situation which is not compatible with perfect foresight.

More formally, the switch time condition discussed above is as follows:

$$b_T = \frac{d}{i^*}(e^{i^*T} - 1) = R_0 - [L(i^*) - L(i^* + \pi)]. \tag{7}$$

The final expression on the right is reserves left over after accounting for the drop in the demand for money. The latter must equal the stock of bonds accumulated up to time T, b_T, since the whole stock of bonds will be redeemed in exchange for international reserves at switch time.

It is interesting to compare switch times with and without bonds. It is easy to verify, by equations (1), (3) and the switch time condition for the Krugman case (no bonds) $R_T = \Delta R$, that the expression corresponding to condition (7) for the Krugman case is as follows:

$$Td = R_0 - [L(i^*) - L(i^* + \pi)]. \tag{8}$$

The right hand sides of equations (7) and (8) are the same, which implies that the balance of payments crisis occurs earlier with than without bonds.

In sum, if individuals redeem their entire stock of bonds at the time of the balance of payments crisis, then inflation after the crisis is the same as in Krugman's case, but the crisis occurs earlier. Covering up the loss of reserves by issuing domestic debt is certainly effective in showing constant reserves during the fixed-rates period, but high inflation takes over earlier. In the present setup the only one that gets fooled by the bonds trick is government because individuals fully anticipate the consequences of this kind of action. Furthermore, it is easy to derive this kind of model from a utility-maximization framework[11] and show that welfare is unambiguously reduced when bonds are used (and are totally redeemed at switch time) instead of fully monetizing the fiscal deficit.[12]

Let us now consider the polar case in which no bond is redeemed at switch time. Thus, the fall in reserves at switch time satisfies equation (3) above. The switch-time condition is $R_0 = \Delta R$, determining π. The same condition for the Krugman case is $R_T = \Delta R$. Hence, since by figure 7.1 $R_T < R_0$, inflation in the Krugman case is less than in the case in which bonds are issued to cover the fiscal deficit during the fixed-rates phase, and bonds are not redeemed at switch time. However, issuing bonds could be an effective device for postponing the balance of payments crisis.

The above analysis could be criticized because it does not offer an explanation of why, when the speculative attack takes place, the government cannot instantly refinance some of the bonds being redeemed. For example, if the rate of inflation implied by equation (5) is less than the one that maximizes revenue from the creation of money, then the government could in principle refinance part of the bonds being redeemed at time T and cover the additional debt service by higher future inflation, that is, the government could borrow against additional future seigniorage. Under those conditions, the timing of the speculative attack would be uniquely determined and correspond to the situation in which inflation maximizes seigniorage. Moreover, one can show that this solution is identical to the one we identified earlier with the case in which there is no bond redemption at time T.

However, the other solutions with partial or total bond redemption would still make economic sense if investors are confident about their knowledge of the demand for money around the time of the crisis (essentially the same knowledge necessary for timing a Krugman crisis) but are much more uncertain about the demand for money over the longer run. The latter is necessary to assess whether the government will be able to service bonds left over after the crisis, that is b_{T+}. Thus, b_{T+} could be interpreted as reflecting investors' estimates about the maximum present discounted seigniorage (net of fiscal deficit d) after the crisis. Given the high volatility and unpredictability of the demand for money in crisis-prone countries, investors' estimates of the maximum present value of seigniorage are likely to be largely idiosyncratic.

A disturbing implication of the above analysis is that equilibrium determination depends, strongly, on speculators' expectations. Furthermore, in a more realistic scenario where speculators cannot perfectly read the minds of the other speculators, the nature of equilibrium will be very sensitive to new information emanating from the market, as opposed to fundamentals. A balance of payments crisis will continue to display catastrophic results, but the latter will occur in a milieu of incessant rumour which (1) leaves the government and economic policy on the sidelines, and (2) can hardly be argued to be welfare enhancing.

5   Variable Deficit: The Talvi Effect[13]

The above examples assumed that the fiscal deficit is constant through time. Recent experience, however, suggests that crisis-prone economies display wide variations in their fiscal deficits, the latter widening sharply after a balance of payments crisis takes place (see Talvi, 1996). A typical pattern is for expenditure (particularly, consumption) to expand during the fixed-rates phase (or, more generally, during the exchange-rate-based stabilization period, see Kiguel and Liviatan, 1992), followed by a sharp decline after the crisis. Thus, to the extent that tax revenue increases with expenditure, the fiscal stance improves before the crisis and deteriorates sharply afterwards.

Consequently, it is possible for variable d (that is, the fiscal deficit) to be time varying and show a marked increase after switch time T. We will illustrate this by an example in which $d_t = 0$, for $0 \leq t < T$, and $d_t = D > 0$, afterwards, where D is a positive constant. Thus, in this example there would be no obvious sign of fiscal imbalance prior to the balance of payments crisis.

As in Calvo (1986), let us assume the existence of a representative individual (total population is normalized to unity) whose time-separable utility depends on consumption, and displays a constant discount rate equal to the international interest rate. Let c and m indicate consumption and real monetary balances held by the representative individual. Assuming:

1. a cash-in-advance type constraint, $c = m$,

2. constant endowment income y,

3. existence of a consumption tax rate, τ, proportional to total consumption and constant over time,

4. endowment taxes that decline with the rate of inflation $\Phi(\pi)$, $\Phi'(\pi) < 0$ (the Olivera–Taniz effect),[14]

5. constant government expenditure g, and

6. the individual holds money as the only type of wealth at time zero,

the representative's individual budget constraint takes the following form:

$$\int_0^\infty [c_t(1 + i^* + \pi_t + \tau) + \Phi(\pi_t) - y]e^{-i^*t} dt - m_0 \leq 0. \tag{9}$$

Therefore, letting $u(c)$ denote the instantaneous-utility index, the first order condition for utility maximization is[15]:

$$u'(c_t) = \lambda(1 + i^* + \pi_t + \tau). \tag{10}$$

where λ is the (constant) Lagrange multiplier.

We will now construct the example so as to yield no fiscal deficit during the fixed-rates period. During fixed exchange rates, inflation is zero. Thus, equation (10) reduces to:

$$u'(c_t) = \lambda(1 + i^* + \tau). \tag{10'}$$

After the crisis, inflation will be constant and higher (its level denoted by π^H, superscript H standing for 'high'); thus, for $t > T$, equation (10) reduces to:

$$u'(c_t) = \lambda(1 + i^* + \pi^H + \tau). \tag{10''}$$

By $(10')$ and $(10'')$ it is clear that consumption during fixed rates will be higher than after the crisis. Thus, their corresponding levels will be denoted by c^H and c^L, respectively (H and L standing for "high" and "low").

For zero fiscal deficit during the fixed-rates phase, we must have:

$$\tau c^H = g - \Phi(0). \tag{11}$$

Furthermore, because of the proportionality between consumption and money holdings, the after-crisis condition (2) above implies:

$$\pi^H = \frac{g - \Phi(\pi^H) - \tau c^L}{c^L} = \frac{g - \Phi(\pi^H)}{c^L} - \tau. \tag{12}$$

The budget constraint for the country as a whole requires that the present discounted value of private and public consumption equals the present discounted value of endowment income *plus* initial international reserves. In the present case, where individuals are assumed to hold no international bonds at time 0, the latter takes the following form:

$$c^H(1 - e^{-i^*T}) + c^L e^{-i^*T} = R_0 i^* + y - g > 0. \tag{13}$$

Consider the case in which the instantaneous utility index is logarithmic and, thus, $u(c) = \log c$. Then, by equations $(10')$, $(10'')$ and (12) we have:

$$\frac{c^H}{c^L} = \frac{1 + i^* + \tau + \pi^H}{1 + i^* + \tau} = 1 + \frac{[g - \Phi(\pi^H)]/c^L - \tau}{1 + i^* + \tau}. \tag{14}$$

To simplify the exposition we further assume that function $\Phi(\pi)$ takes only two values, and $\Phi(\pi) < \Phi(0)$, for all $\pi > 0$. Hence, equations (11) and (14) uniquely determine c^H and c^L, with $c^L < c^{H}$.[16]

Recalling the cash-in-advance constraint assumption, the fall in the demand for money at time T equals $c^H - c^L$. Therefore, to ensure that at time T international reserves are fully depleted, we assume initial international reserves $R_0 = c^H - c^L$. Finally, to ensure that fiscal equilibrium is not sustainable with fixed exchange rates, we choose y such that the value of T that solves (13), given $R_0 = c^H - c^L$, is positive.

Thus, the above example demonstrates the possibility that a balance of payments crisis of the Krugman type will take place *even though there is no fiscal deficit during the fixed-rates period*. This does not mean the absence of basic fiscal problems. Rather it signifies the absence of imbalance from conventional fiscal accounts which do not take into account this cyclical pattern.

Nigel Lawson and E. Walter Robichek have eloquently espoused the theory that government should not be concerned if the private sector runs current account deficits, as long as there is no fiscal deficit. The above analysis shows how wrong this view could be. In the example, there is no fiscal deficit during the fixed-rates phase because of a consumption boom which is fuelled by individuals' expectations that the exchange rate policy is unsustainable!

6   Bonds-Led Speculative Attacks

In all previous examples, the key factor behind balance of payments crises was fiscal disequilibrium. Bonds added serious complications, and variable deficits were shown to make fiscal disequilibrium more difficult to detect. However, a key message emanating from the examples is that to prevent future crises, government will be well-advised to lower its fiscal deficit.

The models that will be discussed in this section represent a complete change of perspective, because they show that the basic cause of a balance of payments crisis may be lenders' behaviour. For instance, in one of the examples, as lenders go into panic, loans are not rolled over, countries are forced into costly, badly designed tax systems to carry out the necessary "adjustment" and, as a result, the economy suffers *real* damage—for example, productivity loss, more tax evasion and corruption, and so on—validating the fears that initially led lenders to withdraw their loans.

6.1 Financial Diversification and Lenders' Information

Both diversification and information are desirable features for an investor. The former because of risk-aversion considerations, and the latter for the obvious reason that a better knowledge of an asset's characteristics makes for a better investment decision, at least at the micro level. However, there may be a significant trade-off between the two.

The discussion will be confined to countries and central points will be illustrated by means of an essentially one-period example. Suppose there are J countries indicated by the index j. We assume that there are investment projects in each and every country.[17] For country j its investment project has return r^j, a random variable. For simplicity, we will assume that if investors do not spend resources in learning more about a specific country, or information filters through the grapevine, the values of r are perceived to be identically and independently distributed with mean ρ and variance σ^2. Under these circumstances, a risk-averse investor will allocate equal amounts of his wealth across all countries. Hence, assuming without loss of generality, that he has one unit of wealth (in terms of output, say), expected return and variance will be ρ and σ^2/J, respectively.

We will now show that diversification exacerbates 'herding' behaviour by making investors more sensitive to 'market' news or rumours. In what follows we assume that the representative individual's von Neumann-Morgenstem utility, U, exhibits constant absolute risk aversion.

Suppose the investor hears a credible rumour that country 1's return has a new mean value r, different from ρ, although its variance is still equal to σ^2 like all other countries, and its distribution is independent from that of each and every other country. Let θ be the share of his portfolio devoted to countries $2, 3, \ldots, J$. Obviously, whatever amount is invested in the latter set of countries, its allocation will be constant across them. Thus, the portfolio's expected return is

$$\theta\rho + (1 - \theta)r. \tag{15}$$

Moreover, portfolio variance satisfies:

$$\left[\frac{\theta^2}{J-1} + (1-\theta)^2\right]\sigma^2. \tag{16}$$

Given our assumptions, expected utility, EU, can be represented as a linear function of expressions (15) and (16) as follows:

$$EU = \theta\rho + (1-\theta)r - \frac{\gamma}{2}\left[\frac{\theta^2}{J-1} + (1-\theta^2)\right]\sigma^2, \quad \gamma > 0. \tag{17}$$

Therefore, maximizing utility (17) with respect to θ (that is, the portfolio share of countries other than country 1) yields the following first order condition:

$$1 + \frac{\rho - r}{\gamma\sigma^2} = \theta\frac{J}{J-1}. \tag{18}$$

The above results are all we need to make our first central point. Let us consider the benchmark case in which starting from a situation where country 1 is *ex ante* identical to all other countries, information filters down to investors that the expected return in country 1 is slightly different from that of the others, ρ_1 while all the other conditions still hold (for example, equality of variance across countries). Then, the change in portfolio composition can be computed taking the implicit derivative of θ with respect to r in equation (18) that is

$$-\frac{\partial\theta}{\partial r} = \frac{J-1}{J}\frac{1}{\gamma\sigma^2} \rightarrow \frac{1}{\gamma\sigma^2} \quad as\ J \rightarrow \infty. \tag{19}$$

Prior to the new information, investment in country 1, as a proportion of total investment, was I/J. Therefore, by making J sufficiently large, the change in investment funds allocated to country 1 as a proportion of the original investment as a result of the new information could be made arbitrary large. Identifying the number of countries, J, with opportunities for diversification, we can then conclude that *as the opportunities for diversification increase, the impact of news on the allocation of investment funds (relative to initial allocation) grows without bound.*

The macroeconomic implications of the above result depend on the type of security held by investors. If securities are stock market shares, then upon hearing the negative news there will be an attempt to pull out from those securities. This will drive down their price until the run stops. By the above reasoning, this could be achieved by just a small drop in stock market prices. However, if securities are composed of short-maturity debt, then investors may ask for full repayment before rolling over the debt. If a country's solvency is not at stake the rollover operation may be carried out without major difficulty. But, as the last model in this section will show, one can build up plausible examples where insolvency is provoked by investors unwillingness to roll over the debt (Calvo and Mendoza (1996a) argue that this case in relevant for understanding the Mexican 1995 crisis).

Let us now introduce the possibility of getting better information. Consider the case in which by spending a fixed sum κ in learning about country j, independently of the amount invested, an individual would be able to know the actual realization of r^j before choosing his portfolio, $j = 1, 2, \ldots J$. Suppose the investor's wealth is one unit of output. Without loss of generality, we will analyze the net return from spending κ to learn about r^1.

As usual, it will be convenient to go backwards and start at the point when r^1 is revealed. Since the latter is known with perfect certainty, we will denote it by r_1 as before. In contrast to the previous example, however, the variance on the return in country 1 is now, by definition, zero. Using the above apparatus, one can show that for interior solutions, the share invested in countries $j = 2, 3, \ldots J$, is given by the following expression:

$$\theta = \frac{\rho - r}{\gamma \sigma^2}(J - 1). \tag{20}$$

Ruling out short sales, if $r \geq \rho$, then investment would be fully concentrated on country 1. This is as expected, because we have assumed that there is no uncertainty about country 1's return. On the other hand, the maximum feasible value for θ is 1. Let $r_{\min}$ be the value of r for which θ in equation (2) equals 1. Then,

$$r_{\min} = \rho - \frac{\gamma \sigma^2}{J - 1}. \tag{21}$$

Thus, interior solutions hold if $r_{\min} < r < \rho$. Furthermore, if $r \leq r_{\min}$ then $\theta = 1$, while if $r \geq \rho$ then $\theta = 0$. Finally, $r_{\min}$ is an increasing function of the degree of diversification, J, and converges to ρ as J grows without bound.

We will now argue that the benefit derived from knowing r eventually declines as the number of diversification opportunities, J, increases. This is the key for the argument that more diversification opportunities eventually imply lower incentives for information gathering.

By (21) in the limit as J becomes very large, information gathering will only pay off (not taking into account the costs of collecting information, κ), if $r \geq \rho$.[18] From the above discussion, however, for small J, information gathering will pay off even though $r \leq \rho$ (but as long as $r \geq r_{min}$). Furthermore, in all cases, information gathering pays off if $r > \rho$. Thus, (1) if *ex post* $r > \rho$, there is a utility gain for both the high- and the low-diversified investor, and (2) if *ex post* $r \leq \rho$, then only the low-diversified investor has a chance to gain from having invested in information about country 1. Therefore, noticing that expected utility increases with diversification opportunities (that is J), and that the utility function is strictly concave, it follows that the *marginal* gain from information gathering eventually falls off as diversification opportunities rise.

In sum, we have shown, in reverse order, that

1. highly diversified investors have lower incentives to learn about individual countries than investors with few diversification opportunities; and

2. investment to or away from a given country could be highly sensitive to news in a world in which investors are highly diversified.

The above characteristics of a highly diversified investors' world look fearsome: diversification encourages ignorance and, in that context, frivolous rumours could result in massive capital flows from the perspective of an individual country. Of course, an optimist would be likely to be able to find a "world" welfare function under which those massive reallocations are socially optimal. However, although holders of internationally mobile capital or highly tradeable goods may not suffer from these swings, those engaged in the production of local, or home, goods could see their fortunes change radically depending on the funds' direction.[19] In addition, fiscal revenue is likely to be an increasing function of capital flows. Hence, their variability would have a negative impact on welfare if, for instance, the government faces convex tax collection costs.[20] Thus, even before introducing direct detrimental effects from the variability of capital flows, a case could be made that herding behaviour under highly diversified portfolios may have seriously detrimental effects on the welfare of individual countries.

The problem of capital flow variability becomes more obvious if investment decisions have an effect on expected rates of return. This topic will be the subject of the next subsection.

6.2   *Additional Costs from the Variability of Capital Flows*

Consider a three period, one good, non-monetary world in which the government issues $b_0 > 0$ units of public bonds in period 0. Let x_t, $t = 1, 2$, denote tax revenue in period t net of government expenditure. We assume that bonds mature in one period, and denote the interest rate in period t by $z_t = 0, 1$. Furtheremore, bonds issued in period 1, b_1, satisfy:

$$b_1 = b_0(1 + z_0) - x_1. \tag{22}$$

Thus, in the last period revenue has to be raised to fully service the outstanding debt, that is

$$x_2 = b_1(1 + z_1). \tag{23}$$

We will assume that the opportunity cost of funds is revealed at the time 0 and, without loss of generality, we assume it to be constant through time. Combining equations (22) and (23) and, once again, denoting the (constant) international interest rate by i^*, the overall budget constraint faced by government takes the following familiar form:

$$b_0(1 + i^*)^2 = x_1(1 + i^*) + x_2. \tag{24}$$

Thus, if revenues raised in periods 1 and 2 are not functionally connected (other than through the budget-constraint equation (24)) then government can choose the optimal configuration of revenues, x, to maximize some social welfare function.

In order to analyze the detrimental effects of runs, we will now assume that revenue raised in period 1 is, after a point, counterproductive to revenue collection in period 2. To simplify, we will postulate that x_1 does not interfere with x_2 if $x_1 \leq X$, where X is a given positive parameter, otherwise, if $x_1 > X$, then $x_2 = 0$. This assumption attempts to capture a situation in which the government is able to collect very high taxes in the short run but, beyond a certain point, high taxes seriously undermine the government's future ability to tax. The following three examples provide some justification for the assumption.

Take a country which has tax legislation in place but needs to collect additional taxes unexpectedly. A popular policy under these circumstances is to raise public sector prices. Since these taxes are seen as temporary and directly affect input prices, production and thus capital accumulation decline, resulting in a smaller tax base tomorrow.

Another possible policy reaction is to impose a wealth tax which, unlike the previous case, is in principle non-distorting. However, if the new tax is large enough, firms and individuals would find it to their advantage to under-report their wealth. This may lead individuals and firms also to under-report *future* income in order not to reveal their previous wealth under-reporting, thus lowering the future tax base.

Finally, let us interpret x_t, $t = 1, 2$, as the difference between taxes and public investment. Thus, x_1 could now go up by simply dropping some public investment projects. Hence, if public investment has a positive effect on private investment, future output will fall, which, once again, will tend to depress the future tax base. This example may be relevant for countries which went through a sharp reduction in public infrastructure investment after the 1982 Debt Crisis (see Easterly, 1989).

By equation (15) if debt is not rolled over in period 1, then revenue in period 1, $x_1 = b_0(l + i^*)$, where the equilibrium interest rate (given our earlier assumptions) is just equal to the international one. Suppose $b_0(1 + i^*) > X$. Then a self-fulfilling run is possible because, if no debt is rolled over, the country could not raise revenue in period 2, and any outstanding debt in period 2 will be defaulted. Thus, there are no incentives to roll over the debt. On the other hand, the first-best equilibrium still exists, so it cannot be claimed that there is anything fundamentally wrong with the country. However, if lenders stage a run: (1) the first-best cannot be achieved and, lamentably, (2) *ex post* no investor will regret having fled. Hence, there is no *ex post* penalty for the panicky investor, no regrets from having run and, thus, no mechanism is set in motion which might help to prevent the same phenomenon from happening in the future.[22]

7   Concluding Remarks

Casual observation suggests that the two views about capital market crises are relevant, and that they could actually magnify the effects implied by the other. Thus, fiscal fragility may make it more likely for self-fulfilling prophecies to exist. And, *vice versa*, a bonds-led crisis may bring about fiscal imbalance.

The view that capital-market crises may be partly the fault of investors, suggests that standard fiscal tightening advice should be complemented by measures that prevent large variations in capital flows, at least in the short run. One such measure is to lengthen the maturity of public debt. In the preceding section's example, this would be the solution to the problem. Let χ_1 and χ_2 be the optimal path of tax revenues. Then, the first-best could be implemented with probability 1 if debt maturing in period 1 amounts to X or less. Furthermore, in the balance of payments model of Section 4, lengthening bond maturity will increase the predictability of crises.

In a more realistic model, however, the long-maturity solution may be harder to implement for the following two reasons: (1) economies have an open-ended horizon (not a fixed number of periods), and (2) fiscal revenue is subject to stochastic shocks. Those two factors combined imply that it will be unlikely for a country to be in a situation in which only prearranged funds are needed. Thus, the expectation that non-prearranged funds are needed opens the door to the kind of problems underlined in the text. Under those circumstances, the longer the maturity of a loan, the higher will be the probability of default, both because of revenue-shortage and lenders' panic. Thus, these two factors could reinforce each other to such an extent that interest rates on long-maturity loans become prohibitively high, and it is optimal for the country to bias the maturity structure of public debt towards the short end of the spectrum—hence exposing the economy to capital-market crises.

Public debt takes many forms, one of which is, in practice, bank deposits. Although no country offers unlimited deposit insurance—and some countries insist on not having any—it is hard to find examples where depositors have not received a sizeable compensation after a banking crisis. Thus, *de facto* the government becomes partially responsible for bank debt, especially short-maturity debt. Therefore, the above discussion suggests that countries which are subject to capital-market crises should be very cautious about liberalizing the banking system (for example by lowering reserve or liquidity requirements), and should give incentives for banks to lengthen deposit maturity.

The chapter also cautions against premature "bond-engineering" where revenue shortfalls are covered by floating new debt. This policy is very attractive in the short run because there is no need to raise additional taxes and it does not call for a loss of reserves or an increase in inflation. However, the chapter has shown that bond-engineering may put the economy at the mercy of the capital market's occasionally whimsical moods.[23]

The problems emphasized in this chapter are likely to be more relevant for countries which undergo basic economic restructuring than for those that have a solid track record. Optimal capital-market policy should reflect that fact and impose stiff restrictions in the short run followed by their eventual relaxation as stability features, like foreign direct investment and long-maturity instruments, are better and more solidly established.

In closing, it is worth recalling that capital-market crises have a tendency to recur, notably in Latin America. In this respect, theories discussed in this paper have little to contribute. It is somewhat hard, however, to imagine rational governments repeatedly falling into Krugman-type crises. In contrast, theories of lenders-led crises appear to need little additional formalization to generate recurrence. Countries could, of course, take measures to prevent business cycles caused by external factors, but these types of measures are costly—like, for instance, lengthening debt maturity—and a rational government weighing benefits and costs may optimally choose to leave itself open to recurring capital-market shocks.

Notes

1. I have benefitted from comments by Michael Kumhof, Saul Lizondo, Nora Lustig, Enrique Mendoza, Michael Mussa, Assaf Razin, and workshop participants at the IMF and MIT.

2. The view that foreign capital could be destabilizing or counterproductive is not new. See, for example, Diaz-Alejandro (1989).

3. In what follows, it is assumed, for simplicity, that either international reserves earn no interest or that the deficit d is inclusive of interest on reserves.

4. Individuals may want to invest these funds in the capital market or increase their expenditure depending on factors that the present discussion need not be specific about. However, see Section 3 below.

5. In case the following equation has more than one solution, we will assume that the economy settles to the one exhibiting the lowest π.

6. A more detailed model should endogenize this maturity structure. However, the latter should not be hard in a context where the central bank provides free deposit insurance.

7. This analysis bears some resemblance to Diamond and Dybvig (1983). However, their bank-run story is essentially non-monetary and relies on technological constraints. In their discussion, the lender of last resort (and the assumption that the fiscal authority is able to raise lump-sum taxes) is part of the solution, whereas here it is part of the problem.

8. Bank runs and, thus, the effect of bank deposits on the timing of balance of payments crises would not exist if banks could credibly offer an interest rate on deposits slightly higher than the ones derived from the zero-profit condition. In our setup, the latter would imply that banks would run at a loss, an unsustainable situation unless banks

receive outside subsidies. However, since the government is likely to be the one providing such subsidies, the timing of the crisis would once again be affected by the presence of banks through the generation of a higher fiscal deficit.

9. This strategy was very common in Latin America during the 1980s after the Debt Crisis. See, for example, Fernandez (1991) and Rodríguez (1994).

10. In the Latin American experiments noted in the preceding note, domestic debt was made highly liquid by intermediating it through the banking system. Thus, another way of modeling this type of debt is equating it to interest-bearing money. In the text, however, we will stick to the assumption of pure bonds.

11. For example, a Sidrauski-type model where utility is separable in consumption and real monetary balances.

12. However, in the unrealistic case in which reserves earn the same interest rates as domestic bonds then, under full bond redemption, social costs and the timing of crisis would be the same as in Krugman's model.

13. This section has greatly benefitted from discussions with Ernesto Talvi who tackles a similar issue in Talvi (1996).

14. This assumption is needed to ensure that there is no fiscal deficit during the fixed-exchange-rate period, if the individual displays an intertemporal elasticity of substitution less than, or equal to, one (which we assume in the example). The size of the Olivera–Tanzi effect is irrelevant for the ensuing example.

15. Function u is assumed to be increasing, strictly concave and twice differentiable.

16. Here is where we need the Olivera–Tanzi effect. Otherwise, if $\Phi(\pi) =$ a constant, then $c^H = c^L$. I wish to thank Michael Kumhof, a graduate student at the University of Maryland, for showing this to me.

17. In this section there is no need to be more specific about the nature of those projects. They could range from foreign direct investment to the purchase of government bonds.

18. If J is large but less than infinity, information gathering will of course be valuable (abstracting from cost κ) for r in the interval $r_{min} < r < \rho$. However, since r_{min} converges to ρ as J grows without bound, the probability of $r_{min} < r < \rho$ goes to zero as J diverges to infinity. Hence, we can disregard the above open interval in our computations as J becomes very large (not just at the limit). See Calvo and Mendoza (1996b) for extensions of these results.

19. For example, assume that there are no state-contingent markets and investment requires local labour in fixed proportions. Labour supply is infinitely elastic at the subsistence wage. Thus, a sudden stoppage of capital inflows may result in a higher starvation index. This extreme example can easily be relaxed to accommodate home goods which would undergo negative but less dire consequences as a result of a change in the flow of capital.

20. These types of costs would exist even though investment projects are, say, land and, initially, land is held by private investors (allowing us to assume that the costs of portfolio reshuffling fall entirely on investors in the form of capital gains and losses), but property taxes are proportional to the value of land.

21. The following example bears the flavours of Calvo (1988). However, equilibrium multiplicity follows from fundamental budget constraint considerations, in contrast with Calvo (1988) in which a key ingredient is the government's policy response function.

22. In the simple example there is no future beyond period 2. However, the model could be extended by assuming a string of three-period economies like the one discussed in the text. Thus, the implication is that country 1000, say, would not be able to avoid a run if investors refuse to roll over the debt, even though everyone had the chance to learn from the experience of the previous 999.

23. In this respect, it is somewhat worrisome that some countries—particularly those in Eastern Europe and former Soviet Union republics—are receiving advice from the technicians of advanced countries (for example, retired Bundesbank officials), with the blessing of leading international financial institutions, on how to develop a market for government bonds.

References

Calvo, G. A. (1986) "Temporary Stabilization: Predetermined Exchange Rates," *Journal of Political Economy*, vol. 94, no. 6, pp. 1319–29.

Calvo, G. A. (1988) "Servicing the Public Debt: The Role of Expectations," *American Economic Review*, vol. 78, no. 4, pp. 647–61.

Calvo, G. A. and Mendoza, E. G. (1996a) "Mexico's Balance-of-Payments Crisis: A Chronicle of a Death Foretold," *Journal of International Economics*, vo. 41, pp. 235–64.

Calvo, G. A. and Mendoza, E. G. (1996b) "Costly Information Aversion to Deviate, and the Incentives for Rational Herd Behavior in Global Securities Markets," manuscript, November, Centre for International Economics, University of Maryland, USA.

Diamond, D. W. and Dybvig, P. H. (1983) "Bank Runs, Deposit Insurance, and Liquidity," *Journal of Political Economy*, vol. 91, pp. 401–19.

Diaz-Alejandro, C. F. (1989) in Velasco, A. (ed.) *Trade, Development and the World Economy* (Oxford and New York: Basil Blackwell).

Easterly, W. R. (1989) "Fiscal Adjustment and Deficit Financing during the Debt Crisis," in Husain, I. and Diwan, I. (eds) *Dealing with the Debt Crisis* (Washington, DC: The World Bank), pp. 91–113.

Fernandez, R. B. (1991) "What Have Populists Learned from Hyperinflation?," in Dornbusch, R. and Edwards, S. (eds) *The Macroeconomics of Populism in Latin America* (Chicago: The University of Chicago Press), pp. 121–50.

Flood, R. P. and Garber, P. M. (1984) "Gold Monetization and Gold Discipline," *Journal of Political Economy*, vol. 92, pp. 90–107.

Keynes, J. M. (1924) *Indian Currency and Finance* (London: Macmillan).

Kiguel, M. and Liviatan, N. (1992) "The Business Cycle Associated with Exchange Rate Based Stabilization," *The World Bank Economic Review*, vol. 6, no. 2, pp. 279–305.

Krugman, P. R. (1979) "A Model of Balance-of-Payments Crises," *Journal of Money, Credit, and Banking*, vol. 11 (August), pp. 311–25.

Obstfeld, M. (1986) "Rational and Self-Fulfilling Balance-of-Payments Crises," *American Economic Review*, vol. 76, March, pp. 72–81.

Rodríguez, C. A. (1994) "Argentina: Fiscal Disequilibria Leading to Hyperinflation," in Easterly, W., Rodríguez, C. A. and Schmidt-Hebbel, K. (eds) *Public Sectors Deficits and Macroeconomic Performance* (Washington, DC: The World Bank).

Talvi, E. (1996) "Exchange-Rate-Based Stabilization with Endogenous Fiscal Response," working paper 324, March, Inter-American Development Bank, Washington, DC, USA.

8   Uncertain Duration of Reform: Dynamic Implications

Guillermo A. Calvo and Allan Drazen

1 Introduction

Although policymakers usually present major economic reforms as permanent structural changes, citizens, on the basis of their past experience, are skeptical about the permanence of such reforms. Doubts about the permanence of reforms not only reflect the nature of the programs—often, drastic breaks with previous policy—but also strongly influence the economic effects that reforms will have.

Price stabilization programs, for example, provide ample evidence that outcomes may very much reflect the degree of credibility enjoyed by the program. Consider the consumption/output boom often observed at the beginning of an exchange-rate-based stabilization program [see Kiguel and Liviatan (1992)].[1] Calvo and Végh (1993) show that initial lack of credibility in the sustainability of the exchange-rate anchor can account for the initial boom, as well as several other stylized facts associated with these programs, such as eventual consumption/output contraction. With the exception of Drazen and Helpman (1988, 1990), however, this type of credibility or limited-policy-durability work has focused mostly on perfect-foresight models in which the timing of the policy switch is fully known at the beginning of the program.[2]

The objective of this chapter is to analyze the effects of uncertain duration of reform, that is, uncertainty about the date a program may be abandoned, on the dynamics of consumption and the current account. The emphasis on consumption and real variables distinguishes our paper from the work of Drazen and Helpman, who concentrated on the dynamics of nominal variables, such as inflation and the nominal exchange rate. Moreover, in contrast to other papers in the literature, we demonstrate how the effects of uncertain duration will depend crucially on the structure of asset markets.

Our primary result is that policies characterized by uncertain duration can generate consumption booms that mirror what has been observed in many economies, even though the same policies would not generate empirically realistic consumption dynamics if their duration were known. For example, a policy that yields an increase in economywide income whose duration is uncertain can generate high and continually rising consumption while the policy is in effect; if the duration of the policy were known, however, it would yield a flat consumption path. A trade liberalization of uncertain duration can generate a number of different consumption paths, depending both on how the government disposes of its tariff revenues and on the elasticity of intertemporal substitution. In the realistic case of the government *not* rebating tariff revenues to consumers and low elasticity of substitution, high and continually rising consumption results, a pattern observed in many countries in which consumers doubted the permanence of trade liberalization. Here too, if the date on which the liberalization would be abandoned were known, the model would not yield this pattern.

The plan of the chapter is as follows. In Section 2, we set up a basic model of a nonmonetary economy that produces a single exportable good and consumes a different importable good. We outline two basic types of policies: an endowment or productivity-increasing policy, by which output of exportables is higher while the program lasts; and a trade liberalization policy, by which tariffs are set to zero while the program lasts, but are expected to be positive afterward. In Section 3, we study the consumption dynamics that would be observed in a model with only one real asset, deriving the paths described above, and compare them with the paths that would obtain if there were a full set of state-contingent markets (or equivalently, if the duration of the policies was certain). Section 4 closes the paper, and an Appendix examines the case of complete markets, which helps more fully to understand the role of capital-market incompleteness.

2   Basic Model

We assume that the timing of the policy switch is the only source of uncertainty. The government announces a policy at time $t = 0$, to which the public assigns an uncertain duration (that is, believes there is a chance of a future policy switch). Let T denote the time of the policy switch. We assume the public has a subjective probability distribution on T, where its c.d.f. is denoted by $H(T)$. Thus, $H(T)$ is the probability that the policy switch occurs at time T or earlier.[3] Function H is assumed to be common knowledge.

The country is endowed with a path of exportables that depends on current economic policy. Residents are assumed to have no taste for exportables and, instead, consume only importables, where the terms of trade in the absence of taxes on imports or exports are assumed to be constant over time and, without loss of generality, are set equal to unity. Import tariffs are represented by $\theta(t)$, equal to one plus the tariff rate.

The economy has a representative individual whose utility is a function of consumption. We assume that the von Neumann–Morgenstern utility function is time-separable. The period utility function $u(\cdot)$ is strictly concave, twice-continuously differentiable, and monotonically increasing. Domestic residents take the international rate of interest, r, as given, and the international bond is the only available financial asset. The representative individual holdings at time t are indicated by $a(t)$. Maximum utility (at T) associated with $a(T)$ is denoted by the value function $V(a(T))$.[4] Therefore, utility at time zero now can be expressed as follows, where r is the rate of discount:

$$\int_0^\infty \left[\int_0^T u(c(t))e^{-rt}\,dt + e^{-rT}V(a(T)) \right] dH(T). \tag{1}$$

To abstract from dynamic considerations that are extraneous to the present discussion, we assume that the international interest rate is constant and equal to the subjective discount rate. Thus, bondholdings evolve according to

$$\dot{a}(t) = y(t) + ra(t) - \theta(t)c(t) + \tau(t). \tag{2}$$

where $\tau(t)$ denotes time-t lump-sum government transfers (in terms of exportables). Therefore,

$$a(T) = a(0)e^{rT} + \int_0^T [y(t) - \theta(t)c(t) + \tau(t)]e^{r(T-t)}\,dt. \tag{3}$$

Condition (3) now stands for the individual's budget constraint.

Maximization of utility yields the following central first-order condition, conditional on the policy switch not having occurred at time t, which can be obtained by pointwise maximization after substituting

(3) into (1):

$$\frac{u'(c(t))}{\theta(t)} = \int_t^\infty V'(a(T)) \frac{dH(T)}{1 - H(t)} \equiv \omega(t). \tag{4}$$

Equation (4) has a clear interpretation. Consider the experiment of increasing consumption at time t by one unit *if the policy switch has not yet occurred at time t.*[5] This increases utility (1) by $u'(c(t))[1 - H(t)]e^{-rt}$, where $[1 - H(t)]$ is the probability that the policy switch will not have taken place by time t. To stay within his budget constraint, the individual is assumed to cut his consumption *after* the policy switch. This implies that the brunt of the adjustment will fall upon $a(T)$, $T \geq t$. By budget constraint (3), an additional unit of $c(t)$ lowers $a(T)$ by $\theta(t)e^{r(T-t)}$. The latter lowers utility (1) by $\theta(t)e^{-rt}V'(a(T))h(T)$, $T \geq t$ [where $h(t)$ is the p.d.f. associated with H], which, adding over $T \geq t$, yields a marginal cost equal to

$$\theta(t)e^{-rt} \int_t^\infty V'(a(T)) \, dH(T). \tag{5}$$

Equating marginal benefit $u'(c(t))[1 - H(t)]e^{-rt}$ to marginal cost, as given by equation (5), results in first-order condition (4).

Differentiating the right-hand side of (4) with respect to time yields

$$\dot{\omega}(t) = \varphi(t)[\omega(t) - V'(a(t))], \tag{6}$$

where $\varphi(t) = h(t)/[1 - H(t)]$ is the hazard rate at time t. Equation (6) represents a basic differential equation associated with the utility maximization problem under no contingent markets, and it applies for every $t < T$. It is in fact the standard Euler equation in continuous time. To see this, note that the return to a unit of assets is the flow return r plus the probability of a policy switch at t, $\varphi(t)$, multiplied by the percentage capital gain in utility that an individual will enjoy if a switch takes place, namely $(V'(a(t)) - \omega)/\omega$. According to the Euler equation, the percentage change in the marginal utility of consumption, ω, is simply the discount rate minus the return to the asset, which is equation (6) because the discount rate is r.

We assume that the economy is stationary after the policy switch, with $y(t) = \underline{y}$, $\theta(t) = \kappa$, and $\tau(t) = $ constant, for all $t \geq T$.[6] Therefore, given the equality between the international interest rate and the subjective rate of discount, consumption after the switch is constant and equals $[\underline{y} + ra(T) + \tau]/\kappa$. Hence,

$$V(a(T)) = \frac{1}{r} u \left(\frac{\underline{y} + ra(T) + \tau}{\kappa} \right),$$

(7)

implying that

$$V'(a(T)) = \frac{u' \left(\dfrac{\underline{y} + ra(T) + \tau}{\kappa} \right)}{\kappa}.$$

(8)

Thus, by equations (3), (6), and (8), we get

$$\dot{\omega}(t) = \varphi(t) \left[\omega(t) - \frac{u' \left(\dfrac{\underline{y} + ra(t) + \tau}{\kappa} \right)}{\kappa} \right].$$

(9)

For each of the policies considered in Section 3, individual maximization and the budget constraint will allow us to represent the economy's dynamics by a system of two differential equations, based on equations (2) and (9).

3   Uncertain Reform and Consumption Dynamics

We now consider the dynamics of consumption (as well as the current account) under different policies of uncertain duration. We first consider the *endowment-increasing policy* which increases output while the policy is in effect. Specifically, we study the case in which $y(t) = \bar{y} > \underline{y}$ if the policy is in effect, $y(t) = \underline{y}$ otherwise, where we assume no tariffs, so that $\kappa = 1$, and zero lump-sum transfers, i.e., $\tau = 0$.

If a full set of state-contingent markets existed, the constant relative price of consumption would imply that after the policy announcement, consumption would be constant across time and states of nature (see the Appendix for details). Consumption would be independent of whether the program was terminated after a week or after a year, even though the longer the program stayed in place, the larger would be the accumulated output of exportables generated by the endowment-increasing policy. Intuitively, it is like fully insuring against a contingency (such as one's house burning down): With perfect insurance, consumption is independent of when or if the event occurs. The same flat pattern of consumption would be observed if T, the date of policy collapse, were known with certainty.

In the absence of state-contingent securities, the story is quite different. By equations (2) and (9), the budget constraint and necessary conditions imply, for $t < T$,

$$\dot{a}(t) = \bar{y} + ra(t) - C(\omega(t)), \tag{10}$$

and

$$\dot{\omega}(t) = \varphi(t)[\omega(t) - u'(\underline{y} + ra(t))], \tag{11}$$

where, recalling (4), function C is defined by the condition

$$u'(C(\omega)) = \omega. \tag{12}$$

By dynamic equations (10) and (11), we have

$$\dot{a} = 0 \Leftrightarrow \omega = u'(\bar{y} + ra), \tag{13}$$

$$\dot{\omega} = 0 \Leftrightarrow \omega = u'(\underline{y} + ra). \tag{14}$$

Therefore, for $\varphi > 0$, dynamic behavior is described by the phase diagram in the (a, ω)-plane as depicted in figure 8.1, in which the locus where $\dot{\omega} = 0$ lies above the one where $\dot{a} = 0$. The direction of movement remains invariant to changes in hazard function φ, as long as $\varphi > 0$.

The initial condition $a(0)$ is given by history. However, $\omega(0)$ is, in principle, free to take any positive value. To pin it down, one works backward. Let T^c be the first point in time at which the policy switch will have occurred with probability 1; that is, let it satisfy the condition (as seen from time 0)[7]

$$H(T^c) = 1, \quad \text{and} \quad H(T) < 1 \quad \text{for all } T < T^c. \tag{15}$$

At T^c, therefore, the consumer faces a perfect-foresight problem and, hence, if the consumption plan is optimal, the marginal utility of wealth, ω, cannot jump at T^c. This imposes a boundary condition on ω at $t = T^c$ which, in terms of figure 8.1, implies that the equilibrium path should reach the $\dot{\omega} = 0$ locus at time T^c. Clearly, the only trajectories compatible with such a condition would be those like the path from A to B in figure 8.1. Consequently, ω falls over time which, by (12), implies that *consumption rises monotonically before the policy switch.* Moreover, if the switch occurs before T^c, say at $T < T^c$, then, right after the switch, $\omega = u'(\underline{y} + ra(T))$. In terms of figure 8.1, this means that, at the time of the switch, ω jumps from E to F. Thus, *if the policy switch is not fully expected, then the switch is associated with a sudden and*

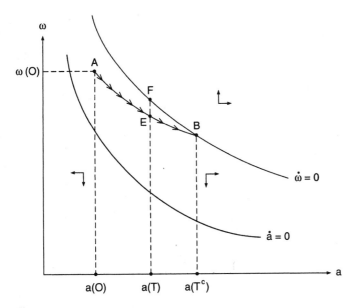

Figure 8.1
Output-increasing policy.

permanent fall in consumption. These results are in sharp contrast with those under complete markets. Finally, bondholdings a accumulate before the policy switch and stay constant afterward. Thus, *the current account is positive as long as the endowment-increasing policy is kept in place.*[8]

The main reason for the difference in results from the complete-markets case is that if the consumer has no access to insurance markets, random shocks produce income effects, i.e., they change the opportunity set faced by the consumer. Suppose the endowment-increasing policy is still in force at t. Just before t, the consumer assigned a probability less than 1 that the program would be in force at t. Hence, since $\bar{y} > \underline{y}$, the choice of $c(t)$ thus reflects a windfall relative to what was expected before: Finding out that the program has not expired at time t is good news; it (marginally) increases the individual's permanent income *after* time t. Hence consumption will be slowly rising over time to reflect a continued windfall as long as the program is in force. Because the consumer assigns a probability less than 1 that the program will be in force after t, some of the excess of $\bar{y}$ over $\underline{y}$ is treated as transitory income and saved, which explains the coexistence of surpluses in the current account. In contrast, the realization of the policy switch at time T (for $T < T^c$) is bad news because, before time T, the event "policy switch" at T had probability less than 1. Furthermore, by assumption, after the policy switch, the economy's endowment goes permanently back to its low level $\underline{y}$. Therefore, it is again plausible that consumption takes a precipitous fall when there is a policy switch. After the switch, the current account is in balance because, by assumption, the economy is fully stationary.

Consider now a *temporary trade liberalization* involving a temporary setting of import tariffs to zero, so that $\theta(t) = 1$ for $T > t \geq 0$; otherwise, $\theta(t) = \kappa$ for some constant $\kappa > 1$. We assume that output of exportables is constant at $\underline{y}$, independent of whether or not the liberalization policy is discontinued. We begin by assuming that tariffs are fully rebated in the form of lump-sum subsidies. Thus, $\tau(t) = 0$, for $t < T$, and $\tau(t) = (\kappa - 1)c(t)$, otherwise.

In the case in which markets are perfect, consumption will be high, but constant, while the trade liberalization is in effect (reflecting the constant price of imports) and will jump down to a lower constant level when the liberal trade policies are abandoned (see the Appendix). In the absence of state-contingent assets, results are quite different. Therefore, by equations (2) and (9), we have

$$\dot{a}(t) = \underline{y} + ra(t) - C(\omega(t)), \tag{16}$$

$$\dot{\omega}(t) = \varphi(t)\left[\omega(t) - \frac{u'(\underline{y} + ra(t))}{\kappa}\right]. \tag{17}$$

Hence, we now have

$$\dot{a} = 0 \Leftrightarrow \omega = u'(\underline{y} + ra), \tag{18}$$

$$\dot{\omega} = 0 \Leftrightarrow \omega = \frac{u'(\underline{y} + ra)}{\kappa}. \tag{19}$$

The economy's dynamics can be represented as in figure 8.2, where the $\dot{a} = 0$ locus lies above the $\dot{\omega} = 0$ line. Therefore, applying earlier reasoning, we conclude that the equilibrium path will look like the curve joining points A and B in figure 8.2. This implies that, *before the policy switch, consumption and bondholdings decrease monotonically over time.* Moreover, if the switch occurs at $T < T^c$, then, at time T, ω falls from E to F in figure 8.2. However, because an instant before the switch $\dot{a} < 0$, it follows from (16) that consumption takes a sudden *fall* at time T (and remains constant forever after).[9]

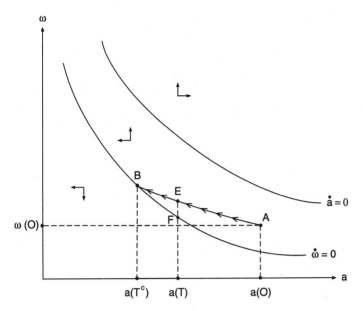

Figure 8.2
Trade liberalization policy.

The basic intuition behind these results follows from the complete-markets case, in which it can be shown (see the Appendix) that equilibrium consumption is higher during the period of trade liberalization than afterward, independently of tariff rebate policy, for the simple reason that consumption is cheaper while trade liberalization lasts. Moreover, the decline in consumption over time before the switch reflects the fact that (as in the preceding example) the individual assigns a probability between 0 and 1 to a policy switch. Suppose, having reached time t, the individual knew for sure that no switch would occur for the next h periods. It then would be optimal to set consumption constant over the interval from t to $t + h$.[10] In contrast, a positive probability of a policy switch in the interval $(t, t + h)$ means that consumption prices may go up in that interval, increasing the individual's incentives to consume more than he would under perfect foresight. If, however, no policy switch occurs in the interval $(t, t + h)$, the individual realizes that he has overconsumed and thus depleted his bond-holdings by more than he would if he knew that there would be no policy switch in the interval. This leads him to revise his consumption downward. (Note also the presence of a current account deficit before the policy switch, corresponding to the fall in bondholdings over time.)

The trade-liberalization experiment discussed so far concentrates on pure substitution effects because tariffs are rebated. In general, however, higher tariffs may be accompanied by higher government expenditure on, e.g., white elephants and, thus, the policy switch will be accompanied by substitution and income effects—which, as shown above, have opposite effects on the pattern of consumption before the policy switch.[11] To examine this type of trade liberalization, let us assume that, contrary to the preceding case, the tariff is not rebated back to the public and thus that lump-sum subsidies are identically equal to zero.

Therefore,

$$\dot{\omega}(t) = \varphi(t) \left[\omega(t) - u'\left(\frac{\underline{y} + ra(t)}{\kappa}\right) \middle/ \kappa \right],$$ (20)

while bondholdings, a, still satisfy equation (16). Hence,

$$\dot{a} = 0 \Leftrightarrow \omega = u'(\underline{y} + ra),$$ (21)

$$\dot{\omega} = 0 \Leftrightarrow \omega = u'\left(\frac{\underline{y} + ra}{\kappa}\right) \middle/ \kappa.$$ (22)

The position of the $\dot{a} = 0$ and $\dot{\omega} = 0$ loci is now ambiguous and depends on the intertemporal elasticity of substitution σ ($\sigma = -u'/u''c$). One can show the following proposition:

PROPOSITION 1. Consider the case of trade liberalization without tariff rebate: (i) if $\sigma = 1$, then consumption is constant over time, and the private sector's current account is always in balance; (ii) if $\sigma < 1$ then the paths of consumption and the private sector's current account follow the patterns associated with the endowment-increasing policy (see figure 8.1); and (iii) if $\sigma > 1$, then the paths of consumption and the private sector's current account follow the patterns associated with trade liberalization when tariffs are fully rebated to the public (see figure 8.2).

Proof of Proposition 1. Case (i) is trivial because the two stationary curves in the phase diagram coincide. By (21) and (22), the phase diagram for case (ii) follows the pattern indicated in figure 8.1. Thus, a and c increase over time. Right before the switch, $u'(c(T)) = \omega(T)$; right after the switch, ω satisfies the rightmost equation in expression (22). Let us indicate such value by $\omega^+(T)$. Then, by figure 8.1,

$\omega^+(T) > \omega(T)$, which implies that $u'(c^+) = \omega^+(T)\kappa > \omega(T) = u'(c(T))$. Hence $c^+ < c(T)$, as asserted. Finally, by (21) and (22), case (iii) is associated with the phase diagram shown in figure 8.2. Therefore, before the policy switch, a and c fall over time. Right before the switch, $\dot{a}(T) < 0$, and after the switch $\dot{a} = 0$, and the consumption price rises from 1 to κ: thus, it is required for consumption to take a discontinuous fall at T, as asserted. ∎

The empirically relevant case appears to be $\sigma < 1$. Thus, under no rebate, all policies studied in this section yield the same pattern: Before the switch, consumption rises over time while the private current account is in surplus; at switch time, consumption collapses, and remains constant forever after.

4 Final Words

This chapter presents an analytical framework in which *lack of credibility* significantly affects the outcome of economic reform programs. We show that uncertain program duration coupled with incomplete markets provides an explanation for the consumption dynamics that often accompany sharp changes in policies. The model could be enriched in several ways. For example, nontraded goods could be introduced into the model, and under some simple assumptions the real exchange rate (defined as the real price of tradables in terms of home goods) will appreciate (depreciate) as c grows (decreases) over time. The model thus could rationalize periods of *gradual* appreciation of the real exchange rate—often observed in temporary price stabilization programs [Végh (1992)]—*even though the fundamental variables show a flat pattern*. These dynamics would characterize an endowment-increasing policy as well as a temporary trade liberalization with no tariff rebate (if the intertemporal elasticity of substitution is less than unity).

Theory can only suggest. Recent empirical work, however, indicates that similar models can help to explain consumption booms in a significant number of stabilization episodes [see Bufman and Leiderman (1992), Reinhart and Végh (1992)]. Nonetheless, we feel that we are just beginning to tap on the large well of empirical evidence connected with recent worldwide reform programs. A thorough and systematic analysis of this evidence should improve the chances of distinguishing between the hypotheses explored in this paper and competing ones such as credit market segmentation [see Calvo and Coricelli (1993)].

APPENDIX: COMPLETE MARKETS

With complete markets, we describe the representative individual's consumption plan by two functions: $c(t)$ and $c^+(t, v)$; where $c(t)$ is consumption at time t if the policy switch has still not occurred at time t, and where $c^+(t, v)$ denotes consumption at time t if the policy switch has occurred at time v, $v \leq t$ (i.e., if the policy switch is of vintage v). Expected utility at time zero can be represented as the sum of discounted utility of consumption in each of the two possible states of nature at each point in time t multiplied by the probability of that state, where, as indicated above, in the case of there having been a policy switch at $v \leq t$, consumption depends on both v and t. We therefore have

$$\int_0^\infty u(c(t))[1 - H(t)]e^{-rt}\,dt + \int_0^\infty \left[\int_0^t u(c^+(t, v))\,dH(v)\right]e^{-rt}\,dt, \qquad (A.1)$$

where r is the constant subjective rate of discount. [To help in understanding (A.1), note that if c^+ were independent of v, the second term in (A.1) would simplify to $\int_0^\infty u(c^+(t))H(t)e^{-rt}\,dt$.]

Prices of importable goods (in terms of exportables discounted to time 0, which we term present prices) are defined by two functions: $q(t)$ and $q^+(t, v)$, where $q(t)$ is the present after-tariff price of importables consumed at time t if the policy switch has not yet occurred at time t, and $q^+(t, v)$ is the present after-tariff price of importables consumed at time t if the policy switch occurred at time v, $v \leq t$; $p(t)$ and $p^+(t, v)$ are the analogous price concepts for exportables. Thus, if initial financial wealth is zero, the representative individual's budget constraint takes the following form:

$$\int_0^\infty q(t)c(t)\,dt + \int_0^\infty \left[\int_0^t q^+(t, v)c^+(t, v)\,dv\right]dt$$

$$= \int_0^\infty p(t)[y(t) + \tau(t)]\,dt + \int_0^\infty \left\{\int_0^t p^+(t, v)[y^+(t, v) + \tau^+(t, v)]\,dv\right\}dt,$$

$$(A.2)$$

where the nonsuperscripted and superscripted variables have the same meaning as in the text.

Assuming the country faces risk-neutral investors, Arrow-Debreu prices satisfy (where θ is 1 *plus* tariff, $t < v$, and θ^+ is the same concept at $t \geq v$):

$$q(t) = [1 - H(t)]\theta(t)e^{-rt}, \tag{A.3a}$$

$$q^+(t,v) = h(v)\theta^+(t,v)e^{-rt}, \tag{A.3b}$$

$$p(t) = [1 - H(t)]e^{-rt}, \tag{A.3c}$$

$$p^+(t,v) = h(v)e^{-rt}. \tag{A.3d}$$

In words, *for each state of nature at time t,* Arrow-Debreu import prices are, by risk neutrality, equal to the present discounted value (after tariffs and in terms of present exportables) at time t of a unit of importables (in the corresponding state of nature) multiplied by the probability of the corresponding state of nature at time, with a similar interpretation for export prices.

The representative individual is assumed to maximize utility (A.1) by choosing contingent paths of consumption, $c(t)$ and $c^+(t,v)$ (for all $t \geq v \geq 0$), such that budget constraint (A.2) is satisfied, given the contingent paths of y, q, and τ, and c.d.f. H. Therefore, in the presence of a risk-neutral (foreign) investor, the first-order conditions for an (interior) optimum are

$$u'(c(t)) = \lambda\theta(t), \tag{A.4a}$$

$$u'(c^+(t,v)) = \lambda\theta^+(t,v), \tag{A.4b}$$

where λ is the (constant) Lagrange multiplier corresponding to budget constraint (A.2).

The results in the text on the endowment-increasing policy leading to flat consumption follow form (A.4) because we assume that the tariff rate was held equal to zero (i.e., $\theta \equiv \theta^+ \equiv 1$). For the case of a trade liberalization, we assumed that tariffs satisfy $\theta(t) \equiv 1$ and $\theta^+(t,v) \equiv \kappa > 1$, for $t \geq v$. Hence, by (A.4), consumption equals a constant $\bar{c}$ while the trade liberalization is still in effect, and a constant $\underline{c} < \bar{c}$ after it collapses. This pattern holds independently of whether tariffs are rebated to the public.

Notes

We wish to thank José DeGregorio, Enrique Mendoza, Pablo Neumeyer, and seminar participants at numerous universities.

1. Eastern Europe provides a counterexample: Reform programs were accompanied by a steep fall in output [see Calvo and Coricelli (1993)].

2. Other papers that have used the framework of Drazen and Helpman to analyze uncertain duration include van Wijnbergen (1988).

3. This formulation is consistent with two different interpretations: either that the policy-maker intends the policy to be temporary, or, more interestingly, that the policy is intended to be permanent, but imperfect policy credibility leads the public to expect a future policy reversal.

4. To simplify the notation, we assume that tariffs, outputs, and subsidies are constant after the policy shift and are independent of the point in time at which the policy switch occurs. This allows us to write the value function as in the text. Without those simplifying assumptions, one should include T as another argument in V—thus writing $V(a(T), T)$.

5. More precisely, the experiment consists of increasing $c(s)$ for s in some small interval around t. Otherwise, t being just a point under the integral, increasing $c(t)$ only would have no perceptible effect on welfare or the budget constraint.

6. Constancy of lump-sum taxes after the policy switch is consistent with the assumptions made in Section 3.

7. Unless otherwise stated, the ensuing discussion assumes $\varphi(t) > 0$, $t \leq T^c$.

8. If $T^c = \infty$, then we define the equilibrium solution to be the limit of solutions corresponding to a sequence of finite T^c distributions converging to the one displaying $T^c = \infty$. Technical convergence issues are not discussed here.

9. Notice that, as compared with the endowment-increasing policy, c is now monotonically declining (instead of monotonically increasing as in the export-oriented policy) over time. However, in both cases, consumption collapses at T if $T < T^c$.

10. A formal proof is obtained noticing that perfect certainty over the interval $(t, t + h)$ is equivalent to saying that the hazard rate $\varphi = 0$ over that interval. Thus, by (25), ω—and, hence, c—is constant over the interval $(t, t + h)$.

11. However, as shown in the Appendix, the pattern of consumption before the policy switch under complete markets is independent of whether or not tariffs are rebated to the public.

References

Bufman, G. & L. Leiderman (1992) Simulating an optimizing model of currency substitution. *Revista de Análisis Económico* 7, 109–124.

Calvo, G. & C. Végh (1993) Exchange-rate based stabilization under imperfect credibility. In *Open Economy Macroeconomics*, New York: Macmillan; reprinted in G. Calvo (1993) *Money, Exchange Rates, and Output*, pp. 365–390. Cambridge, MA: MIT Press.

Calvo, G. & F. Coricelli (1993) Output collapse in Eastern Europe: The role of credit. *IMF Staff Papers* 40, 32–52.

Drazen, A. & E. Helpman (1988) Stabilization with exchange rate management under uncertainty. In E. Helpman, A. Razin & E. Sadka (eds.), *Economic Effects of the Government Budget*, pp. 310–327. Cambridge, MA: MIT Press.

Drazen, A. & E. Helpman (1990) The effect of anticipated macroeconomic policies. *Review of Economic Studies* 57, 147–166.

Kiguel, M. & N. Liviatan (1992) The business cycle associated with exchange-rate based stabilization. *World Bank Economic Review* 6, 279–305.

Reinhart, C. & C. Végh (1992) Nominal interest rates, consumption booms, and lack of credibility: A quantitative investigation. Manuscript, International Monetary Fund.

van Wijnbergen, S. (1988) Inflation, balance of payments crises, and public sector deficits. In E. Helpman, A. Razin & E. Sadka (eds.), *Economic Effects of the Government Budget*, pp. 287–309. Cambridge, MA: MIT Press.

Végh, C. (1992) Stopping high inflation: An analytical overview. *IMF Staff Papers* 39, 626–695.

9 Capital Flows and Capital-Market Crises: The Simple Economics of Sudden Stops

Guillermo A. Calvo

I Introduction

The recent turmoil in emerging and not-so-emerging markets countries has caused a great deal of confusion in the economics profession. The knee-jerk reaction after Mexico's Tequila Crisis was to blame it on fiscal deficits and, above all, current account deficits, CADs (which in Mexico reached 8 percent of GDP in 1994, and was expected to increase to 9 percent in 1995). Tequila brought back memories of the 1982 Mexico's moratorium and the ensuing international debt problems. Since the latter were preceded by CADs, it was tempting to conclude that high CADs and low saving rates lied at the heart of Mexico's difficulties then, and in 1994.

But the 1997/98 Asia Crisis raised serious doubts about the corollary's relevance. In contrast to Mexico and the rest of Latin America (except for Chile), Asian countries exhibited enviably high saving rates and, in some cases, either low CADs (Indonesia) or large surpluses (Taiwan). Moreover, and to add to the profession's confusion, the Asian crisis appears to be deeper and longer-lasting than the Tequila. Of course, confusion will never stop economists from advancing new conjectures or redressing old ones. For example, on the one hand, there is still a sturdy bunch claiming that CADs are the main culprit ("after all, it started in high CAD Thailand").[1] On the other hand, the "floaters" are becoming more conspicuous claiming that the fundamental error was not to allow for greater exchange rate flexibility. Their appeal is increasing because exchange rates have greatly devalued after crises.[2] Finally, in the din of cacophonous voices, the air is pierced with denunciations of "moral hazard," "short-term foreign-exchange denominated debt," "crony capitalism," and so on.

Consequently, time seems to be ripe for going back to basic accounting identities and economic principles. As I will argue, familiar identities still have a wealth of untapped wisdom. In particular, I will use them to discuss the mechanics of a sudden stop in capital inflows (it need not result in capital outflow), and show that this could have large deleterious effects on the economy, validating the pessimistic conjectures that likely led to the initial stop.[3] I will show that the resulting shock need not put into question the country's solvency in order for the pessimistic conjectures to become self-fulfilling. For instance, the shock could be reflected in a downward shift in marginal factor productivities due to associated bankruptcy and financial disruption.

Although debt maturity structure and currency denomination are important, I will show that capital-market crises could take place even though most capital inflows took the form of foreign direct investment.

The chapter is organized as follows. Sections II and III present the core results in the context of a non-monetary economy. Section IV discusses extensions to a monetary framework. Finally, Section V concludes and discusses some policy alternatives. An appendix analyzes a model in which bankruptcies sprout as a result of a anticipated fall in the *CAD*.

A caveat is in order. The chapter aims at laying out some basic mechanisms whereby sudden stops can trigger a crisis, including self-fulfilling prophesy mechanism that help to rationalize sudden stops. However, the paper stops short of providing a framework that could be used to *predict* sudden stop crises. Thus, for instance, although the discussion highlights some early warning indicators, it produces no theory that can help to attach a *probability* of crisis to each of those. This is so because the explicit and implicit models in the chapter display multiple equilibria, and no theory is provided on how those equilibria are actually selected.[4]

II Effects of a Capital Inflows Slowdown: The Non-Monetary Economy

Abstracting from errors and omissions, the following is an accounting identity in a non-monetary economy:

$$KI = CAD, \tag{1}$$

where *KI* and *CAD* stand for capital inflows and current account deficit in, say, tradable goods. Moreover, for both a monetary and non-monetary economy, and distinguishing between tradable and nontradable goods, the following identity holds:

$$CAD = Z - GNP = Z^* - GDP - NFTA, \tag{2}$$

where Z, Z^*, GNP, GDP^*, and $NFTA$ are, respectively, aggregate demand, demand for tradables, gross national product, gross domestic product of tradables and net factor transfers abroad.

A capital-inflows episode is a period during which KI shows a sharp and sustained increase which, by equation (1), is also a period of high CADs. Thus, a sudden stop in KI implies a sudden contraction in CAD which, by equation (2), could be accommodated by lowering the demand for tradable goods with no output cost.

However, this is unlikely to be the case. Given the real exchange rate, lower Z^* is likely to be accompanied by a lower demand for nontradable goods, $Z - Z^*$. In a flexible-prices world, the latter implies a higher real exchange rate (i.e., a decline in the relative price of nontradables with respect to tradables). Sudden stop means that the change is largely unexpected and, therefore, loans to the nontradable sector (e.g., real estate) extended under the expectation that previous relative prices were, on the whole, permanent, could become nonperforming. This, in turn, could lead to across-the-board bankruptcies (see Appendix for an example).

The damage associated with a sudden stop of capital inflows, thus, depends on how easy it is to accommodate the associated fall in the CAD. In this respect, I would advance the following conjecture:

1. The larger is the share of consumption in total expenditure Z and, in particular, on Z^*, the more pronounced will be the damage to the real economy from a fall in the CAD.

Conjecture 1 may not sound terribly new because it brings to mind the warning that economists concerned about a country's solvency use to make, based on the observation that investment makes it easier to repay a country's debt.[5] My conjecture, however, has an entirely different basis. It relies on the guess that consumption of tradable goods is more labor-intensive than investment of tradable goods.[6] Since labor is the nontradable good *par excellence*, this guess implies that the same reduction in aggregate demand for tradable goods will result in a larger cut in the demand for nontradables, the larger is the share of consumption in the demand for tradable goods. And, of course, the larger is the cut in the demand for nontradables, the larger will be the real devaluation B and, therefore, the deeper will be the ensuing financial turmoil.

Sudden Stops and Debt Maturity

The above discussion made no reference to the maturity structure of the country's debt, an issue that has received a lot of attention after the recent crises. The theory of sudden stops is, in principle, independent of the maturity structure. Consider, for example, the case in which the CAD is entirely financed by foreign direct investment, FDI. At one extreme, all of FDI takes the form of new investment and, therefore, by previous reasoning, sudden stops should not be of major concern. At the other end, FDI takes the form of purchases of existing firms. In principle, this need not be translated into a higher CAD. Conceivably, this transaction could give rise to an equal-value asset accumulation in the opposite direction, in which the sellers of domestic assets acquire foreign assets of equal worth, resulting in no change in KI. Thus, if a higher CAD takes place it means that the original owners (or someone else in the domestic chain) are using the proceeds to increase aggregate spending. The fact that the CAD has its origins in FDI is not relevant. *How* it is spent, is (recall conjecture 1 above).

Although previous discussion shows that the impact of a cut in KI is, in principle, independent of the debt maturity structure, the actual size of the cut is not so. Debt maturity structure (more specifically, *residual* debt maturity structure, i.e., the time profile of maturing debt) is relevant in assessing the *potential reversal* of capital flows (in our notation, the largest possible short-run fall in KI). In addition, one would need to determine the probability of debt *refinancing*. The latter, in turn, depends on considerations like the country's standing with the IMF and key G7 countries (recall, Korea and Mexico), and its ability to retaliate if official refinancing is not forthcoming (via trade restrictions, for example). In any case, it appears reasonable to conjecture that

2. The shorter is the residual maturity structure of a country's debt, the more fertile will be the ground for a sudden stop crisis.

III   The *Why* of Sudden Stops

The above discussion assumed a sudden slowdown in capital inflows, and took it as exogenous. The task of this section will be to argue that conjectures that originally lead to a sudden stop may come to be true through a self-fulfilling prophesy mechanism.

I can offer two different lines of reasoning:

1. The capital inflows slowdown could push the economy into insolvency, and/or

2. could drastically lower the "average and marginal productivity of physical capital" as a result of, say, socially-costly bankruptcy battles following sharp, and largely unexpected, changes in relative prices (as discussed in previous section).

Point 1 does not appear to be highly relevant, especially in the case of Asia.[7] Thus, I will focus on point 2. To support the view behind point 2, first recall that sudden stops are likely to generate across-the-board bankruptcies. In addition, I would argue that

• crises that lead to bankruptcies destroy specific human capital (which is complementary with physical capital).

Specific human capital is destroyed for different reasons. For instance, bankruptcy is likely to interfere with the fulfilment of "implicit" contracts. Internal promotion schemes that depend on track records at the firm, for example, may be repudiated after bankruptcy. These schemes are subject to time-inconsistency sustainability problems under the best of circumstances. Hence, it is to be expected that new owners will take advantage of the situation and try to start on a clean slate, writing off implicit contracts and debts. Thus, while bankruptcy procedures take place, incentives inside the firm could be seriously jeopardized, lowering the stock of *effective* human capital. In extreme cases—as after the breakdown of the former Soviet Union—firms are actually cannibalized by employees and managers.

Bankruptcies also produce negative externalities outside individual firms. For example, even in moderately advanced economies, firms rely on interenterprise credit. Thus, the sudden emergence of bankruptcies puts into question not only the solvency of the directly affected firms, but also that of other firms which are—actually or potentially—connected with them through the credit channel. Consequently, all of a sudden more information is needed to assess firms' creditworthiness and, as a result, human capital devoted to production is diverted to financial matters, depressing physical capital's average and marginal productivities. Moreover, even if creditworthiness' assessment were costless, examples can be shown in which credit vanishes until bankruptcy procedures are terminated—as when firms are laid out around a circle and depend on each other for production and credit (see Calvo (1998b)).

Consequently, an exogenous initial slowdown in capital inflows may destroy output, and incentives to rebuild it. In addition, it may destroy credit channels. The latter is conceivably the most devastating feature of this process because it prevents consumption-smoothing, and ensures that the new temporary equilibrium exhibits a sharp decrease of the relative price of nontradables with respect to tradables (i.e., real depreciation).

The self-fulfilling output collapse prophesy can be further deepened by pro-cyclical policy. Thus, many recently affected countries have either adopted or shadowed IMF-sponsored programs which entail tight fiscal and monetary policy. On the one hand, tight fiscal policy would further depress the relative price of nontradables, likely contributing to deeper and more widespread bankruptcies. On the other hand, tight monetary policy aggravates the credit destruction problem.[8]

IV   The Monetary Economy

A monetary economy differs from the "real" one in that, instead of identity (1),

$$KI = CAD + RA, \tag{3}$$

where RA stands for accumulation of international reserves per unit of time.

Previous discussion fully applies to this case. One key difference, however, is that a slowdown in capital inflows (i.e., a cut in KI) could now be met by a loss of reserves (i.e., a fall in RA). Therefore, the output/credit collapse associated with a contraction in the CAD could be cushioned by a loss of international reserves. However, in practice this is largely illusory.

Loss of Reserves

Consider the following central bank balance-sheet identity (in terms of tradable goods):

$$R + NDA = H, \tag{4}$$

where R and H denote international reserves and high-powered money, respectively, and NDA denotes net domestic assets (i.e., the difference between H and RA and, hence, includes with a negative sign, the central bank's certificates of deposit and net worth, and government's deposits at the central bank, among other things). In practice, R is likely to increase as a result of the expansion in high-powered money, H, and certificates of deposit, but also as a result of an increase in government deposits. The latter could be very significant in countries that embark in massive privatization efforts (e.g., Peru after 1991).

Consider now an exogenous fall in KI. If the central bank sticks to its reserves, the economy would essentially go through the same type of adjustment as in the nonmonetary case. To improve over that solution, the central bank would have to find mechanisms that release R and, as a consequence, allow CAD to fall by a smaller amount than KI. A direct way to accomplish this would be to extend loans to those firms and individuals that suddenly found their international credit cut. But this is not easy in practice. Once it is known that the country faces credit rationing, it will be to everyone's advantage to claim that he/she has lost international credit lines.

A capital inflows slowdown is typically associated with an increase in domestic interest rates. Thus, a common procedure is for the central bank to increase NDA (through a discount window, for example) to cushion the interest rate rise. A higher NDA (keeping international reserves constant), in turn, results in an increase in the stock of high-powered money, H, and a devaluation, i.e., a rise in the nominal exchange rate (i.e., the price of foreign in term of domestic currency). However, this does not resolve the adjustment problem because, up to that point, international reserves would not have been lost. Thus, in order for the mechanism to work, the central bank will have to intervene in the foreign exchange market and release international reserves.

If the country is committed to a fixed (or semi-fixed) exchange rate, this mechanism makes the central bank vulnerable to a speculative attack. The moment this is perceived by the public, they will:

1. Lower their demand for assets denominated in domestic currency (most prominently, bonds and bank deposits), and

2. Try to convert dollar-denominated liabilities into domestic-currency denominated liabilities.

Recent experience in Mexico and Indonesia shows that reaction 2 could be very powerful because it is usually conducted by firms and banks with access to the international capital market, which have an above-average in-house financial expertise and information (including *inside* information). Of course, the force of this reaction is likely to increase, the larger is the stock of their dollar-denominated liabilities.

Since reactions 1 and 2 are taking place against a background of tighter international credit, they are likely to further increase all interest rates inside the country: both dollar and domestic currency interest rates. Besides, the rush out of domestic currency assets could exacerbate the fall in capital inflows *KI*.

As noted above, even if the country is not committed to defend the currency, policies that entail reserves losses to cushion the real economy from a slowdown in capital inflows, call for a departure from pure floating, at least momentarily. But, the question arises, could the country release a certain amount of reserves and then go back to floating. Conceivably "yes," but if lower reserves induce a flight from domestic assets, reserves-loss policies could trigger further *KI*'s contraction and, thus, additional downward pressure on the real economy.

In sum, even though the ability to release international reserves could soften the blow of a sudden cut in capital inflows, recent experience, backed by basic economic reasoning, suggests that doing it properly could be a major feat.

Sticky Prices

A monetary economy introduces the realistic possibility of sticky prices and wages. This adds a keynesian channel through which a cut in the current account deficit can have a depressive effect on output, independently of the channels emphasized in previous section. However, keynesian considerations typically conjure up the possibility of avoiding major output loss by means of counter cyclical monetary policy or, more specifically, currency devaluation. However, although this policy could certainly speed up reaching the neoclassical set of relative prices associated with lower *KI*, it does not necessarily help to bypass financial crisis. This is clearly the case if debt is denominated in foreign exchange. The devaluation helps rising the relative price of tradable goods with respect to nontradables, but if nontradables sector took dollar-denominated debt, the problem would be identical to that discussed in previous section.

Would the situation be much better if debt in the nontradables sector was denominated in domestic currency? The answer is likely "no."

Devaluations prompted by crises are usually accompanied by higher nominal and real interest rates (witness Mexico in 1995, and Korea in 1998). This is so because those devaluations are, by and large, involuntary, raising doubts about the government's ability to control over key macro variables.[9] Hence, the real interest rates in terms of both non-tradables and tradables rises, implying a mounting debt burden. Thus, the main difference between dollar and domestic-currency denominated debt is timing: with dollar debts financial distress brought about by devaluation is instantaneous, while with domestic-currency denominated debt it may surface only after several months or even years.[10]

V   What's *International* About All That?

The above discussion could have been carried out in terms of regions within a given country (e.g., Provinces, States). Once identified, each region would have a well-defined *KI* and *CAD*, so the same story could be told with just minor presentation changes. However, although self-fulfilling prophesies can occur in a national context, there are important *international* characteristics that would be absent. As a general rule:

1. Countries, as opposed to regions, are shielded by sovereignty clauses. In particular, countries are less constrained than regions in choosing fiscal and monetary policy, e.g., countries can devalue. Thus, in a way, countries are more able to "repudiate" earlier commitments (e.g., policy commitments).

2. For legal and cultural reasons, labor mobility across countries is markedly less responsive to cyclical fluctuations than across regions and, thus, expected lifetime labor income reflect more local conditions in countries than in regions.

Point 1 implies that, controlling for natural risks,[11] "country risks" are bound to include more non-natural factors (e.g., political factors) than "region risks." Assessing non-natural risks could be more costly in crisis-stricken economies because the political situation in many of them is in a state of flux (recall Mexico, Korea, Indonesia) and, in some cases, because they have a relatively young—and, thus, not much "tried by fire"—economic system (Argentina). As shown in Calvo and Mendoza (1997), high risk-assessment costs makes herding more likely. Moreover, in this context, the probability of herding is even higher if credit runs produce (and/or are expected to produce) negative effects of their own, as discussed in previous sections.

Point 2 implies that national politicians are more likely to be asked by their constituents to implement new policies if hit by crisis, contributing to country risk. Moreover, the higher correlation between a country's cycle and its citizen's expected lifetime income as compared to regions (i.e., the correlation between a region's cycle and its present inhabitant's lifetime income), implies that a country's aggregate demand will have a larger effect on its real exchange rate than in a region. Moreover, lower international labor mobility implies that after-crisis depreciations of the real exchange are likely to be more persistent in countries than in regions. All of which leads to the conjecture that a cut in *KI* contributes to deeper and longer-lasting financial crises in sovereign countries than in regions.

VI   Conclusions and Policy Discussion

Conclusions

1. High negative swings in capital inflows—i.e., sudden stops—are dangerous. They may result in bankruptcies, and destruction of human capital and local credit channels.

2. Large current account deficits are dangerous *independently on how they are financed*. This is so because in order to keep the same current account deficit "new money" is necessary, and the latter is hard to get during sudden stops.

3. The negative effects of a cut in capital inflows are likely to increase, the higher is the marginal propensity to spend on nontradables. Thus, assuming that consumption is more nontradable-intensive than investment, the higher the share of consumption financed by capital inflows, the stronger is likely to be the negative impact of a future sudden stop.

4. Short-term financing may add to those risks to the extent that they contribute to generate larger slowdowns in capital inflows (or downright outflows).

Policy Discussion

1. The financial sector is at the center of the action and directly, or indirectly, must be the key to the solution.

2. Given the different forms that financial transactions can quickly take, partial solutions may be ineffective and highly distorting. Thus, controls on (international) capital flows could be ineffective unless they are accompanied by suitable regulations of the *domestic* capital market.

3. Financial sector policies should cover the whole financial system, including domestic transactions, especially those done through institutions that are under the tutelage of the central bank. This is so because the central bank usually offers free deposit insurance and, thus, a financial crisis could represent a large fiscal burden (recall Chile, Mexico and Venezuela).

4. Financially closed and underdeveloped systems (e.g., India's) should *not* be encouraged to liberalize the financial sector in one fell swoop. Financial reform should be gradual and should not outpace equity financing. Policymakers should keep an eye on firms' leverage ratios (i.e., bond/equity ratios).

5. However, financially open systems (e.g., Argentina's and New Zealand's) should be kept that way and should be complemented with iron-clad rules that make the country resemble a region of a stable country (Argentina's Currency Board is a good example).

6. There is no contradiction between advices 4 and 5. Financial liberalization generates large "capital flows" from, for example, consumers to firms which, since information is limited, are likely to take the form of short-term credit. Thus, these flows are easily reverted, and could cause serious financial trouble. Moreover, financial liberalization may generate large (international) capital inflows through capital repatriation, with similar potentially dangerous results. In contrast, if the financial system is already liberalized, much of the above-mentioned risks may have already been incurred, and the expectation that flows will be taxed or trampled with may generate a run causing, not averting, a crisis.

7. Efficient bankruptcy regulations are essential to prevent liquidity crises to result in major destruction of specific human capital.

8. Policy in the aftermath of crisis. A sudden stop in capital inflows signifies, as a general rule, a serious blow to the economy. Standard offsetting monetary and fiscal policies are likely to be of little use. Large devaluations and easy money are unlikely to be of much use for reasons discussed above. Lax fiscal policy makes no sense when external financing becomes a serious constraint. Thus, it seems that a

reasonable course of action would be a monetary policy aimed at price stability and a fiscal policy that does not further constrain aggregate demand in the short run, and moves towards a balanced budget.[12]

APPENDIX: MECHANICS OF A FINANCIAL CRISIS

A key assumption in the above analysis is that an unanticipated cut in the CAD may result in financial disarray due to the associated decline in the relative price of nontradables. I will now show the assumption's plausibility by means of a simple model.

Consider first a two-period non-monetary endowment economy with one homogeneous tradable good. The economy faces a perfect capital market and a constant real interest rate which, without loss of generality, we assume to be zero. The country is small, both in the output and capital markets, and there are no trade or capital mobility barriers. Denoting y_t endowment at time t, $t = 1, 2$, we assume

$$y_1 = 0, \quad and \quad y_2 > 0. \tag{5}$$

The utility function of the representative individual takes the following form:

$$u(c_1) + u(c_2), \tag{6}$$

where c_t, $t = 1, 2$, stands for consumption in period t, and u is an increasing, strictly concave and differentiable function on the non-negative real line.

Assuming no initial wealth, the relevant Lagrangean for a Social Planner attempting to maximize the representative's individual welfare takes the following form:

$$u(c_1) + u(c_2) + \lambda(y_2 - c_1 - c_2). \tag{7}$$

Hence, at an interior maximum:

$$u < c_1 = c_2 = \frac{1}{2}y_2. \tag{8}$$

Clearly, the planner's optimum is decentralizable into a competitive equilibrium. Therefore, in equilibrium the economy exhibits a $CAD = y_2/2$ in period 1. Under the present circumstances, it is hard to argue that a cut in the CAD in period 1 will cause any damage to the supply side (even if we relax the assumption of exogenous endowments and assume that output is produced). Hence, a momentary loss of international credit in period 1 will quickly be offset by new funds from other credit sources.

I will now introduce nontradable goods, and modify the utility function as follows:

$$u(c_1) + u(h) + u(c_2), \tag{9}$$

where h denotes consumption of nontradables (home goods, houses) in period 1. I assume that one unit of nontradable is produced with one unit of tradable in period 0 (so now the economy exhibits three periods, although nothing momentous happens in period 0, except for the capital market transaction referred to above). Again, the Social Planner's Lagrangean can be written as follows:

$$u(c_1) + u(h) + u(c_2) + \lambda(y_2 - c_1 - c_2 - h). \tag{10}$$

Hence, at interior maximum:

$$0 < c_1 = c_2 = h = \frac{1}{3}y_2. \tag{11}$$

The situation looks very similar to the previous model and, in a sense, it is. For example, the solution described in expression (11) is a competitive equilibrium. There is a CAD at the beginning (here, periods 0 and 1), followed by a current account surplus at the end. However, there is now a capital account transaction in period 0 that may sour if relative prices in period 1 are different from those expected at time 0.

Let us consider the case in which h is borrowed by the representative individual in period 0 to produce h units of nontradables in period 1. At equilibrium, the relative price of nontradables with respect to tradables in period 1, p, satisfies:

$$p = \frac{u'(h)}{u'(c_2)} = 1, \tag{12}$$

where equality to unity holds in the equilibrium described by expression (11). Such an equilibrium requires a $CAD = c_1 = y_2/3$. Thus, if, for example, individuals are unable to borrow as planned in period 1 and, thus, $c_1 < y_2/3$, then $p = u'(y_2/3)/u'(c_1) < 1$. Consider the case in which the individual borrowed under the assumption that equilibrium (11) would hold. Expected profit in period 0, π, satisfies:

$$\pi = (p - 1)h. \tag{13}$$

Hence, given (12), $\pi = 0$. However, as noted, if the individual is unable to borrow as planned, $p < 1$, and, hence, $\pi < 0$. Consequently, if individuals set up limited-liability firms to carry out this project in period 0, those firms would become technically bankrupt in period 1 if the CAD in period 1 were smaller than planned. Moreover, in the present setup, even if individuals were fully liable, they could not repay their debt in full in period 1 because, by assumption, period 1 endowment income is zero.

If bankruptcy carried no social or individual cost, the world capital market should be able quickly to restore credit and allow the representative individual to carry out his/her original plan, preventing bankruptcy. However, aside from the observation that bankruptcies *are* in actuality very costly, bankruptcies involve legal procedures that, at the very least, involve *verification* costs. In the present setup, ensuring that the debt will be repaid in period 2 (instead of period 1 as in the original contract) requires legal paperwork.

To illustrate the effect of bankruptcy cost, consider the simple case in which bankruptcy costs are fixed, independently of size of default.[13] Let the fixed cost (in terms of tradables) be denoted by κ (in addition to the cost of repaying the principal h). This implies that the cost of serving the debt is higher with than without bankruptcy (a sensible assumption). Therefore, after bankruptcy in period 1, the representative individual's budget constraint satisfies (recalling equation (11)):

$$c_1 + c_2 = y_2 - h - \kappa = \frac{2}{3}y_2 - \kappa, \tag{14}$$

Hence, by utility function (9), it follows that

$$c_1 + c_2 = \frac{y_2}{3} - \frac{\kappa}{2} < \frac{y_2}{3}, \tag{15}$$

and

$$p = \frac{u'(h)}{u'(c_1)} = \frac{u'\left(\dfrac{y_s}{3}\right)}{u'\left(\dfrac{y_2}{3} - \dfrac{\kappa}{2}\right)} < 1, \tag{16}$$

implying bankruptcy. Moreover, since c_1 falls relative to the no-bankruptcy solution, bankruptcy is associated with a lower CAD in period 1.

In the present model bankruptcy costs are a black box but the analysis shows the crucial role that financial difficulties may play when a country is forced to lower its *CAD*. Shedding light on the black box appears to be an important area for further research.[14]

It is worth pointing out that bankruptcy costs are, in principle, independent of whether the original investment in the nontradables sector was done by domestic or foreign residents (i.e., foreign direct investment), to the extent that bankruptcy costs cannot be shifted to foreign residents. However, the situation would be different if the original investment was:

• equity financed since, in that case, period 1 losses could be partially shifted to equity holders, lowering bankruptcy probabilities,[15] or

• financed through two-period bonds since, under those circumstances, bankruptcy will only materialize in period 2 when endowment income is positive, possibly cutting on bankruptcy's paperwork.[16]

In any case, these observations suggest that equity financing and long-term loans may help shield the economy from sudden stop crises, as conjectured in Section II.

Notes

I am thankful to Sara Calvo for useful comments on an earlier draft of the paper.

1. The IMF appears to subscribe to that view and is chastising countries like the UK, US, Argentina and Chile for their widening *CADs* (despite, in the same breath, extolling the virtues of an unfettered capital market!).

2. Interestingly, very few commentators realize that if these very same countries had floated their exchange rates a while before crisis hit, their currencies would likely have appreciated, not depreciated.

3. The expression "sudden stops" was inspired by a bankers "adage" it is not speed that kills, it is the sudden stop," quoted in Dornbusch et al. (1995).

4. Hence the expression "Simple Economics" in the subtitle of the paper.

5. For a discussion about the irrelevance of the solvency analysis, see Calvo (1998a).

6. Think of the many retailers wrapping up cheap Taiwan toys, and the few stevedores needed to unload an expensive piece of machinery.

7. It should be noted, however, that even though the shock does not push the economy into bankruptcy, an observationally equivalent situation from the viewpoint of investors could develop if the shock lowers the country's *willingness* to pay. This issue was raised by some Mexico's observers in connection with the PRI's loss of popularity after the 1994/95 crisis.

8. This should not be taken as an indictment of IMF policy in East Asia which, as I understand it, was predicated on the assumption that tight fiscal/monetary policy would enhance policymakers' credibility, and help stem the slowdown of capital inflows. This issue will be revisited in Section VI.

9. However, some observers would claim that higher interest rates are induced by IMF type policy.

10. Thus, for example, according to some reports, Mexico's banking difficulties associated with the Tequila crisis are still simmering in the background.

11. Natural factors include, for instance, floods and earthquakes that are not subject to *short-run* direct human control.

12. These fiscal policy objectives may not be easy to attain. To do so it may be necessary, for instance, to increase taxes and government expenditures in such a way that the former exceeds the latter, but does not revert the expansionary effects of government expenditures—quite a "balancing act" in the aftermath of crisis! It is worth noting that, in contrast, in all crisis-stricken countries government expenditures were cut, and taxes raised.

13. Same implications are obtained if (1) bankruptcy costs are proportional to $(1 - p)h$, i.e., default's size, and the factor of proportionality is greater than unity, and (2) the marginal utility function is iso-elastic, and elasticity is larger than one.

14. For a related discussion, see Calvo (1998b).

15. In the present example equity financing would, by necessity, have to be undertaken by foreign residents because, by assumption, domestic residents have no endowment income in period 0.

16. Notice, however, that bankruptcy may not be prevented if firms are covered by limited-liability clauses.

References

Calvo, G. A. (1998a), "The Unforgiving Market and the *Tequilazo*," in J. M. Fanelli and R. Medhora (eds.) *Financial Reform in Developing Countries*, Macmillan.

Calvo, G. A. (1998b), "Balance of Payments Crises in Emerging Markets: Large Capital Inflows and Sovereign Governments." Paper presented at the NBER Conference on Currency Crises, February.

Calvo, G. A., and E. G. Mendoza (1997), "Rational Herding and the Globalization of Securities Markets," manuscript, University of Maryland.

Dornbusch, R., I. Goldfajn, and R. O. Valdés (1995), "Currency Crises and Collapses," *Brookings Papers on Economic Activity*, 2, pp. 219–293.

10 Rational Contagion and the Globalization of Securities Markets

Guillermo A. Calvo and
Enrique G. Mendoza

If I may be allowed to appropriate the term speculation for the activity of forecasting the psychology of the market, and the term enterprise for the activity of forecasting the prospective yield of assets over their whole life, it is by no means always the case that speculation predominates enterprise. As the organisation of investment markets improves, the risk of the predominance of speculation does, however, increase. . . . Speculators may do no harm as bubbles on a steady stream of enterprise. But the position is serious when enterprise becomes the bubble on a whirlpool of speculation.

—John Maynard Keynes, *The General Theory of Employment, Interest, and Money*, pp. 158–159

1 Introduction

In the aftermath of the Mexican crash of 1994, several emerging stock markets fell as investors "ran for cover," expecting that vulnerable countries like Argentina and Brazil, or even rising stars as Chile or Singapore, would be next in a series of currency crises.[1] Similarly, the spreading of the financial crisis that originated in Thailand across several countries in East Asia in 1997, and the global financial turmoil triggered by Russia's default in 1998, are widely attributed to unprecedented contagion effects across globalized securities markets. In all these instances, investors seemed to follow the "market" rather than take the time and expense to make their own assessments of each country's fundamentals, perhaps guessing that "market" portfolios embodied relevant information, or fearing the consequences of disagreeing with the "market." A similar phenomenon, albeit at a smaller scale, also appears to operate in the recurrent waves of optimism by institutional investors observed in industrial countries.[2]

The extreme volatility of these speculative capital flows, and the costly economic crises that have accompanied recent financial crashes, have led researchers and policy-markers to reconsider the merits of the trend toward the liberalization of global asset trading that prevailed during the last 15 years. The introduction of controversial capital controls, taxes, and other barriers to asset trading is gaining increasing popularity in the wake of the recent financial turmoil. Chile's taxes and timing restrictions on inflows and outflows of short-term capital, which had been in place since the early 1990s, are an often-cited example of the type of controls that could be useful to prevent contagion. Malaysia's decision to suspend foreign trading in its currency and impose widespread capital controls in 1998 is a more radical example. Even at the New York Stock Exchange (NYSE), there are automatic trading halts that stop trading for periods of time during market sessions when stock prices fluctuate too much. However, given that our understanding of the distortions that may produce contagion, and of how these distortions interact with the globalization of capital markets, is very limited, one must remain skeptical about the effectiveness and desirability of these policies. The aim of this paper is, therefore, to contribute to the development of an analytical framework for understanding some of the forces behind contagion effects in global capital markets.

This chapter demonstrates that contagion in securities markets can be an outcome of optimal portfolio diversification that becomes more prevalent as securities markets grow. Contagion is defined as a situation in which utility-maximizing investors choose not to pay for information that would be relevant for their portfolio decision—thereby making them susceptible to react to country-specific rumors—or in which investors optimally choose to mimic arbitrary "market" portfolios. Thus, contagion is reflected in portfolio re-allocations that are not directly related to the "fundamentals" determining the risk and return properties of asset returns.

Using a basic framework of mean-variance portfolio diversification, the chapter shows that two characteristics of imperfect information can produce equilibria in which incentives for contagion grow stronger as capital markets grow:

1. If there is a fixed cost of *gathering* and *processing* country-specific information, and institutional arrangements or government regulations impose binding short-selling constraints, the utility gain of paying the

fixed information cost generally falls as the number of countries where wealth can be invested grows. Portfolio allocations also become more sensitive to changes in asset returns as markets grow, and thus contagion is more likely to prevail and to produce larger capital flows in globalized markets.

2. If portfolio managers face a variable cost or gain that depends on the mean return of their portfolios relative to that of a given market portfolio, and the marginal cost exceeds the marginal gain, there is a range of multiple equilibria inside of which investors rationally choose to mimic market portfolios. When a rumor favors another portfolio in that range, all investors "follow the herd." In this case, globalization exacerbates contagion because the indeterminacy range widens as the market grows.

Since the potential magnitude of contagion effects is largely unknown, and the model proposed here lacks in general tractable analytical solutions, the chapter also examines the model's quantitative implications. The quantitative analysis is based on historical data from equity markets and country credit ratings (CCRs). Equity-market measures of the mean and variance of country asset returns over a historical period are viewed as free information, while the detailed country expertise imbedded in CCRs is assumed to be costly. Two key empirical regularities are identified in these credit ratings: (a) the ratings of both industrialized and least developed countries are very stable, reflecting the fact that new information does not alter much the perception of investment conditions in these countries, whereas the ratings of emerging economies are very volatile, and (b) information gathering generally leads to larger adjustments of the mean and variance of asset returns, compared to historical equity-market moments, for emerging markets than for OECD countries. Thus, the entry of emerging economies into the global market added investment opportunities for which historical equity-market data were not very informative of future asset returns. The model is calibrated to capture these stylized facts, and simulated to assess the magnitude of the maximum fixed cost that agents would pay for country-specific information, and how this maximum is affected by the growth of the global market.

The simulations show that realistic assumptions on the size of the world market, the mean and variance of asset returns, and the information updates provided by CCRs, are consistent with large capital flows driven by contagion. If emerging economies are viewed as a segmented market, our analysis shows that investors rationally choose not to assess the veracity of country-specific rumors if fixed information costs exceed 1/5 of the mean portfolio return prior to the emergence of a rumor. The expected utility gain of information gathering is a steep decreasing function of the number of countries in the portfolio—the full adverse effect of globalization on information gains is transmitted with about a dozen countries.

When variable performance costs are considered, there is a range of portfolio shares, measuring about 2.5 percentage points, that supports contagion equilibria even for small costs. Simulations applied to Mexican data suggest that through both fixed- and variable-cost channels the model can rationalize capital outflows exceeding $15 billion that are unrelated to the country's "fundamentals."

The model examined here does not differentiate global capital markets from domestic stock markets. However, the *key* distinctive feature of global markets is the fact that information frictions play a much larger role in investment decisions than in domestic markets. This is consistent with the empirical regularities we identified in country credit ratings, and is also in line with the detailed warnings that securities firms give investors to highlight the special risks of global investing. Advertisements for U.S.-based international mutual funds typically warn of several risks like fluctuations in exchange rates, imposition of withholding taxes, reduced availability of information on non-U.S. firms, political and economic developments, the imposition of capital and exchange controls, differences in regulatory practices and reporting standards, higher volatility and reduced liquidity of foreign securities, and even the possibility of expropriations and confiscatory taxation. The issues of concern to international investors are thus radically different from those that worry domestic investors, and the costs incurred in gaining an expertise at the same level of that typically acquired for domestic investment are much higher (see Frankel and Schmukler, 1996).

It is worth noting that Keynes' (1936) classic analysis of "rational speculation," which he defined as "the activity of forecasting the psychology of the market," is an important precursor to our work. Keynes argued that speculation is likely to be more pervasive in larger, better organized markets, as eloquently stated in the quotation that opens this paper. He proposed other mechanisms that could drive speculation—changes of opinion driven by mass psychology, perverse incentives of professional investors, and changes in the confidence of lenders that finance speculators—which have been the focus of most of the modern literature on contagion and herding (see, for example, Scharfstein and Stein (1990) and Banerjee (1992)).

The rest of the chapter is organized as follows. Section 2 analyses the relationship between contagion and globalization. Section 3 examines the quantitative implications of the model. Section 4 concludes with a discussion of normative issues and suggestions for further research.

2   Contagion in an Optimizing Framework of Global Portfolio Diversification

Consider a globalized securities market consisting of J countries $(2 \leq J \leq \infty)$ and a large number of identical investors. The portfolio of the representative investor is to be divided between $J - 1$ identical countries and a single country (Country i) which generally has different asset return characteristics. All countries but i pay asset returns that follow i.i.d. processes with mean ρ and variance σ_J^2, which we refer to as the mean and variance of the "world fund." As a result, at equilibrium each one of the $J - 1$ countries will be allocated an identical share of the portfolio. Country i pays expected return r^* with variance σ_i^2, which is correlated with the world fund according to a correlation coefficient η. The share of the portfolio invested in the world fund is defined as θ. The investor's preferences are characterized by the following indirect expected utility function:

$$EU(\theta) = \mu(\theta) - \frac{\gamma}{2}\sigma(\theta)^2 - \kappa - \lambda(\mu(\Theta) - \mu(\theta)), \quad \text{with } \gamma, \kappa > 0. \tag{1}$$

γ is the coefficient of absolute risk aversion, μ and σ define respectively the mean and standard deviation of the portfolio as a function of θ, κ represents a fixed cost of acquiring country-specific information, and $\lambda(\mu(\Theta) - \mu(\theta))$ represents the variable performance cost (benefit) of obtaining a mean portfolio return lower (higher) than the mean return of an arbitrary portfolio Θ. The properties of λ are specified later.

The objective of this section is to show that both the fixed cost and the performance cost introduce frictions that reduce incentives for information gathering as the globalization progresses (i.e., as J rises). This is done by isolating the effects of each cost on the design of optimal portfolios.

2.1   Contagion Driven by Fixed Information Costs and Short-Selling Constraints

Consider an initial equilibrium in which Country i is identical to the rest (i.e. $r^* = \rho$ and $\sigma_i = \sigma_J = \sigma$) and asset returns are uncorrelated ($\eta = 0$), so that the investor allocates equal amounts of wealth across all countries. Assuming, without loss of generality, that he has one unit of wealth, the share of the portfolio invested in each country is $1/J$ and portfolio mean return and variance are ρ and σ^2/J respectively.

The investor then hears a "credible" rumor indicating that Country i's mean return is r, $r \le r^*$, but its variance is still σ^2. The investor can acquire *and* process country-specific information at the fixed cost κ to assess the veracity of the rumor and update the mean and variance of Country i. Assume, for simplicity, that if the investor chooses not to pay κ, the investor believes the rumor—the rumor is indeed "credible." Thus, in this case the portfolio choice involves $J - 1$ countries with asset return moments ρ and σ^2, and Country i with the same variance but expected return r. If he pays κ, asset return characteristics in the $J - 1$ countries are unchanged, but the mean and variance of Country i are updated. For analytical tractability, we focus on the case in which the investor that pays κ learns the "true" return of Country i. Later in the numerical analysis we study the more general case in which he only learns updated values of the mean and variance of Country i returns.[3] The investor knows that by paying κ he will learn a new return r^I with zero variance. Before paying κ, however, the potential update of the return r^I is itself a random variable drawn from a known probability distribution function (p.d.f.).[4] This p.d.f. represents the investor's priors. Clearly, the investor will pay the information cost only if expected utility conditional on costly information, EU^I, exceeds that conditional on free information, EU^U (i.e. the gain from costly information $S \equiv EU^I - EU^U$ must be positive).

Let θ^U and θ^I be the portfolio shares chosen by the investor if he decides to be uninformed or informed respectively. θ^U is chosen so as to maximize:

$$EU^U = \theta^U \rho + (1 - \theta^U)r - \frac{\gamma}{2}\left[\frac{(\theta^U)^2}{J-1} + (1 - \theta^U)^2\right]\sigma^2. \tag{2}$$

For internal solutions, the corresponding first-order condition implies that the optimal portfolio is:

$$\theta^U = \left(\frac{J-1}{J}\right)\left[1 + \frac{\rho - r}{\gamma\sigma^2}\right]. \tag{3}$$

We also assume that optimal portfolios may reflect corner solutions because of short-selling constraints. In particular, we assume that $-a \leq \theta^U \leq b$, for given constants a and b such that $0 \leq a < \infty$ and $1 \leq b < \infty$. The case $a = 0$, $b = 1$ is the extreme case in which short positions in Country i and the world fund are ruled out. Short-selling constraints imply that:

$$\theta^U = b \quad \text{for } r \leq r^{\min},$$

and

$$\theta^U = -a \quad \text{for } r \geq r^{\max},$$

where:

$$r^{\min} = \rho - \frac{\gamma\sigma^2[J(b-1) + 1]}{J-1},$$

$$r^{\max} = \rho + \frac{\gamma\sigma^2[J(1+a) - 1]}{J-1}.$$

Note that as J goes to ∞, the interval of returns that supports internal solutions for θ^U shrinks and converges to $r^{\max} - r^{\min} = \gamma\sigma^2[b + a]$.

The analysis that follows focuses for simplicity on cases in which r is such that the portfolio conditional on free information features internal solutions. For r in the interval $r^{\min} < r < r^{\max}$, EU^U valued at the maximum is:

$$EU^U = \left(r - \frac{\gamma}{2}\frac{\sigma^2}{J} + \frac{(\rho - r)}{2}\frac{J-1}{J}\left[2 + \frac{(\rho - r)}{\gamma\sigma^2}\right]\right). \tag{4}$$

We examine next the portfolio problem under the assumption that the investor pays for information. An investor who paid κ learns the realization r^I. State-contingent utility $U^I(r^I)$ is:

$$U^I(r^I) = \theta^I\rho + (1 - \theta^I)r^I - \frac{\gamma}{2}\left[\frac{(\theta^I)^2}{J-1}\right]\sigma^2 - \kappa. \tag{5}$$

For internal solutions, the optimal, state-contingent portfolio is:

$$\theta^I(r^I) = (J-1)\left[\frac{\rho - r^I}{\gamma\sigma^2}\right]. \tag{6}$$

Short-selling constraints imply: $\theta^I(r^I) = a$ if $r^I \geq r^I_{max}$ and $\theta^I(r^I) = b$ if $r^I \leq r^I_{min}$ where:

$$r^I_{min} = \rho - \frac{b\gamma\sigma^2}{J-1}, \quad r^I_{max} = \rho + \frac{a\gamma\sigma^2}{J-1}. \tag{7}$$

It is important to note that these expressions imply that the interval of returns that supports optimal portfolios of an informed investor with internal solutions vanishes as J grows infinitely large. Thus, as the market grows infinitely large, optimal portfolios conditional on costly information always hit the short selling constraints. This plays a key role in producing the result that S can be decreasing in J.

Let $F(r^I)$ and $f(r^I)$ denote the c.d.f. and p.d.f. of r^I. EU^I is therefore given by:

$$EU^I = \int_{-\infty}^{\infty} \left[\theta^I(r^I)\rho + (1 - \theta^I(r^I))r^I - \frac{\gamma}{2}\left[\frac{(\theta^I(r^I))^2}{J-1}\right]\sigma^2 \right] f(r^I)\,dr^I - \kappa. \tag{8}$$

We show below that, under fairly general conditions, S falls as J rises for any given κ. Thus, globalization can reduce the incentives to gather country-specific information.

PROPOSITION 1.   For any "pessimistic" rumor such that (i) short-selling constraints are not binding for the portfolio of an uninformed investor ($r^{min} < r < r^{max}$) and (ii) the rumor sets the Country i return to be less or equal than the return of the world fund ($r \leq r^* = \rho$), and assuming that both F and f are continuously differentiable, S is decreasing in J (i.e. $dS/dJ < 0$), for $J < \infty$, if the number of countries in the global market is at least $J > 1/\{1 - [F(\rho)(b^2 - a^2) + a^2]^{1/2}\}$.

Proof.   State-contingent utility conditional on costly information can take the following values:
If $r^I \leq r^I_{min}$:

$$U^I(r^I) = b\rho + (1 - b)r^I - \frac{\gamma\sigma^2}{2}\frac{b^2}{J-1} - \kappa. \tag{9}$$

If $r^I_{min} < r^I < \rho$:

$$U^I(r^I) = r^I + \frac{1}{2}\frac{(\rho - r^I)^2}{\gamma\sigma^2}(J - 1) - \kappa. \tag{10}$$

If $r^I \geq \rho$:

$$U^I(r^I) = -a\rho + (1+a)r^I - \frac{\gamma\sigma^2}{2}\frac{a^2}{J-1} - \kappa. \tag{11}$$

Thus, for any rumor in the interval $r^{min} < r < r^{max}$, S is given by:

$$
\begin{aligned}
S = &\left(b\rho - \frac{\gamma\sigma^2}{2}\frac{b^2}{J-1}\right)F(r^I_{min}) + \int_{r^I_{min}}^{r^I_{max}}\left[r^I + \frac{1}{2}\frac{(\rho - r^I)^2}{\gamma\sigma^2}(J-1)\right]dF(r^I) \\
&- \left(a\rho + \frac{\gamma\sigma^2}{2}\frac{a^2}{J-1}\right)(1 - F(r^I_{max})) + \int_{\infty}^{r^I_{min}}(1-b)r^I\,dF(r^I) \\
&+ \int_{r^I_{max}}^{\infty}(1+a)r^I\,dF(r^I) - \kappa \\
&- \left(r - \frac{\gamma}{2}\frac{\sigma^2}{J} + \frac{(\rho - r)}{2}\frac{J-1}{J}\left[2 + \frac{(\rho - r)}{\gamma\sigma^2}\right]\right).
\end{aligned}
\tag{12}
$$

Since $F(r^I)$ is continuously differentiable,

$$
\begin{aligned}
\frac{dS}{dJ} = &\frac{\gamma\sigma^2}{2(J-1)^2}[b^2 F(r^I_{min}) + a^2(1 - F(r^I_{max}))] + \int_{r^I_{min}}^{r^I_{max}}\frac{1}{2}\frac{(\rho - r^I)^2}{\gamma\sigma^2}dF(r^I) \\
&- \frac{\gamma}{2}\frac{\sigma^2}{J^2} - \frac{(\rho - r)}{2J^2}\left(2 + \frac{(\rho - r)}{\gamma\sigma^2}\right).
\end{aligned}
\tag{13}
$$

Setting $r^I = r^I_{min}$ in expression ((13)), it follows that:

$$
\begin{aligned}
\frac{dS}{dJ} \leq &\frac{\gamma}{2}\frac{\sigma^2}{(J-1)^2}\left[b^2 F(\rho) + a^2(1 - F(\rho)) - \left(\frac{J-1}{J}\right)^2\right] \\
&- \frac{(\rho - r)}{2J^2}\left(2 + \frac{(\rho - r)}{\gamma\sigma^2}\right).
\end{aligned}
\tag{14}
$$

Since $r \leq \rho$, it follows that $1/\{1 - [F(\rho)(b^2 - a^2) + a^2]^{1/2}\} < J < \infty$ is sufficient (although not necessary) for $dS/dJ < 0$. $\square$

The intuition of the result is straightforward to explain if $r = \rho$, so that the last terms in (13) and (14) vanish. In this case, there is effectively no rumor and the problem can be restated as studying how the value of acquiring information to eliminate the uncertainty of a single asset changes as the number of assets rises.[5] As J increases, the variance of the world fund falls, making it a more effective means of diversifying risk regardless of whether information about Country i is gathered or not. This can be seen in the right-hand side of (13). The first two terms represent the marginal utility of J conditional on costly information, and the third term is the marginal utility of J conditional on free information. Both are positive but declining functions of J. As long as short-selling constraints are present, however, the marginal utility of J conditional on costly information eventually falls behind that conditional on free information. This occurs because short-selling constraints prevent investors from taking full advantage of costly information. If investors could hold arbitrarily large short positions, the marginal utility of J conditional on costly information would be independent of the size of the market (the first term in the right-hand-side of (13) would vanish and the second would be independent of J). Only the effect of the shrinking marginal utility of J under free information would remain, and hence dS/dJ would be increasing in J.

The key point of Proposition 1 is that, for any given κ and ρ, the utility gain derived from costly information decreases as J rises (i.e., the marginal utility of J is negative). This adverse effect of market growth has "decreasing returns," in the sense that S will fall as J rises but at a declining rate. This is because, as $J \to \infty$, dS/dJ converges to zero, as the world fund becomes a risk-free asset. Hence, S converges to a constant level independent of J as J grows to infinity. Clearly, that constant utility level could be positive or negative depending on the values of κ and ρ, which is not an interesting finding. In contrast, the convergence of S in the presence of costly information and short-selling constraints (for any κ and ρ) is a striking result that deviates sharply from the finding that S grows without bound if short-selling constraints do not exist. Hence, if the cost of information were even trivially increasing in J, short-selling constraints ensure that for a sufficiently large market information is never paid for.

The sufficiency condition, $J > 1/\{1 - [F(\rho)b^2 + (1 - F(\rho))a^2]^{1/2}\}$, established in Proposition 1 to ensure that S is decreasing in J after some critical J merits further clarification. This condition sets restrictions on the relative values of a, b and $F(\rho)$. Roughly speaking, the condition sets lower bounds on the tightness of short-selling constraints relative to the conditional probabilities that costly information will yield updated Country-i returns greater or smaller than the return of the world fund. A natural interpretation emerges if we label $F(\rho)$ the probability of "bad news" (in the sense that $F(\rho) = Pr\{r^I \leq \rho\}$) and $1 - F(\rho)$ the probability of "good news" (since $1 - F(\rho) = Pr\{r^I \geq \rho\}$), keeping in mind that a higher critical J indicates more willingness to pay for costly information since it would take a larger number of countries for S to begin to decrease as J increases. A weaker short-selling constraint on Country i (i.e., higher b) will make critical J larger, the higher the probability of bad news—that is, the more likely is that the investor will face states of nature in which short positions on Country i are optimal. Similarly, a weaker short-selling constraint on the world fund (i.e., higher a) will make critical J larger, the higher is the probability of good news—that is, the more likely it is that the investor will face states of nature in which short positions in the world fund are optimal. It must be recalled, however, that the condition established in Proposition 1 is only a sufficiency condition.

It follows from the previous argument that, in general, assessing the relevance of the result that dS/dJ could be negative can only be determined by assigning values to the model's exogenous parameters, adopting a functional form for $F(\cdot)$ and computing numerically expressions (12) and (13). Numerical simulations are also critical because (12) and (13) reflect a specialized case in which information reveals true asset returns, instead of just updates of the mean and variance of returns, and asset returns are uncorrelated. We lack analytical results for general cases relaxing these assumptions.

A thorough numerical analysis is conducted in Section 3. However, one basic example is still very illustrative of the model's potential. Assume that $a = 0$, $b = 1$ and f is a symmetric p.d.f such that $E(r^I) = r = \rho$ (which, since f is symmetric, implies $F(\rho) = 0.5$). In this case the sufficiency condition of Proposition 1 reduces to $J > 1/[1 - 0.5^{1/2}]$, and dS/dJ is negative with four countries or more. If $F(\rho)$ were smaller (larger) than 0.5, which implies $E(r^I)$ larger (smaller) than ρ, the critical J falls (rises). This shows that when investors are "bullish" on Country i, in the sense that $E(r^I) > \rho$, S begins to decrease with J for a smaller market than when investors are "bearish" on Country i. When costly information is *expected* to produce good news, and short-selling constraints severely limit the gains of learning bad news, incentives for buying information are weak. If we relax the short selling constraint on Country i, so that $b > 1$ while keeping $a = 0$, the sufficiency condition changes to $J > 1/[1 - b0.5^{1/2}]$. With $b = 1.25$, so that the investor can short Country i for up to 25 percent of his wealth, the critical J increases to 9. As b approaches $0.5^{-1/2}$, or 1.41, the critical J goes to infinity, and the sufficiency condition fails for $b > 1.41$.

Expression (13) shows that, in addition to the terms involved in the sufficiency condition, another key determinant of the critical J is the size of the rumor. Consider again the basic case in which f is symmetric, $a = 0$, and $b = 1$. A pessimistic rumor such that $r^{\min} < r < \rho$ implies that dS/dJ may be negative even if $F(\rho)$ is somewhat larger than $1/2$ (i.e. with $r < \rho$, the critical value of J falls for any given $F(\rho)$). This is because expected utility of uninformed investors rises with the difference $\rho - r$. Thus, a bad rumor contributes to reduce the benefits of gathering information on Country i as the market expands even if investors are bearish about Country i (i.e. $E(r^I) < \rho$).

Proposition 1 also has important policy implications. If the proposition holds, globalization works to weaken incentives for information gathering because it takes place against the background of institutional limitations or government regulations that limit the ability of investors to hold short positions. This argument implies, therefore, that policies aimed at containing market volatility by tightening short-selling constraints have at least one channel for being counterproductive: short-selling constraints contribute to reduce an investor's willingness to acquire costly information.

One important remark. As J rises, not only are incentives to gather information diminishing, but the impact of unverified rumors on the portfolio share assigned to a single country (relative to the initial share $1/J$) grows without bound. This is because $-d\theta^U/dr$ converges to $1/\gamma\sigma^2$ as $J \to \infty$. Thus, global market volatility (defined by a shift in $1 - \theta^U$ in response to a pessimistic rumor relative to the initial, rumor-free portfolio share $1/J$) increases as J rises, resulting in larger proportional effects on capital flows.

2.2 Contagion Driven by Performance-Based Incentives

The effects of rumors we examined above could be short-lived to the extent that they could induce a "price correction" in the affected country's securities markets that can drive expected returns high enough to undo the effect of the rumor. There are, however, several reasons why a price correction may fail to undo the effects of rumors. For instance, if the correction is seen as triggering a very distortionary policy response that will cripple the economy, the market collapse can become part of a self-fulfilling crisis (see Calvo, 1998). Another reason is the performance-based incentives we study next. These incentives produce contagion as a result of multiple equilibria in optimal portfolio shares.

Consider investors, or mutual fund managers, that face a variable cost or benefit of obtaining mean returns that deviate from the mean return of an arbitrary market portfolio, and put aside the fixed information cost by setting $\kappa = 0$. The cost function $\lambda(\mu(\Theta) - \mu(\theta))$ satisfies the following properties:

$$\lambda > 0 \quad \text{if } \mu(\theta) < \mu(\Theta), \quad \lambda <= 0 \quad \text{if } \mu(\theta) > \mu(\Theta), \quad \lambda(0) = 0,$$

$$\lambda' \geq 0 \text{ with } \lambda'(x) > \lambda'(-x) \quad \text{for all } x = \mu(\Theta) - \mu(\theta) > 0 \tag{15}$$

$$\lambda' <= 0.$$

It is also assumed that $\lambda'(0)$ does not exist to capture the notion of fixed costs. The conditions in (15) imply that managers pay a cost (earn a benefit) when the mean return of their portfolios is smaller (larger) than that of the market portfolio, and that the marginal cost exceeds the marginal benefit.[6]

The problem of a representative manager is to choose θ, given some Θ, so as to maximize:

$$EU(\theta) = \theta\rho + (1 - \theta)r - \lambda(\mu(\Theta) - \mu(\theta))$$

$$- \frac{\gamma}{2}\left[\frac{(\theta\sigma_J)^2}{J - 1} + ((1 - \theta)\sigma_i)^2 + 2\sigma_J\sigma_i\theta(1 - \theta)\eta\right]. \tag{16}$$

We allow the variances of investing in Country i (σ_i^2) and in all J countries except i (σ_J^2) to differ, and asset returns are correlated according to the coefficient η. Also note that, since $\mu(\theta) = \theta\rho + (1 - \theta)r$ and $\mu(\Theta) = \Theta\rho + (1 - \Theta)r$, it follows that $\lambda(\mu(\Theta) - \mu(\theta)) = \lambda((\Theta - \theta)(\rho - r))$.

This portfolio allocation problem displays contagion in the sense that, for rumors within a certain range of values of Θ, choosing $\theta = \Theta$ is optimal for a representative investor and is also a rational-expectations equilibrium in which all investors select the same portfolio. Any rumor in that range calling for a different Θ results in a herding panic in which all investors re-set their portfolios to that new Θ.

PROPOSITION 2. If in the neighborhood of the optimal portfolio θ^* corresponding to an investor free of performance incentives, the marginal cost (gain) of deviating from the mean return of the market portfolio $\mu(\Theta)$ is sufficiently large (small), there exists a range of global, rational-expectations equilibria of individual portfolio allocations θ, such that investors optimally choose $\theta = \Theta$.

Proof. We prove that, under certain conditions, the optimal response to a market portfolio Θ is to set $\theta = \Theta$ because $EU'(\theta) < 0$ for $\theta > \Theta$ and $EU'(\theta) > 0$ for $\theta < \Theta$. The proof is done in the following steps:

Step 1. The first-order condition for maximization of (16) with respect to θ is:

$$\rho - r - \gamma\left[\frac{\theta\sigma_J^2}{J-1} - (1-\theta)\sigma_i^2 + \eta\sigma_J\sigma_i((1-\theta) - \theta)\right] - \lambda'(\cdot)(r - \rho) = 0.$$

(17)

Step 2. Define $E\hat{U}'(\theta) \equiv \rho - r - \gamma[\theta\sigma_J^2/(J-1) - (1-\theta)\sigma_i^2 + \eta\sigma_J\sigma_i((1-\theta) - \theta)]$ as the marginal utility of θ for an investor that does not face performance incentives, so $E\hat{U}'(\theta^*) = 0$ at the optimum θ^*. Note that the necessary second-order condition for a maximum $E\hat{U}'(\theta) < 0$ requires $\sigma_J^2/(J-1) + \sigma_i^2 > 2\eta\sigma_J\sigma_i$.

Step 3. Given (*Step 2*), rewrite (17) as:

$$E\hat{U}'(\theta) - \lambda'(\cdot)(r - \rho) = 0.$$

(18)

Step 4. The solution(s) to (17) or (18) will depend on the relative returns of Country i and the world fund. Clearly, if $r = \rho$ the solution θ^* will also be the unique solution for the model with performance costs, and there is no contagion. Thus, the relevant cases are those in which r and ρ differ.

Step 5. Consider the case in which $r > \rho$ and assume an arbitrary market portfolio such that $\Theta \leq \theta^*$. Investors will not choose $\theta > \Theta$ if it implies $EU'(\theta) < 0$. There are two options. First, if $\theta > \theta^*$ clearly $EU'(\theta) < 0$ because $E\hat{U}'(\theta) < 0$, as implied by $E\hat{U}'(\theta^*) = 0$ and $E\hat{U}'(\theta) < 0$, and $\lambda'(\cdot)(r - \rho) > 0$. Second, if $\Theta < \theta \leq \theta^*$, a necessary and sufficient condition for $EU'(\theta) < 0$ is $\lambda'(\cdot)(r - \rho) > E\hat{U}'(\theta)$. Since with $r > \rho$ and $\theta > \Theta$ the investor would obtain a mean return smaller than that of the market portfolio, this condition states that the marginal *cost* of producing below-market returns needs to be "sufficiently large" in the vicinity of θ^* for equilibria with contagion to exist. A similar condition ensures that investors will not choose $\theta < \Theta$ (i.e. $EU'(\theta) > 0$ if $\theta < \Theta$). For such a θ, $\theta < \Theta \leq \theta^*$, and $\theta < \theta^*$ implies $E\hat{U}'(\theta) > 0$. Thus, $EU'(\theta) > 0$ if $E\hat{U}'(\theta) > \lambda'(\cdot)(r - \rho)$. Note that in this case the investor would be beating the market by setting $\theta < \Theta$, so this condition states that in the neighborhood of θ^* the marginal *gain* of beating the market must be "sufficiently small" for contagion equilibria to exist. Finally, note there is no contagion for $\Theta \geq \theta^*$ because the condition that $EU'(\theta) > 0$ for $\theta < \Theta$ can never hold if $\theta^* \leq \theta < \Theta$. In this case, $E\hat{U}'(\theta) \leq 0$ and $\lambda'(\cdot)(r - \rho) > 0$, so $EU'(\theta) < 0$.

Step 6. An argument similar to (*Step 5*) shows that for $r < \rho$ there is a range of contagion equilibria for some values of Θ in the region $\Theta \geq \theta^*$, if $E\hat{U}'(\theta) < \lambda'(\cdot)(r - \rho)$ for $\theta > \Theta$ and $E\hat{U}'(\theta) > \lambda'(\cdot)(r - \rho)$ for $\theta^* \leq \theta < \Theta$. In this case, there can be no contagion equilibria for $\Theta \leq \theta^*$. □

The result in Proposition 2 is interesting, although it hinges critically on the assumption that, at the margin, poor performance is punished more than good performance. We are also interested in a second result showing that in the presence of these performance costs it is again the case that globalization strengthens incentives for contagion. The latter is implied by the fact that the range of contagion equilibria widens as the global market grows for a given performance cost function.

PROPOSITION 3. The range of contagion equilibria, defined by values of Θ in the interval $\theta^{\text{low}} < \Theta < \theta^{\text{up}}$ for which Proposition 2 holds, widens as the global market grows (i.e. $\theta^{\text{up}} - \theta^{\text{low}}$ is increasing in J).

Proof. To simplify this proof we consider the case of a linear marginal cost function, so $\lambda'(\Theta - \theta) = 0$, and limit our attention to the case in which $r > \rho$, which are the assumptions adopted in the numerical exercise of the next section. Note that in this case θ^{low} satisfies (17) for $\mu(\Theta) > \mu(\theta)$ and θ^{up} satisfies (17) for $\mu(\Theta) < \mu(\theta)$. The total differential of (17) implies that:

$$\frac{d\theta}{dJ} = \frac{\left(\dfrac{\gamma \theta \sigma_f^2}{(J-1)^2} \right)}{\gamma \left(\dfrac{\sigma_f^2}{J-1} + \sigma_i^2 - 2\eta \sigma_f \sigma_i \right)}. \tag{19}$$

The expression in the denominator of (19) corresponds to $-E\hat{U}'(\theta)$, and thus as long as the second-order condition stated in (*Step 2*) above holds, $d\theta/dJ$ is positive and increasing in θ. It follows that as J rises both θ^{up} and θ^{low} rise, and, since $\theta^{\text{up}} > \theta^{\text{low}}$, θ^{up} rises more than θ^{low}, so the contagion range widens. □

The intuition for this result is simple. Given a marginal cost invariant to J or θ, the growth of the market affects the expected marginal utility of optimal portfolios in two ways. First, as J rises, the effective variance of the world fund $(\sigma_f^2/(J-1)^2)$ falls for given holdings of that fund, and thus the marginal utility of θ rises. This effect is proportional to the portfolio share invested in the world fund, as shown in the numerator of (19). Second, the reduced variance of the world fund makes it a more attractive asset relative to Country i, providing an incentive to increase θ, which in turn reduces marginal utility. This second effect is independent of θ because the rate at which marginal utility falls as θ rises is invariant to portfolio shares, as the denominator of (19) shows. Hence, the optimal portfolio shift induced by an increase in J is larger the larger the initial θ. Notice, however, that $d\theta/dJ$ is decreasing in J and converges to 0 as J goes to infinity because in a large market the world fund becomes virtually riskless. Thus, like the adverse effect of J on S in the fixed-cost case, the magnifying effect of J on the contagion range displays "diminishing returns."

All portfolios inside the contagion range are sub-optimal, except in particular cases in which the Pareto-efficient portfolio θ^* is inside the range.[7] Thus, contagion is generally inefficient. Moreover, the existence of multiple optimal portfolios for a given pair of mean returns r and ρ implies that there can be capital outflows from Country i even in the absence of rumors about country asset returns. This also implies that a price correction following a rumor about r may not prevent persistent contagion effects.

2.3   A Comparison with Game-Theoretic Models of Contagion and Herding

The framework presented above considers a global market consisting of a large number of identical investors formulating simultaneous decisions. This differs sharply from the sequential decision-making setup typical of game-theoretic models of herd behavior.[8] These models show that when information is incomplete, and the signals that transmit it are noisy, agents waiting in line to make a decision may imitate agents ahead of them, rather than use their own information (a situation referred to as an "informational cascade" that leads to herding).

Our framework could be easily incorporated into a sequential decision-making setting. Consider the case in which information can be acquired at a fixed cost.[9] Assume a group of N investors, indexed $h = 1, \ldots, N$, making portfolio choices in sequence. Each draws a noisy signal (i.e. a rumor) about r denoted r_h which cannot be observed by the other $N - 1$ investors, although portfolio choices are public information. Whenever an investor pays the information cost, he learns the true value r^I. Start with the choice of the first investor in a small market. Assume $S > 0$, so that he pays the information cost. In this case the initial rumor does not prevail. Let J rise, so S begins to decline until $S < 0$. Now the first investor does not pay for the information that would discredit the rumor. Moreover, assume that his signal is $r_1 < r^{\min}$, so his portfolio choice is $\theta^U = 1$. This conveys the information that $r_1 < r^{\min}$ to all investors after him. Given an initial negligible prior against Country i, if all investors after the first get signals $r_h > r^{\min}$, for $h = 2, \ldots, N$, and if signals are of the same quality (as in the restaurants example of Banerjee (1992)), all investors go by the prior and choose $\theta = 1$, disregarding private signals favoring Country i. The information cost is never paid and all investors hold the same portfolio reacting to the initial rumor.

The "informational cascades" models require the assumption that investors choose their portfolios in a well-organized sequential setting, which seems at odds with the simultaneous sell offs observed recently in global capital markets. The models also feature equilibria in which private information is not discarded (i.e., depending on the ordering in which sequential decision-makers are lined up, there are "informational cascades" without herding). As a result, the origin of herding is not just in information differences across investors, or in their willingness to acquire new information, but depends critically on the ordering in which a set of investors arrive in the market to make their decisions.

The contagion models examined by Shiller (1995) also have an interesting connection with our model. Contagion by word-of-mouth provides microfoundations for the process leading from one value of Θ to another and for rumors regarding the value of r. There is ample anecdotal evidence of word-of-mouth contagion in the spreading of rumors during the Mexican crisis. One dramatic example was the sharp fall of the peso in November 11, 1995, triggered by the rumors of a coup and the resignation of the finance minister, both of which originated in U.S. capital markets (see Calvo and Mendoza, 1996). The rumors were quickly discredited, but the peso recovered only a small fraction of its losses.

3 Numerical Simulations

This section examines the quantitative implications of the model. The objective of the exercise is not to test the model's ability to explain actual investment behavior, but simply to explore the potential magnitude of the effects that result from the informational frictions we studied analytically in Section 2.

3.1 Benchmark Calibration and Stylized Facts

The numerical analysis starts from a benchmark designed to mimic two sets of stylized facts:

3.1.1 Composition of Global Portfolios and Statistical Moments of Asset Returns

The calibration determines a value of the coefficient of absolute risk aversion, γ, consistent with existing estimates of the mean and variance–covariance structure of asset returns, and data on net holdings of foreign equity by global investors, assuming a conventional mean-variance setup without information or performance costs. The equation that relates γ to θ and the statistical moments of asset returns is derived by solving (17) for γ setting $\lambda'(\cdot) = 0$. We plugged various estimates of the mean and variance–covariance structure of asset returns and the composition of global portfolios from different sources in the resulting expression, and concluded that plausible values of γ range between near 0 and 0.5.[10] We chose the middle point 0.25 for the benchmark. Note, however, that there are also several data combinations that produce negative values of γ, highlighting the flaws of the mean-variance model.

One example of the above calculations is as follows. Consider a two-country world consisting of the United States and "the rest of world" as defined in Bohn and Tesar (1994).[11] This implies the following settings: (1) $\rho = 0.62$ percent and $\sigma_J = 4.46$ percent, which are the mean and standard deviation of monthly excess returns on U.S. equity for the period January 1981–October 1993, (2) $r = 0.69$ percent, $\sigma_i = 5.41$ percent, and $\eta = 0.462$, which are the "rest-of-the-world's" mean, standard deviation and U.S.-correlation of asset returns, measured in U.S. dollars and assuming unhedged currency risk, and (3) $\theta = 0.964$, which reflects the average holdings of foreign equity by U.S. investors measured at less than 4 percent of their portfolios. These parameters imply $\gamma = 0.004$.

3.1.2 Indicators of Information and Their Impact on Asset Return Assessments

The best publicly-available measure of country-specific information is embodied in existing estimates of country credit ratings. In our simulations we use the credit ratings constructed by international banks for their lending operations, and compiled and published every

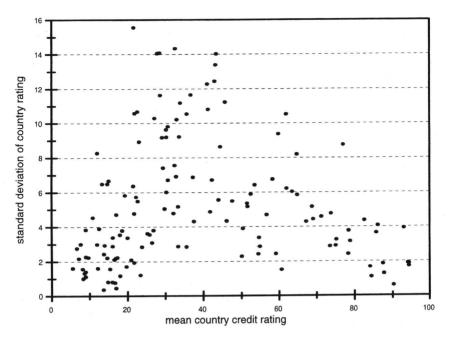

Figure 10.1
Variability of country credit ratings.

six-months, in March and September, by the *Institutional Investor*. We examined these CCRs to assess how much investors may find invest-ment conditions to have changed in individual countries every time they gather new information. Figure 10.1 plots the time-series average of each country's CCR against the corresponding standard deviation, using data for the period September, 1979 to March, 1996. Figure 10.2 is a similar plot that includes only OECD and Latin American countries.

One key stylized fact that emerges from figures 10.1 and 10.2 is that innovations to CCRs at the semestral frequency are much larger in emerging markets than they are in either industrialized or least-developed economies. The variability of credit ratings is very low both in countries that represent "good risks" (i.e. those with average CCRs exceeding 80, as in the OECD) and in countries that are "bad risks" (i.e. those with CCRs lower than 20, as several countries in Sub-Saharan Africa), while the variability of CCRs is much higher in countries that represent "moderate risks" (i.e. emerging markets). This evidence suggests that when asset trading restrictions among indus-trial countries were lifted in the 1980s, the newly-created global market

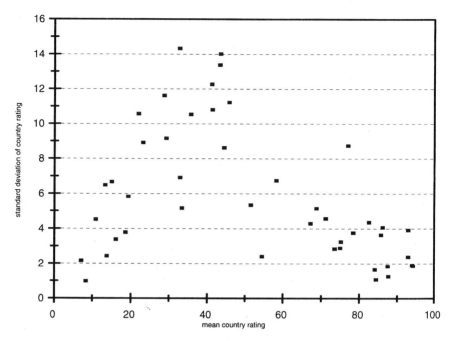

Figure 10.2
Variability of OECD and Latin American country ratings.

consisted of countries of roughly similar risk quality, and where investment conditions were relatively uniform and stable over time. In contrast, the globalization of equity markets in the 1990s expanded to emerging markets where not only asset returns are intrinsically more risky, but where information gathered on economic, social, and political issues results in much larger innovations to credit ratings than in OECD countries.

In order to proceed with the simulations, we also need a framework for mapping the information of the CCRs into probability distributions from which updates of means and variances of asset returns are drawn once κ is paid. This mapping is derived from a framework proposed by Erb et al. (1996) to estimate the mean and variance of asset returns in 80 countries for which CCRs exist but equity markets do not exist. These authors examined the relationship between the mean and variance of asset returns and the information captured by CCRs in countries *with* equity markets. Robust log–linear relationships were estimated and used to forecast moments of asset returns in countries *without* equity markets.

Erb et al. (1996) estimated panel regressions of the form $x_{ht+1} = \alpha^x + \beta^x \text{Ln}(CCR_{ht}) + u^x_{ht+1}$, where $x =$ the semestral mean (μ) or standard deviation (sd) of asset returns in country h. Thus, assuming normal distributions of the variables involved, and standard homogeneity assumptions across country elements in the panel, the moments that describe these distributions are:

$$E[r^I_h] = \alpha^\mu + \beta^\mu E[\text{Ln}(CCR_h)],$$

$$E[\sigma^I_h] = \alpha^{sd} + \beta^{sd} E[\text{Ln}(CCR_h)],$$

$$\sigma^I_{rh} = (\beta^\mu)^2 VAR[\text{Ln}(CCR_h)] + \sigma^{\mu 2}_u, \quad \text{and}$$

$$\sigma^I_\sigma = (\beta^{sd})^2 VAR[\text{Ln}(CCR_i)] + \sigma^{sd2}_u.^{12}$$

The magnitude of the updates of the mean and variance of returns that this framework can produce is illustrated in figure 10.3. This chart plots updates of the mean and standard deviation of returns for each country with an equity market in the sample of Erb et al. (1996) based on the September, 1996 CCRs against each country's CCR. Updates are measured as a difference relative to statistical moments based on historical equity-market data (also from Erb et al.). The chart shows that new information arriving in September, 1996 generally resulted in positive updates of mean returns and reduced estimates of the variability of returns. Emerging markets with CCRs between 20 and 70 showed larger upward adjustments in expected returns, and larger downward revisions in standard deviations of returns, while updates for OECD countries were generally small.

It is important to note that although the *Institutional Investor* provides CCRs at a trivial cost, the information imbedded in them is not free from the perspective of our model. CCRs are costly at the relevant moment in which investors need the information. These costs are incurred by the banks that generate individual credit ratings for leading decisions long before the *Institutional Investor* aggregates and publishes them. Banks act immediately on the information they collect and process, and their individual ratings only become partially public in the aggregate published ratings.

3.2 Fixed Information Costs and the Disincentive for Information Gathering

The quantitative analysis of the fixed cost setup is based on graphs of the expected utility gain of paying for information gross of the fixed

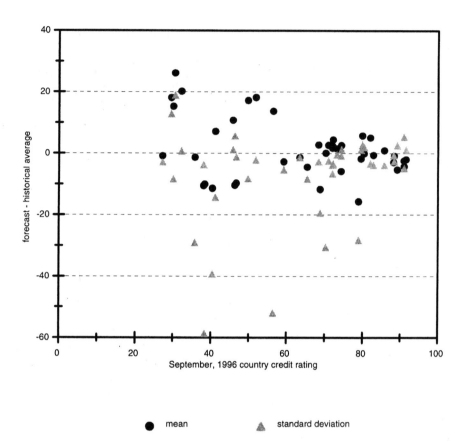

Figure 10.3
Updates of the mean and standard deviation of country returns.

cost, $\hat{S} = S + \kappa$. $\hat{S}$ can also be interpreted as the maximum fixed information cost investors would be willing to pay in terms of mean portfolio return (i.e., κ^{max} such that $S(\kappa^{max}) = 0$). Since we are dealing with a fixed cost, clearly $dS/dJ = d\hat{S}/dJ$.

The simulations proceed using the following expression for EU^I:

$$EU^I + \kappa = \int_{-\infty}^{\infty} \int_{-\infty}^{\infty} \theta^I(r^I, \sigma_i^I)\rho + (1 - \theta^I(r^I, \sigma_i^I))r^I$$

$$-\frac{\gamma}{2}\left[\frac{(\theta^I(r^I, \sigma_i^I)\sigma_J)^2}{J-1} + ((1 - \theta^I(r^I, \sigma_i^I))\sigma_i^I)^2\right.$$

$$\left. + 2\sigma_J\sigma_i^I\eta\theta^I(r^I, \sigma_i^I)(1 - \theta^I(r^I, \sigma_i^I))\right]f(r^I)g(\sigma_i^I)\,dr^I\,d\sigma_i^I, \qquad (20)$$

where f and g are normal probability distribution functions and $\theta^I(r^I, \sigma_i^I)$ is the optimal portfolio conditional on learning updates (r^I, σ_i^I). The simulations allow J to vary from 2 to 3000 countries, and consider three values of rumors about the Country i return, $r = (r^{low}, \rho, r^{high})$, where $r^{low}(r^{high})$ is the minimum (maximum) Country-i return that supports an internal solution for θ^U when $J = 2$ and Country i and the world fund are uncorrelated. The double integral in (20) is computed by Gauss–Legendre quadrature. Integration limits are adjusted gradually, starting from limits equal to $\pm 2\sigma_r^I$ and $\pm 2\sigma_\sigma^I$, until the double integral captures 98 percent of the joint c.d.f. of r^I and σ_i^I. The short-selling constraints are set initially at $a = 0$ and $b = 1$, and the effects of relaxing both constraints are examined later.

3.2.1 Case I—Identical Ex Ante Returns and "Truth-Revealing" Information: The Value of Information

The simulations begin by exploring the quantitative implications of the basic case discussed in Section 2, in which $a = 0$, $b = 1$, and $F(\rho) = 0.5$ (i.e., $E(r^I) = \rho$), calibrated to data for relatively stable OECD markets. The basic case also required the assumptions that: (a) asset returns are uncorrelated, $\eta = 0$, (b) ex ante all countries are identical, $r^* = \rho$ and $\sigma_i = \sigma_J$, and (c) costly information reveals the true Country-i asset return, $E[\sigma_i^I] = \sigma_\sigma^I = 0$. Note that since all countries are identical initially, the scenario in which $r = \rho = r^*$ is the variant of the basic case in which $\hat{S}$ measures simply the value of information to eliminate the uncertainty of one asset in the portfolio (since $r = r^*$, there is in fact no rumor). The basic case also satisfies the consistency condition under rational expectations (i.e., $E(r^I) = r^*$).

The values of ρ, σ_J, and σ_i^I are set to $\rho = 15.31$ percent, $\sigma_J = 22.44$ percent, and $\sigma_i^I = 6.46$ percent respectively. The first two moments are arithmetic averages of the annualized mean and standard deviation of monthly stock returns in U.S. dollars over the period 1979–1995 for OECD countries with "stable markets," and the third moment is an average of the estimates of σ_h^I computed using the regression coefficients from Erb et al. (1996) as explained earlier. "Stable OECD markets" include OECD members during the entire 1979–1995 period for which the standard deviation of returns did not exceed 30 percent. This excludes Greece, New Zealand, Portugal, and Turkey.

Figure 10.4 plots $\hat{S}$ for J up to 50 countries, although the simulations ran to $J = 3000$ to confirm the convergence of $\hat{S}$. The plot confirms

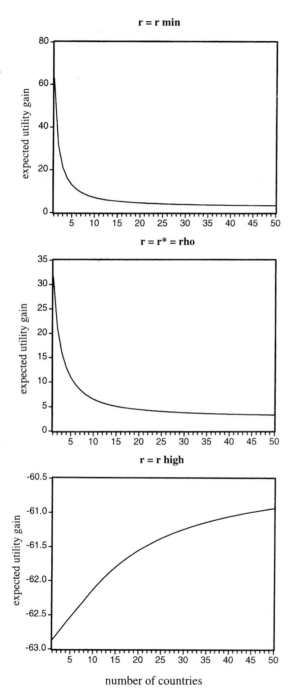

Figure 10.4
Utility gain of costly information: Case I—the value of information.

Proposition 1. $\hat{S}$ is decreasing in J for pessimistic rumors such that $r \leq \rho$ (i.e. $r = r^{\text{low}}, \rho$) and is increasing in J for the optimistic rumor $r = r^{\text{high}}$. $\hat{S}$ is decreasing in J even for $J < 4$ reflecting the fact that the condition established in Proposition 1 is only a sufficiency condition. If, for instance, σ_i^I is increased from 6.46 to 500, $\hat{S}$ is increasing in J for $J < 4$, but for higher J it becomes decreasing as indicated by the sufficiency condition.

In this basic case, investors facing rumors such that $r \leq \rho$ are willing to pay hefty information costs exceeding 30 percent of mean portfolio return for $J = 2$. As J grows to about a dozen countries, $\hat{S}$ falls sharply but still converges to a relatively large amount of 3.7 percent. Thus, for large J, the maximum fixed information cost investors would pay is roughly $1/3$ of the initial mean portfolio return (which was 15.3 percent). Still, only 12 countries are required for the adverse effect of globalization on information gains to be in full force, and this effect cuts information gains by a factor of 8.6.

To assess the sensitivity of these results to the short-selling constraints, a set of simulations were conducted for the $r = \rho$ scenario by setting $a = \varepsilon$, $b = 1 + \varepsilon$, for $\varepsilon = (0, 0.05, 0.1, 0.5, 1, 10, 10^9)$. When $\varepsilon = 0.5$, for example, investors are allowed short positions in which their holdings of the world fund or Country i exceed their total wealth by up to 50 percent. The results showed that figure 10.4 remains essentially unaltered for up to $\varepsilon = 0.5$. When $\varepsilon = 1$, $\hat{S}$ is moderately increasing in J for $50 < J < 100$ and converges to about 8 percent, which is still significantly lower than the starting point of 32 percent for $J = 2$. When $\varepsilon = 10$, the increasing segment of $\hat{S}$ is larger and the rate of increase higher, with $\hat{S}$ converging to about 45 percent. The last case, $\varepsilon = 10^9$, approximates the scenario without short-selling constraints, so $\hat{S}$ converges to a linear function with positive slope. Hence, this analysis suggests that the predictions of the model are fairly robust to the levels of short-selling constraints, unless the latter are assumed to be unrealistically weak.[13]

3.2.2   Case II—Identical Ex Ante Returns with OECD Information Updates

Next we focus on the case in which information cannot reveal true asset returns. Hence, investors only learn updates of the mean and variance of returns when they pay κ. The experiment is calibrated again to "stable" OECD markets, incorporating now the mean and variance of updates of the Country i mean return and its standard deviation. This is done by computing arithmetic averages for the relevant countries again applying the formulae from Erb et al. (1996). This implies setting: $E(r^I) = 15.18$, $E[\sigma_i^I] = 21.81$, $\sigma_r^I = 6.46$, and $\sigma_\sigma^I = 1.84$. We maintain the assumptions that ex ante all countries are perceived to be identical, so $r^* = \rho$ and $\sigma_i = \sigma_J$, and that asset returns are uncorrelated. The first assumption is not too unrealistic for the group of countries considered, but the second is seriously at odds with the data and hence is relaxed below. Figure 10.5 plots $\hat{S}$ for Case II. A comparison with figure 10.4 shows that expected utility conditional on costly information is significantly smaller when information cannot reveal true asset returns. In the case of the neutral rumor $r = r^* = \rho$ (the middle panels of figures 10.4 and 10.5), $\hat{S}$ falls from 32 to 1 percent for $J = 2$, and from about 3.7 to 0.15 percent with $J \geq 20$. A cost of 0.15 percent is 0.6 percent of the ex ante mean return of the portfolio ($r^* = \rho = 15.31$), so in this circumstances investors are significantly more reluctant to pay information costs than in the previous case. Only in the presence of *very* pessimistic rumors in small markets, investors are still willing to pay large information costs—r^{low} for $J = 2$ is -110.6 percent, and in this case $\hat{S}$ exceeds 32 percent, as shown in the top panel of figure 10.5. Moreover, in a market with at least 20 countries, $\hat{S}$ converges to less than 0.45 percent for any rumor $r^{low} \leq r \leq \rho$.

We consider next the fact that the actual correlation of asset returns is not zero, as we have assumed so far. The correlation of returns across stable OECD markets ranges from 0.3 to 0.6 (see Bohn and Tesar, 1994; Lewis, 1995; Erb et al., 1996). Thus, we simulate the model by setting $\eta = 0.35$.[14] Positive correlation in returns across Country i and the world fund yields even smaller gains of information gathering, with the value of $\hat{S}$ for r^{low} and $J = 2$ falling from 32 to 22 percent. This seems natural because of the implicit assumption that the asset returns of the $J - 1$ countries in the world fund are uncorrelated. As a result, when positive correlation between Country i and the world fund is allowed, the assets in the world fund provide better diversification opportunities and this undermines the gains of gathering information on Country i. This finding is not modified significantly if the experiment is altered to introduce also correlation of returns across countries in the world fund at the same level of 0.35. Thus, from a quantitative standpoint, taking into account the fact that returns across OECD countries are positively correlated works to strengthen disincentives to pay country-specific information costs.

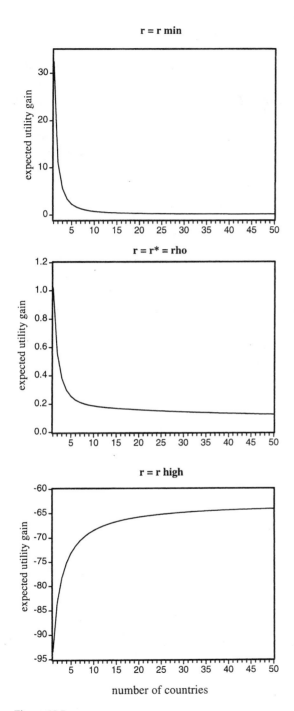

Figure 10.5
Utility gain of costly information: Case II—OECD updates.

3.2.3 Case III—Segmented Emerging Markets

The global capital market includes today a growing list of emerging markets which are often viewed as a group segmented from stable OECD markets. In this context, the question to ask may be whether it is optimal to acquire information about a single country when most of the $J - 1$ countries are also volatile emerging markets. To simulate this scenario, we consider a case in which all countries are identical emerging markets ex ante, with probabilistic parameters set using arithmetic averages for the Latin American countries with equity markets in the sample of Erb et al. (1996)—Argentina, Brazil, Chile, Colombia, Mexico, Peru and Venezuela. The resulting parameterization is: $E(r^I) = 33.12$, $E[\sigma_i^I] = 34.57$, $\sigma_r^I = 49.31$, $\sigma_\sigma^I = 14.04$, $r^* = \rho = 31.21$, and $\sigma_i = \sigma_J = 50.03$.

The plot of $\hat{S}$ in figure 10.6 shows that, when $r = \rho$, the maximum fixed information cost agents are willing to pay declines to about 7 percent for $15 \leq J \leq 300$. This cost represents about $1/5$ of the ex ante mean portfolio return (which is now 31.2 percent). Information gains continue to fall very sharply as the market grows, and the adverse effect of market growth on $\hat{S}$ is nearly fully transmitted with about 20 countries. In sharp contrast with Cases I and II, however, $\hat{S}$ does not converge to a positive constant. It reaches a minimum at $J = 58$ and then it becomes an increasing function of J. Still, it takes a market with at least 500 countries to reach a point where a modest reversal of the initial sharp decline in $\hat{S}$ can be noticed. These results are again robust to a significant relaxation of short-selling constraints. With short-selling constraints set to allow short positions as large as 100 percent of wealth (i.e., $a = 1$, $b = 2$), $\hat{S}$ reaches a minimum of 7.6 percent at $J = 25$, and it takes about 400 countries for a modest reversal of the sharp initial fall to be noticeable.

Case III assumes that new information yields average updates of the mean and standard deviations of returns equivalent to 1.06 and 0.69 of the corresponding moments computed with historical equity market data. However, figure 10.3 showed that updates vary widely across countries. For instance, in the cases of Argentina, Colombia, Philippines, Taiwan and South Africa, information produced sharply lower expected returns than equity market data, while updates of the standard deviation vary from sharp reductions to moderate increases. In Colombia's case, for example, the average update of the mean return is 0.77 of the equity market forecast, while the standard deviation of returns is virtually the same with or without gathering information.

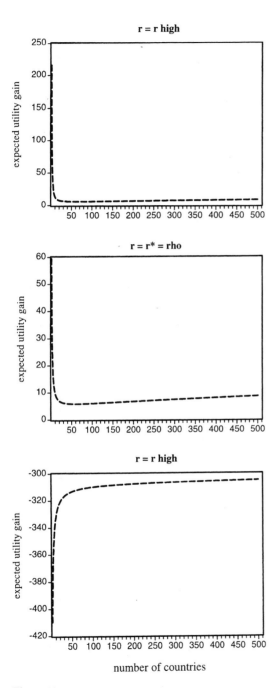

Figure 10.6
Utility gain of costly information: Case III—segmented emerging markets.

Our model predicts that in this case the value of $\hat{S}$ for a neutral rumor $r = r^*$ is 7 percent if $J = 2$. As the market grows to include 20 countries, $\hat{S}$ falls to about 0.5 percent for any rumor $r^{\text{low}} \le r \le r^*$. With the ex ante mean portfolio return at 31.2 percent, this implies that investors in a large market will not pay costs exceeding only 1.6 percent of the ex ante return.

3.2.4   Capital Flows

We quantify next the capital flows that may take place when investors react to rumors. Consider a situation in which investors may liquidate the assets of an emerging market to seek the "safety" of OECD markets. The model is simulated setting parameters so that the $J - 1$ countries represent again stable OECD markets and Country i is calibrated to Mexico using the corresponding data and formulae from Erb et al. (1996). In this scenario, if $\kappa > 6.5$ percent (or about 2/5 of the ex ante mean portfolio return of 15.4 percent), pessimistic rumors about Mexico would prevail. A rumor that reduced the expected return on Mexican equity from the equity market forecast of 22.4 percent to the level of the OECD mean return of 15.3 percent leads to a reduction in the share of the world portfolio invested in Mexico from 1.7 percent to 0.7 percent—a reduction of 40 percent. According to the *Bolsa de Valores de Mexico* (the Mexican stock exchange), direct foreign holdings of Mexican equity exceeded \$50 billion by the end of 1997, so a 40 percent cut implies an outflow of about \$20 billion,[15] a very large amount for a country where central bank foreign reserves exceed that figure by a narrow margin. Note, however, that this calculation does not take into account any correction of prices within the stock market, which would imply that the dollar value of the liquidated stock would likely fall sharply, and hence the ensuing capital outflow would be smaller. Still, even if price adjustments cut the capital outflow by 75 percent, the residual \$5 billion remains a large figure similar in magnitude to the large speculative attacks against the Mexican peso in March, November and December of 1994. Moreover, as argued in Section 2, price corrections may not contain the effects of rumors if there is multiple equilibria in portfolios shares.

3.3   *Performance Costs and Multiple Optimal Portfolios*

The simulations conclude with an analysis of the multiplicity of optimal portfolios resulting from performance costs. We maintain the

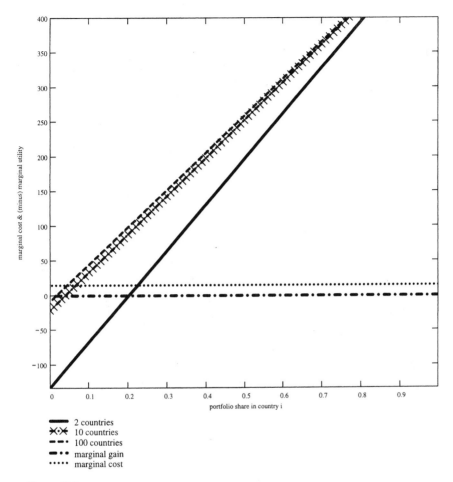

Figure 10.7
The contagion range in the presence of performance costs.

settings of the last example involving Mexico and the OECD. The variable performance cost function is of the form: $\lambda = \phi(\mu(\Theta) - \mu(\theta))$ with $\phi = 15$ for $\mu(\Theta) > \mu(\theta)$ and $\phi = 0$ otherwise. The sensitivity of the results to the value of ϕ is examined later.

The solution is illustrated in figure 10.7. The solid, upward-sloping line is expected marginal utility without performance costs plotted as a function of the share of the portfolio invested in Mexico ($E\hat{U}'(1 - \theta)$ in the notation of Section 2), and for $J = 2$. The horizontal dotted lines represent the constant marginal cost (gain) of producing below-market (above-market) mean returns (i.e., ϕ). The lower and upper bounds of the contagion range are delimited by the intersections of $E\hat{U}'(1 - \theta)$ with the marginal cost and gain lines. If the market calls any portfolio to the right (left) of the lower (upper) bound, Proposition 2 holds and the investor's optimal choice is to mimic the market. The plot shows that, when $J = 2$, the share of portfolio invested in Mexico may fluctuate between 20.2 and 22.5 percent, or about 2.3 percentage points, simply as a result of contagion driven by variable performance costs.

Proposition 3 is illustrated in figure 10.7 by adding more OECD countries. This shifts the line that represents $E\hat{U}'(1 - \theta)$ clockwise (to the crossed lines) and thus widens the contagion range. With $J = 10$ the contagion range widens by about $1/2$ of a percentage point, with the portfolio share invested in Mexico varying between 3.8 percent and 6.6 percent.

The total performance costs avoided by displaying contagion are small. When $J = 20$, and assuming $\Theta = \theta^*$, the maximum cost paid for choosing the largest θ within the contagion range is $1/10$ of the mean portfolio return. Thus, contagion can potentially induce large capital flows in and out emerging markets even in the presence of small performance costs. The marginal cost, however, is large in the sense that it represents a punishment for poor performance equal to 15 times the difference between the mean return paid by the market and that paid by the investor's portfolio. Note also that the size of the contagion range converges to about 2.8 percentage points as J approaches ∞.

Next we measure the capital flows triggered by performance costs. Assume that the investors' total wealth corresponds to the holdings of foreign equity by U.S. investors. The latest *Benchmark Survey of U.S. holdings of Foreign Securities* conducted by the Treasury Department reports that by end-March 1994 the holdings of foreign equity by U.S. investors amounted to $566 billion. The model predicts that with $J = 20$ the fraction of U.S. foreign equity invested in Mexico fluctuates between 2.53 and 5.31 percent.[16] Thus, contagion triggered by performance costs can account for sudden capital flows in and out of Mexico as large as $15.7 billion. Adding investment in bonds, the total foreign security holdings of U.S. investors reach about $870 billion, and thus contagion could account for Mexican capital flows of up to $24.2 billion. As noted earlier, flows of this magnitude can be an important determinant of balance-of-payments crises.

Figure 10.7 also illustrates the role that the assumed properties of the performance cost function play in generating the contagion range.

Without performance costs, the model has a unique solution at the point where $E\hat{U}'(1 - \theta)$ crosses the horizontal axis. Moreover, even if performance costs existed, a unique equilibrium would still prevail if the marginal cost were equal to the marginal gain. The discontinuity of λ' at $\theta = \Theta$ is also critical. If λ were a smooth upward-sloping function, investors would choose a value of θ different from Θ and hence update the market portfolio until the market agrees on a portfolio so that $E\hat{U}'(\theta) = \lambda'(\theta = \Theta) = 0$.

Figure 10.8 examines the sensitivity of the results to changes in different parameters of the model: the marginal cost and gain, ϕ, the correlation of asset returns, η, the coefficient of absolute risk aversion γ, and the variances of asset returns, σ_J and σ_i. The parameter variations are constrained to satisfy the second-order condition specified in Proposition 2. This analysis shows that the results are generally robust to parameter variations. Marginal costs in excess of 15 result in a larger range of contagion equilibria, while lower values obviously reduce it. The opposite holds as we vary the value of the marginal gain. The contagion range is maximized when there is no marginal gain. A higher degree of risk aversion reduces sharply the size of the contagion range, but values of γ higher than 1/2 are grossly inconsistent with data on the composition of actual portfolios. For risk aversion coefficients between the benchmark value (1/4) and 1/2 the reduction in the contagion range is modest, while the range widens considerably for risk aversion coefficients lower than 1/4. The correlation of returns does not affect noticeably the size of the contagion range until it becomes unrealistically high. The contagion range is a declining function of the variances of asset returns in Country i and abroad. However, the effect of the variance of the world fund dissipates with as few as 10 countries, and the range narrows very slightly for values of σ_i above the Mexican estimates used in figure 10.7 (i.e. 46.2 percent). For σ_i below 46 percent and $J = 10$, the size of the contagion range widens very rapidly as σ_i falls.

Despite the large capital flows that contagion can produce, the implied welfare costs are small. We measured welfare costs by the percentage change in consumption needed for a portfolio inside the contagion range to yield the same utility of the Pareto optimal portfolio chosen in the absence of performance costs (i.e. θ^*), making use of the model's direct utility function: $-\exp(-\gamma C)$. The welfare costs are at most 2.5 percent, and for portfolio share variations of 100 basis points around θ^* the costs are actually smaller than 1/4 of a percentage point.

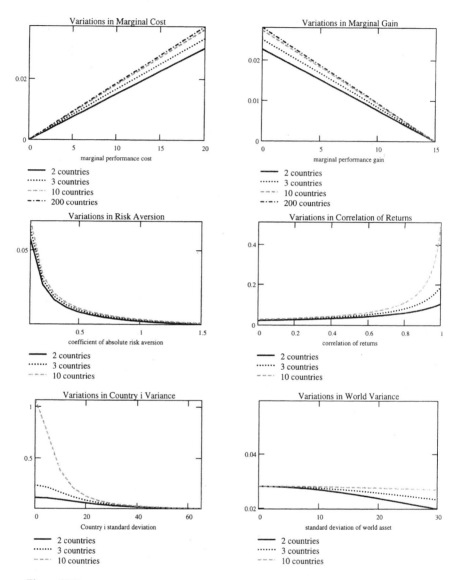

Figure 10.8
Sensitivity analysis of the contagion range.

4   Concluding Remarks

This chapter proposes a model of portfolio choice with imperfect information in which financial globalization may work to strengthen contagion effects. This occurs because: (a) globalization may reduce the gains from paying fixed costs for gathering and processing country-specific information, and (b) in the presence of variable performance costs, globalization widens the range of portfolios inside of which investors find it optimal to mimic market portfolios. Numerical simulations showed that these two frictions can be quantitatively significant and can induce large capital outflows unrelated to country-specific fundamentals.

The analysis shows that informational frictions per se *cannot* produce contagion. Contagion requires that these frictions be combined with particular institutional or regulatory features of financial markets. In the case of fixed information costs, the gain of paying for costly information declines as the market grows only if investors face short-selling constraints. In the case of variable performance costs, a contagion range of multiple optimal portfolios exists only if the structure of incentives is such that the marginal cost of being beaten by the market exceeds the marginal gain of beating the market. In this context, policies that otherwise may seem useful instruments to help contain the volatility of capital flows, such as short-selling constraints or regulations on average returns across institutional investors, can in fact contribute to exacerbate the problem.

The role of fixed information costs deserves further consideration. One could argue that any sensible fixed information cost would be a trivial amount as a fraction of the large absolute wealth invested in securities markets or managed by securities firms. While this point is well taken, it also has a strong potential for complicating the issue further, instead of resolving it. Consider, for example, that clusters of investors group into firms that manage mutual funds up to the point that for them the fixed cost is indeed trivial, and hence become "sophisticated traders," while there remains a group of agents that acting in isolation find the cost prohibitive and thus invest in mutual funds. Aiyagari and Gertler (1998) and Calvo (1999) have shown that in a setting like this, if limits on short bond positions impose binding margin constraints on securities firms, there could be equilibria in which equity prices and equity holdings fluctuate more than predicted by "fundamentals" in response to systemic shocks to "sophisticated traders."

The informational frictions examined here are reminiscent of those driving the models of informational efficiency developed by Grossman and Stiglitz (1976, 1980). Our analysis differed in that we studied the implications of market size for the gain of gathering costly information in a partial-equilibrium setting with exogenous asset returns. In contrast, the Grossman–Stiglitz result that incentives to gather costly information are reduced by the anticipation that prices may reveal that information emphasizes the general equilibrium determination of prices. Their argument suggests, however, that a general equilibrium extension of our model may yield even smaller gains of gathering costly information because endogenous changes in returns would reveal some or all of the costly information at no cost.

The findings of this chapter raise the question of whether globalization is necessarily welfare improving, and suggest that capital controls may be desirable because of the welfare costs induced by contagion. Our model, however, is not well suited for tackling this issue because the inefficiencies produced by contagion (in a setting in which all agents are "globally diversified" investors marginally affected by runs on a particular country) resulted in trivial welfare costs. The welfare costs of volatile capital flows may increase significantly if one departs from this ideal world. One alternative is to consider distortions that lead to self-fulfilling crises. For example, in Calvo (1998) a sudden run on government bonds by global investors forces large tax hikes which in turn cripple the ability of the private sector to yield future tax revenue and lead to a self-fulfilling default on public debt. Another alternative is to consider an economy that depends on capital inflows to finance imports, and uses the latter as inputs in domestic production. Some agents in this economy derive income only from labor services and do not access global capital markets. This model would still have to be carefully studied, however, since welfare costs resulting from ruling out world asset trading to manage country-specific risk in conventional neo-classical models have been found to be trivial (see Mendoza, 1991).[17]

Further research is clearly needed before specific recommendations can be made on the nature and extent of limitations that may be desirable to impose on capital mobility. We need to develop quantitative models that can take into account both the costs and benefits of the globalization of securities markets, and the potentially counterproductive features of instruments that could seem useful to lessen the volatility of capital flows, such as short-selling and margin-call constraints. In the final analysis, the dismal economic performance of the developing world during the 1980s serves as a dramatic reminder of the fact that simply shutting down or limiting access to capital markets can have catastrophic consequences. In light of the events of recent years, however, non-intrusive regulations like the automatic trading halts at work in the New York Stock Exchange are difficult to disagree with.

We started the chapter by quoting Keynes and, given our findings and the above policy discussion, it seems appropriate to end the chapter by quoting Keynes again:

When the capital development of a country becomes a by-product of the activities of a casino, the job is likely to be ill-done.... It is usually agreed that casinos should, in the public interest, be inaccessible and expensive. (Keynes, 1936, p. 159)

Acknowledgements

We thank V. V. Chari, David Bowman, Rudi Dornbusch, Sebastian Edwards, David Howard, Bob Keohane, Peter Lange, Peter Montiel, Maurice Obstfeld, and Matt Pritsker for helpful comments and suggestions. Comments by seminar participants at the Bank of Mexico, the Board of Governors of the Federal Reserve System, the Federal Reserve Bank of Minneapolis, the 1997 Meetings of the Society for Economic Dynamics, the 1998 Meetings of the American Economic Association and the Conference on Globalization, Economic Reform and Capital Markets Crises held at Duke University December 7–8, 1998 are also gratefully acknowledged.

Notes

1. Calvo and Mendoza (1996) review factual evidence of herding by holders of Mexican securities. Calvo and Reinhart (1995) provide some statistical evidence of contagion effects in emerging markets.

2. See the survey data analysis of contagion by word of mouth by Shiller and Pound (1986, 1987).

3. The numerical analysis will also cover more general cases in which $r^* \neq \rho$, $\eta \neq 0$, and $\sigma_i \neq \sigma_j$.

4. A consistency condition under rational expectations implies $E(r^l|\kappa) = r^*$, since r^* is an expectation based on free information and the p.d.f. of r^l is known. This would make rumors $r < r^*$ non-credible. Most of our analysis maintains this condition, but we also examine arbitrary "credible" rumors.

5. For an insightful analysis of the value of information without short-selling constraints see Pritsker (1994). Our results suggest, however, that the value of information differs sharply when these constraints are present.

6. For a real-world example, consider the case of private pension funds in Chile and Colombia. Individual funds are required by government regulation in each country to produce returns within a certain range of the average return for all pension funds.

7. This is because θ^* maximizes $E\hat{U}(\theta)$, and $EU(\theta) = E\hat{U}(\theta)$ whenever $\theta = \Theta$ since $\lambda(0) = 0$.

8. Our analysis shares with the game-theoretic models of Banerjee (1992) and Bikhchandani et al. (1992) the need to assume two sources of uncertainty. They assume uncertainty about outcomes and private signals, while our fixed-cost model assumes uncertainty about ex ante asset returns and about updates of mean and variances of assets returns.

9. A similar example can be constructed for the case with performance costs, if they are viewed as the "sharing-the-blame" reputational effects that induce herding externalities in Scharfstein and Stein (1990).

10. See, for example, Bohn and Tesar (1994), Lewis (1995), and Tesar and Werner (1994).

11. Bohn and Tesar (1994) examined net purchases of foreign stocks by U.S. investors in 17 industrial countries (Australia, Austria, Belgium, Germany, Spain, France, Italy, Netherlands, Switzerland, the U.K., Ireland, Japan, Canada, Denmark, Finland, Norway, Sweden, and South Africa) and 4 emerging markets (Hong Kong, Mexico, Singapore, and Malaysia). They measured returns in dollars relative to the U.S. Tbill.

12. A table listing these moments for a large sample of countries computed using the regression coefficients from Erb et al. (1996) and the actual CCR data is available from the authors on request.

13. Aiyagari and Gertler (1998) report that the maintenance requirement on stocks purchased on margin debt is 0.25 and that the effective margin constraint on futures and options is between 0.15 and 0.2.

14. Given the means and variances of asset returns, and the value of γ, higher correlation coefficients would violate the second-order conditions of the optimization problems of informed and uninformed investors.

15. Quoted in the Mexican newspaper *Reforma*, 1/15/1998, p. 1A, citing as source the Mexican stock exchange.

16. Interestingly, the Treasury's *Survey* estimates the U.S. holdings of Mexican equity at 6.2 percent of the total holdings of foreign equity by U.S. investors.

17. This applies only to models in which growth and fluctuations are unrelated. If volatility affects growth, the gains of diversification can be large (see Obstfeld, 1994; Mendoza, 1997).

References

Aiyagari, S. Rao, Gertler, M., 1999. Overreaction of asset prices in general equilibrium. *Review of Economic Dynamics*, Academic Press for the Society for Economic Dynamics, 2(1), 3–35.

Banerjee, A. V., 1992. A simple model of herd behavior. *Quarterly Journal of Economics* 107, 797–817.

Bikhchandani, S., Hirshleifer, D., Welch, I., 1992. A theory of fads. Fashion, custom, and cultural change as informational cascades. *Journal of Political Economy* 100, 992–1026.

Bohn, H., Tesar, L. L., 1994. Can standard portfolio theory explain international portfolio investment?, mimeo, Department of Economics, University of California–Santa Barbara.

Calvo, G. A., 1998. Varieties of capital market crises. In: Calvo, G. A., King, M. (Eds.), *The Debt Burden and its Consequences for Monetary Policy*, Proceedings of a Conference held by the International Economic Association at the Deutsche Bundesbank, Macmillan, London.

Calvo, G. A., 1999. Understanding the Russian Virus, mimeo, Department of Economics, University of Maryland.

Calvo, G. A., Mendoza, E. G., 1996. Mexico's balance-of-payments crisis: a chronicle of a death foretold. *Journal of International Economics* 41, 235–264.

Calvo, S., Reinhart, C. M., 1995. Capital flows to Latin America: is there evidence of contagion effects, mimeo, World Bank, Washington D.C.

Erb, C. B., Harvey, C. R., Viskanta, T. E., 1996. Expected returns and volatility in 135 countries. *Journal of Portfolio Management* 22, 46–58.

Frankel, J. A., Schmukler, S. L., 1996. Country fund discounts, asymmetric information, and the Mexican Crisis of 1994: did local residents turn pessimistic before international investor?, mimeo, University of California at Berkeley.

Grossman, S. J., Stiglitz, J. E., 1976. Information and competitive price systems. *American Economic Review* 66, 246–253.

Grossman, S. J., Stiglitz, J. E., 1980. On the impossibility of informationally efficient markets. *American Economic Review* 70, 477–498.

Keynes, J. M., 1936. *The General Theory of Employment, Interest, and Money*, Harcourt, Brace, and Co, New York.

Lewis, K. K., 1995. Stocks, consumption, and the gains from international risk-sharing, mimeo, Wharton School of Business, University of Pennsylvania.

Mendoza, E. G., 1991. Capital controls and the dynamic gains from trade in a business cycle model of a small open economy. IMF Staff Papers 38, 480–505.

Mendoza, E. G., 1997. Terms-of-trade uncertainty and economic growth: are risk indicators significant in growth regressions. *Journal of Development Economics* 52, 322–356.

Obstfeld, M., 1994. Risk-taking, global diversification, and growth. *American Economic Review* 84, 1310–1330.

Pritsker, M. G., 1994. The value of information to an individual agent, mimeo, Board of Governors of the Federal Reserve System, Washington, D.C.

Scharfstein, D. S., Stein, J. C., 1990. Herd behavior and investment. *American Economic Review* 80, 465–479.

Shiller, R. J., 1995. Conversation, information, and herd behavior. *American Economic Review*: Papers and Proceedings May.

Shiller, R. J., Pound, J., 1986. Survey evidence on diffusion of interest among institutional investors, NBER working paper No. 1851, Cambridge, MA.

Shiller, R. J., Pound, J., 1987. Are institutional investors speculators? *Journal of Portfolio Management Spring*, 46–52.

Tesar, L. L., Werner, I. M., 1994. U.S. equity investment in emerging stock markets, mimeo, Department of Economics, University of California–Santa Barbara.

11

Balance-of-Payments Crises in Emerging Markets: Large Capital Inflows and Sovereign Governments

Guillermo A. Calvo

1 Introduction

Recent financial crises in emerging markets have shared the following characteristics: (1) They have been preceded by large capital inflows. (2) They evolved through a complicated interaction among the domestic financial and nonfinancial sectors, international investors and banks, and sovereign governments. (3) Few people were able to predict them. (4) They led to a sharp growth slowdown, if not sheer output collapse.

The scientific literature has paid a great deal of attention to point 3 and has generated renewed interest in multiple equilibrium models (see, e.g., Obstfeld 1994; Obstfeld and Rogoff 1995; Eichengreen, Rose, and Wyplosz 1995; Calvo 1998a; Calvo and Mendoza 1996; Cole and Kehoe 1996). However, the models are still highly stylized, and as a result, not much of the richness of detail associated with point 2 has been captured by the models. Finally, points 1 and 4 have not been emphasized (an exception is Calvo 1998b).

Financial analysts (e.g., the financial press and jet-set guru-economists), on the other hand, have singled out the following factors as contributing to crises: large current account deficits (anything larger than 4 percent of GDP is likely to be called "large"); real currency appreciation; and, after the tigers went downhill, fixed or quasi-fixed nominal exchange rates. Of the three points, the only one that has some analytical, as opposed to factual, basis is the first. However, as argued in Calvo (1998b), the current account sustainability theory that provides analytical support for that point leaves much to be desired.

This chapter tries to fill some of the gaps highlighted above. First, it will present a series of conventional representative-individual models in which currency crises can occur in the absence of current account deficits. This is not intended to debunk the view that current account deficits are important but to argue that if they are, one has to bring to the fore features that are not commonly emphasized in the literature. Actually, the chapter will argue that current account deficits, although not a necessary condition for currency or financial crises, play a key role—together with "dollarization"—in the *resolution* of crises. It will be claimed that large current account deficits and dollarization make it more difficult to offset the effects of self-fulfilling crises on the basis of domestic policy alone, raising the need for international cooperation.

The chapter will argue that not bringing the government into the limelight is a major omission. International financial crises have a flavor of their own that is not fully shared by purely domestic episodes (e.g., Orange County, California). Thus the chapter will claim that a key reason for that is the presence of *sovereign* governments. This is a central aspect of the debt crisis literature, but it has been somewhat ignored in the currency-financial crisis literature.[1] The chapter will argue that sovereignty and nonexplicit government policy rules may go a long way toward generating financial vulnerability and multiple equilibria. Sovereignty induces "country risk," and the latter prompts the government—explicitly or implicitly—to favor short-term debt and deposits.

Another aspect that will be highlighted in the paper is large capital inflows. It will be argued that together with sovereignty, large capital inflows magnify the financial vulnerability caused by short-term debt and deposits. In addition, and even more important, the perception that large capital inflows are transitory helps to plant in people's minds the notion that the economy will eventually go back to where it started (before the capital inflow episode). The chapter argues that this could be an important coordinating factor to shift expectations from a good to a bad equilibrium.

Output collapse will be addressed in the context of self-fulfilling prophesies. The chapter will show that output loss can be rationalized in terms of "new classical" and price-stickiness models: in the first one because a crisis changes relative prices and may cause a generalized financial crash and in the second one for textbook-type Keynesian reasons associated with a contraction of aggregate demand. The new classical approach will be complemented by a discussion of "vanishing credit," which shows how a bad shock in a given sector could lead to a credit crunch in the whole economy. The paper will argue that these kinds of spillover effects are crucial for self-fulfilling prophesy theories to be able to give a full—qualitative and quantitative—account of current crises.

Finally, a major part of the chapter will be devoted to providing a rationale for the fact that in Mexico and Argentina current account deficits have fallen but did not turn into surpluses, and yet output suffered a major collapse. This would be no major puzzle in a Keynesian context, but it is in a new classical one. The current account deficit measures net debt accumulation of the country as a whole. Thus, when it suddenly goes down to zero (as in Mexico in 1995), for example, all it means is that new net credit collapses to zero—although no debt repayment is called for. The chapter explores a "time to build" model in which under these circumstances real effects could take place, even in a new classical environment, because curtailment of new credit may imply abandoning ongoing projects.

The chapter is organized as follows. Sections 2 and 3 show models in which crisislike phenomena take place even though the current account is permanently in equilibrium. Section 4 discusses the role of sovereign governments, while section 5 highlights the role of large capital inflows. Section 6 explores factors that could explain growth slowdown or outright output collapse. Section 7 revisits current account deficits and shows their importance for the resolution of currency-financial crises. Section 8 studies the magnification effects of vanishing credit. Sections 9 and 10 analyze the implications of a time-to-build model.

2   Balance-of-Payments Crises with a Balanced Current Account: Full Neutrality

This section introduces money in a conventional model and discusses the relation between balance-of-payments crises and current account deficits.

Consider an infinitely lived representative-individual economy with time-separable utility. There exists one homogenous, fully tradable good. The utility index in period t is denoted by $u(c_t) + v(m_t)$, where c and m stand for consumption and real monetary balances.[2] Existence of commercial banks is not essential to make the following points, and thus, I will assume that money is just high-powered money issued by the central bank.

There is perfect capital mobility, and the real international rate of interest is constant and equal to ρ. To preserve stationarity, we will assume that the subjective rate of discount is also equal to ρ. For the sake of simplicity, we assume that the individual gets a constant flow of endowment income y and a constant flow of government lump-sum transfers (net of lump-sum taxes), g, per unit of time ($g > 0$). Under these conditions, the individuals budget constraint at time zero is given by

$$m_0 + b_0 + \int_0^\infty (y + g - c_t - i_t m_t)e^{-\rho t}\, dt = 0, \tag{1}$$

where b_0 is initial net holdings of the pure foreign bond. Moreover, i denotes the nominal domestic interest rate. Assuming perfect capital mobility, we have

$$i_t = \rho + \varepsilon_t + \pi_t^*, \tag{2}$$

where ε_t and π_t^* denote the instantaneous rate of devaluation and international rate of inflation, respectively, at time t.

Thus, denoting by λ the Lagrange multiplier associated with budget constraint (1), the first-order conditions of the utility maximization problem are

$$u'(c_t) = \lambda, \tag{3a}$$

$$v'(m_t) = \lambda i_t. \tag{3b}$$

An implication of equations (3a) and (3b) is that consumption is constant through time, irrespective of the nominal interest rate.[3] Let the constant optimal consumption rate be denoted by ψ. Then, by equations (3a) and (3b), we have

$$\frac{v'(m_t)}{u'(\psi)} = i_t. \tag{4}$$

Equation (4) implicitly defines a demand for real monetary balances m as a function of the nominal interest rate i.

Let international reserves be defined as the stock of international bonds held by the monetary authority. I denote them by b^g and assume that the government does not consume and rebates all its income to domestic residents in a lump-sum manner. To simplify the exposition, and without loss of generality, we will further assume that discontinuities occur only at time zero.[4] Then the government's budget constraint satisfies[5]

$$b_0^g + (M_{0+} - M_0)/E_0 P_0^* + \int_0^\infty (\dot{M}_t/E_t P_t^*)e^{-\rho t}\, dt = \int_0^\infty g_t e^{-\rho t}\, dt, \tag{5}$$

where E and P^* denote the nominal exchange rate and the international price level, respectively, and M_{0+} denotes the level of nominal monetary balances just after the policy announcement or other event at time zero inducing a discontinuous change in the stock of money. Thus the first term on the left-hand side of expression (5) is net government financial wealth; the second term is the stock seigniorage at time zero; and the integral involving M is the present discounted value of flow seigniorage. Equation (5) states that government lump-sum transfers (properly discounted) will be equal to the government's initial financial wealth, b_0^g, plus the present value of seigniorage from money creation.

Expressing the left-hand side of equation (5) in terms of $m = M/EP^*$, we get

$$b_0^g + m_{0+} - m_0 + \int_0^\infty [\dot{m}_t + (\varepsilon_t + \pi_t^*)m_t]e^{-\rho t}\, dt = \int_0^\infty g_t e^{-\rho t}\, dt, \qquad (6)$$

where $m_{0+} = M_{0+}/E_0 P_0^*$. Moreover, integrating by parts the left-hand side of equation (6), we have

$$b_0^g - m_0 + \int_0^\infty i_t m_t e^{-\rho t}\, dt = \int_0^\infty g_t e^{-\rho t}\, dt. \qquad (7)$$

Consequently, using the government budget constraint (7) in the representative individual's budget constraint (1), we have that at equilibrium (recalling that $c = \psi$)

$$b_0 + b_0^g + y/\rho = \psi/\rho. \qquad (8)$$

Equation (8) just states the commonsensical result that when individuals internalize the government's budget constraint—the government does not consume, and the private and public sectors face the same international interest rate—then the private discounted value of consumption equals initial (private plus public) financial assets plus the present discounted value of endowment income. It follows from equation (8) that at time zero the current account deficit is zero. Thus total financial assets $b + b^g$ do not change at time zero. However, since zero is just a label and could be any calendar time, it also follows that $b + b^g$ is constant over time, implying that *the current account is zero at all points in time.*

Balance-of-payments crisis scenarios are now very easy to set up. For example, following Krugman (1979), one could assume that the exchange rate is kept constant unless crisis hits, in which case the currency is allowed freely to float. By definition, a balance-of-payments crisis takes place when reserves—b^g in our notation—reach a minimum tolerable level and would continue falling unless policy is modified.

Consider first the Krugman case in which international inflation is zero. Hence, in the fixed-exchange-rate phase, reserves accumulate according to the following equation:

$$\dot{b}_t^g = \rho b_t^g - g. \tag{9}$$

Thus a balance-of-payments crisis occurs in finite time if

$$g > \rho b_0^g. \tag{10}$$

The rest of the story is just simple transliteration of Krugman (1979). In particular, since $g > 0$, postcrisis inflation is positive and when crisis hits there is a sudden loss of reserves.[6]

The above scenario can be enriched in an interesting manner by assuming that along the way there is an (expected) rise in the nominal international rate of interest. First, note that by first-order condition (4), we can write the demand for money as follows:

$$m = L(i), \quad L' < 0. \tag{11}$$

Therefore, as the international interest rate rises, the demand for money falls. If the fixed-exchange-rate regime is still sustainable, there will be a sudden loss of reserves (denoted by Δb^g), which—letting the resulting increase in the domestic nominal interest rate be denoted by Δi—is given by

$$\Delta b^g = L(\rho + \Delta i) - L(\rho) < 0. \tag{12}$$

Consider now the following sequence of events. At time zero, the stock of reserves is such that government transfers can be financed out of its yield. Thus, assuming that the inequality in expression (10) is reversed, the government steadily accumulates reserves. However, there are enough degrees of freedom so as to be able to generate a situation in which after the loss of reserves implied by equation (12), we have (denoting by $t_0 > 0$ the time of the interest rate hike)

$$g > \rho b_{t_0}^g. \tag{13}$$

Hence, as in the previous example, the economy is now bound to hit a balance-of-payments crisis. This is an interesting case because the crisis occurs by a combination of domestic and external factors.[7]

3   Balance-of-Payments Crises with a Balanced Current Account: Nontradable Goods

We now introduce a nontradable good, z, and start the analysis assuming that z is in fixed supply. Later the analysis is extended to a production economy.

3.1   Endowment Economy

A straightforward extension of the previous section's model would be to assume the instantaneous utility index to be $u(c_t) + v(m_t) + h(z_t)$, where h is a twice differentiable, increasing, and strictly concave function on the nonnegative real line. Normalizing z so that total supply is one, the market equilibrium condition for nontradables would be

$$z_t = 1, \tag{14}$$

for all t. We denote the relative price of nontradables in terms of tradables (i.e., the *real* exchange rate as measured by the IMF) by p. Under these assumptions (and the other assumptions of section 3.2), one can readily show that both c and z will be constant over time; moreover, $p = h'(1)/u'(\psi)$, where ψ is given by equation (8). Hence, the real exchange rate is also constant over time, irrespective of the existence of a balance-of-payments crisis.

A more empirically relevant version of the model would assume, instead, that the instantaneous utility index depends only on c and z and money is held for cash-in-advance considerations. This type of model is developed in Calvo (1986). There an anticipated balance-of-payments crisis will bring about a real currency appreciation (i.e., p increases) together with a current account deficit before the crisis takes place. Both implications are realistic. However, my purpose is to show that credit problems associated with capital inflows are, in principle, independent of current account deficits. Therefore, I will modify Calvo (1986) and assume that the cash-in-advance constraint applies only to nontradables.[8] More formally, I will assume

$$p_t z_t \leq \alpha m_t, \quad \alpha > 0. \tag{15}$$

The budget constraint for the representative individual becomes

$$m_0 + b_0 + \int_0^\infty (y_t + g - c_t - p_t z_t - i_t m_t)e^{-\rho t}\, dt = 0. \tag{16}$$

Hence, since we will focus on cases in which the nominal interest rate is positive, liquidity condition (10) would be binding and, taking budget constraint (11) into account, the first-order conditions are

$$u'(c_t) = \lambda, \tag{17a}$$

$$h'(z_t) = \lambda p_t(1 + \alpha i_t). \tag{17b}$$

Hence, c is constant over time. Therefore, one can show, once again, that the current account deficit is zero for all times. On the other hand, by equations (14) and (17b), we have

$$\frac{h'(1)}{\lambda} = p_t(1 + \alpha i_t), \tag{18}$$

establishing a negative relation between p and i. Thus along an equilibrium path the real exchange rate p rises as the nominal interest rate declines (or, equivalently, as inflation falls), and vice versa.[9]

3.2 Production Economy

We now enrich the model by assuming that the instantaneous utility function is given by $u(c_t) + h(z_t) + n(l)$, where n is twice differentiable, strictly increasing, and concave function on the nonnegative real line and l stands for leisure. We assume the individual is endowed with one unit of leisure and that z is produced and satisfies

$$z_t = 1 - l_t. \tag{19}$$

Focusing on interior solutions, it is straightforward to show that the crisis scenarios discussed in the previous section will lead, before crisis, to an appreciation of the real exchange rate and an expansion of nontradable output. Thus GDP as conventionally computed will increase during the transition. After the balance-of-payments crisis, however, GDP falls precipitously. All along, however, the current account is undisturbed and in full balance.

3.3 Banks

Banks could easily be accommodated in the present framework. For example, let δ denote the legal minimum reserve requirement ($0 \le \delta \le 1$). We assume that bank deposits and cash are perfect substitutes, but if the return on deposits equals or exceeds that of cash ($= 0$

in terms of domestic currency), then the nonbank sector will exhibit no demand for cash (this is assumed to be the case in what follows).

Let us assume that banks lend at the pure market rate i. Then, under no operating costs for banks, the deposit rate i^D satisfies the following zero-profit condition:

$$i^D = (1 - \delta)i. \tag{20}$$

Incorporating these new aspects into budget constraint (16) and noticing that by equation (20), $i - i^D = \delta i$, we get the following budget constraint (where m now is entirely composed of bank deposits because $i > 0$ and, hence, $i^D > 0$, dominating cash):

$$m_0 + b_0 + \int_0^\infty (y_t + g - c_t - p_t z_t - \delta i_t m_t)e^{-\rho t}\, dt = 0. \tag{21}$$

Thus first-order conditions (17a) and (17b) are now

$$u'(c_t) = \lambda, \tag{22a}$$

$$h'(z_t) = \lambda p_t(1 + \alpha \delta i_t). \tag{22b}$$

Therefore, from a formal point of view, the only change with respect to the cash-only case considered before is that the opportunity cost of money is δi. As expected, the opportunity cost boils down to i when the reserve requirement $\delta = 1$.

If $\delta < 1$, then banks have loanable funds equivalent to $(1 - \delta)m$ in terms of output. These funds are borrowed by depositors to build their stock of deposits to the desired level. Hence, in this simple world, banks are just a device to economize on non-interest-bearing cash: only the share δm is held as cash (indirectly and at banks' vaults).

The crisis scenarios are essentially the same as before, except that when m collapses, so do loans. However, since loans were used to accumulate liquid assets (i.e., bank deposits), no financial crisis takes place—all loans are fully repaid without requiring a central bank bailout. Thus the model is still far from yielding the deep financial troubles that we see in practice. In the remainder of the paper I will try to bring some of those issues into focus.

4 The Role of Sovereign Governments

A successful theory of international financial crises should be able to rationalize the difference between Orange County, California, and

Mexico or Korea. A distinguishing and basic characteristic of *international* financial crises is that as a general rule, countries are sovereign and their governments are subject to loosely defined policy rules. Korea, for example, is much freer to impose taxes on external trade than Orange County is, and both Korea and Mexico can devalue on a moment's notice, while Orange County is bound to fall with the flag (or, rather, the greenback).

The extra degrees of freedom enjoyed by sovereign governments increase the uncertainty about their reaction functions—especially in times of crisis—and enhances the value for the private sector of anticipating future government behavior, inducing present defensive action on the side of the private sector. For example, if in the above models we assume that the government is expected to raise tariffs to stem capital outflows, then anticipated price changes will have real effects, even in the full neutrality case of section 2. Actually, as can readily be shown (see Calvo 1986), an increase in expected future tariffs induces a consumption boom—and thus a current account deficit—as capital flows in, and a sharp fall in consumption once tariffs are raised. The resulting intertemporal substitution of consumption is socially inefficient. It is entirely provoked by the expected policy reaction, and the associated social cost will be paid irrespectively of whether higher tariffs are ever carried out. The *threat* of higher tariffs is bad enough. These costs, incidentally, are magnified in the presence of durable goods (see Calvo 1988).

An interesting feature of the above example is that the deterioration in the current account is due to individuals' perception that the government reaction function opens up utility-enhancing intertemporal trade (i.e., speculation). The associated current account deficit is, in the present context, a clear signal of Pareto inefficiency. The example thus shows a case in which current account deficits are undesirable from a social point of view, even though no sustainability issue would be at stake. *Thus, in more general terms, our discussion so far can be summarized by saying that the large leeway enjoyed by sovereign governments may induce strong and socially costly speculative waves.*

In addition, loosely defined policy rules increase the fixed cost of learning about the profitability of projects in a given country. This is especially relevant for so-called emerging markets with a short track record of market-oriented policy making and, oftentimes, with unstable political institutions. A project's profitability depends on fiscal policy exchange controls, and the like. Sovereign countries have a lot of room to maneuver in this respect, and a potentially attractive project could quickly turn into a loss-making proposition as a result of a policy change. One major problem faced by investors is that in order to keep abreast of the facts for any given country in an effective way, they may have to constantly monitor developments in that country. But perhaps more critical is that macroeconomic-political information—even from the best sources and obtained in a timely fashion—has little predictive power. Thus the expected profitability of investment projects in emerging markets may reflect idiosyncratic factors and be highly sensitive to market "news" and rumors.

As argued in Calvo (1998a) and Calvo and Mendoza (1997), high fixed costs may induce rational herding behavior on the part of investors. This is established by showing that high fixed costs give rise to multiple rational expectations equilibria and, under certain plausible conditions (e.g., limits on short sales), equilibrium multiplicity would be more likely, the larger the number of emerging markets. Under these conditions, any factor that helps to coordinate expectations may cause a change in the economy's equilibrium position. A phenomenon such as "contagion"—which received ample attention during the "tequila" and the recent Southeast Asia crisis episodes—could just be the result of investors drawing parallels between a country undergoing a financial crisis and other countries that on the surface have similar characteristics. Thus, in attempting to protect themselves from potential crises in the other countries, investors could trigger the very same crises they fear and, as a result, contagion takes place. *In sum, the costs of learning about a given country are raised by the existence of a sovereign government that is not tied to clear-cut policy rules, making the country vulnerable to self-fulfilling financial crises.*

The model in Krugman (1979) and the variants discussed in the sections 2 and 3 help to explain some of the mechanics involved in financial crises—and, more specifically, currency crises. In a rudimentary way, these models include a sovereign government that issues its own money. However, those models stop short of exploiting other deleterious implications of sovereign governments from a macromanagement point of view. I will discuss these issues in what follows.

5   The Dangers of Large Capital Inflows: Sketch of a Theory

Abstracting from errors and omissions, the following is an accounting identity:

Capital Inflows (KI) = Current Account Deficit (CAD)

+ Accumulation of Reserves ($\dot{b}^g$).

In the examples discussed in sections 2 and 3, CAD = 0, and, hence, capital inflows were fully reflected in reserve accumulation. Under these conditions, a sharp contraction in capital inflows could just be met by a slowdown in the growth (or outright fall in the level) of international reserves, leaving the real economy unscathed. In actuality, however, accumulation of international reserves is also reflected in an expansion of monetary aggregates (see Calvo, Leiderman, and Reinhart 1996) and, consequently, of bank credit. But, as the last model in section 3 illustrates, even a large credit expansion may not increase the country's vulnerability to a sudden contraction in capital inflows. This is, however, an unrealistic implication of the model and motivates the ensuing discussion.

Governments and central banks, in particular, are very sensitive to any bank credit contraction and, apparently, even to a fall in monetary aggregates. Figure 11.1 shows the case of Mexico around the December 1994 crisis. Clearly, the central bank expanded domestic credit instead of letting the monetary base fall as the crisis unfolded. As a result, there was a massive loss of international reserves, which almost ended

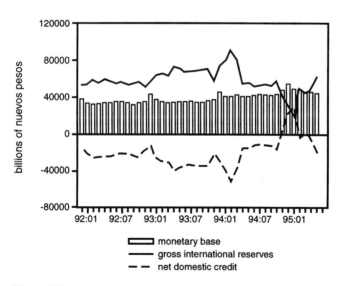

Figure 11.1
Monetary base, foreign reserves, and net domestic credit of the Bank of Mexico

up in a debt moratorium as short-term debt, which had been accumulated through sterilized intervention, started to come due.[10]

Furthermore, central bank sensitivity often reflects the perception that the banking system is highly vulnerable to declining bank deposits or high interest rates, or both. Once again, this would not be the case in the section 3 model because loans are used for highly liquid investments. But the existence of central banks that provide liquidity support in case of massive deposit withdrawals may lead commercial banks to issue loans for illiquid projects. Besides, from an ex ante point of view, lengthening the maturity structure of loans could be socially desirable (see, e.g., Diamond and Dybvig 1983).[11]

To develop a useful theory that helps to address the above issues, one has to be able to answer a key question: *What makes it attractive for sovereign governments in emerging markets to stimulate illiquid projects beyond what the free market will generate?*

Diamond and Dybvig (1983) provide an answer that has paved the road for the introduction of banks in macromodels. Their answer is that by pooling risks banks can finance long-term illiquid projects and, at the same time, ensure the liquidity of bank deposits. Even though this alchemy can be achieved by an unfettered private sector, the government still has a role to play because, otherwise, the economy could land on a "bad" equilibrium in which bank runs are rampant. However, the Diamond-Dybvig answer is not very satisfactory in an international context because, for example, residents of small (in terms of the financial market) countries could have access to large international banks that offer better risk-pooling deals than local banks.[12]

In this chapter I will put forward the notion that the very existence of sovereign governments creates a wedge between domestic and international rates of return for the reasons elaborated in the previous section. This "country risk" factor is generated by the presence of a sovereign government, and thus private insurance markets would be unable to eliminate its negative effect fully.[13] Therefore, governments would have an incentive to offset the country risk factor by, for instance, subsidizing investment and capital inflows, as well as imposing controls on capital outflows (for the experience of East Asian countries in these and other respects, see World Bank 1993). In this connection, a natural policy for a central bank would be to offer deposit guarantees and lower reserve requirements (recall eq. [22]), which leads, in principle, to a higher stock of monetary aggregates and bank credit. Another highly complementary policy would be for the government to offer implicit guarantees on short-term foreign-currency-denominated bonds issued by banks or large firms. Given the important role played by short-term debt and banks in recent crises, I will focus the rest of this section on these guarantees.

To be sure, those guarantees are not a sure recipe for crisis. Under normal circumstances, for example, short-term bonds will automatically be rolled over. However, given the possibly large information costs discussed in the previous section, a change in "market sentiment" may lead to much higher interest rates or outright refusal to roll over short-term debt (including bank deposits). Thus, to the extent that loans take the form of illiquid projects, banks will be unable to honor their debt obligations, and the central bank will be forced to draw on its international reserves (or to obtain fresh funds from the international financial community).

Still, even granting all the above, the question arises, *Why would the government, aware of the above difficulties, stimulate short-term borrowing and deposits?*

In the first place, let us recall that in an expectations-driven world, government guarantees need not be explicit. It is enough that individuals expect them. As for short-term deposits (e.g., sight deposits), they are an essential part of the "payments system." Repudiation of these types of deposits would decrease their liquidity and increase the perceived cost of holding money, thus lowering the stock of monetary aggregates.[14] In terms of the last model in section 3, a fall in monetary aggregates would result in an output and employment contraction. Therefore, a welfare-maximizing government—not bound by a policy rule like a currency board, for example—will likely be tempted to bail out depositors in case of a bank run.

It should be noted, however, that governments concerned about their credibility and eager to avoid future moral hazard difficulties are unlikely to perform bailouts automatically and without any cost for depositors. Therefore, after a crisis episode, the demand for monetary aggregates is likely to fall, implying at least a transitory negative impact on output and employment.

At this juncture the reader is likely to be asking: *What do large capital inflows have to do with all of this?*

The crisis scenarios discussed above are linked to the existence of multiple equilibria. If the economy exhibits a unique equilibrium, then bank runs and the like would be self-defeating. Under uniqueness, for example, if a set of investors refuses to roll over short-term debt, a new set will quickly spring into action wiping out the excess supply of bonds, and the whole episode would amount to just a little financial "hiccup." But on the other hand, the mere existence of multiple equilibria does not provide a convincing crisis theory, unless conditions are such that it can be argued that the economy's agents have developed a distinct feeling that equilibrium multiplicity is in the cards. Here is where large capital inflows have a role to play:

1. Large capital inflows have a strong effect on relative prices (particularly the real exchange rate) and bank credit. This is perceived by everybody.

2. Large capital inflows are usually transitory, leading people to expect that eventually the economy will return to the conditions prevailing before those inflows. The questions are when and how.

3. If individuals are aware of the financial vulnerabilities highlighted above (e.g., large short-term debt), which are magnified by the size of the capital inflows, then they will attach some probability to a sudden reversal (or a "hard landing," as some market analysts like to say).

4. Actually, individuals do not need much information to sense impending trouble. Big and sudden changes in relative prices should alert anyone that there is room for a hard landing. Unless the change in relative prices is prompted by strong and clear technical or natural causes, individuals would infer that some kind of transitory distortion is at play.

Notice, incidentally, that the above difficulties could occur even though the current account is virtually in balance. This is not to deny that current account deficits have been a common feature prior to international financial crises. However, recalling the accounting identity at the outset of this section, current account deficits *not accompanied by capital inflows* can only occur if there is an equivalent loss of reserves. This has not been a feature in recent crises. That is why I feel it is a good research strategy to develop crisis scenarios that are free from current account imbalances. In doing so, it becomes obvious that the issues involved have an essentially *financial* component. In our discussion we have identified a key one, namely, a mismatch between the maturity of assets (long) and of financial obligations (short), partly explained by the nature of banking and the existence of sovereign governments.

6   The Deeper Anatomy of Self-fulfilling Crises: Output Collapse

So far I have conducted a somewhat casual discussion of the impact of a slowdown in capital inflows. This section will offer a more thorough analysis. I will start by examining the impact of a large and sudden capital flow reversal—that is, capital inflows suddenly turning negative and large in absolute value. Later I will study the impact of a simple slowdown in capital inflows.

6.1   Negative Capital Inflows

I will first discuss new classical examples in which prices and wages are fully flexible and then extend the analysis to a sticky price framework.

New Classical Examples
Consider a case similar to that faced by Mexico toward the end of 1994 (see fig. 11.1), in which short-term public debt exceeded available international reserves by a wide margin. Suppose that as in Mexico, creditors refuse to roll over expiring debt. What are the options open to the government? Instant repayment is out of the question because resources are, by assumption, not available.[15] Option 1 is cessation of payments, which could take the form of outright repudiation or involuntary debt rescheduling. Option 2 is obtaining aid from other sovereign countries (an option that requires international cooperation and cannot be taken unilaterally). Option 3 is to persuade the private sector to roll over expiring debt. Leaving option 3 aside for the time being, option 1 is likely to involve direct costs (e.g., lawsuits, strong pressure from creditors' governments, etc.) and indirect costs stemming from more limited access to capital markets.[16] Moreover, option 2 will likely involve tough conditionalities (such as a sharp rise in taxes), which may have deleterious effects on the real economy.

Consequently, in coping with the sudden inability to roll over short-term debt, governments are forced to take actions that have negative effects on output. This sets the stage for self-fulfilling crises.[17] However, I doubt that these effects, by themselves, are quantitatively large enough to generate a "bad" equilibrium that is significantly different from the good one.

Enter the private sector. The government's policies have effects on relative prices. The greater the surprise element in the new policies, the more likely it will be that a significant number of investment projects become unfeasible. And even if feasible, loans contracted to finance such projects may become nonperforming. These unpleasant surprises are also bound to cause reverberations all around the economy. This is so because in most capitalist economies interenterprise credit plays a prominent role (more on this in section 8). Thus, once a significant part of the economy runs into financial difficulties, *much of the rest of the economy becomes suspect*. In this new environment, credits that would have automatically been rolled over are conditioned on passing deeper viability tests. The latter, in turn, are time-consuming exercises (especially during crises) because they require information about the interenterprise credit network to which the firm in question is connected, for example. My conjecture is that the resulting "highway congestion" may signify a major negative supply shock.[18] Once the crisis reaches this point, option 3 above—persuade the private sector to refinance expiring loans—is not an option anymore: the crisis itself has created the conditions that make new loans unattractive to the lender.

Sticky Price Examples
The existence of sticky prices may exacerbate the above effects. Firms have fewer degrees of freedom to respond to the negative shock. Besides, potential lenders now need information about the nature of the price or wage contracts that firms have entered into. However, there is an effect that goes in the opposite direction. The existence of sticky prices may give rise to de facto quasi-monopolistic price setting by firms and, in this fashion, may make them financially less vulnerable in the short run. However, I feel that this positive effect is short lived and unlikely to overturn the negative ones.

6.2 Capital Inflow Slowdown: Time to Build

Debt rollover difficulties are typically associated with financial crises. However, this does not imply that ex post, countries engage in massive net debt repayment. This is typically not possible. Hence, the question arises, Why have we witnessed large output losses in recent crises—6.6 percent in Mexico and 4.4 percent in Argentina during 1995, for example?

One answer is linked to the previous discussion, that is, the highway congestion effect. However, another answer is linked to a version of "time to build." Consider the case in which unfinished projects disintegrate. Thus, if projects were funded on the basis of bank credit lines, for example, an unanticipated capital inflow slowdown could imply a surge of unfinished projects and bankruptcies. This observation helps to explain why the typical bank bailout does not insulate the economy from serious output losses. This is so because a bank bailout provides funds to repay bank *creditors* (e.g., depositors, foreign lenders, etc.) but not to ensure that investment projects are carried to completion. Firms that cannot get the additional funds necessary for that purpose may, therefore, run into serious financial difficulties. This by itself slows growth, while the reverberations from bankruptcies could actually lower output. I will have more to say about this case in sections 9 and 10.

7   Policies to Manage Capital Flows: Current Account Deficits and Dollarization; A Brief Detour

Before proceeding with analytical details, it is worth pausing to discuss some key policy issues. The main result of the section will be to show that taking into account the policies available to deal with a crisis, current account deficits and a dollarized financial sector are more a cause of concern than mere capital inflows (i.e., capital inflows without current account deficits and dollarization).

At the beginning of a capital inflow episode, central banks typically engage in sterilized intervention. In this fashion, the accumulation of reserves is financed by issuing public debt (typically short term). However, sterilization is as a general rule incomplete, and monetary aggregates increase together with bank credit. In the absence of a current account deficit, a sudden unexpected slowdown or fall in capital inflows could be met by an expansion of domestic credit (from the central bank) and a devaluation of the currency. If this is done quickly enough, debtors will benefit from the devaluation, which will give them some extra leeway to negotiate their financial difficulties. Thus monetary policy could be highly effective in offsetting the negative effects stemming from the capital account. It should be stressed, however, that the move has to be quick and decisive. If the monetary authority is slow to react, devaluation expectations will rise and, with it, nominal interest rates. Thus the real value of debt could increase before the currency is devalued. Moreover, to the extent that the devaluation is anticipated by the public, devaluation would fail to lower the real value of debt, and its effect will mostly be on the price level. Actually, passive and slow reaction by the monetary authority, failing to address the debt problem, could lead to gradually increasing inflation, possibly converging to hyperinflation (Argentina in the 1980s is a good example in this respect; see Fernandez 1991).

However, monetary policy is much less effective if the shock involves a cut in a large current account deficit or if the monetary system is highly dollarized.[19] Clearly, dollarization makes the real value of bank debt impervious to devaluation or domestic inflation, rendering the inflation debt repudiation route totally ineffective. On the other hand, if capital inflows are associated with large current account deficits, then, again, debt is as a general rule specified in terms of foreign exchange, and monetary policy becomes ineffective.

How vulnerable is the economy to a given current account deficit? It depends on a myriad of factors, among which are the level of international reserves, the maturity structure of foreign-exchange-denominated debt, the volume of investment projects that will have to be discontinued if the current account deficit has to be sharply reversed, and so forth. A fuller answer is beyond the scope of this paper. However, it should be clear that countries can be very different in this respect and there is no magical number beyond which any current account deficit should be deemed a sure harbinger of crisis. Of course, if prominent people and institutions insist on calling anything greater than 4 percent of GDP, say, "large," then there are enough vulnerabilities out there in the emerging market world that the prophesy could become self-fulfilling. The latter may enhance the worldly reputation of such prophets but, I am afraid, will keep them outside the gates of Heaven!

8 Vanishing Credit

As noted in section 6 I suspect that a major component in emerging market crises has to do with the disarray they create in the private sector and, especially, in the credit and production network of these countries. In this section I will try to illustrate this issue by means of a simple example.

Let figure 11.2 depict a simple economy in which the numbers around the circle indicate "industries," each one composed of a multitude of competitive firms. There are, therefore, four types of firms. Each firm in industry i, $i = 1, 2, 3, 4$, is managed by one individual who is endowed with an initial stock z of industry i's goods (by

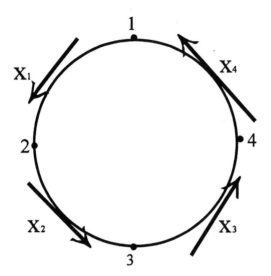

Figure 11.2
Flow of goods

normalization, z is the same for all i). Each firm is an "atom," and we normalize the number of firms in each industry to unity. Individuals in industry i derive utility from their own good and the good of industry $i-1$ (where, if $i = 1$, $i - 1 = 4$). The amount shipped by industry i to individuals in industry $i + 1$ is denoted by x_i ($x_i \leq z$). This pattern is depicted in figure 11.2, where the arrows indicate the direction in which the goods are shipped.

The utility of an individual in industry i is given by

$$z - x_i + kx_{i-1}, \quad k > 1. \tag{23}$$

Thus the marginal utility of goods produced by the preceding industry (ordered in a counterclockwise manner) exceeds that of goods produced by one's own industry. This is a simple way of capturing the mutual dependence among firms for production.

Let p_i be the market price of goods produced by industry i. Then it is readily seen that $p_i = 1$, for all i, is a competitive equilibrium price vector. In this equilibrium, nobody consumes his own good, and therefore, $x_i = z$, for all i. Moreover, utility equals kz for all i, and as expected, the competitive equilibrium is a Pareto optimum.

To make the example more useful for our purposes, let us assume that transactions take time and occur in a predetermined sequential order. First industry 1 ships to 2, then industry 2 ships to 3, and so on. In this context, if all the transactions are contracted "at the beginning of time" and enforced ex post, then the Pareto optimum could be effectively decentralized by a competitive system. Otherwise, these transactions will have to involve some means of payment (money) or credit and trust (C&T), or both. Let us study the workings of C&T since, as will be easy to see, if costless it is likely to dominate money (especially specie money).

Let us take the above equilibrium prices as a reference. Individuals start with zero wealth. Hence, industry 1 ships goods to 2 before industry 2 gets paid by 3. Thus this transaction requires credit in the amount z (i.e., the market value of the goods being shipped). Clearly, the same is true for all the ensuing shipping around the circle. When all shipping is done, each set of individuals has issued and received one IOU in the amount z. But unless there is a market for IOUs, repayment cannot be executed. Individuals in industry 1, for example, will hold IOUs from individuals in industry 4 and will have issued IOUs held by individuals in industry 2.

In the present context, banks can be seen as institutions that facilitate the trading of those IOUs. Actually, a bank can fully substitute for the IOUs by providing credit to individuals in industries 2, 3, and 4. These individuals will later be able to repay the loans from the proceeds of their shipping, which are deposited in their bank accounts.

A fundamental problem arises, however, if individuals realize that it may be optimal for them to consume their own goods after getting credit from the bank. To see the implication of this in a stark way, consider the case in which all the individuals in industry 3 behave that way. If this is anticipated by individuals in industry 1, it is easy to see that they will have no incentive to sell their endowment to those in industry 2 *at any price*. A similar reasoning shows that under those circumstances the only possible equilibrium is full autarky, where utility equals $z < kz$ (the Pareto optimum utility).

Under normal circumstances C&T systems have proved to work smoothly. There are always isolated deviants, but they are as a general rule severely punished. Thus, on the whole, although the Pareto optimum may be hard to achieve, a sufficiently well functioning C&T system could be set in place. A problem arises, though, if the system is subject to a low-probability external (to the system) shock that changes the marginal cost of deviant behavior. Suppose, for example, that industry 3 is forced to repay the principal of an old debt outside the system. If the punishment for not repaying the old debt is high enough, individuals in industry 3 may prefer to use their own goods to effect the repayment. Thus, if anticipated by individuals in industry 1, this behavior will result in full autarky, as before. Interestingly, under these circumstances the potential deviants may not be given the opportunity to default on bank credit because it might instantly dry up for everybody. *Consequently, the above example shows that debt rollover difficulties, even when located in one sector of the economy, can spill over the whole economy and result in vanishing credit and a major welfare loss.*

In practice, of course, banks are not the only form of credit or system that helps to guarantee settlement enforcement. The above economy could use "cash," for example, coupled with some cash-in-advance constraint to ensure an equilibrium positive price of cash in terms of commodities. However, banks are likely to creep back into the picture if the opportunity cost of cash is positive (i.e., if Friedman's optimum quantity of money is not implemented), which is the dominant case in practice.

Another widespread form of credit is "interenterprise credit," that is, credit extended in connection with regular business among firms (see Ramey 1992). Thus, in the above economy, sector i would lend to sector $i + 1$, for all i. Firms as creditors have an advantage over banks in that enforcement may be ensured by the threat of keeping the defaulter away from the stream of goods (and thus forcing him to autarky). This kind of advantage explains the coexistence of interenterprise and bank credit.

A full discussion of interenterprise credit falls outside the scope of the present chapter (see Calvo and Coricelli 1994). However, it should be clear that this type of credit channel will also come to a full stop if just one of its links breaks. Actually, under those circumstances clearinghouses such as banks become more useful because, at the very least, they help net out interenterprise debt. In this fashion, bankruptcy procedures would involve smaller sums of money and could thus lower the cost of legal settlements.[20]

In closing, the reader has to beware that this section is not self-contained because it does not provide an explanation for the external shock. This, however, was discussed in previous sections where the existence of a sovereign government was singled out as a major factor in the creation of financial vulnerability. The main value of this section is to show that the credit channel could greatly magnify external shocks.[21]

9 Time to Build: A Basic Model

I will now discuss the case in which investment projects take time to come to full fruition, which was identified in subsection 6.2 as a possible explanation for the observed high cost of a credit slow-down, as opposed to outright credit cut. To simplify the exposition, I will focus on the non-monetary economy in which, by necessity, $KI = CAD$.

To help fix ideas, consider the case in which it takes two periods to bring an investment project to completion, involving half a unit of output per period. Once completed, the project yields β units of output in the third period, and zero later on. However, if the project is discontinued after the first period, no output is forthcoming, and the project becomes completely useless. Assuming that the riskless international rate of interest is zero and that there is no risk of project discontinuation, the project will be undertaken if

$$\beta \geq 1. \tag{24}$$

In a stationary steady state as many projects will be completed as are started. Thus the total amount of credit outstanding at any point in time will be a constant, implying that as long as total credit does not drop, all projects will see their way to full fruition.

Let us now consider a sudden increase in credit in period t. Denoting the outstanding stock of credit by Z and the sudden increase by ΔZ (in terms of output), it follows that $2\Delta Z$ new projects could be started in period t. However, the new projects will be completed in period $t + 1$ only if the stock of credit rises by at least an additional ΔZ units. Thus total credit must be equal to at least $Z + 2\Delta Z$ in period $t + 1$ if all projects that started in period t will be completed. As a result, if the "capital inflow" in period t is temporary and total credit, say, stays at $Z + \Delta Z$—higher than the level prior to the capital inflow episode, Z, but lower than $Z + 2\Delta Z$—in period $t + 1$ the equivalent of ΔZ loans will become nonperforming. This illustrates the possibility that a *surge of credit may generate future financial difficulties even though total credit does not shrink and, in fact, continues to rise.* More specifically, financial difficulties could just be caused by an *unexpected slowdown* in external credit.

We now move a step further and ask a natural question: *Under what conditions would credit be taken if there was a possibility of credit discontinuation during the second period of the project?*

Suppose the borrower has enough capital to cover all losses, and let the probability of discontinuation be denoted by q. Under these circumstances, creditors undergo no risk and, hence, continue to charge a zero rate of interest. On the other hand, expected return from the project is now

$$(\beta - 1)(1 - q) - \frac{q}{2}. \tag{25}$$

Therefore, the project will be undertaken by a risk-neutral firm if

$$\beta \geq \frac{2 - q}{2(1 - q)} \geq 1. \tag{26}$$

As expected, condition (26) is more stringent than condition (24), but given $\beta > 1$, there are positive values (in fact, an open interval) that the probability of credit discontinuation q could take for which condition (26) is satisfied and, thus, for which the project will be undertaken.

The above example could be criticized on the grounds that the firm undertaking the project could have used its own capital to bring the project to fruition, instead of using it to repay the project's first-period loan. This problem can easily be taken care of by making the realistic assumption that although the firm will eventually be able to repay creditors in full, it cannot liquidate its other assets quickly enough to prevent a meltdown of the project.

In more realistic situations, especially following a big surge of credit (large KI), the firm's capital is not enough to finish all projects. To see the effect of this, let us examine the polar case in which the firm has no capital. Thus, if the project is discontinued during its second period, first-period credit goes unpaid. We will now show that condition (26) still holds if creditors are risk neutral.

We assume that uncertainty is resolved during the project's second period. Thus the only credit subject to risk is that granted during the first period. Let r_{13} denote the interest rate on a loan that is granted during the project's first period and is due for repayment in the project's third period (i.e., when it becomes fully operative). Since repayment occurs with probability $1 - q$, we have

$$(1 - q)(1 + r_{13}) = 1. \tag{27}$$

Moreover, expected net return from the project is

$$(1 - q)\left(\beta - \frac{1}{2}r_{13} - \frac{1}{2}\right). \tag{28}$$

The project will be undertaken if the expression in large parentheses is greater than or equal to zero—which combined with equation (27) implies condition (26). This result is perfectly intuitive. If creditors foresee any chance of default they will charge it on the interest rate paid when there is no default. Since both creditors and borrowers are risk neutral, they value these transfers equally. Hence, the borrower ends up paying the same in expected value. This neutrality proposition can be easily extended to situations of partial default (i.e., when the firm partially shares in the total loss).

10 Time to Build: Large Capital Inflows, Banks, and Financial Vulnerability

The previous section assumed that firms could not secure future financial commitments to bring a project to completion. If capital markets were perfect, however, such a commitment could be secured at the beginning of a project. As a result, expected profits would be $\beta - 1$, which is higher than in any of the other options considered so far. It is interesting to note, however, that in all serious financial crises of the past twenty years, banks have played a prominent role. Thus there are no serious recent balance-of-payments crises in which banks have not suffered heavy losses and the fiscal authority has not borne a significant share of the cost (see Kaminsky and Reinhart 1995).

The conjecture we explore here is that banks can borrow cheaply because their liabilities provide liquidity services (as in the monetary models of sections 2 and 3). In turn, the *quality* of those services is enhanced by implicit or explicit deposit insurance. This allows banks to offer *their clients* interest rates below the bond market, especially for small and medium-size firms and during a surge of capital inflows.

The preceding paragraph contains several implicit assumptions that we need to flesh out. In the first place, we assume that a bank has much better information about its clients than about the rest of potential borrowers.[22] Thus, if bank deposits surge, the bank will in the short run have incentives to lend to its own clients. In the medium term these incentives will tend to subside as the bank has more time to acquire information about other potential borrowers. However, if bank deposits continue to exhibit strong growth, old clients may continue to have the upper hand with the bank (although loans will start spreading to new clients).

Suppose that on account of the associated liquidity services, the international deposit interest rate is lower than the pure international rate, assumed to be equal to zero. Thus the real rate of interest on deposits is negative. We will denote it by $-\kappa$, for some $\kappa > 0$. Let us assume, for the sake of simplicity, that each firm is a client of several banks, so competition will bring down the loan interest rate to its marginal cost.[23] We assume that banks expect to be fully bailed out in case of an economy-wide financial crisis (thus the government plays a key role in the story). Thus a project's first-period rate of interest for a loan that will be repaid in its third period (if no financial crisis occurs), r_{13}, satisfies

$$r_{13} = 1 - \kappa. \tag{29}$$

The latter assumes no transactions costs of extending the loan to the client firm. The "catch" is, however, that banks cannot ensure second-period financing at those rates. Under normal circumstances, depositors have the highest priority claim to a bank's assets. Thus even liquid funds that have been set aside for a customer would have to be used to repay deposits. The best a bank can normally do for a client is to open a credit line, which is, however, instantly closed if the bank undergoes financial stress. This is a key *institutional* assumption.

For the sake of concreteness, let us consider the case in which the firm can either (1) fund the project's first period through a bank and ensure completion by a forward loan contract in the capital market or (2) finance the entire project through a bank, running the risk of having to stop the project if there is a financial crisis.[24] Expected profit during the third period of option 1 would be

$$\beta - \frac{1 - \kappa}{2} - \frac{1}{2}. \tag{30}$$

Expected profit from option 2, the risky one, would be

$$(1 - q)[\beta - (1 - \kappa)]. \tag{31}$$

Therefore, a necessary and sufficient condition for risky option 2 to dominate riskless option 1 is that expression (31) exceed expression (30)—equivalently, that

$$\frac{1}{2}\kappa - q(\beta - 1 + \kappa) > 0. \tag{32}$$

If $\beta \geq 1$, inequality (32) would never hold if banks could not offer a better deal than the bond market, that is, $\kappa = 0$. However, once $\kappa > 0$, no matter how small, there is always an interval of small enough probabilities of financial collapse q (or, more specifically, probabilities that the project cannot be carried to completion) for which inequality (32) holds.

Consequently, we have presented a framework in which the special nature of banks and the treatment they receive from the fisc may induce a sizable share of new deposits to be lent for projects that would not come to fruition in the event of a freeze in the level of bank deposits. Since in such a case all the new loans will become nonperforming, the fisc will be called in to implement a bailout, triggering the series of negative shocks through the economy that we have amply discussed before.

Notes

The author is grateful to Roberto Rigobon and conference participants for useful comments.

1. It should be pointed out, however, that in the multiple equilibrium literature cited above, the government reaction function plays a central role.

2. Functions u and v are assumed to be twice differentiable, strictly increasing, and concave.

3. For simplicity of exposition, we assume interior solutions.

4. Besides, the discontinuity at $t = 0$ is just allowed in order to illustrate that discontinuities do not change the basic result in eq. (8) below.

5. Again for simplicity, we assume that all prices and the exchange rate are differentiable everywhere for $t > 0$.

6. In this model, as in Krugman (1979), the crisis is accompanied by a sudden collapse in monetary aggregates. This is not borne out in a number of recent experiences (see, e.g., fig. 11.1 below). However, Kumhof (1997) shows that this does not imply a fundamental problem with the model, since the stability of monetary aggregates during currency crises can be rationalized by assuming that liquidity is also provided by short-term government bonds.

7. A crisis in which only external factors are at play is also possible. E.g., consider the case in which $g = 0$ and the nominal international interest rate rises gradually over time. One can make assumptions so as to ensure that the minimum tolerable level for international reserves would be reached due to the associated decline in money demand. Thus a crisis must eventually take place.

8. This is in line with the common assumption in ad hoc Mundell-Fleming-type models that the relevant price level is the nominal price of home goods.

9. This relation is the focus of Calvo, Reinhart, and Végh (1995).

10. Why short-term debt was not automatically rolled over, given Mexico's low total debt, is a key question that will be addressed, albeit indirectly, in the following discussion.

11. However, costs would arise ex post if deposit withdrawals exceed the capacity of the central bank to provide the funds (international reserves) that would prevent banks from crashing.

12. For recent papers extending the Diamond-Dybvig approach to an international context, see Goldfajn and Valdés (1997) and Chang and Velasco (1998). It is worth noting that this approach regains some of its appeal when domestic residents are prevented from keeping their deposits in offshore banks.

13. The intuition for this is that the presence of a sovereign government is like a tax distortion. As is well known, tax distortions have a negative effect on welfare even in the context of complete markets.

14. Friedman and Schwartz (1963) assert that repudiation schemes such as cessation of payments on bank deposits have had deleterious effects in the United States.

15. In the case of Mexico total reserves (including credit lines from its NAFTA partners) barely exceeded US$12 billion. See Calvo and Mendoza (1996).

16. It should be noted, however, that indirect costs would be nil if repudiation or involuntary rescheduling is done in such a clean manner that new lenders do not feel threatened by dealing with a country that resorted to such drastic measures (see Bulow and Rogoff 1989). I think this is an unlikely situation, though. In any other scenario at least short-term lending that is not fully collateralized is likely to dry up.

17. This is the type of example worked out in Calvo (1988) and Cole and Kehoe (1996).

18. Needless to say, these effects would never materialize in a complete market context. That is why this discussion is of special significance for emerging markets.

19. Argentina, Bolivia, Peru, and Uruguay are examples of highly dollarized economies. In Uruguay, e.g., dollar-denominated deposits are about 80 percent of the total.

20. Interenterprise debt consolidation, or netting out, has been used in such countries as Russia and Romania on several occasions after interenterprise arrears (or involuntary credit) became large.

21. This is fully in line with the Bernanke-Gertler view of credit in the U.S. economy, although they do not emphasize the interenterprise credit channel.

22. Therefore, we are imbuing banks with a new feature as compared to our earlier discussion about the role of banks; recall section 3.

23. This is in sharp contrast with the model at the end of section 3, in which the loan interest rate is equal to the pure international interest rate.

24. Thus, we are excluding the possibility of financing the project's first period by a bank loan and, if the bank does not extend credit to finance the project's second period, doing it through the bond market. This exclusion captures, in an admittedly crude way, a situation in which being cut off from bank credit to complete the project sends a negative signal to the market about the quality of the project. Under the above assumptions, therefore, the project will not be funded if lenders require one period of time to evaluate it.

References

Bulow, Jeremy I., and Kenneth Rogoff. 1989. Sovereign debt: Is to forgive to forget? *American Economic Review* 79 (March): 43–50.

Calvo, Guillermo A. 1986. Temporary stabilization: Predetermined exchange rates. *Journal of Political Economy* 94 (December): 1319–29.

———. 1988. Costly trade liberalizations: Durable goods and capital mobility. *IMF Staff Papers* 35 (September): 461–73.

———. 1998a. Varieties of capital-market crises. In *The debt burden and its consequences for monetary policy*, ed. G. A. Calvo and M. King. Proceedings of a conference held by the International Economic Association at the Deutsche Bundesbank. London: Macmillan.

———. 1998b. The "unforgiving" market and the *tequilazo*. In *Financial reform in developing countries*, ed. Jose M. Fanelli and Rohinton Medhore. New York: St. Martin's.

Calvo, Guillermo A., and Fabrizio Coricelli. 1994. Interenterprise arrears in economies in transition. *Empirica* 21:37–54.

Calvo, Guillermo A., Leonardo Leiderman, and Carmen M. Reinhart. 1996. Inflows of capital to developing countries in the 1990s. *Journal of Economic Perspectives* 10, no. 2 (spring): 123–40.

Calvo, Guillermo A., and Enrique G. Mendoza. 1996. Mexico's balance of payments crisis: A chronicle of death foretold. *Journal of International Economics* 41 (November): 235–64.

———. 1997. Rational herding and the globalization of securities markets. College Park: University of Maryland. Manuscript.

Calvo, Guillermo A., Carmen M. Reinhart, and Carlos A. Végh. 1995. Targeting the real exchange rate: Theory and evidence. *Journal of Development Economics* 47:97–133.

Chang, Roberto, and Andrés Velasco. 1998. Financial fragility and the exchange rate regime. Atlanta: Federal Reserve Bank of Atlanta, January. Mimeograph.

Cole, Harold L., and Timothy J. Kehoe. 1996. A self-fulfilling model of Mexico's 1994–1995 debt crisis. *Journal of International Economics* 41 (November): 309–30.

Diamond, Douglas W., and Philip H. Dybvig. 1983. Bank runs, deposit insurance, and liquidity. *Journal of Political Economy* 91 (June): 401–19.

Eichengreen, Barry, Andrew Rose, and Charles Wyplosz. 1995. Exchange market mayhem: The antecedents and aftermath of speculative attacks. *Economic Policy* 21:249–312.

Fernandez, Roque B. 1991. What have populists learned from hyperinflation? In *The macroeconomics of populism in Latin America*, ed. R. Dornbusch and S. Edwards. Chicago: University of Chicago Press.

Friedman, Milton, and Anna J. Schwartz. 1963. *A monetary history of the United States, 1867–1960*. Princeton, N.J.: Princeton University Press.

Goldfajn, Ilan, and Rodrigo Valdés. 1997. Capital flows and the twin crises: The role of liquidity. IMF Working Paper no. 97/87. Washington, D.C.: International Monetary Fund.

Kaminsky, Graciela L., and Carmen M. Reinhart. 1995. Twin crises: The causes of banking and balance of payments problems. Paper presented at conference Speculative Attacks in the Era of the Global Economy: Theory, Evidence, and Policy Implications, Center of International Economics, University of Maryland, College Park, December.

Krugman, Paul R. 1979. A model of balance-of-payments crises. *Journal of Money, Credit, and Banking* 11 (August): 311–25.

Kumhof, Michael. 1997. Balance of payments crises: The role of short-term debt. College Park: University of Maryland. Manuscript.

Obstfeld, Maurice. 1994. The logic of currency crises. *Cahiers Economiques et Monétaires* (Bank of France) 43:189–213.

Obstfeld, Maurice, and Kenneth Rogoff. 1995. The mirage of fixed exchange rates. *Journal of Economic Perspectives* 9:73–96.

Ramey, Valery. 1992. The source of fluctuations in money: Evidence. from trade credit. *Journal of Monetary Economics* 30 (November): 171–94.

World Bank. 1993. *The East Asian miracle: Economic growth and economic policy.* New York: Oxford University Press.

12   Contagion in Emerging Markets: When *Wall Street* Is a Carrier

Guillermo A. Calvo

I Introduction

Prior to the Tequila crisis of 1994/5 in Mexico, balance-of-payments crises in emerging-market economies were quickly attributed to macro-economic mismanagement, the first and foremost suspect always being an 'unsustainable' fiscal deficit. The Mexican crisis questioned this conventional view because the country was coming from a long stability period in which important structural reform projects were undertaken and, on the whole, fiscal deficit had been brought under control. After a little while, however, the conventional wisdom started to change, and consensus began to shift in the direction of focusing not just on the fiscal deficit, but on the current account deficit–undoubtedly a more encompassing measure of a country's deficit. Mexico showed some weaknesses in that respect, because its current account deficit was about 8 percent in 1994 and was programmed to rise to 9 percent in 1995. This was considered 'unsustainable' for Mexico, given its poor growth record.[1]

The new crisis paradigm had hardly begun to fly when Asia fell into disarray. The unsustainability flag could not easily be raised in this instance, especially for countries like Korea and Indonesia. It was then that, for the first time, the conventional wisdom started to pay serious attention to what is likely to be central to all recent crises, namely, financial sector weaknesses.

Looking at the financial sector, one begins to find threads that are common to all emerging markets. A salient aspect was the existence of short-term debt which, in most cases, was denominated in foreign exchange (and, thus, could not be liquidated through devaluation) and, in several instances, a weak and poorly supervised domestic financial system. However, before the pieces of the puzzle could be put together, Russia announced (in August 1998) a surprise partial repudiation of its public debt. Russia's trade with most emerging markets is insignificant (particularly with those located in Latin America), and its GDP represents a scant 1 percent of world's output. However, the shock wave spread all over emerging markets, and even hit financial centers. What happened?

The dominant theory is that—due to market incompleteness and financial vulnerabilities—many economies around the globe, and especially emerging-market economies, exhibit multiple equilibria. No one has yet provided a good theory about equilibrium selection, but multiple-equilibrium models allow to make statements like "upon seeing Russia default, investors thought that other emerging-markets countries would follow suit, tried to pulled out and drove those economies into a crisis equilibrium." Moreover, in a formal model exhibiting multiple equilibria, the crisis can be made consistent with rationality (models that can be adapted to provide that kind of explanation are, for instance, Obstfeld (1994), Calvo (1998b), and Cole and Kehoe [1996]).

In this note I will take a different tack, and explore the underpinnings of a model in which a key factor behind the spread of the Russian shock lies at the heart of the capital market. So I will not shift the focus away from the financial sector, but I will explore the possibility that Wall Street could help spread the virus. The basic ideas have been summarized in Calvo (1998c and 1998d) in an informal way. The present note continues the analysis by providing a more formal discussion of the central insights.

The key notion underlying the models is that knowing about emerging-market economies involves large fixed costs relative to the size of investment projects. Learning about an individual country is costly. One has to learn about its economy and politics, which requires a team of experts constantly monitoring those variables. Economies change at a rapid pace, especially in emerging-market economies with incipient political systems. Thus, monitoring has to be frequent and in depth. However, there is no great cost differential between learning about macro variables in the U.S. and, say, a small country like Paraguay. In fact, a large country like the U.S. may exhibit more stability in its macro variables, making frequent monitoring less necessary. Therefore, fixed learning costs may be especially relevant for small emerging-market economies.

Fixed costs generate economies of scale and, hence, the financial industry is likely to organize itself around *clusters of specialists*. This makes it plausible to assume that there exists a set of informed and a set of uninformed investors. The former likely leverage their portfolios (those who know better about a given project have incentives to borrow to finance it) and, thus, are potentially liable to margin calls.[2] In fact, to all accounts, important specialists invested in Russian debt and were subject to margin calls as its value plunged after repudiation. Section II starts from this observation and presents two models for explaining the behavior of the uninformed. In both models, the problem faced by the uninformed is that they can only observe price and, occasionally, some details of the investment strategy followed by specialists. However, if they see the latter selling emerging-market securities, or, more simply, staying out of auctions of new bonds, for example, they could not tell exactly whether it reflects negative information about those securities or that the specialists were subject to margin calls. Thus, they face a "signal extraction" problem. The first model in Section II will show an example in which if the volatility of emerging-markets returns is high relative to, say, margin calls, then it will be rational to attach high probability that the signal received by the uninformed reflects conditions in emerging markets. The second model in Section II gets essentially the same result in terms of a more elementary setup. Thus, these models help to rationalize a situation in which the capital market (the uninformed part of it) took the events surrounding the Russian shock as indication that there were fundamental problems with emerging markets in general, and tried to pull their funds from all of them. The Appendix shows that these phenomena can be captured in terms of a general equilibrium model, patterned after Grossman and Stiglitz (1980). The main difference with the latter is that I assume that the uninformed can observe informed investors' trades, albeit imprecisely.

Section III explores "multiplier" effects that magnify the initial shock. It pursues some ideas developed in Calvo (1998d) according to which a sudden stop in capital inflows (provoked by the Russian shock, for example) can wreak havoc on financial systems, unless financial contracts are indexed to the sudden-stop state of nature (which is unlikely when the shock comes via Russia and margin calls in Wall Street). It will be argued that this channel may give rise to multiple equilibria, but the relatively novel insight is that, even under equilibrium uniqueness, the sudden-stop channel may produce multiplier effects that help to magnify the initial shock. Section IV concludes, and discusses possible extensions.

II   Signal Extraction: Two Simple Models

This section will discuss two simple models in which rational but imperfectly informed individuals may take a signal emitted by informed investors as a good indicator of prospects in emerging markets. The signal is imperfect and sometimes reflects conditions inherent to informed investors—like the margin calls that reportedly took place after Russia decided to repudiate some of its debt—and provide no information on emerging markets. Thus, these models show that emerging markets could be innocent victims of shocks that lie completely outside their realm and control. This insight is further explored in the Appendix in terms of a complete general equilibrium framework.

Model 1

Informed investors take an observable (for the uninformed investors) action y (e.g., buy emerging markets bonds). This action is motivated by a combination of the following two variables: s and m. Variable s is an accurate signal of returns on emerging market securities: the larger is s, the larger is the return. This is the variable that uninformed investors would like to know (not y). In turn, variable m reflects factors that are relevant only for the informed (e.g., margin calls, profitability of investment projects available to informed investors only, see Wang (1994)). For simplicity, we assume that

$$y = s - m. \tag{1}$$

Uninformed individuals are able to observe y, and are assumed to know the unconditional distribution of s and m. Informed individuals know the exact value of the two variables.

Let $s \sim n(\bar{s}, \sigma^2)$, and $m \sim n(0, \tau^2)$, where function n denotes normal distribution and, as usual, the first argument denotes the mean and the second the variance of the associated random variable. These are the *unconditional* distributions of s and m. Upon observing y, however, the uninformed can compute the *conditional* distribution of s and m (conditional on y, of course). In particular, it can be shown that if m and s are stochastically independent, the conditional distribution for s is $n(\theta y + (1 - \theta)\bar{s}, \theta\tau^2)$, where $\theta = \sigma^2/(\sigma^2 + \tau^2)$. The intuitive plausibility of the result can be appreciated in limiting cases.[3] Thus, for example, if τ is very close to zero, the idiosyncratic variable m would be nearly a constant and, hence, it is plausible to attribute most of the change in y to changes in s. That is precisely what the formula implies since in that case $\tau^2 \simeq 0$ and $\theta \simeq 1$. Notice that while the conditional mean of s is a function of the observed variable y, its conditional variance is not.

The case $\theta \simeq 1$ is very interesting because it shows the possibility that uninformed investors will react very strongly even though the change in y is provoked, say, by margin calls. Our formal results imply that one can get $\theta \simeq 1$ even though τ^2 is "large." For, what is actually required is that τ^2 be small *relative to* σ^2. A characteristic of emerging-markets economies is the relatively high volatility of variables like terms of trade (see Hausmann and Rojas-Suarez [1996]), which will be reflected in large σ^2. On the other hand, margin calls and serious liquidity problems in Wall Street are likely to be more the exception than the rule. Consequently, the case for σ^2/τ^2 large is not hard to make. In this context, the Russian shock can be interpreted as the outcome of a large positive shock to m, e.g., large margin calls, which resulted in a sizable cut in observed y.

Model 2

In contrast with previous model, we assume that s and m can take two values indicated by $x^L < x^H$, $x = s, m$. Observable variable y also takes two values $y^L < y^H$, as follows:

$$y = y^H \quad \text{if } s = s^H \quad \text{and} \quad m = m^L,$$
$$y = y^L, \quad \text{otherwise.} \tag{2}$$

This captures a situation in which the informed send a negative signal (i.e., $y = y^L$) if either they get negative information about the profitability of emerging-markets securities (i.e., $s = s^L$), or they are subject to, say, margin calls (i.e., $m = m^H$). Otherwise, they send a positive signal (i.e., $y = y^H$). Again, we assume that variables m and s are stochastically independent.

Hence, the set of possible events $\Omega = \{(s^L, m^L), (s^L, m^H), (s^H, m^L), (s^H, m^H)\}$, and

$$P(s^L/y^L) = \frac{P(s^L)}{1 - P(s^H)P(m^L)}, \tag{3}$$

where P is the probability measure on Ω. As a result, as $P(m^L) \to 1$, we have $P(s^L/y^L) \to 1$. Therefore, again, uninformed investors are going to attach a large probability to the "bad" outcome (i.e., $s = s^L$) after observing $y = y^L$ if the "bad" idiosyncratic shock (i.e., m^H) has low probability.

III   Sudden Stop. Multiplier Effect

Extensions to a dynamic setting could rationalize positive and negative shocks to emerging markets coming from Wall Street but, unless one introduces serial correlation, there will be a quick reversion to the mean. Serial correlation could be introduced through random variables s and/or m, but this is not a satisfactory modeling strategy. Much better would be to obtain serial correlation from fundamental economic considerations. Moreover, if the analysis rested there, large shocks to emerging markets would be predicated on the existence of equivalently large Wall Street shocks. This is possible, but more interesting would be to identify mechanisms that *magnify* Wall Street shocks. The present section will identify "multiplier" effects, and channels that might contribute to serial correlation in dynamic settings.

I have argued elsewhere that a sudden stop (i.e., a sizable and largely unanticipated stop) in capital inflows could result in a collapse of marginal productivity of capital in emerging-markets economies (Calvo [1998c]). One can formalize this situation by postulating that the unconditional mean of s, $\bar{s}$, is decreasing function of the (relative) size of the sudden stop. Let production in emerging-market economies be proportional to their capital stock, k, and the factor of proportionality be given by s. Consider Model 1 above. Suppose that the return on projects outside emerging-market economies is normally-distributed. Thus, in the context of a one-period portfolio choice model, one could write the demand for k as a function of the conditional expectation of s only (recall that the variance of the conditional distribution for s is constant with respect to y and $\bar{s}$). The higher is y or $\bar{s}$, the larger will be the demand for emerging-markets securities. More specifically,

$$k = K(\theta y + (1 - \theta)\bar{s}), \quad K' > 0, \tag{4}$$

for some differentiable function K.

The sudden-stop effect can be captured by postulating that the unconditional expectation of s is a positive function of the difference between k and, say, its expected value from previous period's perspective. Taking the latter as given, one can thus simply write

$$\bar{s} = \Phi(k), \quad \Phi'(k) > 0, \tag{5}$$

for some differentiable function Φ. Function Φ is likely to be concave as a drop in k is likely to have a larger impact than an equivalent rise.

By equations (4) and (5),

$$k = K(\theta y + (1 - \theta)\Phi(k)). \tag{6}$$

The expression on the right-hand side of equation (6) is an increasing function of k. Therefore, the sudden-stop effect is capable of giving rise to *multiplicity of equilibria*. This is possible because, for example, a smaller k lowers the expected marginal productivity of capital (i.e., lowers $\bar{s}$), which induces a lower demand for k. But even in cases where equilibrium is unique, the sudden-stop component implies interesting results. Thus, for instance, assuming $(1 - \theta)K'\Phi' < 1$, we get, by totally differentiating expression (6) with respect to y,

$$\frac{dk}{dy} = \frac{\theta K'}{1 - (1 - \theta)K'\Phi'} > \theta K' > 0. \tag{7}$$

The direct impact of y on k is $\theta K'$ but, by (7), the impact is magnified by multiplier $1/[1 - (1 - \theta)K'\Phi'] > 1$.

Interestingly, the direct impact of y on k increases with θ—which, by last section's analysis is attributed to a larger relative variance of the marginal productivity of capital—while the multiplier is lower as θ rises. The net effect of a rise in θ is ambiguous. To show it, differentiate (7) with respect to θ; thus,

$$\frac{\partial}{\partial \theta}\left(\frac{dk}{dy}\right) = \frac{K'(1 - K'\Phi')}{[1 - (1 - \theta)K'\Phi']^2}. \tag{8}$$

The bracketed expression in the numerator of the right-hand side of expression (8) can be of either sign.

Modeling the Demand for Emerging Markets Securities, K

Calvo (1998b) and Calvo and Mendoza (1998) show that as the capital market gets more globalized, the response of investors to news about expected returns (as a proportion of a country's investment) may increase without bound.

It is worth noting that K'/K will also be large if K is "small" (one way of characterizing emerging markets), and K' is somewhat invariant to

K (i.e., total investment in emerging markets). Thus, for example, this property would hold in a portfolio model in which returns are normally distributed and the utility function exhibits constant absolute risk aversion, because *K* is linear in the rate of return ($= s$, in this paper's notation) and, hence, K' is totally invariant with respect to *K* (see the Appendix).

These examples illustrate the possibility that being small in a globalized capital market may make K'/K large, magnifying the damage caused by a negative signal coming from the capital market. (For further discussion, see the Appendix.)

IV Final Words

The key insight of the above analysis is that under asymmetric information, rational but imperfectly informed investors could react very strongly to signals emitted by informed individuals. Those signals, in turn, may be due to factors that are relevant to informed individuals (e.g., margin calls) but that bear no relationship to fundamentals in emerging-markets economies. Moreover, sudden-stop effects contribute to the existence of multiple equilibria, and may give rise to multiplier effects. These elements help to explain why the Russian shock so virulently spread beyond Russia and still lingers on after a long period in which it has become apparent that much of the global turmoil was caused by problems in the capital market itself (e.g., margin calls), and little or nothing to new problems in emerging-market economies (except Russia).

The chapter does not discuss how the signal is emitted by the informed. This is an important issue that may be left for another occasion. However, it is worth pointing out that specialists may send a negative signal even if they do not run down their stock of emerging-markets securities. This is so because emerging markets exhibit current account deficits that need financing. Thus, absence (or diminished presence) of specialists in the auctioning of new emerging-markets securities is likely to be noticed and taken as a negative signal.

This note places special emphasis on *quantity* signals, while much of the traditional finance literature has focused on *price* signals (e.g., Grossman and Stiglitz [1980], Wang [1994]). I feel that price signals are less relevant in emerging markets because those markets have a relatively short life span and have exhibited sizable volatility, largely unrelated to 'fundamentals.'[4] However, assuming that the uniformed pay attention to price signals will not in general eliminate the effects highlighted in this paper. Actually, price signals could aggravate the effects on margin calls (as shown in Genotte and Leland [1990] and, more recently, Kodres and Pritsker [1998]).

The chapter assumes the existence of one homogeneous emerging-markets security. Extensions are straightforward. A simple extension is to assume that there is a variety of securities, indexed by $i = 1, \ldots, I$. Let us assume that (1) the returns on securities are mutually independent random variables, (2) the unconditional distribution for the return on security i is $n(\bar{s}, \sigma^2)$, the same for all i, and (3) there is an observable variable associated with each security $y_i = s_i - m$. Then, if there exists a large number of securities, uninformed investors could closely estimate m and, in that fashion, approximately pinpoint the value of each s_i.

However, the assumption of a common m shock in all the y_i equations is hard to justify in a context where there are sizable fixed information costs. Under those conditions, there will be few investors who are informed about *all* emerging markets. Most of them are likely to specialize on a few of them. Thus, the polar case in which there exists and m-type shock for each y_i, e.g., $y_i = s_i - m_i$, where m_i are mutually stochastically independent could be a better approximation. Clearly, increasing the number of markets in this case yields no informational bonus. Actually, Calvo and Mendoza (1999) show examples where incentives to collect information declines with the number of markets, which would worsen the forecast-error problem.

The above models are static, while sudden-stop effects are essentially dynamic. An unexpected change in the demand for emerging-markets securities causes disruptions in the financial sector because (in a richer, though straightforward, model) it brings about unexpected changes in relative prices. Thus, in a realistic scenario with incomplete financial contracts (in which, for instance, the loan rate of interest is not made contingent on variables like y), a change in relative prices may cause bankruptcy and, through that channel, bring about a fall in the marginal productivity of capital. However, these effects are likely transitory. As firms are dismantled, new firms will spring to life. Thus, the initial drop in the marginal productivity of capital may be followed by a renaissance in which marginal productivity increases over time and even overshoots its value prior to crisis.

A deeper analysis, of course, will have to rationalize why loan interest rates are not indexed to observables like y. One answer is that y

may be observable but hard to *verify* (Townsend [1976]). Another is that indexation to y is likely to be a function of the indexation rules adopted in other contracts since, for example, a given firm's financial difficulties likely depend on the financial situation of its clients and suppliers (through the interenterprise-credit channel, for example)—the latter, in turn, being a function of the adopted indexation formulas. The complexity of the problem may be so great that one could possibly invoke bounded-rationality considerations for market incompleteness.

APPENDIX

I will show that the asymmetric-information results discussed in Section II can be obtained in a conventional general equilibrium context in which the uninformed make their forecasts on the basis of *quantity* decisions taken by the informed (extensions to the case in which uninformed investors also look at prices are discussed later in the Appendix).

I will borrow the basic framework from Grossman and Stiglitz (1980), GS. There are two periods (*present* and *future*), and two assets: a safe asset (a pure bond, say) yielding ρ units of future output, and a risky asset yielding r units of future output (this asset could be identified as an "emerging-markets assets"). Let us assume

$$r = s + \varepsilon, \quad s \sim n(\bar{s}, \sigma^2), \quad \varepsilon \sim n(0, \omega^2). \tag{9}$$

Informed investors will be assumed to know s but no ε. Thus, contrary to Section II, information is incomplete, even for informed investors. This is a necessary assumption in the present context—in which, following GS, I allow for unlimited short sales—to ensure a well-defined optimal portfolio. Letting $\bar{b}_i$ and $\bar{x}_i$ denote the initial stock of the safe and risky assets, respectively, held by investor i, his budget constraint satisfies:

$$px_i + b_i = p\bar{x}_i + \bar{b}_i, \tag{10}$$

where x_i, b_i, and p stand for the demand for the risky and safe assets by investor i, and the present output price of the risky asset in terms of the safe asset, respectively. Thus, future wealth of individual i, W_i, satisfies:

$$W_i = \rho b_i + rx_i. \tag{11}$$

The utility function exhibits constant absolute risk aversion, CARA, and thus can be expressed as follows:

$$-e^{-\alpha W_i}, \quad \alpha > 0, \tag{12}$$

where α is the coefficient of absolute risk aversion.

As noted, informed investors know s but not ε (only its distribution). On the other hand, uninformed investors know the distribution of both variables, but can directly observe neither. Within each type, investors are identical. Thus, I will use subindex I and U to indicate the per capita portfolio choices of the informed and uninformed investors, respectively.

I will assume that all the random variables defined here are mutually stochastically independent. Under these assumptions, the informed investors' optimal portfolio can be shown to satisfy (see GS):

$$x_I = \frac{s - \rho p}{\alpha \omega^2}. \tag{13}$$

Uninformed investors are not totally in the dark about s. They do not have a long and stable stock market series from which they can infer something about s, but I will assume that they can observe the actions of the informed, subject to some noise z. Formally, I assume that the uninformed can observe $\tilde{x}$, where[5]

$$\tilde{x} = x_I - z, \quad z \sim n(0, \kappa^2). \tag{14}$$

Thus, by (13) and (14),

$$\tilde{x} = \frac{s - \rho p}{\alpha \omega^2} - z. \tag{15}$$

Hence,

$$y \equiv \tilde{x} \alpha \omega^2 + \rho p = s - m, \quad m \equiv \alpha \omega^2 z. \tag{16}$$

Moreover, if we set $\tau^2 = \alpha^2 \omega^4 \kappa^2$, it follows that $m \sim n(0, \tau^2)$. Uninformed investors observe y and, on that basis, infer the statistical properties of s. This is precisely the problem solved in the first model in Section II. Let us denote by r^e random variable r after observing y. Then, it follows that $r^e \sim n(\theta y + (1 - \theta)\bar{s}, \theta \tau^2 + \omega^2)$, where, again, $\theta = \sigma^2/(\sigma^2 + \tau^2)$. Hence, optimal portfolio for the uninformed satisfies:

$$x_U = \frac{\theta y + (1 - \theta)\bar{s} - \rho p}{\alpha(\theta \tau^2 + \omega^2)}. \tag{17}$$

Therefore, by (16) and (17), we get,

$$x_U = \frac{\theta(s - \alpha\omega^2 z) + (1 - \theta)\bar{s} - \rho p}{\alpha(\theta\tau^2 + \omega^2)}. \tag{18}$$

Notice that, as expected, if informed and uninformed have the same information (i.e., $z = 0$, $\kappa^2 = 0$), we have $\theta = 1$, and equation (18) boils down to (13). In all other cases, however, signaling error, represented by z, is a factor in the portfolio decisions of the uninformed.

The model is closed by imposing equilibrium conditions. Assuming a fixed net supply of assets, and assuming total supply of the risky asset equals 1, we can state the general equilibrium condition as follows:

$$\lambda x_I + (1 - \lambda)x_U = 1, \tag{19}$$

where λ is the share of informed investors in total population, and total population is set equal to unity. A brief look at equations (13) and (18) shows that, given s and z, equation (19) determines p. Moreover, p increases with s and declines with z (or m). The impact of z depends positively on the share of uninformed. Thus, given the motivation behind these notes (where m plays a prominent role), it is useful to examine the extreme case in which the informed investors are of measure zero, i.e., $\lambda = 0$. By (18) and (19), we have $x_U = 1$, which implies

$$p = \frac{\theta(s - \alpha\omega^2 z) + (1 - \theta)\bar{s} - \alpha(\theta\tau^2 + \omega^2)}{\rho}. \tag{20}$$

Therefore,

$$\frac{\partial p}{\partial z} = -\frac{\theta\alpha\omega^2}{\rho} = -\frac{\sigma^2}{\sigma^2 + \tau^2}\frac{\alpha}{\rho}\omega^2, \tag{21}$$

which increases in absolute value as κ^2/σ^2 declines. Thus, we have obtained the same type of result that we got in the first model of Section II: misinformation has an increasingly large impact on prices or quantities as the relative volatility of misinformation goes to zero. Notice that, as in the text, the relevant concept is κ^2/σ^2, not just κ^2.

In the present model we also get results about the distribution of prices, which paint a similar picture. Thus, by (20), the unconditional expectation of $p = \bar{s}/\rho$, i.e., it equals (as one would have guessed) the expected return on the risky asset divided by the gross return on the safe asset, while its unconditional variance is

$$\frac{1}{\rho^2} \frac{\sigma^4}{\sigma^2 + \tau^2} = \frac{\theta\sigma^2}{\rho^2}, \tag{22}$$

which, once again, increases as κ^2 declines. However, the existence of uninformed investors *reduces* price volatility. Notice, for instance, that if $\lambda = 1$ and, thus, the uninformed investors are nil, we have, by (13) and (19), that the unconditional variance of p would be

$$\frac{\sigma^2}{\rho^2}, \tag{23}$$

which is larger than the expression in (22).

Sudden Stop effects discussed in Section III are easily captured if one assumes that the unconditional expectation of s, i.e., $\bar{s}$, is an increasing function of p. For instance, assuming $\bar{s} = \hat{s} + \beta p$, where $\hat{s}$ is some fixed parameter, expression (20) becomes

$$p = \frac{\theta(s - \alpha\omega^2 z) + (1 - \theta)\hat{s} - \alpha(\theta\tau^2 + \omega^2)}{\rho - \beta(1 - \theta)}. \tag{24}$$

I will focus on the case in which the denominator is positive, since it (plausibly) implies a positive association between s and equilibrium p. Armed with this result, it is straightforward to show, for instance, that the variance of equilibrium price becomes

$$\frac{\theta\sigma^2}{[\rho - (1 - \theta)\beta]^2}. \tag{25}$$

Thus, the unconditional variance of p is larger, the larger is the SS effect, β. Interestingly, the SS effect vanishes as κ^2/σ^2 goes to zero. This is so because for κ^2/σ^2 small, the uninformed respond almost exclusively to informed investors' behavior, and tend to ignore a priori information about s. However, SS effects are likely to increase the variance of s, σ^2, a channel that is disregarded in this analysis.

Would equilibrium change if the uninformed extracted information from prices? The answer is "no" in the extreme case examined earlier in which the informed are of measure zero. Prices would just reflect what the uninformed learn from the informed investors' *trades*, and nothing else. The information obtained by informed investors does not get reflected in prices because they are insignificant players. However, if $\lambda > 0$, prices will convey additional information. Conceivably, information contained in prices could be so good that the uninformed will altogether stop looking at trades. This would be the case at equilibria in which prices are fully revealing, i.e., p reveals s (an example is shown below). However, if prices are not fully revealing (see, for instance, the examples discussed in GS), the uninformed investors would still have incentives to use information about informed investors' trades. This implies that the effects highlighted in this paper will still hold in the richer model. It would, however, be interesting to gain a deeper understanding about the interaction between price and quantity signals as the share of the informed investors, and other parameters are varied.

It is useful to contrast the equilibrium concept developed above with the one in GS. GS assumes that individuals can observe market prices but not quantities. Interestingly, under the GS assumptions, there exists an equilibrium in which the uninformed would be able have *exactly the same information* as informed investors! To see this, let us assume that the statement holds true. Thus, since both types have the same utility function, the equilibrium condition in the risky-asset market will be, recalling (13) and (19),

$$\frac{s - \rho p}{\alpha \omega^2} = 1. \tag{26}$$

Therefore, in that equilibrium s would be fully revealed by prices (since $s = \alpha \omega^2 + \rho p$).[6] Clearly, as pointed out above, if the economy settles down to this equilibrium, uninformed investors will have no incentive to learn about informed investors' trades.[7]

Notes

A rough version of these notes was presented at the AEA 1999 New York Meetings, and at the Winter Camp in International Finance, organized by the Center for International Economics (University of Maryland) and the Faculty of Economics (Universidad de los Andes, Bogota, Colombia) in Cartagena, Colombia, January 7–11, 1999. I would like to acknowledge with thanks useful comments by Enrique Mendoza, Maury Obstfeld, and other seminar participants.

1. In Calvo (1998a) I have argued that the analysis underlying the sustainability of current account deficits leaves much to be desired, but the topic will not be discussed because it is not central for our purposes here.

2. The economics of margin calls or, more generally, of collaterals will not be discussed in this chapter.

3. The model is isomorphic to that underlying the Lucas Supply Function in Lucas (1976).

4. However, financial analysts seem to pay a great deal of attention to sovereign bonds prices.

5. GS assumes that the total supply of the risky asset is random and the uninformed cannot observe it directly. Our results carry over to that case with just minor formal changes. The present assumption, however, will help to draw a sharp distinction between *quantity* and *price* signals.

6. This equilibrium concept makes sense only if $\lambda > 0$. Otherwise, prices cannot convey information about s. When $\lambda = 0$, the uninformed entirely rely on their prior information. This "discontinuity" at $\lambda = 0$, is key to the GS examples displaying nonexistence of equilibrium when λ is endogenously determined.

7. This is an imprecise statement in a static framework like ours. More precise would be to say that "if investors believe that the other investors believe that equilibrium prices satisfy equation (22), then the uninformed would have no incentive to learn about informed investors' trades, and equation (22) will be satisfied at equilibrium."

References

Calvo, Guillermo A., 1998a, "The 'Unforgiving' Market and the *Tequilazo*," in *Financial Reform in Developing Countries*, edited by J. M. Fanelli and R. Medhora; London: Macmillan Press Ltd.

Calvo, Guillermo A., 1998b, "Varieties of Capital Market Crises," in G. A. Calvo and M. King (editors) *The Debt Burden and its Consequences for Monetary Policy*, chapter 7; London: Macmillan Press Ltd.

Calvo, Guillermo A., 1998c, "Understanding the Russian Virus—with special reference to Latin America," paper presented at the Deutsche Bank's conference "Emerging Markets: can they be crisis free?," Washington, DC, October 3, 1998.

Calvo, Guillermo A., 1998d, "Capital Flows and Capital Market Crises: The Simple Economics of Sudden Stops," *Journal of Applied Economics*, vol. 1, no. 1, November, pp. 35–54.

Calvo, Guillermo A., and Enrique G. Mendoza, 2000, "Rational Contagion and the Globalization of Securities Markets," *Journal of International Economics*, June, pp. 79–113.

Cole, Harold L., and Timothy J. Kehoe, 1996, "A Self-Fulfilling Model of Mexico's 1994–95 Debt Crisis," *Journal of International Economics*, September.

Gennotte, Gerard, and Hayne Leland, 1990, "Market Liquidity, Hedging, and Crashes," *American Economic Review*, vol. 80, no. 5, December, pp. 999–1021.

Grossman, Sanford J., and Joseph E. Stiglitz, 1980, "On the Impossibility of Informationally Efficient Markets," *American Economic Review*, vol. 70, June, pp. 393–408.

Hausmann, Ricardo, and Liliana Rojas-Suarez (editors), 1996, *Volatile Capital Flows: Taming Their Impact on Latin America*, Washington: Inter-American Development Bank.

Kodres, Laura E., and Matthew Pritsker, 1998, "A Rational Expectations Model of Financial Contagion," manuscript, October.

Lucas Jr., Robert E., 1976, "Econometric Policy Evaluation: A Critique," *Carnegie-Rochester Conference Series on Public Policy*, vol. 1.

Obstfeld, Maurice, 1994, "The Logic of Currency Crises," *Cahiers Economiques et Monetaries*, no. 43, Banque de France.

Townsend, Robert M., 1976, "Optimal Contracts and Competitive Markets with Costly State Verification," *Journal of Economic Theory*, vol. 21, October, pp. 265–293.

Wang, Jiang, 1994, "A Model of Competitive Stock Trading Volume," *Journal of Political Economy*, vol. 102, no. 1, February, pp. 127–168.

13

Explaining Sudden Stop, Growth Collapse, and BOP Crisis: The Case of Distortionary Output Taxes

Guillermo A. Calvo

Since Mexico's tequila crisis of 1994/5, emerging market economies (EM) have entered a period of recurrent crises that go far beyond currency crises as experienced in advanced economies. EM crises are characterized by sharp recession, high unemployment, and an alarming rise in the number of people living below the poverty line. A common feature of these episodes is a *sudden stop* (SS), namely, a large reduction in the flow of international capital.[1] This is illustrated in table 13.1 which, incidentally, shows that the phenomenon predates the tequila crisis. Moreover, Calvo and Reinhart (2001) show that, on the whole, SS is absent in advanced countries. This leads me to the conjecture that SS is perhaps the central feature of EM crises from which all the others follow. Developing a theory that rationalizes the conjecture is a challenging task because EM crises have not been preceded by sharply deteriorating fundamentals (see Calvo and Mendoza, 1996a and b, for the case of Mexico). Thus, to model this fact, the theory should ideally be able to display market equilibrium discontinuity as a function of market fundamentals.

The basic model presented at the outset exhibits equilibrium discontinuity. A key assumption is that government expenditure has to be partly financed by output taxes, which, by their nature, lower the after-tax marginal value productivity of capital. Thus, the larger is government expenditure, the lower will be the rate of growth. There is a region, however, where high and low growth equilibria coexist. The intuition for this is straightforward: high (low) growth implies low (high) tax rates, sustaining high (low) growth. The model assumes that international financial institutions (IFIs) will realize that equilibrium indeterminacy is all a matter of expectations, and will help to coordinate the high-growth equilibrium. Thus, equilibrium is unique.[2] A

Table 13.1
Sudden Stop

Country/Episode	SS (percentage of GDP)
Argentina, 1982–83	20
Argentina, 1994–95	4
Chile, 1981–83	7
Chile,[1] 1990–91	8
Ecuador, 1995–96	19
Hungary, 1995–96	7
Indonesia, 1996–97	5
Malaysia,[1] 1993–94	15
Mexico, 1981–83	12
Mexico, 1993–95	6
Philippines, 1996–97	7
Venezuela, 1992–94	9
Korea, 1996–97	11
Thailand, 1996–97	26
Turkey, 1993–94	10

Sources: Calvo and Reinhart (2000) from World Bank, *World Debt Tables*, various issues; and Institute for International Economics, *Comparative Statistics for Emerging Market Economies, 1998.*
1. Sudden stop owing to the introduction of controls on capital inflows.

discontinuity will take place, however, at the point where multiplicity disappears, and only low growth can be sustained. This happens in the model when government expenditure, summarized by the stock of public debt, that has to be serviced by output taxes, reaches a critical level. If the economy is near that critical level, seemingly minor accidents, like a deterioration of the terms of trade or an increase in country risk, could throw the economy into the region where only low growth is sustainable. Moreover, since investment collapses, a SS will take place. The model is then extended to account for nontradable or home goods. In that context, it is shown that if the crisis contains an unanticipated component, then the SS will be accompanied by an increase in the real exchange rate (i.e., *real* devaluation).[3]

Finally, the model is extended to incorporate money in a cash-in-advance fashion. Since money demand is positively correlated with aggregate demand, a collapse of the latter (discussed at the end of last paragraph) would bring about a drop in the demand for money. Thus, if the exchange rate is fixed, international reserves will fall precipitously, resembling a BOP crisis. The monetary economy is then employed to study optimal exchange rate policy in response to SS. Since SS is, after all, a cut in total credit, it may be optimal for the central bank to release some of its international reserves (e.g., through credit subsidy) to relieve the impact of SS on the private sector, especially when the new credit conditions contain an important surprise element. Under the usual rules that dictate the operation of a central bank, the latter can release reserves by expanding domestic credit and pegging the exchange rate; pure floating would not do because, in that case, international reserves will remain intact. This reaction to SS has been quite common in EM. Therefore, the central bank may end up *precipitating* the BOP crisis. This policy, incidentally, is criticized in the paper by indicating that the recipients of central bank largesse may not be the intended target. The paper argues that if policymakers understand this difficulty, they may be driven to experiment with heterodox policies (like directing credit to specific sectors).

I Basic Model

The basic structure of this model is taken from Calvo (1998c) which, in turn, is a dynamic extension of Eaton (1987). I will start by examining the case of an economy that produces tradable output by means of tradable capital, K. The production function is linear homogeneous: one unit of output is produced by means of $1/\alpha$ units of capital. The net cash flow, S, for a firm that accumulates capital at the rate $\dot{K}$ is given by (assuming away capital depreciation):

$$S_t = \alpha(1 - \tau)K_t - \dot{K}_t, \tag{1}$$

where τ, $0 \leq \tau \leq 1$, denotes the constant output tax rate. Thus, denoting the constant international real interest rate (i.e., the own rate of return on output) by r, the value of the firm at time zero, V, is given by:

$$V = \int_0^\infty S_t e^{-rt} \, dt. \tag{2}$$

Hence, assuming that $K_0 = 1$, and setting $z \equiv \dot{K}/K$ yields:

$$V = \int_0^\infty [\alpha(1 - \tau) - z_t] e^{-\int_0^t (r - z_s) \, ds} \, dt. \tag{3}$$

Notice, incidentally, that given linear technology, z equals the rate of output growth.

The firm is assumed to maximize V by choosing the growth path z, taking as given the international interest rate r, the tax rate τ, and the technological constraints. A quick inspection of this problem shows that the optimum can be found among the constant-z paths, in which case equation (3) can be expressed as:

$$V = \frac{\alpha(1 - \tau) - z}{r - z}. \tag{4}$$

Differentiating the right-hand side of equation (4) with respect to z, yields

$$\operatorname{sgn} \frac{\partial V}{\partial z} = \operatorname{sgn}[\alpha(1 - \tau) - r]. \tag{5}$$

As expected, therefore, the firm will grow as fast (slow) as possible if the net of tax marginal productivity of capital exceeds (falls short of) the rate of interest. Thus, in order to obtain well-defined solutions, one must constraint z to a finite interval, and $z < r$. Concretely, I will assume that there exists some $\bar{z} > 0$ such that $0 \leq z \leq \bar{z} < r$. Setting 0 as the lower bound implies that capital cannot be unbolted; thus, the model belongs to the putty-clay family.

The next step is to endogenize the tax rate τ. I will assume that the government inherits a stock of debt D, a share θ of which has to be serviced by means of output taxes. Again, assuming that the government has full access to capital markets, the tax rate τ must be such that:

$$\theta D = \alpha \tau \int_0^\infty K_t e^{-rt} \, dt = \frac{\alpha \tau}{r - z}. \tag{6}$$

Thus, using equation (6) in expression (5), we get the following fundamental relationship:

$$\operatorname{sgn} \frac{\partial V}{\partial z} = \operatorname{sgn}[\alpha - \theta D(r - z) - r]. \tag{7}$$

Notice that the bracketed expression in equation (7) increases with z. Thus, the low-growth equilibrium (LGE), i.e., $z = 0$, is possible if:

$$\alpha - \theta Dr - r < 0. \tag{8}$$

In other words, LGE exists if as firms set $z = 0$, they have no incentive, by expression (8), to revise their choice. It is worth noting, however, that this does not rule out the existence of other equilibria.

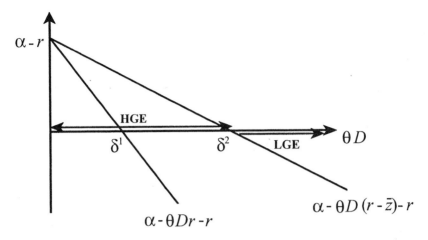

Figure 13.1
Equilibrium determination

On the other hand, by a similar reasoning, the high-growth equilibrium (HGE), i.e., $z = \bar{z}$ exists if:

$$\alpha - \theta D(r - \bar{z}) - r > 0. \tag{9}$$

The left-hand-side functions in expressions (8) and (9) are drawn in figure 13.1.[4] Clearly, LGE exists if $\theta D > \delta^1 = (\alpha - r)/r$, while HGE exists if $\theta D < \delta^2 = (\alpha - r)/(r - \bar{z})$. Thus, indeterminacy exists in the interval (δ^1, δ^2). However, coordination among investors could drive the economy to the HGE. Success of this policy could be greatly aided by strong support from IFIs, requiring, in principle, no public sector resources. For, eliminating the bad LGE in the indeterminacy region is, in principle, a costless operation. Thus, I will assume that if LGE and HGE coexist, the economy will always settle at the HGE.[5]

Consequently, the model implies high growth if $\theta D \leq \delta^2$, and low growth (actually, zero growth) otherwise. Equilibrium discontinuity (see figure 13.2) is a key result because it helps to rationalize situations in which, all of a sudden, a roaring tiger becomes a whining pussycat. This feature is, unfortunately, somewhat clouded in the present model, given that linear production functions generate, as a general rule, corner solutions. Thus, the equilibrium discontinuity highlighted here may appear as a trivial and uninteresting proposition. To dispel that view the Appendix will "smooth the edges" of this model by assuming adjustment costs to investment. As shown there, under uniqueness, growth is a continuous and negative function of D. It takes equilibrium

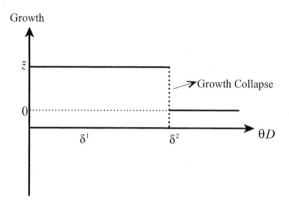

Figure 13.2
Equilibrium growth

multiplicity as depicted in the above model (prior to the equilibrium-selection criterion adopted here, which, in case of indeterminacy, picks the one yielding the highest growth) to generate discontinuity. Growth discontinuity takes place as the systems loses a good equilibrium and plunges to an equilibrium exhibiting lower growth. Notice that, although equilibrium multiplicity is a necessary condition to obtain growth collapse, it is not sufficient. For example, it is easy to construct examples exhibiting two equilibria in which equilibrium solutions converge toward each other as debt goes up. Thus, growth collapse, as depicted in the above model, never takes place. Instead, what one would have is a situation in which, except for a borderline case, the model yields two equilibria or none at all. Therefore, the set of models that yield growth collapse are strictly included in those yielding equilibrium multiplicity (before imposing the equilibrium-selection criterion). Thus, the existence of realistic examples yielding growth collapse cannot be taken for granted, which opens up an interesting research agenda.

In what follows, I will continue the discussion in terms of the present model because SS and other interesting implications are the same as in the more complex model presented in the Appendix (except in the few instances in which it will be explicitly noted).

The model or simple extensions provide interesting insights. For example:

• Variable D represents all-encompassing public debt. Therefore, it should include state-contingent public debt, like the one that surfaces during crises (see Diaz-Alejandro, 1985, for a detailed recount of how contingent public debt became apparent during Chile's 1982/3 crisis; and Calvo, Izquierdo, and Talvi, 2002, for recent estimates). State-contingent debt has proven to be large and to contain a sizable un-anticipated component. Thus, a SS could take place even though the economy appears, to the naked eye, safely ensconced within the high-growth region (i.e., far to the left of critical point δ^2).

• The critical debt level δ^2 is a function of the production parameter α. Recalling figure 13.1, it is clear that δ^2 declines as α falls. A negative terms of trade shock could be captured by a lower α. Thus, a deteriora-tion in the terms of trade could plunge the economy into the LGE, causing, as will be argued in the next section, a SS. This observation, incidentally, shows that for economies that are near their critical debt levels, a relatively minor terms of trade deterioration can bring about a substantial decline in output growth.

• The model assumes that the government and the private sector have access to capital markets. However, D could also stand for country-risk-adjusted public debt, in which case an increase in country risk implies a larger D. Thus, even in the benign case in which the private sector is immune to country risk, θD could jump to the low growth region as a result of an increase in country risk. This is relevant for rationalizing the effects of events like the Russian 1998 crisis (see Calvo, 1998a, and 1999; and Calvo and Mendoza, 2000), which resulted in an increase in country risk all across EM, and appears to have left in its wake a noticeable growth slowdown in Latin America (see Calvo, Izquierdo, and Talvi, 2002).

• Debt levels that can be sustained without inducing low growth, decline with the share of debt that has to be serviced on the basis of distortionary taxes (i.e., as θ increases). Thus, if labor supply were in-elastic, for example, it would be optimal to raise labor taxes and set $\theta = 0$. However, tax evasion may make this impossible or at least im-practical. This suggests the key role of tax reform and adequate fiscal institutions for growth and stability.

II   Sudden Stop and Home Goods

So far our discussion did not require any reference to utility functions because, in the model, there is complete separation between produc-tion and consumption decisions. The latter is, in general, essential information to compute current accounts (and, hence, address the issue of SS) or model the behavior of the real exchange rate, which requires bringing to the picture home or nontradable goods.

Suppose that there exists a representative individual whose utility function is time separable, and the subjective rate of discount is constant and (for simplicity) equal to the international rate of interest r.[6] The instant utility function will be denoted $u(c,h)$, where c and h stand for consumption of tradable and home goods, respectively. Output of home goods is described by a concave production function $f(x)$, where x stands for input of tradables. Functions u and f satisfy the standard regularity conditions. The analysis will be centered on interior solutions.

The above assumptions guarantee that optimal consumption of tradables and nontradables, and production of nontradables will be constant over time. The budget constraint under these conditions boils down to:

$$r[V - (1 - \theta)D] = c + x, \tag{10}$$

where time subscripts are dropped because all paths are constant over time. The square-bracketed expression is net wealth after taking into account distortionary taxes (netted out from V) and nondistortionary taxes, $(1 - \theta)D$. Thus, the optimal (market equilibrium) consumption and production plan is obtained by solving the following problem:

$$\max_c \; u(c, f(r[V - (1 - \theta)D] - c)). \tag{11}$$

Solving equation (11) yields the following familiar first-order condition, equating the marginal rate of substitution between tradables and nontradables and the respective marginal rate of transformation:

$$\frac{u_h(c, f(r[V - (1 - \theta)D] - c))}{u_c(c, f(r[V - (1 - \theta)D] - c))} = \frac{1}{f'(r[V - (1 - \theta)D] - c)} = p, \tag{12}$$

where p is the relative price of home goods with respect to tradables (i.e., the inverse of the *real exchange rate*). By equation (12), equilibrium c and p are functions of net wealth. Moreover, by equations (4) and (6):

$$V - (1 - \theta)D = \frac{\alpha - z}{r - z} - D. \tag{13}$$

Recalling that $\bar{z} < r$, condition (9) for the existence of a HGE requires that $\alpha > r$. Thus, by equation (13), V is an increasing function of z. This can be employed to show, incidentally, that if HGE and LGE coexist, then HGE pareto dominates LGE, as expected.

By equations (10) and (13), the current account (surplus) at time 0, CA_0, satisfies, assuming that $K_0 = 1$ and is entirely owned by domestic residents,

$$CA_0 \equiv \alpha - z - rD - c - x = -\frac{\alpha - z}{r - z}z. \tag{14}$$

Hence, $CA_0 < 0$ on HGE and $CA_0 = 0$ on LGE. Consequently, as the economy switches from high to low growth, the current account deficit exhibits a discontinuous collapse to zero. Thus, SS takes place, since a nonmonetary economy like the present one, $-CA_0$ = capital inflows at time 0. Moreover, assuming that consumption of nontradables is a "normal" good, it follows that, given p, consumption of nontradables falls as net wealth (i.e., $V - (1 - \theta)D$) declines. Therefore, by equation (12), as growth collapses, x falls and $f'(x)$ rises, implying that the SS would be accompanied by real depreciation (i.e., p falls). Clearly, in this case GDP will also collapse because the output of nontradables falls. All of these results are fully in line with empirical observations (see Calvo and Reinhart, 2000; and Calvo, Izquierdo, and Talvi, 2002).

Money

The model can easily be extended to a monetary economy. For example, suppose the demand for money is subject to a cash-in-advance constraint, such that:

demand for nominal money $\equiv M^d = E(c + ph)$, \hfill (15)

where E is the nominal exchange rate (i.e., the price of foreign exchange in terms of domestic currency). Thus, first-order conditions (12) remain intact, and, if the representative individual internalizes the government budget constraint, one can show that money is superneutral in the sense that, along steady states, the *real* side of the economy is invariant to the presence of money.

Thus, recalling that under the crisis scenario highlighted above (i.e., D unexpectedly moves from the high to the low growth region) $c + ph$ declines, it follows that, given E, the demand for money will exhibit a discontinuous fall. Consider the case in which E is fixed. The SS will be associated, therefore, with an unexpected drop in international reserves. If the latter is high enough, a BOP crisis would ensue. Notice that the model gives an anti-Krugman rationale for the BOP crisis (Krugman, 1979). The crisis in the present model is entirely rooted in *real* factors: SS comes first, BOP follows. Policy implications are also very different. For example, Krugman crises can be prevented by following a tighter fiscal policy, whereas in the present model tighter fiscal policy (if based on higher tax rates) could actually trigger the crisis. Not because fiscal balance is undesirable, but because the instruments to achieve it are distorting! Once again, what the present model highlights is the *importance of improving fiscal institutions*.

Anticipated Crises

Although I believe SSs contain a significant unanticipated component, the present model can also rationalize the case in which a SS is fully anticipated. In the first place, notice that, in general, investment decisions are predicated on:

$$\text{sgn}\left[\int_t^\infty \alpha(1 - \tau_s)e^{-r(s-t)} \, ds - 1 \right]. \tag{16}$$

The integral in expression (16) equals the present discounted value of net of taxes return on a unit of investment. Thus, investment will take place when the latter exceeds its cost $(= 1)$, i.e., when the sign in expression (16) is positive; moreover, if expression (16) is negative, no investment will occur. As expected, when τ is constant expression (16) boils down to expression (5). Now consider the situation in which from time 0 to T debt is zero, but everyone knows that at time T the public sector will be loaded with debt $\theta D = \delta^2 + \varepsilon$ (where, it should be recalled, δ^2 is the critical level of distortionary debt beyond which low growth is the only equilibrium solution, recall figures 13.1 and 13.2, and ε is a positive number). Moreover, suppose that on the interval $(0, T]$ the tax rate $\tau = 0$; afterwards, τ is set at a constant level necessary to service debt D. One can easily show that as ε converges to 0, investment will be set at its maximum level in the interval $(0, T]$, and $z_t = 0$, for $t > T$. Thus, a fully anticipated growth collapse at time T would take place. Will this result in a SS? Since the growth crisis is fully anticipated and consumers have access to the capital market (and are not subject to taxes that distort the consumption time profile), consumption will remain undisturbed. However, investment will go from $\bar{z}K_t$ to zero. Therefore, at the onset of the growth crisis, a SS will take place.[7]

In what follows I will show how to construct a *monetary* example that would be a polar opposite to Krugman's (1979). Suppose that the economy starts with zero debt, a positive fiscal deficit, and zero distorting taxes, τ. Clearly, debt will be increasing throughout time and, if policy remains the same, it will eventually reach the critical level δ^2. At this juncture, the government eliminates fiscal deficit by resorting to the inflation tax to cover the primary deficit (as in Krugman, 1979) and services the outstanding debt as in Section I (i.e., employing distorting taxes). Obviously, the economy will display high growth until net output-distorting debt reaches the critical level δ^2, and then switch to low growth forever.[8] The monetary economy under fixed rates will again display a sudden loss of international reserves at crisis, reflecting the effect of *anticipated* inflation (as in Calvo, 1987). One could even generate a BOP crisis à la Krugman (1979) if public debt includes (with a negative sign) international reserves. If, for example, the critical minimum level of reserves is zero, it can be shown that the crisis *coincides* with full depletion of international reserves, in conjunction with a run against the domestic currency. Once again, however, the BOP crisis is inherently *real*.[9]

The following points are worth making:

• As explained, real depreciation follows from an *unanticipated* SS, not the other way around. Given the tendency to focus on exchange rates, however, a casual observer might conclude that the main culprit was currency *over-appreciation*. As "proof" she will likely point out that the real exchange rate shows no sign to return to its prior-to-crisis level.

• Suppose the utility function u is homothetic in tradables and nontradables. Hence, given p, the demand for nontradables, h, is proportional to the demand for tradables, c. In particular, during a SS and, given p, the demand for nontradables falls in the same proportion as the demand for tradables. Let us focus on the case in which the current account deficit, CAD, becomes zero. Then, given CAD, the smaller is the domestic supply of tradables (net of international debt and precommitted transfers) in terms of tradables' consumption, ω, the larger will be the proportional drop in c at SS. Consequently, the smaller is ω, the larger will be the fall in c and h (given p) caused by the SS. Variable ω measures the economy's ability to supply domestic absorption of tradables. In Calvo, Izquierdo, and Talvi (2002), variable ω is called "unleveraged absorption of tradable goods;" ω is shown to vary widely across countries (Argentina and Brazil are shown to have one of the lowest ω). Therefore, the same *CAD* adjustment could have significant differences across countries depending on ω.

• In this model, crises are very tame. There is no room for default, for example. However, this can be easily rectified assuming, for instance, that the government repays only if the default alternative would be more costly. One can show that, abstracting from direct default costs, on the low-growth region the default alternative dominates low growth plus full debt repayment. Thus, (i) even if government is not intent on driving debt beyond the critical level, a bit of uncertainty will generate country risk premia, and (ii) in the anti-Krugman example, in which sooner or later the critical threshold is crossed, the critical threshold will be zero. To see this, note that if it was positive and equal to $\bar{D}$, for example, then investors would stop lending before D reached $\bar{D}$. Otherwise, the "last" loan before reaching $\bar{D}$ will immediately be declared in default, a hardly attractive investment proposition. However, a positive $\bar{D}$ could be generated if there are direct default costs (a realistic assumption).

• The model assumes that output of home goods falls as the cost of raw materials rises or, equivalently, as the real exchange rate rises (i.e., as the relative price of home goods with respect to tradables p falls). In actuality, however, another important factor in nontradables' output contraction during a crisis is *liability dollarization*, i.e., the existence of debt denominated in terms of tradables (*dollar debt*, for short).[10] Under these conditions, for example, an unanticipated SS could give rise to bankruptcies in the home goods sector, resulting in momentarily lower output. How deep and persistent is the output collapse will depend on bankruptcy legislation and the efficiency of the judicial system, and, of course, it will also depend on how much *dollar*-indebted is the home goods sector. The latter, incidentally, could be especially large after a capital inflow episode like the one that occurred in EM during the first half of the 1990s.

• The weaker the enforceability of financial contracts, the more likely will be that loans impose *collateral constraints*, by which the value of attachable assets cannot fall short of a predetermined proportion of the loan. Thus, it has become popular to assume that the loans a firm or individual can take depend on some measure of net worth.[11] Thus, if the collateral constraint is binding, a depreciation of the real exchange rate, i.e., a fall in p, may call for liquidation of productive assets. If we further assume, following Kiyotaki and Moore (1997), that the liquidated assets will go to less efficient hands, then output will suffer a contraction. Thus, a crisis could display a fall in output of nontradables even though, in principle, output would be perfectly price inelastic in absence of the financial shock. Output contraction by this channel does not even require bankruptcy to take place. At any rate, however, these extensions show that the financial channel could add to the depth and persistence of the crisis (see Diaz-Alejandro, 1985). Whereas raw materials are flows, financial obligations are stocks. A stock reversal could actually cause much more damage than a flow cost increase, particularly if the latter is deemed to be temporary.

III   Sudden Stop and Monetary Policy

I will conduct the discussion taking as background the previous section's model, focusing on the case in which the SS is largely unanticipated and causes a credit crunch in the home goods sector (due to, for instance, collateral constraints or margin calls).[12] The analysis will center on policies taken *after* SS and also policies that can be implemented *before* SS to cushion its deleterious effects. Clearly, in this model credit is cut because outstanding credit is too large relative to the economy's capacity to repay. Thus, only policies that have an impact on the latter will have a chance of becoming effective. Monetary policy can influence the ability to repay in at least two different ways: (i) managing international reserves, and (ii) changing relative prices in the face of price/wage stickiness.

Management of International Reserves

A common feature in recent crises is a large expansion of domestic credit from the central bank. As pointed out by Flood, Garber, and Kramer (1996) and Kumhof (2000), this feature is not captured by the first-generation Krugman-Flood Garber models (see Krugman, 1979; and Flood and Garber, 1994). In the latter, the crisis is triggered by a sudden decline in the demand for domestic money. Actually, as illustrated by the tequila crisis (see Calvo and Mendoza, 1996b), in most cases (Argentina and Hong Kong SAR are exceptions) the loss of international reserves is almost entirely driven by domestic credit. The demand for domestic money shows no atypical decline. Can one find a rationale for that?

The following accounting identity is worth recalling:

$$KI = CAD + \Delta R, \qquad\qquad (17)$$

where "errors and omissions" are ignored, and KI, CAD, and ΔR stand for, respectively, capital inflows, current account deficit, and accumulation of international reserves, R. A SS is reflected in a sharp drop in KI. If the central bank lets the exchange rate float, then no reserves will be lost, and the entire adjustment will fall on the current account, calling for a sharp real depreciation (a sharp fall in p, in the model's notation). This, in turn, might provoke sizable income redistribution, including bankruptcies in the nontradable sector. Thus, the central bank will have incentives to follow an expansionary policy that places some of its international reserves in private hands (the nontradable sector's, if the main objective is bankruptcy prevention). Pure floating cannot work, because the central bank would not be able to release its reserves (unless they are directly transferred to the fiscal authority). Therefore, under standard practices the central bank will be forced to adopt some kind of pegging accompanied by domestic credit expansion (hopefully before domestic money holders wise up to the impending crisis). This rationalizes the fact (observed in Mexico in 1994/ 5 and Brazil in 1998/9) that the SS occurs first, and it is later followed by a currency crisis *provoked* by the central bank (not only by panicky domestic money holders).[13] Thus, devaluation follows the SS. Since the latter is contractionary, this analysis also provides a rationale for *contractionary devaluation*, a well known phenomenon in developing countries (see Diaz-Alejandro, 1963; and Sebastian Edwards, 1989). Notice, however, that under this interpretation, output contraction is not the result of devaluation: SS would be.

This discussion highlights the possible desirability of pegging the exchange rate once a SS is detected. Exchange rate pegging allows the central bank to transfer its international reserves to the private sector.[14] Is pegging responsible for the crisis in a deeper sense? I would not deny the possibility, but the present model shows that the roots of a SS may rest on fiscal dysfunction and be totally divorced from exchange rate policy.

Is central bank credit the best way to help the private sector during a SS? I have some serious doubts, because the new domestic credit will likely go to the public sector (slowing down desirable adjustment in government expenditure), and firms that have access to international credit markets (multinationals). The latter, in particular, are likely to use additional domestic credit to unwind their dollar debts, an attractive proposition in view of impending devaluation, and that central bank credit expansion may momentarily push domestic interest rates for prime borrowers below market equilibrium. Thus, it is conceivable that domestic credit expansion drains international reserves from the central bank without substantially relieving the pressure on the current account. This bleak scenario, which unfortunately appears not to be uncommon, helps to explain why, during a SS, governments might be driven to adopt heterodox policies. For example, controls on capital outflows (e.g., Malaysia, 1998), socialization of private debts (e.g., Chile, 1982/3, see Diaz-Alejandro, 1985), or controls on the direction of bank credit (Brazil, 2002).

A serious difficulty with heterodox policies is that, as a general rule, they imply breaking established rules or implicit contracts, opening up the door for *time inconsistency*, and political economy maneuvers, specifically *wars of attrition* where different groups vie to benefit from central bank credit (see Sturzenegger and Tommasi, 1998). Wars of attrition result in policymaking paralysis, becoming very hard to know which side will win. The policy impasse, in turn, increases the *option value of waiting*, which results in further investment and credit contraction—and declining growth (see Calvo, 2002).

One way to get a better outcome might be for the government to offer (or support) *exchange rate hedge contracts* that will be activated the moment a large devaluation takes place. In this fashion, the loss of reserves would be automatic, helping to ameliorate the after-crisis tug of war. It should be noted, however, that government hedges may end up being *underpriced*, because their price reflects, in part, the government's assessment of the likelihood of crisis. Thus, in order to show the authorities' high confidence in current policies, unrealistically cheap hedges may be offered, increasing the fiscal cost of a crisis and, in terms of the above model, also the likelihood of crisis (because contingent net public debt goes up).

Wage/Price Stickiness

This phenomenon lies at the heart of the literature on optimal exchange rate regimes and optimal currency areas (e.g., Flood and Marion, 1982; and Calvo, 2001 for a critical assessment). A standard result is that if the economy is hit by a *real* shock, it is optimal to let the exchange rate free to float. Thus, since a SS is essentially a *real* shock, one might reason that floating would be optimal—at least, until the dust settles.[15]

Let me first note that, in practice, the choice between fixed and floating exchange rate regimes in the aftermath of a SS often turns out to be just an *academic* exercise. Many economies are swept away by events and end up devaluing their currencies before the exchange rate issue is even raised! However, Argentina and Hong Kong SAR in 1995 are interesting counterexamples. These economies were able to maintain their currency board regimes despite massive loss of international reserves. At any rate, the issue that I would like to raise is whether, subject to having enough international reserves, it may be socially desirable to keep a peg a little longer after a SS, in order to slowdown the relative price adjustment.

As noted, SSs call for sharp changes in relative prices (often involving a real currency depreciation, a fall in p). Thus, firms saddled with dollar debts, may be forced into costly asset liquidation or outright bankruptcy. Quick convergence to the new set of equilibrium relative prices will bring this situation into the open, and financial chaos might ensue. Could a temporary peg make a difference? The instinctive answer is probably "no" because, otherwise, sectors that should see their equilibrium relative price fall would instead see their quantities contract—resulting in a wash at best. However, this intuition misses an important point, namely, the microeconomics of price setting. To illustrate, suppose that prices are set in a highly competitive environment, such that, under normal circumstances, profits are near zero. Thus, a shock that set initial home good prices above their new full equilibrium level is observationally equivalent to firms colluding and setting their prices at a higher-than-competitive equilibrium level. Output will fall but firms' profits may rise. This is not always the case, but, in the present context, it is a definite possibility. Therefore, relative price stickiness (brought about by price stickiness plus an exchange rate peg) may help to relieve financial stress.[16] Consequently, the existence of price stickiness may be another reason in favor of pegging in response to a SS.

IV   Final Remarks

The central message of this chapter is that currency crises in EM may just be a sideshow, and that the key factors behind the collapse of economic activity and growth may stem from dysfunctional domestic policies and serious financial vulnerabilities. The latter give rise to sharp changes in market equilibrium in response to relatively minor real shocks. Thus, BOP crises could just be one of the many deleterious effects of a SS.

The model is silent about the factors that trigger a SS. Any shock that pushes the economy beyond the critical debt level would trigger a SS. It could be an external factor, as Calvo, Izquierdo, and Talvi (2002) claimed was the case recently in Argentina, but it could also be an internal factor, like a domestic political or corporate governance scandal.

The main policy lesson from the model is that EM should strive to improve fiscal and financial *institutions*. But, perhaps equally important, policymakers should get ready for the possibility of a SS. They should go through *SS drills*, much as well run buildings go through fire drills. Under normal circumstances, fires are low probability events. If not well managed, however, the resulting stampede may dramatically increase the number of casualties.

As noted, IFIs have a big role to play in coordinating high growth when both high and low growth coexist. Actually, if the model is not misleading, before reaching a SS, there is always a region of indeterminacy in which IFIs could play that role. Outside that region, however, the situation becomes more complicated, because most EM do not qualify for grants (as opposed to loans) from IFIs in response to debt crises (heavily indebted poor countries, HIPCs, are the exception). Moreover, the G-7 have expressed serious concern about the moral hazard implications of bailout packages.[17]

Still, IFIs could play a useful role as coordinators of private sector bail-ins and enforcers of fiscal reform. The former would lower the level of public debt, thus pushing the economy into the high-growth region. Fiscal reform could also be very effective if it helps to lower tax distortions (e.g., θ in the present model). If countries are left on their own, these reforms may be hard to implement, because of political reasons. In the basic model in Section I, for example, fiscal tightening would be effective if it relies on lowering government expenditure in a credible and sustainable manner, which is usually tangled with serious political economy problems. IFIs could help to break the stalemate by offering "loans for reform." If successful, the loans would be fully repaid because fiscal reform would place the economy on the high-growth path.

However, the model suggests that outside the high-growth region, simple minded, belt tightening fiscal programs, relying on higher taxes, could be counterproductive in the short run.

Thus, a literal reading of the model shows that a tax hike will have no effect, given that, in principle, it does nothing about total public debt, D, or its distortionary impact, θ. However, higher taxes may help to bring the economy back to high growth. The hard question in this respect is whether a belt tightening policy will enjoy political support during the transition in which pain is not immediately rewarded by high growth.

Often during crises, tax hikes rely on taxes that are nondistortionary in the *short run* (i.e., wealth taxes and, in general, taxes on "sitting ducks"), but which would be highly distortionary if agents anticipated their continuation in the *future*. Therefore, these taxes are effective if policymakers can credibly ensure the private sector that they will be eliminated as soon as the emergency situation blows over. Conceivably, IFIs could help to reinforce credibility in this context, although I am highly skeptical: in the *future* there will likely be a new set of policymakers both in the world at large, and the country in question—making enforceability extremely difficult.

Finally, a technical note. This chapter shows that SSs can be both anticipated or unanticipated. My conjecture, though, is that SSs contain a large element of surprise, and that the recent episodes have a lot to do with the 1998 Russian crisis, and resulting perception that EM securities constitute a much more risky asset class than previously thought. However, this should not be read as belittling the relevance of domestic factors. On the contrary, as the model shows, the critical debt level is intimately related to domestic institutions. Moreover, given the strong nonlinearities implied by the model, domestic factors could be powerful multipliers of external shocks. The problem for the econometrician is that nonlinearities imply that, faced with the same external shock, some economies enter into deep crisis, while others escape totally unscathed. Moreover, those that are drawn into crisis will likely trigger additional domestic factors that contribute to the depth of the crisis (like political instability). Thus, the econometrician could wrongly infer that domestic factors are the sole determinants of these crises. Furthermore, if the number of crisis countries is small (e.g., at the time of writing, Argentina was the only large Latin American country that went into deep crisis after the Russian shock), empirical estimates will suffer from well known small-sample problems.

APPENDIX

The main purpose of this section is to show that the SS follows from the existence of tax distortions and not from the knife-edge feature of the model in the text. With that in mind, I will modify the previous model and assume that investment is subject to *adjustment costs*. More concretely, I will assume that the output cost per unit of capital associated with capital growth z is portrayed by $\varphi(z)$, where function φ is strictly convex and twice continuously differentiable (implying $\varphi'' > 0$). Notice, incidentally, that in the text I assume $\varphi(z) = z$. Thus, to stay close to that model in a neighborhood of 0, I will further assume $\varphi(0) = 0$, and $\varphi'(0) = 1$; moreover, I will assume that there exists $\underline{z}$ and $\bar{z}$ such that $\underline{z} < 0 < \bar{z} < r$, such that φ is defined on that open interval, and $\lim \varphi'(z) = \infty$ as z converges to $\bar{z}$ from the left, while $\lim \varphi'(z) = -\infty$ as z converges to $\underline{z}$ from the right. Moreover, to simplify the analysis, I make the realistic assumption that $\lim \varphi(z)$ as z converges to $\underline{z}$ from the right is finite (specifically, it does not converge to ∞).

Therefore, the value of the firm at time 0, V, satisfies (see equation (4)):

$$V = \frac{\alpha(1 - \tau) - \varphi(z)}{r - z}. \tag{18}$$

Hence,

$$\operatorname{sgn} \frac{\partial V}{\partial z} = \operatorname{sgn}[-\varphi'(z)(r - z) + \alpha(1 - \tau) - \varphi(z)], \tag{19}$$

and, if $\partial V/\partial z = 0$, then:

$$\operatorname{sgn} \frac{\partial^2 V}{\partial z^2} = -\varphi''(z)(r - z) < 0. \tag{20}$$

Thus, first-order conditions are sufficient for a maximum of V with respect to z because V does not contain a local minimum.

Plugging budget constraint (6) to substitute for τ in expression (19), we get:

$$\alpha - \theta D(r - z) - [\varphi(z) + \varphi'(z)(r - z)] \equiv J(z, D). \tag{21}$$

Previous assumptions ensure that $J(z, D)$ converges to ∞ as z goes to $\underline{z}$ from the right, and to $-\infty$ as z goes to $\bar{z}$ from the left. Hence, equilibrium existence is ensured for all D. It can further be shown, by expression (21), that $J_z(z, 0) < 0$ for all $z \in (\underline{z}, \bar{z})$. Thus, equilibrium is unique for $D = 0$. This result should not surprise us because if $D = 0$, there is no distortionary taxation. Moreover, as a general rule, under uniqueness, equilibrium is a continuous function of D. This shows that in order to get the SS discontinuities discussed in the text, it is, as a general rule, necessary for the model to exhibit multiple equilibria (before imposing the equilibrium-selection principle according to which the economy settles on the highest growth equilibrium).

I will now show an example where equilibrium is not unique (in absence of the equilibrium-selection principle). By expression (21), and recalling that $\varphi(0) = 0$ and $\varphi'(0) = 1$, we have:

$$J(0, D) = \alpha - \theta D r - r. \tag{22}$$

Let D^c be such that $J(0, D^c) = 0$. This implies that if $D = D^c$, then $z = 0$ maximizes the value of the firm V with respect to z. Clearly, by expression (22),

$$\theta D^c = \frac{\alpha - r}{r} > 0. \tag{23}$$

Moreover, by expressions (21) and (22), at $D = D^c$,

$$J_z(0, D_c) = \frac{\alpha - r}{r} - \varphi''(0) r. \tag{24}$$

Hence, given r, for α sufficiently large or $\varphi''(0)$ sufficiently small, we can ensure that $J_z(0, D^c) > 0$. Thus, drawing the J function, given D, under these conditions readily shows that, if $D = D^c$, the economy will exhibit at least three equilibrium solutions (illustrated by the solid line in figure 13A.1). Moreover, by expression (21), the J function shifts down as D increases. Hence, there exists some $\bar{D} > D^c$ such that $J(z, \bar{D}) < 0$ for all $z \in [0, \bar{z}]$. However, the "bad" negative growth equilibrium is never lost (illustrated by the dashed line in figure 13A.1). This implies that there will be some critical D (equivalent to δ^2/θ in the main text's model) such that a growth collapse, SS, etc., will take place even if D suffers a slight increase. Moreover, since the richer model could depict any number of equilibria, there could be succession of SSs as D increases.

In closing, notice that the share of distorting debt in output at time zero, $\theta D^c / \alpha$, satisfies, by expression (23),

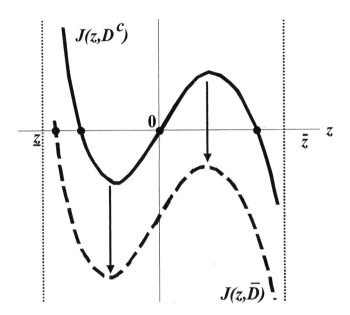

Figure 13A.1
Discontinuous equilibrium mapping

$$\theta D^c / \alpha = \frac{1 - \dfrac{r}{\alpha}}{r}. \tag{25}$$

Thus, distorting debt in the multiple equilibria example can be made as small a share of output as desired by selecting α sufficiently close to r, and $\alpha > r$. This shows that the example does not require unrealistically high debt ratios.

Notes

I am grateful to Fernando Broner, Kevin Cowan, Alejandro Izquierdo, Michael Kumhof, Eduardo Levy-Yeyati, Luis Fernando Mejía, Enrique Mendoza, Ned Phelps, Ernesto Talvi, and seminars participants at IADB, Di Tella University, and the University of Maryland for valuable comments. I would like to dedicate this paper to the memory of Rudi Dornbusch, whose insight, wit, and whip inspired generations of scholars and policymakers in international finance and development economics.

1. The expression sudden stop was first suggested, and the phenomenon highlighted, in Dornbusch, Goldfajn, and Valdés (1995).

2. For an earlier attempt to rationalize SS on the basis of multiplicity of equilibria and in an essentially static nonmonetary framework, see Calvo (1998b).

3. Real depreciation also takes place if the crisis is fully anticipated and, for example, it entails a higher consumption tax.

4. The borderline cases in which expressions (8) or (9) hold with equality are of no interest and will not be discussed here.

5. In my view the IFI's coordination role was successfully carried out in Mexico (1995), Korea (1997), and Brazil (1999), and helps to explain the rapid (V-shaped) recovery of those economies.

6. For a discussion of this model in the more general case in which the rate of discount is different from the international interest rate, see Calvo (1998c). The latter also addresses welfare issues and the impact of controls on capital outflows that will be skipped in the present paper.

7. This does not hold true in the Appendix model because in the latter investment is a continuous function of time. Even though investment does not display a discontinuous fall, however, it will show a declining trend.

8. Again, this does not follow in the Appendix model, in which a lower growth is attained in a continuous manner.

9. Contrary to this scenario, however, most recent BOP crises seem to have been driven more by an expansion of domestic credit from the central bank than by a fall in the demand for monetary aggregates (see Flood, Garber, and Kramer, 1996; Kumhof, 2000; and Calvo, 2001). This issue will be taken up in the next section.

10. This is one of the key new topics in the EM literature. See, for example, Calvo (2001) and Jeanne (2001).

11. This line of research has been pioneered by Kiyotaki and Moore (1997) for the closed economy, and extended to the open economy by Caballero and Krishnamurthy (2001a, b, and c), Izquierdo (2000), and others.

12. Thus, this section departs from the basic model in Section I, and is more speculative than earlier sections.

13. This requires changing the anti-Krugman example in Section II to allow for the central bank to issue domestic credit in response to a SS. Central bank *hyperactivity* during BOP crises, incidentally, is a widely observed fact, as noted by Flood, Garber, and Kramer (1996) and Kumhof (2000).

14. Once again, this policy would be especially relevant if the private sector suffers a credit crunch. Brazil offers a recent example of this kind of central bank policy; see the *Financial Times* (2002).

15. In actuality, however, as shown in the earlier discussion of the monetary economy, a SS gives rise to both real and nominal shocks. Thus, if anything, the standard literature would call for a *dirty float*.

16. For an example in terms of a micro-founded staggered-prices model, see Calvo (2000).

17. For a critical assessment of the moral hazard view in connection with recent EM crises, see Calvo (2002).

References

Caballero, Ricardo J., and Arvind Krishnamurthy, 2001a, "Excessive Dollar Debt: Financial Development and Underinsurance" (unpublished; Cambridge, Massachusetts, MIT).

————, 2001b, "International and Domestic Collateral Constraints in a Model of Emerging Market Crises," *Journal of Monetary Economics*, Vol. 48, No. 3, pp. 513–48.

————, 2001c, "A Vertical Analysis of Crises and Central Bank Interventions" (unpublished; Cambridge, Massachusetts: MIT).

Calvo, Guillermo A., 1987, "Balance of Payments Crises in a Cash-in-Advance Economy," *Journal of Money, Credit, and Banking*, Vol. 19, No. 1, pp. 19–32.

————, 1998a, "Understanding the Russian Virus: With Special Reference to Latin America," unpublished; available at www.bsos.umd.edu/econ/ciecalvo.htm/.

————, 1998b, "Capital Flows and Capital-Market Crises: The Simple Economics of Sudden Stops," *Journal of Applied Economics* (CEMA), Vol. 1 (November), pp. 35–54.

————, 1998c, "Growth, Debt, and Economic Transformation: The Capital Flight Problem," in *New Theories in Growth and Development*, ed. by F. Coricelli, Di Matteo, F. Hahn (Basingstoke: Palgrave Macmillan).

————, 1999, "Contagion in Emerging Markets: When *Wall Street* Is the Carrier," unpublished; available at www.bsos.umd.edu/econ/ciecalvo.htm/.

————, 2000, "Notes on Price Stickiness: With Special Reference to Liability Dollarization and Credibility," unpublished; available at www.bsos.umd.edu/econ/ciecalvo.htm/.

————, 2001, "Capital Markets and the Exchange Rate: With Special Reference to the Dollarization Debate in Latin America," *Journal of Money Credit and Banking*, Vol. 33, Part 2 (May), pp. 312–34.

————, 2002, "Globalization Hazard and Delayed Reform in Emerging Markets," *Economia*, Vol. 2, (Spring), pp. 1–29.

————, Alejandro Izquierdo, and Ernesto Talvi, 2002, "Sudden Stop, the Real Exchange Rate, and Fiscal Sustainability: Argentina's Lessons" (unpublished; Washington: Inter-American Development Bank).

Calvo, Guillermo A., and Enrique G. Mendoza, 1996a, "Petty Crime and Cruel Punishment: Lessons from the Mexican Debacle," *American Economic Review, Papers and Proceedings*, Vol. 86 (May), pp. 170–75.

————, 1996b, "Mexico's Balance-of-Payments Crisis: A Chronicle of a Death Foretold," *Journal of International Economics*, Vol. 41, pp. 235–64.

————, 2000, "Capital Market Crises and Economic Collapse in Emerging Markets: An Informational-Frictions Approach," *American Economic Review, Papers and Proceedings*, Vol. 90 (May), pp. 59–64.

Calvo, Guillermo A., and Carmen M. Reinhart, 2000, "When Capital Flows Come to a Sudden Stop: Consequences and Policy," in *Reforming the International Monetary and Financial System*, ed. by Peter B. Kenen and Alexander K. Swoboda (Washington: International Monetary Fund).

——, 2001, "Fixing for Your Life," in *Brookings Trade Forum*, ed. by Susan M. Collins and Dani Rodrik (Washington: Brookings Institution Press), pp. 1–58.

Diaz-Alejandro, Carlos F., 1963, "A Note on the Impact of Devaluation and the Redistribution Effect," *Journal of Political Economy*, Vol. 71, No. 6, pp. 577–80.

——, 1985, "Good-Bye Financial Repression, Hello Financial Crash," *Journal of Development Economics*, Vol. 19, No. 1, pp. 1–24.

Dornbusch, Rudiger, Ilan Goldfajn, and Rodrigo O. Valdés, 1995, "Currency Crises and Collapses," *Brookings Papers on Economic Activity*, 2, pp. 219–93.

Eaton, Jonathan, 1987, "Public Debt Guarantees and Private Capital Flight," *World Bank Economic Review* (January), pp. 337–95.

Edwards, Sebastian, 1989, *Real Exchange Rates, Devaluation, and Adjustment*, (Cambridge, Massachusetts: MIT Press).

Financial Times, 2002, "Brazil Pledges Loans to Companies," August 13, p. 1.

Flood, Robert P., and Nancy P. Marion, 1982, "The Transmission of Disturbances Under Alternative Exchange-Rate Regimes with Optimal Indexing," *Quarterly Journal of Economics*, Vol. 97 (February), pp. 43–66.

Flood, Robert P., and Peter M. Garber, 1994, *Speculative Bubbles, Speculative Attacks, and Policy Switching* (Cambridge, Massachusetts: MIT Press).

——, and Kramer K., 1996, "Collapsing Exchange Rate Regimes: Another Linear Example," *Journal of International Economics*, Vol. 41, pp. 223–34.

Izquierdo, Alejandro, 2000, "Credit Constraints and the Asymmetric Behavior of Asset Prices and Output Under External Shocks" (unpublished; Washington: Inter-American Development Bank).

Jeanne, Olivier, 2001, "Why Do Emerging Economies Borrow in Foreign Currency?" presented at the 2001 meeting of LACEA, Montevideo, Uruguay, October 18–20.

Kiyotaki, Nobuhiro, and John Moore, 1997, "Credit Cycles," *Journal of Political Economy*, Vol. 105 (April), pp. 211–48.

Krugman, P. R., 1979, "A Model of Balance-of-Payments Crises," *Journal of Money, Credit, and Banking*, Vol. 11 (August), pp. 311–25.

Kumhof, Michael, 2000, "A Quantitative Exploration of the Role of Short-Term Domestic Debt in Balance of Payment Crises," *Journal of International Economics*, Vol. 51, pp. 195–215.

Sturzenegger, Federico, and Mariano Tommasi, 1998, *The Political Economy of Reform* (Cambridge, Massachusetts: MIT Press).

Part IV

The Exchange Rate and All That

Introduction to Part IV

Sometimes I think that the exchange rate is to international finance what sex is to love. Sex is secondary to love, most people would agree, but sex captures much more space than love in everyday conversation, radio, films, and TV. Similarly, economists and the public in general get all worked up about exchange rate regimes, as if the choice made a big difference, or were even truly possible! Until recently the discussion about the optimal exchange rate regime ignored key aspects of EMs, like liability dollarization and other financial vulnerabilities that trouble EMs. Discussing the exchange rate without context is like sex for its own sake, i.e., pornography.

The following chapters attempt to frame the exchange rate debate in a context relevant for EMs. Chapters 14 and 16 were written at about the same time and carry a simple message: floating ain't easy. More specifically, it is very difficult for EMs to ignore the vagaries of the exchange rate as mature economies do. EMs know that and *de facto* peg (witness Russia, China, and Argentina).

Chapter 15 was written in connection with a seminar on dollarization organized by ITAM, Mexico, and the Federal Reserve Bank of Cleveland. Although its main objective was to assess the pros and cons of full dollarization, the chapter focuses rather on the difficulties of assessing alternative exchange rate regimes when key EM characteristics are taken into account. In particular, chapter 15 discusses the incredibly popular optimal currency Area criterion (OCA), for the optimal choice of exchange rate regimes, and concludes that what the OCA leaves out is far more relevant than what it puts in. The discussion is pursued in chapter 17, which reemphasizes the point that the EM context and institutions are critical for choosing the exchange rate regime. Moreover, it dares pro-floating-exchange-rate advocates to meet what might be called the Mundellian challenge: Why stop at countries rather than extending the discussion to regions, as Mundell (1961) proposed? If you take a stroll down 19th Street in Washington, DC, you will find many pro-floaters, but hardly anyone who favors multiple currencies *within* a country. Why?

Let me end this section with a plea: Once and for all, let us take pornography out of international finance!

References

Mundell, Robert A. (1961). "A Theory of Optimum Currency Areas," *American Economic Review* 51(3), pp. 657–665.

14 Fixing for Your Life

Guillermo A. Calvo and
Carmen M. Reinhart

Nearly all the currency crises of the 1990s took place against a background of exchange rate regimes that have been characterized—after the fact—as soft pegs.[1] This has led many analysts to conclude that "the peg did it" and that emerging markets should "just say no" to fixed exchange rates. This advice seems paradoxical in light of the fact that most emerging markets have precarious access to international capital markets during the best of times (and none during the worst), and that access is often contingent on the stability of these nations' currencies.

This chapter argues that in fact "floating" exchange rates are far from a panacea for emerging markets and that this policy advice misses a number of important real-world considerations that are crucial for developing countries. We present evidence that emerging economies are indeed very different from developed economies in several key respects that are bound to play an important role in the choice of exchange rate regime. In emerging market countries, devaluations—or large depreciations for that matter—are contractionary, and the adjustments in the current account are far more acute and abrupt. Currency crises become credit crises when sovereign credit ratings collapse following the collapse of the currency (as they often do), and access to international credit is lost. Lack of credibility also gives rise to a chronic and marked volatility in domestic interest rates. Furthermore, exchange rate volatility appears to be more damaging to trade, and the pass-through from exchange rate swings to inflation is far higher in emerging markets than in developed economies. These differences are significant and may help explain emerging market countries' historic and present reluctance to tolerate large fluctuations in their exchange rates.[2] In the context of a simple framework, we show why devaluations may be contractionary when there is no access to international credit and lead to "fear of floating" and procyclical policies.[3]

In the next section we present evidence on the fear of floating syndrome. We then review the empirical evidence of selected key indicators following currency crashes for emerging and developed economies, take stock of the empirical evidence on the effects of exchange rate volatility on trade for emerging markets, and present some evidence on the extent of pass-through from exchange rates to prices. At pages 377–384 we present an analytical framework that examines circumstances in which credibility loss translates into an inability to borrow from abroad and a devaluation can lead to a contraction in output. We also discuss other reasons for fearing large exchange rate movements, including the role played by liability dollarization and an ineffective lender of last resort. We conclude by examining the implications of this analysis for the choice of exchange rate arrangements in emerging markets.

Fear of Floating: Some Evidence

Despite the relatively recent increase in the ranks of countries classified as "floaters" or "managed floaters," nominal exchange rates in fact show little variation in most emerging markets.

In earlier work we examined the monthly behavior of exchange rates, international reserves, base money, and interest rates for a broad array of countries from 1970 to 1999.[4] In what follows, by contrast, we limit our attention to the time series properties of monthly percentage changes in the exchange rate, measured at the end of period.[5] Despite occasional bouts of foreign exchange market intervention—sometimes even coordinated intervention—the U.S. dollar floated about as freely against the deutsche mark and, more recently, the euro and the Japanese yen as any currency is allowed to float. For this reason, we compare countries with regimes that are classified as freely floating or managed floating against this G-3 benchmark.

We can glean actual policy practices by analyzing the frequency distributions of exchange rates around chosen intervals and comparing these across countries and regimes. The International Monetary Fund (IMF) groups countries into four types of exchange rate arrangements: pegged, limited flexibility, managed floating, and independently floating. Limited flexibility has been used almost exclusively to classify European countries (before the monetary union) with exchange rate arrangements defined in relation to one another (for example, the Snake or the Exchange Rate Mechanism [ERM]). Hence it is possible to evaluate the probability of a particular change or changes in the exchange rate, reserves, or similar factors on the basis of the announced exchange rate regime.

We denote the absolute value of the percent change in the exchange rate by ε. Letting x^c present some critical threshold, we can estimate the probability that ε falls within the prespecified bounds, conditional on a particular exchange rate arrangement.

For example, if $x^c = /1$ percent/ (that is, ε lies within a ± 1 percent band), then

$$P(\varepsilon < x^c|\text{Peg}) > P(\varepsilon < x^c|\text{Float}). \tag{1}$$

That is, the probability that the monthly exchange rate change falls within the 1 percent band is greatest for the fixed exchange regime and lowest for the freely floating arrangement, with the other two types of arrangements falling somewhere in between. Unless otherwise noted, the bilateral rates reported are with respect to the deutsche mark for the European countries, the choice owing to the fact that it was the most prominent reserve currency in Europe before the introduction of the euro, and, since Germany was the lowest-inflation country for many years, currencies in Europe were largely tied to the deutsche mark. For the remaining countries, the U.S. dollar is the usual anchor currency of choice, since the largest share of emerging market countries' external debt is denominated in U.S. dollars, and world trade is predominantly dollar-invoiced.

Table 14.1 presents evidence of the frequency distribution of monthly exchange rate changes (in percent) for recent or current episodes that are classified as freely floating regimes. Our chosen threshold values are $x^c = |1$ percent$|$ and $x^c = 2.5$ percent, which is a comparatively narrow band.[6] For the United States, for example, there is an approximately 59 percent probability that the monthly change in the dollar-deutsche mark exchange rate falls within a relatively narrow ± 2.5 band. For the dollar-yen exchange rate, that probability is slightly higher at 61 percent. By contrast, for Bolivia, Canada, and India (all declared floaters during that period), the probability is approximately 94 percent. An alternative way of stating the same facts is that there is only about a 5 percent probability in those countries that an exchange rate change will exceed 2.5 percent in any given month (versus a more than 40 percent chance for the dollar-deutsche mark exchange). On

Table 14.1
Exchange Rate Volatility in Recent or Current Floating Exchange Rate Regimes

Country	Period	Probability that the monthly percent change in nominal exchange rate falls within:	
		±1 percent band	±2.5 percent band
U.S. dollar/ deutsche mark	February 1973–April 1999	26.8	58.7
Japan	February 1973–April 1999	33.8	61.2
Australia	January 1984–April 1999	28.0	70.3
Bolivia	September 1985–December 1997	72.8	93.9
Canada	June 1970–April 1999	68.2	93.6
India	March 1993–April 1999	82.2	93.4
Kenya	October 1993–December 1997	50.0	72.2
Mexico	December 1994–April 1999	34.6	63.5
New Zealand	March 1985–April 1999	39.1	72.2
Nigeria	October 1986–March 1993	36.4	74.5
Norway	December 1992–December 1994	79.2	95.8
Peru	August 1990–April 1999	45.2	71.4
Philippines	January 1988–April 1999	60.7	74.9
South Africa	January 1983–April 1999	32.8	66.2
Spain	January 1984–May 1989	57.8	93.8
Sweden	November 1992–April 1999	35.1	75.5
Uganda	January 1992–April 1999	52.9	77.9
Average, excluding United States and Japan		51.67	79.27
Standard deviation, excluding United States and Japan		17.83	11.41

Source: Based on Calvo and Reinhart (2000b).

average, for the current set of independently floating exchange rate countries (excluding the United States and Japan), the probability that the exchange rate change will be contained in this moderate ±2.5 percent band is more than 79 percent—significantly above that for the United States and Japan.[7] However, by this metric, postcrisis Mexico approximates a float more closely than any of the other countries—including Canada.[8]

Moderate to large monthly fluctuations in the exchange rate are even rarer among the so-called managed float episodes (table 14.2). For Egypt and Bolivia, the probability of a monthly exchange rate change greater than 2.5 percent is nil; this was also the case for Indone-

Table 14.2
Exchange Rate Volatility in Recent or Current Managed Floating Exchange Rate Regimes

		Probability that the monthly percent change in nominal exchange rate falls within:	
Country	Period	±1 percent band	±2.5 percent band
Bolivia	January 1998–April 1999	100.0	100.0
Brazil	July 1994–December 1998	83.1	94.3
Chile	October 1982–April 1999	45.5	83.8
Colombia	January 1979–April 1999	15.6	86.8
Egypt	February 1991–December 1998	95.7	98.9
Greece	January 1977–December 1997	58.6	85.3
India	February 1979–February 1993	53.6	84.5
Indonesia	November 1978–June 1997	96.4	99.1
Israel	December 1991–April 1999	45.5	90.9
Kenya	January 1998–April 1999	51.0	70.6
Korea	March 1980–October 1997	80.1	97.6
Malaysia	December 1992–September 1998	59.4	81.2
Mexico	January 1989–November 1994	64.3	95.7
Norway	January 1995–April 1999	56.9	90.2
Pakistan	January 1982–April 1999	77.8	92.8
Singapore	January 1988–April 1999	61.5	88.9
Turkey	January 1980–April 1999	12.6	36.8
Uruguay	January 1993–April 1999	22.7	92.0
Venezuela	April 1996–April 1999	60.6	93.9
Average		60.05	87.54
Standard deviation		25.43	14.28

Source: Based on Calvo and Reinhart (2000b).

sia and South Korea until the 1997–98 crisis. Even for self-proclaimed flexible-rate advocates, such as Chile and Singapore, the frequency distribution of their monthly exchange rate fluctuations relative to the U.S. dollar does not vaguely resemble those of the U.S. dollar-deutsche mark or U.S. dollar-yen, and a significantly higher proportion of observations falls within a narrow band; in the case of Singapore, there is an 89 percent probability that monthly exchange rate changes are within a 2.5 percent band, while for Chile that probability is only moderately lower. On average, there is an 88 percent probability that monthly changes in the exchange rate of managed floaters are confined to this

Table 14.3
Exchange Rate Volatility in Recent or Current Limited Flexibility Exchange Rate Regimes

Country	Period	Probability that the monthly percent change in nominal exchange rate falls within:	
		±1 percent band	±2.5 percent band
France	March 1979–April 1999	86.7	97.5
Greece	January 1998–April 1999	40.0	80.0
Malaysia	January 1986–February 1990	71.4	98.1
Spain	June 1989–April 1999	67.0	92.4
Sweden	June 1985–October 1992	58.1	92.1
Average		64.64	92.02
Standard deviation		17.23	7.27

Source: Based on Calvo and Reinhart (2000b).

narrow band. This exchange rate stability is surprising in light of the fact that inflation rates for many of the emerging market countries during these episodes were well above those observed for the United States; terms-of-trade shocks, moreover, were frequent and large.

Not surprisingly, the mean probability that exchange rate changes for limited flexibility arrangements are confined to this band is even greater: 92 percent (see table 14.3). Hence the observed behavior under the exchange rate regime accords with the assumptions stated in equation 1. What is most surprising is the narrowness of the wedge across regimes. Whereas the mean probability that the exchange rate is contained within a 2.5 percent band differs significantly when comparing the fixed exchange rate regime with the freely floating rate regime, other differences across regimes are less pronounced. For example, the average probability that $\varepsilon < 2.5$ percent for freely floating regimes is not significantly different from that for managed floating regimes, which, in turn, is not significantly different from the limited flexibility arrangement. There is, moreover, no statistically significant difference between the limited flexibility category and the pegged exchange rate.[9]

The results presented in our earlier work show that interest rate and reserve variability are significantly higher for most countries than they are for the G-3 countries, attesting to active policies to smooth exchange rate fluctuations, either by direct intervention in the foreign exchange market or by open market operations.[10] Our results suggest that even in many of the countries that are classified as having a high degree of exchange rate flexibility, there is widespread fear of floating.

Emerging Markets Are Different: Some Stylized Facts

Several key differences between emerging market and developed economies may help explain why emerging market countries are often reluctant to allow their currencies to float freely and why policymakers in these countries may be particularly concerned about the consequences of large exchange rate swings. These include the loss of access to international capital markets, the contractionary effects of devaluations or depreciations, and the effects of chronic credibility problems. The adverse impact of exchange rate uncertainty on trade, as well as the problems that emerging market may face as a result of higher inflation pass-throughs may account for why exchange rate variability is so widely resisted.

The Sudden-Stop Problem

In this section we analyze different aspects of the aftermath of currency crises for developed and emerging markets separately, including what happens to growth, the current account, and to sovereign credit ratings. Our sample includes twenty-five countries, which are listed in table 14A.1; the data span the period 1970 through 1999, which includes 96 currency crisis episodes (the dates of these crises are listed in table 14A.2.) Twenty-five of these crises are in developed economies, while the remainder are in emerging markets.

By using national income accounting data and abstracting from errors and omissions, net capital inflows equal the current account deficit plus accumulation of international reserves. Therefore, a sudden stop to capital inflows (that is, a drying up of access to world capital markets) has to be met by reserve losses or by a reduction in the current account deficit. In practice, both can take place. Whereas a loss of international reserves increases the country's financial vulnerability, a forced contraction in the current account deficit usually has serious effects on production and employment.

To visualize this, note that the current account deficit equals aggregate demand minus gross domestic product (GDP). Thus, a sudden contraction in the current account deficit necessitates either a sharp decline in aggregate demand or, in the unlikely case, an offsetting increase in GDP. The decline in aggregate demand, in turn, forces a decline in the demand for both tradable and nontradable goods. The excess supply of tradables thus created can be shipped abroad, but the nontradables are, by definition, bottled up at home. Thus the price of nontradables relative to that of traded goods will have to fall (resulting in a real depreciation of the currency). A prominent example of the process is the real estate sector, where relative prices have exhibited sharp declines in all the crises of the 1990s. From here, what produces a loss of output and employment? Two channels can be identified: (1) the Keynesian channel, and (2) the Fisherian channel (identified, respectively, with John Maynard Keynes and Irving Fisher). The Keynesian channel is straightforward and familiar; it is predicated on the assumption that prices and wages are inflexible downward. Under these conditions, a fall in aggregate demand brings about a fall in output and employment.

The Fisherian channel, by contrast, is less familiar and, in our view, potentially more damaging. Financial contracts are as a general rule contingent on very few "states of nature," that is, objective variables, such as terms of trade, profit, or demand. A bank loan, for example, is typically serviced by a series of fixed installments unless the borrower goes bankrupt. To a first approximation and consistent with the Fisherian channel, loans are made at a fixed, predetermined interest rate that takes into account expected future variables, but they are not conditioned on their future realization. Consider a situation in which the exchange rate is fixed and the international price of tradables is exogenous and constant over time: A decline in aggregate demand that accompanies a sudden stop calls for a lower price of nontradable goods relative to tradable goods. Because the price of tradables is stable, in order to achieve a lower relative price of nontradables, the *nominal* price of nontradables must fall. Thus, since the interest rate is invariant with respect to sudden stops, the ex post real interest rate faced by producers of nontradables surges, increasing the share of nonperforming loans.

Table 14.4 reports averages across the ninety-six currency crises in our sample of the current account deficit as a percent of GDP and the percent change in real GDP before and after the crisis year (T).[11] The fourth column reports the change, or adjustment, that took place between the year immediately preceding the crisis $(T - 1)$ and the year after the crisis $(T + 1)$. The crises episodes were aggregated by classifying the countries as either developed or emerging.

Table 14.4
Current Account Adjustments and GDP Growth before and after Currency Crises[a]

Country Group	$T-1$	T (currency crisis year)	$T+1$	Change from $T-1$ to $T+1$	Change/ precrisis (4)/(1)
	(1)	(2)	(3)	(4)	(5)
Current account deficit as a percent of GDP					
Emerging markets	−4.46	−3.97	−1.39	3.47	−71.4
Developed countries	−2.84	−3.06	−2.10	0.74	−26.1
Difference	−1.62	−0.91	0.71	2.33**	. . .
Percent change in real GDP					
Emerging markets	3.61	1.27	1.62	−1.99	−55.1
Developed countries	1.73	1.49	1.58	−0.15	−8.7
Difference	1.88**	−0.22	0.04	−1.84**	. . .

Sources: Authors' calculations using World Bank data.
a. A total of ninety-six currency crises, of which twenty-five are in developed economies and the remainder are in emerging markets.
**Significant at the 5 percent level.

The general patterns in the current account deficit and economic growth are quite similar for emerging market and developed economies; in both groups, the currency crisis produces a reduction in both the current account deficit and growth. (For developed countries, however, the pre- and post-devaluation difference in growth is not significantly different from zero.) Hence, at least in this sample, devaluations in either group that accompany crises are expansionary, as suggested by most standard textbook models.[12] However, there are also important differences between emerging market and developed countries. The sudden-stop problem in emerging markets, as measured by the current account adjustment between $T-1$ and $T+1$, is almost five times as large as that for developed economies (about 3.5 percent versus 0.7 percent). Furthermore, the difference between the two groups is significant at standard confidence levels. As we show below, the larger adjustment in the current account may be the outcome of emerging markets' involuntary loss of access to international capital markets in the wake of currency crises.[13] Indeed, a simple analytical framework suggests that lack of credibility is likely to be at the heart of this key difference between emerging and developed markets and that this credibility problem may be so severe at times of stress that it results in an abrupt collapse in the country's ability to borrow in international capital markets. (See below.)

In that light, it is not surprising that the magnitude of the recession following the currency crash is also significantly greater for emerging markets (see table 14.4). While the growth slowdown for developed economies is less than 0.2 percent (which is not statistically significant from 0), the recession is far more pronounced among emerging markets, with a reduction in growth of about 2 percent.[14] The difference in growth performance between the developed and emerging markets is also statistically significant; indeed, the last column, which shows the change relative to the precrisis performance, highlights more clearly the gap between the two categories. Furthermore, as shown in our earlier work, recessions appear to grown more severe during the 1990s.[15] Indeed, in the subset of crises in the 1990s there is an actual *contraction* in output—not just a sharp slowdown in growth.

One reason—perhaps a crucial one—for the deeper recessions and larger current account adjustments in emerging markets following currency crises is that these countries do not enjoy the international standing of their developed counterparts; hence emerging market countries may face substantial difficulties in obtaining external financing during the period following a devaluation or depreciation.

Loss of Access to International Capital Markets

One indication of how international credit markets view emerging markets can be gleaned by examining the evolution of sovereign credit ratings (in this instance those issued by Moody's Investor Services and *Institutional Investor* [*II*]) around episodes of financial crisis. The *II* sample begins in 1979 and runs through 1999. For the Moody's ratings, we have an unbalanced panel (that is, we do not have the same number of observations for all the countries). The currency crises examined, as before, are those listed in table 14A.1. For *II*, the ratings are an index that runs from 0 (least creditworthy) to 100 (most creditworthy). The *II* rankings are reported twice a year and are changed frequently. For Moody's, which uses letters to characterize a sovereign's creditworthiness, we map their letter ratings into sixteen possible categories, with zero corresponding to the lowest credit rating and sixteen corresponding to the highest (table 14.5).[16] The ratings may be changed at any time, hence we know in which month any changes took place. Moody's rating changes are far more infrequent than those of *II*.

Table 14.5
Scale for Moody's Foreign Currency Debt Rating

Rating Scale	Assigned Value
Aaa	16
Aa1	15
Aa2	14
Aa3	13
A1	12
A2	11
A3	10
Baa1	9
Baa2	8
Baa3	7
Ba1	6
Ba2	5
Ba3	4
B1	3
B2	2
B3	1
C	0

Sources: Moody's Investors Service and the authors.

Results from the analysis of the *II* and Moody's sovereign ratings are presented in tables 14.6 and 14.7, respectively. We report a variety of statistics in order to capture the various manifestations of the extent and the terms of access to international lending around currency crisis episodes. The statistics reported include the level of the assigned rating at the time of the crisis and at six and twelve months following the currency crisis, the probability of a downgrade for various time horizons following that event, and the probability of multiple downgrades. We also report the percentage change in the ratings at several time horizons. As before, we report the results for emerging and developed countries separately and test for differences among the two groups.

Turning to the *II* results first, as shown in the top panel of table 14.6, we find no significant differences between developed countries and emerging market countries in the probability of a downgrade (or multiple downgrades) following the currency crisis. However, this is where the similarities among the two country groups end. It is worth noting that at the time of the crisis, the average rating for the emerging market countries is 37.6, slightly less than half the average score for developed

Table 14.6
The Probability and Magnitude of Downgrades following Currency Crises: *Institutional Investor* Sovereign Credit Rankings, 1979–99

Country Group	Probability of downgrade in six months (percent)	Probability of downgrade in twelve months (percent)	Probability of more than one downgrade in twelve months (percent)
Emerging	39.0	79.3	31.7
Developed	38.4	73.1	30.8
Difference	0.6	6.2	0.9
	Index level		
	At crisis period	Next six months	Twelve months later
Emerging	37.6	36.0	33.5
Developed	76.0	74.9	74.5
Difference	−38.4**	−38.9**	−41.0**
	Magnitude of downgrade in six months (percent change)	Magnitude of downgrade in next six months (percent change)	Magnitude of downgrade in twelve months (percent change)
Emerging	4.3	6.9	10.8
Developed	1.4	0.5	1.9
Difference	2.8*	6.4**	8.9**

Source: Authors' calculations using data from *Institutional Investor*, 1979–99.
*Significant at the 10 percent level.
**Significant at the 5 percent level.

countries (see table 14.6, middle panel). This, of course, suggests that even in the absence of a crisis, access to international lending is far from even for the two country groupings. Furthermore, that vast gap widens further in the aftermath of the devaluations associated with the currency crises. In the twelve months following the currency crisis, the magnitude of the downgrade is about five times greater for emerging market economies than it is for developed economies. On average, emerging markets' sovereign rating index falls 10.9 percent in the twelve months following the currency crisis. The differences between the postcrisis downgrade for emerging and developed economies is significant at standard confidence levels. The gulf between emerging market and developed economies is even greater when a comparable exercise is performed for the Moody's ratings. As with the *II* ratings, the level of the ratings at the outset of the currency crisis is signifi-

Table 14.7
The Probability and Magnitude of Downgrades following Currency Crises: Moody's Sovereign Credit Rankings, 1979–99

Country Group	Probability of downgrade in six months (percent)	Probability of downgrade in twelve months (percent)	Probability of more than one downgrade in twelve months (percent)
Emerging	20.0	26.7	6.7
Developed	10.0	10.0	0.0
Difference	10.0**	16.7**	6.7*

	Index level		
	At crisis period	Next six months	Twelve months later
Emerging	4.9	4.5	4.3
Developed	15.0	14.9	14.9
Difference	−10.1**	−10.4**	−10.6**

	Magnitude of downgrade in six months (percent change)	Magnitude of downgrade in next six months (percent change)	Magnitude of downgrade in twelve months (percent change)
Emerging	8.2	4.4	12.2
Developed	0.7	0.0	0.7
Difference	7.5**	4.4**	11.5**

Source: Authors' calculations using data from Moody's Investors Service, 1979–99.
*Significant at the 10 percent level.
**Significant at the 5 percent level.

cantly lower for emerging market economies—the sovereign rating level is about a third of that assigned to developed economies. Furthermore, as in the *II* results, the magnitude of the downgrade in six months is far greater for emerging markets—about 9 percent versus less than 1 percent for developed countries. However, as shown in table 14.7, in the case of Moody's sovereign ratings, the probabilities of a downgrade in the twelve months following the crisis *and* of multiple downgrades is significantly higher for the emerging economies in our sample.

To complement the preceding analysis, we examine whether knowing that there was a currency crisis helps to predict sovereign credit rating downgrades for emerging and developed economies. In the case of the *II* ratings, for which there is a continuous time series, we regress the six-month change in the credit rating index on a currency crisis dummy variable, which takes on the value of one when there is a crisis and zero otherwise; the crisis dummy enters with a six-month lag.[17] The method of estimation is generalized least squares, correcting both for generalized forms of heteroskedasticity and for serial correlation in the residuals. In the case of the Moody's ratings, the dependent variable is three-month changes in the rating, while the explanatory variable is the crisis dummy three months earlier. The latter specification allows us to glean more precisely whether downgrades follow rapidly after crises take place. In the case of Moody's, the sovereign rating dependent variable is allowed to assume the value of -1, 0, or 1 depending on whether there was a downgrade, no change, or an upgrade. We estimate the parameters of interest with an ordered probit technique that allows us to correct for heteroskedastic disturbances.

The results of the estimation for both II and Moody's ratings are summarized in table 14.8. For developed countries, there is no conclusive evidence that ratings react to currency crises in a systematic and significant way. In the case of emerging markets, by contrast, currency crises help predict downgrades, irrespective of which rating index is used: the coefficients are significant at standard confidence levels—even though their marginal predictive contribution remains small. For

Table 14.8
Reactive Credit Ratings: Developed and Emerging Markets

Dependent variable: *Institutional Investor* six-month changes in sovereign rating. Estimation method: Ordinary least squares with robust standard errors.

Independent variable is a currency crisis dummy	Coefficient (1)	Standard error (2)	Probability value (3)	R^2 (4)
Developed	−0.009	0.019	0.61	0.01
Emerging	−0.04**	0.014	0.005	0.07

Dependent variable: Moody's three-month changes in sovereign rating. Estimation method: Ordered probit.

Independent variable is a currency crisis dummy	Coefficient (1)	Standard error (2)	Probability value (3)	Pseudo R^2 (4)
Developed	−0.08	0.90	0.901	0.001
Emerging	−0.27**	0.14	0.048	0.04

Source: Authors' calculations, using data from *Institutional Investor* and Moody's Investors Service.
**Significant at the 5 percent level.

example, in the case of Moody's, a currency crisis increases the likelihood of a downgrade by 5 percent. The difference between developed and emerging market economies in the reaction of sovereign ratings is not entirely surprising given the finding that slowdowns following currency crises are more severe in emerging markets. To the extent that the downturn in economic activity is perceived to increase the risk of difficulties in meeting debt obligations, credit ratings have tended to behave in a reactive manner.

These results are also in line with those of other authors, who find evidence of two-way causality between sovereign ratings and market spreads.[18] Hence not only do international capital markets react to changes in the ratings, but the ratings systematically react (with a lag) to market conditions, as reflected in the sovereign bond yield spreads.

Exchange Rate Volatility and Trade: Emerging Markets Are Different

The preceding analysis focused on the differences between emerging markets and developed countries during periods of market stress. In this section we turn our attention to differences that are always present—crisis or no crisis. Given the outwardly oriented growth strategy pursued by many emerging market countries and, more generally, the prominent role played by international trade, we revisit the literature that has examined the links between exchange rate uncertainty and trade. The aim of this exercise is not to provide an exhaustive review of this vast literature; rather, our focus is on what these studies reveal about the differences between emerging markets and developed economies.

A large number of studies have attempted to examine the link between exchange rate uncertainty and trade with respect to industrialized countries. Some observers have found that real exchange rate volatility has adverse consequences for the imports of several developed economies.[19] Others have found little evidence of any systematic effects.[20] In general, the findings of this literature are quite mixed—at least as far as industrial countries are concerned. Although the body of work that examines the link between exchange rate volatility and trade is thinner with respect to emerging markets, most of the existing studies appear to find more consistent patterns in the data. In general, this literature (summarized in table 14.9) seems to point in the direction that exchange rate variability has deleterious effects on trade,

Table 14.9
Summary of the Empirical Literature on the Effects of Exchange Rate Variability on Trade with an Emphasis on Emerging Markets

Study	Period and country coverage	Volatility/risk measure	Estimation method and approach	Key findings
Mixed sample of emerging and developed economies				
Brada and Mendez (1988)	Thirty countries, of which fourteen are emerging markets, 1973–77	Dummy variable was assigned to designate whether a country has a fixed or flexible exchange rate	Cross section	Mixed results. For emerging markets exchange rate uncertainty inhibits bilateral exports.
Frankel and Wei (1993)	Sixty-three countries, annual data for 1980, 1985, 1990	Standard deviation of the first difference of log of nominal and real exchange rate	Gravity model of bilateral trade. Cross section ordinary least squares and instrumental variables	Mixed results. Small negative significant effect in 1980; positive significant effect in 1990.
Savvides (1993)	Sixty-two developed and emerging economies, 1973–86	Attempts to separate expected and unexpected variability of the real exchange rate	Two-step procedure for cross-sectional exports	Only the unexpected variability measure has a negative and significant effect on export volumes; result is robust when the countries are disaggregated into developed and emerging market groups.

Emerging economies only

Study	Sample	Measure	Method	Results
Arize, Osang, and Slottje (2000)	Thirteen emerging market countries, quarterly data, 1973–96: Ecuador, Indonesia, Korea, Malaysia, Malawi, Mauritius, Mexico, Morocco, Philippines, Sri Lanka, Taiwan, Thailand, and Tunisia	Moving standard deviation of real effective exchange rate volatility	Johansen's cointegrating VARs. Country-specific error correction models are estimated for exports	Increases in volatility of the real effective exchange rate exert a significant negative effect on exports in both short and long run in all thirteen countries.
Caballero and Corbo (1989)	Six emerging market countries: Chile, Colombia, Peru, Philippines, Thailand and Turkey	Real bilateral exchange rate variance	Koych-type model is used to estimate export demand equations	Strong, negative and significant effect of real exchange rate uncertainty on the exports of all the countries in the sample.
Coes (1981)	Brazil, 1957–74, annual data	Real exchange rate variability and also dummy for crawling peg period	Log-linear demand for Brazilian exports	Reduction in exchange rate uncertainty during the crawling peg period significantly increased exports.
Grobar (1993)	Ten emerging market countries, 1963–85: Argentina, Brazil, Colombia, Greece, Malaysia, Mexico, Philippines, South Africa, Thailand, and Yugoslavia	Four uncertainty indexes capturing different measure of real exchange rate volatility	Export supply by SITC category. Pooled time-series, cross-sectional data, fixed effects	Most export categories were adversely affected by exchange rate uncertainty.
Medhora (1990)	West African Monetary Union	Real exchange effective rate variance	Import demand equations	Found no evidence that exchange rate variability affected African imports.
Paredes (1989)	Brazil, Chile, and Peru	Various measures	Manufactured exports, log-linear specification for individual countries	Volatility has a significantly adverse effect on exports.

either on emerging market exports or imports.[21] Taken together, these findings would seem to support those of Andrew Rose, who, using data for 186 countries over the 1970–90 period, finds that countries that share a common currency trade three times as much with each other as those that lack a common currency.[22]

The more conclusive evidence that trade is adversely affected by exchange rate volatility in emerging markets is not entirely surprising and may owe to several features of the emerging market countries themselves. First, as Ronald McKinnon (among others) has shown, the patterns of trade invoicing in emerging market countries are markedly different from those in industrial countries.[23] In explaining what he calls the East Asian dollar standard, McKinnon observes that nearly all trade with the United States—including East Asia's trade—is dollar denominated. About 98 percent of United States exports and nearly 90 percent of its imports are dollar invoiced. Furthermore, he notes, "on a worldwide basis, manufactured and brand name goods tend to be invoiced in the home currency of the exporting country even though primary commodities remain overwhelmingly dollar invoiced."[24] McKinnon's observation is particularly relevant for emerging market countries, even those that have little trade with the United States, since many of these countries' exports have a high primary commodity content. Indeed, the evidence presented in some studies on developed countries reveals that invoicing patterns matter in determining the effects of exchange rate volatility on exports.[25]

Although emerging markets may fear depreciations or devaluations, as the case may be, as well as exchange rate volatility, these countries also tend to fear (and as a consequence, to resist) the consequences of large real appreciations not only for the obvious reason that they erode international competitiveness but also because of concerns about Dutch disease–type problems.[26] Such concerns are especially commonplace when countries are attempting to diversify their export base.[27]

A second feature of emerging economies that may explain why real exchange rate volatility has a negative effect on trade is the incomplete nature of their capital markets. Exporters and importers in developed countries, where futures markets are relatively well developed, have the tools to hedge exchange rate risk. In emerging economies, futures markets are either illiquid or non-existent; out of fear of large exchange rate swings, central banks may attempt to replicate the conditions for exporters and importers that capital markets provide in the developed world.

Inflation and Exchange Rate Pass-Through Issues

Another reason why emerging market countries may fear floating in general and devaluations or depreciations in particular may be traced to concerns about the effects of large currency swings on domestic inflation. This exchange rate pass-through issue merits attention, especially in the context of countries that have adopted or are thinking of adopting inflation targets.[28]

Estimates of exchange rate pass-through should be grounded on a well-defined, micro-founded model. However, in the absence of such a model (or models) for this hybrid group of countries we rely, as a first pass, on simple techniques that allow us to glean what the temporal relationship between exchange rate changes and inflation looks like.

For each exchange rate regime, we estimate a bivariate vector autoregressive (VAR) model in inflation and exchange rate changes. The number of regimes covered in this exercise totals forty-one and covers the cases shown in tables 14.1–14.3.[29] Although the exercise is a simple one, it has several appealing features. First, because our delineation of the sample for each case is dictated by the exchange rate arrangement, it is less likely to be subject to Lucas critique–type problems—to the extent that pass-through may depend on the type of exchange rate arrangement. Second, the VAR approach treats both variables as potentially endogenous. This is particularly important where emerging market countries are concerned, as tables 14A.3 to 14A.5 attest. In several instances, the relationship runs from inflation to exchange rates, as countries follow a purchasing power of parity rule.[30] Third, it allows the data to reveal the dynamic relationship between the two variables of interest, since the lag length for the VAR is selected on a case-by-case basis according to the Schwarz information criterion. This is particularly valuable when it comes to comparing high- and low-inflation countries; in the case of the former, the pass-through tends to be more immediate.

Table 14.10 summarizes the incidence and magnitude of exchange rate pass-through (the results are based on tables 14A.3 to 14A.6). Two features of the results are noteworthy. First, the percentage of cases in which the block-exogeneity tests indicate that the lagged exchange rate change has a statistically significant effect on inflation is 43 percent for emerging markets versus 13 percent for developed countries. Second, the average pass-through is about four times as large for emerging

Table 14.10
A Summary of the Incidence and Magnitude of Exchange Rate Pass-Through[a]

Country group	Proportion of cases where there was a statistically significant pass-through
Emerging	0.43
Developed	0.13
	Average pass-through coefficient
Emerging	0.228
Developed	0.065
Difference	0.163**

Sources: Authors' calculations, using International Monetary Fund, *International Financial Statistics.*
a. Details of the country and period coverage are provided in tables A-3 to A-6.
**Significant at the 5 percent level or higher.

markets as it is for developed economies. Taken together, these results may also help explain emerging markets' intolerance to large exchange rate fluctuations—especially devaluations or depreciations.[31]

Emerging Markets: The Chronic Credibility Problem

Even in the absence of a crisis, emerging economies have precarious access to capital markets. This credibility problem is reflected in sovereign credit ratings that are vastly inferior to those that prevail for developed countries—even before a devaluation. This chronic lack of credibility also affects the magnitude and abruptness of the sudden-stop problem.

Interest rates are an intertemporal price and for that reason heavily influenced by expectations; high and volatile interest rates are indicators of lack of credibility. As shown in table 14.11, interest rates are about five times more volatile in emerging markets as in developed economies, and that gap widens even further if we include countries with a history of chronic inflation.[32] This gap between the low- and chronic inflation emerging market countries is hardly surprising. Many emerging economies have a weak revenue base and a rudimentary tax collection system, a combination that has driven many a country, particularly in Latin America, to use and abuse the inflation tax (Calvo dubs this problem the "political fiscal gap").[33] As firms and households take into account the possibility of being taxed in this manner, credibility problems are exacerbated and translate into high and

Table 14.11
Credibility Problems and Financial Volatility

Country Group	Average Variance in Monthly interest rates[a]
Emerging	758.19
Emerging excluding high inflation	80.15
Developed	16.78
Difference excluding high inflation	63.37**

Sources: IMF, *International Financial Statistics,* various central banks.
a. Calculations based on Calvo and Reinhart (2000b).
**Significant at the 5 percent level.

volatile interest rates. This interest rate volatility may be the outcome of procyclical policies that are responding to unstable expectations.

The evidence of the preceding discussion suggests that emerging markets may have solid grounds for resisting and fearing devaluations and exchange rate variability. Not only are currency crises contractionary, but they are associated with large and significant changes in countries' ability to borrow from international sources. The marked and systematic declines in credit ratings for emerging market economies following currency crashes, in contrast to the relatively unscathed developed economies, suggest that the large adjustments in the current account—the sudden-stop problem—that we observe in the data may be largely owing to an abrupt and involuntary loss of access to international capital markets. If such is the dire outcome of a currency crisis for emerging market countries, one might expect to observe a generalized tendency among these economies to try to limit exchange rate fluctuations, at least when compared to the currency swings evident among the developed economies that allow their exchange rate to float freely.

Varieties of Fear of Floating

The widespread fear of large exchange rate swings is made understandable by the fact that devaluations (or depreciations) in emerging markets tend to be contractionary. For emerging economies, moreover, these appear to be accompanied by an erosion of credibility (as revealed by deteriorating credit ratings) that may be so severe as to result in a loss of access to international capital markets. In this section, we present an analytical framework that examines the link between lack of credibility and fear of floating (or, more generally, allowing the exchange rate to adjust); we also consider the more extreme case where the credibility loss translates into an inability to borrow from abroad and a contraction in output. Other reasons for fearing exchange rate swings, including the role played by liability dollarization and an ineffective lender of last resort, are also discussed.

Managing Monetary Policy

Despite their heterogeneity, emerging market countries tend to share a common characteristic: they appear to be reluctant to let their currencies fluctuate freely. This leads us to conjecture that there may be at least one common cause—lack of credibility. If credibility is not conferred, the monetary authority has no authority. Expectations will rule the day. These credibility problems may be manifested in multiple ways, including volatile interest rates and sovereign credit ratings. Furthermore, lack of credibility may give rise to liability dollarization and limit the central bank's ability to act as an effective lender of last resort, all of which feed the fear of exchange rate fluctuations.

We can use a simple version of a conventional monetary model to put more structure on the lack of credibility conjecture. Let us assume that the demand for money satisfies the following Cagan form:[34]

$$m_t - e_t = \alpha E_t(e_t - e_{t+1}), \quad \alpha > 0, \tag{2}$$

where m and e are the logs of the money supply and the nominal exchange rate, and E_t is the mathematical expectations operator conditional on information available in period t (which includes money supply and exchange rate in period t). The interest–semi-elasticity parameter is denoted by α.

For simplicity, consider the case in which money supply in period 2 onward takes a constant value $\bar{m}$. Then one can show that in a rational expectations equilibrium we have

$$e_1 = \frac{m_1 + \alpha \bar{m}}{1 + \alpha}. \tag{3}$$

Thus the exchange rate in period 1 (which we can identify with the *present*) is a weighted average of present and future money supply. Moreover, and by the same token, $e_t = \bar{m}$, for $t = 2, 3, \ldots$. On the other hand, assuming (again, for simplicity) perfect capital mobility and that the international interest rate equals zero, we have the nominal interest rate $i_t = e_{t+1} - e_t$ satisfying

$$i_1 = e_2 - e_1 = \frac{\bar{m} - m_1}{1 + \alpha}. \tag{4}$$

Case 1: Permanent Increase in Present m

Suppose that the economy was at steady state (that is, money supply constant at $\bar{m}$ and it is shocked by an unanticipated once-and-for-all increase in the supply of money in period 1. By equations 3 and 4, the exchange rate suffers a permanent devaluation accompanied by *no* interest rate volatility.

Case 2: Permanent Increase in Future m

By equations 3 and 4, a permanent increase in future money supply $\bar{m}$ (keeping m_1 constant) results in an increase in both the current exchange rate and interest rate.

Under circumstances of poor credibility, a policymaker faced with currency devaluation, and who does not intend to increase future money supply, faces a serious dilemma: if money supply in period 1 is not adjusted upward, the ex post *real* interest rate will increase, possibly generating difficulties in the real and financial sectors. On the other hand, if m_1 is jacked up to stabilize interest rates, credibility could be impaired and future expectations could become more unruly and arbitrary.[35]

To increase realism, let us assume that the central bank pays interest m on money, and that the demand for money satisfies

$$\tilde{m}_t - e_t = \alpha E_t(e_t - e_{t+1} + i_t^m), \quad \alpha > 0, \tag{5}$$

where "$\sim$" on variable m is a reminder that it refers to interest-earning money. It can readily be verified that equations 3 and 4 are still valid for the present version, if one defines

$$m_t = \tilde{m}_t - \alpha i_t^m. \tag{6}$$

Hence, under this interpretation, raising central bank–controlled interest rates would be equivalent to lowering money supply. In this context, the currency devaluation that would be caused by a positive shock on future money supply $\bar{m}$ could be partially or fully offset by raising central bank–controlled interest rates (recall equation 3), a typical policy followed in emerging markets when the exchange rate threatens to rise sharply. Interestingly, by equation 4, the associated fall in m_1 raises market interest rates even more than if the central banks had stayed put. So this analysis suggests that in practice emerging markets have exhibited a pro-interest-rate-volatility bias.

If policymakers were faced with the choice between stabilizing i or stabilizing e, then the decision would be clear: stabilize the exchange rate. Exchange rate stabilization provides the economy with a clear-cut nominal anchor, while stabilizing i does not. In general, policymakers will find it optimal to allow for some volatility in both variables, while always steering clear from perfect interest rate stability. Therefore, credibility problems may bias the outcome toward lower exchange rate and higher interest rate volatility, as borne out by the facts.

Before examining that scenario, we turn to the case in which lack of credibility is so intense that the country loses access to capital markets.

The Role of Loss of Access to International Capital Markets

A loss of credibility so intense as to exclude access to capital markets approximates the serious capital market difficulties that emerging markets underwent during recent crises, especially during the Russian crisis of August 1998. Indeed, the evidence of more frequent and significantly more severe downgrades in sovereign credit ratings in the aftermath of devaluations for emerging market countries presented above suggests that this capital market problem is far more generalized than the examples provided by the recent crises in East Asia and Russia.[36]

Consider an economy with tradables and home goods but without physical capital. Let c and h denote the consumption of tradables and home goods, respectively. The instantaneous utility index is given by $u(c) + v(h)$, where u and v are increasing, strictly concave, and twice differentiable over the positive real line. The intertemporal utility function is time-separable and exhibits a positive rate of time preference r, which for convenience is set equal to the (constant) international interest rate. The output of tradables is exogenously given. In contrast, home-good prices are staggered, and the output of home goods is demand determined. Government rebates all income to the representative individual in a lump sum. Moreover, consumption is subject to a cash-in-advance constraint that takes the following form:

$$m_t = e_t c_t + h_t, \tag{7}$$

where m denotes real monetary balances in terms of home goods and e is the real exchange rate, that is, the ratio of the nominal exchange rate to the price of home goods (the international price of tradables is set equal to unity).[37]

We examine the impact of a once-and-for-all devaluation of the currency under two polar regimes: perfect capital mobility and no capital mobility. Recent devaluations in advanced economies have not impaired these countries' ability to borrow abroad. Sweden, for example, has even been able to externally finance domestic bank rescue packages. In contrast, devaluations in emerging markets have been accompanied by a serious interruption of external financing. Therefore, the analysis of the two polar cases will help us to better understand why devaluations in emerging markets are linked to output loss, while the opposite happened in developed economies.

Assume that the economy starts at a steady state and has zero foreign assets or liabilities. Let y denote the supply of tradables and, for simplicity, assume y constant over time. Thus, under the above assumptions, at the steady state we have $c = y$. Moreover, given the separability of the instantaneous utility index, and the equality between the subjective rate of discount and the international rate of interest, a once-and-for-all devaluation does not affect tradables' consumption. Hence $c = y$ after devaluation. Furthermore, the following static first-order condition is satisfied (interior solutions are assumed throughout):

$$\frac{u'(c_t)}{v'(h_t)} = e_t, \tag{8}$$

which is the familiar equality between marginal rate of substitution and relative price. Hence before and after devaluation the following condition holds under perfect capital.

$$\frac{u'(y)}{v'(h_t)} = e_t. \tag{9}$$

Therefore, since a devaluation entails an increase in e (recall that home-goods prices are sticky), on impact a devaluation is always expansionary (that is, it leads to a rise in h and, hence, in the output of home goods).[38]

Consider now the case of no capital mobility. Under this condition, the stock of nominal money cannot be changed instantaneously.

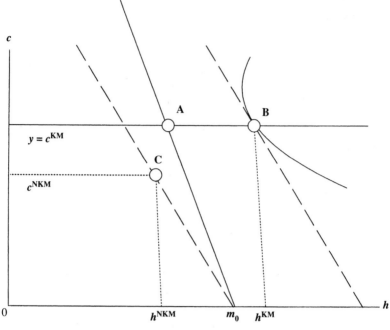

Consumption of tradable goods

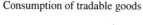

Consumption of home goods

Figure 14.1
Devaluation with and without Capital Mobility.

Thus, since homegoods prices are sticky, m is a predetermined variable. Moreover, with positive nominal interest rates (as in the present model), the cash-in-advance constraint is binding. Hence

$$m_0 = e_\infty y + h_\infty = e_0 c_0 + h_0, \tag{10}$$

where the subindex "∞" denotes steady state, and time $t = 0$ is, by definition, the point in time at which devaluation takes place. Figure 14.1 illustrates the determination of c and h at time $t = 0$ under the two regimes, where superscript KM and NKM refer to perfect capital mobility and no capital mobility, respectively. Point A corresponds to the steady state prior to devaluation, where the slope of the line passing through A corresponds to the real exchange rate prior to devaluation. After devaluation, relative prices are given by the slope of the dashed lines. With capital mobility, on impact the economy shifts to a point such as B and, as noted above, home-good output rises. Thus, given that tradables' consumption remains the same while their price goes up and that consumption of home goods rises, it follows from equation 2 that, on impact, real monetary balances have to increase and be larger than m_0. However, by condition 5, under no capital mobility, expenditure cannot exceed m_0. Hence the no-capital-mobility equilibrium, point C, is reached from point B as if the consumer in the standard textbook analysis had suffered a negative income effect. Consequently, if goods are normal (which holds under the present static separability assumption), consumption (and hence production) of home goods is larger with than without capital mobility. Therefore, *devaluation is more expansionary with than without capital mobility.* This is the central proposition. As a subsidiary result, note that if the income effect dominates the substitution effect, *devaluation with no capital mobility would be contractionary* (although, of course, it is always expansionary under perfect capital mobility). This income-effect dominance condition is empirically plausible given that home goods largely comprise services, which are likely to be highly complementary with tradables.

Consequently, the analysis shows that losing access to capital markets when a country devalues tends to suppress the expansionary effects of devaluation. Moreover, if market access is not lost, devaluation is always expansionary. This analysis suggests the following explanation for why output in developed economies and emerging markets reacted so differently to speculative attack on their currencies. Devaluation in advanced countries came as a result of an attack on their currencies, but there is no evidence that their creditworthiness was put into question. By contrast, in all recent emerging market crises, the attack was first and foremost on bonds issued by the country in question, making debt rollover impossible or very difficult. Thus the key to the explanation may lie in loss of capital market access.

In terms of our central discussion in this section, the model gives a rationale for the reluctance of countries with poor access to capital markets to devalue in order to relieve balance-of-payments difficulties.[39] Moreover, Mexico's Tequila crisis suggests that a devaluation *may trigger* a loss of access to capital markets, especially if it is seen as breaking a policy commitment.[40] This is an additional motivation for emerging markets to exhibit devaluation aversion and thus generate a smoother exchange rate path.

Consequently, losing access to capital markets when a country devalues tends to suppress the expansionary effects of devaluation.

Moreover, if market access is not lost, devaluation is always expansionary. This is at the root of why output in advanced economies and emerging markets reacted so differently to speculative attack on their currencies. Devaluation in developed countries came as a result of an attack on their currencies that did not put their creditworthiness into question. The key to the explanation may lie in loss of access to capital markets.

Ineffective Lender of Last Resort

A widespread view is that adoption of a currency board or dollarization significantly detracts from the central bank's ability to operate as a lender of last resort. This view is based on the conjecture that, since sums involved in bank bailouts are usually staggering, an effective lender of last resort should be able to issue its own money.

Typically, bank regulation allows banks to hold fractional reserves against deposits and imposes nonprohibitive costs on a maturity mismatch between assets and liabilities. As a result, banks' liabilities are more liquid than bank assets, which makes them liable to successful bank runs. One way to prevent self-fulfilling bank-run prophecies is for the central bank to step in and bail out the banking system if a run takes place. If expected by the public, the bailout may never have to be activated, thus making lender-of-last-resort capabilities costless to the central bank and beneficial to the private sector.

Douglas Diamond and Philip Dybvig, in a widely quoted paper, formalized self-fulfilling bank runs in terms of a *nonmonetary* model.[41] They give welfare grounds for the liquidity mismatch and show that, as a result, banks are liable to self-fulfilling runs. However, if the government announces that it will step in so that every depositor will come out whole, no bank run ever takes place. This operation captures the notion behind the existence of a lender of last resort. To make it credible, however, the government has to be able to raise enough taxes to finance the operation. Given the sums involved, this normally requires issuing government debt, which will eventually be serviced by higher taxes. However, this may not be possible for a country that has lost access to the capital market.[42]

Another drawback of the Diamond-Dybvig model is that it is a *real* model and, hence, cannot directly address the issue of whether a sovereign country's relinquishing the issuance of its own money could seriously impair the effectiveness of the lender of last resort. Suppose that deposits are denominated in domestic money, and that the central bank guarantees that depositors will be able to withdraw 100 percent of their deposits, if they so wish. A mechanical application of the Diamond-Dybvig model might suggest that this would be effective in preventing self-fulfilling bank runs. But this is wrong. In a monetary economy, the above guarantee does not ensure depositors that their deposits' *purchasing power* will remain intact.

Consider first the simple case in which bank-deposit interest rates are subject to a statutory ceiling (for example, the Federal Reserve's Regulation Q). Under those circumstances, if depositors expect a balance-of-payments crisis, there will be a bank run that the government will be unable to stop by the mere artifact of issuing money. Indeed, the act of issuing money will actually worsen the balance-of-payments crisis. This example is not very relevant in modern economies, because a large share of deposits earns interest (this will also be the equilibrium outcome of the Diamond-Dybvig model in a monetary economy). Under those circumstances, though, bank runs could cause balance-of-payments crises. First, depositors are unlikely to switch their deposits entirely into non-interest-bearing domestic cash. Instead, they are likely to try to hold alternative interest-earning assets (land, for example) or foreign exchange. As a result, if the central bank is unable to sterilize the extra bailout liquidity, the price level and exchange rate are bound to take a sharp upturn, unless the central bank has sufficient reserves to back up a large aggregate such as M2.[43] Consequently, if depositors expect a bank run, either depositors will withdraw their deposits— validating the run—or interest rates on bank deposits will have to become sharply higher.

If higher interest rates are successful in stopping bank runs, a lender of last resort would not be needed, because this operation could be undertaken by the banks without the help of the central bank. However, we cannot be very hopeful about the high-interest strategy: to compensate for a sharp price rise, interest rates may have to be so large that *if the run is stopped, banks will go bankrupt* (for fundamental reasons now). Banks will go under either because interest rates on their liabilities have risen substantially more than on their assets or, if that kind of interest-rate mismatch is avoided, because their loans have become nonperforming.

To keep depositors from fleeing the banking system, deposits can be indexed to prices (for example, UDIs in Chile) or exchange rates. The latter—"dollarization" of deposits—is a widespread practice in emerging market countries. Indexation provides an automatic mechanism to implicitly raise deposit interest rates when expectations of a bank run arise. Its advantage over deposits denominated in domestic currency is that the inflation or devaluation component of the interest rate is paid only if inflation or devaluation occurs. Thus banks' fundamentals are less likely to be undermined. This helps to explain, incidentally, why deposit indexation is so popular in emerging market countries. However, indexation increases the burden on the lender of last resort because deposits are now denominated in real terms. In fact, if all deposits are indexed to the exchange rate, for example, there would not be a major difference between this case and full dollarization.

How do advanced countries such as the United States manage to have an effective lender of last resort? The answer suggested above is simple: advanced countries never lose access to capital markets.[44] Was it critical for those countries to be able to print their own currencies? We doubt it.

In terms of the exchange rate volatility issue, this discussion shows that, contrary to popular belief, fixing the exchange rate may not entail a substantial loss of lender-of-last-resort capabilities in countries that are credit-constrained. Moreover, a limited lender of last resort gives rise to indexation of deposits. Aside from Chile, where UDIs have been a very successful vehicle for indexing debt to indexation to a domestic price level, and Brazil for a limited period, all other cases involve indexation to a hard currency (typically the U.S. dollar). This, in turn, induces banks (sometimes for regulatory reasons) to extend dollar loans. Given that domestic banks have a comparative advantage in lending to domestic residents, these loans will likely be channeled to them (and not recycled to the rest of the world).[45] However, not all domestic residents' earnings are denominated in dollars. In the services sector, for example, the dominant invoice currency is mostly domestic. Therefore, a devaluation may create serious financial problems in some sectors of the economy. This is an additional reason for the fear of floating.

Liability Dollarization

It could be argued that liability dollarization is partly a result of pegging, magnified by the overconfidence and moral hazard problems that pegging may foster. As the argument usually goes, if the exchange rate was free to float, domestic investors, especially those in the non-tradables sector, would shy away from loans denominated in foreign currency. This is so because they will now face a larger currency risk than under a fixed regime. This sounds convincing, but it misses two important points: (1) most emerging markets start from a situation of partial dollarization (at the very least, liability dollarization), and (2) it is exceedingly difficult to find instances in which an emerging market country completely ignores exchange rate volatility. These points reinforce one another. Partial dollarization increases the cost of exchange rate volatility (through the Fisherian channel, for example), inducing the central bank to intervene in the foreign exchange markets to prevent fluctuations in the nominal exchange rate. In fact, as the cases of El Salvador, the Philippines, and Venezuela attest, this "fear of floating" may be so severe that the exchange rate spends long stretches of time at a fixed level, making it observationally equivalent to a soft peg.[46] This fear of floating induces more liability dollarization, creating a vicious circle from which it is very hard to exit.[47]

Fear of floating and the lack of the discipline that underlies fixed exchange rates may drive authorities to adopt additional control measures, such as dual exchange rates and controls on capital mobility. Even when fear of floating does not lead to capital controls and countries adopt "market-friendly" ways of stabilizing the exchange rate through open market operations, such policies have significant costs both in terms of the associated interest rate volatility and their procyclical nature. Thus, contrary to the view that floating provides authorities with an extra degree of freedom to guarantee a market-friendly environment, the opposite may happen.

Concluding Remarks

If the past is any guide to the future, promises and statements by countries to move in the direction of a floating exchange rate may be devoid of real consequences. There appears to be a widespread "fear of floating" that is closely linked with credibility problems.

The root causes of the marked reluctance by emerging market countries to allow for much fluctuation in their exchange rates are multiple. When circumstances are favorable (such as capital inflows or positive terms-of-trade shocks), many emerging market countries are reluctant to allow the nominal (and real) exchange rate to appreciate.[48] This probably stems from fears of loss of competitiveness and setbacks to export diversification. When circumstances are adverse, the case against allowing large depreciations (or a devaluation if the exchange rate is explicitly pegged) becomes even more compelling. The fear of a collapse in the exchange rate derives from pervasive liability dollarization, since in most emerging markets the debt of both the government and the private sector are largely denominated in hard foreign currency. Devaluations or depreciations may also result in the loss of access to international capital markets. For this and other reasons, devaluations or depreciations in developing countries have a history of being associated with recessions—not export-led booms. Our theoretical framework illustrates this point. Furthermore, financial regulatory authorities may resist large swings in the exchange rate because of the inflationary consequences of such changes and the credibility problems these may feed. Even in the best of times, exchange rate volatility appears to hinder trade, which is so essential to emerging market countries. We have shown that the pass-through from exchange rates to prices is higher for emerging markets. Similarly, our review of the literature on the consequences of exchange rate volatility on trade suggests that developing countries' trade appears to be more systematically impacted by exchange rate volatility.

If the fear of significant exchange rate swings continues to be the serious policy issue it has been in the past, and if, as the stylized facts suggest, emerging market countries remain dollarized both in terms of their debt and the invoicing of trade receipts and if their prices continue to be more predominantly linked to the fate of the exchange rate, it would appear that there is little solid basis on which to expect that emerging markets will "simply float." Indeed, as the dust settles following the Asian crisis and capital flows aggressively return to that region, we are seeing many of the old ways resurface—foreign exchange intervention rules the day and currency appreciations are actively resisted. Alas, it sounds a great deal like the early 1990s. Other countries, such as Brazil and Mexico, have embraced "inflation targeting." But in countries where the pass-through from exchange rates to prices is high, inflation targeting often starts to resemble a soft peg, as swings in the exchange rate are resisted.

Much of the glitter of "flexible" exchange rates disappears upon closer examination. The degrees of freedom provided by exchange rate flexibility are fallacious or can be substituted by fiscal policy. In reality, it appears that in emerging markets what prevails are varieties of soft pegs—despite their poor track record—which raises the issue of dollarization: Why bother having a national currency in the first place?

One point to remember in the debate over whether dollarization is appropriate for emerging markets is that these economies are still "emerging." They are setting policy in a world in which their own financial markets remain underdeveloped, their trade is invoiced predominantly in dollars, their corporate and financial institutions have a limited ability to hedge exchange rate risk, and their governments, more often than not, lack credibility. Exchange rate movements are costly in this environment. If policymakers take a hard look at the options for exchange rate regimes in emerging economies, they may find that floating regimes may be an illusion and that fixed rates—particularly, full dollarization—might emerge as a sensible choice for some countries, especially in Latin America or in the transition economies in the periphery of Europe and Asia.

APPENDIX

Table 14A.1
Country Coverage, January 1970–December 1999

Africa	Norway
South Africa	Spain
Asia	Sweden
Indonesia	Turkey
South Korea	*Latin America*
Malaysia	Argentina
Philippines	Bolivia
Thailand	Brazil
Europe and the Middle East	Chile
Czech Republic	Colombia
Denmark	Mexico
Egypt	Peru
Finland	Uruguay
Greece	Venezuela
Israel	

Table 14A.2
Currency Crisis Dates

Country	Month and year
Argentina	June 1975, February 1981*, July 1982, September 1986*, April 1989, February 1990
Bolivia	November 1982, November 1983, September 1985
Brazil	February 1983, November 1986*, July 1989, November 1990, October 1991, January 1999
Chile	December 1971, August 1972, October 1973, December 1974, January 1976, August 1982*, September 1984
Colombia	March 1983*, February 1985*, August 1998*
Czech Republic	May 1997
Denmark	May 1971, June 1973, November 1979, August 1993
Egypt	January 1979, August 1989, June 1990
Finland	June 1973, October 1982, November 1991*, September 1992*
Greece	May 1976, November 1980, July 1984
Indonesia	November 1978, April 1983, September 1986, August 1997
Israel	November 1974, November 1977, October 1983*, July 1984
Malaysia	July 1975, August 1997*
Mexico	September 1976, February 1982*, December 1982*, December 1994*
Norway	June 1973, February 1978, May 1986*, December 1992
Peru	June 1976, October 1987
Philippines	February 1970, October 1983*, June 1984, July 1997*
South Africa	September 1975, July 1981, July 1984, May 1996
South Korea	June 1971, December 1974, January 1980, October 1997
Spain	February 1976, July 1977*, December 1982, February 1986, September 1992, May 1993
Sweden	August 1977, September 1981, October 1982, November 1992*
Thailand	November 1978*, July 1981, November 1984, July 1997*
Turkey	August 1970, January 1980, March 1994*
Uruguay	December 1971*, October 1982*
Venezuela	February 1984, December 1986, March 1989, May 1994*, December 1995

*designates episodes of twin crises.

Table 14A.3
Significance Levels for Block Exogeneity Tests: Inflation and Exchange Rate Changes in Floating Exchange Rate Regimes

Country	Exchange rate equation		Inflation equation	
	ε	t statistic	ε	t statistic
U.S. dollar/yen	0.703	0.574	0.906	0.000*
Japan	0.294	0.889	0.313	0.000
Australia	0.389	0.158	0.045	0.000
Bolivia	0.000	0.459	0.000	0.015
Canada	0.024*	0.065*	0.246	0.000
India	0.151	0.342	0.723	0.000
Indonesia	0.786	0.743	0.000	0.000
Mexico	0.880	0.967	0.000	0.000
New Zealand	0.048	0.009	0.001	0.000
Nigeria	0.475	0.797	0.741	0.003*
Norway	0.027	0.319	0.153	0.297
Peru	0.004	0.000	0.000	0.000
Philippines	0.237	0.829	0.267	0.000
South Africa	0.013	0.004	0.059	0.000
South Korea	0.329	0.268	0.000*	0.795
Spain	0.219	0.788	0.792	0.916
Sweden	0.167	0.490	0.592	0.703
Thailand	0.335	0.924	0.668	0.281
Uganda	0.539	0.046	0.022	0.000
Venezuela	0.861	0.956	0.560	0.000*

*Significant at the 10 percent level or higher.

Table 14A.4
Significance Levels for Block Exogeneity Tests: Inflation and Exchange Rate Changes, Managed Floating Exchange Rate Regimes

Country	Exchange rate equation		Inflation equation	
	ε	t statistic	ε	t statistic
Bolivia	0.487	0.814	0.091*	0.942
Brazil	0.275	0.297	0.279	0.000
Chile	0.918	0.000	0.849	0.000
Colombia	0.000	0.240	0.739	0.000
Egypt	0.025	0.004	0.575	0.303
Greece	0.673	0.343	0.214	0.000
India	0.398	0.081*	0.557	0.000*
Indonesia	0.999	0.100*	0.403	0.000*
Israel	0.833	0.269	0.315	0.000
Kenya	0.706	0.904	0.764	0.962
Malaysia	0.524	0.269	0.050*	0.141
Mexico	0.358	0.419	0.702	0.000
Norway	0.746	0.426	0.526	0.951
Pakistan	0.907	0.278	0.905	0.002
Singapore	0.084	0.045	0.138	0.040
South Korea	0.000*	0.851	0.000	0.000
Turkey	0.135	0.298	0.000	0.000
Uruguay	0.691	0.010*	0.021	0.000
Venezuela	0.264	0.055*	0.000	0.000

*Significant at the 10 percent level or higher.

Table 14A.5
Significance Levels for Block Exogeneity Tests: Inflation and Exchange Rate Changes, Limited Flexibility Exchange Rate Regimes

Country	Exchange rate equation		Inflation equation	
	ε	t statistic	ε	t statistic
France	0.042	0.605	0.297	0.000
Germany	0.587	0.275	0.390	0.000
Greece	0.724	0.476	0.111	0.827
Malaysia	0.899	0.085	0.123	0.688
Spain	0.036	0.139	0.173	0.000
Sweden	0.589	0.708	0.521	0.509

Table 14A.6
Exchange Rate Pass-Through Coefficients[a]

Country	Exchange Rate Arrangement and Dates	Coefficient of inflation equation
Emerging Markets		
Bolivia	Float, September 1985–December 1997	0.474
Bolivia	Managed float, January 1998–November 1999	1.001
Indonesia	Float, August 1997–November 1999	0.062
Malaysia	Managed float, December 1992–August 1998	0.02
Mexico	Float, January 1995–November 1999	0.076
Peru	Float, August 1990–November 1999	0.149
South Africa	Float, January 1989–November 1999	0.098
South Korea	Managed float, March 1980–November 1997	0.014
South Korea	Float, December 1997–November 1999	0.085
Turkey	Managed float, January 1980–November 1999	0.256
Uganda	Float, January 1992–November 1999	0.147
Uruguay	Managed float, January 1993–November 1999	0.468
Venezuela	Managed float, April 1996–November 1999	0.114
Average		0.228
Standard deviation		0.276
Developed Economies		
Australia	Float, January 1984–November 1999	0.059
New Zealand	March 1985–November 1999	0.071
Average		0.065
Standard deviation		0.008

a. This table reports only coefficients for those cases where the estimated pass-through was statistically significant at the 10 percent level (or higher).

Table 14C.1
Evidence of Fear of Floating

	International reserves/M2		Volatility of depreciation/volatility of: International reserves		Interest rate	
Country	Level	Rank	Level	Rank	Level	Rank
Australia	0.06	25	6.91	5	90.21	3
Brazil	0.25	14	2.92	8	12.13	24
Canada	0.06	26	3.37	7	23.46	12
Chile	0.49	3	0.42	25	7.96	27
Colombia	0.41	5	0.93	19	8.48	26
Czech Republic	0.31	8	1.26	16	13.97	20
Dominican Republic	0.09	23	1.58	14	11.57	25
Germany	0.11	21	2.84	9	157.91	2
Greece	0.36	6	0.39	28	25.02	9
Guatemala	0.30	9	0.42	26	24.94	10
India	0.13	20	1.21	17	3.70	29
Indonesia	0.34	7	2.15	13	23.38	13
Israel	0.26	12	0.76	21	21.38	15
Jamaica	0.25	15	0.27	30	2.75	30
Japan	0.05	28	30.45	1	377.26	1
South Korea	0.24	16	1.35	15	14.14	19
Mexico	0.30	10	0.84	20	6.99	28
New Zealand	0.06	27	12.68	4	23.78	11
Norway	0.29	11	0.36	29	12.34	23
Paraguay	0.26	13	0.62	23	12.38	22
Peru	0.64	2	0.51	24	13.13	21
Philippines	0.24	17	2.32	11	38.50	8
Poland	0.45	4	0.42	27	14.58	18
Singapore	0.88	1	0.69	22	20.00	16
South Africa	0.06	24	2.47	10	22.80	14
Sweden	0.14	19	0.98	18	62.59	5
Switzerland	0.09	22	2.27	12	40.43	7
Thailand	0.23	18	6.62	6	15.16	17
United Kingdom	0.02	29	17.95	3	46.54	6
United States	0.01	30	19.38	2	69.63	4
Averages by country grouping						
G-3	0.06		17.55		201.60	
Other industrialized countries[a]	0.15		5.07		38.42	
Emerging market countries[b]	0.37		1.76		15.65	

Table 14C.1
(continued)

	International reserves/M2		International reserves		Interest rate	
Country	Level	Rank	Level	Rank	Level	Rank
Other developing[c]	0.21		0.82		11.06	
Latin American and Caribbean countries[d]	0.42		1.12		9.74	
East Asia[c]	0.39		2.63		22.23	
All countries	0.25		4.18		40.57	

Header spanning: Volatility of depreciation/volatility of:

Source: Hausmann, Panizza, and Stein (2000).
a. Australia, Canada, Greece, Israel, New Zealand, Norway, Sweden, Switzerland, and the United Kingdom.
b. Brazil, Chile, Colombia, Czech Republic, Indonesia, South Korea, Mexico, Peru, the Philippines, Singapore, South Africa, and Thailand.
c. Dominican Republic, India, Guatemala, Jamaica, and Paraguay.
d. Brazil, Chile, Colombia, Dominican Republic, Guatemala, Jamaica, Mexico, Paraguay, and Peru.
e. South Korea, the Philippines, Indonesia, Singapore, and Thailand.

Table 14C.2
Ability to Borrow in Domestic Currency

Country or country group	Country debt as share of debt issued by country residents (bond and money market instruments)
Australia	0.437
Brazil	0
Canada	0.273
Chile	0
Colombia	0
Czech Republic	0
Dominican Republic	0
Germany	0.872
Greece	0.245
Guatemala	0
India	0
Indonesia	0
Israel	0
Jamaica	0
Japan	1.522
South Korea	0

Table 14C.2

(continued)

Country or country group	Country debt as share of debt issued by country residents (bond and money market instruments)
Mexico	0
New Zealand	1.048
Norway	0.053
Paraguay	0
Peru	0
Philippines	0.019
Poland	0.324
Singapore	0
South Africa	1.173
Sweden	0.076
Switzerland	2.055
Thailand	0
United Kingdom	0.943
United States	2.325
Regional average	
G-3	1.57
Other industrialized countries[a]	0.57
Emerging market countries[b]	0.13
Other developing[c]	0
Latin American and Caribbean countries[d]	0
East Asia[e]	0
All countries	0.443

Source: Bank for International Settlements detasets on bonds and money market instruments.

a. Australia, Canada, Greece, Israel, New Zealand, Norway, Sweden, Switzerland, and the United Kingdom.

b. Brazil, Chile, Colombia, Czech Republic, Indonesia, South Korea, Mexico, Peru, the Philippines, Singapore, South Africa, and Thailand.

c. Dominican Republic, India, Guatemala, Jamaica, and Paraguay.

d. Brazil, Chile, Colombia, Dominican Republic, Guatemala, Jamaica, Mexico, Paraguay, and Peru.

e. South Korea, the Philippines, Indonesia, Singapore, and Thailand.

Notes

The authors wish to thank Susan Collins, Ricardo Hausmann, Michael Kumhoff, Vincent Reinhart, Dani Rodrik and participants in *Brookings Trade Forum 2000* for helpful comments and suggestions and Ioannis Tokatlidis for superb research assistance.

1. At the time of the East Asian crisis, South Korea and Malaysia were self-classified as managed floats, Indonesia had an exchange rate band, and the Philippines' de jure label was "freely floating."

2. See Hausmann, Panizza, and Stein (2000), for a discussion of these issues.

3. "Fear of floating" refers to the fact that countries with exchange rate regimes that are classified as flexible, more often than not, maintain their exchange rates within a narrow band with respect to some anchor currency—usually the U.S. dollar. More broadly, however, emerging markets display a chronic fear of large swings in their currencies, as evidenced by the lengths countries go to avoid a devaluation when their exchange rates are pegged.

4. These data are monthly and cover thirty-nine countries in Africa, Asia, Europe, and the Western Hemisphere during January 1970–April 1999. The countries are Argentina, Australia, Bolivia, Brazil, Bulgaria, Canada, Chile, Colombia, Côte d'Ivoire, Egypt, Estonia, France, Germany, Greece, India, Indonesia, Israel, Japan, Kenya, Korea, Lithuania, Malaysia, Mexico, New Zealand, Nigeria, Norway, Pakistan, Peru, the Philippines, Singapore, South Africa, Spain, Sweden, Thailand, Turkey, Uganda, Uruguay, the United States, and Venezuela. The sample covers 154 exchange rate arrangements. Calvo and Reinhart (2000b).

5. In an earlier paper, we analyzed international reserves, nominal and real interest rates, base money (nominal and real), prices, and a broad array of commodity prices that are relevant for a particular country. See Calvo and Reinhart (2000b).

6. For instance, following the ERM crisis many European countries adopted (at least, in principle) ± 15 percent bands for the exchange rate. Similarly, until recently Chile had comparably wide bands. Other examples include Mexico before December 1994 (the country's exchange rate had an "ever-widening" band: the lower end [appreciation] of the band was fixed, and the upper ceiling [depreciation] was crawling) and Israel and Colombia from 1994 to 1998.

7. The t-statistic for the difference-in-means test is 3.38, with a probability value of (0.00) under the null hypothesis of no difference.

8. The variance of the monthly changes in the Mexican peso-U.S. dollar exchange rate is about twice as large as the variance of the monthly changes in the yen-U.S. dollar exchange rate.

9. For the freely floating-pegged exchange means test the probability value is (0.00); for the freely floating-managed floating means test it is (0.04); for the managed floating-limited flexibility means test the probability value is (0.32); and for the limited flexibility-pegged exchange means test it is (0.44).

10. See Calvo and Reinhart (2000b).

11. We define a currency crisis as in Kaminsky and Reinhart (1999), who construct an index of exchange market pressure that captures losses and depreciation; it is a weighted

average of these two indicators with weights such that the two components have equal sample volatility. Because changes in the exchange rate enter with a positive weight and reserves enter with a negative weight, large positive readings of this index indicate speculative attacks. Readings of this index that are three standard deviations above its mean are classified as crises.

12. The textbook account emphasizes the influence of a change in relative prices in shifting the composition of a given level of aggregate demand. Both the Keynesian and Fisherian channels provide mechanisms to account for why total demand might fall.

13. Recall that $CA + KA + \Delta R \equiv 0$, where CA denotes the current account balance, KA is capital account balance, and ΔR denotes changes in reserves, and where a negative number indicates an accumulation of reserves by the monetary authority.

14. For the contractionary consequences of devaluations in developing countries, see also Edwards (1986, 1989) and Morley (1992). Each of these studies focuses on devaluation episodes, even when they was not associated with crises.

15. See Calvo and Reinhart (2000b).

16. This approach follows the procedure adopted in Cantor and Packer (1996a; 1996b).

17. It would be interesting to ascertain whether the rating change follows immediately after a crisis, but as the index is published only twice a year, it is not possible to make that determination from the *II* data.

18. See Larraín, Reisen, and von Maltzan (1997).

19. See, for example, Kenen and Rodrik (1986).

20. See, for example, Mann (1989).

21. Only one of the papers that focuses on emerging markets—Medhora (1990), which examines the imports of the West African Monetary Union—finds no link between exchange rate volatility and trade.

22. Rose (1999).

23. McKinnon (1979).

24. McKinnon (2000).

25. See Qian and Varangis (1994).

26. Such problems exacerbate a country's dependence on a single primary commodity export.

27. See Reinhart and Wickham (1994).

28. See, for example, Mishkin and Savastano (2000).

29. For an alternative approach to this issue, see Hausmann, Panizza, and Stein (2000).

30. On this issue see Calvo, Reinhart, and Végh (1995).

31. Of course, although a high pass-through is undesirable from the vantage point of controlling inflation, it helps cushion the effects of a devaluation (or depreciation) when there is extensive liability dollarization—an issue that we examine below.

32. The results are based on the episodes shown in tables 14.1–14.3. For country-specific details, see Calvo and Reinhart (2000b).

33. Calvo (1999a).

34. This section draws heavily from Calvo and Reinhart (2000b).

35. Moreover, as shown in Sargent and Wallace (1975) and Calvo (1983), interest rate targeting may leave the system without a nominal anchor, even in the case where credibility is not an issue.

36. For further evidence about the sizable credit cut in emerging markets during recent crises, see Calvo and Reinhart (2000a).

37. Thus the economy exhibits all the characteristics of the model in Calvo and Végh (1993), which permits us to pass over the technical discussion of cash-in-advance constraints.

38. Over time, e will return to its initial steady state, and hence initial expansion will vanish. This analysis will not be pursued because we focus solely on impact effects here.

39. What happens as a result of currency *appreciations*? A mechanical extension of the above model shows that credit-constrained economies would suffer a smaller contraction. However, this extension is misleading because it implies that credit-constrained economies cannot *lend* abroad. If, instead, we assume that there are no constraints to lending, then we obtain the same contractionary effects from currency appreciation in constrained and unconstrained economies. An insight of this analysis is that in credit-constrained economies any exchange rate fluctuation is contractionary. Exchange rate volatility is harmful.

40. See Calvo and Mendoza (1996).

41. Diamond and Dybvig (1983).

42. The Diamond-Dybvig model is a two-period model, and thus the issue of how to finance the bank bailout does not arise. Moreover, that paper does not discuss the critical issue of whether government is capable of raising the necessary additional taxes.

43. This should be ruled out in this example, however; otherwise the country would not be credit constrained.

44. This may well change in the case of Japan if forecasters are correct in their projection of domestic public debt reaching 130 percent of GDP in the next several months!

45. Since the 1998 Russian crisis, however, banks in Latin America have exhibited a much diminished appetite for lending to the domestic private sector.

46. This was also the case for Mexico during the years before the 1994 assassination of Luis Donaldo Colosio Murrieta, the presidential candidate of the Partido Revolucionario Institucional (PRI), despite an announced ever-widening band.

47. Fear of floating may arise as well when domestic firms use imported raw materials. In this case, floating is less destructive than in the previous example, but it can still cause financial difficulties over the medium term.

48. In the context of fixed exchange rates, revaluations are indeed rare.

References

Arize, Augustine C., Tomas Osang, and Daniel J. Slottje. 2000. "Exchange Rate Volatility and Foreign Trade: Evidence from Thirteen LDCs." *Journal of Business and Economic Statistics* 18 (January): 10–17.

Borensztein, Eduardo, and Jeromin Zettelmeyer. 2000. "Monetary Independence in Emerging Markets: Does the Exchange Rate Regime Make a Difference?" (May 2000) (www.worldbank.org/research [November 2000]).

Brada, Josef C., and José Mendez. 1988. "Exchange Rate Risk, Exchange Rate Regime and the Volume of International Trade." *Kyklos* 41 (2): 263–80.

Broda, Christian. 2000a. "Terms of Trade and Exchange Rate Regimes in Developing Countries." Massachusetts Institute of Technology, Department of Economics (unpublished).

———. 2000b. "Coping with Terms of Trade Shocks: Pegs versus Floats." *American Economic Review* (forthcoming *Paper and Proceedings*).

Caballero, Ricardo J., and Vittorio Corbo. 1989. "The Effect of Real Exchange Rate Uncertainty on Exports: Empirical Evidence." *World Bank Economic Review* 3 (May): 263–78.

Calvo, Guillermo A. 1983. "Staggered Prices in a Utility-Maximizing Framework." *Journal of Monetary Economics* 12 (September): 383–98.

———. 1999a. "Capital Markets and the Exchange Rate: With Special Reference to the Dollarization Debate in Latin America." Paper presented at the ITAM conference on Optimal Monetary Institutions for Mexico, Mexico City, December 3–4, 1999.

———. 1999b. "On Dollarization." University of Maryland, Department of Economics (April) (www.bsos.umd.edu/econ/ciecpn.htm [November 2000]).

Calvo, Guillermo A., and Enrique G. Mendoza. 1996. "Mexico's Balance-of-Payments Crisis: A Chronicle of a Death Foretold." *Journal of International Economics* 41 (November): 235–64.

Calvo, Guillermo A., and Carmen M. Reinhart. 2000a. "When Capital Flows Come to a Sudden Stop: Consequences and Policy Options" (www.bsos.umd.edu/econ/ciecpp6 .pdf ([November 2000]) (forthcoming in *Reforming the International Monetary and Financial System*, edited by Peter B. Kenen and Alexander K. Swoboda. Washington: International Monetary Fund).

———. 2000b. "Fear of Floating" (www.puaf.umd.edu/papers/reinhart/fear.pdf [November 2000]).

Calvo, Guillermo A., Carmen M. Reinhart, and Carlos A. Végh. 1995. "Targeting the Real Exchange Rate: Theory and Evidence." *Journal of Development Economics* 47 (June): 97–133.

Calvo, Guillermo A., and Carlos A. Végh. 1993. "Exchange-Rate-Based Stabilisation under Imperfect Credibility." In *Open-Economy Economics: Proceedings from a Conference Held in Vienna by the International Economic Association*, edited by Helmut Frisch and Andreas Wörgötter, 3–28. Basingstoke, U.K.: Macmillan. Reprinted as chapter 18 of Guillermo A. Calvo, *Money, Exchange Rates, and Output* (MIT Press, 1996).

Cantor, Richard, and Frank Packer. 1996a. "Determinants and Impact of Sovereign Credit Ratings." *Federal Reserve Bank of New York Economic Policy Review* 2 (October): 37–53.

———. 1996b. "Sovereign Risk Assessment and Agency Credit Ratings." *European Financial Management* 2 (2): 247–56.

Cespedes, Luis Felipe, Roberto Chang, and Andrés Velasco. 2000. "Balance Sheets and Exchange Rate Policy." Working Paper 7840. Cambridge, Mass.: National Bureau of Economic Research (August).

Coes, Donald V. 1981. "The Crawling Peg and Exchange Rate Uncertainty." In *Exchange Rate Rules*, edited by John Williamson, 113–36. St. Martin's Press.

Côté, Agathe. 1994. "Exchange Rate Volatility and Trade: A Survey." Bank of Canada Working Paper 94-5. Ontario (May).

Diamond, Douglas W., and Philip H. Dybvig. 1983. "Bank Runs, Deposit Insurance, and Liquidity." *Journal of Political Economy* 91 (June): 401–19.

Edwards, Sebastian. 1986. "Are Devaluations Contractionary?" *Review of Economics and Statistics* 68 (August): 501–08.

———. 1989. *Real Exchange Rates, Devaluation, and Adjustment: Exchange Rate Policy in Developing Countries*. MIT Press.

Frankel, Jeffrey A. 1999. "No Single Exchange Rate Regime Is Right for All Countries or at All Times," Graham Lecture, Princeton University. Essays in International Finance 215, Princeton University, Department of Economies, International Finance Section.

Frankel, Jeffrey A., and Shang-Jin Wei. 1993. "Emerging Currency Blocs." Working Paper 4335. Cambridge, Mass.: National Bureau of Economic Research (April).

Grobar, Lisa Morris. 1993. "The Effect of Real Exchange Rate Uncertainty on LDC Manufactured Exports." *Journal of Development Economics* 41 (August): 367–76.

Hausmann, Ricardo, Ugo Panizza, and Ernesto Stein. 2000. "Why Do Countries Float the Way They Float?" Inter-American Development Bank Research Paper 418. Washington (November).

Kaminsky, Graciela, and Carmen Reinhart. 1999. "The Twin Crises: Causes of Banking and Balance-of-Payments Problems." *American Economic Review* 89 (June): 473–500.

Kenen, Peter B., and Dani Rodrik. 1986. "Measuring and Analyzing the Effects of Short-Term Volatility in Real Exchange Rates." *Review of Economics and Statistics* 68 (May): 311–15.

Larraín, Guillermo, Helmut Reisen, and Julia von Maltzan. 1997. "Emerging Market Risk and Sovereign Credit Ratings." OECD Development Center Technical Paper 124. Paris: Organization for Economic Cooperation and Development (April).

Larrain, Felipe, and Andrés Velasco. 1999. "Exchange Rate Arrangements for Emerging Market Economies." Group of Thirty Occasional Paper 60. Washington.

Mann, Catherine L. 1989. "The Effects of Exchange Rate Trends and Volatility on Export Prices: Industry Examples from Japan, Germany, and the United States." *Weltwirtschaftliches Archiv* 125 (3): 588–618.

McKinnon, Ronald I. 1979. *Money in International Exchange: The Convertible Currency System*. Oxford University Press.

———. 2000. "The East Asian Dollar Standard: Life after Death?" *Economic Notes* 29 (February): 31–82.

Medhora, Rohinton. 1990. "The Effect of Exchange Rate Variability on Trade: The Case of the West African Monetary Union's Imports." *World Development* 18 (February): 313–24.

Mishkin, Frederick, and Miguel A. Savastano. 2000. "Monetary Policy Strategies for Latin America." Working Paper 7617. Cambridge, Mass.: National Bureau of Economic Research (March).

Morley, Samuel A. 1992. "On the Effect of Devaluation during Stabilization Programs in LDCs." *Review of Economics and Statistics* 74 (February): 21–27.

Paredes, Carlos E. 1989. "Exchange Rate Regimes, the Real Exchange Rate and Export Performance in Latin America." Brookings Discussion Papers in International Economics 77. Washington (August).

Powell, Andrew, and Federico Sturzenegger. 2000. "Dollarization: The Link between Devaluation and Default Risk." Central Bank of Argentina and Business School of the Universidad Torcuato di Tella (October 23) (www.utdt.edu/~fsturzen/powell.pdf [November 2000]).

Qian, Ying, and Panos Varangis. 1994. "Does Exchange Rate Volatility Hinder Export Growth? Additional Evidence." *Empirical Economics* 19 (3): 317–96.

Reinhart, Carmen M. 2000. "The Mirage of Floating Exchange Rates." *American Economic Review* 90 (May, *Papers and Proceedings*): 65–70.

Reinhart, Carmen M., and Peter Wickham. 1994. "Commodity Prices: Cyclical Weakness or Secular Decline?" *International Monetary Fund Staff Papers* 41 (June): 175–213.

Rose, Andrew K. 1999. "One Money, One Market: Estimating the Effects of Common Currencies on Trade." Working Paper 7432. Cambridge, Mass.: National Bureau of Economic Research (December).

Sargent, Thomas J., and Neil Wallace. 1975. "'Rational' Expectations, the Optimal Monetary Instrument, and the Optimal Money Supply Rule." *Journal of Political Economy* 83 (April): 241–54.

Savvides, Andreas. 1993. "Pegging the Exchange Rate and the Choice of a Standard by LDCs: A Joint Formulation." *Journal of Economic Development* 18 (December): 107–25.

Williamson, John. 1995. *What Role for Currency Boards?* Policy Analyses in International Economics 40. Washington: Institute for International Economics.

―――. 1996. *The Crawling Band as an Exchange Rate Regime: Lessons from Chile, Colombia, and Israel*. Washington: Institute for International Economics.

15

Capital Markets and the Exchange Rate with Special Reference to the Dollarization Debate in Latin America

Guillermo A. Calvo

The central focus of this chapter is the optimal choice of a foreign exchange system for emerging market economies, EMs, taking into account the conditions under which these countries operate, and that have been revealed to us as a byproduct of recent financial crises. The issues involved are very complex, and cannot be dealt in a purely analytical fashion. Thus, I will start the discussion, first, in section 1 examining the "initial conditions" (a "where-do-we-stand" exercise). Then, in section 2, I will take a cursory look at received theory and try to identify the lessons that are still valid, while at the same time pinpoint areas for future research. One key observation in section 1 will be that several EMs are already partially dollarized. In that respect, *liability dollarization*, that is, sizable dollar-denominated debts, is especially worrisome because exchange rate flexibility in that context could bring about massive bankruptcy. The theory and implications of liability dollarization are analyzed in section 3. The objective is to gain a better understanding of the phenomenon. Does it arise spontaneously, or is it a result of government policy (maybe dollarization of public debt, as the famous Mexican *tesobonos*)? I find good reasons for both.

Section 4 analyzes an extreme case of fixing: full dollarization (that is, adoption of a foreign currency for all transactions). The bottom line is that although dollarization is a serious commitment that calls for hard preconditions to work, it could be advantageous when taking into consideration the "initial conditions" which are relevant to many EMs.

If dollarization is not good enough, then what? This is the topic of section 5. The alternative is a system of flexible exchange rates. The analysis reiterates and expands on the issue that in practice flexibility is subject to narrow bounds, especially if credibility is at stake. Moreover, the section discusses *inflation targeting*, a system that is gaining the serious consideration of academics and policymakers worldwide.

The main thrust of the chapter is that there are compelling reasons for EMs to stay away from exchange rate flexibility. Dollarization may be costly, but it may put the EMs on the fast track toward monetary and financial stability which, otherwise, may take years to achieve.

The chapter is closed with conclusions in section 6. The more technical material is relegated to two Appendixes.

1 Initial Conditions: Financial Globalization and Partial Dollarization

This section will present evidence that EMs have been operating under sharply different global financial conditions than those prevailing before 1989. The central conjecture is that the surge of capital flows to EMs partly resulted from new market structures and conditions, combined with imperfect policy and policymakers' credibility. Moreover, these very structures could have set the stage for the ensuing financial turmoil that took place after 1994. Understanding these conditions is essential for the design of the optimal foreign exchange system. To organize the discussion, I will subdivide the discussion between external and domestic factors.

External Factors

The integration of EMs into the world (private) financial markets could be dated to 1989. Figure 15.1 shows a sharp increase in capital inflows to emerging markets around 1989, accompanied by an also sharp rise in net portfolio flows (especially to Latin America; see figures 15.2 and 15.3, where Asia refers to countries in the region that recently underwent financial turmoil, excluding Japan). I conjecture that these phenomena are partly linked to the development of the Brady bonds market, and the launching of a major U.S. campaign to push open the Asian capital market.

The Brady bond market developed as a result of securitizing nonperforming sovereign debt. This meant taking debt entries in banks' books and placing them on the capital market to be traded. The amounts were significant (their market value was around U.S. $25 billion in 1990 and reached almost U.S. $100 billion in 1996/7). Trading fixed-income sovereigns requires knowledge about fundamentals such as

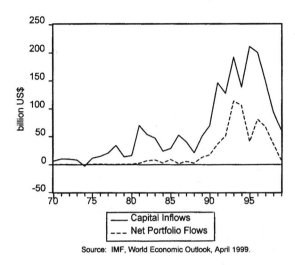

Source: IMF, World Economic Outlook, April 1999.

Figure 15.1
Capital flows to emerging markets

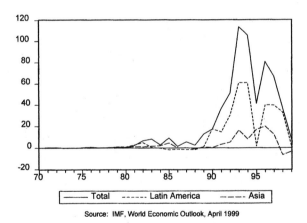

Source: IMF, World Economic Outlook, April 1999

Figure 15.2
Portfolio flows to EMs

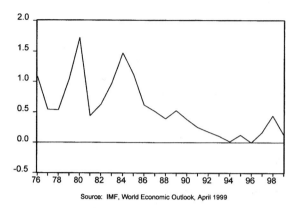

Source: IMF, World Economic Outlook, April 1999

Figure 15.3
Share of official capital in total flows to emerging markets

macroeconomic performance, political trends, and, especially, willingness to pay. This type of information is not easy to acquire but, once
acquired, can be utilized to assess other securities emanating from the
same country, because the return to private sector investment also
depends on those variables. Thus, for instance, the imposition of controls on capital flows (as in Malaysia, recently) could drastically change
a project's "dollar" rate of return.[1]

The above observation supports a key conjecture, namely, that
issuers of Brady bonds opened up the market for other types of bonds
and securities originating from their countries.[2] Moreover, if this view
is accepted, other important implications follow. As noted, information
about sovereigns' fundamentals is subject to (possibly large) economies of scale. Under those conditions, a likely capital market configuration is one in which there are just a few *specialists* (informed
investors) surrounded by a sea of (mostly) uninformed investors. The
latter will be clients of the specialists, mimicking their behavior, or
investing on the basis of their own priors, market rumors, etc., which
do not involve the use of first-hand information.

This type of market structure is consistent with the models in Cross-
man and Stiglitz (1980), Gennotte and Leland (1990), Kodres and
Pritsker (1998), Calvo and Mendoza (2000), and Calvo (1999a). Under
these circumstances, rational herding is possible and market prices
could be highly sensitive to the actions of specialists. In particular, if
specialists are subject to a liquidity crunch [as presumably was the
case during the August 1998 Russian crisis; see Calvo (1998a) and

Yuan (2000)], EMs' security prices could collapse. Thus, as specialists are forced to download their positions in EMs' securities (or, more simply, are unable to acquire the flow of securities coming from EMs to finance their current account deficits), uninformed investors mistakenly (but rationally) interpret it as a negative signal on those securities' expected return.

Domestic Factors: Credibility and Partial Dollarization

Financial globalization has not hit all EMs to the same degree. Africa, for example, has been largely spared (Calvo and Reinhart 1998). Pull factors are, thus, also relevant. However, pull factors are not always beneficial. There is an extensive literature showing that under incomplete policy or policymakers' credibility, capital inflows could lower social welfare (see, for example, Calvo 1986 and 1996). This literature is especially relevant during periods in which EMs' access to capital markets shows a sizeable increase (due to lower international interest rates or better country-specific information). This is so because no matter how well an EM was run in the past, the sudden access to substantial additional funds will likely raise serious questions about the policymakers' ability to handle the boom. These questions range from ability to keep fiscal discipline, to effectiveness of bank supervision, to maintenance of political stability. Assessment of those risks is not easy. For example, during a capital-inflow episode there is a surge in fiscal revenue (Talvi effect) and international reserves, helping to give a semblance of improved financial conditions. In most cases, economic advisors are unable to control the politician's drive to spend and, as a result, large fiscal deficits materialize when the capital-inflow episode comes to an end (see Talvi 1997). Thus, as rational agents become aware that, eventually, present policies may have to be abandoned, they engage in intertemporal speculation which, as a general rule, have led to higher present private sector expenditure and current account deficit. These imbalances are unsustainable because higher expenditure occurs as a reaction to perceived *policy* unsustainability [or temporariness; see Calvo (1986)].[3]

I will now turn to discuss the phenomenon of *partial dollarization*. There exists a large number of EMs in which foreign-exchange-denominated deposits, FXDs, exceeds 30 percent of the total (IMF 1999). In those countries bank loans are also heavily dollarized (a phenomenon that is associated with what I will call *liability dollarization*,

LD, that is, sizable dollar debts) due to the standard regulation that requires banks to match the currency denomination of their assets and liabilities in order to avoid currency risk.

LD has sprung into prominence since the recent financial crisis in Indonesia. On all accounts, Indonesia passed the traditional tests of sustainability (for example, low current account and fiscal deficits, stable and not overappreciated currency, etc.) with flying colors. However, Indonesia's Achilles' heel was private sector exposure to short-term foreign-exchange-denominated debt. Since those loans were largely invested in nontradeables, and exceeded the country's stock of international reserves, the inability to refinance them during the Asian crisis faced Indonesia with a serious balance-of-payments problem. Why would firms expose themselves to bankruptcy by engaging in LD? This is a question that has scarcely received any attention in the literature [however, see Calvo (1999b)]. It will be further discussed in section 3.

2   Choosing a Foreign Exchange System: the Traditional Approach

The traditional approach follows Mundell (1961), and has recently been reviewed and summarized by De Grauwe (1994). Development of the theory has relied heavily on Poole (1970) (see, for instance, Flood and Marion 1982 and Aizenman and Frenkel 1985). The main thrust of the theory can be captured by a simple example.

Consider the following equilibrium conditions:

$$y = \alpha e + g + u, \tag{1}$$

and

$$m = y + v. \tag{2}$$

Equation (1) represents equilibrium in the output market (the IS curve), while (2) denotes equilibrium in the money market (the LM curve), where y, e, g, and m denote the logs of output, nominal exchange rate, autonomous demand (a shift parameters which could be interpreted as government expenditure or external demand factors) and money supply, respectively. The domestic and foreign price levels are assumed constant for the time being, and equal to 0 (in logs). Variables u and v are random shocks, and α is a positive constant. For simplicity, I will not explicitly model interest rates. Aggregate demand is represented on the right-hand side of equation (1) and is an increasing function of the real exchange rate. Moreover, without loss of generality, the demand for money is assumed to be unit elastic with respect to output.

For the present purposes it is enough to focus on two polar cases: fixed and (pure) flexible exchange rates. Under fixed (which I will call Fix), $e =$ constant and m is determined by the market. Under flexible exchange rates (which I will call Flex), $m =$ constant and e is determined by the market.

Solving for y in equations (1) and (2), we get under Fix

$$\text{var } y = \text{var}(u + g), \quad \text{and} \quad \text{var } e = 0. \tag{3}$$

Moreover, under Flex

$$\text{var } y = \text{var } v, \quad \text{and} \quad \text{var } e = \frac{1}{\alpha^2} \text{var}(u + g + v). \tag{4}$$

Following Poole (1970), this literature focuses on output volatility, var y. Therefore, abstracting momentarily from g, the following familiar proposition follows immediately: Fix is better (alt. worse) than Flex, if the volatility of nominal shocks (that is, var v) is larger (alt. smaller) than the volatility of real shocks (that is, var u).

This setup helps to rationalize the often-heard concern that Fix may not be attractive if the country to which the currency is pegged (the United States, say) exhibits shocks which are "asymmetric" with respect to those suffered by the pegging country. Although the word "asymmetric" is usually loosely defined, the focus is on shock u, and by "asymmetric" it is meant to say that there is a negative covariance between the us of the two countries. Let variable g in equation (1) capture the effect of U.S. policy. Moreover, let us assume that the United States engages in counter-cyclical policy (that is, g is negatively correlated with U.S. u shock). Thus, under asymmetric shocks, $\text{cov}(g, u) > 0$. Clearly, by equation (3), the larger is the latter, the larger will be var $y = \text{var}(u + g)$ under Fix.

Variable Rules and Time Inconsistency

Given that capital flows are volatile and involve both real and nominal shocks, policymakers guided by the above model are not likely to choose either one of the two extremes, Fix or Flex. The choice is likely to fall somewhere in the middle, *and depend very much on current circumstances.* One day nominal shocks will dominate, another day real shocks will, and yet another day both shocks will share the limelight.

Therefore, I am afraid that the traditional approach—which, it is worth saying, has still a strong influence on the profession—will lead policy-makers to adopt *a highly discretionary foreign exchange system*. This kind of system may work reasonably well in advanced economies (see Blinder 1998). However, I cannot be hopeful about its effectiveness in EMs, since I suspect that a discretionary foreign exchange system (dirty float, managed float, etc.) is likely to lead to serious credibility problems for countries that have not yet reached a *national accord* on the size and nature of the public sector.[4]

Volatility of the Real Exchange Rate

Why the exclusive focus on var y? Why not also take into account var e, the volatility of the real exchange rate? The nominal exchange rate in the present context entails a relative price the volatility of which has effects on sensitive areas of the economy like income distribu-tion and poverty. Moreover, as pointed out in the previous section, unexpected relative price changes could have devastating financial effects, especially when they are large and lead to lower relative prices for indebted sectors.[5]

Ranking systems by var e yields very different answers. In the first place, Fix wins hands down. Second, recalling equation (4), shock asymmetry increases the volatility of the real exchange rate under Flex.[6]

Price Indexation

I will now extend the model in a conventional manner in order to take explicit account of the domestic price level, p (in logs). Equations (1) and (2) become

$$y = \alpha(e - p) + g + u, \tag{5}$$

and

$$m - p = y + v. \tag{6}$$

This setup can be used to examine the role of indexation. In the limit when prices are perfectly indexed to the exchange rate, that is, $e = p +$ a constant, either exchange rate system will yield the same output volatility. This suggests that for economies exhibiting high pass-through coefficients like Mexico (see Carstens and Werner 1999), adoption of Fix may not much increase output variability. On the other hand, under both Fix and Flex the volatility of the real exchange rate is zero. Thus, perfect indexation makes the traditional approach useless.

Endogenous Random Shocks

A major omission of this approach lies in the assumption that random shocks are exogenous to the foreign exchange regime. According to this approach, for example, Fix with low international reserves is equivalent to full dollarization, or the intermediate system Currency Board. In contrast, for instance, those who see the advantages of dollarization focus on the *endogeneity* of random shocks (see Calvo 1999a and b). This endogeneity is supported by the discussion in section l, where it was argued that recent crises reflect the existence of imperfect and asymmetric information. Thus, systems that lower the need for information (as a fully dollarized system would) could help to alleviate the information problem, and lower the incidence of contagion (which would be reflected in lower volatility of random shocks u and v in the above analytical framework).[7]

3   Liability Dollarization

This section will present a discussion of liability dollarization, LD, and the effect that LD may have in the event that the currency suffers a large devaluation.

Theory

Some progress has been made by Calvo and Guidotti (1990) (see also Calvo 1996, ch. 12) for public debt and in the context of time inconsistency. Let the public debt be denominated in pesos (the local currency) and, for the sake of simplicity, let us assume that PPP prevails. Under these conditions, a devaluation lowers the real value of outstanding debt. This gives rise to time inconsistency because a welfare-maximizing government would be tempted to devalue more than what would be optimal to announce in the previous period. However, if individuals are rational and fully understand this situation, they will not be taken by surprise: in a perfect-foresight context, the ex post real interest rate will equal the international interest rate, but inflation will be too high. One solution to this problem is to dollarize the public debt (which in this case is equivalent to indexing the debt to the price level). By removing the incentive to devalue, authorities could keep inflation at its ex ante optimal level.[8]

I was not able to extend Calvo-Guidotti approach in a straightforward manner to account for LD in the *private sector* (which, for the sake of this discussion, I will assume to be completely atomistic). Risk-averse individuals whose income is in pesos will have an incentive to borrow in pesos, not in dollars, unless their peso income is highly correlated with the exchange rate (see Appendix A for further discussion). However, if the latter correlation is high, sharp devaluations under LD need not provoke serious financial difficulties. Since it is the connection between LD and financial difficulties that motivates this discussion, I conclude that one must look elsewhere for an explanation.

Consider the case in which external private sector peso debt is positive. Then, the government will have incentives to devalue giving rise to excessive inflation, as in the previous case. However, this does not necessarily lead the private sector to change its debt currency denomination to dollars. The reason is that the private sector is atomistic and, therefore, does not internalize the government's reaction function. Thus, again, the model falls short of target.

An alternative hypothesis is that domestic firms have better information about the exchange rate than foreign investors (especially those foreign investors not operating within the country's confines on a regular basis). Why would domestic residents have superior information? First, learning about the exchange rate is a costly exercise because it involves keeping a close tab on monetary policy and relevant random shocks in a relatively unstable institutional environment. Thus, such costs will likely be incurred by firms and individuals that have a chance to apply that knowledge to other substantial purposes. A firm that operates in an EM is a candidate to incur in those costs because it will regularly be buying or selling tradeable goods and, if subject to foreign ownership, it will be sending profit remittances abroad. Another incentive is provided by currency substitution, CS [that is, domestic and foreign currencies concurrently being used for transactions purposes; see Calvo (1996, ch. 8) and IMF (1999)]. In contrast, for the pure foreign investor who just buys bonds issued by the EM firm, there will be little use for exchange rate information, beyond helping to evaluate the dollar return on those bonds. Thus, devaluation expectations between the local firm and foreign lenders may differ. If lenders expect a higher devaluation rate than borrowers, LD may occur, despite borrowers' risk aversion. However, if the difference of opinion went in the opposite direction, no LD will be exhibited (except for the cases discussed in Appendix A). So the theory, as it stands, gives an ambiguous answer.

Suppose the economy suffers from a *peso problem* stemming, for example, from several past episodes of surprise devaluations (for example, the *sexenio* phenomenon in Mexico). If we assume that domestic firms can better assess the timing of the devaluation than the uninformed foreign investors, then it may be optimal for the former to borrow in foreign exchange, giving the desired result. Incentives for LD would be further enhanced if the private sector expects that, when devaluation looms, it can refinance its dollar debts in pesos at "low" nominal interest rates (that is, interest rates that are far lower than expected rates of devaluation). This happened in several recent crisis episodes as central banks tried to keep nominal interest rates from skyrocketing, and expanded domestic credit (Mexico 1994 is an example).[9]

A more straightforward explanation for LD is based on institutional constraints associated with currency substitution, CS. Several countries that have undergone CS have eventually allowed their banks to issue dollar deposits (for example, Argentina, Bolivia, Peru), since allowing for dollar deposits lowers banks' vulnerability to changes in currency composition. Notice that, if dollar deposits are not allowed, a sudden expansion in the demand for foreign currency—for instance, as a result of an increase in the expected rate of devaluation—may bring about a bank run, as individuals try to buy foreign exchange with bank deposits. In contrast, if dollar deposits are allowed, the change in currency composition can be carried out simply by modifying the denomination of bank deposits without altering its total.[10]

Under standard regulations, banks have to match the denomination of assets and liabilities. Therefore, if in equilibrium there is a stock of dollar deposits, banks will have to invest those sums in dollar assets. Assuming that domestic banks have a comparative advantage in assessing domestic borrowers, LD might develop. However, the interest rate differential between peso and dollar loans may be less than the expected rate of devaluation. Otherwise, nontradeable sectors might not be willing to borrow in dollars (see Appendix A).[11]

Finally, public sector LD may induce private sector LD. For example, consider a government that is subject to time-inconsistency problems and, as pointed out above, engages in LD. This lowers incentives to devalue, inducing a risk-averse private sector to increase LD, further reducing devaluation incentives.

I conjecture that large private sector LD occurs in response to (1) government's actions that generate substantial CS (for example, high inflation), (2) public debt dollarization, or (3) the expectation of peso refinancing of private sector dollar debt at attractive interest rates.

4 Dollarization

I will define dollarization or full dollarization as a situation in which a country abandons its own currency and adopts another country's currency (generically called the dollar) as a means of payment (except perhaps for small change, as in Panama) and unit of account.[12] It is an extreme case of Fix and, by its nature, is fully shielded from BOP crises. However, banking and financial sector crises are still possible. Thus, to the extent that banks' money is used as means of payment, a banking crisis could break the equivalence of bank money with dollar currency, and the economy might end up operating in a two-currency system. This is one reason, incidentally, why a dollarized system may have to ensure mechanisms that mimic the operation of a lender of last resort, LOLR.[13]

I will return to the LOLR issue at the end of this section. For the time being I would like to discuss the basic economics of a dollarized economy abstracting from banking difficulties. There are three positive features of a dollarized system that I would like to highlight: (1) credibility, (2) lower information costs, and (3) providing a cushion for sharp relative price changes (in comparison with flexible exchange rates).

Point (1) is less trivial than it may at first look. Obviously, a dollarized system is immune to devaluation, so "exchange rate" credibility is ensured.[14] But, from a policy perspective, an economy is much like a "pressure cooker" in which if one valve is obstructed (a policy variable is set at a fixed level, for example), pressure increases on the other valves (that is, the other policies), fiscal policy, for example. Thus, dollarization removes the ability to raise seigniorage but, if push comes to shove, the inflation tax can be substituted by a wealth tax or a tax on bank checks. The main difference, however, is *predictability*. Collecting the inflation tax in the context of Flex, for example, may generate high volatility because the exchange rate is highly sensitive to expectations and is subject to overshooting. Thus, the effective tax *rate* may turn out to be highly volatile.[15] In contrast, the same average tax revenue could be collected through a wealth tax. Wealth is a relatively stable variable and, therefore, the fiscal authority can collect the desired amounts by setting a very stable tax *rate*. To be true, wealth taxes could change in the future to finance higher government expenditure, introducing some degree of uncertainty, but under normal circumstances, the hand of the legislator is noticeably steadier than inflation or devaluation rates, especially when there is no firm exchange rate commitment on the part of the monetary authority. Part of the reason for this hand-steadiness is that, as a general rule, regular taxes have to go through Congress, entailing time-consuming political compromise.

Point (2), lowering information costs, has been discussed before. It acquires special significance when combined with point (3)— cushioning relative price changes—because relative price changes are a major factor behind financial vulnerability in EMs. (This issue is further discussed below.)

On the negative side of the ledger for dollarization, an often-mentioned issue is the costs associated with nominal price and wage rigidities. Critics claim that these rigidities make unemployment more likely to happen and to exhibit a high degree of hysteresis. The situation gets worse under downward *public* sector price/wage inflexibility (a very common feature) because it becomes more costly for the private sector to lower its own prices. Moreover, inflexibility of public sector wages switches the burden of fiscal adjustment during recessions mostly to the taxpayer.[16]

However, the above difficulties can be partially offset by appropriate fiscal policy. For example, one can increase labor subsidies financed by a higher income tax, or impose uniform export subsidies and import tariffs (which mimics devaluation without affecting the dollar value of peso-denominated assets and liabilities). These are *cyclical* policies and, therefore, they must be phased out accordingly. Otherwise, they are bound to be counterproductive as they remove incentives for price and wage adjustment.[17]

There is, however, a silver lining to nominal stickiness and it is related to financial considerations (point 3 above). With price/wage flexibility, a shock that requires downward nominal adjustment will take place very quickly, implying that *nominal* profits will fall. This may generate financial difficulties to firms that have taken the typically rigid (non-state-contingent) loans. In contrast, if prices/wages are sticky, the nominal adjustment will be slower which, on that account, facilitates debt repayment. Of course, the final effect has to take into consideration the greater output contraction that price/wage rigidity may bring about. However, slow nominal adjustment may facilitate a more orderly debt recontracting. Moreover, in economies that undergo Keynesian-type recession, a rise in unemployment helps to give a clear signal that financial problems are not specific to a given firm. As a consequence, banks may become more willing to refinance loans under more lenient or longer-maturity terms.[18] At this juncture, however, it is no longer possible to ignore the role of LOLR (that is, lender of last resort). Without it, a Keynesian-type recession, for example, may trigger fears of financial collapse, making it hard for banks to refinance debt in an orderly fashion as suggested above.

Lender of Last Resort

First let me dispose of a common red herring. It is sometimes said that a dollarized economy lacks a LOLR because it cannot print its own money. This is false. A LOLR has just to be able to lend. In advanced countries, the LOLR does not issue money to finance the operation, it issues bonds, public debt. This may be more difficult to achieve for an EM but what this suggests is that EMs may have to engage in more planning than advanced economies. Credit lines, for instance, may have to be negotiated in advance (the recent IMF CCL points in that direction). In addition, EMs will likely have to muster a relatively large stock of international reserves. All of this adds to the cost of running a dollarized system. But those costs should not be overdone because, under these conditions, restoring the powers of a LOLR via the printing press is also costly. If the central bank can freely turn the wheels of the money-printing machine, a Damocles sword will hang on the economy every time there is a slight suspicion that the LOLR is preparing for action. And the sword is, of course, an inflationary explosion. Therefore, as soon as suspicion arises about the health of the banking system, interest rates will sharply rise, further weakening the banking system.

5 The Dollarization Debate: Summary and Realistic Alternatives

The opening of the capital market for EMs has brought about new complications for macroeconomic management. The chapter has argued that at the heart of this problem may lie imperfect information, inexperience in handling suddenly larger capital inflows, flaky political equilibrium, etc., which lead to seriously questioning the credibility of policy and policymakers. In some cases, this situation resulted in partial dollarization and, most worrisome, in liability dollarization. This is the background from which, I believe, any useful discussion of dollarization in EMs should start.

Against this background, it is not obvious that greater *policy* flexibility is a sound idea. While flexibility is welcome in a context in which policymakers can make credible policy announcements, it could magnify distortions otherwise. Not surprisingly, then, even though several EMs have opted for more flexible exchange rates, in practice their exchange rates are closely managed. In addition, since imperfect credibility detracts from the effectiveness of open market operations, EMs that opt for exchange rate flexibility usually carry (or aim to carry) a large stock of international reserves. In this fashion, if juggling the domestic interest rate to stabilize the exchange rate proves ineffective, the monetary authorities can always intervene by "issuing" advanced-country securities (for example, U.S. Treasury Bills), that is, running down international reserves.

Therefore, dollarization has to be compared, not with the textbook paradigm of pure floating (Flex as I called it in section 2), but with a closely managed flexible-rates system, in which explicit, implicit, or even potential foreign exchange intervention play a central role. Thus, the range of realistic possibilities is not huge. The chapter argues that the larger the degree of liability dollarization and lack of credibility, the greater will be the attractiveness of dollarization. On the other hand, the more adamant are nominal rigidities, the more attractive may be to have some degree of exchange rate flexibility (although, as noted above, slow adjustment may lower the incidence of financial crises).[19]

In the previous discussion, however, I took for granted the traditional open-economy model with tradeables and nontradeables. In that context, the exchange rate is a very powerful instrument because it can help to avoid exchange rate misalignment (again, assuming that the country has enough reserves to place the exchange rate where it wants it to be, and that exchange rate indexation is low). This "nominal" solution to a real problem works only under price stickiness. However, it is worth recalling (theorist: pay attention) that we do not live in a world with a single nontradeable good. Thus, if price stickiness is a relevant issue, we are bound to encounter misalignment in several directions. Not just between tradeables and nontradeables, but between, say, nontradeables No. 173 and No. 18112. In other words, the exchange rate is not good enough to take care of misalignment across the prices of nontradeables goods. This is obvious (although systematically forgotten). More interesting is the following question: If the exchange rate will be managed to minimize misalignment, which sectors will be privileged by the policymaker? The urban or the rural, skilled workers or unskilled workers, etc.? These are never easy issues for a politician, especially in EMs subject to the above-mentioned political fiscal gaps, and impair policy credibility.

Inflation Targeting

This monetary system has caught the fancy of politicians and some academic economists (see Bernanke et al. 1999). In Latin America, Chile has taken the lead years ago, followed, more recently, by Brazil and Colombia (or so it seems at the time of writing). Inflation targeting is equivalent to pegging the currency to a basket of goods. If the basket is composed of tradeable goods, inflation targeting is essentially equivalent to fixed exchange rates. Naturally, if a basket containing nontradeables is targeted, then the exchange rate will be flexible—or, more precisely, it will move. A very common conceptual error, however, is to identify inflation targeting with flexible exchange rates. True, the exchange rate is flexible, but the situation is very far from the Flex case discussed in section 2. And it is very different from the exchange rate flexibility envisaged by the Optimal Currency Area literature (see De Grauwe 1994). Moreover, pegging to a basket does not shield the economy from large fluctuations in the real exchange rate, or insulate the EM from U.S. monetary policy, for example. As shown in Appendix B, inflation targeting is also subject to distortions generated by imperfect credibility, much like it happens under not fully credible pegged exchange rates.

A possible advantage of inflation targeting (assuming that the target rate is positive or zero) is that it prevents *deflation* of the basket's price index, which, as a general rule, includes nontradeable goods. Thus, under price stickiness, this policy may give rise to a lower incidence of Keynesian-type unemployment.[20] However, compared to dollarization, this advantage could be minimal in countries exhibiting a high pass-through coefficient (as seems to be the case in Mexico).[21] Moreover, inflation targeting does not shield the economy from sharp relative-price changes, like a collapse in real estate prices and, thus, may give rise to major financial difficulties.

The credibility problem under inflation targeting may be quite seri-ous because authorities are allowed to use a whole battery of instru-ments to achieve their inflation objectives. Since instruments come first and inflation later, the public will have to infer whether authorities are committed to the targets from the instruments they utilize. Thus, I am afraid that this will increase the "fear of floating." Exchange rates are easily observable variables and a devaluation is usually taken as a har-binger of higher inflation. As a result, fear of floating is likely to be exhibited, especially during periods of global financial turmoil (for ex-ample, Chile narrowed the exchange rate band right after the Russian default in August 1998). Since high-frequency changes in fiscal policy are hard to implement, the instrument of choice (or, *instrument of last resort*) will likely be the interest rate.

This discussion leads me to conjecture that credibility-riddled EMs that adopt inflation targeting are likely to place a lot of weight on interest rate policy and exchange rate stability. These two policies are, in principle, inconsistent unless there are controls on capital mobility, like in Chile (presently discontinued). But controls on capital mobility have been shown, by and large, to be ineffective in changing aggregate flows. They can at best be claimed to have an effect on maturity com-position of capital inflows (Edison and Reinhart 1999). Thus, this some-what tortuous policy mix (inflation targeting cum controls on capital mobility) may have the desired effects only in the short run. Eventu-ally, inflation targets may have to be changed or, at least, momentarily broken–enhancing the persistence of the credibility problems.

6   Conclusions

The chapter highlights the importance of credibility issues for the design of optimal macroeconomic policy in EMs, particularly for the choice of the foreign exchange regime. Credibility is a highly country-specific characteristic. A credible policymaker can steer the economy by a subtle turn of phrase (witness Alan Greenspan), and make unanti-cipated policy changes without creating confusion. In contrast, a non-credible policymaker may have to tie himself firmly to the mast to get any results. In my opinion, most policymakers in Latin America are, unfortunately, of the second type because they are faced with "a politi-cal fiscal gap." This explains why without strong monetary commit-ments, interest rates remain high and highly volatile [actually, orders of magnitude higher and more volatile than in the United States, for example; see Calvo and Reinhart (2000)].

In addition, the chapter argues that the subtle arithmetic of the traditional approach for the choice of the optimal exchange rate system could still be useful, but it ignores key relevant features for EMs. In particular, it assumes that random shocks are independent of the foreign exchange regime, and the institutions that support them. Moreover, there is scant or no reference to the role of the financial sector and currency substitution or liability dollarization, and most of the literature takes policy credibility for granted.

When those missing aspects are incorporated into the analysis, a totally different picture arises. Thus, dollarization, an extreme form of fixed exchange rates, begins to look like a plausible choice. True, dollarized systems must meet stringent conditions, but they hold the promise of putting EMs on a fast track to much greater policy credibility and effectiveness.

APPENDIX A: NOTES ON THE MICROECONOMICS OF LIABILITY DOLLARIZATION

I will conduct the analysis in terms of a mean-variance framework. The objective is to study incentives for LD when the price faced by the firm is not highly correlated with the exchange rate, because it is under those conditions that a sharp change in the exchange rate can provoke serious financial disruption.

Consider a risk-averse firm. Peso revenue (net of operating costs), accruing "next" period, is proportional to its price P, in pesos. The firm has a stock of debt $B > 0$ in pesos which has to be refinanced today. The problem is to choose between exchange rate indexation, or no indexation at all. Without indexation, next-period peso profit will be

$$\beta P - (1 + i)B, \quad \beta > 0, \tag{A1}$$

where i is the one-period peso interest rate. On the other hand, if debt is denominated in dollars, peso profit will be

$$\beta P - XB, \quad \beta > 0, \tag{A2}$$

where the present exchange rate is set equal to unity, X denotes next-period peso-dollar exchange rate and, without loss of generality, I assume that the international dollar interest rate is zero.

Since the country is small, it is reasonable to assume that lenders are risk neutral (in dollars).[22] Therefore, at equilibrium

$$E \frac{1+i}{X} = 1, \tag{A3}$$

where E denotes the mathematical expectation operator conditional on present information.

By Jensen's Inequality,

$$E \frac{1}{X} \geq \frac{1}{EX}, \tag{A4}$$

with strict inequality if X displays any volatility. Thus, by (A3) and (A4),

$$1 + i \leq EX. \tag{A5}$$

Therefore, by (Al), (A2), and (A5), expected profit is smaller under LD. The ranking of variances is ambiguous if P and X are positively correlated. In all other cases LD displays higher variance. Therefore, for LD to dominate, the correlation between P and X must be sufficiently high.

The situation is somewhat different if the dollar is also the relevant unit of account for the domestic firm.[23] Under those circumstances, expressions (Al) and (A2) become, respectively,

$$\beta \frac{P}{X} - \frac{1+i}{X} B, \tag{A6}$$

and

$$\beta \frac{P}{X} - B. \tag{A7}$$

Clearly, by (A3), (A6), and (A7), expected dollar profit is the same in the two cases. Unfortunately, I could not obtain general analytical results for ranking profit variances, but examination of two polar cases makes me confident that in this case also adoption of LD requires sufficiently high correlation between X and P. First, suppose P is nonstochastic (hence, the correlation between P and X is zero). Thus, if expected profit and i are positive (the normal case), then profit variance is larger under LD. Second, suppose P is proportional to X (hence, the correlation between P and X is one). Thus, LD exhibits the lowest profit variance.

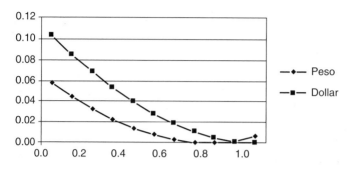

Figure 15.4
Profit Variance (exponential distribution)

To check intuition and to get some sense for the conditions under which LD dominates, I used Mathcad random number generators under the assumption that $P = \theta X$, where $0 \leq \theta \leq 1$ is the pass-through coefficient. Figure 15.4 shows results for ten thousand trials in the case in which X is $1 +$ exponentially distributed variable, where the exponent is set equal to 0.1. In the simulation, the equilibrium interest rate $i = 0.093$. Variables $peso(\theta)$ and $dollar(\theta)$ are the profit variances for peso and dollar loans, respectively, when the pass-through coefficient is equal to θ. Clearly, peso loans dominate dollar loans for most θs, except for very high θ (more specifically, $\theta > 0.935$). All cases examined shared this feature, that is, LD dominates only for very high pass-through coefficients.

APPENDIX B: INFLATION TARGETING AND CREDIBILITY PROBLEMS

In this section I will show that inflation targeting under imperfect credibility could produce distortionary effects similar to those encountered in not fully credible fixed exchange rate regimes. The model utilized follows closely on Calvo (1986).

To simplify, I will assume a representative (price-taker) individual whose utility function from the perspective of time 0 (identified as "the present") satisfies

$$\int_0^\infty [u(c_t) + v(z_t)]e^{-\rho t}\, dt, \tag{B1}$$

where c and z stand for consumption of tradeable and nontradeable goods, respectively, and ρ is a positive subjective discount rate. Instant utility indexes u and v are increasing, strictly concave and twice-continuously differentiable.

The individual is subject to a cash-in-advance constraint,

$$m_t = c_t + p_t z_t,\tag{B2}$$

where p is the relative price of nontradeables with respect to tradeables, and m is the stock of money held by the individual expressed in terms of tradeables. The assumption behind (B2) is that individuals are constrained to hold monetary balances for their planned consumption.[24] In what follows, I will assume that the international price of tradeables is constant and equal to unity. Therefore, m also stands for the ratio of nominal money balances to the exchange rate (the foreign exchange market is totally free and there are no controls on capital mobility). Moreover, the total number of individuals is normalized to one and, hence, individual variables also stand for their corresponding aggregates.

Following Calvo (1986), the representative individual's budget constraint can be written as follows:

$$\int_0^\infty [y + p_t h + g_t - (c_t + p_t z_t)(1 + i_t)]e^{-rt}\, dt = 0,\tag{B3}$$

where, to save on notation, I assume that initial financial wealth is zero, and y, h, g, r, and i stand for endowment flow of tradeables and nontradeables (assumed constant, for simplicity), government lump-sum transfers, and the instantaneous international and nominal interest rates, respectively. For simplicity and to stay away from uninteresting dynamics, the international interest rate r is assumed constant through time and equal to the subjective rate of discount ρ.

Maximization of utility (B1) subject to budget constraint (B3) with respect to the paths of c and z, yields the following familiar first-order conditions (interior solutions are assumed throughout):

$$u'(c_t) = \lambda(1 + i_t),\tag{B4}$$

and

$$v'(z_t) = \lambda p_t(1 + i_t),\tag{B5}$$

where λ is the time-invariant Lagrange multiplier.

Suppose the government targets the price level P (identified with the price of nontradeables in terms of domestic currency), such that $P_t = 1$, for all times t.[25]

Given the assumption of perfect capital mobility, we get

$$i_t = r + \frac{\dot{E}_t}{E_t},$$ (B6)

where E is the nominal exchange rate (that is, the price of foreign in term of domestic currency). Under these circumstances, one can show that along a perfect-foresight equilibrium E is not expected to jump after $t = 0$. It can also be shown that differentiability of E also holds on open intervals where the target is fully credible.

At equilibrium, we have, for all t,

$$z_t = h.$$ (B7)

Thus, by (B4), (B5), and (B7), we have

$$p_t = \frac{v'(h)}{u'(c_t)},$$ (B8)

and, moreover, by (B5), (B6), and (B7), on open intervals where the target is credible, we have (recalling that $p = P/E$, and that target $P = 1$)

$$i_t = \frac{\dot{E}_t}{E_t} + r = v'(h)\frac{E_t}{\lambda} - 1.$$ (B9)

This defines an ordinary differential equation for E.

Assuming that the government's consumption is nil and that revenue from seigniorage is given back to the public as lump-sum transfers, the overall budget constraint takes the following form:

$$\int_0^\infty c_t e^{-rt}\, dt = \frac{y}{r}.$$ (B10)

In words, equation (B10) simply states that present discounted value of the economy's consumption of tradeables must be equal to the present discounted value of the endowment flow of tradeables (recall that the economy is assumed to start with no initial financial wealth).

The steady state of equation (B9) is unstable. Hence, if the target is credible at all points in time, equilibrium nominal exchange rate E must be constant over time, implying that $p \equiv 1/E$ is constant through time. Thus, by (B8) and (B10), at equilibrium $c_t = y$, for all t.

Consider now the standard paradigm of noncredible targeting in which individuals expect that the target will be satisfied for an initial interval, but that it will be followed by higher inflation afterward. More precisely, I will assume that individuals expect

$$P_t = 1, \quad \text{for } 0 \leq t < T, \quad \text{and}$$

$$\frac{\dot{M}_t}{M_t} = \mu, \text{ a positive constant,} \quad \text{for } t \geq T, \tag{B11}$$

where M is nominal monetary balances and the credibility horizon $T > 0$. To anchor the system, I will assume that M is continuous with respect to t at $t = T$, which rules out a jump of M at T.

By (B2) and (B7), we have

$$M_t = E_t c_t + P_t h. \tag{B12}$$

Question: Can the price level P jump at T, in spite of the nominal exchange rate E and money supply M being continuous at T? I will show that the answer is "no." Suppose, for instance, that P jumps up at T, then since M and E are continuous, c has to jump down, contradicting (B8). The contradiction is intuitive because when P jumps up, nontradeable goods become more expensive, and satisfaction of (B12) would require that the individual consumes *less* tradeable goods, while keeping constant the consumption of nontradeables.

Furthermore, one can show that from T on, the rate of inflation is constant and equal to μ (the proof is omitted). Therefore, recalling (B6),

$$i_t = r + \mu, \quad \text{for all } t \geq T. \tag{B13}$$

Continuity of P implies that equation (B9) holds at T. Hence, by (B9) and (B13), initial conditions in (B9) must be such that i converges to $r + \mu$ at T. Furthermore, by (B9), it is easy to see that there exists a unique E_0/λ that ensures that condition, and that E will rise over the credibility interval $[0, T)$. Since over that period P is constant, equilibrium condition (B8) implies that the consumption of tradeables will be falling over time. For this to be consistent with the overall budget constraint (B10), there must exist some t_0, such that $0 < t_0 < T$, and

$$c_t > y, \quad t < t_0, \quad \text{and}$$

$$c_t < y, \quad t > t_0. \tag{B14}$$

As in Calvo (1986), one can show that this consumption fluctuation is not optimal. Moreover, compared to the full-credibility case in which $c \equiv y$, the currency exhibits real appreciation in the first stages of the program (more specifically, on the interval $[0, t_0)$), and depreciation beyond t_0. Finally, it can be shown that there will be a current account deficit over all the interval $[0, T)$.

Consequently, noncredible inflation-target programs may suffer from much the same maladies that afflict noncredible currency pegs. Moreover, readers familiar with the earlier literature will notice that noncredible inflation-target programs give rise to richer consumption and real exchange rate dynamics than noncredible currency pegs.

It will be interesting to study the implications of imperfect credibility in richer scenarios displaying price stickiness, for example, and also to get a better sense of the costs of noncredible inflation-target programs compared to noncredible currency pegs [Michael Kumhof (2000) makes important inroads in this matter].

Notes

This is a shortened version of a paper with similar title that was sponsored by Instituto Tecnológico Autónomo de México (ITAM) as part of the project Optimal Monetary Institutions for Mexico. The author acknowledges very helpful comments by Sebastian Edwards, Francisco Gil-Díaz, Elisabeth Huybens, Enrique Mendoza, Marco del Negro, Carmen Reinhart, Kurt Schuler, Alan Stockman, and an anonymous referee.

1. In what follows the dollar will be identified with foreign exchange. Thus, "dollarization" stands for the adoption of a foreign currency, not necessarily the U.S. dollar.

2. As shown in figure 15.2, portfolio flows went mostly to Latin America. This supports the conjecture in the text, since Latin America is a major issuer of Brady Bonds.

3. It should be noted, however, that for the mechanism of intertemporal substitution to operate, agents must feel that current policies will be maintained for a reasonable span of time. Thus the theory is not contradicted by the fact that capital has not flowed to some countries in which policymakers have no credibility at all.

4. A typical problem of EMs is tax evasion, which keeps the size of the public sector below target, and results in a lopsided tax burden across individuals. This creates a tension, a *political* fiscal gap, which politicians promise to close when campaigning for office, and fail to fulfill when they get elected. This sows the seeds for time inconsistency, since when honesty fails trickery's charms are hard to resist.

5. Irving Fisher (1933) was one of the first to identify this problem, and he called it Debt Deflation [although Keynes (1963), originally published in 1931, appears to have preceeded him].

6. A more satisfactory model would continue focusing on y, but make output a negative function of var e. Results would be similar in that Fix will be given more weight than in the traditional models. However, there will be a larger range of ambiguity.

7. It is interesting to note that the traditional literature abstracts from credibility and financial considerations. For example, in the subject index of De Grauwe's (1994) compendium there is no entry under Finance or Banking.

8. It should be noted that Calvo and Guidotti (1990) show that full LD may not be optimal if there are shocks to government expenditure (a result that could easily be extended to any real shock in the sense of the model of section 2), and the government cannot issue bonds contingent on those shocks. However, the point remains that time inconsistency is one possible explanation for government's LD.

9. This case is discussed in Burnside, Eichenbaum, and Rebelo (1999).

10. This shift in the composition of deposits may still create banking problems if reserve requirements have to be kept in the currency in which deposits are denominated. It is worth noting, incidentally, that Argentina solved this problem by allowing banks to hold reserves in either pesos or dollars. This was facilitated by the fact that there is a fixed parity between the two currencies.

11. In addition, similar regulations prevent foreign-located banks to lend in pesos. Thus, foreign borrowing from banks would necessarily involve LD.

12. For a recent policy discussion on dollarization, see Chapman (1999), Hanke and Schuler (1999), and Moreno-Villalaz (1999).

13. According to Eichengreen (1998) during the gold standard period, LOLR capabilities were limited, and banks were forced to declare inconvertibility of bank deposits. Interestingly, this phenomenon operated as an automatic stabilizer because gold flowed in as a result of the liquidity crunch provoked by deposit inconvertibility.

14. I am assuming that it would be very costly, if not impossible, to de-dollarize once dollarization has been adopted. Treaties with the United States, for example, would be one way to make the system virtually impermeable to de-dollarization attempts.

15. As a point of some theoretical interest, I would like to note, however, that there are cases in which exchange rate volatility is totally harmless (see Calvo and Guidotti (1993) or Calvo (1996) Chapter 2). However, my sense is that inflation or exchange rate volatility is highly undesirable in EMs, given the fragility of their financial markets, an issue that is not accounted for in Calvo and Guidotti (1993).

16. Argentina attempted to lower public sector wages in response to the Tequila crisis, but the decision was overturned by the labor courts. Moreover, some privatizations have contributed to nominal rigidity by guaranteeing U.S. dollar prices on their services.

17. This represents a major practical difficulty for the implementation of this type of fiscal policy because tariffs and subsidies lead to the formation of lobbies that make their eventual removal politically hard to achieve.

18. Banks have to solve a signal-extraction problem when faced with a nonperforming loan. Is the borrower a deadbeat, or a casualty of recession and macroeconomic malfunctioning? The rise of unemployment—a variable that is easily observable, in contrast to nonperforming loans in the banking sector, which banks keep hidden from the public's eye—leads banks to put more weight on the possibility that the borrower is an innocent bystander. One can think of several reasonable models in which unemployment makes banks more reluctant to sue the delinquent borrower and more willing to offer better terms on nonperforming loans.

19. The Optimal Currency Area literature suggests that fixed exchange rates could still be attractive despite nominal rigidities if there is enough factor (especially labor) mobility across countries or regions (De Grauwe 1994). However, factor mobility cannot realistically be a very relevant issue because exchange rate flexibility helps to deal with

high-frequency imbalances, while labor mobility decisions are dictated by relatively low-frequency considerations. Even in the United States it is hard to imagine that labor will move massively across states in response to a temporary real wage disparity, thus making exchange rate flexibility totally unnecessary.

20. As argued above, however, unemployment may have a silver lining in terms of improved information.

21. Reader be warned: pass-through coefficients could be endogenous to monetary policy.

22. Departure from risk neutrality by lenders may contribute to LD because lenders would welcome the opportunity of risk diversification provided by peso loans. However, I believe that the information and time-inconsistency arguments in the text ought to play a bigger role for LD. Thus, the risk-neutrality case emphasized here appears to be a useful benchmark for the discussion in the text, irrespective of its factual accuracy.

23. The reader should recall that the unit of account matters in incomplete-markets models like the one we are discussing here.

24. This constraint has a more natural interpretation in discrete time, but its use in continuous time makes the analysis more elegant without distorting the implications of the model.

25. Alternatively, one could assume that authorities only set a target for the rate of inflation (zero in this case). To anchor the system, however, one would have to make some assumption about initial money supply. The results are unchanged, and I chose the present formulation for its directness.

References

Aizenman, Joshua, and Jacob A. Frenkel. "Optimal Wage Indexation, Foreign Exchange Intervention, and Monetary Policy." *American Economic Review* (June 1985), 402–23.

Bernanke, Ben S., Thomas Laubach, Frederic S. Mishkin, and Adam S. Posen. *Inflation Targeting—Lesson from the International Experience.* Princeton, N.J.: Princeton University Press, 1999.

Blinder, Alan S. *Central Banking in Theory and Practice,* Cambridge, Mass.: The MIT Press, 1998.

Burnside, Craig, Martin Eichenbaum, and Sergio Rebelo. "Hedging and Financial Fragility in Fixed Exchange Rate Regimes." National Bureau of Economic Research, Working paper 7143 (May 1999).

Calvo, Guillermo A. "Temporary Stabilization: Predetermined Exchange Rates." *Journal of Political Economy.* (December 1986), 1319–29.

———. *Money, Exchange Rates, and Output.* Cambridge, Mass.: The MIT Press, 1996.

———. "Understanding the Russian Virus, with Special Reference to Latin America." October 13, 1998 (a); online www.bsos.umd.edu/econ/ciecalvo.htm.

———. "Capital Flows and Capital-Market Crises: The Simple Economics of Sudden Stops." *Journal of Applied Economics* (November 1998) (b), 35–54.

———. "Contagion in Emerging Market: When Wall Street Is the Carrier." Manuscript, February 1999 (a); online www.bsos.umd.edu/econ/ciecalvo.htm.

———. "On Dollarization." April 20, 1999 (b); online www.bsos.umd.edu/econ/ciecalvo.htm.

Calvo, Guillermo A., and Pablo Guidotti. "Indexation and Maturity of Government Bonds: An Exploratory Model." In *Capital Markets and Debt Management*, edited by R. Dornbusch and M. Draghi, pp. 52–82. New York: Cambridge University Press, 1990.

———. "On the Flexibility of Monetary Policy: The Case of the Optimal Inflation Tax." *Review of Economic Studies* (June 1993), 667–87.

Calvo, Guillermo A., Leonardo Leiderman, and Carmen M. Reinhart. "Inflows of Capital to Developing Countries in the 1990s." *Journal of Economic Perspectives* (Spring 1996), 123–40.

Calvo, Guillermo A., and Enrique G. Mendoza. "Rational Contagion and the Globalization of Securities Markets." *Journal of International Economics* (June 2000), 79–114.

Calvo, Guillermo A., and Carmen M. Reinhart. "The Consequences and Management of Capital Inflows: Lessons for Sub-Saharan Africa." EGDI, distributed by Almqvist & Wicksell International, P.O. Box 7634, SE-103 94 Stockholm, Sweden, 1998.

Calvo, Guillermo A., and Carmen M. Reinhart. "Fear of Floating: Theory and Evidence." Manuscript, Center for International Economics, University of Maryland, 2000.

Carstens, Agustin G., and Alejandro M. Werner. "Mexico's Monetary Policy Framework under a Floating Exchange Rate Regime." Documento de Investigacion No. 9905, Banco of Mexico, May 1999; online www.banxico.org.mx.

Chapman, Guillermo. "La Experiencia de Dolarizacion en Panama." Paper presented at the conference on Opciones Cambiarias para la Region sponsored by the IADB, July 23–24, 1999, Panama City, Panama.

De Grauwe, Paul. *The Economics of Monetary Integration*, second revised edition. New York: Oxford University Press, 1994.

Edison, Hali, and Carmen M. Reinhart. "Stopping Hot Money: On the Use of Capital Controls during Financial Crises." Manuscript, 1999.

Eichengreen, Barry. *Globalizing Capital: A History of the International Monetary System*. Princeton, N.J.: Princeton University Press, 1998.

Fisher, Irving. "The Debt-Deflation Theory of Great Depressions." *Econometrica* (October 1933), 337–57.

Flood, Robert P., and Peter M. Garber. *Speculative Bubbles, Speculative Attacks, and Policy Switching*. Cambridge, Mass.: The MIT Press, 1994.

Flood, Robert P., and Nancy P. Marion. "The Transmission of Disturbances under Alternative Exchange-Rate Regimes with Optimal Indexing." *Quarterly Journal of Economics* (February 1982), 43–66.

Gennotte, Gerard, and Hayne Leland. "Market Liquidity, Hedging, and Crashes." *American Economic Review* (December 1990), 999–1021.

Grossman, Sanford J., and Joseph E. Stiglitz. "On the Impossibility of Informationally Efficient Markets." *American Economic Review* (June 1980), 393–408.

Hanke, Steve H., and Kurt Schuler. "A Monetary Constitution for Argentina: Rules for Dollarization." *CATO Journal* (Winter 1999), 405–19.

IMF. *International Capital Markets: Developments, Prospects, and Policy Issues*. Washington D.C., August 1995.

———. "Monetary Policy in Dollarized Economies." Occasional Paper no. 171, Washington, D.C., 1999.

Keynes, John Maynard. "The Consequences to the Banks of the Collapse of Money Values." Reprinted in his *Essays in Persuasion*. New York: W.W. Norton & Company, 1963.

Kodres, Laura E., and Matthew Pritsker. "A Rational Expectations Model of Financial Contagion." Manuscript, October 1998.

Kumhof, Michael. "Inflation Targeting under Imperfect Credibility." Manuscript, Stanford University, January 10, 2000.

Moreno-Villalaz, Juan Luis. "Lessons from the Monetary Experience of Panama: A Dollarized Economy with Financial Integration." *CATO Journal* (Winter 1999), 421–39.

Mundell, Robert A. "A Theory of Optimum Currency Areas." *American Economic Review*, 51:4 (1961), 657–65.

Poole, William. "Optimal Choice of Monetary Policy Instruments in a Simple Stochastic Macro Model." *Quarterly Journal of Economics* (May 1970), 197–216.

Talvi, Ernesto. "Exchange-Rate Based Stabilization with Endogenous Fiscal Response." *Journal of Development Economics* (October 1997), 59–75.

Yuan, Kathy. "Asymmetric Price Movements and Borrowing Constraints: A REE Model of Crisis, Contagion, and Confusion." Manuscript, MIT, January 24, 2000.

16

Fear of Floating

Guillermo A. Calvo and
Carmen M. Reinhart

I Introduction

After the Asian financial crisis and the subsequent crises in Russia, Brazil, and Turkey, many observers have suggested that intermediate exchange rate regimes are vanishing and that countries around the world are being driven toward corner solutions. The bipolar solutions are either hard pegs—such as currency boards, dollarization, or currency unions—or freely floating exchange rate regimes.[1] On the surface, at least, this statement accords with recent trends. Twelve countries in Europe chose to give up their national currencies, while Ecuador was the first of what may be several countries in Latin America to adopt the United States dollar as its official national tender. More recently, El Salvador has also moved in that direction. At the other end of the spectrum, South Korea, Thailand, Brazil, Russia, Chile, Colombia, Poland, and, more recently, Turkey have announced their intentions to allow their currencies to float. Hence, on the basis of labels, at least, it would appear that currency arrangements are increasingly bipolar.

In this chapter we investigate whether countries are, indeed, moving as far to the corners as official labels suggest. Since verifying the existence of a hard peg is trivial, our focus is on the other end of the flexibility spectrum. Specifically, we examine whether countries that claim they are floating their currency are, indeed, doing so. We analyze the behavior of exchange rates, foreign exchange reserves, and interest rates across the spectrum of exchange rate arrangements to assess whether the official labels provide an adequate representation of actual country practice. The data span monthly observations for 39 countries during the January 1970–November 1999 period. One-hundred-and-fifty-five exchange rate arrangements are covered in this sample.

The chapter proceeds as follows. In Section II we provide descriptive statistics for exchange rates, foreign exchange reserves, and money market interest rates. We then compare the behavior of these variables across different exchange rate arrangements. In Section III we present a simple model that replicates several of the key stylized facts in these data; this framework explains why a country might prefer a smooth exchange rate as a result of the combined roles of inflation targeting and low credibility. In Section IV we introduce an exchange rate flexibility index motivated by the model. This index is meant to provide a multivariate summary measure of the degree of exchange rate flexibility in each episode—hence, it enables us to compare each episode with the benchmark of some of the more committed floaters to see whether the actual country practices match official labels. The concluding section touches on some of the implications of our findings.

II Fear of Floating: The Stylized Evidence

Our data are monthly and span January 1970–November 1999. Thirty-nine countries in Africa, Asia, Europe, and the Western Hemisphere constitute our sample. The countries are Argentina, Australia, Bolivia, Brazil, Bulgaria, Canada, Chile, Colombia, Cote D'Ivoire, Egypt, Estonia, France, Germany, Greece, India, Indonesia, Israel, Japan, Kenya, Korea, Lithuania, Malaysia, Mexico, New Zealand, Nigeria, Norway, Pakistan, Peru, Philippines, Singapore, South Africa, Spain, Sweden, Thailand, Turkey, Uganda, Uruguay, the United States, and Venezuela. One-hundred-and-fifty-five exchange rate arrangements are covered in this sample. Our analysis, however, does not give equal attention to all regimes. In the earlier part of the sample, there were pervasive capital controls that make these episodes less relevant for the purposes of comparison to the present environment of high capital mobility. Also, a few of the floating exchange rate episodes occur during hyperinflations, which also complicate comparisons. Our choice of countries was, in part, constrained by the need to be able to parallel official exchange arrangements as reported by the International Monetary Fund, and by data limitations, particularly as regards market-determined interest rates.[2] However, most regions have adequate coverage, and both developed and developing countries are well represented in the sample.[3]

In addition to bilateral exchange rates and foreign exchange reserves, we also focus on the time series properties of nominal and real ex post interest rates. The bilateral exchange rate is end-of-period. Whenever possible, the interest rate used is that most closely identified with monetary policy; if that is not available, a treasury bill rate is used. The Data Appendix provides the details on a country-by-country basis. Our desire for a long sample covering many countries precludes using higher frequency data. Relatively few countries report foreign exchange reserve data on a daily or weekly basis, and for many of those that do it is a relatively recent phenomenon. Interest rates are included in the analysis because many countries, particularly in recent years, routinely use interest rate policy to smooth exchange fluctuations—the use of interest rate policy to smooth exchange rate fluctuations in the context of an inflation target is an issue we take up in the next section. We focus on the behavior of monthly percent changes (unless otherwise noted) of each variable, one at a time, and compare these across regimes.[4]

II.1   Methodology Issues

It is widely accepted that a "pure float" is an artifact of economics textbooks. Yet, despite occasional instances of foreign exchange market intervention, sometimes even in a coordinated fashion, the United States dollar (US$) floated about as freely against the German deutsche mark (DM) (and now the euro), and the Japanese Yen (¥), as any currency has ever been allowed to float. Thus, if the only criterion was the extent of commitment to float their currencies, the G-3 are the best candidates to serve as a benchmark for comparing whether countries that claim they float are indeed doing so. However, the wealthy G-3 countries all share the common feature that (in varying degrees) their currencies are the world's reserve currencies, which somewhat reduces their value as benchmarks for smaller industrial nations and, especially, for emerging market economies. However, another comparator is also available: Australia, with a credible commitment to floating, shares some features of the other smaller industrial nations and developing countries that make up the lion's share of our sample. For example, the Australian dollar is not a world reserve currency, and Australia continues to rely heavily on primary commodity exports, like many of the developing countries in our sample. As a consequence of the latter, its terms of trade exhibit a higher volatility than those of the G-3, and it is more representative of the characteristics of many of the non-G-3 countries in our study. Giving weight to both criteria (commitment to floating and shared characteristics), we opted to use both Australia and the G-3 as benchmarks.

Our strategy is to compare what countries say and what they do. What they say is reported to the IMF, which classifies countries into four types of exchange rate arrangements: peg, limited flexibility, managed floating, and freely floating. Limited flexibility has been used, almost exclusively, to classify European countries (prior to the monetary union) with exchange rate arrangements vis-à-vis one another (i.e., the Snake, the Exchange Rate Mechanism, etc.).

What countries do can be described by the movement in their asset prices. Unless otherwise noted, the bilateral exchange rates are reported with respect to the DM for European countries and with respect to the United States dollar for everyone else. The choice of the DM owes to the fact that this was the most prominent reserve currency in Europe and, because Germany was the low inflation country for many years, the anchor for currencies in that region. For the remaining countries, the dollar is the usual anchor currency of choice. Indeed, the largest share of emerging market's external debt is denominated in US dollars, and world trade is predominantly invoiced in US dollars.

We denote the absolute value of the percent change in the exchange rate and foreign exchange reserves by ε, $\Delta F/F$, respectively. The absolute value of the change in the interest rate, $i_t - i_{t-1}$, is given by Δi. Letting x^c denote some critical threshold, we can estimate the probability that the variable x (where x can be ε, $\Delta F/F$, and Δi), falls within some prespecified bounds, conditional on a particular type of exchange rate arrangement. For example, if x^c is arbitrarily set at 2.5 percent, then the probability that the monthly exchange rate change falls within the 2.5 percent band should be greatest for the fixed exchange regimes and lowest for the freely floating arrangements, with the other two types of currency regimes positioned in the middle. In our notation, for $x = \varepsilon$, we should observe

$$P(x < x^c | \text{Peg}) > P(x < x^c | \text{Float}) \quad \text{for } x = \varepsilon.$$

Because shocks to money demand and expectations when the exchange rate is fixed are accommodated through purchases and sales of foreign exchange reserves, the opposite pattern should prevail for changes in foreign exchange reserves. Hence, for $x = \Delta F/F$,

$$P(x < x^c | \text{Peg}) < P(x < x^c | \text{Float}).$$

Thus, the probability that changes in reserves fall within a relatively narrow band is a decreasing function of the degree of exchange rate rigidity, as money demand shocks and changes in expectations are accommodated to prevent a change in the exchange rate.

Theory provides less clear-cut predictions as to how the volatility of interest rates could covary with the extent of exchange rate flexibility. Interest rates could fluctuate considerably if the monetary authorities actively use interest rate policy as a means of stabilizing the exchange rate—an issue that we will explore more formally in a simple setting in the next section. But policy is only a partial source of interest rate volatility. Interest rates are bound to be volatile if expectations about future inflation or exchange rate changes are unanchored, as is the case when the authorities lack credibility. Hence, the likelihood of observing relatively large fluctuations in interest rates would depend on both the degree of credibility and on the policymakers' reaction function.

While we also consider other statistical exercises in Section IV, examining the probabilities that the variable of interest stays within a prespecified band has some definite advantages over alternative descriptive statistics. First, it avoids the problem of outliers that can distort variances. For example, it is not uncommon in this sample (particularly for countries with capital controls or in the earlier part of the sample) to have a crawling peg exchange rate for an extended period of time (hence, some degree of exchange rate flexibility), with some periodic large devaluations (upward of 100 percent is not unusual) and return to a crawl. Brazil in the 1970s is a good example of this type of policy.[5] Short-lived inflationary spikes create similar problems for interest rates. Second, the probabilistic nature of the statistic conveys information about the underlying frequency distribution that is not apparent from the variance.

II.2   Measuring Volatility: Exchange Rates and Reserves

Tables 16.1 and 16.2 present evidence on the frequency distribution of monthly percent changes in the exchange rate, foreign exchange reserves, and nominal money-market interest rates for recent or current exchange rate regimes that are classified as freely floating regimes and managed floaters; Appendix 1 presents the comparable statistics for limited flexibility arrangements and peg episodes. The first column lists the country, the second the dates of the particular exchange

Table 16.1
Volatility of Selected Indicators in Recent or Current "Floating" Exchange Rate Regimes

			Probability that the monthly change is	
			Within a ±2.5 percent band:	Greater than ±4 percent (400 basis points):
Country (1)	Period (2)	Exchange rate (3)	Reserves (4)	Nominal interest rate (5)
Australia	**January 1984–November 1999**	**70.3**	**50.0**	**0.0**
Bolivia	September 1985–December 1997	93.9	19.6	14.8
Canada	June 1970–November 1999	93.6	36.6	2.8
India	March 1993–November 1999	93.4	50.0	23.8
Kenya	October 1993–December 1997	72.2	27.4	15.7
Japan	February 1973–November 1999	61.2	74.3	0.0
Mexico	December 1994–November 1999	63.5	28.3	37.7
New Zealand	March 1985–November 1999	72.2	31.4	1.8
Nigeria	October 1986–March 1993	74.5	12.8	1.4
Norway	December 1992–December 1994	95.8	51.9	4.1
Peru	August 1990–November 1999	71.4	48.1	31.4
Philippines	January 1988–November 1999	74.9	26.1	1.5
South Africa	January 1983–November 1999	66.2	17.4	0.5
Spain	January 1984–May 1989	93.8	40.1	4.1
Sweden	November 1992–November 1999	75.5	33.3	1.3
Uganda	January 1992–November 1999	77.9	32.9	3.6
United States$/DM	February 1973–November 1999	58.7	62.2	0.3

Source: International Financial Statistics, International Monetary Fund.

arrangement, and the remaining columns the relevant probability for changes in the exchange rate, international reserves, and interest rates, in that order. For exchange rates and foreign exchange reserves, our chosen threshold value is $x^c = 2.5$ percent, which is a comparatively narrow band. For instance, following the Exchange Rate Mechanism crisis, many European countries adopted a ±15 percent band for the exchange rate. Chile, until recently, had comparable bands. Other examples include Mexico (prior to December 1994) which had in place an "ever-widening" band, as the lower end (appreciation) of the band

Table 16.2
Volatility of Selected Indicators in "Managed Floating" Exchange Rate Regimes

| | | Probability that the monthly change is | | |
| | | Within a ± 2.5 percent band: | | Greater than ± 4 percent: |
Country (1)	Period (2)	Exchange rate (3)	Reserves (4)	Nominal interest rate (5)
Bolivia	January 1998–November 1999	100.0	12.5	0.0
Brazil	July 1994–December 1998	94.3	51.8	25.9
Chile	October 1982–November 1999	83.8	48.2	51.2
Colombia	January 1979–November 1999	86.8	54.2	2.9
Egypt	February 1991–December 1998	98.9	69.4	0.0
Greece	January 1977–December 1997	85.3	28.9	0.7
India	February 1979–November 1993	84.5	36.7	11.2
Indonesia	November 1978–June 1997	99.1	41.5	5.2
Israel	December 1991–November 1999	90.9	43.8	1.1
Kenya	January 1998–November 1999	70.6	14.3	1.1
Korea	March 1980–October 1997	97.6	37.7	0.0
Malaysia	December 1992–September 1998	81.2	55.7	2.9
Mexico	January 1989–November 1994	95.7	31.9	13.9
Norway	January 1995–November 1999	90.2	42.3	0.0
Pakistan	January 1982–November 1999	92.8	12.1	14.1
Singapore	January 1988–November 1999	88.9	74.8	0
Turkey	January 1980–November 1999	36.8	23.3	61.4
Uruguay	January 1993–November 1999	92.0	36.5	60.1
Venezuela	April 1996–November 1999	93.9	29.4	n.a.

Source: International Financial Statistics, International Monetary Fund.

was fixed and the upper ceiling (depreciation) was crawling; Israel and Colombia (during 1994–1998) also had fairly wide bands.[6]

For the United States, for example, as shown in column (3) of table 16.1, there is about a 59 percent probability that the monthly US\$/DM exchange rate change would fall within a relatively narrow plus/minus $2\frac{1}{2}$ percent band. For the US\$/¥ exchange rate, that probability is slightly higher, at 61 percent. By contrast, for Bolivia, Canada, and India (all declared floaters during that period), the probability of staying within the band is around 95 percent—significantly above the benchmark of Australia, where the comparable probability is about 70 percent (see note 5). Put in another way, there is only about a 5 percent probability in those three countries that the exchange rate will change more than $2\frac{1}{2}$ percent in any given month. On average, for this group of floaters, the probability that the exchange rate change is contained in this moderate plus/minus $2\frac{1}{2}$-percent band is over 79 percent—significantly above that for Australia, Japan, and the United States. The t-statistic for the difference in means test is 3.38 with a probability value of (0.00) under the null hypothesis of no difference. By this metric, post-crisis Mexico approximates a float more closely than any of the other cases—including Canada.[7]

Moderate-to-large monthly fluctuations in the exchange rate are even rarer among the so-called "managed float" episodes (table 16.2). For Egypt and Bolivia the probability of a monthly exchange rate change greater than 2.5 percent is nil—as was the case for Indonesia and Korea up to the 1997 crisis. Even for self-proclaimed flexible-rate advocates, such as Chile and Singapore, the frequency distribution of their monthly exchange rate fluctuations relative to the US dollar do not vaguely resemble that of Australia, let alone the US$/DM or US$/¥. Even a casual inspection reveals that a significantly higher proportion of observations falls within the $2\frac{1}{2}$ percent band. On average, there is an 88 percent probability that managed floaters' monthly changes in the exchange rate are confined to this narrow band. This exchange rate stability versus the US dollar (or DM if it is a European country) is surprising in light of the fact that for many emerging market countries during these episodes, inflation rates were well above U.S. or German levels, terms-of-trade shocks were frequent and large, and macroeconomic fundamentals were markedly more volatile than in any of the benchmark countries. Not surprisingly, the evidence presented in Appendix 1 shows that for limited flexibility arrangements and for pegs the probabilities that exchange rate changes are confined to this band are even greater, at 92 and 95 percent, respectively. Hence, the observed behavior accords with the priors that exchange rate variability is least for pegs and greatest for floaters. For the Float-Peg difference, the probability value from the means test is (0.00); for the Float-Managed, it is (0.04); for the Managed-Limited flexibility, the means test of the probability value is (0.32) while for the Limited flexibility-Peg it is (0.44).

Yet, we cannot glean from exchange rates alone what would have been the extent of exchange rate fluctuations in the absence of policy interventions; that is, we do not observe the counterfactual. To assess the extent of policy intervention to smooth out exchange rate fluctuations, we next examine the behavior of foreign exchange reserves. In principle, the variance of reserves should be zero in a pure float. In reality, however, it is not that simple, as reserves may change because of fluctuations in valuation and the accrual of interest earnings.[8] However, even absent these, there are other factors that influence changes in reserves. First, there are "hidden" foreign exchange reserves transactions. Credit lines may be used to defend the exchange rate during periods of speculative pressures. Indeed, several European countries made ample use of their lines of credit during the Exchange Rate Mechanism (ERM) crisis of 1992–1993. Central banks may engage in derivative transactions, much along the lines of Thailand in 1997, which borrowed dollars in the futures market, or issue debt denominated in a foreign currency, such as Brazil among others. These transactions hide the true level and variation in reserves. Second, even in the absence of any "hidden" reserve transactions, countries may rely more heavily on domestic open market operations and interest rate changes to limit exchange rate.

Column (4) of tables 16.1 and 16.2 summarizes the frequency distribution of monthly foreign exchange reserve changes (in US dollars). With the exception of the United States and the few European countries in the sample, most countries represented in tables 16.1 and 16.2 hold most of their foreign exchange reserve holdings in dollar-denominated assets—hence, for this group valuation changes are not much of an issue.[9] As table 16.1 shows, there is about a 74 percent probability that Japan's monthly changes in foreign exchange reserves fall in a plus/minus 2.5 percent band, while for Australia the comparable probability is 50 percent. Yet, in the case of Mexico, there is only a 28 percent probability that changes in foreign exchange reserves are that small, while in the case of Bolivia that probability is even lower; note that for post-crisis Thailand there is only a 6 percent probability that reserves changes are inside the band.[10] Indeed, for all other countries, large swings in foreign exchange reserves appear to be commonplace, consistent with a higher extent of intervention in the foreign exchange market—relative to what is to be expected a priori from a freely floating exchange rate regime. Nor is this exclusively an emerging market phenomenon—Canada's reserve changes are about seven times as volatile as those of the United States. For the group of "floaters" the average probability (shown in the right-hand panel of figure

16.1) is about 34 percent—about one-half the Japan-United States average and significantly below the Australian benchmark. The difference is statistically significant. Indeed, the observed behavior of international reserves runs counter to our priors—$P(\Delta F/F, < x^c|\text{Peg}) < P(\Delta F/F, < x^c|\text{Float})$. We find that reserve variability is highest for the "floaters" and least for the limited flexibility arrangements. This point is made starkly in the top panel of figure 16.1, which plots the probability that the monthly exchange rate change lies within a $2\frac{1}{2}$ percent band (along the horizontal axis) and the probability that foreign exchange reserves change more that $2\frac{1}{2}$ percent (along the vertical axis) for the four currency regimes and our three comparators. Two points are evident. First, the range of observed exchange rate variation is quite narrow, with all four regimes associated with a higher chance of changing in a narrow band than any of the three benchmarks. Second, the smoothness in the exchange rate seems to be the result of explicit policy choice: international reserves move more from month to month for those countries with the more stable exchange rates.

II.3   Interest Rate Volatility, Lack of Credibility, and Monetary Policy

As discussed earlier, policy intervention to dampen exchange rate fluctuations is not limited to purchases and sales of foreign exchange. Interest rates in the United States, Japan, Australia, and other developed economies are usually set with domestic considerations in mind. Yet, in many of the other countries in our sample, the authorities who set domestic interest rates accord a much higher weight to the stabilization of the exchange rate—particularly when there are credibility problems or a high passthrough from exchange rates to prices. This is also the case for countries which have inflation targets and have a high passthrough from exchange rates to prices, which is the case we model in Section III. For evidence that pass-through tends to be higher for emerging markets, see Calvo and Reinhart [2001]. This policy, coupled with credibility problems, may help explain the high relative volatility of interest rates in these countries. As shown in table 16.1, while the probability that interest rates change by 400 basis points (4 percent) or more on any given month is about zero for Australia, Japan, and the United States, that probability is close to 40 percent for Mexico and about 30 percent for Peru and India (among the floaters). Nominal and real interest rates in India are about four times as variable

Averaged across exchange rate regimes

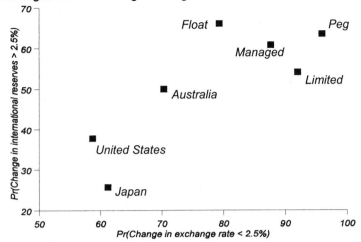

Averaged across exchange rate regimes

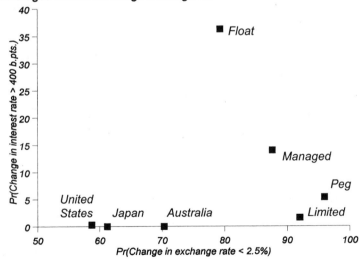

Figure 16.1
Source: Tables 16.1 and 16.2 and Appendix 1.

as in the United States; for Mexico, interest rates are about twenty times as variable—Peru holds the record.[11] A recent example of Chile and Mexico's use of high interest rates as a means to limit exchange rate pressures (despite a markedly slowing economy and an adverse terms-of-trade shock) comes from the aftermath of the Russian crisis in August 1998. At the time of this writing, Brazil's central bank hiked interest rates in the midst of a recession and an energy crisis to halt the slide of its currency, the real.

These examples, however, are not unique in emerging markets. Among the managed floaters (table 16.2), other emerging markets, including Brazil, Turkey, and Uruguay have an equally high or higher incidence of large fluctuations in interest rates. While in the case of Turkey and Uruguay, it is at least partially due to their comparatively high inflation rates, this is not the case for the others. The picture painted by the volatility of real ex post interest rates is quite similar.[12]

When comparing the four types of exchange rate regimes, interest rates are the most stable for the limited flexibility group—which is almost exclusively made up of European developed countries—and least stable for the managed floating group, which is comprised predominantly of developing countries.[13] Indeed, Calvo and Reinhart [2001] show that the variance of interest rates in low inflation in emerging markets is about four times that of developed economies, and that gap is far greater for countries with a history of inflation.

Moreover, such interest volatility is not the result of adhering to strict monetary targets in the face of large and frequent money demand shocks. In reality, most of these countries do not have explicit or implicit money supply rules. Interest rate volatility would appear to be the byproduct of a combination of trying to stabilize the exchange rate through domestic open market operations and lack of credibility. These findings are summarized in the lower panel of figure 16.1, which plots the relative probabilities of small changes in the exchange rate (again, along the horizontal axis) and large changes in the nominal interest rate (the vertical axis). As is evident, the countries that move their interest rates the most are those that, by self-identification, would seem to have to move them the least—those that follow a float or a managed float.

II.4   General Observations about the Findings

In this section we have presented evidence that the variability in international reserves and interest rates is high relative to the variations in the exchange rate. Taken together, these findings would suggest that in many cases the authorities are attempting to stabilize the exchange rate through both direct intervention in the foreign exchange market and open market operations. Furthermore, "fear of floating" does not appear to be limited to a particular region. Indeed, it would appear that in emerging markets floating has been largely confined to brief periods following currency crises or chaotic episodes of high inflation —an issue we examine in greater detail in Section IV. In the next section we develop a simple framework that replicates these stylized facts and provides a rationale for fear of floating.

III   Inflation Targeting, Lack of Credibility, and Fear of Floating

There are multiple reasons why countries may be reluctant to tolerate much variation in their exchange rates.[14] Liability dollarization, which is pervasive in emerging markets, may produce a fear of floating. In Lahiri and Végh's [2001] model, fear of floating arises because there is an output cost associated with exchange rate fluctuations; in the Caballero and Krishnamurthy [2001] setting, an inelastic supply of external funds at times of crises explains exchange rate overshooting and fear of floating. Calvo and Reinhart [2001] stress concerns about lack of credibility and loss of access to international capital markets.

In this chapter we present a simple model where fear of floating arises from the combination of lack of credibility (as manifested in large and frequent risk-premiums shocks), a high passthrough from exchange rates to prices, and inflation targeting. It is worth pointing out that lack of credibility in this setting is not manifested in first moments. Lack of credibility is associated with the (higher) variance of the risk premiums shocks. This setting is motivated by the recent trend in emerging markets to couple floating with explicit inflation targets. Indeed, at present, this combination appears to have become the most popular alternative to fixing the exchange rate.[15]

Explanations of a central bank's choice of the expansion of nominal magnitudes have often been framed as some variant of Barro and Gordon's [1983] rules-versus-discretion model, whether allowing for uncertainty (as in Canzoneri [1985]), heterogeneity among potential central bankers (as in Rogoff [1985]), or even electoral choice among central bankers (as in Alesina and Grilli [1992]). Policy is cast as attempting to reconcile the long-run benefits of low inflation with the temptation to get extra output in the near term by generating an inflation surprise that works through a Phillips curve.

It could be argued that a formulation that describes discretionary monetary policy as attempting to exploit a Phillips curve is of little practical relevance for most emerging markets. A history of high and variable inflation in many emerging markets has eroded any meaningful trade-off between unemployment and inflation surprises. Furthermore, even in the absence of a notorious inflation history, the evidence suggests that monetary policy is often procyclical—as central banks raise interest rates in bad states of nature to restore investor confidence and stem capital outflows. Yet, this does not imply that the central bank is indifferent to inflation surprises. Indeed, in many emerging markets there has been a tendency to use inflation surprises to improve the government's fiscal position. Overreliance on the inflation tax (and other easy-to-implement taxes, such as tariffs) may be due to the fact that in many emerging markets tax collection is inefficient and evasion is rampant. That is, the benefits to the monetary authority are that surprise inflation generates additional revenue from money creation and erodes the real value of nominal government debt and public sector wages.

It could also be argued that the focus on a closed economy controlling the domestic inflation rate limits the seeming relevance of Barro-Gordon models for many developed and emerging market countries alike. In fact, central bankers in emerging market economies appear to be extremely mindful of external factors in general and the foreign exchange value of their currency, in particular. In what follows, the policy choice explicitly considers the problem of a small open economy setting its nominal interest rate.

Consider one period of an infinitely lived sequence.[16] Households make two sets of decisions at the start of the period based on incomplete information; that is, before shocks are realized. As workers, they bargain for nominal wages that will prevail over the period in anticipation that goods and service price inflation will equal π^e. As investors, they place part of their assets at banks in deposits that do not bear interest, implying an opportunity cost that is expected to be i^e, the market-based return on domestic government debt.

Foreign investors also hold domestic debt, with the home interest rate linked to the foreign interest rate i^*, by uncovered interest parity. Defining s to be the price of foreign currency in terms of domestic currency so that when s rises (falls), the home currency depreciates (appreciates). If ε is the expected rate of change in the exchange rate, then the uncovered interest parity condition holds up to a risk premium ρ:

$$i = i^* + \varepsilon + \rho. \tag{1}$$

The risk premium is assumed to be a random shock, drawn from a distribution with mean $\mu_\rho = 0$ and variance σ_ρ^2. To keep notational clutter to a minimum, we will assume that the mean to the risk premium shock equals zero.

From the government's perspective, the public's willingness to hold money balances must be supported by noninterest-bearing domestic reserves, issued in the amount R. Because a central bank's balance sheet must balance, these domestic reserves can also be expressed in terms of their asset counterparts, foreign exchange reserves, and domestic credit. Since the central bank can issue R, this implies that it can issue less interest-bearing obligations. This interest saving is one measure of the seigniorage from money creation,

$$i(R/p), \tag{2}$$

where p is the domestic price level.[17] Our simplification of a fractional banking system is to assume a constant money multiplier k, so that

$$M = kR. \tag{3}$$

The demand for domestic real balances is written as a linear approximation,

$$M/p = c - \eta i^e + \zeta, \tag{4}$$

where ζ represents a random shock with mean zero and variance σ_ζ^2. As before, the assumption is that households place their balances at banks before the outcome of financial market clearing is known. Thus, the opportunity cost of holding money must be forecasted rather than known with certainty.

As a consequence of this specification of the financial sector, seigniorage can be written as

$$i\frac{c - \eta i^e + \zeta}{k}. \tag{5}$$

Notice the key wedge between anticipations and actions opened up in this product: seigniorage depends on both the expected interest rate (which determines the real stock of reserves) and the actual interest rate (which determines the earning rate of those reserves).

We also assume that foreign and domestic goods, prices at p^* and p, respectively, are perfect substitutes:

$$p = sp^*,\tag{6}$$

so that purchasing power parity prevails, which completes the description of economic behavior that the central bank takes as given. This, of course, implies a pass-through of unity from exchange rate to prices. This assumption can be relaxed without altering the qualitative results of the model. Here we assume that purchasing power of parity holds for "the" relevant country in the region; if there were more currencies, the analysis could also be extended to include less-than-unit pass-through.

Each period, the central bank is assumed to maximize its welfare, which is increasing in its seigniorage and decreasing in the deviation of the inflation rate from its target, with the target taken to be zero to save on notation. This welfare function can be written as

$$W = i\frac{R}{p} - \frac{b}{2}\pi^2,\tag{7}$$

where b is a coefficient representing the welfare loss (relative to one unit more of seigniorage) from inflation deviating from its target in either direction.

The two parity conditions combine to explain domestic inflation in terms of domestic nominal interest rates and variables from the external sector. As a result,

$$\pi = i - i^* - \rho + \pi^*.\tag{8}$$

Assuming that the foreign nominal interest rate and inflation rate equal zero, the objective function of the central bank can be written as

$$W = i\frac{c - \eta i^e + \zeta}{k} - \frac{b}{2}(i - \rho)^2.\tag{9}$$

First, we find the welfare-maximizing interest rate taking expectations as given. From the first-order condition we get,

$$i = \rho + (c - \eta i^e + \zeta)/bk.\tag{10}$$

As is evident, in setting the nominal interest rate, the central bank responds one for one to risk premium shocks but proportionally to money demand shocks. The key tension that produces time inconsistency is that the central bank's desired setting of the ex post nominal interest rate depends negatively on interest rate expectations, which are formed earlier in the period.

Second, on average, those expectations should be correct. This places the condition on the model that

$$i^e = c/(bk + \eta).\qquad(11)$$

Even though both the real interest rate and the inflation target are zero, households will expect a positive nominal interest rate, implying that they expect some inflation. This is due to the presence of seigniorage in the objective function. The greater the weight on the inflation target, the smaller will be this inflation premium (as $b \to \infty$, then $i^e \to 0$).

It is important to note that there are two elements to this premium due to the importance of seigniorage itself in the objective function and the temptation to generate surprise inflation to get extra seigniorage because money demand depends on the expected interest rate. If money demand were to depend on the actual interest rate, that second element would be eliminated, although the first alone would still produce inflation in the long run. It can be shown in that circumstance that the expected nominal interest rate would equal

$$c/(2\eta + bk),\qquad(12)$$

which is smaller than that in the baseline model. The difference between the two represents, in Rogoff's [1985] term, the premium paid to investors because the central bank succumbs to the temptation to cheat systematically. The irony, of course, in all these models is that systematic cheating yields no return.

The representation for interest rate expectations in the baseline model can be substituted into the interest rate equation. This yields an expression for the optimal setting of the nominal interest rate in the presence of shocks to asset holding—namely the risk premium and money demand,

$$i = \rho + \frac{\zeta}{bk} + \frac{c}{bk + \eta}.\qquad(13)$$

Given our assumption that the shocks are uncorrelated, the variance of the domestic nominal interest rate is given by

$$\sigma_i^2 = \sigma_\rho^2 + \sigma_\zeta^2 / b^2 k^2.\qquad(14)$$

Note that the variance of the nominal interest rate declines as the commitment to the inflation target rises (b is larger) but increases when credibility is low; that is, when the variance of risk premium shocks are large. Emerging markets are routinely buffeted by large swings in risk premiums. This is evident, for example, in the volatility of emerging market sovereign credit ratings (see Reinhart [2001]). But still, even under an extreme commitment to an inflation target, nominal interest rates will vary as the central bank finds it optimal to offset risk premium shocks.

The other variables of interest follow directly. The expected change in the exchange rate will be, $i - \rho$, or

$$\varepsilon = \frac{\zeta}{bk} + \frac{c}{bk + \eta}. \tag{15}$$

That is, in setting its nominal interest rate, the central bank will completely offset the effects on the exchange rate of foreign risk premium shocks and partially offset money demand shocks. The greater the importance of the inflation target, the greater will be the offset of money demand shocks.

As a result, the variance of the change in the exchange rate can be written as

$$\sigma_\varepsilon^2 = \sigma_\zeta^2 / b^2 k^2. \tag{16}$$

Because risk premium shocks are offset completely, the variance of the exchange rate is independent of the variance of the risk premium. Moreover, the greater the commitment to an inflation target, the smaller will be the variance of the change in the exchange rate. Hence, in this setting inflation targeting can explain fear of floating.

The real domestic monetary base will equal

$$\frac{R}{p} = \frac{cb}{bk + \eta} + \frac{\zeta}{k}. \tag{17}$$

The level of real balances increases directly with the weight on inflation, in that a stronger commitment to low inflation generates a greater willingness to hold real balances. Real reserves also vary one for one with the money demand shock but are invariant to the risk premium shock. The reason, of course, that real reserves are invariant to the risk premium shock is that the decision by domestic investors to hold money balances depends on the expected, not actual, domestic interest rate.

Given this, the variance of the real monetary base will equal

$$\sigma_{R/p}^2 = \sigma_\zeta^2/k^2. \tag{18}$$

As Calvo and Guidotti [1993] point out, the cost of discretionary policy is due to its effect on expectations, which induce households to change their behavior regarding real magnitudes. The cost of a policy that alters expectations has to be weighed against the possibility of reducing the variance of real magnitudes by offsetting shocks realized after expectations are formed. In our framework, smoothing the exchange rate reduces the variation in real outcomes. Offsetting risk premium shocks and thereby damping fluctuations in the exchange rate limits unnecessary variations in domestic inflation. For an inflation targeter, this may be an end that appears particularly attractive.

It is useful to define a variance ratio that captures the variation in the exchange rate relative to policy instruments—the domestic nominal interest rate and reserves—a form of exchange rate flexibility index. In particular,

$$\lambda = \sigma_\varepsilon^2/(\sigma_i^2 + \sigma_{R/p}^2). \tag{19}$$

In this model, this term reduces to

$$\lambda = \frac{\sigma_\zeta^2}{(1 + b^2)\sigma_\zeta^2 + b^2k^2\sigma_p^2} < 1. \tag{20}$$

Note that this variance ratio goes to one as the weight on the inflation target declines. Conversely, as the weight on the inflation target increases, the variance ratio tends to zero. In the next section we examine the empirical relevance of this issue by contrasting the readings of the variance ratio given by equation (19) with the actual inflation performance for the various exchange rate arrangement episodes in our sample.

IV   An Exchange Rate Flexibility Index: Basic Tests and Comparisons

We begin this section by conducting some basic tests to assess the extent of foreign exchange market intervention (as measured by variability in foreign exchange reserves) in the 155 episodes that make up our study. We then proceed to construct an exchange rate flexibility index, along the lines suggested by the model in Section III. In both of these exercises, we compare those cases classified as floaters and managed floaters to the benchmark of the committed floaters (here taken to be Australia, Japan, and the United States).

IV.1 F-tests

As noted in Section II, with regard to exchange rates, interest rates, and other nominal variables in the local currency, outliers can significantly distort the variances of some of these variables. In the case of international reserves, which are reported in dollars and are less affected by periodic mega-devaluations or inflationary spikes, the outlier problem is somewhat less severe. Hence, in what follows, our emphasis will be on the variability of international reserves—although in the next subsection we construct a flotation index that is multivariate, as it includes the variances of the exchange rate and an interest rate.

As to the F-tests, the null hypothesis being tested is the equality of variances between the committed floaters and the particular country/ episode in question; the alternative hypothesis is that, if there is fear of floating, the variance of reserves for the episode in question will exceed that of the more committed floaters serving as a benchmark. Hence, it is a one-tailed test. The results of the F-tests are summarized in table 16.3.[18] If the Australian benchmark is used, in those episodes classified as floaters, the null hypothesis of the equality of variances in favor of the alternative hypothesis (consistent with the fear of floating phenomenon) is rejected in 73 percent of the cases. If, instead, Japan is used as a benchmark, the null hypothesis can be rejected for 97 percent of the cases. For the managed floaters, there is a similarly high incidence of

Table 16.3
Proportion of Cases Where the Volatility of Reserves Significantly Exceeds that of the Benchmark Country: Summary of the F-tests

Regime according to IMF classification	Number of cases	Australia	Benchmark is Japan	United States
Peg	70	81.4	95.7	92.9
Limited flexibility	11	72.7	100	90.9
Managed floating	43	76.2	88.4	88.4
Floating	31	73.3	97.3	87.1
All	155	77.8	93.5	90.9

The alternative hypothesis, if fear of floating is present, is that the variance in reserves for country and episode I is greater than that for the benchmark country, b. Denoting the variance of reserves by σ_R^2, the alternative hypothesis is thus, $\sigma_{Ri}^2 > \sigma_{Rb}^2$. The individual case-by-case results of the F-tests are available from the authors upon request.

rejection of the null hypothesis. In effect, in the majority of cases, the variance of foreign exchange reserves is several orders of magnitude greater than for Australia, Japan, or the United States. It is also noteworthy that the results of these tests reveal that rejection of the null hypothesis is not appreciably different for the floaters than for those with fixed exchange rates or more limited flexibility arrangements. While on the surface this result seems paradoxical, it is consistent with both a high incidence of fear of floating among the group classified as floaters and a higher incidence of capital controls among the fixers. If binding, the controls can help stabilize the exchange rate without the need for large fluctuations in international reserves.

IV.2 An Exchange Rate Flexibility Index

As discussed above, there is no single all-encompassing indicator that provides an adequate measure of the extent of exchange rate flexibility allowed by the monetary authorities. Yet from the model developed in Section III, we can motivate the construction of a multivariate index that captures different manifestations of the extent of exchange rate variability relative to the variability of the instruments that are at the disposal of the monetary authorities to stabilize the exchange rate.

As noted earlier, domestic reserves R can also be expressed in terms of their asset counterparts, which includes foreign exchange reserves F. As the results of the F-tests attest, reserve variability is significantly higher for the less committed floaters than for the benchmark countries. Furthermore, it is well-known that foreign exchange market intervention is commonplace in many of the cases studied here. For this reason, in the empirical application of the model, we focus on a variance ratio that looks at the central bank balance sheet from the asset side, implying that equation (19) should be modified to

$$\lambda = \sigma_\varepsilon^2 / (\sigma_i^2 + \sigma_F^2). \tag{21}$$

The values λ can range from zero, when there is a peg or a very high degree of commitment to inflation targeting, to one when seignorage has a high weight in the policymaker's objective function. As shown in table 16.4, in about 83 percent of the cases the index of exchange rate flexibility is below that of Australia—for Japan and the United States the share of cases below these two benchmarks is 95 and 90, respectively. When we disaggregate the advanced economies from the emerging market countries, no obvious differences emerge on the

Table 16.4
Probabilities of "Floating" in Comparison to the Benchmark Country: A Composite Index
of Exchange Rate Flexibility

Proportion of total case where	Australia	Benchmark is Japan	United States
All countries			
Index is below benchmark	83.0	95.0	90.0
Index is above benchmark	17.0	5.0	10.0
Advanced economies			
Index is below benchmark	78.0	100.0	90.0
Index is above benchmark	22.0	0.0	10.0
Of which: high inflation: 30 percent cutoff	0.0	0.0	0.0
Of which: post-crisis	0.0	0.0	0.0
Emerging market economies			
Index is below benchmark	85.7	91.4	90.0
Index is above benchmark	14.3	8.6	10.0
Of which: high inflation	33.0	42.9	42.9
Of which: post-crisis	30.0	50.0	42.9

Source: The authors. The indices for the individual country episodes are not reported
here to economize on space but are available at www.puaf.umd.edu/papers/reinhart
.htm.
The high inflation cutoff is 30 percent or higher during the episode in question; this is in
keeping with the threshold used by Easterly [1998] and others.
For, the United States, the index uses the US$/DM (subsequently euro) exchange rate;
very similar results obtain if the US dollar/yen exchange rate is used.
a. Another 22 percent of the cases above the Australian benchmark were accounted for
by the G-3 countries.

proportion of cases that lie below and above the three benchmarks.
Separating the two groups does shed light on the "causes" behind the
high readings. For the advanced economies, there is no obvious link
between a high flexibility index reading and high inflation or rising inflation, as is usually the case following a currency crisis. For emerging
markets, however, between 66 and 93 percent of the cases (depending
on whether the Australia or Japan benchmark is used) recording a
"higher degree of variability" either had inflation rates above 30 percent per annum or the period in question is immediately following a
currency crisis. This finding is broadly consistent with the model's
predictions that the higher the weight placed on seignorage relative to
the inflation target, the more variable the exchange rate relative to the
instruments of policy, as the shocks to the risk premiums will not be

offset to the same degree if the commitment to an inflation target is not binding.

Furthermore, the mode index level for emerging markets is well below the mode for the advanced economies group. This is also in line with the predictions of the model. The variance of nominal interest rates is determined on a one-to-one basis by the variance of risk premium shocks, σ_p^2 (equation (14))—as discussed earlier, risk premiums are far more volatile in emerging markets than in developed economies.

V   Concluding Remarks

Announcements of intentions to float, to be sure, are not new. The Philippines announced it would float on January 1988, yet less than ten years later, following its 1997 currency crises, its exchange rate policy would be lumped together with the rest of the affected Asian countries, under the commonly used (but ill-defined) label of a "soft peg." Bolivia announced it would float on September 1985, because of its hyperinflation—despite this announcement its exchange rate so closely tracked the United States dollar that the regime was reclassified as a managed float on January 1998. Korea and Thailand, despite their relatively new floating status, seem to amass reserves at every possible opportunity.[19]

While these episodes provide anecdotal evidence that countries may be reluctant to allow their currencies to float, the systematic evidence presented in this paper suggests that the fear of floating phenomenon is, indeed, widespread and cuts across regions and levels of development. Fear of floating—or more generally, fear of large currency swings—is pervasive for a variety of reasons, particularly among emerging market countries. The supposedly disappearing middle account makes up the predominant share of country practices. Indeed, one of the hardest challenges trying to draw lessons from the experiences of countries that are at the corners is that there are so few to study. The experiences of some of the floaters like the United States and Japan may not be particularly relevant for developing countries. Similarly, the number of countries with hard pegs is so small (excluding small islands) that it is difficult to generalize.

We have presented evidence in this chapter that, when it comes to exchange rate policy, the middle has not disappeared. Yet, there is an apparent change in the conduct of monetary-exchange rate policy in many emerging markets—interest rate policy is (at least partially) replacing foreign exchange intervention as the preferred means of smoothing exchange rate fluctuations. This is evident in the high variability of interest rates in developing economies and in the practices of countries like Mexico and Peru. The use of interest rate policy to smooth exchange rate fluctuations has received considerable attention in recent years; see, for example, Lahiri and Végh [2000] and references therein.

Our finding that so many of the episodes that come under the heading of floating exchange rates look similar to many of the explicit less flexible exchange rate arrangements may help explain why earlier studies, which relied on the official classifications of regimes, failed to detect important differences in GDP growth rates and inflation, across peg and the floating regimes.[20]

In sum, economic theory provides us with well-defined distinctions between fixed and flexible exchange rate regimes, but we are not aware of any criteria that allow us to discriminate as to when a managed float starts to look like a soft peg. Indeed, the evidence presented in this chapter suggests that it is often quite difficult to distinguish between the two. On the basis of the empirical evidence, perhaps, all that we can say is that, when it comes to exchange rate policy, discretion rules the day.

Data Appendix: Definitions and Sources

This appendix describes the data used in this study and their sources. IFS refers to the International Monetary Fund's *International Financial Statistics*.

1. Exchange rates. Monthly end-of-period bilateral exchange rates are used. For the European countries it is bilateral exchange rates versus the deutsche mark, except pre1973, where it is bilateral rates versus the US dollar. For selected African countries (as noted) bilateral exchange rates versus the French franc are used, while for the remaining countries, which constitute the majority, it is bilateral rates versus the US dollar. We focus on monthly percent changes. Source: IFS line ae.

2. Reserves. Gross foreign exchange reserves minus gold. As with exchange rates, we use monthly percent changes. Source: IFS line 1L.d.

3. Nominal interest rates. Where possible, policy interest rates were used. As these vary by country, the table below summarizes for each country which interest rate series is used and its source.

4. Real ex post interest rates. The nominal interest rates listed above, deflated using consumer prices (IFS line 64), expressed in percentage points. The real interest rate is given by $100 \times [((1 + i_t) p_t / p_{t+1} - 1,$ where I is the nominal interest rate and p are consumer prices.

Table 16A.1

Country	Interest rate series used	IMF/IFS code
Argentina	Interbank	60B
Australia	Interbank	60B
Bolivia	Deposit	60L
Brazil	Interbank	60B
Canada	Interbank	60B
Chile	Deposit	60L
Colombia	Discount	60
Egypt	Discount	60
France	Interbank	60B
Germany	Interbank	60B
Greece	T-bill	60C
India	Interbank	60B
Indonesia	Interbank	60B
Israel	T-bill	60C
Ivory Coast	Discount	60
Japan	Interbank	60B
Kenya	T-bill	60C
Malaysia	Interbank	60B
Mexico	Interbank	60B
New Zealand	Interbank	60B
Nigeria	T-bill	60C
Norway	Interbank	60B
Pakistan	Interbank	60B
Peru	Discount	60
Philippines	T-bill	60C
Singapore	Interbank	60B
South Africa	Interbank	60B
South Korea	Interbank	60B
Spain	Interbank	60B
Sweden	Interbank	60B
Thailand	Interbank	60B
Uganda	T-bill	60C
United States	Federal funds	60B
Uruguay	Discount	60
Venezuela	Discount	60

Table 16A.2
Volatility of Selected Indicators in "Limited Flexibility and Fixed" Exchange Rate Regimes

| | | Probability that the monthly percent change is | | |
| | | Within a ±2.5 percent band: | | Greater than ±4 percent: |
Country	Period	Exchange rate	Reserves	Nominal interest rate
"Limited flexibility"				
France	March 1979–November 1999	97.5	54.9	0.8
Greece	January 1998–November 1999	80.0	31.3	0.0
Malaysia	January 1986–February 1990	98.1	35.9	3.9
Spain	June 1989–November 1999	92.4	64.7	0.0
Sweden	June 1985–October 1992	92.1	39.3	3.4
"Fixed"				
Argentina	March 1991–November 1999	100.0	36.7	18.4
Bulgaria	June 1997–November 1999	93.1	48.2	3.57
Cote D'Ivoire	January 1970–November 1999	99.4	8.7	0.0
Estonia	June 1992–November 1999	100.0	32.6	5.7
Kenya	January 1970–September 1993	85.6	20.8	1.5
Lithuania	April 1994–November 1999	100.0	37.3	19.4
Malaysia	March 1990–November 1992	96.9	39.4	0.0
Nigeria	April 1993–November 1999	98.6	8.9	1.4
Norway	December 1978–November 1992	86.8	35.1	6.5
Singapore	January 1983–December 1987	96.6	83.3	0.0
Thailand	January 1970–June 1997	98.5	50.2	2.4

Recent pegs episodes with few monthly observations are Malaysia in September 1998 and Egypt in January 1999.
Source: International Financial Statistics, International Monetary Fund.

Notes

The authors wish to thank Alberto Alesina, Enrique Mendoza, Vincent Reinhart, Juan Trevino, Carlos Végh, seminar participants at the Hoover Institution conference on "Currency Unions," Stanford, California, Summer Camp, Paracas, Peru, International Monetary Fund, and the NBER's Summer Institute 2000 in International Finance and Macroeconomics, and two anonymous referees for very useful suggestions, and Facundo Martin, Ioannis Tokatlidis, and Juan Trevino for superb research assistance.

1. For recent interesting discussions of the corner solution hypothesis, see Frankel, Schmukler, and Servén [2001] and Fischer [2001]. Obstfeld and Rogoff [1995], who stress

the increased difficulty of maintaining a peg in the face of rising capital mobility, also anticipate many of these issues.

2. While data on exchange rates and reserves are readily available for a much larger set of developing countries, data on interest rates pose a problem in many cases, as they are riddled with large gaps and discontinuities.

3. Many small countries in Africa and the Western Hemisphere with a long history of fixed exchange rates (for instance, the CFA Franc Zone) are not well represented in our sample. As we are primarily interested in verifying whether countries that are currently (or previously) classified as floaters or managed floaters behave like the truly committed floaters, this does not seem like a serious omission.

4. In a longer working paper version of this chapter, we also studied the behavior of the monetary aggregates, real ex post interest rates, and primary commodity prices (see Calvo and Reinhart [2001]).

5. As another example, the variance of the monthly exchange rate change over Pakistan's pegged episode, which ended in December 1981, was 119.42; excluding a single monthly observation (the devaluation of May 1972), the variance plummets to 0.85. Some of the problems with the alternative exchange rate classification proposed by Levy Yeyati and Sturzenegger [1999] rest on their heavy reliance on second moments distorted by outliers.

6. In a longer working paper version, we also report comparable statistics for a ± 1 percent band.

7. The variance of the monthly changes Mexican peso/US$ is about twice as large as the variance of the monthly changes in the ¥/US$ exchange rate (see Calvo and Reinhart [2001]).

For a study of Peru's fear of floating, see Morón, Goñi, and Ormeño [1999], who estimate an implicit intervention band. For a discussion on East Asia's Dollar Standard, see McKinnon [2001].

8. For instance, in the case of New Zealand, reserves fluctuate due to the Treasury's management of its overseas currency debt rather than foreign exchange market intervention. We thank Governor Brash (in personal correspondence) for pointing this out.

9. One may also want to construct an estimate of interest earned by the reserve holdings and adjust the reported stocks accordingly. This is work in progress.

10. So while monthly changes in the Mexican peso/US$ exchange rate are almost twice as variable as monthly changes in the ¥/US$ rate—changes in Mexico's reserves are 18 times as volatile as changes in U.S. reserves and 25 times as variable as changes in Japan's reserves and more than four times as volatile as Argentina's reserves.

11. See Calvo and Reinhart [2000] for details.

12. See the working paper version of this chapter.

13. It is important to note that some countries with a highly regulated financial sector and limited capital mobility simultaneously show exchange rate and interest rate stability; examples include Egypt, India (in the earlier managed floating period), Kenya, and Nigeria.

14. See also Hausmann, Panizza, and Stein [2001].

15. Inflation targeters include Australia (September 1994), Brazil (June 1999), Canada (February 1991), Colombia (September 1999), Czech Republic (January 1998), Finland

(February 1993–June 1998), Israel (January 1992), South Korea (January 1998), Switzerland (January 2000), Mexico (January 1999), New Zealand (March 1990), Peru (January 1994), Poland (October 1998), South Africa (February 2000), Spain (November 1994–June 1998), Sweden (January 1993), Thailand (April 2000), and United Kingdom (October 1992). The dates in parentheses, which indicate when inflation targeting was introduced, highlight that for most of the emerging markets the policy change is relatively recent.

16. We will suppress time subscripts where possible.

17. In a growing economy, seigniorage would also include the increase in real balances induced as income expands.

18. The individual country and episode (there are 155 of these) results are available in the background material to this paper at www.puaf.umd.edu/papers/reinhart.htm.

19. Of course, one interpretation of these developments is that, burned by the liquidity shortage faced during the 1997–1998 crisis, these countries are seeking to build a "war chest" of international reserves in order to avoid having similar problems in the future.

20. See, for instance, Baxter and Stockman [1989], Ghosh, Gulde, Ostry, and Wolf [1997], and Edwards and Savastano [2000] for a review of this literature.

References

Alesina, Alberto, and Vittorio Grilli, "The European Central Bank: Reshaping Monetary Politics in Europe," in *Establishing a Central Bank: Issues in Europe and Lessons from the U.S.*, M. Canzoneri, V. Grilli, and P. Masson, eds. (Cambridge, UK: Cambridge University Press, 1992), pp. 49–77.

Barro, Robert J., and David Gordon, "Rules, Discretion and Reputation in a Model of Monetary Policy," *Journal of Monetary Economics*, XII (1983), 101–122.

Baxter, Marianne, and Alan C. Stockman, "Business Cycles and the Exchange-Rate Regime: Some International Evidence," *Journal of Monetary Economics*, XXIII (1989), 377–400.

Caballero, Ricardo, and Arvind Krishnamurthy, "A "Vertical" Analysis of Crises and Intervention: Fear of Floating and Ex-Ante Problems," mimeograph, Massachusetts Institute of Technology, 2001.

Calvo, Guillermo A., and Pablo E. Guidotti, "On the Flexibility of Monetary Policy: The Case of the Optimal Inflation Tax," *Review of Economic Studies*, LX (1993), 667–687.

Calvo, Guillermo A., and Carmen M. Reinhart, "Fear of Floating," NBER Working Paper No. 7993, 2000.

Calvo, Guillermo A., and Carmen M. Reinhart, "Fixing for Your Life," in *Brookings Trade Forum 2000. Policy Challenges in the Next Millennium*, S. Collins and D. Rodrik, eds. (Washington, DC: Brookings Institution, 2001), pp. 1–39.

Canzoneri, Matthew B., "Monetary Policy Games and the Role of Private Information," *American Economic Review*, LXXV (1985), 1056–1070.

Edwards, Sebastian, and Miguel Savastano, "Exchange Rates in Emerging Economies: What Do We Know? What Do We Need to Know?" in *Economic Policy Reform: The Second Stage*, A. Krueger, ed. (Chicago: University of Chicago Press, 2000), pp. 453–510.

Fischer, Stanley, "Exchange Rate Regimes: Is the Bipolar View Correct?" *Journal of Economic Perspectives*, XV (2001), 3–24.

Frankel, Jeffrey A., Sergio Schmukler, and Luis Servén, "Verifiability and the Vanishing Exchange Rate Regime," in *Policy Challenges in the Next Millennium*, S. Collins and D. Rodrik, eds. (Washington, DC: Brookings Institution, 2001), pp. 59–109.

Ghosh, Atish, Anne-Marie Gulde, Jonathan Ostry, and Holger Wolf, "Does the Nominal Exchange Rate Regime Matter?" NBER Working Paper No. 5874, 1997.

Hausmann, Ricardo, Ugo Panizza, and Ernesto Stein, "Why Do Countries Float the Way They Float?" *Journal of Development Economics*, LXVI (2001), 387–417.

Lahiri, Amartya, and Carlos A. Végh, "Living with the Fear of Floating: An Optimal Policy Perspective," in *Preventing Currency Crises in Emerging Markets*, S. Edwards and J. Frankel, eds. (Chicago: University of Chicago Press for the National Bureau of Economic Research, 2001).

Levy Yeyati, Eduardo, and Federico Sturzenegger, "Classifying Exchange Rate Regimes: Deeds versus Words," mimeograph, Universidad Torcuato Di Tella, 1999.

McKinnon, Ronald I., "After the Crisis, the East Asian Dollar Standard Resurrected," in *Rethinking the East Asian Miracle*, J. Stiglitz and S. Yusuf, eds. (Washington, DC: World Bank and Oxford University Press, 2001), pp. 197–246.

Morón, Eduardo, Edwin Goñi, and Arturo Ormeño, "Central Bankers' Fear of Floating: The Peruvian Evidence," mimeograph, Universidad del Pacifico, 1999.

Obstfeld, Maurice, and Kenneth Rogoff, "The Mirage of Fixed Exchange Rates," *Journal of Economic Perspectives*, IX (1995), 73–96.

Reinhart, Carmen M., "Sovereign Credit Ratings Before and After Financial Crises," mimeograph, University of Maryland, College Park, 2001.

Rogoff, Kenneth, "The Optimal Degree of Commitment to an Intermediate Monetary Target," *Quarterly Journal of Economics*, C (1985), 1169–1190.

17   The Mirage of Exchange Rate Regimes for Emerging Market Countries

Guillermo A. Calvo and
Frederic S. Mishkin

In recent years, a number of emerging market countries have experienced devastating financial crises and macroeconomic turbulence, including Argentina (2001–2002), Turkey (2000–2001), Ecuador (1999), Russia (1998), east Asia (1997), Mexico (1994–1995) and even Chile (1982). In the ensuing postmortems, an active debate has followed over how the choice of exchange rate regime might have contributed to macroeconomic instability—and conversely, how a shift in exchange rate regime might have improved macroeconomic performance. Should an emerging market economy prefer a floating exchange rate, a fixed exchange rate or some blend of the two, like an exchange rate that was usually fixed but might sometimes shift?

Many countries used to choose an intermediate path: that is, an exchange rate that was often stabilized by the central bank, but might sometimes shift, often known as a "soft peg." However, in the aftermath of the macroeconomic crisis across east Asia in 1997–1998, a view emerged that this exchange rate regime was in part responsible for the depth of the macroeconomic crisis. The governments of Thailand, Malaysia, South Korea and other nations in that region had kept exchange rates fixed. There was no explicit institutional guarantee that the exchange rate would remain fixed, but the rates had been stable for long enough that local financial institutions borrowed in dollars abroad and then loaned freely in U.S. dollars to domestic borrowers. But when a surge of foreign investment stopped, the existing exchange rate became unsustainable. For example, when the Thai baht collapsed against the U.S. dollar, Thai borrowers were unable to repay their dollar-denominated loans—and in turn many Thai financial institutions were insolvent. This meltdown of the financial sector led to an enormous economic contraction.

Thus, one often-told lesson of the east Asian experience is that nations must make a bipolar choice: either choose a framework for credibly guaranteeing a fixed exchange rate, known as a "hard peg," or else accept a freely floating exchange rate.[1] Yet neither of these extreme exchange rate regimes has an unblemished record, either.

There are two basic ways a government can offer a credible guarantee of a fixed exchange rate: a currency board and full dollarization. In a currency board, the note-issuing authority, whether the central bank or the government, fixes a conversion rate for this currency vis-à-vis a foreign currency (say, U.S. dollars) and provides full convertibility because it stands ready to exchange domestically issued notes for the foreign currency on demand and has enough international reserves to do so. Full dollarization involves eliminating the domestic currency altogether and replacing it with a foreign currency like the U.S. dollar, which is why it is referred to as "dollarization," although it could instead involve the use of another currency, like the euro. This commitment is even stronger than a currency board because it makes it much more difficult—though not impossible—for the government to regain control of monetary policy and/or set a new parity for the (nonexistent) domestic currency.

Argentina, for example, chose the currency board approach for ensuring a fixed exchange rate. Indeed, Argentina even recognized that full backing of the monetary base may not be enough, because that would leave the banking system without a lender of last resort or a situation where the government might need additional credit, so the Argentines also paid for contingent credit lines. From a legal perspective, the central bank of Argentina was highly independent. But in 2001, large budget deficits (including contingent government obligations, like supporting state-owned banks) forced the Argentine government to look for a new source of funds. After Domingo Cavallo became Minister of the Economy in April 2001, the supposedly independent central bank president, Pedro Pou, was forced to resign. Soon after, Argentina's prudential and regulatory regime for its financial sector, which had been one of the best in the emerging market world, was weakened. Banks were encouraged and coerced into purchasing Argentine government bonds to fund the fiscal debt. An attempt was made to reactivate the economy via expansive monetary policy. With the value of these bonds declining as the likelihood of default on this debt increased, banks' net worth plummeted. The likely insolvency of the banks then led to a classic run on the banks and a full-scale banking crisis by the end of 2001. Because most debt instruments in Argentina were denominated in U.S. dollars, the depreciation of the Argentinean currency made it impossible for borrowers to earn enough Argentinean currency to repay their dollar-denominated loans. The Argentine financial sector melted down, and the economy, as well. Argentina's experiment with its currency board ended up in disaster.

The remaining option of freely floating exchange rates is also problematic. Without further elaboration, "floating exchange rate" means really nothing other than that the regime will allow for *some* exchange rate flexibility. It rules out a fixed exchange rate regime, but nothing else. A country that allows a floating exchange rate may pursue a number of very different monetary policy strategies: for example, targeting the money supply, targeting the inflation rate or a discretionary approach in which the nominal anchor is implicit but not explicit (the "just do it" approach, described in Mishkin, 1999b, 2000, and Bernanke, Laubach, Mishkin and Posen, 1999). But regardless of the choice of monetary regime, in many emerging market economies, exports, imports and international capital flows are a relatively large share of the economy, so large swings in the exchange rate can cause very substantial swings in the real economy. Even a central bank that would prefer to let the exchange rate float must be aware that if the country's banks have made loans in U.S. dollars, then a depreciation of the currency versus the dollar can greatly injure the financial system. Under these circumstances, the monetary authority is likely to display "fear of floating" (Calvo and Reinhart, 2002), defined as a reluctance to allow totally free fluctuations in the nominal or real exchange rate, which Mussa (1986) showed are very closely linked.

Thus, the literature on exchange rate regimes seems to have backed itself into a corner where none of the available options is without problems. In this paper, we argue that much of the debate on choosing an exchange rate regime misses the boat. We will begin by discussing the standard theory of choice between exchange rate regimes, and then explore the weaknesses in this theory, especially when it is applied to emerging market economies. We discuss a range of institutional traits that might predispose a country to favor either fixed or floating rates and then turn to the converse question of whether the choice of exchange rate regime may favor the development of certain desirable institutional traits. Overall, we believe that the key to macroeconomic success in emerging market countries is not primarily their choice of exchange rate regime, but rather the health of the countries fundamental macroeconomic institutions, including the institutions associated with fiscal stability, financial stability and monetary stability. In general, we believe that less attention should be focused on the general question of whether a floating or a fixed exchange rate is preferable and more on these deeper institutional arrangements.

The Standard Theory of Choosing an Exchange Rate Regime

Much of the analysis of choosing an exchange rate regime has taken place using the theory of optimal exchange rate regimes—and its close relative, the theory of optimal currency areas—which owes much to Mundell (1961) and Poole (1970). Models of choosing an exchange rate regime typically evaluate such regimes by how effective they are in reducing the variance of domestic output in an economy with sticky prices.

If an economy faces primarily nominal shocks—that is, shocks that arise from money supply or demand—then a regime of fixed exchange rates looks attractive. If a monetary shock causes inflation, it will also tend to depreciate a floating exchange rate and thus transmit a nominal shock into a real one. In this setting, the fixed exchange rate provides a mechanism to accommodate a change in the money demand or supply with less output volatility.

On the other hand, if the shocks are real—like a shock to productivity, or to the terms of trade (that is, if the relationship between export prices and import prices shifts due to movements in demand or supply)—then exchange rate flexibility of some sort becomes appealing. In this case, the economy needs to respond to a change in relative equilibrium prices, like the relative price of tradables with respect to nontradables. A shift in the nominal exchange rate offers a speedy way of implementing such a change and, thus, ameliorating the impact of these shocks on output and employment (De Grauwe, 1997). On the other hand, if a downturn is driven by real factors in an economy with a fixed exchange rate, the demand for domestic money falls and the central bank is forced to absorb excess money supply in exchange for foreign currency. The result is that (under perfect capital mobility) the decrease in the demand for domestic money leads to an automatic outflow of hard currency and a rise in interest rates. In this case, the hard peg contributes to increasing the depth of the downturn.

This standard model of choosing an exchange rate regime offers some useful insights. However, it ultimately fails to address a challenge issued by Mundell himself in his original 1961 paper, and many of the underpinnings of the model do not apply especially well to emerging market economies.

The Mundell Challenge

In Robert Mundell's (1961) original paper on optimum currency areas, he pointed out that this theory implies that the optimality of fixed exchange rates *within* a given country cannot be taken for granted. Why should Texas and New York in the United States, or Tucuman and Buenos Aires in Argentina, share the same currency? These regions are hit by different real shocks and would, according to the standard theory, benefit by the extra degree of freedom provided by having their own currencies and allow them to float against each other. We will call this deep observation the "Mundell challenge."

The usual response to the Mundell challenge is that a country has internal mechanisms that can substitute for regional exchange rate variability, including labor mobility between regions and compensatory fiscal transfers from the central government. However, these arguments are only partially persuasive. Fiscal transfers, in contrast to currency devaluation, do not change relative prices. Moreover, labor mobility is a poor substitute for exchange rate flexibility. Imagine the social costs of having to ship people from Texas to New York, when a simple movement in the exchange rate would have restored equilibrium.

Indeed, the Mundell challenge cuts even more deeply. After all, why should exchange rate flexibility be limited to large regions like New York or Texas? Why not have differing exchange rates between cities or neighborhoods? Indeed, why not move to a world of complete contingent contracts, with no money at all, and thus in effect have a different flexible exchange rate for every transaction? Of course, no one has pushed the theory to this implausible extreme. However, *not* pushing the theory in this way implies acknowledging the existence of other factors that are key and, actually, that dominate the factors emphasized by the theory of exchange rate regimes.

An important set of such factors relate to the observation that modern economies have not yet been able to function without some kind of money. The fundamental functions of money are to reduce transactions costs and to address liquidity concerns, functions that are especially valuable in a world with seriously incomplete state-contingent markets. A common currency is a useful coordinating mechanism within a national economy, even if it can sometimes go awry. Similarly, a fixed exchange rate may be a useful mechanism for an economy, even if that country faces differential real shocks, because the gains from reducing transactions costs and providing liquidity are great enough. Thus, in choosing an exchange rate regime, it is not enough to analyze the nature of the shocks. The potential benefits from fixed exchange rates must be taken into account, too.

The Realities of Emerging Market Economies

The standard framework for choosing an exchange rate regime is based on a number of implicit assumptions that do not apply well to many emerging economies. The standard theory presumes an ability to set up institutions that will assure a fixed exchange rate, but after the experience of Argentina, this assumption of an institutional guarantee seems improbable. The standard theory assumes that a time-consistent choice is made on the exchange rate regime, when in many countries the exchange rate regime may frequently shift. In the standard model of exchange rate choices, the focus is on adjustments in goods and labor markets and the financial sector is thoroughly ignored. However, no recent macroeconomic crisis in an emerging market has been free from financial turmoil of one form or another. Finally, as mentioned a moment ago, the standard exchange rate model pays no attention to transaction costs and liquidity considerations, which are essential to explain why money should exist in the first place. This issue is especially severe for emerging market economies, where the lack of contingent contracts is more severe than in advanced economies.

To illustrate the shortcomings of the standard model of choosing an exchange rate regime for emerging markets, and also to highlight some of the main issues in making such a choice, it is useful to identify several institutional features that are common in emerging market economies: weak fiscal, financial and monetary institutions; currency substitution and liability dollarization; and vulnerability to sudden stops of outside capital flows.

Weak fiscal, financial and monetary institutions make emerging market countries highly vulnerable to high inflation and currency crises. A key lesson from the "unpleasant monetarist arithmetic" discussed in Sargent and Wallace (1981) and the recent literature on fiscal theories of the price level (Woodford, 1994, 1995) is that irresponsible fiscal policy puts pressure on the monetary authorities to monetize the debt, thereby producing rapid money growth, high inflation and downward pressure on the exchange rate. Similarly, poor regulation and supervision of the financial system can result in large losses in bank balance sheets that make it impossible for the monetary authorities to raise interest rates in a way that holds down inflation or to prop up the exchange rate because doing so would likely lead to a collapse of the financial system (Mishkin, 2003). Also, a frail banking system can produce fiscal instability, and hence high inflation and devaluations, because the need for a bailout can imply a huge unfunded government liability (Burnside, Eichenbaum and Rebelo, 2001). Weak monetary institutions in which there is little commitment to the goal of price stability or the independence of the central bank mean that the monetary authorities will not have the support or the tools to keep inflation under control or to prevent large depreciations of the currency. Thus, in an economy where the government may run up enormous fiscal deficits, banks are poorly regulated and the central bank may recklessly expand the money supply, the real value of money cannot be taken for granted.

Firms and individuals in emerging market countries react to the threat that their money may dramatically change in value—either through inflation or the exchange rate—by turning to *currency substitution*, where they use a foreign currency for many transactions (Calvo and Végh, 1996). Currency substitution is likely to be due not only to past inflationary experience resulting from weak monetary, fiscal and financial institutions, but also to the fact that a currency like the U.S. dollar is a key unit of account for international transactions. This phenomenon induces the monetary authority to allow banks to offer foreign exchange deposits—that is, a firm in Argentina can deposit U.S. dollars directly in an Argentine bank without converting to local currency.[2]

Foreign exchange deposits induce banks—partly for regulatory reasons that prevent banks from taking exchange rate risk—to offer loans denominated in foreign currency, usually U.S. dollars, leading to what is called *liability dollarization*. Liability dollarization leads to an entirely different impact of a sharp currency devaluation in an emerging market (Mishkin, 1996; Calvo, 2001). In emerging market countries, a sharp real currency depreciation creates a situation where those who have borrowed in U.S. dollars are unable to repay. The money they are

Table 17.1
The Incidence of Sudden Stops, 1992–2001

Number of episodes

Event type	Emerging markets	Developed economies
Devaluations associated with sudden stop	12	4
Of which: First sudden stop, then devaluation	8	2
First devaluation, then sudden stop	4	2
Devaluations not associated with sudden stop	7	19

Percentage of total

Event type	Emerging markets	Developed economies
Devaluations associated with sudden stop	63	17
Of which: First sudden stop, then devaluation	42	9
First devaluation, then sudden stop	21	9
Devaluations not associated with sudden stop	37	83

Notes: A sudden stop is defined as a reversal in capital inflows that i) exceeds the mean minus two standard deviations of the annual change in capital inflows observed since 1990, and ii) is associated with a decline in output. The exercise also considers rises in the real exchange rate that i) exceed the mean plus two standard deviations of the annual change in the real exchange rate observed since 1990, and ii) are greater than 20 percent. The sample consists of 15 emerging economies and 17 developed countries. See Calvo, Izquierdo and Mejía (2003) for further details and some sensitivity analysis.

earning is in local currency, but their debts are in U.S. dollars. Thus, the net worth of corporations and individuals falls, especially those whose earnings are primarily in local currency. The result is many bankruptcies and loan defaults, a sharp decline in lending and an economic contraction. Liability dollarization may become a major problem for countries where the level of dollar borrowing has been especially high and where the economy is relatively closed so that most parties earn only in local currency, as has recently been the case in several emerging market countries (Calvo, Izquierdo and Talvi, 2002). However, not all emerging market countries suffer from liability dollarization in a serious way; for example, Chile and South Africa, which have stronger monetary, fiscal and financial institutions, are commonly cited exceptions (Eichengreen, Hausmann and Panizza, 2002).

Vulnerability to large negative changes in capital inflows, which often have a largely unanticipated component (Calvo and Reinhart, 2000), also contributes to susceptibility to currency and financial crises.

Table 17.1 shows the incidence of these *sudden stops* over the last decade. It shows that this phenomenonis mostly confined to emerging market countries and is more likely to be associated with large currency devaluations in these countries, probably because of their weak fiscal and financial institutions. (The precise definition of a "sudden stop" and "large" devaluations are found in the note to the table.) In addition, preliminary evidence suggests that there is a high degree of bunching of sudden stops across emerging market countries. This bunching is especially evident after the Russian 1998 crisis and also after the recent Wall Street scandals that included Enron and other firms. This pattern leads us to conjecture that, to a large extent, sudden stops have been a result of factors somewhat external to emerging market countries as a group.[3]

The links from weak institutions and sudden stops to currency substitution and liability dollarization—and then the links from liability dollarization to collapsed balance sheets and economic downturn—naturally differ from country to country.[4] But currency depreciations and sudden stops bring about large changes in relative prices and have a deep impact on income distribution and wealth (Calvo, Izquierdo and Talvi, 2002). In addition, the sudden stop is typically associated with a sharp fall in growth rates, if not outright collapse in output and employment. A floating exchange rate is clearly the wrong prescription for this situation, since it allows the sharp depreciation that cripples balance sheets and the financial sector. But under the dual stresses of weak institutions and sudden stops, it is not clear that a fixed exchange rate is sustainable, either. Rather than focusing on the choice of exchange rate regime, the appropriate answer to this situation would seem to be an improvement in fiscal, financial and monetary institutions. Such an improvement would limit the amount of currency substitution and liability dollarization and also make the economy more resilient in reacting to sudden stops when they occur. In more graphic terms: "It's the institutions, stupid."

Choosing Between Exchange Rate Regimes

No exchange rate regime can prevent macroeconomic turbulence. But the choice of exchange rate regime can be better- or worse-suited to the economic institutions and characteristics of an economy. In the discussion that follows, we will focus primarily on the overall choice between fixed and floating exchange rates. However, it is worth remembering that exchange rate regimes come in a wide variety of arrangements: currency boards, dollarization, soft pegs, crawling bands, free floating and many others. Moreover, a floating exchange rate regime can be accompanied by a number of different domestically oriented monetary policies (inflation targeting, monetary targeting or a "just do it" discretionary approach).

The Ability to Have Domestic Monetary Policy

The strongest argument in favor of a floating exchange rate regime is that it retains the flexibility to use monetary policy to focus on domestic considerations. In contrast, a hard exchange rate peg leaves very narrow scope for domestic monetary policy, because the interest rate is determined by monetary policy in the anchor country to which the emerging market country has pegged. However, in emerging market economies, this argument is more relevant in some institutional contexts than in others.

One difficulty that emerging market economies face is that their capital markets are geared to interest rates set in major financial centers. Frankel, Schmukler and Servén (2002) show, for example, that in Latin America, all interest rates reflect changes in U.S. interest rates and, furthermore, that countries that do not peg to the dollar see their interest rates change by a larger factor than those that do. In addition, emerging market economies may be hit as a group with financial contagion, as noted earlier, which will affect their interest rates. The central bank in an emerging market country thus faces real practical difficulties.

Moreover, although a floating exchange rate raises the theoretical possibility for domestic monetary authorities to pursue countercyclical monetary policy, the central bank may not possess this capability in practice. If the monetary authorities have little credibility in terms of their commitment to price stability, then monetary policy may be ineffective. For a central bank without inflation-fighting credibility, an expansionary monetary policy will only lead to an immediate jump in interest rates and/or the price level.

Building credible monetary institutions is a difficult task. It requires a public and institutional commitment to price stability. Some of this commitment can be expressed through laws and rules that assure the central bank will be allowed to set the monetary policy instruments without interference from the government, that the members of the monetary policy board must be insulated from the political process and that the central bank is prohibited from funding government deficits. There is a large literature on the forms that central bank independence can take (for example, Cukierman, 1992), but what is written down in the law may be less important than the political culture and history of the country. The contrast between Argentina and Canada is instructive here. Legally, the central bank of Canada does not look particularly independent. In the event of a disagreement between the Bank of Canada and the government, the minister of finance can issue a directive that the bank must follow. However because the directive must be specific and in writing and because the Bank of Canada is a trusted public institution, a government override of the bank is likely to cost the ruling party heavily in the polls. Thus, in practice, the Bank of Canada is highly independent. In contrast, the central bank of Argentina was highly independent from a legal perspective. However, this did not stop the Argentine government from forcing the resignation of the highly respected president of the central bank and replacing him with a president who would do the government's bidding. It is unimaginable in countries like Canada, the United States or in Europe that the public would tolerate the removal of the head of the central bank in such a manner, and, indeed, we do not know of any case of this happening in recent history.[5]

Many emerging market countries, like Argentina, have had a history of poor support for the price stability goal, and laws supporting central bank independence in these countries are easily overturned. It is therefore important for such countries to develop genuine public and political support for central bank independence as well as legal independence in order to have the ability to conduct domestic monetary policy successfully.

If an emerging market country is able to develop fiscal, financial and monetary institutions that provide credibility for society's pursuit of price stability, then monetary policy can be used to stabilize the economy. However, not all emerging market countries are up to this task, and so they may decide to choose a hard exchange rate peg instead. (However, the absence of strong institutions may make it difficult for them to sustain the hard peg.)

This interdependence between institutions and exchange rate regimes helps to explain the general empirical finding that whether a country has a fixed or flexible exchange rate tells us little about whether it has higher economic growth or smaller output fluctuations. Indeed, when you look more closely at which emerging market countries have successful macroeconomic performance, the exchange rate regime appears to be far less important than deeper institutional features of the economy relating to fiscal stability, financial stability and the credibility of monetary institutions that promote price stability.[6] However, there is some evidence that floating exchange rate regimes can help countries cope with terms-of-trade shocks and might promote economic growth (Broda, 2001; Levy-Yeyati and Sturzenegger, 2003).

Reducing Inflation

Just as the main advantage of a floating exchange rate may be that it allows the monetary authorities some discretion and flexibility to use monetary policy to cope with shocks to the domestic economy, the main weakness of a floating exchange rate may be that it allows too much discretion to monetary policy and so may not provide a sufficient nominal anchor (for example, Calvo, 2001; Calvo and Mendoza, 2000).

Of course, many emerging market countries have been able to keep inflation under control with flexible exchange rate regimes, which is why the evidence on whether fixed versus floating exchange rate regimes are associated with lower inflation rates on average is not clear-cut (for example, Edwards and Magendzo, 2001; Reinhart and Rogoff, 2002). But a central bank can only work to reduce inflation if it is supported by the public and the political process. In some countries, giving the central bank an explicit focus on inflation targeting can help focus the public debate so that it supports a monetary policy focus on long-run goals such as price stability (Bernanke, Laubach, Mishkin and Posen, 1999). However, these benefits require excellent communication skills on the part of the central bank in what can be a swirling political environment in emerging market countries.

A Misaligned Exchange Rate?

One danger of a hard exchange rate peg is the risk of being locked into a misaligned exchange rate, which can be defined as a sizable difference between its actual level and the one to which "fundamentals" would dictate. This possibility supports the case for flexible exchange rates, but again, the situation is more complex than it may at first seem.

Even in a country with a fixed nominal exchange rate, it is possible to use taxes and subsidies on imports and exports to alter the effective real exchange rate. For example, a uniform tax on imports accompanied by a uniform subsidy on exports of the same size is equivalent to a *real* currency depreciation—even though the nominal exchange rate stays unchanged. Moreover, a tax-and-subsidy-induced fiscal devaluation has one built-in advantage over nominal denomination. The fiscal devaluation has an upper bound, determined by the fact that beyond a certain point, tax evasion becomes rampant. Nominal devaluation, on the other hand, has no upper bound and can lead to high inflation.

But fiscal devaluation may be difficult to implement in a timely and effective manner without well-run fiscal institutions. For example, politicians may be quick to impose a tax on imports out of protectionist sentiment, happy to use a fiscal devaluation as an excuse, but then slow to remove that import tax later when the reason for the devaluation has evaporated.

Expanding the Gains from Trade

A hard exchange rate peg will tend to promote openness to trade and economic integration (Frankel and Rose, 2002; Rose, 2000). For example, an exchange rate fixed to the U.S. dollar will likely promote trade with the United States and other countries tied to the U.S. dollar. Fixed exchange rates or even a common regional currency as in the European monetary union may help regional economic integration (this point is also discussed further below in connection with the effect of exchange rate regimes on institutions). Thus, countries that are seeking to expand trade would naturally place a higher value on some form of a fixed exchange rate with a trading partner.

Along with gains from trade, an economy that is more open to trade may also be less susceptible to sudden stops. An expansion of trade means that a greater share of businesses are involved in the tradable sector. Because the goods they produce are traded internationally, they are more likely to be priced in foreign currency, which means that their balance sheets are less exposed to negative consequences from a devaluation of the currency when their debts are denominated in foreign currency. Then, a devaluation that raises the value of their debt in terms of domestic currency is also likely to raise the value of their assets as well, thus insulating their balance sheets from the devaluation.[7] Moreover, the more open is the economy, the smaller will be the required real currency depreciation following a sudden stop (Calvo, Izquierdo and Talvi, 2002).

Reducing the Risk Premium in Interest Rates

Advocates of hard exchange rate pegs suggest that it can reduce the currency risk component in domestic interest rates, thus lowering the borrowing costs for both the government and the private sector and improving the outlook for financial deepening, investment and growth. Some, such as Schuler (1999), have even gone so far as to suggest that dollarization will allow domestic interest rates in emerging market countries to converge to those in the United States.

However, the risk of government default and the related risk of confiscation of private assets denominated in both domestic and foreign currency are more likely to be the source of high interest rates in emerging market countries than is currency risk. The experience of Ecuador serves to illustrate this point. The spread between Ecuador's sovereign bonds and U.S. Treasury bonds remained at high levels in the first half of 2000, even though the government had already dollarized in January of the same year. Spreads came down considerably only after the government reached an agreement with its creditors in August 2000 that resulted in a substantial debt reduction of 40 percent. Sound fiscal policies that make government defaults extremely unlikely are thus essential to getting interest rates to approach those in advanced countries. Indeed, Chile, with its flexible exchange rate regime, has been able to achieve lower interest rates on its sovereign debt than Panama, which is dollarized (Edwards, 2001).

Flexibility in Wages and Prices

It is possible that emerging market economies, with their large informal sectors, have greater price and wage flexibility than developed economies. An economy with highly flexible wages and prices has less need of a flexible exchange rate.

To some extent, the degree of flexibility in wages and prices is controlled by government regulation. For example, public sector wages are often a component of the economy that is quite inflexible. However, it may be politically palatable to index public sector wages to their comparable private sector wages and thus create greater flexibility. In general, an emerging market economy with a greater degree of flexibility in wages and prices will benefit less from the additional flexibility of a floating exchange rate.

Widespread Loans in a Foreign Currency

Liability dollarization makes a policy of freely floating exchange rates more difficult to sustain. When the monetary authority knows that a currency devaluation can lead to extreme stress on the financial sector, it cannot turn a blind eye to exchange rate fluctuations (Mishkin and Savastano, 2001). A large devaluation when there is extensive liability dollarization raises the value of the foreign-denominated debt, deals a heavy blow to balance sheets and therefore can lead to a full-fledged financial crisis (Mishkin, 1996).[8]

The extent of liability dollarization is partly affected by government financial regulatory policy. For example, banking regulations can help to ensure that financial institutions match up any foreign-denominated liabilities with foreign-denominated assets and thus reduce currency risk. But even when the banks have equal foreign-denominated (dollar) assets and liabilities, if banks' dollar assets are loans to companies in dollars who themselves are unhedged, then banks are effectively unhedged against currency devaluations because the dollar loans become nonperforming when the devaluation occurs; for discussion of how this problem occurred in Mexico, see Mishkin (1996) and Garber (1999). Thus, limiting currency mismatches may require additional government policies to limit liability dollarization or at least reduce the incentives for it to occur. If a country wishes to choose a floating exchange regime, it would be wise to implement financial regulatory policies to discourage currency mismatches and liability dollarization.[9] For example, both Chile and Argentina experienced a sudden stop after the 1998 Russian crisis, but the impact on the Chilean economy was relatively small because Chile's stronger fiscal, financial and monetary institutions have resulted in much less liability dollarization.

International Reserves

A hard peg exchange rate system, like a currency board, may require a substantial war chest of international reserves. It may seem that a floating exchange rate system could avoid the cost of these reserves, but this conclusion would be too simple.

Many large emerging market economies like Mexico, Chile and Brazil, which have a floating exchange rate and have announced a domestic monetary policy aimed at targeting inflation, also have large international reserves. Indeed, they occasionally hold international reserves in excess of monetary base. Because of these large reserves, it could be said that such countries "float with a large life jacket." Why do large reserves appear to be necessary even with floating exchange rates? One explanation is that international reserves provide collateral for public bonds issued in connection with open market operations. Another explanation is that even a nation with a floating exchange rate must be concerned about the possibility of a run on its currency. Finally, policymakers in emerging market economies are very sensitive to the exchange rate because many such economies often exhibit a high pass-through coefficient; that is, devaluation often leads to inflation (González, 2000; Hausmann, Panizza and Stein, 2001).

Thus, nations with a domestically oriented monetary policy and floating exchange rates also have good reasons to carry high reserves, and it does not appear that they typically have much smaller reserves than nations with fixed exchange rates.

Lender of Last Resort

A hard exchange rate peg is sometimes said to be at a disadvantage relative to a floating exchange rate regime because it cannot accommodate a money-printing lender of last resort. While this argument would seem to weaken the case for fixed exchange rates, the scope for a lender of last resort for emerging market countries with floating rates is oversold (Calvo, 2001; Mishkin, 1999a, 2001).

In advanced economies, the monetary authority can issue liquidity to bail out the banking system, but this extra liquidity is expected to be soaked up by open market operations in the near future, so that bank bailouts can stabilize the banking system with little if any inflationary consequence. In contrast, in emerging market countries, central bank lending to the banking system in the wake of a financial crisis—characterized by a sudden stop in capital inflows—is likely to unleash fears of an inflationary explosion and produce a sharp exchange rate depreciation. If there is substantial liability dollarization, the depreciation will then have a major negative impact on private sector balance sheets, which will then promote even more financial instability.

This discussion reemphasizes an earlier lesson. If monetary institutions are well developed and the central bank has sufficient credibility, only then can the central bank act as a lender of last resort. Alternatively, a government can secure contingent credit lines (like the central bank of Argentina did during the so-called Convertibility Program), but these credit lines can be very expensive and may not be sufficient when a crisis hits.

Shifts from Fixed to Floating Regimes

Even if a country might be better served in the long run by adopting a floating exchange rate regime, the timing of the shift from a peg can have serious economic consequences. The costs of shifting from a fixed exchange rate regime to a floating regime under conditions of economic stress, like a sudden stop, are especially striking. As discussed earlier, a move from a fixed to a floating exchange rate regime in the midst of a sudden stop is likely to exacerbate the crisis. The initial devaluation that raises the value of foreign-denominated debt can cause widespread destruction of corporation and household balance sheets, which sends the economy into a devastating downward spiral. Recent papers by Caballero and Krishnamurthy (2003) and Jeanne (2002) also suggest that de-dollarization (the reestablishment of a domestic currency) may require a major overhaul of the domestic financial sector. Development of the necessary institutions to support a successful domestically oriented monetary policy takes time.

Can Exchange Rate Regimes Improve Economic Institutions?

The discussion in the preceding section focuses on what institutional traits or policy concerns should cause a country to prefer fixed or floating exchange rates. But the possibility of reverse causation also deserves consideration. Perhaps the choice of exchange rate regime should not be analyzed as a response to existing institutional traits, but instead as a potential cause of preferred institutional outcomes. Research on theories of institutional development in emerging market countries is in its early stages, but is developing rapidly (for example, see La Porta, Lopez-de-Silanes, Shleifer and Vishny, 1998; Shleifer and Vishny, 1999; Boone, Breach, Friedman and Johnson, 2000). Several intriguing hypotheses about how exchange rate regimes may improve institutions have been proposed.

Advocates of hard exchange rate pegs argue that they improve fiscal institutions and trigger sounder budgetary management, because if the central bank is focused on a fixed exchange rate, then the government no longer has access to the money printing press to finance its spending (for example, Hanke and Schuler, 1994). As the recent example of Argentina suggests, where the fiscal tensions between the provinces and the central government were not solved by the currency board, hard pegs may be less effective at constraining fiscal policy than was previously believed. Hard pegs may even weaken incentives for governments to put their fiscal house in order, because the hard peg may make it easier for governments to borrow foreign funds, thus allowing them to delay necessary reforms to fix fiscal imbalances. For example, Panama (which has been dollarized for close to 100 years) has had poor fiscal performance, with fiscal deficits over 7 percent in the 1970s and averaging 5 percent in the 1980s—it is just in recent years that the fiscal position has improved to the point that the fiscal surplus averaged 1.4 percent during the 1990s. On the other hand, it is not clear that in floating exchange rate systems, the conduct of monetary policy has any particular impact in promoting fiscal responsibility. However, one might argue that a floating exchange rate, particularly if it involves the government in setting an inflation target, has the potential to promote government transparency and fiscal responsibility.

Advocates of hard pegs also suggest that dollarization promotes a healthier financial system because it avoids currency mismatches and deepens the financial system, making it less prone to crisis (for example, Hausmann, 1999). However, there is little evidence to support this view (Eichengreen, 2002). On the other hand, a hard exchange rate peg in the form of a currency board might encourage unhedged dollar (foreign-denominated) liabilities that nonfinancial and financial firms might be willing to undertake, thus making the financial system more vulnerable in case the system has to be abandoned, as illustrated by Argentina in 2002. The hard peg might also encourage the issuance of dollar liabilities because financial firms would believe that the government would feel responsible for any devaluation and would, thus, be more likely to offer a bailout (McKinnon and Pill, 1999; Broda and Levy-Yeyati, 2000). However, the evidence that floating rate regimes lead to less liability dollarization is quite weak (Honig, 2003). After all, on its face, a floating exchange rate would seem to encourage holding some assets in several different currencies as a form of diversification. For example, Peru, with its floating exchange rate regime, has a tremendous amount of liability dollarization, while Brazil, when it had a quasi-fixed exchange regime rate in the period of 1994 to 1999, did not.

Can the choice of exchange rate regime help improve monetary institutions that enable the monetary authorities to build credibility? If a fixed exchange rate regime is constructed with a full array of supporting institutions, then it would seem to offer at least a gain in credibility—although after the collapse of Argentina's fixed rate system, such credibility will always remain incomplete. Moreover, a floating exchange rate can be a mechanism for monetary credibility as well, Tornell and Velasco (2000) argue, because the foreign exchange market will anticipate the effects of policy inconsistency by devaluing the exchange rate, providing a clear signal that something is rotten. Moreover, the signal itself could help establish some discipline in government's quarters and possibly lead to a timely rectification of policy inconsistencies (Mishkin, 1998).

Although at the outset, the credibility of the monetary authorities might be weak and the public support for central bank independence may not be all that strong, adoption of inflation targeting might help the central bank to work to produce "constrained discretion" (Bernanke and Mishkin, 1997) in which transparent discussion of the conduct of monetary policy and accountability of the central bank for achieving its inflation target might make it more difficult for the central bank to follow overly expansionary monetary policy. In addition, over time it may help obtain credibility for the central bank as it did in Chile, and it may also increase support for the central bank independence. Indeed, Mishkin and Posen (1997) and Bernanke, Laubach, Mishkin and Posen (1999) suggest that the support for central bank independence in the United Kingdom was a direct result of the inflation targeting regime. However, although inflation targeting might help with central bank credibility and support for central bank independence to some extent, a fair degree of support for good monetary institutions already needs to be present if inflation targeting is to have a chance of success.

There is some evidence that hard exchange rate pegs, particularly those in currency unions, do encourage openness to trade and integration with the countries to which the currency is pegged (Frankel and Rose, 2002; Rose, 2000). As we mentioned earlier, trade openness can reduce the vulnerability of emerging markets to financial crises, while economic integration with an anchor country reduces the cost of the loss of domestic monetary policy with a hard peg.

The possible connections between exchange rate regimes and the improvement of economic institutions is a potentially important topic for future research.

The Choice of Exchange Rate Regimes in Context

When choosing between exchange rate regimes, one size does not fit all (or always). This argues against international financial institutions like the International Monetary Fund, the World Bank and other development banks having a strong bias toward one type of exchange rate regime. Instead, an informed choice of exchange rate regime requires a deep understanding of a country's economy, institutions and political culture.

Indeed, we believe that the choice of exchange rate regime is likely to be of second order importance to the development of good fiscal, financial and monetary institutions in producing macroeconomic success in emerging market countries. Rather than treating the exchange rate regime as a primary choice, we would encourage a greater focus on institutional reforms like improved bank and financial sector regulation, fiscal restraint, building consensus for a sustainable and predictable monetary policy and increasing openness to trade. A focus on institutional reforms rather than on the exchange rate regime may encourage emerging market countries to be healthier and less prone to crises than we have seen in recent years.

Notes

We are grateful to Luis Fernando Mejía for excellent research assistance and to Jose De Gregorio, Linda Goldberg, the editors of this journal (especially Timothy Taylor) and participants in the Macro Lunch at Columbia University for helpful comments. The views expressed in this paper are exclusively those of the authors and not those of the Inter-American Development Bank, the University of Maryland, Columbia University, nor the National Bureau of Economic Research.

1. For a discussion of why soft pegs have fallen out of favor and the rise of the bipolar view, see Obstfeld and Rogoff (1995), Eichengreen and Masson (1998) and Fischer (2001) in this journal.

2. In this fashion, a sudden switch away from domestic and into foreign money need not result in a bank run, since in the presence of foreign exchange deposits, such a portfolio shift could be implemented by simply changing the denomination of bank deposits. Otherwise, deposits would be drawn down to purchase foreign exchange, resulting in a bank run.

3. In this symposium, Kaminsky and Reinhardt discuss how the process of contagion occurs.

4. Among the factors that differ across countries, we would mention the problem of tax evasion. As a result of tax evasion, the tax base of many emerging market economies is very small, the informal sector large and, thus, any adjustment to shocks causes major distortion in the formal part of the economy, leading to capital flight. Effects could be large if resulting externalities give rise to multiple equilibria (Calvo, 2002).

5. The stability of the central bank in advanced countries may be partly explained by the size of the shocks, rather than by some advantage in the political culture. After all, except for the Great Depression, advanced countries have not been hit by equally large shocks as in Argentina and other emerging market economies.

6. Indeed, Tommasi (2002) has argued that even deeper institutions, relating to politico-institutional rules as reflected in the constitution, electoral rules and informal practices of the polity, are crucial to the development and sustainability of strong fiscal, financial and monetary institutions. Also, Acemoglu, Johnson, Robinson and Thaircharoen (2003) provide evidence that deeper, fundamental institutions are more crucial to lowering economic volatility and raising growth than are specific macroeconomic policies.

7. If traded goods are not denominated in the same foreign currency as the debt, then this insulation may be incomplete unless the currency used for denominating debt moves very closely with the currency used for denominating traded goods.

8. Furthermore, it may induce the government to provide subsidized hedging instruments, which could substantially increase fiscal imbalance (this was the case in Brazil after the 1999 large devaluation of the *real*), impairing credibility.

9. However, the possible costs of pursuing such a policy also have to be taken into account. The literature on liability dollarization is still in its infancy, and, thus, it is hard to tell whether these costs are significant (Eichengreen, Hausmann and Panizza, 2002; Jeanne, 2002).

References

Acemoglu, Daron, Simon Johnson, James A. Robinson and Yunyong Thaicharoen. 2003. "Institutional Causes, Macroeconomic Symptoms: Volatility, Crises and Growth." *Journal of Monetary Economics*. 50:1, pp. 49–123.

Bernanke, Ben S. and Frederic S. Mishkin. 1997. "Inflation Targeting: A New Framework for Monetary Policy?" *Journal of Economic Perspectives*. 11:2, pp. 97–116.

Bernanke, Ben S., Thomas Laubach, Frederic S. Mishkin and Adam Posen. 1999. *Inflation Targeting: Lessons from the International Experience*. Princeton: Princeton University Press.

Boone, Peter, Alasdair Breach, Eric Friedman and Simon Johnson. 2000. "Corporate Governance and the Asian Crisis." *Journal of Financial Economics*. 58:1–2, pp. 141–86.

Broda, Christian. 2001. "Coping with Terms-of-Trade Shocks: Pegs versus Floats." *American Economic Review*. 91:2, pp. 376–80.

Broda, Christian and Eduardo Levy-Yeyati. 2000. "Safety Nets and Endogenous Financial Dollarization." Mimeo, Universidad Torcuato Di Tella.

Burnside, Craig, Martin Eichenbaum and Sergio Rebelo. 2001. "Prospective Deficits and the Asian Currency Crisis." *Journal of Political Economy*. 109:6, pp. 1155–197.

Caballero, Ricardo J. and Arvind Krishnamurthy. 2003. "Excessive Dollar Debt: Financial Development and Underinsurance." *Journal of Finance*. 58:2, pp. 867–94.

Calvo, Guillermo A. 2001. "Capital Markets and the Exchange Rate: With Special Reference to the Dollarization Debate in Latin America." *Journal of Money, Credit, and Banking*. 33:2, pp. 312–34.

Calvo, Guillermo A. 2002. "Explaining Sudden Stop, Growth Collapse and BOP Crisis: The Case of Distortionary Output Taxes." Mundell-Fleming Lecture, 3rd IMF Annual Research Conference, Washington, D.C., November 7.

Calvo, Guillermo A. and Enrique G. Mendoza. 2000. "Capital-Market Crises and Economic Collapse in Emerging Markets: An Informational-Frictions Approach." *American Economic Review*. 90:2, pp. 59–64.

Calvo, Guillermo A. and Carmen M. Reinhart. 2000. "When Capital Flows Come to a Sudden Stop: Consequences and Policy," in *Reforming the International Monetary and Financial System*. Peter B. Kenen and Alexander K. Swoboda, eds. Washington, D.C.: IMF, chapter 5.

Calvo, Guillermo A. and Carmen M. Reinhart. 2002. "Fear of Floating." *Quarterly Journal of Economics*. 117:2, pp. 379–408.

Calvo, Guillermo A. and Carlos A. Végh. 1996. "From Currency Substitution to Dollarization and Beyond: Analytical and Policy Issues," in *Money, Exchange Rates, and Output*. Guillermo A. Calvo, ed. Cambridge, Mass.: MIT Press, pp. 153–75.

Calvo, Guillermo A., Alejandro Izquierdo and Luis-Fernando Mejía. 2003. "On the Empirics of Sudden Stops." IADB working paper.

Calvo, Guillermo A., Alejandro Izquierdo and Ernesto Talvi. 2002. "Sudden Stops, the Real Exchange Rate and Fiscal Sustainability: Argentina's Lessons." IADB Working Paper No. 469; Available at ⟨http://www.iadb.org/res/publications/pubfiles/pubWP-469.pdf⟩.

Cukierman, Alex. 1992. *Central Bank Strategy, Credibility and Independence: Theory and Evidence*. Cambridge, Mass.: MIT Press.

De Grauwe, Paul. 1997. *The Economics of Monelary Integration, 3rd Edition*. London: Oxford University Press.

Edwards, Sebastian. 2001. "Dollarization: Myths and Realities." *Journal of Policy Modeling*. 23:3, pp. 249–65.

Edwards, Sebastian and I. Igal Magendzo. 2001. "Dollarization, Inflation and Growth." NBER Working Paper No. 8671.

Eichengreen, Barry. 2002. "When to Dollarize." *Journal of Money, Credit and Banking*. 34:1, pp. 1–24.

Eichengreen, Barry and Paul Masson. 1998. "Exit Strategies: Policy Options for Countries Seeking Greater Exchange Rate Flexibility." IMF Occasional Paper No. 168.

Eichengreen, Barry, Ricardo Hausmann and Ugo Panizza. 2002. "Original Sin: The Pain, the Mystery, and the Road to Redemption." Presented at the conference *Currency and Maturity Matchmaking: Redeeming Debt from Original Sin*, IADB, Washington, D.C., November 21–22.

Fischer, Stanley. 2001. "Distinguished Lecture on Economics in Government—Exchange Rate Regimes: Is the Bipolar View Correct?" *Journal of Economic Perspectives*. 15:2, pp. 3–24.

Frankel, Jeffrey A. and Andrew K. Rose. 2002. "An Estimate of the Effect of Common Currencies on Trade and Income." *Quarterly Journal of Economics*. 117:2, pp. 437–66.

Frankel, Jeffrey A., Sergio L. Schmukler and Luis Servén. 2002. "Global Transmission of Interest Rates: Monetary Independence and Currency Regime." NBER Working Paper No. 8828.

Garber, Peter. 1999. "Hard-Wiring to the Dollar: From Currency Board to Currency Zone," in *Global Markets Research*. London: Deutsche Bank.

González, José A. 2000. "Exchange Rate Pass-Through and Partial Dollarization: Is There a Link?" CREDPR Working Paper No. 81, Stanford University.

Hanke, Steven and Kurt Schuler. 1994. *Currency Boards for Developing Countries: A Handbook*. San Francisco: ICS Press.

Hausmann, Ricardo. 1999. "Should There be 5 Currencies or 105?" *Foreign Policy*. Fall, 116, pp. 65–79.

Hausmann, Ricardo, Ugo Panizza and Ernesto Stein. 2001. "Why Do Countries Float the Way They Float?" *Journal of Development Economics*. 66:2, pp. 387–414.

Honig, Adam. 2003. "Dollarization, Exchange Rate Regimes and Government Myopia." Mimeo, Columbia University, March.

Jeanne, Olivier. 2002. "Why Do Emerging Economies Borrow in Foreign Currency?" Presented at the conference *Currency and Maturity Matchmaking: Redeeming Debt from Original Sin*. IADB, Washington, D.C., November 21–22.

La Porta, Rafael, Florencio Lopez-de-Silanes, Andrei Shleifer and Robert W. Vishny. 1998. "Law and Finance." *Journal of Political Economy*. 106:6, pp. 1113–1155.

Levy-Yeyati, Eduardo and Federico Sturzenegger. 2003. "To Float or Fix: Evidence on the Impact of Exchange Rate Regimes on Growth." *American Economic Review*. Forthcoming.

McKinnon, Ronald and Huw Pill. 1999. "Exchange Rate Regimes for Emerging Markets: Moral Hazard and International Overborrowing." *Oxford Review of Economic Policy*. 15:3, pp. 19–38.

Mishkin, Frederic S. 1991. "Asymmetric Information and Financial Crises: A Historical Perspective," in *Financial Markets and Financial Crises*. R. Glenn Hubbard, ed. Chicago: University of Chicago Press, pp. 69–108.

Mishkin, Frederic S. 1996. "Understanding Financial Crises: A Developing Country Perspective." *Annual World Bank Conference on Development Economics*. pp. 29–62.

Mishkin, Frederic S. 1998. "The Dangers of Exchange Rate Pegging in Emerging-Market Countries." *International Finance*. 1:1, pp. 81–101.

Mishkin, Frederic S. 1999a. "Lessons from the Asian Crisis." *Journal of International Money and Finance*. 18:4, pp. 709–23.

Mishkin, Frederic S. 1999b. "International Experiences with Different Monetary Policy Regimes." *Journal of Monetary Economics*. 43:3, pp. 579–606.

Mishkin, Frederic S. 2000. "What Should Central Banks Do?" *Federal Reserve Bank of St. Louis Review*. 82:6, pp. 1–13.

Mishkin, Frederic S. 2001. "The International Lender of Last Resort: What are the Issues?" in *The World's New Financial Landscape: Challenges for Economic Policy*. Horst Siebert, ed. Berling: Springer-Verlag, pp. 291–312.

Mishkin, Frederic S. 2003. "Financial Policies and the Prevention of Financial Crises in Emerging Market Countries," in *Economic and Financial Crises in Emerging Market Countries*. Martin Feldstein, ed. Chicago: University of Chicago Press, pp. 93–130.

Mishkin, Frederic S. and Adam Posen. 1997. "Inflation Targeting: Lessons from Four Countries." *Economic Policy Review*. August, 3:3, pp. 9–110.

Mishkin, Frederic S. and Miguel Savastano. 2001. "Monetary Policy Strategies for Latin America." *Journal of Development Economics*. 66:2, pp. 415–44.

Mundell, Robert A. 1961. "A Theory of Optimum Currency Areas." *American Economic Review*. 51:3, pp. 657–65.

Mussa, Michael. 1986. "Nominal Exchange Rate Regimes and the Behavior of Real Exchange Rates: Evidence and Implications." *Carnegie-Rochester Conference Series on Public Policy*. 25, pp. 117–213.

Obstfeld, Maurice and Kenneth Rogoff. 1995. "The Mirage of Fixed Exchange Rates." *Journal of Economic Perspectives*. 9:4, pp. 73–96.

Poole, William. 1970. "Optimal Choice of Monetary Policy Instruments in a Simple Stochastic Macro Model." *Quarterly Journal of Economics*. 84:2, pp. 197–216.

Reinhart, Carmen M. and Kenneth S. Rogoff. 2002. "The Modern History of Exchange Rate Arrangements: A Reinterpretation." NBER Working Paper No. 8963, June.

Rose, Andrew K. 2000. "One Money, One Market: Estimating the Effect of Common Currencies on Trade." *Economic Policy*. April, 15, pp. 7–46.

Sargent, Thomas and Neil Wallace. 1981. "Some Unpleasant Monetarist Arithmetic." *Federal Reserve Bank of Minneapolis Quarterly Review*. Fall, 5:3, pp. 1–17.

Schuler, Kurt. 1999. "Encouraging Official Dollarization in Emerging Markets." Joint Economic Committee Staff Report. Washington, D.C.: United States Senate.

Shleifer, Andrei and Robert Vishny. 1999. *The Grabbing Hand: Government Pathologies and Their Cures*. Cambridge, Mass.: Harvard University Press.

Tommasi, Mariano. 2002. "Crisis, Political Institutions, and Policy Reform: It is not the Policy, it is the Polity, Stupid." Mimeo, University of San Andres; forthcoming in *Annual World Bank Conference on Development Economics*.

Tornell, Aaron and Andrés Velasco. 2000. "Fixed versus Flexible Exchange Rates: Which Provides More Fiscal Discipline?" *Journal of Monetary Economics*. 45:2, pp. 399–436.

Woodford, Michael. 1994. "Monetary Policy and Price Level Determinacy in a Cash-in-Advance Economy." *Economic Theory*. 4:3, pp. 345–80.

Woodford, Michael. 1995. "Price Level Determinacy without Control of a Monetary Aggregate." *Carnegie-Rochester Conference Series on Public Policy*. 43:3, pp. 1–46.

Part V   Parting Shots

18 Globalization Hazard and Delayed Reform in Emerging Markets

Guillermo A. Calvo

Capital inflows to emerging market economies rose to unprecedented heights in the first part of the 1990s and then collapsed very rapidly in the second. Such volatility could partly be explained by financial vulnerability in the emerging markets themselves, but the global nature of the phenomenon raises the suspicion that the world financial market is wrought with systemic problems that are largely independent of the individual countries affected. This chapter puts forward the conjecture that phenomena such as contagion could stem from the way the capital market operates (for example, crises generated by margin calls). These systemic phenomena require systemic instruments. Unfortunately, few are available. The International Monetary Fund (IMF) operates more like a fire department than like a central bank. Liquidity is sprayed where fire is found, not on the system as a whole in the manner of a central bank faced with a liquidity crisis.[1]

The combination of domestic financial vulnerability and the lack of a worldwide safety net gives rise to what I call globalization hazard, that is, risk generated by the sudden large expansion of credit to emerging market economies in the first half of the 1990s, probably as a result of imperfect information and underdeveloped financial institutions. Several recent financial crises were low-probability events that were uninsured and perhaps uninsurable in the private sector, and they called for ex post government intervention. Government intervention, however, represents a major roadblock in the presence of delayed reform, a condition in which the government delays the implementation of socially desirable reform and wealth redistribution. Delayed reform may thus exacerbate the impact of low-probability events and possibly help to coordinate expectations on "bad" equilibria, contributing to the severity of globalization hazard.

The policy implications of the globalization hazard view are diametrically opposed to those of the moral hazard view recently popularized by Meltzer.[2] This makes the present discussion greatly relevant for the design of a new financial architecture, an issue of enormous urgency and importance.

Moral Hazard versus Globalization Hazard

A salient characteristic of currency crises after the 1994 Mexican crisis (the so-called tequila crisis) is their frequent recurrence. The tequila crisis was followed by massive crises in Asia (1997), Russia (1998), Ecuador (2000), and Turkey (2001), as well as the protracted crisis in Argentina (2000–02). With the exception of Argentina, these crises have been relatively short-lived, especially compared to the debt crisis in the 1980s. However, they followed each other domino fashion. Why?

A leading explanation is moral hazard. According to this point of view, large and timely bailout packages, orchestrated by the IMF, allowed fixed-income investors to exit the market following the occurrence of each crisis without suffering major capital losses, even though the rate of return on these assets far exceeded those of safe assets like U.S. Treasury bills. The expectation that future crises would be resolved in the same manner emboldened fixed-income investors to take high risks in other emerging market economies, thereby increasing the probability of a crisis. Plausible as it sounds, however, this view has slim empirical support. In the first place, as shown in figure 18.1, net private capital flows to emerging markets started to subside after 1995, a trend that is even sharper for portfolio flows (see figure 18.2).[3] Second, after the tequila crisis the composition of capital flows shifted in favor of foreign direct investment (FDI) (see figure 18.3). Investors in those and related assets (stocks) suffered major losses during crises and thus cannot easily be claimed to have greatly benefited from bailout packages.

Questioning the moral hazard view is not tantamount to saying that policymakers and investors will not take advantage of generous giveaways, but the existence of distortion-driven behavior does not prove that distortions are seriously costly. The moral hazard view claims that bailouts by the Group of Seven (G-7) countries are a major cause of both the succession of crises and their high cost. To uphold this view, one has to be able to argue, among other things, that moral

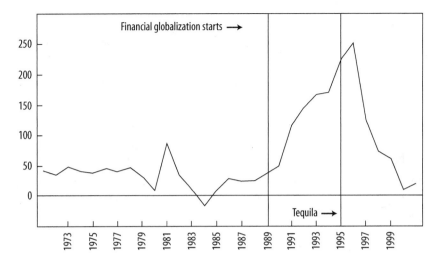

Figure 18.1
Net private capital flows to emerging markets, 1971–2001. Source: IMF (2001).

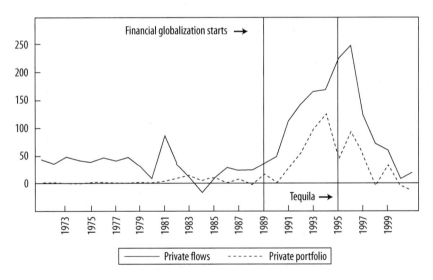

Figure 18.2
Net private portfolio and total capital flows to emerging markets, 1971–2001. Source: IMF (2001).

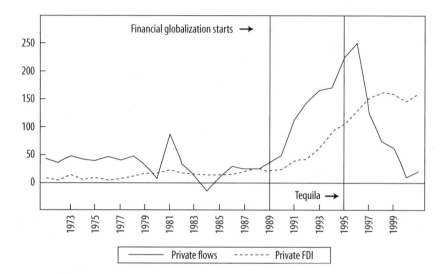

Figure 18.3
Private foreign direct investment and total capital flows to emerging markets, 1971–2001.
Source: IMF (2001).

hazard led to the large output and employment losses suffered during the crises. At equilibrium, this would imply either that emerging market policymakers deliberately brought their economies into a painful maelstrom (in exchange, perhaps, for a brief affluence mirage) or that they exhibited a fantastic lack of judgment, bordering on the insane. Since there is no scientific evidence that those characteristics are the monopoly of emerging market policymakers, however, and given that the empirical evidence reviewed above is not supportive, the moral hazard view must be classified, at least momentarily, as an intellectually appealing but unsubstantiated conjecture.

An alternative hypothesis is that the recent crises are the result of the surge in capital flows to emerging markets in the early 1990s, their subsequent decline, and their volatility. Neither 20-20 vision nor sophisticated econometrics is needed for one to realize from figure 1 that something truly extraordinary happened after 1989. In 1996, for example, net private capital flows to emerging market economies were about ten times as large as their average in the period 1970–89. This sharp climb took place in the span of a few years, and it was followed by an equally swift reversal. The result was major economic disruption.

Table 18.1
Sudden Stop of Capital Inflows

Country	Episode	Reversal of capital inflows (percent of GDP)
Argentina	1982–83	20
Ecuador	1995–96	19
Korea	1996–97	11
Mexico	1981–83	12
Thailand	1996–97	26
Turkey	1993–94	10

Source: Calvo and Relnhart (2000).

By definition, and abstracting from errors and omissions, the following accounting identity holds:

Capital inflows = Current account deficit

+ Accumulation of international reserves.

Sharp fluctuations in capital inflows thus result in equally sharp fluctuations in current account deficits and reserve accumulation. Both could give rise to serious difficulties, the former because it brings about sharp, possibly unanticipated changes in aggregate demand, and the latter because international reserves are still perceived as an indicator of financial health. A sizable fall in international reserves, for example, is commonly seen as a harbinger of serious financial trouble in the official sector. The mere fact that capital flows exhibit large fluctuations suggests that at least part of the problem may reside in the new features of the capital market after 1989.

One can get a better sense of the importance of capital flow fluctuations by examining capital flow reversals (that is, the drop in capital inflows) during crises. This is illustrated in table 18.1, which shows the reversals to have been sizable. Thailand, one of the Asian Tigers, holds the record in the table, with a reversal equivalent to 26 percent of gross domestic product (GDP). This is quite remarkable given the long period of growth enjoyed by its economy prior to the crisis. Moreover, these magnitudes are unheard of in advanced countries. Table 18.2 illustrates the difference between emerging markets and advanced countries around crisis periods, focusing on changes in the current account deficit.[4] In the table, T denotes the year the crisis takes place, $T - 1$ is the year before, and $T + 1$ the year after. "Change" corresponds

Table 18.2
Change in Current Account

Country group	$T-1$	T	$T+1$	Change
Emerging markets	−4.86	−3.97	−1.39	3.47
Advanced economies	−2.84	−3.06	−2.10	0.74
Difference	−2.02	−0.91	0.71	2.73*

Source: Calvo and Reinhart (2001).
*Statistically significant at the 5 percent level.

to the difference between the current account in $T+1$ and $T-1$. Two points are worth making. First, change in advanced countries is insignificant compared to that in emerging market economies. In emerging markets, the average current account adjustment corresponds to a sizable 3.5 percent of GDP, whereas the adjustment in advanced countries represents less than 1 percent. Second, during periods of crisis, that is, T, the current account deficit contracts in emerging markets, while it shows a slight increase in advanced countries. Thus the overall flow credit to emerging markets declines during crises, while that of advanced countries increases. This observation, incidentally, suggests that emerging market crises contain a credit contraction element that is, on the whole, absent in advanced countries.

Where was the public sector during the financial globalization episode that started in 1989? As shown in figure 18.4, all the action took place in the private sector. Official flows were essentially flat throughout the period 1971–2001.

This evidence leaves little doubt that the phenomenon in question is unprecedented in recent history, and it is associated with the globalization of finance. The private sector initiated a large increase in the flow of savings from advanced to emerging market economies, and the investments were protected by a flimsy official safety net. A plausible conjecture, then, is that financial globalization may bear the seeds of its own fragility, a phenomenon that I call globalization hazard. The sheer size and unprecedented nature of the flows could be the simple explanation. For example, temporary flows could have been mistaken for permanent flows. As a result, investment projects that were undertaken with the expectation that the relative prices prevailing during the boom would be permanent became unsustainable under the relative prices that prevailed as the capital flows subsided. The term globalization hazard is thus justified, as it suggests that this is a case of market

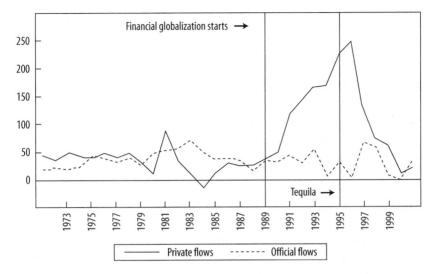

Figure 18.4
Net private foreign and public capital flows to emerging markets

failure, not moral failure—a case in which the market suffers from too little, instead of too much, protection and harnessing. As shown in the figure, the public sector did little to offset the collapse of private sector flows after 1996. This lack of response could indicate that what the world needs is a central bank of global dimensions coupled with more, not less, global financial cooperation.

Globalization Hazard: A Closer Look

Establishing the globalization hazard view as a serious alternative to the moral hazard view requires presenting non-moral-hazard arguments for the surge, decline, and volatility of capital flows to emerging market economies, including the so-called sudden stop phenomenon highlighted above (that is, the sharp drops in capital flows shown in table 18.1). In that respect, my conjecture is that the key factors accounting for globalization hazard are institutional and informational, both in the global capital market and in the emerging markets.

An example of an institutional factor at the global level is the development in the early 1990s of the market for Brady bonds, which increased investors' incentives to collect information on emerging market economies and led to the development of the bond markets of emerging market economies.[5] Examples of institutional factors at the local level of the emerging markets themselves include a weak local financial sector (such as weak banks initially controlled by the public sector) and liability dollarization (that is, the denomination of external debt in terms of foreign exchange).[6] The latter places severe bounds on exchange rate policy, and it is one possible explanation for what has been termed the fear of floating in emerging market economies, that is, a reluctance to let the exchange rate fluctuate as freely as in advanced countries.[7] When fear of floating is combined with an underdeveloped local financial system, it gives rise to an economy that is highly vulnerable to shocks. The existence of limited monetary policy instruments and rigid financial institutions (such as limited access to state-contingent financial contracts) could be deadly. In that context, downward price and wage flexibility may prove to be the only available adjustment mechanism short of bankruptcy and financial disruption. Price and wage flexibility could be harmful, however, if not supported by state-contingent financial contracts.

This point was highlighted long ago by Irving Fisher.[8] To illustrate the Fisher effect, take the case in which loans specify a constant stream of nominal interest payments. A sharp, unanticipated fall in prices and wages would result in an equally sharp increase in the ex post real interest rate, as well as a possibly large contraction in the capital of borrowing firms. A direct and obvious effect of downward price and wage flexibility would be a higher incidence of bankruptcies, which, under imperfect information, could give rise to negative spillover effects, such as through the interfirm credit network.[9] Another channel (not emphasized by Fisher) is that the resulting decapitalization of indebted firms, associated with an unanticipated ex post rise in real interest rates, lowers those firms' collateral and may trigger a strong credit reversal, such as a cut in indebted firms' credit lines.[10] If credit to firms goes partly to finance working capital, then a credit reversal could result in a sudden drainage of funds available to pay for labor services and raw material. The Fisher effect (which Fisher called debt deflation) will be especially strong for highly indebted economies. In the context of the recent crises, emerging market economies may have become much more vulnerable to negative shocks after the 1989–95 capital flows.

Why should emerging market economies be more vulnerable than advanced countries? This is a key question because all of the above considerations should, in principle, also be applicable to advanced economies. A plausible conjecture is that institutional changes around the start of the 1990s gave rise to a stock reallocation of loanable funds, which, by its nature, was bound to be transitory. Policymakers attributed the larger flows to good domestic policies, an opinion that was shared in report after report by the Washington establishment. Several emerging market economies were depicted as being on the road to joining the first world as a result of having heeded the Washington Consensus. Many individual investors may have been led to believe that the capital inflow episode had a large permanent component—larger than a more balanced analysis would have found.[11] Wall Street establishments, on the other hand, may have joined the bandwagon because they shared the opinion of the Washington Consensus—and perhaps also for moral hazard considerations: seeing the blind support that the emerging markets received from Washington, they may have softened their lending stance in the expectation that Washington would send timely rescue teams if trouble arose.[12]

From this perspective, the tequila episode becomes the tip of the iceberg. The market had made wrong investment decisions, and it was bound to go through a correction. Given the policy and market rigidities highlighted above, the adjustment was abrupt in Mexico and Argentina (a sudden stop), and it gave rise to suspicions that the market may have been operating under false expectations. At first, the problems were confined to Argentina and Mexico, and funds emigrated to other emerging market economies. However, the Asian crisis of 1997 started a sharp contraction for emerging markets as a whole (see figure 18.1).

Prima facie, the Russian crisis of 1998 appears to be the best case for the moral hazard argument. Russia was loaded with nuclear weapons, making it too dangerous to fall and perhaps leading investors to take higher risks in the expectation that the IMF would bail them out. However, the IMF funds to Russia were not sufficient to prevent default on domestic public debt, part of which was held directly or indirectly abroad. The default took Wall Street by surprise and reportedly caused a serious liquidity crunch, together with a consequent liquidation of emerging market securities. This, it could be argued, generated rational confusion in the market. Informed investors sold emerging market securities to uninformed investors, depressing their price below their fundamental levels. All emerging market economies were affected, which indicates that emerging market securities, as an asset class, were more risky than previously thought. The demand for emerging market securities shrunk as a result, putting further down-ward pressure on capital flows to those countries.[13] The shock can thus be seen as a sort of reverse-moral-hazard effect—in that the bail-out was smaller than expected—that was magnified by confusion and imperfect information in the capital market.

Even if it is true that investors' mood reversals are similar across all economies, they are likely to have a larger impact on emerging market economies than on advanced countries, owing to differences in infor-mation and institutions. In the case of the former, for example, finan-cial globalization could lead investors to invest in securities about which they have very limited information.[14] This may be especially true for emerging market securities, which, by their nature, do not have a long or reliable track record. These securities are highly suscep-tible to rumors: a negative rumor, for example, could drive investors to chuck them out of their portfolios almost entirely.[15]

Finally, a formal model of globalization hazard might be defined in terms of a multiple-equilibrium model stemming from financial rigidities.[16] Increased financial flexibility (that is, the existence of a wide array of state-contingent financial transactions) could help to eliminate bad equilibria, thereby avoiding a major collapse. Arguably, a salient feature of emerging markets is financial inflexibility. This kind of model thus helps to rationalize the view that emerging markets are more vulnerable to shocks than are financially mature markets, even in the absence of the perception errors referred to above.[17]

In short, my answer to the question of why emerging market econo-mies were more vulnerable centers on two factors: overly optimistic (though not necessarily irrational) expectations during the capital inflow period, kicked off by structural change in the global capital market, and relatively poor information about emerging market econo-mies, including political conditions. Informational and institutional problems also help explain the severity of the crises.

Why do crises recur? This question has implicitly been answered above. The crises themselves, including their systemic nature, in-creased the perception of risk on the part of investors. This resulted in a lower demand for emerging market securities and higher interest rate spreads, which increased the probability of crisis and thus its recent recurrence. One implication of this analysis is that crisis recur-rence may slow down once investors reach their new steady-state portfolio allocation.

If this were the whole story, then episodes like those of the 1990s would be unlikely to be repeated in the near future. One hopes that investors have learned their lesson and that their memories are not too short. However, some emerging market economies (particularly in Latin America) suffer from a serious case of what I call delayed reform, a condition in which government delays the implementation of socially desirable reform or wealth redistribution. This condition may give rise to future episodes of excessive borrowing and financial turmoil. I return to this topic later in the paper, after exploring the role of global policy in the next two sections.

Global Policies after Crisis

Emerging market financial crises have a negative impact on growth and income distribution. Consequently, there is a general consensus that something has to be done about them. This section discusses global policies, that is, policies that can primarily be implemented by advanced G-7 countries when a crisis hits one or several emerging markets. The welfare justification for these kinds of policies is taken up in the next section.

Global policies require multilateral institutions. The institutions exist, but unfortunately their size has shrunk relative to potential global capital flows (recall figure 18.4). Their effectiveness has thus become questionable. Recent bailout packages required the collaboration of several of these institutions, as well as bilateral aid and, as in the case of Ecuador, private sector involvement. The sums were large, but the procedures were clumsy and far from transparent or automatic. The world has reached for policies on an ad hoc basis; nothing predictable or systematic has been established. The popularity of the moral hazard view leads me to suspect that multilateral institutions will be slow to respond to crises in the future, and private sector involvement will rule the day. In what follows, I briefly comment on the role of private sector involvement and discuss the creation of an emerging market fund to prevent financial contagion.

Private Sector Involvement

The idea behind private sector involvement is straightforward, namely, to make the private sector (creditors, mostly) play an active role in solving financial difficulties. If left to its own devices, the private sector is unlikely to help solve solvency problems unless creditors are com-pelled to cooperate among themselves.[18] Otherwise, it will be hard to achieve a solution. It is always optimal for a creditor to claim 100 per-cent of what is owed to it after all the other creditors have negotiated a cut in debt obligations to prevent bankruptcy. This may be a serious problem in the present circumstances, given the large share of bonds in total emerging market debt.[19] Private sector involvement would still be effective for handling liquidity problems, however, because these could be solved by debt swaps that do not necessarily lower (and may actually increase) the present discounted value of debt (as in the case of Argentina's 2001 debt swap).

Private Sector Involvement plus Guarantees from International Financial Institutions

Loans from multilateral institutions are senior to other credit obliga-tions. A bond issued under that kind of guarantee, for example, is de facto senior to the other obligations. Suppose the debtor country declares a cessation of payments. This triggers the loan guarantee, automatically making the country a debtor of the corresponding multi-lateral institution for the full amount of the guarantee. This type of guarantee thus serves as a roundabout way of endowing debt instru-ments with seniority. Senior instruments could be very effective in coordinating creditors in case of insolvency. To illustrate, let the stock of debt obligations be 100 units (of output, say), while the maximum amount that the country can and is willing to repay is 50 units. If the country offers to swap the entire outstanding debt for a new senior bond paying 50 units, then each unit of the senior debt would be swapped for 2 units of the old debt, which in other words represents a discount of 50 percent over the old debt. In addition, the government announces that if less than 50 units of the new senior bond are issued in the swap (which would happen if some creditors did not want to participate in the swap), then the remainder will be offered in the open market. The government will thus issue 50 units of the new senior debt under all circumstances, be it as a result of the swap or through sales to new investors. Clearly, the market value of the new senior debt is 1 unit, because the government can repay 50 units with full certainty. Moreover, the market value of the old debt falls automatically to zero, since the debtor country would have no funds left over for repayment after servicing the new senior debt. Consequently, investors will have no incentive to keep the old debt, the swap will be successful, and solvency will be fully restored by means of market-friendly mechanisms.[20]

Emerging Market Fund

In each crisis episode, the crisis has spread to other emerging market economies. As noted above, a dominant explanation for this phenomenon is based on imperfect information. One way to attack this problem is to try to stabilize an emerging market index like the J. P. Morgan Emerging Markets Bond Index Plus (EMBI+). The idea is to stop contagion resulting from a financial crisis in an individual country by making a credible announcement that some global institution will stand ready to buy bonds from the other emerging markets in order to prevent a collapse in bond prices. This could be accomplished by setting up an emerging market fund (EMF) endowed with G-3 debt instruments (for example, G-3 Treasury bills). To illustrate, emerging market bonds listed in the J. P. Morgan EMBI+ (around U.S.$160 billion in 2001) are equivalent to about 3 percent of G-3 public debt (around U.S.$5 trillion in 2001).[21] If the EMF were to be endowed with 1 percent of G-3 public debt (around U.S.$50 billion), the fund's capital would represent around 30 percent of emerging market bonds (listed in the EMBI+). This significant backing of emerging market bonds involves a small risk for the G-3. The level of G-3 exposure is actually smaller than these numbers suggest because the EMF is intended only to forestall a total collapse in emerging market bond prices, not to prevent run-of-the-mill fluctuations. The EMF need only intervene in special circumstances, such as a price meltdown. It is not supposed to fight trends. For example, a meltdown could be defined as a situation in which the bond price index falls by more than x percent relative to a moving average. If prices do not recover from the initial x percent drop, the moving average will decline over time and the EMF will start selling emerging market bonds, reversing its portfolio back to G-3 bonds. If the initial price drop reflected a fundamental deterioration of emerging market fundamentals, then the EMF would eventually sell all its stock of emerging market bonds even though prices would have exhibited a substantial decline. On the other hand, if the EMF intervention is successful and prices recover, the EMF will quickly undo the initial intervention. In all cases, the EMF will converge to a situation in which its holdings of emerging market bonds would be negligible. If the large swings in emerging market bond prices are due to liquidity considerations, the EMF is likely to make a profit. The fund could incur a loss, however, by buying high and selling low. This occurs when the initial sell-off signals a permanent deterioration in emerging market fundamentals. The EMF would therefore have to decide on a case-by-case basis when it is appropriate to intervene.[22]

The EMF is a relative of the contingent credit line (CCL) recently created by the IMF. Both mechanisms pump liquidity into the market to prevent a liquidity crisis from triggering the deterioration of fundamentals and, possibly, insolvency. However, the CCL goes to the epicenter of the crisis, while the EMF aims at preventing contagion. Moreover, the EMF is less subject to the moral hazard criticism because it supports the asset class, rather than the bonds of an individual country. Finally, the EMF does not stigmatize emerging markets, whereas the CCL does. A key reason why the CCL has not yet gotten off the ground is that eligible countries feel that applying for such a facility would give a clear signal to the market that policymakers are worried about a possible sudden stop, for example.

Another close relative to the EMF is the Lerrick-Meltzer proposal that the IMF stand ready to buy all of a country's debt at a large discount.[23] Unlike the EMF, this proposal does not prevent liquidity-based contagion, and it is aimed at stopping a meltdown at the epicenter of the crisis.

A Rationale for Public Sector Involvement

The moral hazard view cautions against public sector involvement (recall the discussion above). Although empirical evidence does not support this view in the context of recent international financial crises, it would be hard to dismiss the argument that an indiscriminate and systematic bailout of loss-making investment projects will eventually induce undue risk taking by the private sector, thereby contributing to the recurrence of crisis episodes. However, this argument does not imply that every kind of bailout is bound to have negative consequences.

The issue discussed in this section is more general than the one at hand. It has to do with the advisability of public sector intervention ex post, that is, after the state of nature is revealed. In an ideal Arrow-Debreu setup with complete markets, there is no Pareto-improving ex post government intervention. This proposition is no longer true under incomplete markets, since government intervention could help to substitute for missing markets. For example, in an economy with two risk-averse farmers with uncorrelated outputs, it would be optimal for these farmers to write an ex ante insurance contract that redistributes output from the winner to the loser for each state of nature. This contract may not be feasible for a variety of reasons, in which case it would be optimal ex ante if the government could implement the corresponding transfers ex post. Winners will oppose the action ex post, so this type of transfer would have to be cloaked in a politically acceptable garment (such as a solidarity program). The optimal arrangement under these circumstances thus involves systematic bailouts, yet it need not give rise to moral hazard.

The relevance of this example could be criticized by noting that the same factors that prevent the emergence of markets or institutions for implementing the optimal insurance arrangement are also likely to impair the effectiveness of government intervention. For example, the state of nature may be hard to observe or verify.[24] The farmers might thus prefer to live in isolation and suffer the vagaries of the weather rather than writing a contract that would be very difficult to verify. The government would face the same difficulties, and thus the net benefits of government intervention are no longer apparent. This type of consideration has led many modern policymakers to take the command "Thou shalt not intervene" as their guiding principle.

Although I would not quarrel with this guiding principle for regular situations, the principle may break down for states of nature that have low probability ex ante. Since observability is not at stake, I assume for the sake of the argument that these low-probability events are perfectly observable. Consider, once again, the case of the two farmers. Suppose that under catastrophic circumstances they are able to obtain information about output free of cost, while otherwise information costs are prohibitive. I also assume that catastrophic circumstances are low-probability events. Let $k > 0$ denote the output cost of writing a clause in the insurance contract that specifies the transfer received by the victim in a low-probability event. Clearly, if k is high enough or, more interestingly, if the probability of the event is low enough, it may not be optimal to include that type of clause in the insurance contract between the two farmers. Suppose the government is subject to the same cost k if the transfer is executed ex post. Ex post government intervention clearly has a smaller ex ante cost, because it will be incurred only if conditions are catastrophic. To make this point even more obvious, notice that if the farmers write the clause into the insurance contract, the expected cost is k, whereas if the transfer is implemented by the government ex post, the expected cost would be pk, where p is the probability of the low-probability event: pk could be substantially smaller than k.[25]

A possible objection to the relevance of the example is that ex post transfers could be much more expensive than a mere clause in an insurance contract. The objection is well taken. Let the cost of ex post intervention be denoted by K and let us assume that K is significantly larger than k. First, the comparison of expected values is now between k and pK. Thus, if p is small enough, ex post intervention could still dominate the writing of an ex ante clause. Furthermore, in reality there are many low-probability events. Let the cost of each clause be the same and equal to k, and let N be the number of mutually exclusive low-probability events. If written as ex ante clauses, the social cost is Nk, whereas if the government makes the optimal ex post transfer, the cost is still pK, which reinforces the case for ex post intervention.[26]

I now return to the central thread of the discussion. Several recent crises could be claimed to be low-probability events, at least from the perspective of 1994. I would even be prepared to argue that the spread of the Russian 1998 crisis across emerging market economies was also a low-probability event from the standpoint of July 1998.[27] The attack on the Twin Towers and the resulting increase in aversion to air travel is undoubtedly another low-probability event.[28] Writing contracts contingent on these events would hardly be justified ex ante. The events, however, are quite clear, as are their consequences. This establishes a basis for the kinds of post-crisis intervention outlined in the previous section.

An open economy presents new and challenging issues. The two farmers in the story are now residents of different countries. Thus ex post transfers cannot be implemented by a single authority. Transfers become an international issue involving (at least) two sovereign nations. To complicate matters even further, authorities in country A, say, are elected by the residents of that country. Policymakers in the country that got lucky may be highly reluctant ex post to carry out the corresponding international transfers.

Thus far, the discussion has not touched on the debt issue. Consider the point-input-point-output Ricardian case in which labor is employed one period in advance, and the labor cost is financed by loans. It may be individually optimal in some cases not to make loan repayment contingent on certain low-probability events, even though both parties would benefit from writing a contingency clause to that effect if transaction costs were nil. Under certain circumstances, ex post government intervention can also generate ex ante Pareto improvement. Such intervention, for example, could take the form of debt forgiveness in catastrophic low-probability events. These transfers, as noted above, could be difficult to implement when international loans are involved. Negotiations are time-consuming. In the meantime, output losses occur as a result of bankruptcy procedures—a situation that is particularly damaging if key sectors like banking or airlines are involved, since their failure would be detrimental to many other sectors of the economy. There are thus circumstances in which it would be socially beneficial for the government to socialize private debts by, for instance, extending low-interest loans to the affected sectors, while financing the operation through new public debt obligations.[29] This policy implies a transfer from the domestic economy as a whole to the damaged sector, which is, in principle, inferior to a transfer from the creditor to the damaged sector. But the policy may be justified if externalities are large enough. Debt socialization may also help to implement Pareto-improving international transfers, because governments have direct access to international financial institutions and are in a better position than the private sector to obtain bilateral official aid or credit.

Delayed Reform

Transfers associated with low-probability events are common in a large country like the United States, where catastrophic shocks occur every year. Floods, hurricanes, and tornadoes are recurring events that trigger immediate federal transfers, and the government takes on the role of transferrer of last resort. To be able to perform this task effectively, the government should be capable of generating the necessary resources through higher taxes, donors' contributions, or lower expenditure on other items. In this context, I define delayed reform as a situation in which the government is unable or unwilling to articulate clear-cut policies to fund its transfer activities. Consequently, when faced with a low-probability event that calls for a transferrer of last resort, people are uncertain as to how the transfer operations will be funded or whether they will be funded at all.[30] Here I take delayed reform as an assumption and do not address the underlying political economy considerations.[31]

A typical case is a country that suffers a large low-probability deterioration of its terms of trade (for example, Nicaragua after the recent collapse of coffee prices caused by Vietnam's large crops). As a result, the equilibrium price of nontradables relative to tradables falls (that is, the equilibrium real exchange rate depreciates), and if interest rates are not indexed to nontradables prices, then massive bankruptcies are likely to follow (especially if the country has recently experienced a large capital inflow episode)—unless the government comes to the rescue as a transferrer of last resort.[32] The immediate fiscal effect of the terms-of-trade deterioration is lower fiscal revenue. Moreover, if the country is highly specialized, there will be few healthy sectors from which to collect rescue funds. This situation will likely drive the government to issue new debt without making it explicit how repayment will be engineered. Since default would be a real possibility, investors will charge a hefty country risk premium.

Who will eventually foot the bill? Precisely because that question remains unanswered, everyone will run for cover the moment they realize that a low-probability event of major dimensions has taken place. Investors postpone decisions as they wait for the dust to settle, which further reduces growth rates and weakens the fiscal stance. The deleterious impact of delayed reform thus becomes stronger by the day once the economy is hit by a large low-probability event that calls for government intervention. The private sector is seriously tarnished, too. Fiscal uncertainty increases the uncertainty of the net (after tax) return on private sector projects. Moreover, running for cover in an open economy implies, among other things, capital flight and a run on the domestic banking system, which creates the need for even bigger government transfers. What will governments do under such circumstances? The likely approach is Plan B, as Krugman recently called it in connection with the crisis in Malaysia: namely, controls on capital outflows.[33] Plan B is typically carried out through foreign currency controls. Floating exchange rates are no solution under these circumstances because what is involved is a debt problem, and emerging market debt is typically either of very short maturity or indexed to a foreign currency.[34]

The successful IMF program in connection with the tequila crisis proves that rapid action on the part of multilaterals can be highly effective. True, Mexico's economy suffered a contraction in output exceeding 6 percent in 1995, but recovery was fast, strong, and lasting.[35] The medicine? A U.S.$50 billion package that helped to refinance short-term debts at below-market rates.[36] From this perspective, there is nothing wrong with large bailout packages in the context of low-probability events.[37] If the packages are clearly predicated on the existence of verifiable low-probability events, then they will trigger no moral hazard problems.

What is the role of tight fiscal policy during crises? As argued above, low-probability accidents that unduly increase the burden of external debt should trigger fiscal laxity. The problem under delayed reform is that fiscal laxity increases fiscal uncertainty, with nefarious consequences. Tighter fiscal policy is not likely to solve the problem either, however, unless it helps to reverse the initial negative shock. This is not likely to happen if the event is a trade account shock, such as a deterioration of the terms of trade. Fiscal tightening could help if the low-probability event involves a credibility shock provoked by, for instance, a crisis in another emerging market, even though the economies are not linked by fundamental factors (such as trade and financial flows). In that context, tighter fiscal discipline could send a strong signal that the country in question is different, which could serve to keep interest rates from skyrocketing. In practice, it is very hard to know what is the appropriate action. Large G-7 support for countries suffering from delayed reform may therefore be crucial. Under that umbrella, the IMF doctor can operate with confidence, knowing that a large supply of blood and oxygen is available for offsetting policy errors (some of them his own, no doubt) without killing the patient.[38]

Governments suffering from delayed reform could themselves take measures that help to prevent low-probability events, in particular events involving other sovereign countries. One strategy is to ensure that debt service obligations are not bunched. This helps to eliminate self-fulfilling expectations equilibria of the type discussed by Calvo and by Cole and Kehoe.[39] Another approach is to impose controls on capital inflows, especially during capital inflow episodes. This policy, which has been implemented in Chile and Colombia, for example, can help prevent maturity bunching by lengthening debt maturity.[40]

Exchange Rate Policy: Delayed Reform in a Global Environment

The financial globalization episode that started in 1989 may be coming to an end, and the end may be unpleasant as the stock of emerging market fixed income assets held in advanced countries' portfolios starts to unravel. This is far from inevitable, however. International cooperation may get a strong boost from the new security concerns, and the emerging market economies may again become an attractive destination for FDI and other types of capital flows. What have emerging market economies learned about macroeconomic policy that will help them cope with a future wave of capital inflows and prevent, or at least ameliorate, future crises? I started to discuss this issue at the end of the previous section. I now focus on the exchange rate.

As one examines the monumental problems that arise in connection with deep financial crisis, the exchange rate looks like a minor distraction. And it actually is, during a crisis. The exchange rate could play a key destabilizing role, however, under the delayed reform syndrome. Changes in the exchange rate have a direct effect on relative prices. This can, for example, be due to signaling considerations, coupled with wage and price stickiness. Governments are constantly under suspicion of creating new sources of fiscal uncertainty. A devaluation could be read as a signal that the government is relying more heavily on the inflation tax, fueling devaluation and inflation expectations. Expected higher future devaluation could have an impact on today's relative prices, possibly causing financial difficulties (more on this below).[41] If large swings in the exchange rate are common, then individuals will incorporate them in their contracts, and the associated transfers might be handled by the market. However, complete markets could be suboptimal when the government's credibility is at stake.[42] The simple intuition is that credibility problems involve intertemporal distortions, which are magnified by market completeness. On the other hand, if large exchange rate fluctuations are not common and become low-probability events, then they would prompt government intervention and—under the delayed reform assumption—cause fiscal uncertainty. This is just one of several reasons why emerging market economies show a marked preference for stable exchange rates, or fear of floating.[43]

Recently, some emerging market economies appear to have relaxed their foreign currency anchor by instead adopting an inflation targeting regime. It is still too soon to know whether the new anchor will prove effective. Brazil, a recent convert, already seems to be reeling back to the old dollar anchor. In any case, a strict inflation targeting regime is not that different from exchange rate targeting. The two regimes would be identical if the exchange rate was the only item in the basket on which the inflation index is based. Moreover, both regimes are orthogonal to pure floating, in which the monetary authority sets the money supply and there is no feedback from the exchange rate to the money supply.

It is, therefore, quite misleading to say that the post-tequila world bifurcates into pure floating and pure fixed foreign exchange regimes. While Hong Kong pursues a currency board regime pegged to the U.S. dollar and Bulgaria to the Euro, I could not point to any emerging market economy that has adopted pure floating. In practice, the choice is not fixed versus floating, but rather which basket to use in targeting one's currency.

Highly dollarized economies like Argentina and Uruguay peg to the U.S. dollar.[44] Bolivia and Peru, which are also highly dollarized, have mostly followed a system that would be difficult to differentiate from pegging.[45] On the other hand, inflation targeting was first adopted in Latin America by Chile, followed by Brazil and Colombia; dollarization is not an issue in these economies. Exchange rate pegging thus appears to be the favorite of dollarized economies. Chile features a highly indexed economy: all financial transactions are expressed in UFs (Unidades de Fomento), which is a price index involving tradable and nontradable goods. Inflation targeting appears to complement the type of indexation prevailing in the Chilean financial system. More generally, the optimal basket might be linked to the type of indexation prevailing in the corresponding financial system.

The theory of the optimal exchange rate system ranks systems according to a loss function, which in many papers is given by output variance.[46] According to this welfare criterion, fixed exchange rates come out ahead when money supply and money demand shocks are dominant, while floating exchange rates are preferable when the dominant shocks are real, that is, originating in output demand and supply considerations. Standard theory ignores balance sheet shocks, like those discussed earlier. If those shocks are taken into account in an economy with a highly dollarized financial system, for example, the case for fixed rates becomes stronger. On the other hand, if dollarization is not an issue and, say, the financial system is indexed à la Chile, then balance sheets are much more insulated from fluctuations in the nominal exchange rate. To the extent that not all prices and wages are fully indexed, abrupt changes in the inflation rate would cause balance-sheet trouble in the excluded sectors, and inflation targeting becomes an attractive system.

Balance-sheet shocks are important under delayed reform because they trigger uncertainty-generating government intervention. As noted, a highly dollarized financial system increases the appeal of fixed exchange rates. But dollarization is not the only relevant consideration. For example, all countries are linked to the rest of the world through trade. Abrupt changes in the exchange rate may bring about other, more subtle balance-sheet problems stemming from the impact that fluctuations in the nominal exchange rate have on earnings. This is most apparent for firms that produce nontradables by means of imported raw materials. If the associated fluctuations in the real exchange rate have some degree of persistence, shocks to the nominal exchange rate will also have balance-sheet effects. Moreover, as noted above, credibility problems could also provoke changes in the real exchange rate, which could be quite sharp under flexible exchange rates.[47] Consequently, balance-sheet considerations may strongly bias governments subject to delayed reform toward fixed exchange rates.

General Policy Considerations

Previous sections demonstrated the limited scope of policy in economies that are afflicted by delayed reform, as well as the desirability of lowering the number and potential intensity of balance-sheet shocks. This is especially pertinent given the present lack of systemic instruments for dealing with global crises. Emerging market economies are visited by highly disruptive phenomena like sudden stops, which can wreak havoc on an otherwise well-run economy.

A safe strategy seems to be the adoption of policies that help offset the effects of delayed reform, such as trade agreements with large developed economies, which then have an incentive to assist the emerging market country in developing advanced institutions. Another example is full dollarization.[48] If the crisis has already hit, however, debt restructuring may be necessary. This represents a serious complication for governments subject to delayed reform. Exclusively relying on domestic solutions is likely to be costly, leading to situations in which social objectives are held back, while husky lobbyists take control. Multilateral institutions could play a useful role by helping to de-politicize the decisionmaking process. No new institutions are necessary for that purpose, but more funding and innovative financial products (such as guarantees) may be appropriate. One can only hope that prejudice and sheer intellectual inertia will not undermine the creativity necessary for dealing with these important issues.

A final note. Empirical knowledge in macroeconomics derives mostly from the experience of developed economies. However, the little that is known about emerging market economies suggests that they are financially more fragile and more vulnerable than their developed counterparts. Their relatively short track record, small size, and political instability seem to militate against the existence of institutions and informational bases comparable to those found in developed economies. Policies that work for developed economies may not transport well into emerging market territory. This is an important insight. Unfortunately, the scant available empirical work leaves the field open to wildly different interpretations that appear equally valid on the surface. This could provoke the policymakers' paralysis I warned about above. There is thus an urgent need for serious, convincing empirical work in this field.

Notes

This version of the paper has greatly benefited from incisive and exhaustive comments by Allan Meltzer, Enrique Mendoza, and Andrés Velasco. I would also like to acknowledge useful comments by Ricardo Caballero, Sara Calvo, Ricardo Hausmann, Alejandro Izquierdo, Luis Fernando Mejía, and Guillermo Mondino. To all of them, my heartfelt thanks, as well as my apologies for not having heeded all their good advice.

1. The IMF's contingent credit line (CCL) is, in fact, an attempt to prevent fires—not quite a central bank, but at least a fire department that is trying to increase the available water supply in case of fire.

2. Meltzer (2000).

3. Some supporters of the moral hazard view claim that the decline of capital flows to emerging market countries is the result of Russia not getting a bailout package in 1998, which supposedly made investment in emerging market securities less attractive. However, flows started to decline prior to that (in 1997; see figure 18.1), and Brazil got a large bailout package soon after the Russian crises, followed by equally large packages for Argentina and Turkey in 2001.

4. For further details, see Calvo and Reinhart (2001).

5. Calvo (2001).

6. See Calvo (2001); Hausmann, Stein, and Panizza (2001).

7. See Calvo and Reinhart (2002). Liability dollarization could reflect institutional factors in both global and domestic capital markets; see Caballero and Krishnamurthy (2001b) and Jeanne (2001).

8. Fisher (1933). See also Keynes ([1931] 1963), who appears to have anticipated Fisher's ideas on this subject.

9. See Calvo (2000a).

10. This effect is studied in Kiyotaki and Moore (1997); Izquierdo (2000); Caballero and Krishnamurthy (2001b); Céspedes, Chang, and Velasco (2001).

11. See Calvo, Leiderman, and Reinhart (1993).

12. I would not place a lot of weight on this conjecture. First, the world was extricating itself from the 1980s debt problem, for which Washington had taken a good number of years to find an effective cure. Second, debt difficulties were significantly more complicated to negotiate in the 1990s than in the 1980s, given that there was a myriad of lenders (such as bond holders), as opposed to a handful of large banks holding the bulk of the loans extended to the countries in trouble.

13. For further discussion, see Calvo (2001) and Guillermo Calvo, "Understanding the Russian Virus, with Special Reference to Latin America," (www.bsos.umd.edu/econ/ciecalvo.htm [October 1998]).

14. This discussion takes its lead from Calvo (1998b) and Calvo and Mendoza (2000a, 2000b).

15. See Calvo (1998a) for a simple example in which a sudden stop caused by rumors could bring about an output loss.

16. See, for example, Calvo (1998b).

17. The existence of equilibrium multiplicity is not a necessary condition for generating a severe crisis, whereas financial frictions appear to be essential. For a recent rational expectations dynamic model of this sort, see Mendoza and Smith (2001).

18. See, for example, Krugman (1992).

19. This constraint could be relaxed if a critical number of bondholders were able to modify some key clauses in the bond contract, as in the recent debt restructuring in Ecuador.

20. A market-friendly mechanism does not break explicit contracts, although implicit contracts might be trounced. This is likely to be the case in debt restructuring during a crisis, as when some clauses in the bond contract are modified following strictly legal procedures. However, breaching implicit contracts could seriously impair the resumption of credit flows.

21. See J. P. Morgan, "Government Bond Index Monitor," (www2.jpmorgan.com/MarketDataInd/GovernBondIndex/Publications/bim.html [31 July 2001]).

22. Technical details are yet to be worked out. It is clear, however, that countries protected by the EMF should submit to new rules in order to prevent moral hazard, among other things.

23. Lerrick and Meltzer (2001).

24. Under asymmetric information, this situation gives rise to the classical moral hazard problem discussed in the insurance literature (see Kreps, 1990).

25. I conduct the discussion in terms of expected values, although a rigorous approach would be based on utility functions. However, the substantive implications in the text carry over to the more general case of risk aversion.

26. The cost of writing clauses encompassing low-probability events need not be proportional to N. In the example of the farmers, one clause could specify the transfers in terms of output corresponding to each low-probability event, which could arguably be less costly than writing separate clauses.

27. See Guillermo Calvo, "Understanding the Russian Virus, with Special Reference to Latin America," (www.bsos.umd.edu/econ/ciecalvo.htm [October 1998]) and "Contagion in Emerging Market: When Wall Street Is the Carrier," (www.bsos.umd.edu/econ/ciecalvo.htm [February 1999]).

28. For example, tourist cancellations in Jamaica right after the attack exceeded 80 percent!

29. Diaz-Alejandro (1985) discusses socialization of private debts in Chile during the 1982–83 crisis.

30. I do not imply that delayed reform afflicts only emerging market economies. As pointed out to me by Allan Meltzer, recent U.S. economic history exhibits clear episodes reflecting that characteristic. Delayed reform may be devastating, however, if the body politic is hit by sufficiently large undiversifiable shocks, as the previous discussion suggests may have been the case in the recent emerging market crises.

31. For further discussion on the political economy of delayed reform, see, for example, Sturzenegger and Tommasi (1998, part 1).

32. Irving Fisher (1933) identifies bankruptcies following a sharp change in relative prices as a key factor in explaining the depth of the Great Deflation. He focuses on the case in which loans specify a fixed nominal interest rate, and the nominal price level suffers a sharp unexpected drop. However, this kind of financial shock would hold whenever a debtor is faced with a sharp, unexpected deterioration of a product price, on which the loan's interest rate is not being indexed. I pick up this topic in connection with the dollarization debate in Calvo (2001).

33. *Fortune*, "Saving Asia: It's Time to Get Radical," 9 August 1998.

34. See Hausmann, Stein, and Panizza (2001).

35. Part of that fast recovery could be due to the North American Free Trade Agreement (NAFTA).

36. The package was never fully used, and it was wholly repaid before schedule. Moreover, the United States, a key donor, made a substantial profit from its U.S.$25 billion loan—no doubt benefiting many U.S. "carpenters and plumbers."

37. Was the tequila crisis a low-probability event? Evidence is strongly in favor. Mexico was the poster child of multilateral institutions in 1994, and the risk premium on Mexico's debt was very low just weeks before the crisis. Moreover, although some analysts warned about current account sustainability problems well before the crisis, few, if any, imagined that it would spread so wildly across emerging market economies.

38. An important caveat: systemic external aid could contribute to the persistence of the delayed reform syndrome. Assessing this possibility, however, requires models that flesh out the political economy of delayed reform (see Sturzenegger and Tommasi, 1998).

39. Calvo (1998b); Cole and Kehoe (1996). The Greenspan-Guidotti proposal runs along these lines (see Guidotti, 2000).

40. See Calvo and Reinhart (2000).

41. See Calvo (1983).

42. Calvo (2000b).

43. Liability dollarization is another possible cause. The fear of floating literature is in its infancy, but early efforts in this area of research include Hausmann, Stein, and Panizza (2001); Calvo and Reinhart (2000, 2002); Lahiri and Végh (2001); Caballero and Krishnamurthy (2001a).

44. A country is highly dollarized if it shows a high incidence of foreign-exchange-denominated deposits and bank loans. As argued by Hausmann, Stein, and Panizza (2001), most emerging market economies exhibit dollarized external debt.

45. See Calvo and Reinhart (2002) and Morón, Goñi, and Ormeño (1999). Peru let its currency devalue quite sharply starting in the second half of 1998. At the same time, however, the share of nonperforming loans doubled, a phenomenon that appears to have made policymakers more cautious about using this instrument. One leading conjecture is that borrowers take dollar-denominated loans to finance projects in the nontradables sector. A large devaluation could thus contribute to the spread of bankruptcy in that sector.

46. For recent discussions focusing on emerging market economies, see Calvo (2001) and Hausmann, Stein, and Panizza (2001).

47. Recall the literature on exchange rate overshooting, including Dornbusch (1976) and Calvo and Rodriguez (1977).

48. See Calvo (2001) for further discussion.

References

Caballero, Ricardo J., and Arvind Krishnamurthy. 2001a. "A Vertical Analysis of Crises and Central Bank Interventions." Massachusetts Institute of Technology.

———. 2001b. "International and Domestic Collateral Constraints in a Model of Emerging Market Crisis." *Journal of Monetary Economics* (48)3: 513–48.

Calvo, Guillermo A. 1983. "Temporary Stabilization: Predetermined Exchange Rates." *Journal of Political Economy* 94 (December): 1319–29.

———. 1998a. "Capital Flows and Capital-Market Crises: The Simple Economics of Sudden Stops." *Journal of Applied Economics* (CEMA) 1(1): 35–54.

———. 1998b. "Varieties of Capital-Market Crises." In *The Debt Burden and Its Consequences for Monetary Policy*, edited by Guillermo Calvo and Mervyn King, 181–202. Macmillan.

———. 2000a. "Balance-of-Payments Crises in Emerging Markets: Large Capital Inflows and Sovereign Governments." In *Currency Crises*, edited by Paul R. Krugman, 71–104. University of Chicago Press for National Bureau of Economic Research.

———. 2000b. "Betting against the State: Socially Costly Financial Engineering." *Journal of International Economics* 51 (June): 5–20.

————. 2001. "Capital Markets and the Exchange Rate, with Special Reference to the Dollarization Debate in Latin America." *Journal of Money, Credit and Banking* 33 (May, part 2): 312–34.

Calvo, Guillermo A., Leonardo Leiderman, and Carmen M. Reinhart. 1993. "Capital Inflows and Real Exchange Appreciation in Latin America: The Role of External Factors." *IMF Staff Papers* 40(1): 108–51.

Calvo, Guillermo A., and Enrique G. Mendoza. 2000a. "Capital Market Crises and Economic Collapse in Emerging Markets: An Informational-Frictions Approach." *American Economic Review* (May, *Papers and Proceedings, 1999*): 59–64.

————. 2000b. "Rational Contagion and the Globalization of Securities Markets." *Journal of International Economics* 51(1): 79–113.

Calvo, Guillermo A., and Carmen M. Reinhart. 2000. "When Capital Flows Come to a Sudden Stop: Consequences and Policy." In *Reforming the International Monetary and Financial System*, edited by Peter B. Kenen and Alexander K. Swoboda. Washington: International Monetary Fund.

————. 2001. "Fixing for Your Life." In *Brookings Trade Forum*, edited by Susan M. Collins and Dani Rodrik, 1–58. Brookings.

————. 2002. "Fear of Floating." *Quarterly Journal of Economics* 117(2): 379–408.

Calvo, Guillermo A., and Carlos A. Rodriguez. 1977. "A Model of Exchange Rate Determination under Currency Substitution and Rational Expectations." *Journal of Political Economy* 85 (April): 617–25.

Céspedes, Luis F., Roberto Chang, and Andrés Velasco. 2001. "Dollarization of Liabilities, Net Worth Effect, and Optimal Monetary Policy." Paper prepared for the Sixth Annual Meeting of the Latin American and Caribbean Economic Association (LACEA). Montevideo, Uruguay, 18–20 October.

Cole, Harold L., and Timothy J. Kehoe. 1996. "A Self-Fulfilling Model of Mexico's 1994–1995 Debt Crisis." *Journal of International Economics* 41(3–4): 309–30.

Diaz-Alejandro, Carlos F. 1985. "Good-bye Financial Repression, Hello Financial Crash." *Journal of Development Economics* 19(1). Reprinted in *Trade, Development and the World Economy*, edited by Andrés Velasco, chap. 17. Basil Blackwell.

Dornbusch, Rudiger. 1976. "Expectations and the Exchange Rate Dynamics." *Journal of Political Economy* 84 (December): 1161–76.

Fisher, Irving. 1933. "The Debt-Deflation Theory of Great Depressions." *Econometrica* 1(4): 337–57.

Guidotti, Pablo E. 2000. "Toward a Liquidity Risk Management Strategy for Emerging Market Economies." Universidad Torcuato Di Tella.

Hausmann, Ricardo, Ernesto Stein, and Ugo Panizza. 2001. "Why Do Countries Float the Way They Float?" *Journal of Economic Development* 66(2): 387–414.

IMF (International Monetary Fund). 2001. *The World Economic Outlook (WEO) Database, December 2001*. Washington.

Izquierdo, Alejandro. 2000. "Credit Constraints and the Asymmetric Behavior of Asset Prices and Output under External Shocks." Washington: Inter-American Development Bank.

Jeanne, Olivier. 2001. "Why Do Emerging Economies Borrow in Foreign Currency?" Paper prepared for the Sixth Annual Meeting of the Latin American and Caribbean Economic Association (LACEA). Montevideo, Uruguay, 18–20 October.

Keynes, John Maynard. [1931] 1963. "The Consequences to the Banks of the Collapse of Money Values." Reprinted in *Essays in Persuasion*. W. W. Norton & Company.

Kiyotaki, Nobuhiro, and John Moore. 1997. "Credit Cycles." *Journal of Political Economy* 105(2): 211–48.

Kreps, David. 1990. *A Course in Microeconomic Theory*. Princeton University Press.

Krugman, Paul R. 1992. *Currencies and Crises*. MIT Press.

Lahiri, Amartya, and Carlos A. Végh. 2001. "Living with the Fear of Floating." Paper prepared for the Sixth Annual Meeting of the Latin American and Caribbean Economic Association (LACEA). Montevideo, Uruguay, 18–20 October.

Lerrick, Adam, and Allan H. Meltzer. 2001. "Blueprint for an International Lender of Last Resort." Carnegie Mellon University.

Meltzer, Allan H. 2000. "Report of the International Financial Institution Advisory Commission." U.S. Senate Committee on Banking, Housing, and Urban Affairs.

Mendoza, Enrique, and Katherine Smith. 2001. "Margin Calls, Trading Costs, and Asset Prices in Emerging Markets: The Financial Mechanics of the 'Sudden Stops.'" Duke University.

Morón, Eduardo, Edwin Goñi, and Arturo Ormeño. 1999. "Central Bankers' Fear of Floating: The Peruvian Evidence." Lima: Universidad del Pacífico.

Sturzenegger, Federico, and Mariano Tommasi. 1998. *The Political Economy of Reform*. MIT Press.

19

Sudden Stop,
Contractionary
Devaluation, and Time
Inconsistency

Guillermo A. Calvo

After a decade of looking at financial crises in EMs, intensive discussions with policymakers here and there, and some research, I feel that much of what I have learned I would have known beforehand, if only I had thought more deeply on received theory. This makes me think that macroeconomics is much like a large collection of lenses in the optometrist's office. The art is to combine just a few of them to improve the patient's vision. The optometrist need not invent new lenses. They are all lying on the table; the trick is to find the right ones. The right ones, in turn, depend on what the glasses are intended for. The right macro model equally depends on what one wants to focus on.[1]

In this chapter I present a set of lenses that I find particularly useful in order to focus on three central topics. Topic 1 is the distinction between debt sustainability and sudden stop, which leads to switch the focus from the *level* of the current account to its *potential change*—although I will argue that the level of the current account could still be a sufficient statistic for the *intensity* of sudden stop.

Topic 2 is a clear example of how a change of lenses can give a very different perspective on a classical issue. I will be referring to currency devaluation, but in a context in which the initial shock comes from the credit market, specifically a sudden stop. As a result, currency devaluation will be accompanied by output contraction, a puzzling combination when seen from the standard perspective—relevant for Advanced economies—in which currency devaluation is not associated with a disruption in credit markets (see Krugman and Taylor [1978]).

Finally, Topic 3 is on the tradeoff between flexibility of intertemporal (e.g., credit) contracts and time inconsistency. This is a fundamental issue for EMs that operate in a highly volatile environment, and has received inadequate attention in the literature.[2] Examples will confirm the intuitive conjecture that flexibility is more valuable the larger is volatility. Given the institutional rigidities imposed in standard bank credit and bond market contracts, flexibility may on occasion be obtained through the "back door," for example, through debt default and banking crises, and facilitated by weak creditor-protection schemes. Thus, for example, the empirical association between volatility and weak creditor-protection may run from the former to the latter. In other words, high volatility may call for weak creditor protection.

High Current Account Deficit: Level or Potential Change?

The current account deficit, CAD, is a central piece of information for debt sustainability analysis (recall the introduction). As a result, its *level* prominently figures in policy debates. However, recent EM crises show that their devastating effects can be tracked to a sudden *contraction* in the CAD (sometimes called current account *reversals*; see Edwards (2004)). The contraction in the CAD is associated with sudden stops, while its deleterious effects can be attributed to: (1) downward price/wage inflexibility and (2) sizable (real) currency depreciation.

Reason (1) is straightforward and can be formalized in terms of standard Keynesian models. Moreover, its recessionary effects could, in principle, be offset by floating the exchange rate and expanding the money supply. Currency devaluation will ensue, restoring relative-price equilibrium without requiring a drop in nominal prices or wages. This is, incidentally, an example of the benefits of flexible exchange rates emphasized in a highly influential paper by Friedman (1953). Put differently, the argument is that if the economy is faced with nominal price/wage inflexibilities, the exchange rate provides an escape valve by which relative-price disequilibrium can be attenuated. Notice, incidentally, that the argument does not take into account the possibility that devaluation may bring about further adjustment in the current account—as may be the case if devaluation lowers the credibility of policymakers (recall discussion of the Tequila crisis in the introduction)—and causes further disruption.

However, a sudden stop calling for sizable real currency depreciation could be disruptive even though prices are perfectly flexible or monetary supply could be adjusted to substitute for downward price inflexibility. This is effect (2) listed above. As noted, an increase in the current account surplus (unaccompanied by an equivalent increase in income) requires a drop in aggregate demand; thus, given the real exchange rate, the demand for tradables and nontradables will likely contract. The consequent increase in the excess supply of tradables causes no serious disruption because international markets will absorb it. The situation is entirely different for nontradables. Their excess supply has no outlet outside the domestic market. Real currency devaluation is normally required. Under price flexibility, relative prices could quickly accommodate the shock. However, an aspect that has been left out of macro textbooks is that the change in relative prices may cause *financial* difficulties.[3] For example, if the debt of firms producing nontradables is denominated in terms of tradables (*liability dollarization*), real currency depreciation may seriously impair their ability/willingness to repay debt.

The relative-price effect is associated, among other things, with the *change* in the *CAD*, not its *level* as emphasized by debt sustainability analysis. I will now argue, however, that the level of the *CAD* may be informative about a potential disruptive change.

By definition (and ignoring errors and omissions), the current account deficit, *CAD*, equals *increase in net international indebtedness*. Consider now an economy subject to sudden stops (of capital inflows). Under those circumstances, no fresh capital may be available (or its price may be prohibitive), driving *CAD* to zero (after international reserves are exhausted). In fact, the *CAD* could be driven to negative territory if debt obligations come due and have to be fully amortized. However, there is an asymmetry here. *CAD* can be driven to zero by foreign investors refusing to extend new credit. But, to make *CAD* negative, that is, generate a current account surplus, the country must be willing to repay.[4] As shown in the recent case of Argentina, there is little that foreign creditors can do to force repayment of public sector debt. Actually, this difficulty could also apply to the private sector if, for example, the government imposes foreign exchange restrictions, such as controls on capital outflows. Therefore, a plausible indicator of a potential *effective* credit crunch would be *CAD*. In other words, the level of the current account deficit is an indicator of its potential change, in which case it should be a cause of concern for post-Keynesians and post-Fisherians alike. Calvo, Izquierdo, and Mejía (2004) confirms this conjecture by showing that the *CAD* and a measure of domestic liability dollarization appear to determine the probability of sudden stops.

Sudden Stop First, Devaluation Later

The typical experiment in the theory of currency devaluation is a once-and-for-all rise in the exchange rate in isolation from other shocks. The theory has been extended to examine other experiments—like a once-and-for-all increase in the rate of devaluation, as in Calvo (1981)—but the common feature of these experiments is that the credit market remains invariant. Thus, the theory has been developed under the assumption of perfect capital mobility as well as no international capital mobility, but the feedback from devaluation to capital mobility and vice versa has been largely ignored.

The standard approach to the theory of currency devaluation makes perfect analytical sense. What makes much less sense, however, is to expect that the insights from the standard theoretical experiment can be directly applied to actual devaluation episodes, since it is not easy to find examples in which policymakers devalue the currency on a whim. Usually, devaluation follows a period of stress in which some key variables are misaligned (e.g., the real exchange rate), or devaluation follows a sudden stop (of capital inflows). Thus, in most cases, currency devaluation is a result of other shocks or misalignments.

The standard approach leads to the conclusion that, as a general rule, devaluation is expansionary, contradicting a large body of empirical research on EMs (see Edwards [1991]), and flying in the face of recent EM crises in which large devaluations were accompanied by deep recession. This suggests that one has to look elsewhere for the initial shock—for example, the ubiquitous sudden stop. Once the central bank stops selling international reserves in response to a sudden stop, currencies typically devalue. Thus, empirically there seems to be little doubt that most likely the sequence is from sudden stop to devaluation.[5] Building a theory that yields these results also seems straightforward, because, given international reserves, a sudden stop implies contraction in aggregate demand, which, under a cash-in-advance assumption, for example, would result in a fall in the demand for domestic money, and currency devaluation. It is also plausible to conjecture that sudden stop should result in output contraction, but that is a little less straightforward. The reason is that, under sticky prices, currency devaluation makes nontradable goods less expensive, stimulating their demand. Thus, the exchange rate may help undo the damage caused by sudden stop.

In what follows I will sketch out a sticky-price model to cast some light on these issues.

A Model of Sudden Stop and Contractionary Devaluation

Consider a representative-individual economy where the instantaneous time-separable utility index is a function of consumption of tradables, c, and nontradables, h. I will indicate it by $u(c,h)$, and assume that function u satisfies all the usual regularity conditions (e.g., strict concavity), including that optimal solutions are interior, i.e., optimal $c, h > 0$. The individual is endowed with an exogenous path of tradables. Full-capacity supply of nontradables is a given constant (over time), but current output is demand-determined. Price of nontradables is sticky, and money demand satisfies a cash-in-advance constraint.

The cash-in-advance constraint takes the following form:

$$h + ec = m, \tag{1}$$

where e stands for the relative price of tradables in terms of nontradables, and m denotes real monetary balances in terms of nontradables.

At optimum

$$\frac{u_c(c,h)}{u_h(c,h)} = e, \tag{2}$$

i.e., the familiar real-economy relationship between marginal rate of substitution and relative price, which in this case also holds because the cash-in-advance constraint (1) equally applies to tradables and nontradables.

By equation (2), the excess demand for nontradables can be expressed by some function $\Phi(c,e)$. I will assume that tradables and nontradables are normal goods, and gross substitutes, implying that $\Phi_j > 0$, $j = c,e$.

Thus, by equations (1) and (2), one gets

$$h - H = \Phi(c,e) = \Phi\left(c, \frac{m-h}{c}\right), \tag{3}$$

where H is the constant supply of nontradables. Solving for h in equation (3), one obtains

$$h = f(c,m), \quad f_m > 0, \ f_c \text{ ambiguous.} \tag{4}$$

Ambiguity of h with respect to c is the result of the following facts: (a) by normality, a rise in c induces h to go up; however, (b) by the cash-in-advance-constraint (1), a rise in c will be associated with a fall in e (i.e., real currency appreciation), which lowers the demand for h (given that h and c are gross substitutes).

I will now discuss the impact effects of a sudden stop experiment under the assumption that money supply is predetermined and the nominal exchange rate is free to float (dynamic implications will be left for another paper). First, notice that price-stickiness implies that m (i.e., real monetary balances in terms of nontradables) is a predetermined variable. Consider the realistic case in which $f_c > 0$. Thus, if sudden stop results in a lower current account deficit, c falls, implying a contraction in the demand for nontradables h and, hence, output.

Let us now turn to the exchange rate. By equation (1),

$$e = \frac{m - h}{c}.$$ (5)

Since the sudden stop implies a fall in c and h, it follows, by equation (5), that on impact e jumps up. However, since the price of nontradables are sticky and cannot change on impact, the jump in the real exchange rate, e, calls for an increase in the *nominal* exchange rate, i.e., currency devaluation. Consequently, by turning the tables and starting from sudden stop, an otherwise standard model can display contractionary devaluation.

Time Inconsistency, Flexibility and Volatility

Currency crises and breaching of credit contracts go hand in hand. For example, Kaminsky and Reinhart (1999) show that currency crises in EM are often accompanied by banking crises, a phenomenon labeled twin crises. Why is that? A possible reason is moral hazard. Banks know that they are central for ensuring a working payments system and, hence, conclude that the central bank will bail them out if they run into financial difficulties. This drives banks to take excessive risk and in that fashion create contingent government liabilities, which become evident during a crisis episode. In fact, those contingent liabilities may give rise to crisis in a Krugman-type model (see Velasco [1987] and chapter 7 in this book).

In this section I will discuss an entirely different mechanism for the twin crises and other related issues like poor creditor protection in

EMs. I will show the possibility that these phenomena may result from high Volatility. Volatility is much greater in EMs than in advanced economies (see IADB [1995]). Since many credit contracts are not *explicitly* state-contingent, high volatility is likely to create incentives for contract breaching. This point is straightforward. Less obvious is the proposition, shown below in terms of a couple of examples, that higher volatility may make it socially optimal to lower the cost of default or contract breaching. This is a novel reason for the incidence of twin crises in EM. Furthermore, the example suggests that a phenomenon like poor creditor protection—which is especially prevalent in high-volatility economies, see Galindo and Micco (2001)—is not an unmitigated curse, as the existing literature seems to suggest, since it may help to increase flexibility.

I will start with some general considerations that may help to clarify the difference between state-contingent intertemporal contracts and the *black sheep*: time inconsistency. The distinction between these two concepts is sometimes blurred in the policy debate.

Consider a two-period economy. The two periods will be called *today* and *tomorrow*. Let $A(s)$ denote the action that an economic agent (an individual, the government, etc.) *wishes to take tomorrow* if the state of nature is s. Furthermore, let $a(s)$ be the action that the same agent *will take tomorrow* if the state of nature is s. These actions could refer to credit contracts, but the discussion is more general and, thus, I will keep it that way. I will say that the vector of actions is *time consistent* if $a(s) = A(s)$ for all states of nature s. Otherwise, the vector of actions is *time inconsistent*. Kydland and Prescott (1977) and Calvo (1978) suggest that time inconsistency is the rule rather than the exception in macroeconomic policy.

Obviously, state-contingency is an instrument for optimality; there is nothing negative about it for social welfare. On the contrary, rigid policy rules are rarely going to be optimal. However, modern macro policymaking is full of examples of rigid rules. Even the European Union has shackled its members by the stability pact, imposing a series of rules that make it difficult for governments to adjust to new circumstances, e.g., independent central banks stick to inflation targets irrespective of the business cycle. Why is that? The most likely reason is that contingent policymaking opens the door to the black sheep, TI, since TI lowers *today's* social welfare (although it helps to maximize *tomorrow's* welfare).[6]

A Detour

Is TI a big factor in financial crises? This issue will not be discussed at
any length in this section, but the reader may find it instructive to
think about the issue in the context of the 2001–2002 crisis in Argentina. Before the crisis struck, the government emphatically insisted that
public debt would be repaid in full. As of the time of writing, on the
other hand, the government is equally insistent and emphatic about
repaying only 25 percent of a large chunk of outstanding public obligations. Does this reflect a significant TI problem? To answer this question one should be able to assess whether in, say, December 2000,
social welfare would have been substantially higher if the government
could ensure that, under the circumstances leading to financial crisis,
the government would repay, say, 50 percent of certain public obligations. If the answer is Yes, then TI played a major aggravating role in
the crisis *from the perspective of December 2000*. However, the 25 percent
current offer is, in principle, optimal from the perspective of 2001
(assuming that the government is maximizing social welfare). My conjecture is that the answer to the above question is Yes and, more generally, that small economies benefit from tying their hands through
international treaties to hold back massive default, but I will not pursue this issue here.[7]

A Basic Example

Without loss of generality, I will focus on TI at the individual level.
Consider an individual whose utility from *today's* perspective satisfies

$$\mathbf{E}\left[sl - \frac{\gamma}{2}(l - L)^2 - l \right],$$ (6)

where $\mathbf{E}$ is the expectations operator conditioned on the information
available *today*; s, a positive number, is the state of nature (which will
be revealed *tomorrow*); γ is a positive parameter; l is *tomorrow's* effort or
labor supply; and L is a labor-supply commitment made *today*. Interpretation: think of s as the marginal = average labor productivity; the
last term, l, as the marginal disutility of labor; and the quadratic middle term as adjustment cost, which is a function of the difference between labor supply *tomorrow*, and the level committed *today*, L. As will
become clear in the following discussion, *tomorrow's* utility function
will differ from (6) in a significant way, so that *tomorrow* the "same" in-

dividual will chose a level of labor supply that will not coincide with his *today's* best wishes. However, *today* the individual can set L, in a way anchoring his future labor-supply decision l. This is a rough commitment device given that it does not take into account the state of nature s. The motivation for this kind of non-state-contingent commitment device is that this is how many bank credit and bond contracts are stipulated.

Utility from the *tomorrow's* perspective satisfies

$$sl - \frac{\gamma}{2}(l - L)^2 - \kappa l, \quad \kappa > 1. \tag{7}$$

The difference between utility indexes (6) and (7) is the parameter $\kappa > 1$. Thus, the marginal disutility of labor is higher *tomorrow* than it is from the perspective of *today*. Looking at himself *tomorrow* from the perspective of *today*, our individual realizes that he is going to become lazier. This sets the stage for TI. Notice that the problem is isomorphic to a principal-agent problem. The principal would be the individual *today*, and the agent is the same individual *tomorrow*.

I will now characterize the solution to this problem under the assumption that the individual behaves in an optimal manner under the above constraints. The only variable that can be chosen *today* is L; *tomorrow* the individual is free to set l given state of nature s. Thus, maximizing *tomorrow's* utility (7) with respect to l, we get (at interior solutions)

$$l = L + \frac{s - \kappa}{\gamma}. \tag{8}$$

Hence, labor supply increases with the marginal productivity of labor, and it pivots around the rigid level L set *today*. Pivoting is smaller the larger is the adjustment-cost parameter γ.

One can rig up the model so that it is possible to abstract from natural bounds to labor supply. For example, if labor supply cannot exceed 1 (and is non-negative), then one could choose the support of the probability distribution of s, parameters γ and κ, and set bounds on L in order to ensure that l, given by equation (8), lies strictly between 0 and 1. Under those conditions, utility from the perspective of *today* (the Principal's utility, expression (9)) becomes, recalling equation (8),

$$\mathbf{E}\left[(s - 1)\left(L + \frac{s - \kappa}{\gamma}\right) - \frac{1}{2\gamma}(s - \kappa)^2\right]. \tag{9}$$

Determination of optimal L is a trivial problem because function (9) is linear in L. Thus, except in a borderline case, optimal L will lie on one of its bounds (depending on the sign of $\mathbf{E}(s - 1)$).

Suppose now that the individual *today* can determine the cost of adjustment γ in order to maximize expected utility (9). This also has an easy answer because the terms multiplying $1/\gamma$ are:

$$\mathbf{E}\left[(s - \kappa)\left(\frac{s + \kappa}{2} - 1\right)\right] = \frac{\text{var } s}{2} + \left(\frac{\bar{s}^2}{2} - \bar{s}\right) - \left(\frac{\kappa^2}{2} - \kappa\right), \tag{10}$$

where $\bar{s} = \mathbf{E}s$. Clearly, if expression (10) is positive, optimal γ is the lowest possible (i.e., adjustment cost is set as low as possible). On the other hand, if expression (10) is negative, optimal adjustment cost γ is as high as possible. For example, if the individual *today* and *tomorrow* share the same utility function, i.e., $\kappa = 1$, then expression (10) is positive; hence, optimal γ is set as low as possible. This makes sense because once TI ceases to be a problem, flexibility has no drawback: the more flexible, the better. On the other hand, κ can be set high enough that expression (10) is negative, and optimal adjustment cost γ is the largest possible, which, again, makes a great deal of sense. Finally, and most interesting, expression (10) can always be made positive by setting the variance of s large enough. This can be expressed by saying that *volatility puts a premium on flexibility*.

The last result deserves further discussion. First, notice that it is eminently plausible and, thus, likely to have much wider applicability. Volatile environments tend to increase the cost of rigid policies. Thus, in the absence of TI one would like future policymakers to have ample flexibility to adapt to varying circumstances. However, the tradeoff of flexibility is TI. The example suggests that as volatility becomes more prevalent, one should privilege flexibility and care less about TI. To illustrate, let us take the stylized fact that Latin America is much more volatile than advanced economies. Thus, the example suggests that creditors' protection mechanisms should be laxer in Latin American than in advanced economies, which is in line with empirical findings (see Galindo and Micco [2001]). Moreover, the example questions the generality of the conventional wisdom, according to which poor creditor protection *causes* greater volatility (see Galindo et al. [2004]). The example suggests that actually poor creditor protection could be an *optimal policy response* of high volatility. Under this optic, solving the credit-market problems that have troubled Latin America in recent times may lie more in offsetting volatility than in enforcing creditors' legal rights.[8]

Another related implication of the above finding is that credit-market arrangements such as CACs (collective action clauses) may become especially attractive in highly volatile environments. The fact that the private sector appears to have spontaneously embraced these types of clauses is an indication that greater flexibility may be seen as an improvement in EM credit contracts.

Related Literature

Townsend (1979) is the first to study limited contract enforceability by assuming that state verification is costly. Contracts have a clause specifying the set of states of nature in which there is contract-verification and the contract is made state-contingent (and displays time consistency). State verification is socially costly, that is, it represents deadweight loss. In the other states of nature there is no state verification and the borrower is free to choose an action within pre-specified bounds, which are not state-contingent. The competitive contract is written before the state of nature is revealed. At that early stage principal and agent specify the subset of states of nature where there will be state verification. In terms of the above example, the Townsend setup could take the following form: (a) set $l = L$ for $s \in S$, where S is the set of states of nature where there is *no* state verification; and (b) for $s \notin S$, l is made state-contingent. Townsend (1978) pins down a solution by assuming that principals are competitive, an assumption that has no obvious correlate in the present setup. A possibility in our case would be to assume that the agent has the upper hand and the contract is designed such for each $s \notin S$, $l(s)$ maximizes the agent's utility (7), without the quadratic term (i.e., $(s - \kappa)l$). The principal chooses L and S, subject to the previous constraint. Under these assumptions the Townsend (1978) analog implies that flexibility is costly, as in our example. Notice that the contract is time consistent by construction (since it maximizes utility (7) for each $s \notin S$ and L and, hence, internalizes potential TI).

In our example, there is no reference to a verification region. However, one could interpret our example as saying that there is no such a thing as a no-verification region. All states of nature are verified, and the cost is a quadratic function of $l - L$. Therefore, under this interpretation, our example belongs to the family of models that Townsend analyzed in his seminal paper.

The macro literature has also toyed with related ideas. For example, Flood and Isard (1994) divide the states of nature into two subsets: subset S in which the agent is free to choose any action—and its complement in which the agent's actions are rigid (e.g., where rigid rules prevail). Thus, implicitly Flood and Isard (1994) assume that all states are publicly observed and that contracts are costless to enforce. In terms of our example, this amounts to assuming that the principal sets L and $l = L$ for all $s \notin S$; and, if $s \in S$, l is set to maximize the agent's utility (7), without the quadratic term.

In a recent paper Athey, Atkeson, and Kehoe (2004) study optimal bounds on the agent's actions assuming that the state of nature is not publicly observable, implicitly assuming prohibitive non-compliance costs. In terms of our example, their assumptions amount to saying that instead of setting L, the Principal sets an interval where l is allowed to lie, and the agent is free to choose l within that interval in order to maximize the agent's utility (7), without the quadratic term. The maximization problem faced by the principal is a simple one, and a brief discussion is warranted.

Abstracting from the quadratic term in utilities (6) and (7), and recalling that $\kappa > 1$, it is clear that the agent will never want to work harder than the principal wishes the agent did. Hence, assuming that labor endowment is equal to 1, the upper bound for l set by the utility-maximizing Principal *today* will be 1. However, since the Agent is lazier than the Principal, it may be optimal for the latter to set a positive lower bound. I will denote the lower bound on l by $\underline{L}$. Therefore, recalling expression (9) without the quadratic term, the Principal's expected utility is given by the following expression:

$$\int_{\kappa}^{\infty} (s - 1)\, dF(s) + \underline{L} \int_{-\infty}^{\kappa} (s - 1)\, dF(s), \tag{11}$$

where F is the (continuous) cumulative probability distribution function for state of nature s. Left to his own devices, the agent would set $l = 0$ if $s < \kappa$. The principal would set $l = 0$ only if $s < 1 < \kappa$. Thus there is a region of disagreement between principal and agent where $s \in (1, \kappa)$. This is the reason why the principal could find it optimal to set a lower bound $\underline{L} > 0$. Clearly, if $s < \kappa$, the agent will set $l = \underline{L}$, giving rise to the second term in expression (11). Thus, by expression (11), the principal's utility will be maximized by setting

$$\underline{L} = 1, \quad \text{if} \int_{-\infty}^{\kappa} (s-1)\, dF(s) \geq 0,$$

$$\underline{L} = 0, \quad \text{otherwise.} \tag{12}$$

By definition,

$$\int_{-\infty}^{\kappa} (s-1)\, dF(s) = \int_{-\infty}^{1} (s-1)\, dF(s) + \int_{1}^{\kappa} (s-1)\, dF(s). \tag{13}$$

The first term in the right-hand side of expression (13) is negative, while the second one is positive. Moreover, for κ sufficiently close to 1, expression (13) is negative, implying, by expression (12), that $\underline{L} = 0$. Thus, in other words, if the agent is sufficiently similar to the principal, the agent is subject to no constraint in his choice of labor supply, l. However, if $\bar{s} > 1$, then expression (13) becomes positive for sufficiently large κ.[9] This case is the polar opposite of the previous example. The result indicates that if principal and agent are sufficiently dissimilar, then $\underline{L} = 1$, and the agent is given no room for discretion. This is a plausible implication, which is in line with the results in our original example.[10]

What about greater volatility of s? Expression (13) can alternatively be written as follows:

$$\int_{-\infty}^{\kappa} s\, dF(s) - F(\kappa) = -\int_{-\infty}^{\kappa} F(s)\, ds + (\kappa - 1)F(\kappa). \tag{14}$$

Equality in expression (14) involves integration by parts. I will say that random variable s becomes more volatile if its distribution function puts more weight on its tails, as defined by Rothschild and Stiglitz (1970). This is equivalent to saying that "as s becomes more volatile, $\int_{-\infty}^{\kappa} F(s)\, ds$ grows larger" (see Rothschild and Stiglitz [1970]). Therefore, greater volatility increases the chances that expression (14) will be negative, which, by expression (12), implies that optimal $\underline{L} = 0$, i.e., that principal gives agent total leeway to choose labor effort l. This result is also in line with earlier results in terms of our original example.

It is worth noting once again here that the literature appears not to have explored the relation between volatility and flexibility highlighted here. I think this issue deserves further attention given that EMs, particularly Latin American economies, exhibit substantially higher volatility than advanced economies.

Notes

I am thankful to Andres Rodriguez-Clare for useful comments, and to Rudy Loo-Kung for research assistance at the speed of light.

1. The wise optometrist also knows, incidentally, that placing lots of high-tech lenses on the patient's nose—showing off his lens power, so to speak—will surely drive off the patient in utter disgust. So, Young Turk, you have been warned!

2. There is a large literature dealing with the *sources* of volatility and their policy implications, starting with the seminal work of Poole (1970). In open-economy macro the discussion has centered on whether the shocks are "real" or "nominal" (see chapter 15 in this volume). In contrast, it is only recently that the policy implications of *large* volatility, irrespective of source, in EMs has been underscored (e.g., IADB [1995], IMF [2003, chapter 3]).

3. Fisher (1933) discussed this issue in the context of price deflation with nominal, non-state-contingent financial obligations, a situation which he called debt deflation. Debt deflation is a problem because prices are *flexible*, not inflexible like in the typical Keynesian textbook model. Maybe that is the explanation why debt deflation has been largely ignored until recently. Incidentally, multifaceted Keynes (1931) was fully aware of this issue, and appears to have independently discovered it.

4. This is reminiscent of asymmetries that appeared to fascinate Keynes and his disciples, exemplified by statements like: "you can a take horse to the river, but you cannot make him drink," or "you can pull on a string, but you can't push on a string," etc. See also Keynes's quotation at the start of chapter 7, which is even more akin to the discussion here.

5. Calvo, Izquierdo and Mejia (2004) show that an ample majority of large devaluation episodes in EMs coincide or are preceded by Sudden Stop. This stands in sharp contrast with advanced economies in which Sudden Stop is absent or follows devaluation.

6. In a two-period economy TI is an irresistible temptation because there is no future penalty. However, this is an artificial feature of the example, which does not extend to longer horizons.

7. This discussion links up with the issue of Reform of the International Financial Architecture. If one were to conclude that Argentina would have profited from more rigid credit-market discipline, then it follows that there is room for more or better International Financial Institutions.

8. Let me hasten to add, in order to avoid unnecessary confusion, that poor institutional arrangements can never be a first-best solution. All the example does is to show that simply making institutions more like those in Advanced economies may not be enough to increase social welfare, unless those institutions are adapted to the economy's prevailing objective conditions.

9. $\hat{s} > 1$ implies that if the Principal could set l constant and non-state-contingent, then it would set $l = 1$. This assumption is much more plausible than the alternative $\hat{s} < 1$, because the latter implies $l = 0$. Moreover, notice that if $\hat{s} < 1$, expression (13) never becomes positive.

10. These results are also in line with Athey, Atkeson and Kehoe (2004). For example, the abstract of the paper states: "The more severe the time inconsistency problem, the more

tightly the cap constrains policy and the smaller is the degree of discretion. As this problem becomes sufficiently severe, the optimal degree of discretion is none."

References

Athey, Susan, Andrew Atkeson, and Patrick J. Kehoe, 2004, "The Optimal Degree of Discretion in a Monetary Economy," NBER Working Paper 10109.

Calvo, Guillermo A., 1978, "On the Time Consistency of Optimal Policy in a Monetary Economy," *Econometrica* 46: 1411–1428. Reprinted as chapter 1 in Calvo (1996).

Calvo, Guillermo A., 1981, "Devaluation: Levels vs. Rates," *Journal of International Economics* 11, pp. 165–172. Reprinted as chapter 5 in Calvo (1996).

Calvo, Guillermo A., 1996, *Money, Exchange Rates, and Output*; Cambridge, MA: The MIT Press.

Calvo, Guillermo A., Alejandro Izquierdo and Luis-Fernando Mejia, 2004, "On the Empirics of Sudden Stops: The Relevance of Balance-Sheet Effects," NBER Working Paper No. 10520, May.

Edwards, Sebastian, 1991, *Real Exchange Rates, Devaluation, and Adjustment*; Cambridge, MA: The MIT Press.

Edwards, Sebastian, 2004, "Thirty Years of Current Account Imbalances, Current Account Reversals, and Sudden Stops," NBER Working Paper No. 10276.

Fisher, Irving, 1933, "The Debt-Deflation Theory of Great Depressions," *Econometrica*, 1, 4, October, pp. 337–357.

Flood, Robert P., and Peter Isard, 1994, "Monetary Policy Strategies," chapter 20 in R. P. Flood and P. M. Garber (editors) *Speculative Bubbles, Speculative Attacks, and Policy Switch*; Cambridge, MA: The MIT Press.

Friedman, Milton, 1953, "The Case for Flexible Exchange Rates," in M. Friedman (editor) *Essays in Positive Economics*; Chicago, IL: University of Chicago Press.

Galindo, Arturo and Alejandro Micco, 2001, "Creditor Rights and Credit Cycles," Research Network Working Paper. Washington, DC: Inter-American Development Bank, Research Department.

Galindo, Arturo, Alejandro Micco and Gustavo Suárez, 2004, "Credit Cycles and Financial Protection," mimeo Inter-American Development Bank.

IADB, 1995, *Overcoming Volatility*, Inter-American Development Bank, Washington, DC.

IMF, 2003, *World Economic Outlook*, International Monetary Fund, Washington, DC, September.

Kaminsky, Graciela L., and Carmen M. Reinhart, "The Twin Crises: The Causes of Banking and Balance of Payments Problems," *American Economic Review* 89, No. 4, pp. 473–500.

Keynes, John Maynard, 1931, "The Consequences to the Banks of the Collapse of Money Values," reprinted in his *Essays in Persuasion*, W. W. Norton & Company, New York, 1963.

Krugman, Paul, and Lance Taylor, 1978, "Contractionary Effects of Devaluation," *Journal of International Economics* 8, pp. 445–456.

Kydland, Finn E., and Edward C. Prescott, 1977, "Rules Rather then Discretion: The Inconsistency of Optimal Plans," *Journal of Political Economy* 85, pp. 473–493.

Poole, William, 1970, "Optimal Choice of Monetary Policy Instruments in a Simple Stochastic Macro Model," *Quarterly Journal of Economics*, 84, 2, May: 197–216.

Rothschild, Michael, and Joseph E. Stiglitz, 1970, "Increasing Risk: I. A Definition," *Journal of Economic Theory* 2, September, pp. 225–243.

Townsend, Robert, 1979, "Optimal Contracts and Competitive Markets with Costly State Verification," *Journal of Economic Theory* 21, No. 2, October, pp. 265–93.

Velasco, Andres, 1987, "Financial Crises and Balance of Payments Crises," *Journal of Development Economics*, October, pp. 263–283.

Sources

Chapter 1. "Capital Inflows and Real Exchange Rate Appreciation in Latin America: The Role of External Factors" (with L. Leiderman and C. Reinhart), *Staff Papers*, March 1993.

Chapter 2. "Capital Inflows to Latin America: The 1970s and the 1990s" with (L. Leiderman and C. Reinhart), in E. L. Bacha (ed.), *Economics in a Changing World*, Proceedings of the Tenth World Congress of the International Economic Association, vol. 4, London: Macmillan, 1994.

Chapter 3. "Capital Flows and Macroeconomic Management: Tequila Lessons," *International Journal of Finance Economics* 1:207–223, 1996.

Chapter 4. "Petty Crime and Cruel Punishment: Lessons from the Mexican Debacle" (with Enrique Mendoza), *American Economic Review* 86, no. 2 (2000):170–175.

Chapter 5. "Capital Market Contagion and Recession: An Explanation of the Russian Virus," in *Wanted: World Financial Stability*, Baltimore: Johns Hopkins University Press, 2000.

Chapter 6. "Sudden Stops, the Real Exchange Rate and Fiscal Sustainability: Argentina's Lessons" (with E. Talvi and A. Izquierdo), in *Monetary Unions and Hard Pegs: Effects on Trade, Financial Development and Stability*, ed. George M. von Furstenberg.

Chapter 7. "Varieties of Capital-Market Crises," in G. Calvo and M. King (eds.) *The Debt Burden and its Consequences for Monetary Policy*, Macmillan, 1998.

Chapter 8. "Uncertain Duration of Reform: Dynamic Implications" (with A. Drazen), *Macroeconomic Dynamics*, December 1998.

Chapter 9. "Capital Flows and Capital-Market Crises: The Simple Economics of Sudden Stops," *Journal of Applied Economics*, November 1998.

Chapter 10. "Rational Contagion and the Globalization of Securities Markets" (with Enrique Mendoza), *Journal of International Economics*, June 2000.

Chapter 11. "Balance of Payments Crises in Emerging Markets: Large Capital Inflows and Sovereign Governments," in Paul Krugman (ed.) *Currency Crises*, Chicago: University of Chicago Press, 2000.

Chapter 12. "Contagion in Emerging Markets: When Wall Street Is a Carrier," proceedings from the International Economic Association Congress, vol. 3, Buenos Aires, Argentina, 2002. The version that will be reprinted in the book contains a mathematical appendix that was dropped from IEA publication.

Chapter 13. "Explaining Sudden Stops, Growth Collapse and BOP Crises: The case of distortionary output taxes," IMF Mundell-Fleming Lecture, forthcoming special issue *IMF Staff Papers*.

Chapter 14. "Fixing for your Life" (with C. Reinhart), *Brookings Trade Forum*, 2000.

Chapter 15. "Capital Markets and the Exchange Rate: With Special Reference to the Dollarization Debate in Latin America," *Journal of Money, Credit and Banking* 33, no. 2 (2001):312–334.

Chapter 16. "Fear of Floating" (with C. Reinhart), *Quarterly Journal of Economics*, 2002.

Chapter 17. "The Mirage of Exchange Rate Regimes for Emerging Markets Countries" (with F. Mishkin), *Journal of Economic Perspectives*, 2003.

Chapter 18. "Globalization Hazard and Delayed Reform in Emerging Markets," *Economia*, 2002.

Chapter 19. "Sudden Stop, Contractionary Devaluation, and Time Inconsistency," previously unpublished.

Index